Lecture Notes in Computer Science 5060

Commenced Publication in 1973
Founding and Former Series Editors:
Gerhard Goos, Juris Hartmanis, and Jan van Leeuwen

T0190005

Chunming Rong   Martin Gilje Jaatun
Frode Eika Sandnes   Laurence T. Yang
Jianhua Ma (Eds.)

Autonomic and Trusted Computing

5th International Conference, ATC 2008
Oslo, Norway, June 23-25, 2008
Proceedings

 Springer

Volume Editors

Chunming Rong
University of Stavanger, Stavanger, Norway
E-mail: chunming.rong@uis.no

Martin Gilje Jaatun
SINTEF ICT, Trondheim, Norway
E-mail: martin.g.jaatun@sintef.no

Frode Eika Sandnes
Oslo University College, Oslo, Norway
E-mail: frodes@hio.no

Laurence T. Yang
St. Francis Xavier University, Antigonish, NS, Canada
E-mail: ltyang@stfx.ca

Jianhua Ma
Hosei University, Tokyo 184-8584, Japan
E-mail: jianhua@hosei.ac.jp

Library of Congress Control Number: 2008929348

CR Subject Classification (1998): D.2, C.2, D.1.3, D.4, E.3, H.4, K.6

LNCS Sublibrary: SL 2 – Programming and Software Engineering

ISSN   0302-9743
ISBN-10   3-540-69294-0 Springer Berlin Heidelberg New York
ISBN-13   978-3-540-69294-2 Springer Berlin Heidelberg New York

Springer is a part of Springer Science+Business Media

springer.com

© Springer-Verlag Berlin Heidelberg 2008

Typesetting: Camera-ready by author, data conversion by Scientific Publishing Services, Chennai, India
Printed on acid-free paper   SPIN: 12277896   06/3180   5 4 3 2 1 0

Preface

This volume contains the proceedings of ATC 2008, the 5th International Conference on Autonomic and Trusted Computing: Bringing Safe, Self-x and Organic Computing Systems into Reality. The conference was held in Oslo, Norway, during June 23–25, 2008.

ATC 2008 is a successor of the First IFIP Workshop on Trusted and Autonomic Ubiquitous and Embedded Systems (TAUES 2005, Japan), the International Workshop on Trusted and Autonomic Computing Systems (TACS 2006, Austria), the Third International Conference on Autonomic and Trusted Computing (ATC 2006, China), and the 4th International Conference on Autonomic and Trusted Computing (ATC 2007, Hong Kong).

Computing systems including hardware, software, communication and networks are growing dramatically in both scale and heterogeneity, becoming overly complex. Such complexity is getting even more critical with the ubiquitous permeation of embedded devices and other pervasive systems. To cope with the growing and ubiquitous complexity, Autonomic Computing (AC) focuses on self-manageable computing and communication systems that exhibit self-awareness, self-configuration, self-optimization, self-healing, self-protection and other self-x operations to the maximum extent possible without human intervention or guidance. Organic Computing (OC) additionally emphasizes natural-analogue concepts like self-organization and controlled emergence.

Any autonomic or organic system must be trustworthy to avoid the risk of losing control and to retain confidence that the system will not fail. Trust and/or distrust relationships in the Internet and in pervasive infrastructures are key factors in enabling dynamic interaction and cooperation of various users, systems and services. Trusted/Trustworthy Computing (TC) aims at making computing and communication systems as well as services available, predictable, traceable, controllable, assessable, sustainable, dependable, persistable, security/privacy protectable, etc.

A series of grand challenges remain before practical self-manageable autonomic systems with truly trustworthy services become a reality. ATC 2008 addressed the most innovative research and development in these challenging areas, and covered a multitude of technical aspects related to autonomic/organic computing (AC/OC) and trusted computing (TC).

The ATC 2008 conference provided a forum for engineers and scientists in academia, industry, and government to exchange ideas and experiences in developing AC/TC theory and models, architectures and systems, components and modules, communication and services, tools and interfaces, services and applications. There were 75 papers submitted, representing 22 countries and regions, from Asia, Europe, North America and the Pacific. All submissions were reviewed by at least three Technical Program Committee members or external reviewers.

In order to allocate as many papers as possible and keep the high quality of the conference, we finally decided to accept 25 regular papers for presentation, which reflected a 33% acceptance rate. In addition, there were 26 special session papers included in the proceedings. We believe that all of these papers and topics not only provided novel ideas, new results, work in progress and state-of-the-art techniques in this field, but also stimulated the future research activities in the area of autonomic and trusted computing.

Organization of conferences with a large number of submissions requires a lot of hard work and dedication from many people. We would like to take this opportunity to thank numerous people whose work made this conference possible and ensured its high quality. We wish to thank the authors of submitted papers, as they contributed to the conference technical program. We wish to express our deepest gratitude to the Program (Vice) Chairs for their hard work and commitment to quality when helping with paper selection. We would also like to thank all Program Committee members and external reviewers for their excellent job in the paper review process, the Steering Committee and Advisory Committee for their continuous advice, and Erik Hjelmås for organizing a panel on the important question: "Do we need a secure element in hardware?" A special thanks to Yo-Ping Huang and Tsun-Wei Chang for organizing a special session on "Sensor Networks, VoIP, and Watermarking." We are also in debt to the Publicity Chairs for advertising the conference, to the Local Organizing Committee for managing registration and other conference organization-related tasks, and to Oslo University College for hosting the conference. We are also grateful to Son T. Nguyen for the hard work on managing the conference website and the conference management system.

Chunming Rong

Martin Gilje Jaatun

Frode Eika Sandnes

Laurence T. Yang

Jianhua Ma

Organization

Executive Committee

General Chairs   Chunming Rong, University of Stavanger, Norway
Jianying Zhou, Institute for Infocomm Research, Singapore
Frode Eika Sandnes, Oslo University College, Norway

Program Chairs   Martin Gilje Jaatun, SINTEF, Norway
Xiaolin (Andy) Li, Oklahoma State University, USA
Geng Yang, Nanjing University of Post and Telecommunications, China

Program Vice Chairs   Tadashi Dohi, Hiroshima University, Japan
Hein Meling, University of Stavanger, Norway
Jean-Marc Seigneur, University of Geneva, Switzerland
Stephen R. Tate, University of North Texas, USA

Honorary Chairs   Christian Müller-Schloer, University of Hannover, Germany
Tosiyasu L. Kunii, Kanazawa Institute of Technology, Japan
Javier Lopez, University of Malaga, Spain

Steering Committee   Jianhua Ma (Chair), Hosei University, Japan
Laurence T. Yang (Chair), St. Francis Xavier University, Canada
Hai Jin, Huazhong University of Science and Technology, China
Jeffrey J.P. Tsai, University of Illinois at Chicago, USA
Theo Ungerer, University of Augsburg, Germany

International Advisory Committee   Jiannong Cao, Hong Kong Polytechnic University, Hong Kong
Chin-Chen Chang, Feng Chia University, Taiwan
Jingde Cheng, Saitama University, Japan
Zhong Chen, Peking University, China
Petre Dini, Cisco Systems, USA
Jadwiga Indulska, University of Queensland, Australia
Victor C.M. Leung, University of British Columbia, Canada
David Ogle, IBM, USA
Manish Parashar, Rutgers University, USA
Franz J. Rammig, University of Paderborn, Germany

Executive Committee(continued)

International Advisory Committee	Omer F. Rana, Cardiff University, UK
	Kouichi Sakurai, Kyushu University, Japan
	Hartmut Schmeck, Karlsruhe Institute of Technology, Germany
	Xinmei Wang, Xidian University, China
	Stephen S. Yau, Arizona State University, USA
	Mazin Yousif, Intel, USA
Publicity Chairs	Jinhua Guo, University of Michigan-Dearborn, USA
	Ting-Wei Hou, National Cheng Kung University, Taiwan
	Jan Newmarch, Monash University, Australia
	Fangguo Zhang, Sun Yat-Sen University, China
International Liaison Chairs	Ho-Fung Leung, Chinese University of Hong Kong, Hong Kong
	Yi Mu, University of Wollongong, Australia
	Benno Overeinder, Vrije University, The Netherlands
	Nguyen Huu Thanh, Hanoi University of Technology, Vietnam
	Huaglory Tianfield, Glasgow Caledonian University, UK
	George Yee, National Research Council, Canada
Industrial Track Chairs	Leif Nilsen, Thales Norway
	Josef Noll, UniK/Movation, Norway
Publication Chairs	Tony Li Xu, St. Francis Xavier University, Canada
	Son Thanh Nguyen, University of Stavanger, Norway
Award Chairs	Bjarne E. Helvik, Norwegian University of Science and Technology
	Bin Xiao, Hong Kong Polytechnic University, Hong Kong
Panel Chair	Erik Hjelmås, Gjøvik University College, Norway
Financial Chair	Kari Anne Haaland, University of Stavanger, Norway
Web Administration Chair	Son Thanh Nguyen, University of Stavanger, Norway
Local Arrangement Chairs	Siri Fagernes, Oslo University College, Norway
	Simen Hagen, Oslo University College, Norway
	Kirsten Ribu, Oslo University College, Norway
	Kyrre Begnum, Oslo University College, Norway
	Jie Xiang, Simula Research Laboratory, Norway
	Qin Xin, Simula Research Laboratory, Norway
	Hai Ngoc Pham, University of Oslo, Norway

Program Committee

Ahmed Al-Dubai	Napier University, UK
Richard Anthony	University of Greenwich, UK
Bernady Apduhan	Kyushu Sangyo University, Japan
Irfan Awan	University of Bradford, UK
Bernhard Bauer	University of Augsburg, Germany
Russell Beale	University of Birmingham, UK
Christophe Birkeland	NorCERT, Norway
Jürgen Branke	Karlsruhe Institute of Technology, Germany
Sergey Bratus	Dartmouth College, USA
Uwe Brinkschulte	Universität Karlsruhe, Germany
Lawrie Brown	ADFA, Australia
Tony Chan	The University of Akureyri, Iceland
Yuanshun Dai	Indiana University-Purdue University, USA
Olivia Das	Ryerson University, Canada
Murat Demirbas	SUNY Buffalo, USA
Feico Dillema	University of Tromsø, Norway
Dietmar Fey	Friedrich Schiller University of Jena, Germany
Noria Foukia	University of Otago, New Zealand
Xinwen Fu	Dakota State University, USA
Silvia Giordano	University of Applied Science, Switzerland
Bok-Min Goi	Multimedia University, Malaysia
Jinhua Guo	University of Michigan-Dearborn, USA
Tor Helleseth	University of Bergen, Norway
Jiman Hong	Soongsil University, Seoul, Korea
Runhe Huang	Hosei University, Japan
Michel Hurfin	Irisa, INRIA, France
Jörg Hähner	Leibniz University of Hannover, Germany
Xiaolong Jin	University of Bradford, UK
Audun Jøsang	Queensland University of Technology, Australia
Hidenori Kawamura	Hokkaido University, Japan
Engin Kirda	TU Wien, Austria
Satoshi Kurihara	Osaka University, Japan
Geir Køien	Telenor, Norway
Jiang (Leo) Li	Howard University, USA
Zhuowei Li	Indiana University at Bloomington, USA
Maria B. Line	SINTEF ICT, Norway
Luigi Lo Iacono	NEC Laboratories Europe, Germany
Seng Wai Loke	La Trobe University, Australia
Antonio Maña Gomez	University of Malaga, Spain
Geyong Min	University of Bradford, UK
Chris Mitchell	RHUL, UK
Alberto Montresor	University of Trento, Italy
Gero Mühl	Technical University of Berlin, Germany
Simin Nadjm-Tehrani	Linköping University, Sweden

Program Committee(continued)

Nidal Nasser	University of Guelph, Canada
Dimitris Nikolopoulos	Virginia Tech, USA
Jong Hyuk Park	Kyungnam University, Korea
Günther Pernul	University of Regensburg, Germany
Huaifeng Qin	Platform Computing, China
Aaron Quigley	University College Dublin, Ireland
Indrakshi Ray	Colorado State University, USA
Wolfgang Reif	University of Augsburg, Germany
Burghardt Schallenberger	Siemens CT IC 6, Germany
Ali Shahrabi	Glasgow Caledonian University, UK
Kuei-Ping Shih	Tamkang University, Taiwan, Taiwan
Einar Snekkenes	Gjøvik University College, Norway
Luca Spalazzi	Universitá Politecnica delle Marche, Italy
Gritzalis Stefanos	University of the Aegean, Greece
Ketil Stølen	SINTEF ICT/UiO, Norway
Willy Susilo	University of Wollongong, Australia
Wolfgang Trumler	University of Augsburg, Germany
Peter Urban	Google Inc., USA
Athanasios Vasilakos	University of Western Macedonia, Greece
Javier Garca Villalba	Complutense University of Madrid, Spain
Antonino Virgillito	Istat, Italy
Guojun Wang	Central South University, China
Xingang Wang	University of Plymouth, UK
Yan Wang	Macquarie University, Australia
Thomas J. Wilke	Technische Agentur Lehr, Germany
Liudong Xing	University of Massachusetts Dartmouth, USA
Lu Yan	University College London, UK
Shuang-Hua Yang	Loughborough University, UK
George Yee	National Research Council, Canada
Noriaki Yoshikai	Nihon University, Japan
Sherali Zeadally	University of the District of Columbia, USA
Zonghua Zhang	INRIA POPS Research Group, Lille, France
Sheng Zhong	SUNY Buffalo, USA
Norbert Zisky	PTB, Germany
Deqing Zou	Huazhong University of Science and Technology, China

Table of Contents

Trusted Systems and Crypto

Autonomic Computing

Organic Computing

Special Session Papers

Routing and Reliable Systems

Special Session on Sensor Networks, VoIP, and Watermarking

Sensor Network Applications Implemented by Industry and Their Security Challenges

Erdal Cayirci

NATO JWC & University of Stavanger, Norway

Wireless sensor networks (WSN) have many security and safety applications. BODAS, TADAS and TEDAS are three examples for WSN security applications implemented and deployed recently.

BODAS detects threats against the security and safety of pipelines. TADAS is a tactical sensing system to detect and classify the intruders. It is developed for surveillance along borders, through approach routes and around critical facilities. Finally TEDAS detects the intruders passing over, through or under a perimeter fence. All three applications are based on the deployment of a large number of unattended nodes for extended time periods. Therefore, scalability and power awareness are critical design parameters for them. They are also susceptible to security threats different from typical military and commercial systems.

We first introduce briefly these applications, and then elaborate the security threats and required security mechanisms for them. We also give our practical solutions for some of these security challenges and experimental results for them obtained through the implementation and deployment of BODAS, TADAS and TEDAS.

C. Rong et al. (Eds.): ATC 2008, LNCS 5060, p. 1, 2008.
© Springer-Verlag Berlin Heidelberg 2008

Detecting Stepping-Stone Intrusion and Resisting Evasion through TCP/IP Packets Cross-Matching

Jianhua Yang and Byong Lee

Department of Mathematics & Computer Science, Bennett College for Women,
900 E. Washington St., Greensboro, NC 27401, USA
{jhyang,blee}@bennett.edu

Abstract. In this paper, we propose a cross-matching algorithm that can detect stepping-stone intrusion. The theoretical analysis of this algorithm shows that it can completely resist intruder's time-jittering evasion. The results of the experiments and the simulation show that this algorithm can also resist intruders' chaff-perturbation with chaff-rate up to 80%. Compared with A. Blum's approach, which can resist chaff-perturbation with every x inserted packets out of 8*(x+1), this approach has promising performance in terms of resistance to intruders' manipulation.

1 Introduction

It is not a secret that intruders usually attack other computers through stepping-stones [1]. One obvious reason is that using stepping-stone could make the intruders safe from being detected, even captured. Along with the development of computer technologies many approaches to detect stepping-stone intrusion were proposed [1]. Some of the known approaches are Content-Based Thumbprint [3], Time-Based Approach [1], Deviation-Based Approach [4], Round-Trip Time Approach [5, 2], and Packet Number Difference-Based Approach [6, 7]. Usually intruders take advantage of the vulnerabilities of TCP/IP in manipulating TCP sessions in order to avoid detection. Most commonly used manipulation methods are time-jittering and chaff-perturbation [6].

Staniford-Chen and Heberlein proposed a method that identifies intruders by comparing different sessions for suggestive similarities of connection chains [3]. The major weakness of this method is that it cannot be applied to encrypted sessions in which the contents that are crucial for making thumbprint are not available. Zhang and Paxson proposed the Time-Based Approach that can be used to detect stepping-stone or trace back intrusion even if a session is encrypted [1]. However, this method has three major problems. First, it can be easily manipulated by intruders. Second, it requires that the packets of connections have precise and synchronized timestamps in order to correlate them properly. This makes it difficult or impractical to correlate the measurements taken at different points in the network. Third, it is observed that a large number of legitimate stepping-stone users routinely traverse a network for a variety of purposes. Yoda and Etoh proposed the Deviation-Based Approach, a network-based correlation scheme [4]. It defines the deviation as the minimum average delay gap between the packet streams of two TCP connections. This method is based

C. Rong et al. (Eds.): ATC 2008, LNCS 5060, pp. 2–12, 2008.

on the observation that the deviation of two unrelated connections is large enough to be distinguished from that of connections in the same connection chain. The Deviation-Based Approach has the following problems in addition to the problems that the Time-Based Approach has: 1) computing deviation is not efficient; 2) it is not applicable for a compressed session because it depends on the size of a packet; 3) it cannot correlate connections where padding is added to the payload because it can correlate only the TCP connections that have one-to-one correspondences in their TCP sequence numbers; 4) correlation measurements are applicable only to the post-attack traces because the correlation metrics are defined over the entire duration of the connections. The Round-Trip Time (RTT) approach proposed by Yung [2] detects stepping-stone intrusion by estimating the downstream length using the gap between a request and its corresponding response, and the gap between the request and its corresponding acknowledgement. The problem of the RTT approach is that it makes inaccurate detection because it cannot compute the two gaps precisely.

The Packet Number Difference-Based Approach (PND-based) proposed by Blum [7] detects stepping-stones by checking the difference between the Send packet numbers of an incoming connection and those of an outgoing connection. The method is based on the idea that if the two connections are relayed, the difference should always be bounded, otherwise, it should not. It is claimed that this method can resist intruders' evasions such as time-jittering and chaff-perturbation to an extent. Donoho, et al. [6] showed that there are theoretical limits on the ability of attackers to disguise their traffics using evasions during a long interactive session. Using wavelet and multiscale methods they proved that even if the session is jittered by time and chaff perturbation, stepping-stone detection is still possible by monitoring a session for a long time. However, Donoho, et al. did not show how much time a session needs to be monitored in order to detect a stepping-stone. Blum [7] continued Donoho's work and proposed a PND-based algorithm for stepping-stone detection using Computational Learning Theory. Blum achieved provable upper bounds on the number of packets required to be monitored in an interactive session in order to achieve a given confidence. A major problem with the PND-based approach is due to the fact that the upper bound of the number of packets required to monitor is large, while the lower bound of the amount of chaff needed to evade this detection is small. This fact makes Blum's method weak in terms of resisting intruders' chaff evasion. J. Yang proposed a couple of methods that match TCP/IP packets to detect stepping-stone intrusion [5, 8, 9]. The main idea of these methods is to detect stepping-stone intrusion by estimating the length of a connection chain between the stepping-stone and the victim host. The longer the connection chain is, the higher the probability that the session is a stepping-stone intrusion.

As we can see, most approaches that have been developed to detect stepping-stone intrusion are vulnerable in resistance to intruders' evasion. In this paper, we propose a new algorithm, TCP/IP Packets Cross-Matching, to detect stepping-stone intrusion and to resist intruders' time-jittering and chaff-perturbation evasions. The main idea of the TCP/IP Packet Cross-Matching is to match the send and echo packets of not only the same session, but also the different sessions. To determine whether a stepping-stone intrusion occurs, the TCP/IP packet matching rates between different sessions are compared. The results of the experiments and the simulations we conducted showed that this method can not only detect stepping-stone intrusion, but also resist intruders' evasions such as time-jittering and chaff-perturbation to a significant extent.

Section 2 introduces intruders' evasion approaches; time-jittering, and chaff-perturbation, and our assumptions. Section 3 explains TCP/IP Packets Matching method and the TCP/IP Packet Cross-Matching Algorithm. Section 4 covers the experimental setup, simulation, and the analysis of the experimental and simulation results. Section 5 summarizes our work with a conclusions and possible directions for the future work.

2   Intruder's Evasion Approaches and Assumptions

As we discussed before, intruders usually evade stepping-stone detection by manipulating the TCP session. The purpose of the manipulation is either to make two unrelated connections look like related or two unrelated connections look like related. Time-jittering and chaff-perturbation are the methods most frequently used by intruders to manipulate TCP sessions. Before we discuss the TCP/IP Packet Cross-Matching Algorithm, we would like to explain these two evasion approaches first.

2.1   Time-Jittering

Intruders can evade detection by holding some of the Send packets of a session. This method is called time-jittering. Different packets are held for different time gaps. Usually intruder's randomly generates time gaps for the Send packet delays. But the Send packets original order must be kept and guaranteed. Suppose we have n send packets $\{s_1, s_2, s_3, ..., s_n\}$ and their corresponding time stamps are: $\{t_1, t_2, t_3, ..., t_n\}$. The following relations must be satisfied if these packets belong to one interactive session,

$$t_n > t_{n-1} > ... > t_3 > t_2 > t_1 \qquad (1)$$

If the ith packet is held for a time gap Δt_i, the time stamps of the jittered Send packets would be: $\{t_1 + \Delta t_1, t_2 + \Delta t_2, t_3 + \Delta t_3, ..., t_i + \Delta t_i ..., t_n + \Delta t_n\}$. Regardless of the size of Δt_i, the following relations must be satisfied to guarantee the original send packets' order,

$$t_n + \Delta t_n > t_{n-1} + \Delta t_{n-1} > ... > t_3 + \Delta t_3 > t_2 + \Delta t_2 > t_1 + \Delta t_1 \qquad (2)$$

This is required by TCP/IP protocol. Many of the approaches proposed to detect stepping-stone [1, 3, 4] are vulnerable in terms of resistance to Time-Jittering evasion.

Intruders could manipulate either incoming connections or outgoing connections using time-jittering. Generally, intruders cannot hold Echo packets. The reason is that each Echo packet is the response to a Send packet and holding an Echo packet may cause resending the corresponding Send and this complicates the network communication beyond the control. That is why holding Send packet is the usual way used to manipulate an interactive session by intruders. Another fact is that intruders cannot hold Send packets indefinitely. In other words, an intruder can hold a Send packet only for a limited time [6]. Therefore, we can make the following two assumptions:

Assumption 1: Intruders can apply time-jittering manipulation to Send packets only.

Assumption 2: The time that an intruder can hold a Send packet must be bounded, i.e. $\Delta t_i < T_b$, where T_b represents an upper boundary.

2.2 Chaff-Perturbation

Another way to evade detection is to insert meaningless packets to an interactive session. This method is called chaff-perturbation. With chaff-perturbation, intruders can manipulate connections, either making two relayed connections un-relayed or making two un-relayed connections relayed. The methods that detect stepping-stone intrusion by counting the number of Send packets fail to resist this chaff-perturbation evasion because the packet number could be easily changed with the chaff-perturbation. Chaff-perturbation is more difficult to implement than time-jittering. There are two issues to consider in chaff-perturbation evasion. They are chaff rate and chaff removing.

Intruders usually do not insert too many packets into an interactive TCP/IP session for two reasons: It is difficult to control and it is inefficient. The purpose of chaff-perturbation is to evade detections by the methods in which the number of Send packets in incoming connection and the one in outgoing connection are compared to see if the two numbers are close enough. In other words, it checks if the relative difference (the rate between the difference of the two numbers and the minimum of the two numbers) is within ε where $0 < \varepsilon < 1$. If we use δ to represent the relative difference, then the following equation must be satisfied,

$$| \delta | < \varepsilon \tag{3}$$

The smaller the ε is, the more accurate the detection. If an intruder wants to evade the detection, he/she would chaff the session with a rate that is just a little bit higher than ε. Our conclusion is that intruders do not need to insert a large number of packets into a session to evade the detection.

Another important fact is that intruders must remove all the chaffs before they reach the target host of an interactive session because the meaningless packets cannot be executed at the end host. Further more if the chaffs arrive at the end host, they will interfere with the execution of the normal packets. So we make the third and fourth assumptions.

Assumption 3: All the chaffs do not have any corresponding Echo packets because the chaffs will be removed before it goes to the end host.

Assumption 4: Intruders can chaff any send or echo packets, and if the chaffs are removed, they will be removed completely rather than partially.

3 TCP/IP Cross-Matching Algorithm

3.1 Motivation

The basic idea employed in the algorithms that detect stepping-stone intrusion is to compare a feature of an incoming connection with the same feature of the corresponding outgoing connection to see if the two features are the same or close enough. The main reason why the previous approaches are weak or fail in resisting intruders' evasion is that the features used in those approaches are easy to be manipulated by either delaying send packets or inserting some meaningless packets. For example, the ON-OFF feature used by Zhang [1] is easy to be changed by holding different send packets for different time gaps; the send packet number used by A. Blum [7] is also uncomplicated to be changed by inserting some meaningless packets even though A. Blum proved that his method would work if less than x packets are inserted in $8*(x+1)$ packets.

We believe that only the methods that use a characteristic that is not easy to be manipulated will have the ability to resist intruders' evasion. The method proposed by J. Yang [8] to detect stepping-stone intrusion uses an estimation of the length of the connection chain. Unlike other approaches that use only send packets, J. Yang used send and echo packets together to detect stepping-stone. The key to estimate the length of a connection is to match the send and echo packets of an outgoing connection. J. Yang [8] showed that the matched packets always form the largest cluster, i.e. among the clusters formed the matched packets produce the highest matching rate, which is defined as the ratio between the number of element of a cluster and the number of send packets. We found that matching rate is very promising indicator to determine if two connections are relayed. If two connections are not relayed, the matching rate between the send packets of one connection and the echo packets of the other connection is close to zero. However, if two connections are relayed, that rate would be close to one. The most important fact regarding this matching rate is that it is not inclined to be affected by manipulation. That is, the probability that chaff packets are involved in a matched cluster is very low unless they are strictly controlled. Even if some chaffed packets are involved in a matched cluster, it still cannot affect the matching result significantly unless all the chaffed packets form a new cluster which has the matching rate higher than the real one. To make this happen, the intruder would need to insert more than 100% meaningless packets into an interactive session. It is not easy for an intruder to implement it as what Donoho [6] proved. The TCP/IP Cross-Matching algorithm is based on the packets matching idea proposed by J. Yang [8].

3.2 TCP/IP Packets Cross-Matching Algorithm

In the cross-matching algorithm the send packets of an outgoing connection is matched to the echo packets of the same connection and to the echo packets of an incoming connection, and then the two matching rate are compared to see how close they are. We use matching rates of an incoming connection and its corresponding outgoing connection as the bench mark to decide if a stepping-stone intrusion occurs. Fig. 1 illustrates this idea.

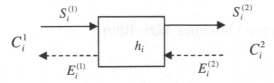

Fig. 1. Illustration for Cross-Matching

As Fig.1 shows, h_i is a host to be determined if it is a stepping-stone. This host has two connections; C_i^1 and C_i^2. C_i^1 is the incoming connection that contains two streams: the send packet stream $S_i^{(1)}$, and the echo packet stream $E_i^{(1)}$. C_i^2 is the outgoing connection that also includes the send packet stream $S_i^{(2)}$ and the echo packet stream $E_i^{(2)}$.

The packets in $S_i^{(2)}$ are matched to the packets in $E_i^{(2)}$ using the packet matching method in [8] and produce a matching rate ρ_{22}. The packets in $S_i^{(2)}$ match the packets in $E_i^{(1)}$ and produce a matching rate ρ_{21}. If the two connections C_i^1 and C_i^2 are relayed, the following inequality must be satisfied.

$$| \rho_{21} - \rho_{22} | < \varepsilon,$$

where $0 < \varepsilon < 1$ The lower the value of ε is, the higher probability that the two connections are relayed. The ideal value of $| \rho_{21} - \rho_{22} |$ is equal to zero.

In addition to the matching rate difference, we also check the similarity between two matched sequences. The two packet matching rates ρ_{21} and ρ_{22} come from one send packet sequence. Not always all the packets of $S_i^{(2)}$ match all the echo packets in sequence $E_i^{(2)}$, as well as those packets in sequence $E_i^{(1)}$. We define S_{22} as the set of the packets in $S_i^{(2)}$ that match with $E_i^{(2)}$ and N_{22} as the number of packets in S_{22}; S_{21} as the set of the packets in $S_i^{(2)}$ that match $E_i^{(1)}$ and N_{21} as the number of packets in S_{21}. The similarity between two sequences can be measured by checking how many packets are the same between S_{21} and S_{22}. We use λ to represent the similarity and then λ is defined as follow.

Similarity: $\lambda = \dfrac{\Delta}{\max(N_{21}, N_{22})}$, where Δ is the number of the packets in the intersection of S_{21} and S_{22}.

3.3 Resistance Analysis

3.3.1 Time-Jittering

An intruder could perform time-jittering either in the incoming connections by holding $S_i^{(1)}$ or in the outgoing connections by holding $S_i^{(2)}$ as Fig.1 shows. Based on Assumption 1, an intruder cannot hold Echo packets. To simplify our analysis, we assume that the Send packets $S_i^{(2)}$ in outgoing connection are held randomly. We assume there are n Send packets S: $\{s_1, s_2, s_3, ..., s_n\}$ with time stamps $\{ t_{s1}, t_{s2}, t_{s3}, ..., t_{sn} \}$ passing through the outgoing connection before time-jittering is implemented. We also assume that there are m Echo packets E: $\{ e_1, e_2, e_3, ..., e_m \}$ with time stamps $\{ t_{e1}, t_{e2}, t_{e3}, ..., t_{em} \}$ generated by the target host of the session in the incoming connection. We also assume that s_i with time stamp t_{si} matches e_j with time stamp t_{ej} if the two connections are relayed. After time-jittering, the two time stamps should become to $t_{si} + \Delta t$, and $t_{ej} + \Delta t$, where Δt is the time-jittering. The round-trip time (RTT) before time-jittering is RTT1 = $t_{ej} - t_{si}$, and after time jittering is RTT2 = $(t_{ej} + \Delta t) - (t_{si} + \Delta t) = t_{ej} - t_{si}$. Therefore, we can say that time-jittering does not affect the round-trip time which is used to match Send and Echo packets. Consequently, we can conclude that the matching rate cannot be affected by time-jittering. Therefore, we can justify the Assumption 1: an intruder will hold Echo packets. It means that the time stamps of packets in $E_i^{(1)}$ are very close to the ones in $E_i^{(2)}$. The matching rate ρ_{21} is also not affected by the time-jittering imposed on the send packets of the outgoing connection. If the two connections are relayed, these two matching rate should be very close. In other words, if ρ_{21} and ρ_{22} are very close, we may induce that the possibility that the two connections are relayed is very high. So cross-matching can be used to detect stepping-stone intrusion, and can resist intruder's time-jittering evasion.

3.3.2 Chaff-Perturbation

To determine if cross-matching could resist intruders' chaff-perturbation evasion, we need to analyze the effect of chaff-perturbation on packet matching rate or on RTT which is used to match Send and Echo packets. Unlike time-jittering, intruders can perform chaff-perturbation on Send packets, on Echo packets, or on both. We analyzed two cases. First, chaff-perturbation is performed in only Send packets. Second, chaff-perturbation is performed in both Send and Echo packets. The analysis was based on the Assumption 4: when the chaffs are removed, they must be removed completely, rather than partially.

Case 1: Chaff on Send packets only
We assume that the Send packet stream has n packets $\{s_1, s_2, s_3, ..., s_n\}$ with time stamps $\{t_{s1}, t_{s2}, t_{s3}, ..., t_{sn}\}$, and Echo packet stream has m packets $\{e_1, e_2, e_3, ..., e_m\}$ with time stamps $\{t_{e1}, t_{e2}, t_{e3}, ..., t_{em}\}$ before chaff perturbation. If a packet (we call it k^{th} packet with time stamp t_{sk}) is inserted between i^{th} and $(i+1)^{th}$ Send packets, then this Send packet will not have corresponding Echoed packet because this k^{th} packet will be removed before it goes to the end host (Assumption 3). When t_{sk} is very close to t_{si}, this packet will merge to the ith packet. When t_{sk} is very close to t_{si+1}, this packet will merge to the $(i+1)^{th}$ packet.. If it is close to neither i^{th} packet nor $(i+1)^{th}$ packet, this packet will exist independently and match nothing. Therefore, theoretically the round-trip time cannot be affected by chaffs inserted in Send packets. Obviously packet matching rate cannot be affected either. So cross-matching can resist intruders' evasion with only Send packets chaffed.

Case 2: Chaff on both Send and Echo packets
Assume that two Send packets s_i, s_{i+1} are matched by two Echo packets e_j, e_{j+1}, respectively before chaff-perturbation. After chaff-perturbation, they become s_i, s_p, s_{i+1}, and e_j, e_q, e_{j+1}, where s_p and e_q are chaffs. If s_p is either close to s_i or to s_{i+1}, it would not affect the round trip time computation as shown in the Case 1. If s_p is close to neither s_i nor s_{i+1}, then e_q may match s_p to form a different RTT and interfere the packet matching. As a result it may make either two un-relayed connections look like relayed or two relayed connections look like un-relayed. This happens only when the following two conditions are met. First, there are a large number of chaffs and second,

the chaffs can form RTTs which are very close and these RTTs can interfere with the real RTTs. This, however, happens with very low probability because it is almost impossible to meet the both conditions. For the first condition, as we stated before it is impractical and inefficient to insert a large number of meaningless packets into an interactive session. For the second condition, even if an intruder could handle everything and would not care about the efficiency of the network communication, it is still very hard to affect the packet matching rate because the intruder must control the interactive session so that all the packets inserted can be matched and form a different set of fake RTTs that can interfere with the real RTTs. The more packets are inserted, the more difficult for intruders to control. The point is that a small number of packets inserted does not affect packet matching rate significantly. If intruders randomly insert some meaningless packets into an interactive session, it is unlikely that the chaffs matched each other. Our conclusion is that packet matching rate cannot be affected by randomly inserted chaff and therefore, the cross-matching method can resist chaff-perturbation to an extent.

3.4 The Algorithm

Based the discussions we had in the previous sections, we propose the cross-matching algorithm that could detect stepping-stone intrusion, as well as resisting time-jittering and chaff-perturbation evasions. We assume there are n Send packets captured and ε is a given threshold which determines the detection accuracy. This threshold is determined by the tradeoff between the false positive rate and the false negative rate of intrusion detection.

Cross-Matching ($S_i^{(1)}, E_i^{(1)}, S_i^{(2)}, E_i^{(2)}, \varepsilon$):

1. Call the matching algorithm in [8] to match the packet between $S_i^{(2)}$ and $E_i^{(1)}$, as well as $S_i^{(2)}$ and $E_i^{(2)}$, and compute the matching rate ρ_{21} and ρ_{22}, respectively;

2. Determine if $|\rho_{21} - \rho_{22}| < \varepsilon$ is satisfied. If it is, then got to Step 3, otherwise go to Step 4;

3. Check the similarity λ. If it is over 90%, then terminate and output "stepping-stone intrusion"; if it is over 60%, then terminate and output "highly doubted"; otherwise, go to Step 4.

4. If the inequality in Step 2 is not satisfied, then change the incoming connection and repeat Steps 1 to 3 until all the incoming connections are checked.

End

The computation cost of this algorithm is dominated by the computations in Step 1 which is used to match Sends and Echoes. J. Yang pointed out that the time complexity of the efficient clustering algorithm is $O(nm^2)$, where n is the number of Sends, and m is the number of Echoes [8]. If there are p incoming connections and q outgoing connections at a host, in the worst case, the time complexity of detecting stepping-stone would be $4*O(nm^2)*p*q \approx O(pqnm^2)$ [8].

In this algorithm, we employed the thresholds for the similarity; 90% to indicate stepping-stone intrusion and 60% to indicate highly doubted stepping-stone intrusion.

These two numbers were selected purely based on our experience and our experimental context. Different similarity threshold may be selected based on the detecting context.

4   Experimental Results

4.1   Experimental Setup

We established two connections using OpenSSH. They went through the host computer at Bennett College. One connection connects to Mexico, and the other connects to California. We have two incoming connections C_1^1 and C_2^1, and two outgoing connections C_1^2 and C_2^2. C_1^1 and C_1^2 are relayed and C_2^1 and C_2^2 are relayed. We monitored these four connections, and collected the send and echo packets from the outgoing connections C_1^2 and C_2^2, as well as the echo packets from the incoming connections C_1^1 and C_2^1. We call the cross-matching algorithm to compute the matching rates and the similarities. Obviously, the experimental results showed that C_1^1 and C_1^2, C_2^1 and C_2^2 are in the same session respectively. We do not want to get in details at this point, but we want to show how the cross-matching algorithm behaves when the connections are manipulated. Is it strong in resisting intruders' evasion? We justify this through simulation with $\varepsilon = 0.1$.

4.2   Resisting Time-Jittering and Its Analysis

As we discussed in section 3.3.1, what we monitor is the timestamps of the send packets of the outgoing connections. Whatever how long an intruder holds the send packets, it does not affect the timestamps of the packets. That is it does not affect the matching rates if Assumption 1 is met. So we do not have to do any justification at this point. Under Assumption 1, cross-matching can resist intruders' time-jittering completely.

4.3   Resisting Chaff-Perturbation and Its Analysis

In this section, we ponder two questions. First, when the two connections are relayed, is it possible to make them not relayed by chaff-perturbation? Second, when the two connections are not relayed, is it possible to make them relayed by chaff-perturbation? We took the packet sequence as the mother sample, and inserted some meaningless packets into both echo and send sequences with the different ratios, 10%, 20%, ...100%. Here we assumed that the original timestamps would not be changed with chaff inserted. For each inserting ratio, we simulated 100 times, and took the worst result. Fig. 2 shows the matching rate difference and the matching rate similarity at different inserting rates under the assumption that the two connections are relayed.

According to Fig. 2 the two connections are in highly doubted relayed status when the chaff-rate is over 80% because the similarity is lower than 90% but higher than 60%. The cross-matching can resist intruders' chaff-perturbation with chaff-rate up to 80%.

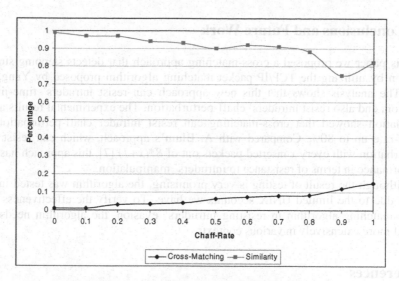

Fig. 2. Two relayed connections with Chaff-Perturbation

Fig. 3 shows the case when two connections are not relayed. We chaffed both the send and echo sequence with different chaff-rate from 10% to 100%. The simulation results show that the similarities are always under 10% whatever how the connections were chaffed. And the matching rate difference is always over 90%. The results drive us to believe that chaff-perturbation cannot escape from the detection of cross-matching.

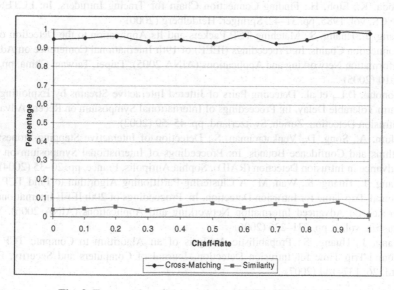

Fig. 3. Two unrelayed connections with Chaff-Perturbation

5 Conclusions and Future Work

In this paper we proposed a cross-matching approach that detects stepping-stone intrusion by utilizing the TCP/IP packet matching algorithm proposed by Yang, et al. [8]. The analysis shows that this new approach can resist intruders' time-jittering evasion, and also resist intruders' chaff-perturbation. The experimental results and the simulation showed that cross-matching can resist intruder chaff-perturbation with chaff-rate up to 80%. Compared with A. Blum's approach, which can resist chaff-perturbation with every x inserted packets out of $8*(x+1)$ [7], this approach has better performance in terms of resistance to intruders' manipulation.

Although the result of testing is very promising, the algorithm was tested in small scale due to the limited UNIX accounts we have. To verify the effectiveness of the cross-matching algorithm in resisting intruders' evasion, the algorithm needs to be tested more extensively in various contexts.

References

[1] Zhang, Y., Paxson, V.: Detecting Stepping Stones. In: Proc. of the 9th USENIX Security Symposium, Denver, CO, USA, pp. 171–184 (2000)
[2] Yung, K.H.: Detecting Long Connecting Chains of Interactive Terminal Sessions. In: Wespi, A., Vigna, G., Deri, L. (eds.) RAID 2002. LNCS, vol. 2516, pp. 1–16. Springer, Heidelberg (2002)
[3] Staniford-Chen, S., Todd Heberlein, L.: Holding Intruders Accountable on the Internet. In: Proc. IEEE Symposium on Security and Privacy, Oakland, CA, USA, pp. 39–49 (1995)
[4] Yoda, K., Etoh, H.: Finding Connection Chain for Tracing Intruders. In: LCTES 2000. LNCS, vol. 1985, pp. 31–42. Springer, Heidelberg (2000)
[5] Yang, J., Huang, S.: Matching TCP Packets and Its Application to the Detection of Long Connection Chains. In: Proceedings (IEEE) of 19th International Conference on Advanced Information Networking and Applications (AINA 2005), Taipei, Taiwan, China, pp. 1005–1010 (2005)
[6] Donoho, D.L., et al.: Detecting Pairs of Jittered Interactive Streams by Exploiting Maximum Tolerable Delay. In: Proceedings of International Symposium on Recent Advances in Intrusion Detection, Zurich, Switzerland, pp. 45–59 (2002)
[7] Blum, A., Song, D., Venkataraman, S.: Detection of Interactive Stepping-Stones: Algorithms and Confidence Bounds. In: Proceedings of International Symposium on Recent Advance in Intrusion Detection (RAID), Sophia Antipolis, France, pp. 20–35 (2004)
[8] Yang, J., Huang, S., Wan, M.: A Clustering-Partitioning Algorithm to Find TCP Packet Round-Trip Time for Intrusion Detection. In: Proceedings of 20th IEEE International Conference on Advanced Information Networking and Applications (AINA 2006), Vienna, Austria, vol. 1, pp. 231–236 (2006)
[9] Yang, J., Huang, S.: Probabilistic Analysis of an Algorithm to Compute TCP Packet Round-Trip Time for Intrusion Detection. Journal of Computers and Security, Elsevier Ltd. 26, 137–144 (2007)

Preventing DDoS Attacks Based on Credit Model for P2P Streaming System

Jun Yang[1], Ying Li[2], Benxiong Huang[1], and Jiuqiang Ming[1]

[1] Dept. of E. I. E, Huazhong University of Science and Technology, Wuhan, China
cody.yang@gmail.com, huangbx@mail.hust.edu.cn,
mingjiuqiang@hotmail.com
[2] State Key Lab. of ISN, Xidian University, Xi'an, China
yli@mail.xidian.edu.cn

Abstract. Distributed Denial of Service (DDoS) attack is a serious threat to the Internet communications especially to P2P streaming system. P2P streaming system is vulnerable to DDoS attacks due to its high bandwidth demand and strict time requirement. In this paper, we propose a distributed framework to defense DDoS attack based on Credit Model(CM) which takes the responsibility to identify malicious nodes and categorize nodes into different credit level. We also introduce a Message Rate Controlling Model (MRCM)to control the message rate of a node according to its credit level. Combining CM and MRCS together, our framework can improve the resistibility against DDoS for P2P streaming system.

Keywords: Distributed Denial of Service (DDoS), peer-to-peer (P2P), Credit.

1 Introduction

Peer-to-peer networks, especially P2P file sharing networks, have been quickly adopted by many Internet communities in the past few years. Recently, the popularity of P2P streaming service demonstrates its ability to deliver high quality media streams to a large number of audiences. The Thriving of P2P networks starts to attract distributed denial of service (DDoS) attacks. Compared with the widely applied file-sharing networks[1][2], P2P streaming networks are more vulnerable to DDoS attacks for the following three reasons. Firstly, streaming usually requires high bandwidth such that a certain amount of data loss could make the whole stream useless. Secondly, Streaming applications require their data to be delivered before a deadline. Otherwise data with a missed deadline is useless. Thirdly, a streaming network usually consists of a limited number of data sources which are easily attacked[3].

In P2P streaming network, the attacks on data sources and part of the network may cause DDoS. A P2P streaming network consists of a limited number of data sources which are easily attacked by some malicious nodes when they send amounts of requests[4]. Then other well-behaving nodes will not download media stream from data sources which means a DDoS attack to data sources has happened. On the other hand, since receivers can make unrestricted requests in such a system, if many nodes request a large number of media streams and consume too much bandwidth that all of

C. Rong et al. (Eds.): ATC 2008, LNCS 5060, pp. 13–20, 2008.
© Springer-Verlag Berlin Heidelberg 2008

the available upload bandwidth in part of P2P media streaming system is exhausted[5]. A DDoS attack to part of the network has happened because other well-behaving nodes will be prevented from downloading media streams.

In this paper we propose a generic DDoS resilience framework for preventing both attacks to data sources and part of the network. To identify DDoS attackers and prevent the system from being corrupted by malicious nodes, our framework employs a CM to allow nodes to evaluate other nodes' behaviors and introduces a MRCM to control the message rate of a node according to its credit level MRCM accomplishes prevention of DDoS by enforcing maximum message rate (the numbers of requests a node sends in a time unit) limits for each participating node. Each node in the P2P streaming network has different message rate limits according to its credit level. In order to prevent both attacks to data sources and part of the network we limit the total message rate and the message rate to data sources for each node. In this framework, MRCM consists of a subset of trusted nodes from the P2P streaming network. The nodes in MRCM will dynamically store message rate information about each node in the P2P streaming network. When the message rate of a node surpasses its message rate limit, MRCM will prevent it from sending more requests until the message rate is below its limit.

Nodes in MRCM are also participants in the underlying P2P streaming overlay. Unlike a solution that uses a central database sever[6] to control nodes' message rate, we provides an approach that avoids a central bottleneck, avoids a central point of failure[7] and provides scalability. According to limiting each node's message rate to data sources and part of the network, we can detect malicious nodes immediately and control the system efficiently. The network can recover quickly even if a few of DDoS attacks have happened.

The rest of the paper is structured as follows: We first introduce the categorization of DDoS attacks in P2P streaming network and propose a novel framework to solve these security problems in Section 2. Section 3 discusses the performance of our framework at preventing DDoS attacks. Section 4 presents a brief summery of this paper.

2 System Design

In this section we first introduce the categorization of DDoS attacks in P2P streaming network. Then we propose a novel framework to prevent these DDoS attacks and then present its two key components: CM and MRCM.

We categorize the DDoS attacks in P2P streaming networks into attacks to data sources and attacks to part of the network. Attacks to data sources may happen because P2P streaming network consists of a limited number of data sources. It is easy to attack data sources for some malicious nodes by sending amounts of requests to data sources. Then other well-behaving nodes will not download media stream from data sources. Attacks to part of the network happen since users can make unrestricted requests in such a system, if many nodes behave selfishly by requesting a large number of media streams and consuming too much bandwidth, then well-behaving nodes might not be able to access media streams that would otherwise be available if all nodes were well-behaved. When one or more nodes exhaust all of the available upload bandwidth in part of P2P media streaming system due to malice, a DDoS attack has occurred because other well-behaving nodes will be prevented from downloading media streams.

In order to prevent both attacks to data sources and attacks to part of the network we propose an interconnection framework consists of CM and MRCM. As shown in Fig. 1, the credit model nodes (CMNs) collect the credit information of each node and inform the information to the MRCM nodes (MRCMNs). The MRCM nodes control the behaviors of the P2P streaming nodes (PSNs) based on their credit level obtained from CMNs. We will discuss CM and MRCM in detail in the following sections.

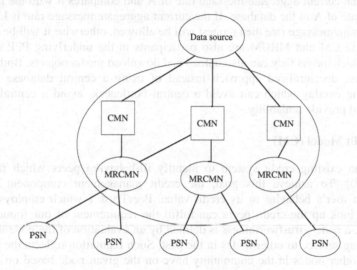

Fig. 1. Internet Interconnection Framework

2.1 Framework

As mentioned above it is important to realize that DDoS could exist in a large-scale P2P media streaming system where attackers are capable of consuming a lot of resources with just a small amount of effort, that is, sending a few requests that take a small amount of bandwidth could lead to receiving several high bandwidth streams that exhaust resources. In order to solve this problem we can maintain a decentralized database that stores the current aggregate message rate of each node in the system as well as the maximum message rate allowed for each node in the system. Meanwhile, we introduce a CM to evaluate the behaviors of each node and calculate their credit level. The node whose credit level is below some value will be referred to as a malicious node. Finally, the essential idea of our proposed framework is to combine an existing credit system to limit the message rate of each node. In our framework, nodes have different maximum message rate based on their credit level. The higher the credit level, the larger the maximum message rate a node can have. Then ill-behaving nodes can not send amounts of requests to both data sources and other nodes.

Our framework consists of two key components: CM and MRCM. CM defines the interface between overlay events or transactions and the underlying credit system. It evaluates each node's credit level dynamically based on some principles which will be described later and informs this value to MRCM. MRCM defines credit-constrained node control mechanism. It maintains a database which stores each node's maximum message rate based on its credit level obtained from CM. When a node A joins the overlay, it first obtains a list of nodes with low credit from a bootstrap mechanism. After joining the overlay, A accumulates credit by fulfilling its duties. When A sends a request to data sources or other nodes, MRCM nodes compute the current aggregate message rate of A and compares it with the maximum message rate of A in the database. If the current aggregate message rate is lower than the maximum message rate then request will be allowed, otherwise it will be cut off.

Nodes in CM and MRCM are also participants in the underlying P2P streaming overlay which means they can also upload and download media objects. Both CM and MRCM use decentralized approach instead of using a central database server to manage the overlay which can avoid a central bottleneck, avoid a central point of failure, and provide scalability.

2.2 Credit Model (CM)

We use an existing credit system to identify ill-behaving peers which mentioned in[8][9][10]. To achieve this goal, the credit management component needs to translate a user's behavior to its credit value. PeerTrust 1 which employs DHT to store and look up the credit peers can fulfill the requirement of our framework. In PeerTrust, a node's trustworthiness is defined by an evaluation of the node it receives in providing service to other nodes in the past. Such reputation reflects the degree of trust that other nodes in the community have on the given node based on their past experiences. It identifies five important factors for credit evaluation: the feedback a node obtains from other nodes, the feedback scope, such as the total number of transactions that a node has with other nodes, the credibility factor for the feedback source, the transaction context factor for discriminating mission-critical transactions from less or noncritical ones and the community context factor for addressing community related characteristics and vulnerabilities. PeerTrust defines the following trust metric:

$$T(u) = \alpha * \sum_{i=1}^{I(u)} S(u,i) * Cr(p(u,i)) * TF(u,i) + \beta * CF(u) \tag{1}$$

In this equation, $T(u)$ denotes the credit of node u, $I(u)$ is the total number of transactions performed by u, $S(u,i)$ is the normalized amount of satisfaction u gets from transaction i, $p(u,i)$ represents the other peer in transaction i, and $Cr(p)$ stands for the credibility of feedbacks from node p. $TF(u,i)$ is the transaction context factor. $CF(u)$ is the community factor of node u, and α and β are normalized weight factors for the collective evaluation and the community context factor.

CM is the fundamental defense mechanism of MRCM. It requires nodes to report their experience to CM. CM works with the underlying overlay to aggregate nodes' experience and calculates their credibility. The credibility will be used by MRCM to classify nodes into different level.

2.3 Message Rate Control Model (MRCM)

The main idea behind MRCM is that selfishness and DDoS attacks in P2P media streaming systems can be prevented by consisting of a subset of trusted nodes form a separate overlay that stores node request information objects. These trusted nodes will be referred to as MRCM nodes and the remaining nodes will be referred to as ordinary nodes. We assume that each ordinary node knows the IP address of the MRCM node that stores its request information. Treating node identifiers from the streaming application overlay as node request information object keys in MRCM, Mj (current message rate for node j) and $Mmax_j$ (maximum message rate for node j) for node j will be stored at the MRCM node to which key j maps according to the P2P lookup protocol. When a node i sends a streaming request, it must query its known MRCM node c about whether or not the request should be allowed. MRCM node c will retrieve Mj and $Mmax_j$ from either its local database of node request information objects or retrieve those values by requesting the node request information object from the MRCM node c ' responsible for storing key j . The underlying P2P lookup protocol can be used to locate and retrieve these objects. Upon receiving Mj and $Mmax_j$, MRCM node c will only gives permission to node j to upload the media object if the additional stream's message rate will not cause Mj to exceed $Mmax_j$.

MRCM consists of a separate overlay of trusted nodes. How can we determine whether or not a node can be trusted to be a MRCM node? In our framework CM is used to evaluate each node's reputation. At the beginning a single node could be the first MRCM node. As time goes on, the MCRM node could collect information from CM that would allow it to determine whether or not other untrusted nodes could be upgraded to trusted node status in order to participate in the MRCM overlay. MRCM nodes may be degraded to ordinary nodes when their credit level becomes lower than some value.

3   Performance Evaluation

In this section, we evaluate the performance of our framework with respect to its effectiveness at preventing DDoS attacks. To evaluate the performance of our framework, we execute two types of simulations of a P2P media streaming application: one where our framework is used and another one where our framework is not used. In each simulation, we observe the ratio of requests allowed for benign and malicious nodes when our framework is used and compare that to the ratio of requests allowed for benign and malicious nodes when our framework is not used. When our framework is not used, each node decides whether or not to grant a request based on whether its upload limit will be exceeded.

In our simulations, we assume that each media object request has a data rate of 400Kbps. We chose to give each node an upload limit of 1 Mbps. Each benign node makes five total requests at most for media objects during each simulation. These requests are spaced between three and five minutes apart. The number of requests from each benign node, the spacing between requests, and the media object keys requested are all random values. Each attacker makes 10 requests for random media object keys that are spaced 100 milliseconds apart. Based on these specified behaviors in our simulation, no benign node will attempt to exceed its message rate limit and every attacker will attempt to exceed its message rate limit.

For the results that appear in Fig. 2, the P2P network had a total of 200 nodes with 10 of those 200 nodes being MRCM nodes. For the results that appear in Fig. 3, the P2P network had a total of 400 nodes with 10 of those 400 nodes being MRCM nodes. In both cases, we varied the number of attackers in our simulations to see how they would affect the fraction of requests allowed for the following categories:

NRA = ratio of normal requests allowed for benign nodes without our framework
NRAF = ratio of normal requests allowed for benign nodes with our framework
MRA = ratio of malicious requests allowed for attackers without our framework
MRAF = ratio of malicious requests allowed for attackers with our framework

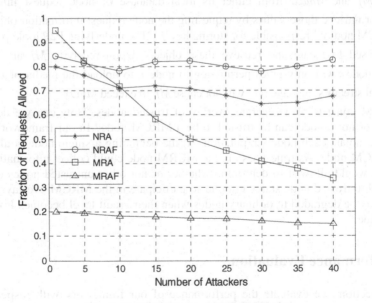

Fig. 2. 200 Total Nodes, 10 MRCM Nodes

As Fig. 2 and Fig. 3 show, a larger ratio of well-behaving nodes' requests are allowed when our framework is used compared to when our framework is not used. More importantly, Fig. 2 and Fig. 3 show that our framework only limits malicious requests from attackers compared to when our framework is not used.

When our framework is not used, each node decides whether a request is upload based on whether its upload limit will be exceeded.

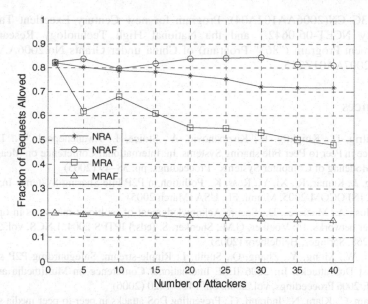

Fig. 3. 400 Total Nodes, 10 MRCM Nodes

Fig. 2 and Fig. 3 also indicate that not all of benign nodes' requests are allowed. This case happens because each has and upload limit of 1 Mbps which can not be exceed. If three benign nodes simultaneously request media objects that happen to be stored at the same node, then at least one benign node will be denied due to upload rate limits.

4 Conclusion

In this paper we present a credit-based supporting framework, which includes CM and MRCM for limiting nodes' message rate to both data source and P2P streaming network. CM and MRCM are implemented decentralized over a structured P2P overlay net work. The benefit of our framework is that it provides a scalable solution while also avoiding the drawbacks of having a bottleneck and central point of failure.

As our simulation shows, these benefits come at the cost of increased overhead because nodes in CM and MRCM must store node credit and request information. However, the benefit of paying these costs is preventing malicious nodes from exhausting the resources of and entire P2P media streaming system. Our evaluations show that our framework can effectively stabilize the overlay and improve the streaming quality under DDoS attacks.

Acknowledgement

This work was supported by National Natural Science Foundation of China under Grant No.60572047, China Hubei Science & Technology Department through project

SBC in 3G CN(2006AA102A04), Program for new Century Excellent Talents in University NCET-06-0642.1 and the National High Technology Research and Development Program ("863" Program) of China under Grants No.2006AA01Z267 and No. 2007AA01Z215.

References

1. Dumitriu, D., Knightly, E., Kuzmanovic, A., Stoica, I., Zwanenepoel, W.: Denial of Service in Peer to Peer File sharing Systems. In: International Conference on Measurement and Modeling of Computer Systems - Proceedings, pp. 38–49 (2005)
2. Liang, J., Kumar, R., Xi, Y., Ross, K.: Pollution in P2P File Sharing Systems. In: Proc. of IEEE INFOCOM 2005, Miami, FL, USA (March 2005)
3. Nicolosi, A., Mazieres, D.: Secure Acknowledgment of multicast messages in open peer-to-peer networks. In: Voelker, G.M., Shenker, S. (eds.) IPTPS 2004. LNCS, vol. 3279, pp. 259–268. Springer, Heidelberg (2005)
4. Wang, W., Xiong, Y., Zhang, Q., Sugih, J.: Ripple-stream: Safeguarding P2P streaming against DoS attacks. In: 2006 IEEE International Conference on Multimedia and Expo, ICME 2006 Proceedings, vol. 2006, pp. 1417–1420 (2006)
5. William, C., Klara, N., Indranil, G.: Preventing DoS attacks in peer-to-peer media streaming systems. In: Proceedings of SPIE-IS and T Electronic Imaging, p. 607–610D (2006)
6. Cao, F., Bryan, D., Lowekamp, B.: Providing secure services in peer-to-peer communications networks with central security servers. In: Proceedings of the Advanced International Conference on Telecommunications and International Conference on Internet and Web Applications and Services, AICT/ICIW 2006, p. 105 (2006)
7. Wang, H., Zhu, Y., Hu, Y.: An efficient and secure peer-to-peer overlay network. In: Proceedings of The IEEE Conference on Local Computer Networks - 30th Anniversary, LCN 2005, pp. 764–771 (2005)
8. Sorge, C., Zitterbart, M.: A reputation-based system for confidentiality modeling in Peer-to-Peer networks. In: Stølen, K., Winsborough, W.H., Martinelli, F., Massacci, F. (eds.) iTrust 2006. LNCS, vol. 3986, pp. 367–381. Springer, Heidelberg (2006)
9. Yu, B., Singh, M.P., Sycara, K.: Developing trust in large-scale peer-to-peer systems. In: 2004 IEEE 1st Symposium on Multi-Agent Security and Survivability, pp. 1–10 (2004)
10. Xiong, L., Liu, L.: PeerTrust: Supporting Reputation-Based Trust for Peer-to-Peer Electronic Communities. IEEE Transactions on Knowledge and Data Engineering 16(7), 843–857 (2004)

Design, Prototype, and Evaluation of a Network Monitoring Library

Karl-André Skevik, Vera Goebel, and Thomas Plagemann

Department of Informatics, University of Oslo,
P.O. Box 1080 Blindern, N-0316 Oslo, Norway
{karlas,goebel,plageman}@ifi.uio.no

Abstract. This article describes a library for customization of overlays. The *custcom* library optimizes and maintains the results of network measurement operations, allowing applications to specify requests for how to prioritize overlay nodes in an abstract manner, without having to implement network measurements operations in order to achieve network awareness.

The library is used in the context of the Autonomic Network Architecture (ANA) project where application functionality is implemented in independent units called *bricks*. A network latency measurement brick and a node monitoring brick have been implemented using the *custcom* library. The *custcom* optimization code has been tested with a real-world dataset, demonstrating how it can reduce network overhead and measurement time.

1   Introduction

Overlay networks can be constructed from geographically distributed nodes with possibly highly variable link and CPU capacity. For applications where network parameters such as peer throughput, latency, or link error rate are important for performance, nodes need some way of obtaining information about the network. The current Internet does not provide any mechanisms for doing this in a simple and reliable manner; applications need to either actively or passively probe the network. Many techniques, some of which are listed below, have been proposed for obtaining these values for Internet applications, but these techniques generally require applications to implement code that makes significant assumptions about network behavior and does not relate to the purpose of the application.

This article describes the core of a monitoring system for the Autonomic Network Architecture (ANA) project[1]. The *custcom* library allows customization of overlay networks based on application specified criteria for ordering and prioritizing participating nodes.

Section 2 gives an overview of work related to network monitoring and peer selection techniques. Section 3 introduces relevant ANA concepts. Section 4 presents the design of the *custcom* library that allows applications to integrate

C. Rong et al. (Eds.): ATC 2008, LNCS 5060, pp. 21–35, 2008.

network awareness and application level information without implementing network monitoring directly in the application. Section 5 describes how the *custcom* library can be integrated into the ANA system. An evaluation of the core optimization function of the *custcom* library is given in Section 6. Section 7 concludes this article.

2 Related Work and Network Awareness

Overlay networks can consist of many nodes, of which a client is only interested in communicating with a small subset based on criteria such as latency or node throughput. Identifying this subset will often involve the same challenges as the peer selection and server selection problem. A look at research in this field reveals the complexity that network aware Internet based applications need to implement.

Popular content is often replicated on multiple servers, and the goal of server selection is to identify the server that offers the shortest download time. Randomly selecting a server is possible but inefficient [2,3]. Instead, many server selection techniques use active probing, and these can be divided into three categories [3]: static, statistical and dynamic. Static server selection techniques use network characteristics that stay relatively stable over time, such as hop count, geographic distance, or Autonomous System (AS) count. These values are generally not affected by current network conditions, causing static server selection techniques to be inefficient [2,4,5]. Statistical approaches consider past behavior, but while they may generally have good performance [5], they do not adapt well to variable network conditions [3]. Best performance is achieved with a dynamic approach, but at the cost of high network overhead and time spent on active probing.

The most direct approach for dynamic selection is to download some data from all available servers and then choose the server with shortest download time. However, because transmitting data is time consuming and not scalable to a large number of servers, many dynamic techniques use latency estimation rather than data transfers. Simply using the mean latency of five 100 Byte ping packets can work well according to Carter et al. [2]. Latency estimation is efficient, but there is no reliable correlation between the measured latency and the transfer time of files larger than 1 MB [4]. The same is the case for estimation techniques based on the transfer of short files: results cannot be assumed to apply for larger files [4]. The difficulty lies in finding an appropriate trade-off between accuracy and overhead.

There are many similarities between server selection and peer selection in P2P networks, but there are also some important differences. Dedicated servers are more likely to be always available, whereas clients in a P2P system may only be active for a few hours. Certain characteristics of end user access technologies are another source of potential problems. The relationship between RTT and throughput for machines using broadband Internet connections is less reliable than for well-connected servers [6]. However, the RTT value, especially the last-hop RTT value, can give an accurate estimate of peer access speeds for access technologies such as dial-up modems, ADSL modems, and cable connections [7].

Work on peer selection includes that by Ng et al.[7], who have examined the efficiency of RTT probing, 10 KB TCP transfers, and bottleneck bandwidth probing in P2P streaming systems. These lightweight techniques can be used to identify fast peers, but they are less effective with respect to differentiating between peers when used alone. The best results were found to be obtainable by combining multiple techniques, such as first using RTT estimation to find the five closest peers and then using bottleneck bandwidth probing or 10 KB transfers to choose from these peers. A similar approach is recommended by Zhang et al. [8]. The authors observe that relying solely on latency distance prediction can lead to significantly reduced application performance. Instead, a subset of close peers is chosen, and then active probing is used on this subset. With this combination of techniques, even simple distance estimation algorithms work well.

It is evident that network monitoring is nontrivial and dependent upon changing factors such as node and link hardware; having code related to this in applications would in the worst case require updates to be made as network technologies change. As discussed below, application design for ANA leads itself naturally to having these operations implemented as services used by network aware applications rather than as part of an application.

The Network Weather Service[9] offers similar functionality as our solution, but the *custcom* library makes it possible to combine application level and network level information in order to achieve network awareness efficiently. The large number of participants in some overlay networks make optimization of active measurements important and the *custcom* library can achieve this while simultaneously reducing application complexity.

3 ANA: Autonomic Network Architecture

ANA is a project that examines legacy free future networking architectures, with a focus on autonomicity. The programming model used in ANA dispenses with the rigid layers of the OSI model and instead uses *bricks* that can be combined to build a *compartment* offering the functionality required by an application. Restrictions such as TCP always being layered on top of IP do not exist, with e.g., arbitrary bricks offering transport functionality being usable to communicate with other nodes in a compartment. Application functionality is divided among specialized bricks, giving a clean and non-monolithic design. This article describes a library that has been designed to be used both in applications directly, and in a specific brick for network monitoring.

4 Library Design

The *custcom* C library is designed for applications that require network awareness and can be used to manage a set of nodes on behalf of an application. Application requirements are specified via a high level query language. The library hides the implementation of network measurement and monitoring operations from applications, but can still be integrated with application specified functions. Since there is no need for applications to implement network awareness, code development is simplified and the library can optimize the order and type of monitoring operations performed. The library has been designed to be usable both with ANA and the current Internet, but only the ANA part has been fully developed at the time of writing.

4.1 Library Interface

An application that uses the *custcom* library first specifies the nodes that constitute the nodeset that it wishes to operate on. It is possible for an application to specify multiple different *queries* that manipulate the nodes in the nodeset. The following pseudocode illustrates these steps:

```
cc_nodeset cc;
cust_init(&cc);

cust_addnode(&cc, "foo.org", "www", NULL);
...

cc_query query;
cust_queryinit(&query, "sort node_rtt;");

cust_ordernodes(&cc, &query);
```

The nodeset is initialized with the function *cust_init()* and one or more nodes are added to the nodeset with *cust_addnode()*. The nodes are initialized with the node identity ("*foo.org*" in the example above), a service name ("*www*"), and an optional pointer to a data structure maintained by the application, in this case *NULL*. The *cust_queryinit()* function initializes a query for the nodeset, and the *cust_ordernodes()* function arranges the nodes in the nodeset according to the specified query. The query is submitted by the application as a text string with one or more query statements. In this example, the query specifies that the nodes are to be sorted based on the ordering specified by the function *node_rtt*. The library supplies several predefined functions for ordering nodes, but applications can provide their own functions using *cust_funcadd()*. The query can include both application supplied functions and library functions in the same query, allowing nodes to be ordered based on both application and network parameters in a single query.

4.2 Query Specification

Each line of the query specification contains a single semicolon terminated command. Three different commands are currently supported. The *sort* command orders all nodes in the nodeset using the specified sorting function. Sorting functions consist of three different types, depending on how they sort nodes: *rank sorting*, *value sorting*, or *full sorting*. A rank sorting function gives each node an integer rank value that is used to order the nodes. A value based sorting function sorts nodes by comparing e.g., the latency of each node. A full sorting function is free to order the nodes in any way.

The most significant difference between rank and value sorting is that a rank based sorting can result in many nodes with the same rank. The *subsort* command can then be used to rearrange the order of nodes with the same rank value based on another criteria. By combining *sort* and *subsort* operations it is possible to rank nodes based on multiple criteria. An application that wishes to identify nodes with low latency and a high available bandwidth value might specify a ranking function that gives nodes a rank value between zero and three, based on whether the ranking function deems the node to be on the same LAN, in the same neighborhood, in the same country, or further away. As long as there are more than four nodes there will in this example be multiple nodes with the same rank. For example, the following query can be used to order nodes based on throughput and an application defined node ranking function:

```
sort app:node_rank;
subsort node_throughput;
```

The third command that can be used in queries is *trim*, and as the name indicates, this command results in a subset of the nodes being returned. The format of a trim command is *"trim param op val"*, where *param* is a parameter such as RTT or throughput, *op* is an operation such as less than (<) or greater than (>), and *val* is a numeric value. To eliminate slow nodes from the ordered set, the query above can be extended as follows:

```
sort app:node_rank;
subsort node_throughput;
trim mbps < 0.1;
```

The trim command only reduces the number of nodes that is returned by a query, it does not change the composition of the full nodeset specified with *cust_init()*.

4.3 Network Measurements

The preceding examples use values such as node throughput and RTT to order nodes, but this cannot be done without obtaining these values in some way. The library keeps track of measurement data for each node, and it can either obtain these values itself through network measurements, or the information can be provided by the application. Typically, the library will obtain the necessary network information by itself using measurement functions implemented in the library, but an application can provide additional values[1]. In the case of ANA, these functions are wrappers around calls to bricks that implement the network measurement operations.

---

[1] Applications that perform operations such as file transfers obtain information about peer throughput during normal program execution. This information can be added to the data maintained by the library.

4.4   Optimizations

The *custcom* library gives applications a simple interface for choosing among a potentially large number of nodes based on criteria such as throughput or latency, but obtaining these values can be time and resource consuming. As discussed in Section 2, there is neither any guarantee that the result will be accurate. The library hides these details, but the measurement operations still need to be performed, ideally as efficiently as possible. To reduce query time and network overhead, the library attempts to optimize submitted queries.

The *cust_ordernodes()* function can be used to sort all the nodes in the nodeset, but for an application that is only interested in, for example, the single node with most available bandwidth, or the ten nodes with lowest latency, the exact ordering of the other nodes is not interesting. The *trim* command can be used to remove uninteresting nodes and, by examining the *trim* commands in a query, the library can in many cases reduce the number of measurement operations needed.

```
sort app:node_rank;
subsort node_throughput;
trim index > 10;
```

For example, in the query above the nodes are first sorted by rank, then the ordering of the nodes with the same rank are sorted internally. Finally, all but the ten first nodes are removed. The resulting ordering gives the ten nodes with lowest latency and highest throughput, but executing these steps sequentially results in a large number of wasted measurement operations if the number of nodes is large. Avoiding the first sorting operation is not possible in this case because RTT information is required for all nodes[2], but the second command can be optimized.

With *subsort*, nodes with a different rank value cannot change place, meaning that in this case it is only necessary to obtain node throughput information for the nodes that can appear among the first ten nodes. If the rank values of the first 20 nodes are as specified below, the nodes with rank three or higher can never be returned, so it is not necessary to perform an internal ordering of these nodes. As a result, the library can reduce the number of required operations quite significantly if there are many nodes in the nodeset.

```
0123456789 0123456789
0001111222|2222333344
          ^^^^^^^^^
```

This *trim index* optimization looks at the effect of the trim statement on the preceding commands, but in some cases it is possible to reorder commands in order to obtain the same result. The statement below sorts the nodes in the node-set by throughput and eliminates the nodes slower than 100 Kbit/s. The *trim* statement is placed at the end, but it is possible to perform this operation first

---

[2] By using an Internet coordinate latency estimation system such as Vivaldi[10], it is possible to obtain these values arithmetically, if the coordinates of all nodes are known.

without changing the result; nodes that have an estimated throughput of less than 100 Kbit/s will never be returned and it is not necessary to include these nodes during sorting. Furthermore, it is possible to use a latency based TCP model[11] to eliminate nodes without actually estimating the node throughput, if the application is willing to sacrifice accuracy for speed. For real-time applications such as VoD streaming systems, a fast answer might be preferable to a very accurate answer.

```
sort node_throughput;
trim mbps < 0.1;
```

An application can still specify queries that cannot be optimized, or queries that will take a long time to complete with a large number of nodes. By itself, the library does not currently provide an interface that allows applications to specify statements such as "return the fastest/closest node". Programmers of applications that use the library still need an understanding of network issues and the potential cost of queries, but the library is designed to be a building block for providing this kind of high level interface.

4.5   Examples

There are many different application types that can benefit from network awareness and that can use the *custcom* library to achieve this. Server selection is one of the more simple scenarios, with a client choosing between a small number of servers offering the same service. For transfers of large files from FTP servers, throughput is the most interesting parameter, so the query below can be used in this case. For server selection, measurement time will not be a problem unless there is a high number of servers.

```
sort node_throughput;
```

BitTorrent and similar P2P file distribution applications generally try to request the rarest blocks of a file first, but using fast peers will usually result in shorter download time. Assuming that the application provides a function *app:rank_blockfreq* that ranks nodes based on the rarity of the blocks on a given node, it is possible to construct the following query, which uses throughput information in order to prefer the fastest nodes that have the rarest blocks.

```
sort app:rank_blockfreq;
subsort node_throughput;
```

4.6   Implementation

The primary challenge for implementing the library is the need to present a simple interface to applications while at the same time being able to perform the necessary measurement operations in an unobtrusive way. For the Internet, measuring network parameters such as throughput, latency, and router hop counts requires the transmission of data, maintenance of timers and timeouts, and possibly blocking operations such as DNS lookups. Furthermore, the node data must be accessible to application provided functions in order to be able to integrate both application level and network level information in queries.

This problem is somewhat similar to the one faced by implementations of *Secure Sockets Layer* (SSL), such as OpenSSL[3]. Establishing and maintaining a SSL protected stream over an already existing connection can involve data being transmitted over the connection in both directions, independently of the data transmitted by the application. A non-blocking socket will require testing for both readability and writeability depending on the SSL state. The SSL library functions handle this by returning an error when an operation would block. Applications can then obtain a status value which indicates whether the SSL library needs to wait for the socket to become readable or writable. The *custcom* library can use a similar approach, but might additionally need to perform operations such as the simultaneous initiation of multiple connections, which cannot be done through the testing of only a single descriptor in a single process.

Instead, the *custcom* implementation has been structured to use a separate process for operations that cannot be performed in a simple manner from the application process. This extra worker process initiates connections, maintains timers, etc., but is controlled by the *custcom* library which is executed in the application process. To initiate an operation in the worker process the library obtains a control socket to the worker process and sends the request over this socket. Control is then returned to the application with a request for testing of readability on the supplied descriptor, in a manner similar to the operation of the OpenSSL library. When the worker process has completed the submitted task it sends the results over the control socket to the application process where the application again calls the library. This separation results in a tight integration between the application and the library that allows application supplied functions that access application state to be used by the library, while still isolating potentially timing sensitive operations from the application.

The design of ANA gives a more natural division of code elements and simpler code. Rather than implementing the monitoring operations directly in the library, they are accessed via bricks that perform these operations. For applications, the benefits from the optimizations described in Section 4.4 will be less directly observable as ANA is designed to have monitoring as a integral function of the system. This is however only as the library can be used at two levels; as a general monitoring brick used to optimize monitoring operations by all bricks, and inside applications, in order to integrate application level and network level information through a high-level interface.

4.7 Summary

The *custcom* library gives applications a simple interface to network level information about nodes. However, the primary strength of the library is not in simply removing the need for implementing techniques for estimating latency or available bandwidth, even though this also is beneficial.

---
[3] See http://www.openssl.org

The library allows network measurement operations implemented in the library to be combined with application specified functions in the same query specification. The resulting query can then be optimized by the library in order to reduce the number of measurement operations and the total execution time. Furthermore, the text based query specification is simple to modify, simplifying experimentation with different ordering mechanisms in order to achieve better application performance.

5   Custcom Monitoring Brick

To demonstrate how *custcom* can be integrated in an ANA monitoring architecture we have implemented a monitoring brick that can be used by other bricks to monitor or perform *custcom* queries on a specified nodeset. As there is currently no available ANA brick that offers network transport service, apart from an Ethernet brick for LAN communication[4], it is still not possible to build a system where the *custcom* optimization features can be put to proper use, but we have created an implementation based on a brick offering Ethernet based communication to verify that it is possible to integrate the *custcom* library in ANA. As more ANA functionality becomes available, more complicated usage scenarios will be tested.

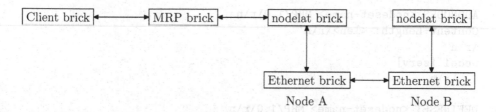

Fig. 1. Brick structure

The brick composition has the structure given in Figure 1. The *nodelat* brick offers a simple latency estimation service on top of the Ethernet brick. The *nodelat* brick is called by the Monitoring Request Protocol (MRP) brick, which contains the *custcom* functionality. A simple client brick makes application-like requests from the MRP brick.

5.1   MRP Overview

The Monitoring Request Protocol allows clients to request monitoring or ordering of a set of nodes using the following seven commands: *DEFINESET, ORDER, MONITOR, STATUS, ADDNODES, RMNODES, DELETESET.*

---

[4] The drawback with a legacy free, start-from-scratch approach to network research is that all the functionality that is taken for granted on the current Internet must be reimplemented.

The client application lists the nodes in the nodeset and specifies how they are to be monitored. In ANA, there is currently no generic way of obtaining a list of nodes participating in a compartment, but support for compartments that support this might be added later, removing the need for applications to specify each node.

A set of nodes is defined with the DEFINESET command along with a nodeset name. The ADDNODES and RMNODES commands modify the members of a named nodeset, and DELETE removes the defined nodeset entirely. The ORDER command is used to request an ordering of nodes, based on either a named function for node ordering or using a *custcom* query directly. Long-term monitoring of nodes based on various criteria such as node availability (liveliness), RTT, and transfer rate can be requested using the MONITOR command. The STATUS command returns a text listing of the status of each node.

5.2 MRP Syntax

The statements below show the syntax of the MRP commands. The general syntax is similar to the HTTP protocol. Lines are terminated by two carriage return and newline characters and a blank line ends a request. Supplementary data can follow some of the commands, with the length of this data given by a *Content-Length* header.

```
ADDNODES <nodeset-name> MRP/1.0\r\n
Content-Length: <len>\r\n
\r\n
node1 [serv]
...\r\n

DEFINESET <nodeset-name> MRP/1.0\r\n
Content-Length: <len>\r\n
\r\n
node1 [serv]\r\n
node2 [serv]\r\n
...\r\n

DELETESET <nodeset-name> MRP/1.0\r\n
\r\n

MONITOR <nodeset-name> MRP/1.0
Value: liveliness|rtt|rate|hops\r\n
Interval: <seconds>
\r\n

ORDER <nodeset-name> MRP/1.0
Rank: lowest-rtt <N>|highest-rate <N>\r\n
\r\n
```

```
ORDER <nodeset-name> MRP/1.0
Rankspec: "sort by rank_rtt;
           trim index > 10;"\r\n
\r\n

RMNODES <nodeset-name> MRP/1.0\r\n
Content-Length: <len>\r\n
\r\n
node1 [serv]
...\r\n

STATUS <nodeset-name> MRP/1.0\r\n
\r\n
```

5.3   MRP Brick Implementation

An MRP brick has been implemented which supports latency based monitoring, ordering, and status reporting of a specified set of nodes. The functionality is demonstrated in a MRP client brick that uses broadcast via the Ethernet brick to discover the members of the *nodelat* compartment. This discovery operation is performed at regular intervals and the discovered nodes are added to a nodeset defined at the MRP brick. At regular intervals the client brick requests a status report and a latency based ordering of the compartment nodes. Nodes that become unavailable are eventually marked as *down* if they fail to reply to multiple latency requests.

6   Evaluation

The current lack of WAN network transport functionality in ANA makes it difficult to test the MRP brick in any meaningful environments, but we have tested the core of the *custcom* library which is used in the MRP brick.

6.1   Library Optimizations

To illustrate the operation of the optimization function in the *custcom* library, we have used latency data from the *Hourglass project*[5]. The first node in this dataset is used to represent a client node running the *custcom* library, and the 432 other nodes represent the other participants in the overlay network. The distribution of RTT values from the client node to these nodes is shown in Figure 2. The figure also shows the ranking values given by a *custcom* ranking function, where each increase in rank roughly corresponds to a 50% reduction in the throughput predicted by a TCP model[12], assuming low packet loss and an *MSS* of 1448 bytes.

Table 1 shows the results of using optimization for the *trim index* command in following query:

---

[5] http://www.eecs.harvard.edu/~syrah/nc/

```
sort rank_rtt;
subsort node_throughput;
trim index > 10;
```

The number of RTT estimates cannot be reduced but the optimization is able to eliminate almost 90% of the throughput measurement operations. The benefits from the *custcom* optimization technique will clearly depend on the contents of a given query statement and the node composition of the overlay, but the results show the potential for reducing the query execution time and the resources spent on measurements.

6.2   MRP Brick

Section 5.3 describes the MRP demo brick, which locates and monitors ANA nodes on an Ethernet. Every 11 seconds it requests an RTT based node ordering from the MRP brick, and every 13 seconds it requests the current status of the known nodes. Table 2 shows the status output from the demo brick, generated during an experiment on April 1, 2008. The values correspond to the RTT in microseconds.

The test network was configured with the ANA software running on three nodes: the node running the demo brick, *Node A*, and *Node B*. The ANA software

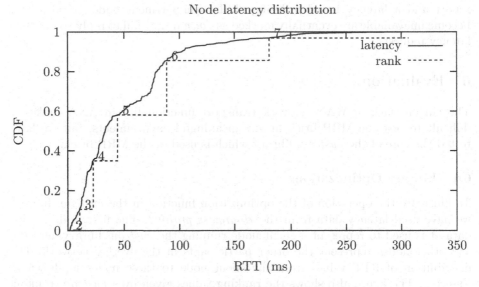

Fig. 2. Node latency distribution

Table 1. Optimization effects

Optimization	Node total	RTT estimates	Throughput estimates
None	432	432	432
Enabled	432	432	45

Table 2. MRP brick status output

Node A	-	-	-	-	-	-	11 .00
Node B	UNKNOWN	148.00	148.00	349.00	349.00	494.00	494.00
Node A (cont.)	11.00	319.00	319.00	352.00	352.00	364.00	364.00
Node B (cont.)	494.00	370.00	370.00	345.00	345.00	373.00	373.00
Node A (cont.)	364.00	14.00	14.00	10.00	10.00	11.00	11.00
Node B (cont.)	373.00	373.00	373.00	373.00	373.00	DOWN	DOWN
Node A (cont.)	250.00	250.00	250.00				
Node B (cont.)	DOWN	DOWN	DOWN				

on *Node B* is already running when the demo brick is started, while *Node A* is started after the demo brick. *Node B* is terminated at the end of the session. The four rows show the status values for the entire run. The *UNKNOWN* value indicates that the first status output is requested before the monitoring has started, while the *DOWN* values indicate that the MRP brick has detected the brick as being unavailable. This occurs after the timeout of multiple RTT estimation attempts.

The MRP demo requests monitoring of the known nodes every 15 seconds. The same values are repeated several times in the table because the status output is requested more frequently than the nodes are monitored.

The limitations of the test environment prevent any extensive experiments, but the results serve to demonstrate a simple application based on the *custcom* library.

6.3 Compartments

The compartment concept is central to ANA and the MRP brick is meant to utilize this by allowing applications to rank compartment nodes. A practical problem encountered during design of the MRP brick was the need to have the client brick manage the list of nodes in a compartment. This requires the client brick to notify the MRP brick of changes in the compartment, resulting in increased client complexity and potentially runs the risk of having the MRP brick operate on outdated information.

The ideal solution would be to have the node composition of a compartment available to the MRP brick on demand, allowing it to be requested only when needed. We plan to examine possible ways of achieving this, either through a generic interface, or if this is not possible, by adding a specific interface for compartments that can benefit from use of the MRP brick.

7   Conclusion

It is not trivial to add support for network awareness in Internet applications. The *custcom* library described in this article represents a way of optimizing network measurement operations in applications, whether on the Internet or in ANA. We have implemented an ANA brick that accepts requests for monitoring operations. The brick does not implement these operations itself, but optimizes requests in order to limit the total number of measurement operations that are performed. The brick can be used by any other brick that needs network information, leading to reduced overhead when similar operations are requested from different bricks. The MRP brick stores the results of measurement operations and can reuse this information in multiple requests. The MRP brick is not needed on all nodes in order to use this system, only monitoring bricks such as *nodelat* must run on all nodes.

The current implementation and evaluation shows that it is possible to integrate the *custcom* library in ANA, but more work is planned in this area. Two main directions are planned for further work. First, on the *custcom* code, in order to examine the possibility of simplifying the query language by allowing more abstract queries by application. Second, through the implementation and testing of a WAN overlay video streaming application scenario where network awareness is important for performance.

Acknowledgment

This work has been funded by the EC-funded ANA Project (FP6-IST-27489), and supported by the CONTENT Network-of-Excellence.

References

1. Sestinim, F.: Situated and autonomic communication an ec fet european initiative. SIGCOMM Computer Communication Review 36(2), 17–20 (2006)
2. Carter, R.L., Crovella, M.E.: Server selection using dynamic path characterization in wide-area networks. In: INFOCOM 1997: Proceedings of the Sixteenth Annual Joint Conference of the IEEE Computer and Communications Societies. Driving the Information Revolution, p. 1014 (1997)
3. Dykes, S.G., Robbins, K.A., Jeffery, C.L.: An empirical evaluation of client-side server selection algorithms. In: INFOCOM 2000: Proceedings of the Nineteenth Annual Joint Conference of the IEEE Computer and Communications Societies, pp. 1361–1370 (2000)
4. Hanna, K.M., Natarajan, N., Levine, B.N.: Evaluation of a novel two-step server selection metric. In: ICNP 2001: Proceedings of the 9th International Conference on Network Protocols, pp. 290–300 (2001)
5. Sayal, M., Breitbart, Y., Scheuermann, P., Vingralek, R.: Selection algorithms for replicated web servers. SIGMETRICS Performance Evaluation Review 26(3), 44–50 (1998)
6. Lakshminarayanan, K., Padmanabhan, V.N.: Some findings on the network performance of broadband hosts. In: IMC 2003: Proceedings of the 3rd ACM SIGCOMM conference on Internet measurement, pp. 45–50. ACM Press, New York (2003)
7. Ng, T.S.E., Chu, Y.H., Rao, S.G., Sripanidkulchai, K., Zhang, H.: Measurement-based optimization techniques for bandwidth-demanding peer-to-peer systems. In: INFOCOM 2003: Proceedings of the Twenty-Second Annual Joint Conference of the IEEE Computer and Communications Societies (2003)

8. Zhang, R., Tang, C., Hu, Y.C., Fahmy, S., Lin, X.: Impact of the inaccuracy of distance prediction algorithms on internet applications: an analytical and comparative study. In: INFOCOM 2006: Proceedings of the 25th Annual Joint Conference of the IEEE Computer and Communications Societies (April 2006)
9. Wolski, R., Spring, N.T., Hayes, J.: The network weather service: a distributed resource performance forecasting service for metacomputing. Future Generation Computer Systems 15(5-6), 757–768 (1999)
10. Dabek, F., Cox, R., Kaashoek, F., Morris, R.: Vivaldi: a decentralized network coordinate system. SIGCOMM Computer Communication Review 34(4), 15–26 (2004)
11. Mathis, M., Semke, J., Mahdavi, J.: The macroscopic behavior of the tcp congestion avoidance algorithm. SIGCOMM Computer Communication Review 27(3), 67–82 (1997)
12. Padhye, J., Firoiu, V., Towsley, D., Kurose, J.: Modeling tcp throughput: a simple model and its empirical validation. SIGCOMM Computer Communication Review 28(4), 303–314 (1998)

Real-Time IP Checking and Packet Marking for Preventing ND-DoS Attack Employing Fake Source IP in IPv6 LAN

Gaeil An and Kiyoung Kim

Network Security Research Division,
Electronics and Telecommunications Research Institute (ETRI),
161 Gajeong-dong, Yuseong-gu, Daejon, 305-350, Korea
{fogone,kykim}@etri.re.kr

Abstract. IPv6 has been proposed as a basic Internet protocol for realizing a ubiquitous computing service. An IPv6 LAN may suffer from a Neighbor Discovery-Denial of Service (ND-DoS) attack, which results in network congestion on the victim IPv6 LAN by making a great number of Neighbor Discovery protocol messages generated. A ND-DoS attacker may use a fake source IP address to hide his/her identity, which makes it more difficult to handle the attack. In this paper, we propose an IP checking and packet marking scheme, which is applied to an IPv6 access router. The proposed scheme can effectively protect IPv6 LAN from ND-DoS attack employing fake source IP by providing the packets suspected to use fake source and/or destination IP addresses with a poor QoS.

1 Introduction

IPv6 has been proposed as a basic Internet protocol for realizing a ubiquitous computing service [1]. Even though IPv6 is much better than IPv4 in the point of view of network scalability and functionality such as address space, routing, QoS, and etc., IPv6 is not stronger than IPv4 in the point of view of security [2].

For example, one of the most common forms of network attacks is an IP spoofing attack [3] in which an attacker forges the source IP address of a network packet, the destination IP, or both of them. As a way for preventing the attack, an ingress filtering scheme [4] has been popularly used in current IPv4 networks. The schemes check the validity of the source IP address of an incoming packet at an edge router. The demerit of the ingress filtering scheme is that it can not detect an attack packet spoofed to the source IP address of any other node on the same local area network (LAN) as the attacker. This is because the schemes use a routing table that stores location information not by a host, but by a group of hosts, thereby allowing an attacker to spoof a packet to the IP address of a non-working host on the same LAN (i.e., unoccupied IP address). As it is well known, the address space of IPv6 is still larger than that of IPv4 because IPv6 uses 128-bit IP address while IPv4 uses 32-bit IP address. So, the number of IP addresses unoccupied by an IPv6 LAN will be greater than by a IPv4 LAN. This makes the schemes used in IPv4 more difficult to protect IPv6 LAN from IP spoofing attack.

C. Rong et al. (Eds.): ATC 2008, LNCS 5060, pp. 36–46, 2008.

IP spoofing attack has been typically used being combined with Denial of Service (DoS) attack [5]. In IPv6 LAN, there is an attack called Neighbor Discovery-DoS (ND-DoS) attack [6][7], which is a kind of IP spoofing attack combined with DoS attack and can cause more severe damage to a victim IPv6 LAN. An attacker can result in ND-DoS attack by fabricating attack packets composed of the randomly generated suffix IP part and the right prefix IP part of the victim IPv6 LAN and by continuously sending the packets to the victim IPv6 LAN. The last IPv6 access router is obligated to resolve these abnormal IP addresses by broadcasting a Neighbor Discovery protocol (NDP) [8][9] message on the victim IPv6 LAN. The enormous number of ND protocol messages result in consuming network resources, thereby degrading the quality of service (QoS) for normal network traffic. A ND-DoS attacker may use a fake source IP address to hide his/her identity, which make it more difficult to detect the attack.

This paper focuses on ND-DoS attack employing fake source IP address. In this paper, we propose an IP checking and packet marking scheme, which is applied to an IPv6 access router to effectively prevent ND-DoS attack from paralyzing an IPv6 LAN. The IP checking is used to check if the IP address of an incoming packet is a working or a non-working IP. In our architecture, the packet with working IP gets a high-priority of service while the packet with non-working IP get low-priority of service in packet forwarding service. The packet marking is used to mark a packet with non-working IP as a suspicious packet at the ingress IPv6 access router. The marked packet may be discarded or forwarded using low-priority of service by the egress IPv6 access router.

The rest of this paper is organized as follows. Section 2 introduces IP spoofing attack and ND-DoS attack. Section 3 describes our scheme. The performance of the proposed scheme is evaluated in section 4. Finally, conclusion is given in section 5.

2 IP Spoofing Attack and ND-DoS Attack

An IP spoofing attack is one of the most common forms of network attacks. An IP spoofing attack can be divided by a source IP spoofing attack [3] that forges a source IP address and a network scan attack [10] that forges a destination IP address.

The source IP spoofing attack is generally done to hide attacker's identity. It can be commonly found in DoS attack that generates a huge volume of traffic to paralyze a victim system or network. To check if a source IP address is valid, an ingress filtering technology has been currently used in edge router. The technology checks the validity of the source IP address of a packet coming from a LAN by using a routing table. The demerit of the technology is that it can not detect an attack packet spoofed to the source IP address of any other node on the same LAN as the attacker. This is because the technology uses a routing table that stores location information not by a host, but by a group of hosts.

A network attacker may accidentally spoof the destination IP address in the process of a network scan attack, which is used to know the configuration of a victim network because an attacker is interested in identifying active hosts and application services that run on those hosts. For example, a worm virus, such as Limda and Slammer, randomly scans a network to find victim systems with weak point. To detect the network scan attack, the previous research has observed whether TCP connection request succeeds or fails [11]. If the failure count/rate of the connection requests initiated by a source is very high, then the source is regarded as the network scanner. The approach is a kind of passive defense scheme in that it could not notice the network scan attack until the failure count/rate of the connection requests is calculated. So it is not easy to provide a real-time reaction against the attack because an attacker can generate attack packets using each different abnormal IPs including fake source IP.

A network scan attack may cause more severe damage to a victim network in case that it is combined with DoS attack. There is a Neighbor Discovery Protocol (NDP) [8][9], which is known as one of the most significant protocols in IPv6 because it provides IP auto-configuration [1]. NDP is used by IPv6 nodes on the same link to discover each other's presence and link layer addresses, to find default routers, and to maintain reachability information about the paths to active neighbors. NDP defines five types of messages, Neighbor Solicitation (NS), Neighbor Advertisement (NA), Router Solicitation (RS), Router Advertisement (RA), and Redirect. NS message is used to request link-layer address of a neighbor node. The node that receives a NS message sends back a NA message giving its link-layer address. RS message is used to discover default routers and to learn the network prefixes. The router that receives a RS message sends back a RA message. Redirect message is used by router to inform other nodes of a better first hop toward a destination.

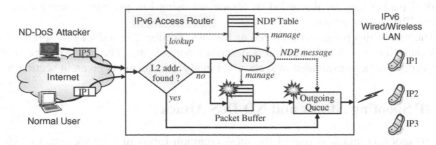

Fig. 1. Architecture of IPv6 access router and ND-DoS attack: ND-DoS attack raises congestion in the packet buffer and the outgoing queue

The NDP is very vulnerable to a mutative network scan attack called ND-DoS attack despite having defined a Secure Neighbor Discovery (SEND) protocol [12][13] proposed to protect the NDP from attacks to spoof NDP messages. In the ND-DoS attack, an attacker continuously sends a great number of packets with fake destination IP address of which prefix address is a real prefix address of the victim IPv6 LAN, but suffix address is a fake. The access router of the victim IPv6 LAN is obligated to resolve these fake addresses by broadcasting NDP signaling messages on the LAN. The enormous numbers of NDP messages cause network congestion on the LAN, thereby degrading QoS for the normal network traffic.

Fig. 1 shows the architecture of an IPv6 access router for processing NDP. When an IPv6 access router receives a data packet, if the link-layer address of the packet is founded in NDP table, then the router just forwards the packet to its destination node using its link-layer address. Otherwise, the router stores the packet in a packet buffer, sends out a NS message, and waits for a NA message. If the router receives a NA message, it looks for the packets in the packet buffer that correspond to the link-layer address included in the NA message, forwards them to their destination nodes. For example, in Fig. 1 when a IPv6 access router receives a packet with destination IP address IP1, if it does not know its link-layer address then it stores the packet in the packet buffer and performs NDP. Subsequently, NDP sends out a NS message and after a while it receives a NA message from the IP1 node. The NA message includes the link-layer address of IP1 node. Finally, the router forwards the packet with the destination IP address, IP1 to the IP1 node using its link-layer address.

The attacker can execute a ND-DoS attack on an IPv6 wire/wireless LAN by bombarding the IPv6 access router with packets with fictitious destination addresses, causing the router to busy itself by performing address resolution for non-working destination IP addresses. For example, in Fig. 1 when the IPv6 access router receives a packet with destination IP address IP5, it sends out a NS message to discovery the link-layer address of the packet. But, the router will never receive any NA message in response to the NS message because the destination IP address of the packet is a fictitious address that does not exist on the IPv6 LAN.

ND-DoS attack results in congestion at the following two points: packet buffer and outgoing queue. Generally, an attacker brings about a great number of NS messages on the target IPv6 LAN by generating a large number of abnormal data packets with non-working destination IP address and by sending them to the target IPv6 LAN. A large number of abnormal data packets may make the packet buffer of the IPv6 access router full, causing drop of normal data packets that waits for NA message. A great number of NS message may also result in network congestion on the target IPv6 LAN and cause normal data packet to experience congestion at outgoing queue. As a result, the QoS for the normal data packet is degraded.

There have been proposed a rate-limit scheme [14] and a compact neighbor discovery scheme [7], which are able to prevent outgoing queue congestion by reducing the volume of NS messages. The rate-limit scheme limits the bandwidth for NDP messages to a threshold. But, the scheme is likely to have a problem that normal packets are dropped because not only NS message for abnormal packet but also NS message for normal packet can be dropped under ND-DoS attack. The compact neighbor discovery scheme uses only a single NS message instead of multiple NS messages in discovering the link-layer addresses of multiple packets. It is said that the scheme can achieve a bandwidth gain around 40 percent in the target IPv6 LAN. However, this scheme does not address the issue of protecting normal packets from congestion.

3 Prevention of ND-DoS Attack Employing Fake Source IP

In this session, we propose an IP checking and packet marking scheme that is able to effectively defeat ND-DoS attack employing fake source IP.

3.1 Real-Time IP Checking and Packet Marking

In dealing with ND-DOS attack, one of the most important things is to draw a clear line between a normal packet and an abnormal. We pay attention to a fact that a non-working (unoccupied) IP is occasionally used in an IP spoofing attack. This happens because an attacker has no perfect knowledge on topology of his/her own LAN and the victim's LAN. Our strategy for detecting ND-DoS attack is to check whether the source and the destination IP addresses of the incoming packet really exist on the source and the destination LANs, respectively. If yes, the packet is regarded as a normal packet. Otherwise, it is suspected as an abnormal packet. To collect the topology information of the source and the destination LAN, the IPV6 access router of each LAN monitors all the packets coming from its own LAN.

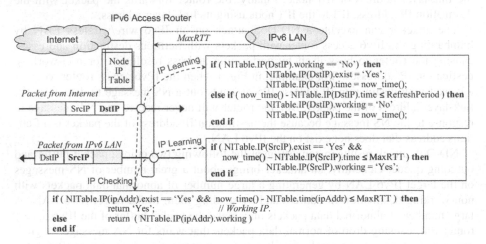

Fig. 2. Real-time IP learning and checking at IPv6 access router

In this paper, we propose algorithms for a real-time IP learning and checking as shown in Fig. 2. The IP learning is used to allow an IPv6 access router to construct a Node IP table composed of the IP addresses of the working nodes on the LAN and to check the validity of the IP address of an incoming packet by looking up the Node IP table. If an IPv6 access router receives a packet from an external network (i.e., Internet), it register its destination IP in the node IP table because it makes sure that the destination IP exists on the LAN, even if it has no idea whether there is a real owner of the destination IP on the LAN. If the IPv6 access router find that the registered destination IP is used as the source IP of a packet coming from the LAN within a predefined time (i.e., *MaxRTT*: a maximum round trip time between the IPv6 access router and the IPv6 LAN), then it regards the destination IP as a working IP being actually used by someone on the LAN. To handle the case that working nodes become not working, the IP learning algorithm refreshes the Node IP table every predefined time period, *RefreshPeriod*, as shown in Fig. 2.

The packet using a working IP is regarded as a normal packet and the packet using a non-working IP as a suspicious packet. Our IP checking scheme is not a hundred percent correct because it requires IP learning. To weaken the problem, we use a differentiated packet forwarding service and a packet marking when handling the suspicious packets. In our scheme, IPv6 access router provides the normal packet with a high-priority packet forwarding service and the suspicious packet with a low-priority service. At the same time, the suspicious packet is marked by an ingress IPv6 access router to notify the egress IPv6 access router which one is a suspicious packet with fake source IP.

To support our packet-marking concept proposed in this paper, we need a field in IPv6 header. There is a 'traffic class' field in IPv6 header to show priority or class for a packet. The six most signification bits of the 'traffic class' byte are now used by Differentiated Service (DiffServ) [15]. The last two bits are now reserved for use of Explicit Congestion Notification (ECN) [15]. Until now, DS5 in DiffServ has been always 0 [16]. We are thinking that to use the DS5 bit as a marking is better than to use the ECN bit.

3.2 Architecture of IPv6 Access Router Supporting Our Scheme

Fig. 3 shows the architecture of an IPv6 access router supporting our scheme, which can defeat ND-DOS attack. Our architecture consists of an IP learning module that collects the IP addresses of the working nodes and constructs the Node IP table introduced in section 3.1, a packet marking that marks a suspicious packet with a non-working source IP address, a NDP modified by this paper, and a packet buffer that stores a NDP-requested data packets and its priority.

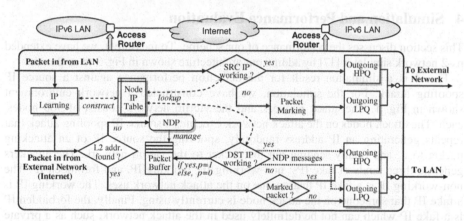

Fig. 3. Architecture of IPv6 access router supporting our scheme against ND-DoS attack

A ND-DoS attacker may spoof the source IP address of the attack packets to hide his/her identity. To detect such source IP spoofing attack, if an ingress IPv6 access router receives an IP packet from its own LAN, it checks whether the source IP address of the incoming packet is a working IP or a non-working by looking up the node IP table. If its source IP is a working IP, it is regarded as a normal packet, otherwise it is regarded as a suspicious packet with fake source IP address. The suspicious packets are forwarded to the next node using the low-priority queue after being marked as 'suspicious' while the normal packets are forwarded using the high-priority queue. The marked packet may be differently handled according to the security policy of its destination IPv6 access router. For example, an IPv6 access router might discard the marked packet in case of network congestion or forward it using a low-priority of queue. In this paper, we provide the marked packet with a low-priority of queue, instead of discarding it.

The egress IPv6 access router takes the responsibility of mitigating the ND-DoS attack by checking the destination of an incoming packet and by checking whether it is marked. From now, we will explain how the egress IPv6 access router supporting our scheme operates to prevent ND-DoS attack, in details. As shown in Fig. 3, when the egress IPv6 access router receives a packet from the external network, if it does not know the link-layer address of the packet, then it checks whether the destination IP address of the packet is a working by looking up the Node IP table. If yes, the packet is regarded as a high-priority packet. Otherwise, it is regarded as a low-priority packet and dealt badly by NDP. NDP stores the packet in the packet buffer until it knows its link-layer address. The Packet buffer may experience congestion which results in dropping normal packets. To prevent it, we employ a priority-based buffer management in which if the packet buffer is full, NDP discards the oldest one among low-priority packets. Subsequently, NDP needs to broadcast a NDP signaling message including the destination IP address of the packet to know the link-layer address of the packet. The signaling message for a high-priority packet is sent out using high-priority of queue while the signaling message for a low-priority packet is sent out using low-priority of queue. Finally, if NDP receives a replay message, it sends out all the data packets corresponding to the link-layer address that the reply message includes.

4 Simulation and Performance Evaluation

This section discusses the performance of our scheme. To measure it, we have extended ns-2 network simulator [17] by adding our architecture shown in Fig. 3 to ns-2 node.

Fig. 4 is a simulation result for the detection performance against a source IP spoofing attack. For the simulation, we have constructed a network environment shown in Fig. 1. The attack network and the victim network consist of 500 nodes, each. The attack nodes on the attack network executes a source IP spoofing attack that repeats generating an IP address randomly, spoofing the source IP of an attacking packet to it, and finally sending out the packet to the victim network. The attackers generate three kinds of fake IPs: non-working IP, working IP, and forbidden IP. The non-working IP is a fake IP that no one on the attack network uses. The working IP is a fake IP that someone on the attack node is currently using. Finally, the forbidden IP is a fake IP which can not be definitely used in the attack network, such as a private IP or an IP being used in other networks.

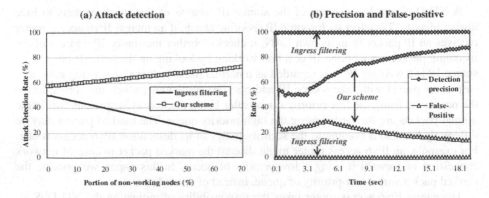

Fig. 4. Detection performance against source IP spoofing attack

Fig. 4-(a) shows the detection rate of the ingress filtering scheme and our scheme against a source IP spoofing attack of when we increase the portion of the non-working IP address among the fake IP addresses. Our scheme is better than the ingress filtering scheme in detection rate and its performance is directly proportional to the number of the non-working nodes. This is because our scheme can detect an attack packet spoofed to a non-working IP. When the portion of non-working nodes is zero percent in Fig. 4-(a), the detection rate of our scheme is not same as that of the ingress filtering. This is because in the experiment some of the 500 nodes started network communication late, and their IP was late registered in the Node IP table. For this reason, our scheme could detect attack packets spoofed to even working IP, even though the ability did not last long.

As explained in the previous section, our IP checking scheme needs IP learning to construct the node IP table. So, our scheme suffers from false-positive error (i.e., to judge a normal packet to be an attack packet) and is worse than the ingress filtering scheme in detection precision, as shown in fig. 4-(b). However, the more IP learning time our scheme has, the more the false-positive error of our scheme decrease and the more the detection rate of our scheme increase. Moreover, our scheme marks packets judged suspicious instead of dropping them. This can make it possible to weaken the false-positive problem.

Fig. 5 and Fig. 6 are simulation results for the reaction performance of our scheme against a ND-DoS attack using fake source IP address. As the network topology for the simulation of ND-DoS attack, we have constructed the networks shown in Fig. 1. In the simulation networks, a ND-DoS attacker and normal users are connected to an external network using a link with the bandwidth of 3Mbps and the delay of 5ms. The victim LAN has the bandwidth of 3Mb and the delay of 20ms, and uses a MAC 802.3 Ethernet protocol. The access router on the victim LAN is connected to the external network using a link with the bandwidth of 3Mbps and the delay of 2ms. Even though the default queue of the router is FIFO queue, when it employs our scheme it uses a priority queue instead of FIFO. In the simulation, normal users generate UDP packets at 1 Mbps, and then send them to the victim LAN. A malicious user generates UDP packets of which source IP and/or destination IP is spoofed increasing by 6Kbit per second, and then sends them to the victim LAN to results in ND-DoS attack.

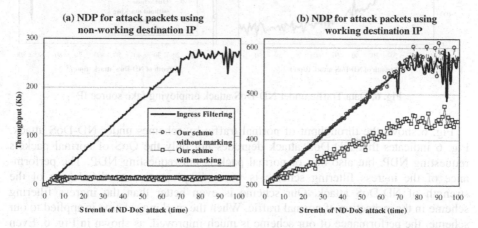

Fig. 5. NDP messages under ND-DoS attack employing fake source IP

Fig. 5 shows the throughput of NDP messages triggered by attack packets. Fig. 5-(a) and (b) are the simulation results of when attack packets are spoofed to non-working destination IP and when attack packets are spoofed to working destination IP, respectively. Once ND-DoS attack starts, it cause a great number of NDP messages to be generated on the victim LAN. The ingress filtering scheme does not control the NDP messages for the ND-DoS attack, as shown in Fig. 5-(a), because it can not detect attack using non-working IP. On the other hand, our scheme distinguishes whether the IP address of an incoming packet is a non-working or a working, and also provides the NDP message for a suspicious packet using non-working IP with a low-priority of service and the NDP message for a normal packet using working IP with a high-priority of service. Our scheme chocks the throughput of the NDP messages for the ND-DoS attack, as shown Fig. 5-(a).

In case of the ND-DoS attack that attack packets are spoofed to working destination IP, even though our scheme can not defeat it perfectly, it can block or weaken the attack. If the ND-DoS attack node does not spoof its source IP, it is not difficult to find out who the attack node is because the attack node among source nodes is typically one who generates the most packets. If the ND-DoS attack employs source IP spoofing attack, our scheme can weaken the attack by using packet marking proposed in this paper, as shown in Fig. 5-(b). The packet marking scheme improves the security performance of our scheme by notifying the access router which one is a suspicious packet with fake source IP.

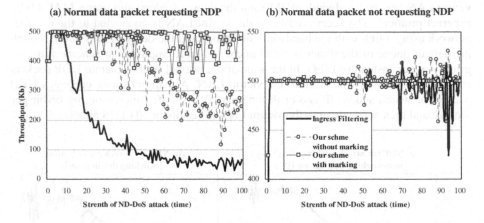

Fig. 6. Data Traffic under ND-DoS attack employing fake source IP

Fig. 6 shows the throughput of normal traffic by schemes under ND-DoS attack. Fig. 6 indicates that ND-DoS attack degrades not only the QoS of normal packets requesting NDP, but also that of normal packets not requesting NDP. The performance of the ingress filtering scheme is worse in proportion to the degree of the strength of ND-DoS attack. Our scheme is even better than the ingress filtering scheme in the protection of normal traffic. When the marking scheme is applied to our scheme, the performance of our scheme is much improved, as shown in Fig. 6. Even though our scheme is able to defeat ND-DoS attack using non-working IP address, it does not perfectly guarantees the bandwidth of the normal data traffic requested, as shown in Fig. 6-(a). This is because the ND-DoS attacker in this simulation has used not only a non-working IP, but also a working IP.

5 Conclusion

IPv6 has been proposed as a basic Internet protocol for realizing a ubiquitous computing service.

This paper deals with ND-DoS attack employing fake source IP address, which can give an IPv6 LAN trouble. In this paper, we have proposed and simulated the real-time IP checking and packet marking scheme that can effectively protect IPv6 LAN from ND-DoS attack employing fake source IP by providing the packets suspected to use fake source and/or destination IP addresses with a poor QoS. The simulation results demonstrates that our scheme protect QoS of normal packet from not only a simple ND-DoS attack, but also a crafty ND-DoS attack employing fake source IP address.

Even though our scheme can defeat ND-DoS attack using abnormal IP very excellently, it is weak in handling DoS attack using working IP. Our future work is to make our scheme stronger so as to be able to mitigate such DoS attack.

Acknowledgement

This work was supported by the IT R&D program of MIC/IITA [2007-S-023-01, Development of the threat containment for all-in-one mobile devices on convergence networks]".

References

1. Altug, R.O., Akinlar, C.: Unique Subnet Auto-configuration in IPv6 Networks. In: Parr, G., Malone, D., Ó Foghlú, M. (eds.) IPOM 2006. LNCS, vol. 4268, pp. 108–119. Springer, Heidelberg (2006)
2. DeNardis, L.: Questioning IPv6 Security. Business Communications Review Magazine, 51–53 (2006)
3. Templeton, S.J., Levitt, K.E.: Detecting Spoofed Packets. In: Proc. Of DISCEX 2003, pp. 164–175 (2003)
4. Ferguson, P., Senie, D.: Network Ingress Filtering: Defeating Denial of Service Attacks which employ IP Source Address Spoofing. IETF, RFC 2827 (2000)
5. Geng, X., Whinston, A.B.: Defeating Distributed Denial of Service Attacks. IT Professional 2(4), 36–41 (2000)
6. Nikander, P., Kempf, J., Nordmark, E.: IPv6 Neighbor Discovery (ND) Trust Models and Threats. IETF, RFC 3756 (2004)
7. Mutaf, P., Castelluccia, C.: Compact Neighbor Discovery: a Bandwidth Defense through Bandwidth Optimization. In: Proc. of INFOCOM 2005, pp. 2711–2719 (2005)
8. Narten, T., Nordmark, E., Simpson, W.: Neighbor Discovery for IP Version 6 (IPv6). IETF, RFC 2461 (1998)

9. Tseng, Y., Jiang, J., Lee, J.: Secure Bootstrapping and Routing in an IPv6-Based Ad Hoc Network. In: Proc. of ICPP Workshops, pp. 375–383 (2003)
10. Leckie, C., Kotagiri, R.: A Probabilistic Approach to Detecting Network Scans. In: Proc. NOMS 2002, pp. 359–372 (2002)
11. Schechter, S., Jung, J., Berger, A.W.: Fast Detection of Scanning Worm Infections. In: Jonsson, E., Valdes, A., Almgren, M. (eds.) RAID 2004. LNCS, vol. 3224, pp. 59–81. Springer, Heidelberg (2004)
12. Arkko, J., Kempf, J., Zill, B., Nikander, P.: SEcure Neighbor Discovery (SEND). IETF, RFC 3971 (2005)
13. Arkko, J., Aura, T., et al.: Securing IPv6 Neighbor and Router Discovery. In: Proc. of the 3rd ACM workshop on Wireless security, pp. 77–86 (2002)
14. Cisco Systems: Strategies to Protect Against Distributed Denial of Service (DDoS) Attacks. White paper (2000), http://www.cisco.com/warp/.../newsflash.html
15. Bradner, S., Paxson, V.: IANA Allocation Guidelines For Value. In: the Internet Protocol and Related Headers. IETF, RFC 2780 (2000)
16. Grossman, D.: New Terminology and Clarifications for Diffserv. IETF, RFC 3260 (2002)
17. UCB/LBNL/VINT: ns Notes and Documentation, http://www.isi.edu/nsnam/ns

A Semantic-Aware Ontology-Based Trust Model for Pervasive Computing Environments⋆

Mohsen Taherian, Rasool Jalili, and Morteza Amini

Network Security Center, Department of Computer Engineering,
Sharif University of Technology, Tehran, Iran
{taherian,m_amini}@ce.sharif.edu,
jalili@sharif.edu

Abstract. Traditionally, to handle security for stand-alone computers and small networks, user authentication and access control mechanisms would be almost enough. However, considering distributed networks such as the *Internet* and *pervasive environments*, these kinds of approaches are confronted with flexibility challenges and scalability problems. This is mainly because open environments lack a central control, and users in them are not predetermined. In such ubiquitous computing environments, issues concerning security and trust become crucial. Adding *trust* to the existing security infrastructures would enhance the security of these environments. Although many trust models are proposed to deal with trust issues in pervasive environments, none of them considers the semantic relations exist among pervasive elements and especially among *trust categories*. Employing *Semantic Web* concepts, we propose a computational trust model based on the *ontology* structure, considering the mentioned semantic relations. In this model, each entity can calculate its trust in other entities and use the calculated trust values to make decisions about granting or rejecting collaborations. Using ontology structure can make the model extendible to encompass other pervasive features such as *context awareness* in a simple way.

1 Introduction

Nowadays, with the immense growth of available data and information which motivates moving toward distributed environments, security of users and information is getting more important than ever. With these distributed environments, existing challenges about security and data integrity in centralized environments, must be investigated more extensively. Many authentication and access control mechanisms have been proposed to deal with security issues in distributed environments. However, by increasing the distribution of information, and the arising open environments such as *pervasive computing environments*, existing security infrastructures are not adequate for new requirements of users from now on [6,14].

⋆ This research is partially supported by Iran Telecommunication Research Center (ITRC).

C. Rong et al. (Eds.): ATC 2008, LNCS 5060, pp. 47–59, 2008.

Pervasive computing environments, as a new generation of computing environments after distributed and mobile computing, were introduced in 1991 with a new look at the future of computing environments. The aim of pervasive computing is to move computers and computing devices to the background and place them in human living environments such that they were hidden from humans. To this aim, computing devices must be designed in small sizes to locate in apartments, walls, and furnitures [15]. In pervasive computing environments, users expect to access resources and services anytime and anywhere, leading to serious security risks and problems with access control as these resources can now be accessed by almost anyone with a mobile device. Adding security to such open models is extremely difficult with problems at many levels. An architecture with a central authority can not be assumed and access control is required for external users. The portable hand-held and embedded devices have severe limitations in their processing capabilities, memory capacities, software support, and bandwidth characteristics. Existing security infrastructures deal with authentication and access control. These mechanisms are inadequate due to the increasing flexibility required by pervasive environments.

Trust, which is similar to the way security is handled in human societies, plays an important role in enhancing security of pervasive environments. However, it is not considered in traditional access control models seriously [7]. Till now, several trust models have been proposed for pervasive environments including computational models and none-computational ones. In a computational trust model, the entity's trust to another one is estimated. On the other hand, the aim of a non-computational trust model is only to find out if an entity is trusted or not. It is worthwhile to note that an entity can trust another one in different categories. For example, the device A may trust the device B in the category of reading a file, but A may give up trusting B in the category of writing a file. The semantic relations exist among pervasive devices and specially trust categories may significantly affect security policies. For instance, if we know a special device belongs to the family of PDAs, and also if we have a subsumption relation between PDAs and mobile devices, we can generalize the security rules defined for mobile devices to this particular device. Semantic relations among trust categories mean the security relevance of categories to each other. For example, If an entity A has a high degree of trust to an entity B in getting a web service, we expect A to have a high degree of trust to B in getting a mail service as a consequence.

None of published trust models for pervasive environments have considered the mentioned semantic relations yet. Employing *ontology* structure propounded in *Semantic Web*, we propose a new trust model for pervasive environments. This model, in addition to being a computational trust model, considers semantic relations among devices and among trust categories. Each entity can calculate its trust degree to other entities and make security decisions based on the calculated trust values. In fact, each entity can accept or reject collaboration with other entities with regard to their trust values. Also, each entity can vote for another entity after a direct collaboration with it. Furthermore, this model satisfies autonomy which is an important property of pervasive entities. A pervasive device can define its security rules independently using the *SWRL* language [1], which is a semantic language for defining rules on ontology structures. The use of ontology structure, makes the model capable of encompassing other pervasive concepts such as *context awareness* in a simple way.

The rest of the paper is organized as follows; In section 2, previous trust models proposed for pervasive environments are reviewed. The structure of our trust model and its main components are discussed in section 3. Section 4 is devoted to explain the trust inference protocol and updating trust values. Finally, we conclude the paper and introduce some future work in section 5.

2 Related Work

Many trust models have been proposed for distributed environments. A small number of them, such as the one proposed by Abdul-Rahman in [3], were designed with such generality to be applicable in all distributed environments. Other cases concentrated on a particular environment. The trust models for *web-based social networks* [8,9,12] and the ones for *peer-to-peer networks* [10,16] are examples of these trust models. In this section, our review focuses on the trust models have been already suggested for pervasive computing environments. In almost all distributed trust models, there must be some basic services and facilities. *Trust inference* and *trust composition* are examples of such facilities. By trust inference, we mean calculating our belief to a statement based on the believes of some other people to whom we trust. Trust composition is a necessary part of a trust inference algorithm to combine the believes obtained from different sources.

The trust model proposed by Kagal *et al.* in 2001 [13,14] is one of the well-known trust models for pervasive computing environments. This model is not a computational trust model and uses certificates to determine whether an entity is trusted or not. In the Kagal's suggested architecture, each environments is divided into some security domains and for each security domain a *security agent* is leveraged. The security agent is responsible for defining security policies and applying them in the corresponding domain. Interfaces of available services in a domain are also provided by its security agent. When an external user requests a service offered in a domain, he must provide a certificate from the agents which are trusted for the security agent of the domain. Then, he must send its request accompanying the acquired certificates to the security agent. The security agent checks the validity of the certificates and responses the user's request. In fact, the Kagal's trust model is more likely to be a certificate-based access control model. In this model, an entity can be trustworthy or not from the security agent's point of view. An entity is not capable of calculating trust values of other entities and collaboration with inter-domain entities which are trusted for a security agent are not supervised.

Among the existing trust models for pervasive environments, the model proposed by Almenarez *et al.* in [4,5], called PTM^1, is so popular. This trust model is a computational trust model and it is implemented on a wide range of

---

[1] Pervasive Trust Management.

pervasive devices. Considering two kinds of trust, *direct trust* and *recommendation trust* [4], the architecture of this model is divided into two parts; 1) *belief space*, which assigns an initialize trust value to new arriving entities, and 2) *evidence space*, which updates the trust values of entities with respect to their behaviors over the time. To combine trust values, the weighted average operator (WAO) is used and values in the belief space are presented as fuzzy values. A recommendation protocol is defined to recommend an entity the trust values of other entities. If an entity wishes to collaborate with another one, it uses this protocol to acquire that entity's trustworthy degree. In the first collaboration of an entity, its initial trust value, which is assigned in the belief space, is considered. However, over the time, the entity's trust value changes with respect to the entity's behavior. The implementation of this model is added to security infrastructure of some pervasive devices to enhance their security [2].

The above mentioned approaches present drawbacks for open pervasive environments. Perhaps, the main drawback of them is not taking into account the semantic relations among pervasive devices and among trust categories. We have defined a pervasive trust model based on ontology structure between autonomous entities without central servers. Considering mentioned semantic relations makes the model capable of defining security rules with more flexibility. The model is also simple enough to implement in the very constrained devices which have strict resource constraints.

3   The Trust Model

In our proposed model, in addition to calculating the trust values from each entity to other entities, the semantic relations among pervasive devices and trust categories are considered using an ontology structure. In this section, the basic components of this model are introduced.

3.1   Trust Ontology

In this model, to represent trust relations among pervasive devices, a particular ontology is defined, called *trust ontology*. As known, each ontology O contains a set of concepts (classes) C and a set of properties P. The formal notation of trust ontology is defined as follows:

```
O={C,P}

C={Device, Category, TrustValue, DirectTrust, RecTrust,
   CategoryRelation, RelevanceValue, Time}

P={hasDirectTrust, hasRecTrust, initialTrustValue,
   trustedDevice, trustedCategory, hasTrustValue,
   trustRelated, relatedCategory, hasRelevanceValue,
   updateTime, collaborationNo}
```

Classes of the Trust Ontology. The class *Device* represents the available devices of pervasive environment such as users, sensors and PDAs. The class *Category* includes individuals which represent trust categories, e,g., login access or reading file. In fact, the trust category describes the semantics of a trust relation. The class *TrustValue* contains the valid values of trust degrees. The float numbers in the range of [0..1] can be an example of these values.

Similar to many other trust models, two kinds of trust are considered in our model. First, *direct trust* which is given by the knowledge of an entitys nature or its past interactions in the physical world, without requesting information from other entities. Second trust type is *indirect trust* or *recommendation trust*. When two entities, unknown to each other, are willing to interact, they can request other entities to give information about the other party. This process of asking other entities and calculating the final trust value from the received answers is called *trust inference*.

To model the trust relations, for both direct trust and recommendation trust, some properties must be defined in the ontology. These properties have some attributes themselves. In Semantic Web languages, such as RDF and OWL, a property is a binary relation; it is used to link two individuals or an individual and a value. However, in some cases, the natural and convenient way to represent certain concepts is to use relations to link an individual to more than just one individual or value. These relations are n-ary relations. For instance, it might be required to represent properties of a relation, such as our certainty about it, relevance of a relation, and so on. One solution to this problem is creating an individual representing the relation instance itself, with links from the subject of the relation to this instance and with links from this instance to all participants that represent additional information about the instance. In the class definition of the ontology, an additional class is required to include instances of this n-ary relation itself. Classes *DirectTrust* and *RecTrust* are of such classes.

One of the main features of our model is considering semantic relations among trust categories. Like direct trust and indirect trust relation, the semantic relation among trust categories is n-ary relation. The class *CategoryRelation* is defined to include instances of this n-ary relation.

The class *RelevanceValue* defines the valid values for the relevance values among trust categories. Finally, the class *Time* characterizes the time values in the model. Individuals of this class are used to hold the time of inferring trust values.

Properties of the Trust Ontology

– **initialTrustValue:** An instance of this property assigns to a new arriving entity an initial trust value. This assignment is done by special agents called *trust managers* which are described in the next section. One way is to assign different initial trust values to the new entity corresponding to different trust categories. Another way is to assign only one initial trust value for all trust categories. Concentrating on simplicity of the model, the latter one is considered in this paper. The criteria of assigning this value is dependent to

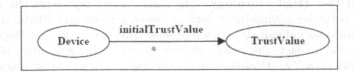

Fig. 1. *initialTrustValue* property

the policies of the trust manager. The schema of this property is shown in Fig. 1.

- **hasDirectTrust:** When an entity collaborates with another one, it gains a degree of trust about that entity. This type of trust is called *direct trust*. Since this relation is not a binary relation and it has some attributes, the pattern described before to define n-ary relations is used. Fig. 2 shows the schema of *hasDirectTrust* property. The class *DirectTrust* includes instances of the relation. The property *trustedDevice* determines the device that the trust relation is established with. The class N includes the natural numbers and the property *collaborationNo* identifies number of collaborations which are already done between these two entities. The property *hasTrustValue* assigns a trust value to the trust relation and the property *trustedCategory* characterizes the trust category in which the trust relation is set up.

- **hasRecTrust:** If an entity wants to begin a collaboration with another one, it may want to know the opinions of other entities about the other party. The trust value derived in this way is called *indirect trust* or *recommendation trust*. Like *hasDirectTrust*, this relation is also an n-ary relation. The

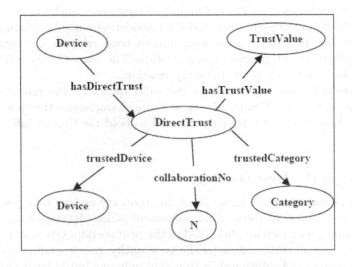

Fig. 2. *hasDirectTrust* property

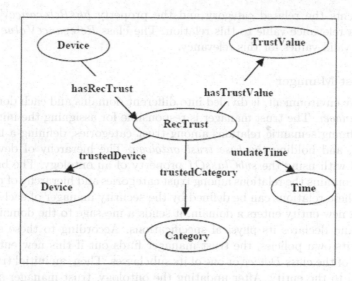

Fig. 3. *hasRecTrust* property

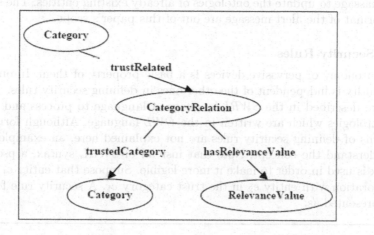

Fig. 4. *trustRelated* property

schema of this relation is illustrated in Fig. 3. The class *RecTrust* includes individuals of the relation. All attributes of this relation is similar to the direct trust relation except that instead of property *collaborationNo*, the property *updateTime* is added. This property determines the time of last trust inference. Details of the inference algorithm is discussed in section 4.

- **trustRelated:** The semantic relation between two categories of trust is modeled with this property. According to Fig. 4, the class *CategoryRelation* contains individuals of the relation itself. The property *trustedCategory* represents the related category and the property *hasRelevanceValue* assigns a relevance value to this relation. The class *RelevanceValue* consists of the valid values for this relevancy.

3.2 Trust Manager

A pervasive environment, is divided into different domains and each domain has a *trust manager*. The trust manager is responsible for assigning the initial trust values, defining semantic relations among trust categories, defining a hierarchy of devices, and holding the *base trust ontology*. The hierarchy of devices can be defined with using the *subClassOf* property of an ontology. The base trust ontology, contains the relations among trust categories and hierarchy of pervasive devices. These relations can be defined by the security manager of each domain.

When a new entity enters a domain, it sends a message to the domain's trust manager and declares its physical specifications. According to these specifications and its own policies, the trust manager finds out if this new entity is an individual of the class *Device* or one of its subclasses. Then, an initial trust value is assigned to the entity. After updating the ontology, trust manager sends the file of ontology to the new entity. Thus, all entities receive the domain's base trust ontology when they enter the domain. The trust manager also broadcasts a new massage to update the ontologies of already existing entities. The structure and format of the alert message are out of this paper's scope.

3.3 Security Rules

The autonomy of pervasive devices is a basic property of them. In our model, each entity is independent of the other ones in defining security rules. The policies are described in the *SWRL* language, a language to process and to query the ontologies which are written in the *OWL* language. Although formats and patterns of defining security rules are not explained here, an example is given to understand the concept. Note that instead of SWRL syntax, a pseudocode syntax is used in order to make it more legible. Suppose that entity e_1 begins a collaboration with entity e_2 in the trust category c_1. A security rule for e_1 can be represented as:

```
if e₂ is a sensor
 and

 ([hasDirectTrust(e₁)=X and        [hasRecTrust(e₁)=Y and
   trustedDevice(X)=e₂ and           trustedDevice(Y)=e₂ and
   trustedCategory(X)=c₁ and    and  trustedCategory(Y)=c₁ and
   hasTrustValue(X) ≥ 0.6]           hasTrustValue(X) > 0.7 and
                                     updateTime(Y) ≥ (now-20s)])

 then collaboration with e₂
 in the category c₁ is granted.
```

Before beginning the collaboration, e_1 looks up in its security rules to find the matching rules. In this case, the mentioned security rule is matched with the collaboration properties. If the found rules are satisfied, the entity begins the collaboration. If no rule is matched with an interaction, granting or denying the interaction can be decided according to the security policies. In this approach, a possible problem is conflicting the rules, matched with a collaboration. Conflict resolution is out of the scope of this paper.

4   Trust Inference

In any trust model, one of the main parts is the algorithm of inferring trust. Trust inference means calculating indirect trust value (or recommendation trust value). In addition to indirect trust, the way in which direct trust values are created is important too. In this section, trust inference protocol and the method of updating both direct and indirect trust values are discussed. The approach of applying semantic relations among trust categories is also described in the following subsections.

4.1   Trust Inference Protocol

Suppose that device e_1 does not have any information about entity e_2 and it is willing to interact with e_2. Consider that this type of interaction needs a degree of trust in the trust category c_1. Now, c_1 needs to derive the trust value of e_2 by asking other entities. Thus, e_1 broadcasts a query message to other entities. The query part of this message is expressed in the SWRL language. Although the format and structure of messages are not discussed in this paper, an example of broadcasting query is illustrated below using pseudocode.

```
hasDirectTrust(x)=X and trustedDevice(X)=e₂ and
trustedCategory(X)=c₁ and hasTrustValue(X)= ?
```

In the above query, x matches with each entity that receives the message. It is clear that to answer the sender, address of sender must be located in the message. Also, a timeout must be declared by sender to ignore indefinite waiting. Each entity which has a direct trust to e_2 in the category c_1, replies e_1. After finishing the declared timeout, e_1 calculates the derived trust value with respect to delivered answers. The equation 1 shows this operation.

$$T_{infer}(e_1, e_2, c_1) = \frac{\sum_{i=1}^{n} T(e_i, e_2, c_1) \times T(e_1, e_i, c_1)}{T(e_1, e_i, c_1)} \qquad (1)$$

The entities who reply e_1 are denoted by e_i. $T(e_i, e_2, c_1)$ is the value of direct trust from entity e_i to e_2 in the trust category c_1 and $T(e_1, e_i, c_1)$ is the direct trust value from e_1 to e_i in the trust category c_1. Considering trust value of sender to repliers causes that answers from more reliable entities, having more impact on the inferred trust value. Note that if e_1 does not have a direct trust to e_i (e_1 has not done any interaction with e_i in the trust category c_1 yet.), it considers the initial trust value of e_i ($initialTrustValue(e_i)$) instead of $T(e_1, e_i, c_1)$. As it is mentioned before, this initial trust value is assigned by the trust manager. It is obvious that the inferred trust value will be located in the valid range of trust values defined by class $TrustValue$ of trust ontology. After computing the inferred trust value, e_1 updates its ontology. The time of inferring trust (t_{infer}) will be also located in the ontology using $updateTime$ property. Updating the trust ontology of e_1 includes the following items:

---

hasRecTrust(e_1)=X and trustedDevice(X)=e_2 and
trustedCategory(X)=c_1 and updateTime(X)=t_{infer} and
hasTrustValue(X)=$T_{infer}(e_1,e_2,c_1)$

In our inference method, the weighted average operator (WAO) is used to combine the trust values. Although other distributed trust models use alternative operators to combine trust values which may cause getting more accurate results, like the *consensus operator* [11] used in [12], for pervasive devices which have considerable limitations on battery life, memory capacities, size, and performance, the simplicity is preferred to accuracy.

4.2   Updating the Trust Values

To update indirect trust values, different approaches can be used. One way is that each entity recalculates its trust value to another entity after a predefined time periods. Another way is to derive the trust value whenever a rule consisting the time constraint is fired up. A combination of these two approaches can be used too. In a pervasive domain, the security manager can choose one of the above methods.

Now, the question is that how direct trust values can change. In this model, after completing a transaction, entities can vote for each other. The new direct trust value can be computed by the equation 2.

$$T_{new}(e_1, e_2, c_1) = \frac{T_{old}(e_1, e_2, c_1) \times collaborationNo + vote(e_1, e_2, c_1)}{collaborationNo + 1} \quad (2)$$

In this equation, $T_{old}(e_1, e_2, c_1)$ represents the direct trust value from e_1 to e_2 in the category c_1 before beginning the transaction. The term $vote(e_1, e_2, c_1)$ represents the opinion of e_1 about e_2 in the category c_1 after completing the transaction and $collaborationNo$ is the number of transactions between e_1 and e_2 which have taken place in the category c_1 before this transaction. $T_{new}(e_1, e_2, c_1)$ is the new direct trust value from e_1 to e_2 in the category c_1. Updating the trust ontology of e_1 includes the following items:

```
hasDirectTrust(e₁)=X and trustedDevice(X)=e₂ and
trustedCategory(X)=c₁ and
collaborationNo(X)=collaborationNo(X)+1 and
hasTrustValue(X)=T_new(e₁,e₂,c₁)
```

Note that the new direct trust values can be alerted to the trust manager to take these values into account in its later decisions.

4.3 Semantic Relations among Trust Categories

Defining the *trustRelated* property in the trust ontology provides this possibility for the trust model to represent semantic relations among trust categories. Considering these relations, provide us security rules with more flexibility and higher security level. For example, assume that e_1 wishes to begin an interaction with e_2 which requires satisfaction of the following security rule:

```
hasDirectTrust(e₁)=X and trustedDevice(X)=e₂ and
trustedCategory(X)=c₁ and hasTrustValue(X) ≥ 0.6
```

Now, suppose that e_1 would collaborate with e_2 if it has the same degree of trust to e_2 in other categories which are related to c_1 with the relevancy value of 0.8. The security rule to support this requirement is shown below:

```
hasDirectTrust(e₁)=X and trustedDevice(X)=e₂ and
trustedCategory(X)=Y and trustRelated(Y)=Z and
relatedCategory(Z)=c₁ and hasRelevanceValue(Z) > 0.8
hasTrustValue(X) ≥ 0.6
```

5 Conclusions and Future Works

In this paper, we have introduced a new semantic-aware trust model for pervasive environments based on ontology concepts. A standard ontology, called *trust ontology*, is defined to support trust in pervasive environments. The trust ontology is represented with the OWL language and queries on the ontology can be expressed in existing rule languages such as SWRL. Using the ontology structure, the model provides a standard trust infrastructure for pervasive devices.

Using the weighted average operator (WAO), a simple inference protocol is proposed to calculate the indirect trust values. For pervasive devices which have significant limitations on battery life, memory capacities, size, and performance, the simplicity of inference protocol offers many benefits to calculate the indirect trust values. Another advantage of the model is taking into account the autonomy of pervasive devices. Each device can define its private security rules independent of other devices. There exist such flexibility for devices to employ both direct and indirect trust values in defining their security policies.

Considering the semantic relations among trust categories and defining hierarchical structure of pervasive devices, provides us more flexibility to define security rules. With this feature, a wide range of security policies can be expressed in a simple way. Adding more attributes of pervasive environments such as *context-awareness* is possible with making a little extension to the model. For example, suppose that we want to add a context variable such as the *location*. The property *hasLocation* and a class *validPlaces* can be defined in the trust ontology to support this context variable. New security rules can use this new concept to enhance their expressiveness.

Future work includes defining the structure of messages and patterns of security rules. Moving toward implementing this model on pervasive devices like PDAs and evaluating the performance impacts are also in our future plans.

References

1. Swrl: A semantic web rule language combining owl and ruleml,
   http://www.w3.org/Submission/SWRL
2. Ubisec project, pervasive trust management model (ptm),
   http://www.it.uc3m.es/~florina/ptm
3. Abdul-Rahman, A., Hailes, S.: A distributed trust model. In: New Security Paradigms Workshop, pp. 48–60. ACM Press, New York (1998)
4. Almenarez, F., Marin, A., Campo, C., Garcia, C.: Ptm: A pervasive trust management model for dynamic open environments. In: First Workshop on Pervasive Security, Privacy and Trust PSPT (2004)
5. Almenarez, F., Marin, A., Diaz, D., Sanchez, J.: Developing a model for trust management in pervasive devices. In: Fourth Annual IEEE International Conference on Pervasive Computing and Communications Workshop (PERCOMW 2006) (2006)
6. Blaze, M., Feigenbaum, J., Keromyts, A.D.: The role of trust management in distributed systems security. In: Secure Internet Programming, pp. 185–210 (1999)
7. English, C., Nixon, P., Terzis, S., McGettrick, A., Lowe, H.: Dynamic trust models for ubiquitous computing environments. In: Ubicomp Security Workshop (2002)
8. Golbeck, G.A.: Computing and Applying Trust in Web-Based Social Networks. PhD thesis, University of Maryland (2005)
9. Golbeck, G.A., James, H.: Inferring binary trust relationships in web-based social networks. ACM Transactions on Internet Technology 6(4), 497–529 (2005)
10. Griffiths, N., Chao, K.M., Younas, M.: Fuzzy trust for peer-to-peer systems. In: P2P Data and Knowledge Sharing Workshop (P2P/DAKS 2006), at the 26th International Conference on Distributed Computing Systems (ICDCS 2006), Lisbon, Portugal, pp. 73–73. IEEE Computer Society Press, Los Alamitos (2006)
11. Josang, A.: The consensus operator for combining beliefs. Artificial Intelligence Journal 142(1-2), 157–170 (2002)
12. Josang, A., Hayward, R., Pope, S.: Trust network analysis with subjective logic. In: Australasian Computer Science Conference (ACSC 2006), Hobart, Australia, pp. 85–94 (2006)
13. Kagal, L., Finin, T., Joshi, A.: Trust-based security in pervasive computing environments. IEEE Computer 34(12), 154–157 (2001)

14. Kagal, L., Finin, T., Joshi, A.: Moving from security to distributed trust in ubiquitous computing environments. IEEE Computer (2001)
15. Satyanarayanan, M.: Pervasive computing: Vision and challenges. IEEE Personal Communications 8(4), 10–17 (2001)
16. Wang, Y., Vassileva, J.: Trust and reputation model in peer-to-peer networks. In: 3rd International Conference on Peer-to-Peer Computing (P2P 2003), pp. 150–157. IEEE Computer Society, Los Alamitos (2003)

Using Automated Planning for Trusted Self-organising Organic Computing Systems

Benjamin Satzger, Andreas Pietzowski, Wolfgang Trumler, and Theo Ungerer

Department of Computer Science
University of Augsburg,
D-86135 Augsburg, Germany
{satzger,pietzowski,trumler,ungerer}@informatik.uni-augsburg.de
http://www.informatik.uni-augsburg.de/sik

Abstract. The increasing complexity of computer-based technical systems require new ways to control them. The initiatives *Organic Computing* and *Autonomic Computing* address exactly this issue. They demand future computer systems to adapt dynamically and autonomously to their environment. In this paper we propose a new approach based on automated planning to realise self-organising capabilities for complex distributed computing systems. The user/administrator only defines objectives describing the conditions which should hold in the system, whereas the system itself is responsible for meeting them using a planning engine. As many planning algorithms are known to be sound and complete, formal guarantees can be given. Thus we aim at building trusted self-organising distributed computer system which are suitable to control real technical systems. Our approach is demonstrated and evaluated on the basis of a simulated production cell with robots and carts. We propose and evaluate two optimisations.

Keywords: Organic Computing, self-organisation, automated planning.

1 Introduction

Organic Computing (OC) [14,12,15] and Autonomic Computing (AC) [8,10,9] both identified the increasing complexity of distributed computing systems as a major challenge to future management of computer systems and postulate so-called self-x properties (i.e. self-organisation, self-configuration, self-optimisation, self-healing, and self-protection) for these systems. Thus, the system is able to manage itself in order to hide the complexity from users, administrators, and programmers. In highly complex systems it is unfeasible or even impossible for humans to care about details. A way to manage such systems is to use policies describing just their objectives. These objective policies only specify *what* is expected from the system - the way it should behave. The way *how* this is managed should be determined automatically. Policies are an important technique used to specify the desired behaviour of AC and OC systems, respectively. Policies normally are rules consisting of a condition and zero or more actions [1]. During runtime, a policy engine will verify the conditions and take the stipulated action.

C. Rong et al. (Eds.): ATC 2008, LNCS 5060, pp. 60–72, 2008.

However, for self-organisation in distributed systems the enumeration of all conditions, e.g. all possible types of failures is often impracticable. Also, the actions to recover the system can be too arduous to be specified manually. Furthermore many different ways to reconfigure a system from one certain fail state may exist what raises the complexity even more.

A methodology that is better in line with the visions of OC and AC is policies only describing the desired conditions of a system, leaving it to the system itself to meet these conditions. Automated planning is a concept to enable computer systems to reason about actions in order to automatically compute plans to follow the policies. This has also been identified by Srivastava et al. [16] who argue that planning is an evolutionary next step for AC systems that use procedural policies. Other approaches used to develop self-organising computer systems like AI-learning or bio-inspired techniques with emergent effects are too unreliable for many domains. The behaviour of such systems often cannot be predicted nor understood. In contrast, planning is similar to human reasoning and thus more comprehensible. Actually, many planning algorithms are known to be formally sound and complete.

The contributions of this work are the proposal of a new approach for trusted self-organising distributed systems, based on an automated planning engine we have developed to guide self-healing after a component failure in an OC-managed system. Our approach is explained, demonstrated, and evaluated on the basis of a simple scenario, a small production cell. This scenario has been introduced by Güdemann et al. [7] to motivate their work.

The paper is subdivided into seven sections. Section 2 gives a short introduction to automated planning and related work. Section 3 describes our scenario, a self-organising production cell. Then, Section 4 clarifies how the self-organisation process works while Section 5 proposes some optimisations for that process. Section 6 presents the results of the conducted evaluation. Finally, Section 7 gives an overview of future work and concludes the paper.

2 Automated Planning

Automated planning is a branch of artificial intelligence. The primary problem of planning is the computation of sequences of actions which will achieve specified objectives from specified initial conditions. Domain-independent planning is concerned with the fundamental principles of planning as an activity. Basically, an automated planning problem can be described as follows: Given a description of the domain and the initial state, find a sequence of actions that transforms the system from the initial state to a state that satisfies defined objectives. A formalisation provides a formal description of all relevant information of planning problems. The system's state, the objectives, the actions, and its causalities have to be covered by such a formalisation. The STRIPS (STanford Research Institute Problem Solver) [4] representation has been devised by Fikes and Nilsson. STRIPS is probably the most famous planning language and is still widely used today. PDDL [11] is an attempt to standardise planning languages and was developed primarily to make planning competitions possible. PDDL is inspired by the STRIPS formulation, and basically a first-order logic language. The syntax is inspired by Lisp, so much of the structure of a domain description is a Lisp-like list of parenthesised expressions.

Basically, planning can be seen as a search problem. Planning algorithms vary in the space that is searched, how the search is performed, in which way the plans are constructed, and so on. In the following an overview of different planning techniques is given. The simplest classical planners are based on *state space planning* where the search space is a subset of the state space. A state space planning problem can be represented as a graph: Every node is an element of the set of states of the system. The edges are elements of the set of possible actions. The edges connect a state and the state that results from the application of the corresponding action at this state. A plan can be represented as a path within the graph. A path from the initial state to a goal state is a solution of the planning problem. It is possible that multiple paths lead from the initial to a goal state. An alternative to the search through the state space is to search through the space of plans, called *plan space planning*. In this space, the nodes represent partially specified plans, the start node is an empty plan which has no actions. The edges correspond to refinements of the partial plans, called *plan refinements*, that expand them until a complete plan has been created that solves the stated planning problem. For a more detailed introduction in the field of automated planning see [6].

Distributed and coordinated planning problems have been studied within the context of multi-agent systems (MAS). Multi-agent planning can be seen as planning together with coordination. Partial Global Planning (PGP) [3] is perhaps one of the most influential approaches in distributed AI [2]. In contrast to most MASs where agents are self-interested, PGP uses cooperative agents. It is particularly suited for the use in sensor networks and is applied to distributed vehicle monitoring, whereby the goal is to provide a consistent view of vehicle movement.

For this work, a planner has been developed in JAVA, based on a plan space planning approach [18] which has been extended to work with numerical resources. It takes a subset of PDDL as input, and uses heuristics to guide the search. Furthermore a technique has been incorporated to allow distributed planning, i.e. the coordinated planning of entities within a distributed system. We chose to build our planner based upon a plan space planning approach, because it performs very effectively in parallel, distributed domains and the generated plans have a better execution flexibility compared with other approaches [13]. The high execution flexibility is mainly based on the fact that e.g. state based planners typically output a totally ordered plan what means that all plans have to be executed sequentially also in distributed domains. However, our planner outputs partially ordered plans which allow a parallel execution of actions. This makes plan execution much more efficient and flexible, especially in distributed systems.

3   Self-organising Production Cell

In this section, first the production cell scenario is introduced, then it is presented how it can be controlled by our approach.

3.1   Scenario

The scenario we are using to demonstrate and evaluate our planner, a small automated production cell, has been introduced by Güdemann et al. [7]. It consists of three robots and two carts. Each robot has three tools which can be switched during runtime: (1) a drill to drill holes into workpieces, (2) an inserter to insert a screw into a drilled hole, and (3) a screw driver to tighten an inserted screw. The carts transport workpieces from one robot to another. All workpieces must be processed in the order drill, insert, and tighten. Figure 1 illustrates this scenario. The arrows represent the flow of the workpieces, the tools below the robots are the available tools for the robot, tools marked with a dot indicate the robot's tasks, i.e. the processing steps it is responsible to execute.

Now, this scenario is mapped to our approach. The robots and carts of the production cell are understood as nodes of a special distributed system. As a prerequisite, these nodes need to be able to send messages and it is assumed that each of them runs an instance of our planning engine. The planning is distributed over the entities, however, in an instance only one entity is coordinating the planning. There are three different scopes, information are needed about. The first one is knowledge about the current state of the system. In order to control the system properly, it is of course necessary to know about its current condition. The *system state* is gathered from a constant monitoring process of the nodes of the system.

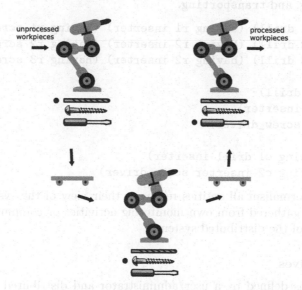

Fig. 1. Production cell

The *objectives* define desired system properties whereas it is the task of the system to meet these properties. The objectives determine the behaviour of the system. The third component is an *action description* which basically informs every entity of the distributed system which actions it is able to perform and what effects they have. In the following, these three topics are introduced in more detail.

3.2   System State

Based on monitoring and potentially previous knowledge all entities form their view of the world. With entities, we denote all components of the system able to perform actions. In the production cell example robots and carts form these entities. The state of the world is composed of the relevant objects and their states which are expressed with predicates.

The production cell consists of three robots r1, r2, and r3, two carts c1 and c2, and three tools `drill`, `inserter`, and `screw_driver`. The entities represent these objects as follows, whereas the source of this information is either previous knowledge or monitoring of the environment:

```
r1 r2 r3 - robot
c1 c2 - cart
drill inserter screw_driver - tool
```

It is supposed that all three robots have the tools `drill`, `inserter`, and `screw_driver`, whereas r1 is currently using the `drill`, r2 the `inserter`, and r3 the `screw_driver`. Furthermore assume that c1 is transporting workpieces from the robot using the `drill` to the robot using the `inserter` and c2 is transporting workpieces from the robot using the `inserter` to the robot using the `screw_driver`. The representation of these conditions is based on the predicates `having`, `using`, and `transporting`.

```
(having r1 drill) (having r1 inserter) (having r1 screw_driver)
(having r2 drill) (having r2 inserter) (having r2 screw_driver)
(having r3 drill) (having r2 inserter) (having r3 screw_driver)

(using r1 drill)
(using r2 inserter)
(using r3 screw_driver)

(transporting c1 drill inserter)
(transporting c2 inserter screw_driver)
```

With this formalism all entities represent their view of the system. The information are gathered from own monitoring activities or communication with other entities of the distributed system.

3.3   Objectives

An objective is defined by a user/administrator and distributed to the nodes of the system. It provides a statement of the requirements about the system's condition and determines its behaviour. Thus, one instance exists whose change yields a behavioural change in the whole system. An objective defines which conditions always should hold within the system. The planning engine is responsible to control the system in order to meet these conditions. In the scenario of the production cell a reasonable objective is: For every tool (drill, inserter, screw_driver) a robot is required using this tool. Furthermore carts are required, first a cart transporting workpieces from the robot using the drill to the robot using the inserter, and a second cart transporting workpieces from the robot using the inserter to the robot using the screw driver. This objective is shown in the following:

```
(forall (?t - tool) (exists (?r - robot) (using ?r ?t)))
(exists (?c - cart) (transporting  drill inserter))
(exists (?c - cart) (transporting  inserter screw_driver))
```

However, the above objectives do not cover the equal distribution of tasks, i.e. it is also a valid configuration if one robot is using all three tools whereas the others are doing nothing. To prevent such situations the objectives can be extended as follows:

```
(forall (?r - robot) (<= (#tools ?r) N))
(forall (?c - cart) (<= (#paths ?c) M))
```

where $N = \lceil \frac{3}{\#robot} \rceil$ and $M = \lceil \frac{2}{\#carts} \rceil$. Thus, no robot is allowed to use more than N tools, no cart is allowed to serve more than M paths. If everything in the production cell is working properly then $N = 1$ and $M = 1$. If e.g. one cart fails then $M = 2$ and the remaining cart is allowed to serve two paths. Now, at last the action description is discussed.

3.4 Action Description

Each entity needs information about what it is able to do, i.e. what actions it can execute and how these actions affect the system. The two fundamentally different types of entities - robots and carts of the production cell scenario - result in two different types of action descriptions. The action description for robot r1 looks as follows, whereas the descriptions for the robots r2 and r3 are defined analogue:

```
:action startTool
   :parameters  (r1  ?t - tool)
   :precondition (and  (having r1 ?t)
   :effect       (and  (using r1 ?t))

:action stopTool
   :parameters  (r1  ?t - tool)
   :precondition (and  (using r1 ?t))
   :effect       (and  (not (using r1 ?t)))
```

Thus, robots can start and stop tools. Being able to start a tool `?t` the corresponding tool must be available for the robot (`having r1 ?t`). The effect of the action `startTool` is that the robot is using the tool afterwards (`using r1 ?t`). A robot can also use two tools simultaneously what is especially important if another robot completely fails and the remaining ones have to take over its tasks. The action `stopTool` can be seen as the complementary action to `startTool` and stops using a tool. Carts transport workpieces from one robot to another. Similar to robots they also start and stop these tasks.

```
:action startTransport
   :parameters   (c1   ?from ?to - robot)
   :precondition ( )
   :effect       (and  (transporting c1 ?from ?to))


:action stopTransport
   :parameters   (c1   ?from ?to - robot)
   :precondition (and  (transporting ?c ?from ?to))
   :effect       (and  (not (transporting ?c ?from ?to)))
```

4 Planning Process

In this section the planning process is explained which is the core of the self-organisation feature. All entities in the distributed system, in our case the production cell, constantly monitor their environment. If one entity observes a violation of an objective it initiates a reconfiguration process. This entity now serves as coordinator for a distributed planning process with the goal to recover the system to a state in line with the system's objectives. In a nutshell, the coordinator manages an agenda with open conditions that have to be addressed in order to recover the system. The open conditions are announced, while all entities communicate what they can contribute to resolve an open condition to the coordinator. Thus, the coordinator is able to generate a plan where the abilities of other entities are included. The result is a parallel executable plan that recovers the system from the unwanted state.

Consider an example where all robots have all tools while `r1` is using the drill, `r2` the inserter, and robot `r3` the screw driver. Unfortunately, the inserting tool of `r2` is breaking. This situation, shown in Figure 2(a), results in a violation of the objectives as no robot is using the inserter. It is reasonable to assume that `r2` is the first to detect this violation. Therefore it initiates the reconfiguration process starting with an initial partial order plan. The initial plan consists of two dummy steps representing the current state of the system and the goal state of the system. During the planning process the initial plan is refined until a valid plan, as illustrated in Figure 2(c), is found that transforms the invalid state into a goal state. Figure 2(b) represents the system after the reconfiguration process.

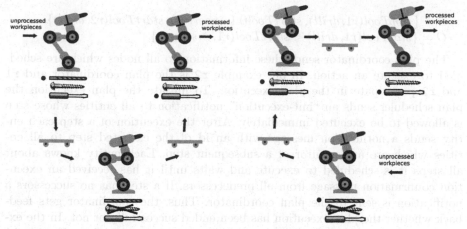

(a) Invalid situation due to broken inserter   (b) Valid situation after planning/plan execution

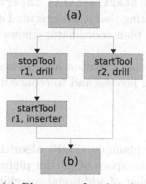

(c) Plan transforming invalid situation to valid situation according to the objectives

Fig. 2. Recovery process of the production cell

Note that the resulting plan is a partial ordered plan which allows a parallel execution of the actions. During the planning process the coordinator announces open conditions, e.g. the condition not (exists (?r - robots) (using (?r inserter))). Based on the responses and its own capabilities the coordinator computes all possible refinements of the current plan. These refined plans are the successors of the current plan. Thus, the planning process can be seen as a special tree search within the space of plans. The initial plan is the root node of the search tree, refinements lead to children, the search ends when a valid plan is found.

If such a plan has been generated it needs to be executed in order to recover the system. The plan contains a set of steps S and a partial ordering on this steps O:

$$S = \{stopTool(r1, drill), startTool(r1, inserter), startTool(r2, drill)\}$$
$$O = \{stopTool(r1, drill) < startTool(r1, inserter)\}$$

The plan coordinator sends these information to all nodes which are scheduled to execute an action. In our example r2 is the plan coordinator and r1 and r2 participate in the plan execution. To initiate the plan execution the plan scheduler sends an "init-execution" notification to all entities whose step is allowed to be executed immediately. After the execution of a step each entity sends a notification message with an id of the executed step to all entities which are an executor of a subsequent step. Each entity knows about all steps it is scheduled to execute and waits until it has received an execution confirmation message from all predecessors. If a step has no successors a notification is sent to the plan coordinator. Thus, the coordinator gets feedback whether the plan execution has been ended successfully or not. In the example above, r2 sends an "init-execution" message to r1 and itself executes step startTool(r2, drill). After the receipt of this message, r1 executes stopTool(r1, drill) and startTool(r1, inserter) afterwards. Then, r1 sends a message to r2 indicating that it has executed startTool(r1, inserter) (cp. Figure 2(c)). Now the plan coordinator knows that the plan execution is completed successfully.

In the next section some optimisation approaches are presented, which aim at speeding up the planning process and to reduce its complexity.

5   Optimisations

The standard partial order planning (POP) algorithm uses a breadth first approach to search through the space of partial plans. The planner we have developed incorporates a number of additional searching algorithms. Using an A^* search algorithm, a heuristic function $f(P)$ can be used to guide the search. This distance-plus-cost heuristic function consists of two parts: the costs from the initial plan to the currently examined partial plan P, called $g(P)$, and an estimate of the distance of P from the final plan, called $h(P)$. As an estimate for h the number of open conditions in the agenda is used, which is a well-known approach [5]. To compute $g(P)$ every step of the plan must have a value assigned representing the step costs, i.e. the costs it takes an entity to execute a step. When an entity receives a request containing an open condition, it checks whether it can contribute to solve this open condition. If it is able to contribute it sends an offer back to the plan coordinator consisting of an action together with the costs that are caused by its execution. This costs are set according to the principle: "The more tasks an entity is already executing the more expensive is it to take on another one". For example, consider the two robots r1 and r2 are asked to contribute to solve the open condition not (exists (?r - robots) (using(?r drill))) while r1 uses the tools inserter and screw_driver and r2 nothing. Then r1 sends as his contribution [startTool(r1, drill), 4] where the latter are the costs. Node r2 sends [startTool(r2, drill), 1] which is interpreted as a step with less costs. The cost heuristic function $g(P)$ is set as the sum of the step costs of a plan. Thus, the A^* search ranks plans with a balanced burden-sharing higher than unbalanced ones. If the reasoning of automated planning is compared to human reasoning a heuristic function can be seen as experience that also allows to rank options of actions.

Another approach which we consider crucial to enable scalable systems based on automated planning is to form groups. The planning within each group works independently from the other groups. Only if a group is unable to find a valid plan to reconfigure the group properly, members of other groups are requested to help. This has the advantage that nodes only need to know about the current state within the scope of their group which represents an enormous reduction in complexity if applied to more complex distributed systems.

6 Evaluation

This section presents results of performance measurements of our distributed planning approach. As testbed a distributed system with five nodes has been used to model the production cell. The nodes can communicate by passing messages, which has been realised using a middleware called "Organic Computing Middleware for Ubiquitous Environments" $OC\mu$, formerly called AMUN [17], which is based on Java and JXTA. But note that any other environment/setting that allows to pass messages could have been used equally.

As objectives the following requirements have been stated which do not only ensure the functional correctness but also the fair sharing of tasks.

```
(forall (?t - tool) (exists (?r - robot) (using ?r ?t)))
(exists (?c - cart) (transporting  drill inserter))
(exists (?c - cart) (transporting  inserter screw_driver))
(forall (?r - robot) (<= (#tools ?r) N))
(forall (?c - cart) (<= (#paths ?c) M))
```

To investigate the behaviour of the planner under all circumstances, a script has been written which puts the system into a random state. It simulates the outage of robots and carts, broken tools, and unbalancedly assigned tasks, but is restricted to states where it is at least possible to recover the system. With this approach 1000 random states have been generated where it has been the task of our self-organisation approach to recover the system. Three variations of the underlying planning engine have been tested:

Basic algorithm: The planning is based on the standard POP algorithm with breadth first search. Additional features, compared to standard POP, are basically planning with resources, distributed planning, and a richer input language.

Heuristic: This variation refers to the application of an A^* together with the heuristic function stated in Section 5.

Heuristic & Grouping: Additional to the usage of a heuristic guided search, two groups have been formed what refers to the second proposed optimisation in Section 5. One group consists of the three robots the other consists of the two carts. The robot group has the objectives:

```
(forall (?t - tool) (exists (?r - robot) (using ?r ?t)))
(forall (?r - robot) (<= (#tools ?r) N))
```

while the cart group has the objectives:

```
(exists (?c - cart) (transporting  drill inserter))
(exists (?c - cart) (transporting  inserter screw_driver))
(forall (?c - cart) (<= (#paths ?c) M))
```

Thus the maintenance of the objectives has been shared among the groups.

Because the planning is based on the POP algorithm, which is *sound* and *complete*, the system could obviously find a valid plan in all cases. Furthermore, we assumed that the plan execution does not fail. This could happen in real systems, if e.g. the startTool action fails because an arm of the robot is locked. In this case a replanning had to occur incorporating this information. However, such scenarios have been neglected. Table 1 gives indicators for the efficiency of the self-organisation process. It contains the average number of visited partial plans until a final valid plan has been found. Each refinement of a plan leads to a successor plan. These refinements can be the addition of a step offer received from another node but also internal changes of a partial plan like a different ordering of steps and so on. Lower numbers of visited partial plans are better and represent a more efficient and sophisticated planning process.

Table 1. Average number of visited partial plans

Basic algorithm	Heuristic	Heuristic & Grouping
144.644	17.853	13.247

The results show that the usage of heuristics in the distributed planning process dramatically reduce the costs for the planning process. The grouping of robots and carts into two groups further improves the performance. By the way, to have an idea about the temporal dimensions to generate a plan, using the basic algorithm it took in our setting on average 2.3 seconds to generate a plan, communication time included.

7   Conclusions and Outlook

We have presented a planning-based approach to enable self-organisation of distributed systems. Therefore, objectives are provided to the system which defines its desired properties. Thus, the administrator/user only has to define *what* must hold in the system. It is left to the planning engine to generate plans *how* to recover the system if necessary. As the planning engine is based on a sound and complete algorithm it can be trusted in the behaviour of the system: If there exists a solution it is guaranteed that the system finds it, and all successful executions of generated plans lead to a desired state. The functionality of the proposed self-organising approach has been applied to a production cell. The evaluation showed that the approach is suitable to autonomically manage such a production cell. Using heuristics and grouping, the efficiency of the self-organisation could be dramatically improved.

We are planning to apply and evaluate our approach within much more complex domains. Furthermore we are working on extensions to integrate our planner into an organic controller geared amongst others to human perception, decision processes, and social communities/capabilities to cope with highly complex, dynamic, and distributed domains.

References

1. Bahat, R.M., Bauer, M.A., Vieira, E.M., Baek, O.K.: Using policies to drive autonomic management. In: WOWMOM 2006: Proceedings of the 2006 International Symposium on on World of Wireless, Mobile and Multimedia Networks, Washington, DC, USA, pp. 475–479. IEEE Computer Society, Los Alamitos (2006)
2. de Weerdt, M., ter Mors, A., Witteveen, C.: Multi-agent planning: An introduction to planning and coordination. In: Handouts of the European Agent Summer School, pp. 1–32 (2005)
3. Durfee, E.H., Lesser, V.R.: Partial global planning: A coordination framework for distributed hypothesis formation. IEEE Transactions on Systems, Man, and Cybernetics 21(5), 1167–1183 (1991)
4. Fikes, R., Nilsson, N.J.: STRIPS: A new approach to the application of theorem proving to problem solving. Artificial Intelligence-4, 1971 2, 189–208 (1971)
5. Gerevini, A., Schubert, L.K.: Accelerating partial-order planners: Some techniques for effective search control and pruning. CoRR cs.AI/9609101 (1996)
6. Ghallab, M., Nau, D., Traverso, P.: Automated Planning: Theory and Practice. Morgan Kaufman, San Francisco (2004)
7. Güdemann, M., Ortmeier, F., Reif, W.: Formal modeling and verification of systems with self-x properties. In: Yang, L.T., Jin, H., Ma, J., Ungerer, T. (eds.) ATC 2006. LNCS, vol. 4158, pp. 38–47. Springer, Heidelberg (2006)
8. Horn, P.: Autonomic computing: Ibms perspective on the state of information technology (2001), http://www.research.ibm.com/autonomic/
9. Kephart, J.O.: Research challenges of autonomic computing. In: Inverardi, P., Jazayeri, M. (eds.) ICSE 2005. LNCS, vol. 4309, pp. 15–22. Springer, Heidelberg (2006)
10. Kephart, J.O., Chess, D.M.: The vision of autonomic computing. Computer 36(1), 41–50 (2003)
11. McDermott, D.: Pddl — the planning domain definition language (1998)
12. Müller-Schloer, C., von der Malsburg, C., Würtz, R.P.: Organic computing. Informatik Spektrum 27(4), 332–336 (2004)
13. Nguyen, X., Kambhampati, S.: Reviving partial order planning. In: Nebel, B. (ed.) Proceedings of the seventeenth International Conference on Artificial Intelligence (IJCAI 2001), August 4–10, 2001, pp. 459–466. Morgan Kaufmann, San Francisco (2001)
14. Schmeck, H.: Organic computing-vision and challenge for system design. In: Proceedings of the Parallel Computing in Electrical Engineering, International Conference on (PARELEC 2004), Washington, DC, USA, pp. 3–3. IEEE Computer Society Press, Los Alamitos (2004)

15. Schmeck, H.: Organic computing. Künstliche Intelligenz 05(3), 68–69 (2005)
16. Srivastava, B., Kambhampati, S.: The case for automated planning in autonomic computing. In: ICAC, pp. 331–332. IEEE Computer Society, Los Alamitos (2005)
17. Trumler, W., Bagci, F., Petzold, J., Ungerer, T.: AMUN - autonomic middleware for ubiquitous environments applied to the smart doorplate. ELSEVIER Advanced Engineering Informatics 19(3), 243–252 (2005)
18. Weld, D.S.: An introduction to least commitment planning. AI Magazine 15(4), 27–61 (1994)

A Trusted Group Signature Architecture in Virtual Computing Environment*

Deqing Zou, Yunfa Li, Song Wu**, and Weizhong Qiang

Services Computing Technology and System Lab, Cluster and Grid Computing Lab,
School of Computer Science and Technology,
Huazhong University of Science and Technology, China

Abstract. Nowadays coordinated applications become more and more popular in network computing environments, and group is the basic unit of task processing for such applications. Members in a group exchange data with each other. Group signature is used to guarantee the integrity of exchanged data and provide source authentication. In a Virtual Machine (VM) based computing system, a Virtual Machine Monitor (VMM) allows multiple applications to run in different virtual machines, and each virtual machine runs in its own hardware protection domain, and is strongly isolated from each other. A Trusted VMM can provide stronger security protection to build group signature architecture than traditional computing platforms. In this paper, we first introduce a trusted group signature architecture in virtual computing environment and how the Trusted VMM (TVMM) provides security guarantee for group signature components. Then we propose a group signature scheme with the function of message checking based on the discrete logarithm problem (DLP). Finally, we prove the security of the group signature scheme and architecture.

1 Introduction

Nowadays coordinated applications become more and more popular in network computing environments. Several entities are required to be involved in a task at the same time, and group is the basic unit of task processing for such applications. Group security is one of the most important issues for some important coordinated applications, such as e-commerce, military command system. In traditional computing environments, an operating system directly runs on the hardware, and it is hard for the operating system to protect itself from being attacked because of its complication and vulnerability. Applications running on an untrusty operating environment might be attacked. In addition, a suspicious application can easily attack other applications because there is no effective isolation mechanism among them. Consequently, if coordinated applications with group security function is implemented on an untrusty operating environment, sensitive information will be easily disclosed by the attackers even if group management itself can provide strong security functions.

---

* The project is supported by National Base Research Program of China (2007CB310900), and National Natural Science Foundation of China (60503040, 60673174). The project is also supported by Program for New Century Excellent Talents in University honored by Chinese Ministry of Education (NECT-07-0334).
** Corresponding author.

C. Rong et al. (Eds.): ATC 2008, LNCS 5060, pp. 73–85, 2008.
© Springer-Verlag Berlin Heidelberg 2008

In a Virtual Machine (VM) based computing system, a Virtual Machine Monitor (VMM) allows multiple applications to run in different virtual machines, and each virtual machine runs in its own hardware protection domain, providing strong isolation between virtual machines. Furthermore, migration can be easily implemented based on the VMM architecture. As the main work of the VMM platforms, such as VMWare and XEN, is virtual machine management and physical resource allocation for each virtual machine, they are more simple and with less vulnerability than traditional operating systems. With the development of information technology, the trusted computers, taking advantage of the functions of the underlying trusted computing hardware, become more and more important to provide security support for applications. Based on the VMM architecture, the trusted computers can provide a more flexible, isolated environment for each application than the ones based on the traditional architecture.

Group signature technology is adopted to guarantee the integrity of exchanged data and provide source authentication. There are a lot of group signature schemes, such as the group signature scheme based on the discrete logarithm [13], the threshold group signature scheme [14], the group blind signature scheme [15] and the forward-secure group signature scheme [16]. Although these group signature schemes can meet the security requirement of coordinated applications in different aspects, they didn't consider the situation of the underlying platform. For some coordinated applications, the group signature method that only one member is responsible for group signature is more efficient and secure than the one that several members are needed for group signature if the member of the front method and its platform are trusty. Based on the discrete logarithm problem (DLP), we propose a group signature scheme with the function of message checking, which allows an individual group member to sign a message on behalf of the group and only the specified receiver can recover, verify and check the message. Moreover, in case of disputes, the group controller can reveal the identity of the signer. Although the existing group signature schemes can be used for group-oriented communication, they do not provide the checking function. The group controller and group members are required to be located on a trusted platform, and its sensitive information, such as private key, can be protected by the platform.

The rest of this paper is organized as follows: we discuss the related work in section 2. In section 3, we mainly introduce the group signature architecture in the virtual computing environment. In section 4, we present a group signature scheme with the function of message checking. We proof the correctness and security of this group signature scheme in section 5. Finally, the conclusions and future work are drawn in section 6.

2   Related Work

In 1970s, virtual machine concept was proposed and defined in [1], which is a software replica of an underlying real machine and multiple virtual machines can operate on the same host machine concurrently, and be isolated from each other [1] [2]. In the past several years, with the appearance of muti-core technologies, virtual machines have gained a lot of attention again. In [3], the VM/370 Time-Sharing System was proposed by Creasy. In the VM/370 environment, an exclusive environment was created as a virtual machine for each user. With the progress of virtual machine technology, the virtual machine monitor (VMM) comes into being as a software-abstraction layer that partitions a hardware platform into one or more virtual machines [4]. In fact, a virtual machine environment is created by a Virtual Machine Monitor (VMM), also called an "operating system for operating systems" [5]. The monitor creates one or more virtual machines on top of a single real machine. Each VM provides facilities for an application or a "guest system" that believes to be executing on a normal hardware environment.

There are two different methods to build a virtual machine system. One is that the virtual machine monitor is implemented between the hardware and the guest systems, such as Xen [6] and VMware ESX Server [7]. The other is that the virtual machine monitor is implemented as a normal process of an underlying real operating system, such as VMware Workstation [8] and User-Mode Linux [7]. Some security research work was conducted based on the VMM architecture, for example, an experience of use of virtual machines for the security of systems was described in [9]. In the paper, Revirt is defined as an intermediate layer between the monitor and the host system, and the captured data is sent to the host system through the syslog process (the standard UNIX logging daemon) of the virtual machine. However, if the virtual system is compromised, the log messages can be manipulated by the invader and consequently are no more reliable. A VMI-IDS (Virtual Machine Introspection Intrusion Detection System) is described for searching intrusion evidences in [10]. In the system, the virtual machine executes directly on top of the hardware and the intrusion detection system executes in a privileged virtual machine and scans data extracted from the other VMs. The Secure Hypervisor (sHype) project [11] aims to support controlled sharing of resources between VMs on a platform, such as memory, CPU cycles, and network bandwidth. The above mentioned projects didn't consider the security of the VMM itself.

The Trusted Computing Group (TCG) is an international industry organization to define a set of specifications aiming to provide hardware-based root of trust and a set of primitive functions to propagate trust to application software as well as across platforms [12], [13]. The root of trust in TCG is a hardware component on the motherboard of a platform called the Trusted Platform Module (TPM). TPM provides protected data (cryptographic secrets and arbitrary data) by never releasing a root key outside the TPM. In addition, TPM provides some primitive cryptographic functions, such as random number generation, RSA key generation and RSA asymmetric key algorithms. Most important, a TPM provides mechanism of integrity measurement, storage, and reporting of a platform, from which strong protection capabilities and attestations can be achieved. To utilize the functions provided by TPM, TCG set TSS specification [14]. This specification defines a TCG Software Stack (TSS) that is an integral part of each platform, and provides functions that can be used by enhanced operating systems and applications. TSS supplies one entry point for applications to the TPM functionality.

In [15], the design and implementation of a virtual trusted platform Module (TPM) facility is presented. In this Module, TPM is virtualized and can supports higher-level services. Moreover, it can also support suspend and resume operations, as well as migration of virtual TPM instances with their corresponding virtual machine across platforms. In [16], a flexible architecture for trusted computing is presented that is called Terra. On Terra, applications with a wide range of security requirements are allowed to run simultaneously on commodity hardware. At the same time, Terra supports today's operating systems and applications. Terra realizes this union with a trusted virtual machine monitor (TVMM), that is, a high-assurance virtual machine monitor that partitions a single tamper-resistant, general-purpose platform into multiple isolated virtual machines.

Group signature is first introduced by Chaum and van Heyst in [17], allows each group member to sign messages on behalf of a group anonymously and unlinkably. However, in case of later disputes, a designated group manager can open a group signature and then identify the true signer.

In 1998, Lee and Chang presented an efficient group signature scheme based on the DLP [18]. Since two same pieces of information are included in all group signatures generated by the same group member, their scheme is obviously linkable. Therefore, although this scheme is efficient, it needs to be improved. To provide unlinkability, an improved group signature scheme is proposed in [19]. Regretfully, the improved group signature scheme is still linkable [20]. Therefore, based on Shamir's idea of identity (ID)-based cryptosystems [21], Tseng and Jan proposed an ID-based group signature scheme in [22]. In this ID-based group signature scheme, anyone (not necessarily a group member) is able to generate a valid group signature on any message, which cannot be opened by the group manager. Therefore, this scheme is forgeable. In order to solve the question, in [23] and [24], Tseng and Jan revised their schemes, and Popescu presented a modification to the Tseng-Jan ID-based scheme [25]. After that, Xian and You proposed a new group signature scheme with strong separability [26] such that the group manager can be split into a membership manager and a revocation manager. In addition, based on the above group signature schemes, Wang presented a security analysis for these group signature schemes [27]. In this paper, we design a trusted VMM based group signature schemes, and propose a group signature scheme with the function of message checking.

3   Trusted VMM Based Group Signature Architecture

In this section, we will describe Trusted VMM (TVMM) based group signature architecture, as depicted in Figure 1, and introduce a group signature scheme. The TVMM is the heart of the system architecture, and it can virtualize machine resources and allow VMs to run independently and concurrently.

3.1   Group Signature Architecture

We will introduce the main components of group signature architecture based on TVMM in this sub-section.

- **Hardware Platform**

Hardware is the basement of TVMM. In the process of attestation, hardware embedded with cryptographic keys is the trust base of the attestation chain. Furthermore, hardware also assists in following aspects: Hardware Support for Virtualization; Hardware Support for Secure I/O; Secure Counter (against roll back or re-play attack); and Device Isolation. In order to prevent leaking of privacy through the hardware private key in the process of attestation, it's suggested that the hardware vendor signs their products.

Normally, security chipsets, such as TPM, are embedded in the platform. This module is a security specification defined by the Trusted Computing Group. It provides cryptographic operations such as asymmetric key generation, decryption, encryptions, signing and migration of keys between TPMs, as well as random number generation and hashing. It also provides secure storage for small amounts of information such as cryptographic keys. Because the TPM is implemented in hardware and presents a carefully designed interface, it is resistant to software attacks.

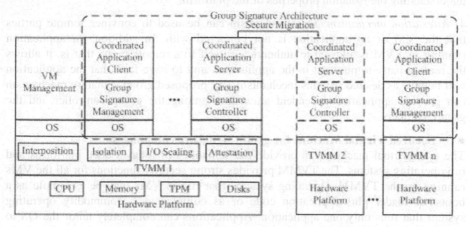

Fig. 1. TVMM based group signature architecture

• **Trusted Virtual Machine Monitor**

The VMM provides the VM management with interfaces to create and manage VMs, and to connect them through virtual devices. Besides the functions of the VMM, the TVMM provide functions as Interposition, I/O Sealing, isolation, and attestation for VM security considerations. We introduce these functions in detail as follows:

1) *Interposition mechanism.* This mechanism intercepts all kernel-user transitions for the TVMM to protect sensitive information. In the mechanism, the VMM interposes all the transition between user space and kernel space in order to protect CPU context. Upon the interception of a transition, the VMM is responsible for saving and restoring the CPU context owned by a trusted process. The VMM also conceals some general purpose registers from the OS kernel. No replay attack is possible since the OS kernel cannot set malicious CPU context that resumes the execution of a trusted process in a previous execution.

2) *I/O Sealing mechanism.* From the start, the TVMM must allocate the physical storage (i.e. hard disk space) into different parts and distribute them to VMs. This mechanism transparently encrypts and decrypts sensitive I/O data to prevent the OS kernel from observing the data. Sensitive data of a trusted process, when to be input from or output to persistent storage, will be protected by cryptographic means. In the TVMM layer, sensitive I/O data can be transparently encrypted. Generally, I/O operations are made using system calls or memory-mapped I/O. For system calls, the TVMM intercepts each I/O related system call and encrypts the data before passing it

to the OS kernel. For memory-mapped I/O, the TVMM intercepts the page table updating requests and decrypts the data on the first page fault.

3) *Isolation mechanism.* The TVMM allows multiple applications to run in different virtual machines. Each virtual machine runs in its own hardware protection domain, providing strong isolation between virtual machines. Therefore, secure isolation is essential for providing the confidentiality and integrity required by VMs. Also, the abstraction of separate physical machines provides an intuitive model for understanding the isolation properties of the platform.

4) *Attestation mechanism.* This mechanism can be used to convince remote parties that the VM or an application is not tampered with. In addition, an application running in a VM is allowed to authenticate itself to a remote party, that is, it allows the remote party to put trust in the application, and to have faith that the application will behave as desired. By this mechanism, our proposed group signature mechanism can provide application dependent attestation among the group controller and the group members.

- **Secured Virtual Machine for group signature components**

The open virtual machine can provide the semantics of today's open platforms and run operating systems. The TVMM provides strong security functions for all the VMs running on the TVMM. Operating systems that run in VMs may be as simple as a bootstrap loader plus application code or as complex as a commodity operating system that runs only one application. Applications can completely tailor the OS to their security needs.

There are two kinds of VMs, including privileged VM and normal VM, for example, Dom 0 is a privileged VM and Dom U is a normal VM in the virtual machine platform, XEN. The privileged VM can manage other normal VMs, for example, a privileged VM can create, pause, resume, and destroy a normal VM. Normally, the privileged VM utilizes a tailored OS, and an application with high-security requirements runs in a normal trusted VM with an embedded, tailored OS.

Group signature is implemented to provide message integrity and source authentication for coordinated applications. The normal trusted VM provides a secure environment for group signature components, including group signature controller, and group signature management. Normally, group signature controller is used to support coordinated application server, and group signature management is used to support coordinated application client. A group member of the client side can join a group managed by the group controller in the server side. If peer-to-peer architecture is adopted for a coordinated application, the above two components can be located at the same VM, and any peer can be selected to take the functionality of a group controller. Group signature management can be used by group members to sign or verify the message. Group signature controller can be used by the group controller to manage the message exchanged among the group members.

- **Secure Migration for group signature controller**

In order to guarantee the availability of group controller, the VM where the group controller is located should be migrated from one trusted platform to another trusted platform securely. In our secure migration mechanism, we enable VM secure migration by using asymmetric and symmetric keys to encrypt the image file on the source platform, and decrypt and resume it in the destination. There are four steps: 1) Attestation between the two platforms, with the trusted computing technology, platforms can authenticate each other with Attestation Identity Certificates; 2) VM image secure transportation, after VM image data with group signature controller has been serialized and a symmetric key created, the image encrypted with this symmetric key is then retrieved from the source platform. For integrity validation on the target side, an internal migration digest is updated with the data's hash and embedded. Besides the encrypted VM image, the symmetric key encrypted with the public key of the destination platform also needs to be migrated; 3) Verify VM image in the target side, after the decryption of the symmetric key and the VM image on the destination platform, the source VM image is retrieved and the migration digest recalculated; 4) Restart the VM image after the verification in the target side. XEN supports live migration that shortens downtimes by replicating the running system's image on a destination machine. We extend its migration function with our secure migration protocol, but will extend the downtime of the migrated system a little longer than the original.

3.2 Group Signature Scheme

Based on the architecture in section 3, we propose a group signature scheme in this section, which contains four phases, including the parameters generating phase, the signature generating phase, the verification signature phase and the opening signature phase. The group signature scheme is described in detail as follows:

(1) The parameters generating phase
Suppose p and q are two large prime numbers such that $q|p-1$, and g is a generator with order q in $GF(p)$.

Step 1: Each group member GM_i randomly chooses an integer x_i and computes the public keys $y_i = g^{x_i} \bmod p$ ($i=1, 2, 3, \ldots, n$).

Step 2: The group controller randomly chooses an integer x_c and computes the public key $y_c = g^{x_c} \bmod p$.

Step 3: For each group member GM_i, the group controller randomly chooses an integer a_i in Z_q^*, and computes $r_i = a_i * ID_i - x_c \bmod q$, $s_i = y_i^{a_i} \bmod p$ ($i=1, 2, 3, \ldots, n$).

Step 4: The group controller sends (r_i, s_i) to the group member GM_i secretly.

Step 5: After receiving (r_i, s_i), GM_i verifies the validity by checking the following equation

$$s_i = (g^{r_i} * y_c)^{x_i / ID_i} \bmod p \tag{1}$$

(2) The signature generating phase
Step 1: The GM_i computes $M = M_{check} \| M_{original}$, where M_{check} is a short checking message, $M_{original}$ is the message that the group member GM_i wants to sign, and $\|$ denotes the concatenation.

Step 2: The GM_i randomly chooses three integers b_1, b_2 and b_3 in Z_q^*.

Step 3: The GM_i computes

$$\beta = x_i * b_1 \ mod \ q \qquad (2)$$

$$\delta = s_i^{b_1 * ID_i} \ mod \ p \qquad (3)$$

$$\xi = g^{b_2} \ mod \ p \qquad (4)$$

$$\psi = M * y_j^{-b_1 * \beta * h(\beta \| \delta \| \xi) * b_3} \ mod \ p \qquad (5)$$

$$\rho = b_1 - r_i * h(\psi) - b_2 \ mod \ p \qquad (6)$$

Where $h()$ is a publicly known hash function

Step 4: The group signature for message M is η, where $\eta = \{\beta, \delta, \xi, \psi, \rho, M_{check}\}$.

(3) The verification signatures phase
The group member GM_j can verify the validity of the group signature by using the following steps.

Step 1: Recover the message

$$M = \psi * [(g^\rho * y_c^{-h(\psi)} * \xi)^\beta * \delta^{h(\psi)}]^{x_j * h(\beta \| \delta \| \xi) * b_3} \ mod \ p \qquad (7)$$

Step 2: Check the following congruence relation

$$M_{check} = head(M, L) \qquad (8)$$

Where L is the bit number of the checking message M_{check} and $head(M, L)$ is a function which returns the first L bits of M. If the above relations hold, GM_j accepts the group signature η. Otherwise, the group signature η is rejected by GM_j.

(4) The opening signature phase
In case of a dispute, the signature must be opened to reveal the identity of the signer. Because the group controller has an access to the (ID_i, y_i, a_i) of each group member GM_i, the group controller can acquire the (ID_i, y_i, a_i) of GM_i. So, in case of disputes, the group controller can reveal the identity of the signer by using the equation $\delta = g^{\beta * a_i * ID_i} \ mod \ p$.

4 The Analysis of Group Signature Scheme in Virtual Computing Environment

In this section, we will analyze the security of our group signature scheme first, and we will analyze the security of group signature architecture based on TVMM.

4.1 Security Analysis of Group Signature Scheme

The security of our proposed scheme is based on the DLP. In this section, we will analyze the security of our proposed scheme. Some possible attacks against the proposed scheme are presented below.

Attack 1: If an adversary intercepts a valid membership (r_i, s_i), he/she tries to forge a group signature.

Analysis of Attack 1: If an adversary intercepts a valid membership (r_i, s_i), he/she can compute δ and ξ by Equation (3) and (4). Although he/she can forge an integer x_i^* to compute β, ψ, and ρ by Equation (2), (5) and (6), he/she can not forge a group signature making Equation (7) and (8) holds. The main reason is he/she does not have the secret key x_i. Therefore, even if an adversary intercepts a valid membership (r_i, s_i), he/she does not forge a group signature.

Attack 2: If an adversary does not intercept any information, he/she tries to forge a group signature.

Analysis of Attack 2: If an adversary does not intercept any information, he/she who tries to forge a group signature will have to face the DLP. For the adversary who does not intercept any information, there are five situations if he/she wants to forge a group signature. The analyses about the five situations are described as follows:

1. An adversary chooses a message $M=M_{check}\|M_{original}$ and randomly selects β, δ, ξ, ψ. According to the DLP, it is difficult to calculate parameter ρ in Equation (7) when ψ, A, B, θ and g are knowable
2. An adversary chooses a message $M=M_{check}\|M_{original}$ and randomly selects β, δ, ξ, ρ. According to the DLP, it is difficult to calculate parameter ψ in Equation (7) when we know A, B, D, β, θ and g.
3. An adversary chooses a message $M=M_{check}\|M_{original}$ and randomly selects β, δ, ψ, ρ. According to the DLP, it is difficult to calculate parameter ξ in Equation (7) when A, B, ψ, β and θ are knowable.
4. An adversary chooses a message $M=M_{check}\|M_{original}$ and randomly selects δ, ξ, ψ, ρ. According to the DLP, it is difficult to calculate parameter β in Equation (7) when A, δ, ξ, ψ and θ are knowable.
5. An adversary chooses a message $M=M_{check}\|M_{original}$ and randomly selects β, ξ, ψ, ρ. According to the DLP, it is difficult to calculate parameter δ in Equation (7) when A, β, ξ, ψ and θ are knowable.

Based on the above analyses, we can conclude if an adversary does not intercept any information, it is difficult for the adversary to forge a group signature.

Attack 3: The verifier GM_j who does not have any information except his/her secret key x_j tries to forge a group signature.

Analysis of Attack 3: If the verifier GM_j does not have any information except his/her secret key x_j, he/she tries to forge a group signature. For the verifier GM_j, there are five situations if he/she wants to forge a group signature.

1. The verifier GM_j chooses a message $M=M_{check}\|M_{original}$ and randomly selects β, δ, ξ, ψ. It is difficult to calculate parameter ρ in Equation (7) when ψ, A, B, θ and g are knowable.
2. The verifier GM_j chooses a message $M=M_{check}\|M_{original}$ and randomly selects β, δ, ξ, ρ. It is difficult to calculate parameter ψ in Equation (7) when A, B, D, β, θ and g are knowable.
3. The verifier GM_j chooses a message $M=M_{check}\|M_{original}$ and randomly selects β, δ, ψ, ρ. It is difficult to calculate parameter ξ in Equation (7) when A, B, ψ, β and θ are knowable.
4. The verifier GM_j chooses a message $M=M_{check}\|M_{original}$ and randomly selects δ, ξ, ψ, ρ. It is difficult to calculate parameter β in Equation (7) when A, δ, ξ, ψ and θ are knowable.
5. The verifier GM_j chooses a message $M=M_{check}\|M_{original}$ and randomly selects β, ξ, ψ, ρ. It is difficult to calculate parameter δ in Equation (7) when A, β, ξ, ψ and θ are knowable.

Based on the above analyses, we know: if the verifier GMj does not have any information except his/her secret key x_j, it is very difficult for the verifier to forge a group signature.

Attack 4: If an adversary intercepts a valid group signature $\eta=\{\beta, \delta, \xi, \psi, \rho, M_{check}\}$, he/she tries to identity the actual signer.

Analysis of Attack 4: If an adversary intercepts a valid group signature $\eta=\{\beta, \delta, \xi, \psi, \rho, M_{check}\}$, he/she will have to compute y_i by Equation $y_i= g^{x_i} \bmod p$ and $s_i = y_i^{a_i} \bmod p$ in order to find out the identity of actual signer. But b_1 is an unknown number, the adversary can not find out the signer. In addition, a_i, b_1 and ID_i are unknown. Based on Equation $s_i = y_i^{a_i} \bmod p$ and $\delta = s_i^{b_1*ID_i} \bmod p$, It is very difficult to calculate parameter ID_i. Therefore, the adversary can not find out the identity of actual signer.

Attack 5: If an adversary intercepts two valid group signatures, he/she tries to identity whether the two group signatures were generated by the same signature or not.

Analysis of Attack 5: Assume an adversary intercepts two valid group signatures $\eta=\{\beta, \delta, \xi, \psi, \rho, M_{check}\}$ and $\eta'=\{\beta', \delta', \xi', \psi', \rho', M_{check}'\}$, he/she can compute $\dfrac{g^\beta}{g^{\beta'}}=\dfrac{g^{x_i*b_1}}{g^{x_i*b_1'}} \bmod \mathrm{p}$ and $\dfrac{\delta}{\delta'}=\dfrac{s_i^{b_1*ID_i}}{s_i^{b_1'*ID_i}}=\dfrac{(g^{x_i*b_1})^{a_i*ID_i}}{(g^{x_i*b_1'})^{a_i*ID_i}} \bmod \mathrm{p}$. Thus, he/she can get $\dfrac{\delta}{\delta'}=\dfrac{s_i^{b_1*ID_i}}{s_i^{b_1'*ID_i}}=\dfrac{(g^\beta)^{a_i*ID_i}}{(g^{\beta'})^{a_i*ID_i}} \bmod \mathrm{p}$ and check whether the equation holds or not. If the equation holds, the two valid group signature η and η' were generated by the same signer. But the integer a_i and ID_i are unknown, hence, the adversary can not identity whether the two group signatures were generated by the same signature or not.

Based on the above analytic results, we can draw a conclusion: our proposed scheme satisfies the requirement of unforgeability, anonymity, unlinkability and exculpability [27]. In addition, the group controller can acquire the (ID_i, y_i, a_i) of GM_i

because he/she has an access to the (ID_i, y_i, a_i) of each member GM_i. So, the group controller can determine the signer. Therefore, our proposed scheme also satisfies the requirement of traceability [27].

4.2 Security Analysis of Group Signature Architecture

Sensitive information of a group member or group controller, when to be input from or output to persistent storage, will be protected by cryptographic means. For coordinated applications, the TVMM intercepts each related system call and encrypts the data before passing it to the OS kernel. On fetching these data from the OS kernel, the TVMM will also decrypt the data before passing them to the user spaces. Moreover, in order to prevent information leakage during the process that the coordinated applications are loaded, a key provided by the TVMM platform is used to encrypt the relation program code and data. Meanwhile, the TVMM assists the process creation to decrypt the code and data. In addition, the architecture can transparently encrypt sensitive information above the TVMM layer by using our proposed group signature mechanism. Because there are the TVMM and our proposed group signature mechanism that can decrypt the code and data during process creation, there is no leakage of sensitive information during this process. So, it is very secure for sensitive information of group member and group controller.

In this TVMM, attestation enables a coordinated application to authenticate themselves to remote parties. The group controller can judge for itself the correctness and security of each group member, which is based on the trusted platform. By receiving the attestation, the group controller can know the remote party which group member was started to send a message on the TVMM platform. In this TVMM, a certificate chain is first build for the attestation. This chain begins with the hardware, whose private key is permanently embedded in a tamper resistant chip and signed by the vendor providing the machine. The tamper-resistant hardware certifies the system firmware (e.g. PC BIOS). The firmware certifies the system boot loader, which certifies the TVMM, which in turn certifies the VMs that it loads. In the following step, a group certificate is built for the group attestation. In the group certificate, the group controller uses the group private to sign a message, and each group member can use the group public to verify the correctness and security of the message. By using the certificate chain and the group certificate, the group controller can judge for itself the correctness and security of each group member.

In this trusted VMM based group signature architecture, the group controller first chooses a public key for the coordinated applications and sends the message (r_i, s_i) to the group member GM_i secretly. The message (r_i, s_i) and the corresponding VM image data are encrypted by the symmetric key, which is created by the source platform. Then, the encrypted messages are sent to the destination and only the destination platform can resume it by using TPM. Thus, it is impossible for any adversary to decrypt these messages. So, it is secure when the key component migrates from the source platform to the destination platform.

5 Conclusions and Future Work

In this paper, we propose a TVMM based group signature architecture, and design a novel group signature scheme with the function of message checking. Under this architecture, coordinated applications with high-security requirement can be supported.

We analyze how the TVMM provides security guarantee for group signature components. In order to provide the availability of the coordinated application server and group signature controller, secure migration is adopted. We analyze the security of our proposed group signature scheme, and the security of the group signature architecture. In our future work, we will integrate our group signature architecture into some coordinated application with high-security requirement, such as online game, coordinated military command system.

References

[1] Popek, G., Goldberg, R.: Formal Requirements for Virtualizable Third Generation Architectures. Communications of the ACM 17(7), 412–421 (1974)

[2] Goldberg, R.P.: Survey of Virtual Machine Research. Computer, 34–45 (June 1974)

[3] Creasy, R.J.: The Origin of the VM/370 Time-Sharing System. IBM J. Research and Development, 483–490 (September 1981)

[4] Whitaker, A., Shaw, M., Gribble, S.D.: Denali: lightweight virtual machines for distributed and networked applications., University of Washington (Technical Report 02-02-01)

[5] Kelem, N., Feiertag, R.: A Separation Model for Virtual Machine Monitors. In: Research in Security and Privacy. IEEE Computer Society Symposium, pp. 78–86 (1999)

[6] Barham, P., Dragovic., B., Fraser, K., Hand, S., Harris, T., Ho, A., Neugebauer, R., Pratt, I., Warfield, A.: Xen and the Art of Virtualization. In: 9th ACM Symposium on Operating Systems Principles – SOSP 2003, October 19-22, 2003, pp. 164–177 (2003)

[7] VMware Inc. VMware Technical White Paper, Palo Alto–CA-USA (1999)

[8] Dike, J.: A User-mode port of the Linux Kernel. In: Proceedings of the 4th Annual Linux Showcase & Conference, Atlanta – USA, pp. 63–72 (2000)

[9] Dunlap, G., King, S., Cinar, S., Basrai, M., Chen, P.: ReVirt: Enabling Intrusion Analysis through Virtual-Machine Logging and Replay. In: Proceedings of the 2002 Symposium on Operating Systems Design and Implementation (OSDI) (December 9-11, 2002)

[10] Garfinkel, T., Rosenblum, M.: A Virtual Machine Introspection Based Architecture for Intrusion Detection. In: Proceedings of the Network and Distributed System Security Symposium (NDSS) (2003)

[11] Sailer, R., Jaeger, T., Valdez, E., Caceres, R., Perez, R., Berger, S., Griffin, J.L., van Doorn, L.: Building a mac-based security architecture for the xen open-source hypervisor. In: Proceeding of the 2005 Annual Computer Security Applications Conference, December 2005, pp. 276–285 (2005)

[12] Trusted Computing Group, TCG Specification Architecture Overview, Version1.2 (2003), April 2004, http://www.trustedcomputinggroup.org

[13] Trusted Computing Group, Trusted Platform Module Main Specification, Part 1: Design Principles, Part 2: TPM Structures, Part 3: Commands, March 2006, Version 1.2, Revision 94 (2003)

[14] Trusted Computing Group (2003), TCG Software Stack (TSS) Specification, Version 1.2 (January 6, 2006)

[15] Berger, S., Caceres, R., Goldman, K.A., Perez, R., Sailer, R., van Doorn, L.: vTPM: Virtualizing the Trusted Platform Module. In: Proceedings of the 15th conference on USENIX Security Symposium, July 31-August 4, Vancouver, B. C, Canada (2006)

[16] Garfinkel, T., Pfaff, B., Chow, J., Rosenblum, M., Boneh, D.: Terra: a virtual machine-based platform for trusted computing. In: Proceedings of the 19th ACM Symposium on Operating Systems Principles 2003 (SOSP 2003),October 19-22, 2003, Bolton Landing, NY, USA, pp. 193–206 (2003)

[17] Chaum, D., van. Heyst, E.: Group Signatures. In: Davies, D.W. (ed.) EUROCRYPT 1991. LNCS, vol. 547, pp. 257–265. Springer, Heidelberg (1991)

[18] Lee, W., Chang, C.: Efficient Group Signature Scheme Based on the Discrete Logarithm. In: IEE Proceedings Computers & Digital Techniques, January 1998, vol. 145(1), pp. 15–18 (1998)

[19] Tseng, Y.M., Jan, J.K.: Improved Group Signature Based on Discrete Logarithm Problem. Electronics Letters 35(1), 37–38 (1999)

[20] Sun, H.: Comment: Improved Group Signature Scheme Based on Discrete Logarithm Problem. Electronics Letters 35(16), 1323–1324 (1999)

[21] Shamir, A.: Identity-based Cryptosystem and Signature Schemes. In: Blakely, G.R., Chaum, D. (eds.) CRYPTO 1984. LNCS, vol. 196, pp. 47–53. Springer, Heidelberg (1985)

[22] Tseng, Y.M., Jan, J.K.: A Novel ID-based Group Signature. In: International Computer Symposium, Workshop on Cryptology and Information Security, Tainan, pp. 159–164 (1998)

[23] Tseng, Y.M., Jan, J.K.: Reply: improved group signature scheme based on discrete logarithm problem. Electronics Letters 35(20), 1324 (1999)

[24] Tseng, Y.M., Jan, J.K.: A Novel ID-based Group Signature. Information Sciences 120(1-4), 131–141 (1999)

[25] Popescu, C.: A Modification of the Tseng-Jan Group Signature Scheme. Studia Universitatis Babes-Bolyai Informatica XLV(2), 36–40 (2000)

[26] Xia, S., You, J.: A group signature scheme with strong separability. The Journal of Systems and Software 60(3), 177–182 (2002)

[27] Wang, G.L.: Security Analysis of Several Group Signature Schemes. In: Johansson, T., Maitra, S. (eds.) INDOCRYPT 2003. LNCS, vol. 2904, Springer, Heidelberg (2003)

SepRep: A Novel Reputation Evaluation Model in Peer-to-Peer Networks

Xiaowei Chen, Kaiyong Zhao, and Xiaowen Chu

Department of Computer Science, Hong Kong Baptist University
{xwchen,kyzhao,chxw}@comp.hkbu.edu.hk

Abstract. In a heterogeneous peer-to-peer network, different peers provide different qualities of service. It will be very helpful if a peer can identify which peers can provide better services than others. In this paper, we design a novel reputation model which enables any peer to calculate a reputation value for any other peer that reflects the quality of service provided by that peer, so as to differentiate peers providing good quality of service from those peers providing poor service. Furthermore, to overcome the problem of malicious recommendations, we propose an auxiliary trust mechanism which calculates a trust value for each peer. Experimental results show that our reputation model achieves a fast convergence speed, and it is also robust against a large portion of malicious peers that provide fraud recommendations.

1 Introduction

Network development shows a new trend towards large scale content distribution, global computing, and global storage. Meanwhile, the networking system has been shifting from Client/Server model to the Peer-to-Peer (P2P) model. The large-scale deployment of P2P software (such as KaZaA, BitTorrent, eMule, Skype, etc.) provides strong evidence to the success of P2P model, especially in the area of content distribution. Recent Internet traffic statistics indicate that P2P traffic accounts for more than 60% of the total Internet traffic since 2004 [1]. Along with the popularity of P2P model, many problems are becoming more complex and different from Client/Server computing environment, due to the anarchic nature of P2P systems such as decentralization, autonomous, and dynamics. In this paper, we are specifically interested in the issue of reputation and trust management in P2P networks.

1.1 Background

The objective of reputation and trust system in P2P network is to allow two sides of a transaction to judge the reliability and/or quality of transaction by studying the peer's history behavior. As pointed out by Jøsang, the efficiency of a trust mechanism should cover three factors: long time availability of attribution-entity object, acquirement and distribution of trust information, and decision-making by creditable information [2].

Currently, a number of reputation models or systems have been proposed to enhance the robustness, scalability and efficiency of P2P computing model, such as

C. Rong et al. (Eds.): ATC 2008, LNCS 5060, pp. 86–99, 2008.

EigenTrust [3], P2Prep [4], Credence [5], NICE [6], PeerTrust [7], LIP [8], P-Grid [9] and PowerTrust [10]. In reality, Amazon, eMule, eBay, Epinions and BitTorrent, etc. are using their proprietary P2P reputation systems. In fact, the origin of reputation and trust in P2P comes from free-riding [11]. Recent research results also indicate that it is not uncommon to see bad behaviors in P2P systems due to the lack of efficient incentive and reputation mechanism [12]. Examples of bad behaviors are spreading virus, worm and Trojan horse [13], dissemination of fake files into P2P file-sharing network [14], index poisoning in P2P file-sharing network [15].

1.2 Motivation

The concepts of reputation and trust are always ambiguous in the research literature. Different people have different understandings on the terms "reputation" and "trust". Some researchers take them as the same meaning, while some others think they are quite different.

We should take a new perspective to see what a peer really needs. In a P2P content distribution network, a peer wants to retrieve genuine files with fastest speed, so it is apt to choose peers which can provide high quality of service (QoS). It is worthwhile to point out that a high QoS implicitly means a successful service. E.g., providing a fraud file is regarded as the worst service. Traditionally, the reputation or trust systems are built to detect which peers fail to provide genuine files. But, the quality of the service has not been considered into the reputation system. Consider another scenario: a peer M intentionally sets the outbound bandwidth to be very low, and it takes several days for other peers to download a small file from peer M, then the quality of service of M is very low. If this information is publicly available, other peers would avoid acquiring services from M, and as a penalty, they may stop providing services to M.

In this paper, we propose a novel reputation model named SepRep that explicitly defines reputation as the quality of service provided by a peer. A peer keeps a reputation value for every other peer. Every time a peer X has received a service from peer Y, X updates the reputation value of Y based on the quality of this service. If we assume that every peer consistently provides the service around a quality level in a time window, it will be critical to converge the calculated reputation values in a short time. Obviously it is not efficient to update reputation values only through direct transaction. A peer can actually ask other peers about the reputation of some peer to speed up the convergence. In the course of gathering reputation values from the P2P network, some malicious peers may collude to provide fraud recommendations for the purpose of increasing someone's reputation or decreasing someone's reputation adversely. To resolve this issue, we propose to deploy an auxiliary trust system that measures the trustworthiness of peers when propagating reputation values. It is worthwhile to clarify that the trust system is used to detect malicious peers that report fraud reputation values, not for detecting peers that provide fraud services. The peers providing fraud services can be detected as peers providing very low quality of service.

We designed and implemented a simulation model to evaluate the performance of our SepRep reputation model. The experimental result validates that SepRep reputation model can converge quickly and it is robust against a large portion of malicious peers.

The remaining parts of this paper are organized as follows: Section 2 reviews existing work on P2P reputation and trust systems. In Section 3, we present the SepRep model in detail. We evaluate the performance of SepRep model in section 4. Finally, Section 5 concludes the paper.

2   Related Works

Many literatures try to exactly define the concepts of reputation and trust. Due to the universality of the concepts, the understandings to them appear diversity. According to the ITU-T X.509, Section 3.3.54, trust is defined as follows: "Generally an entity can be said to 'trust' a second entity when the first entity makes the assumption that the second entity will behave exactly as the first entity expects." That means, trust is an indicator of credibility to content, and it is comparable. Another very similar concept is reputation. According to a formal definition of reputation given by Wilson [16], together with P2P environment, it is "a characteristic or attribute ascribed to one peer (or peers) A by another person (or peers) B". On the other hand, the reputation is also considered as a service provider which can be formed by means of a collection of ratings by different users, each such rating is intuitively equivalent to user satisfaction. Besides, Jøsang distinguishes the trust and reputation: trust is divided into reliability trust and decision trust, and reputation is viewed as a collective measure of trustworthiness based on the referrals or ratings from members in a community [2].

Though reputation and trust have various definitions, they are interrelated tightly, have some common features, so some researchers take the two concepts as the same meaning. But the biggest difference between reputation and trust is that reputation is an objective concept, and that trust is a subjective concept. We can use one sentence to describe them: I trust you because you have good reputation; I trust you despite your bad reputation [2].

There are some new reputation systems in P2P in recent years. They provide different approaches to evaluate reputation.

Credence is a subjective, independent and local reputation mechanism based on Gnutella. It defines polling mechanism, which let users vote for whether the sharing file matches the file description or not. Credence exchanges reputation table among the selected high reputation value users, extends reputation relationship by reputation transitivity, and chooses the path with highest reputation value as the peer's reputation value. Credence uses file as the basis of building reputation relationship. It can avoid dynamic feature of users' behaviors and can judge the essential attribution of file. But peer's reputation value will be affected in users' voting because of users' subjectivity, especially in collusion attack. And it needs to solve the problem about how to prompt users' spontaneity.

TrustGuard is a secure reputation mechanism framework based on PeerTrust. The major goal of TrustGuard focuses on the vulnerabilities of a reputation system itself. The authors identify three types of threats, that is, strategic oscillations, fake transaction and dishonest feedback, and provide corresponding countermeasures. In this framework, each peer has a transaction management unit, a reputation evaluation engine and a feedback data storage unit. The three components' computing uses strategic oscillation guard and dishonest feedback guard to ensure the correctness. TrustGuard uses modular design, it does not need to worry about the other parts of system when adding new guard module or modifying current module.

LIP is an objective, global reputation mechanism. LIP discovered and proved that "users are apt to remain real files in a long time, and delete polluted files in a short time". It gives statistics automatically about file's remaining time in each user's computer, and then computes the number of holders to each file and the file's average remaining time in user's computer. The objective statistics feature of LIP can make it get more reliable information, and it can collect complete information without adopting incentive mechanism.

PowerTrust is a global, robust and scalable reputation system based on power-law. It uses trust overlay network (TON) model to analyze the power-law distribution of peer feedbacks. The system offers very fast global reputation aggregation, ranking and updating, together with robustness and wide applicability. PowerTrust does not solve collusion problem well and it has not supported unstructured P2P system currently.

3   SepRep Model Methodology

3.1   The SepRep Model Concept

In SepRep model, reputation is an objective concept. It is a measure of quantified Quality of Service (QoS) provided by a peer to another peer in P2P networks, which can be formed by all the aspects of service quality. For file-sharing applications, QoS can be evaluated by considering a peer's available outbound bandwidth, the number of sharing contents, content validity, the online duration time, etc. For P2P computing applications, QoS can be evaluated by the time of completing the computing task. In the following, we consider a P2P network with n nodes which are labeled from 1 to n.

Each peer has an inherent global reputation (GR) which depends on that peer's characteristics such as CPU and dedicated network bandwidth for this P2P system. The GR determines the level of QoS provided by a peer. For simplicity, we further make the following assumptions: (1) a peer's GR is constant in a long time window; (2) The value of GR ranges between 0 and 1, where a higher value of GR means a higher QoS; (3) the QoS received by a peer is GR plus a random disturbance; this requires that all the peers agree with a set of rules for quantifying the QoS. This issue is important but beyond the scope of this paper.

Each peer keeps a local reputation (R) for every other peer: $R_{i \to j}$ represents the opinion of peer i on peer j's reputation in the P2P system. It is this set of local reputations that provides useful references for the action of a peer, e.g., how to select the peer(s) for a service. To calculate the values of local reputations, we make use of direct reputation (DR) and indirect reputation (IR). Direct reputation $DR_{i \to j}$ represents the direct opinion of peer i on peer j's service in a transaction. As mentioned previously, we assume that $DR_{i \to j}$ is close to the value of GR_j. It will be very slow to get all the local reputation values convergent by using direct reputations only. Hence we incorporate the indirect reputation $IR_{i \to j}$ which represents the opinions collected by peer i from other peers on peer j's reputation, in order to speed up the convergence.

If a reputation system is deployed in the P2P networks, it is not uncommon that some malicious nodes will try to adversely increase or decrease other peer's reputation value, by reporting fraud reputation values when they are consulted. To overcome this issue, we incorporate a trust system into SepRep. We define trust as the quantified credibility hold by a peer to another peer in P2P networks. The credibility represents the opinion of a peer on how honest another peer is in the propagation of reputation values. The trust value is also ranged from 0 to 1: a higher value means a higher credibility. The trust value of peer i on j is denoted by $T_{i->j}$.

In summary, each peer i maintains two rating vectors, namely, the reputation rating $R[R_{i->1}, R_{i->2}, \ldots, R_{i->n}]$ and the trust rating $T[T_{i->1}, T_{i->2}, \ldots, T_{i->n}]$. We can therefore build a hybrid reputation and trust overlay network (HRTON) on top of the physical network, as shown in Fig. 1.

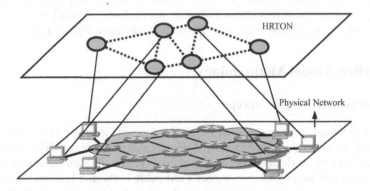

Fig. 1. Hybrid Reputation and Trust Overlay Network

Globally we have two matrices, reputation matrix M_R and trust matrix T_R:

$$M_R = \begin{bmatrix} R_{1->1} & R_{1->2} & \cdots & R_{1->n} \\ R_{2->1} & R_{2->2} & \cdots & R_{2->n} \\ \cdots & \cdots & \cdots & \cdots \\ R_{n->1} & R_{n->2} & \cdots & R_{n->n} \end{bmatrix}, \quad T_R = \begin{bmatrix} T_{1->1} & T_{1->2} & \cdots & T_{1->n} \\ T_{2->1} & T_{2->2} & \cdots & T_{2->n} \\ \cdots & \cdots & \cdots & \cdots \\ T_{n->1} & T_{n->2} & \cdots & T_{n->n} \end{bmatrix}$$

In the above two matrices, we can ignore the values of $R_{i->i}$ and $T_{i->i}$. Our SepRep model updates the two matrices after each transaction, and the matrix M_R converges to the global reputation matrix.

3.2 Initial Reputation and Trust Model

In HRTON, all peers are not familiar with each other at the beginning. Their reputations will be set an initial value and their trust values will also be set to some initial value.

Then we will explain the computing model in detail. First, we consider a simple situation. In one transaction, there exist three kinds of peers: service receiver peer i, service provider j, consultant peer k. Figure 2 is the sketch map.

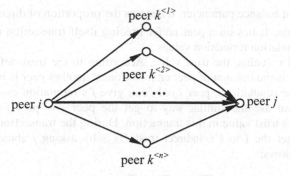

Fig. 2. Transaction between peer i and j

Peer i receives a service from peer j. It will give evaluation to j according to j's QoS. If necessary, it will consider peer k's suggestion to judge whether it should transact with j or not. In fact, peer i can consult a set of random peers about peer j's reputation. After the transaction, peer i will compare the recommendations from the consultant peers with the direct reputation, and adjust the trust values on these consultant peers accordingly.

Initial reputation computing will combine the direct transaction evaluation and indirect evaluations from agency peers. Direct reputation is calculated as follows:

$$DR_{i->j}^{<n>} = \alpha(t)DR_{i->j}^{<n-1>} + (1-\alpha(t))R_{Evaluation}^{<n>} \qquad (1)$$

$DR_{i->j}^{<n>}$ means the n-th direct reputation of i on j. The above formula means the current direct reputation will be decided by the last direct reputation, time factor $\alpha(t)$ and the current evaluation $R_{Evaluation}$. Obviously, if the transaction scale is the same, then the reputation of a peer in a transaction a year ago should be lower than in a transaction a week ago, so time is the necessary factor.

Next we will compute the indirect reputation. Peer i will ask peer k to about peer j's reputation. Peer k's trust will be counted in it. It is calculated as follows:

$$IR_{i->j} = T_{i->k} \cdot R_{k->j} \qquad (2)$$

Apparently, it is not sufficient to ask only peer j, so we will ask multiple peers. Here we define a set $K^{<n>}$ to denote peer i's random neighbors. Instead of simple addition, we adopt a normalized integration as follows:

$$IR_{i->j} = \sum_{k \in K^{<n>}} R_{k->j} \cdot t_{i->k} \qquad (3)$$

$$t_{i->k} = T_{i->k} / \sum_{k \in K^{<n>}} T_{i->k} \qquad (4)$$

After we get $DR_{i->j}$ and $IR_{i->j}$, we can calculate local reputation $R_{i->j}$ as follows:

$$R_{i->j} = \beta DR_{i->j} + (1-\beta) \cdot IR_{i->j} \qquad (5)$$

β is a weight balance parameter. It denotes the proportion of direct reputation and indirect reputation. It lies on a peer prefer trusting itself transaction records or other peers' recommendation reputation values.

Then we will calculate the trust value. According to the trust definition given in this model, trust is the opinion of peer on how honest another peer is in the distributed computing of the reputations, peer i only can give j's reputation evaluation, but not the trust. We can use the similar way to get the peer i to peer j's trust. We can calculate peer k's trust value in this transaction. During the transaction between peer i and j, we can get the i to k's indirect trust $IT_{i\to k}$ by asking j about k's trust. It is calculated as follows:

$$IT_{i\to k} = T_{j\to k} \cdot T_{i\to j} \tag{6}$$

Then the local trust $T_{i\to k}$ is calculated as follows:

$$T_{i\to k}^{<n>} = \gamma(t)T_{i\to k}^{<n-1>} + (1-\gamma(t)) \cdot IT_{i\to k}^{<n>} \tag{7}$$

$\gamma(t)$ has the same purpose as $\alpha(t)$. In order to fasten the convergence speed, we add feedback function to make the trust value reach the real value faster. So the trust value is updated as follows:

$$T_{i\to k}' = \frac{\sum_{transaction} T_{i\to k} + feedback}{\sum_{transaction} +1} \tag{8}$$

$$feedback = \begin{cases} 1-2\mid R_{i\to j} - R_{k\to j} \mid & if \mid R_{i\to j} - R_{k\to j} \mid \leq 0.5 \\ 0 & if \mid R_{i\to j} - R_{k\to j} \mid > 0.5 \end{cases} \tag{9}$$

The feedback function is to update $T_{i\to k}$ according to the difference between $R_{i\to j}$ and $R_{k\to j}$. The bigger the difference value is, the smaller the $T_{i\to k}'$ will be.

3.3 Reputation Propagation Model

We then discuss our reputation propagation model. Based on the above explanation, the second hand reputation is defined as $R_{i\to j}^{<2>} = \sum_k R_{k\to j} \cdot t_{i\to k}$, i.e., $R^{<2>} = T \cdot R$. Similarly, the h-th reputation is defined as follows:

$$R^{<h>} = T \cdot R^{<h-1>} \ (h>2) \tag{10}$$

This approach guarantees that the learned reputation $R_{i\to k}^{<h>}$ of peer i on any peer k (via at most h-hop queries) is bounded by max $R_{i\to k}$.

This reputation model has the "loss goes shares" effect. Let peer j be a malicious peer that offers high quality services with 10% probability. If peer i requests direct transaction with j, then the interactive times will be at least 10 to get j's correct reputation value, and i will get 9 low quality services (or suffer losses) in the 10 transactions. But by taking our approach, i only needs to use information provided by 10 trust buddies who have transaction history with j. The difference is that loss goes shares by other 9 peers.

4 Experiment and Analysis

4.1 Simulation

For ease of presentation, in all our simulations we assume peers provide either "high" quality of service or "low" quality of service. Normal peers have a "high" trust value, whereas malicious peers will result in a "low" trust value. In our simulations, the mapping of reputation value and trust value to the rank is shown in Table 1. Hence we can classify all peers as four kinds in HRTON:

- HRHT: an HRHT peer can provide high quality of service, and its recommendations are trustful.
- HRLT: an HRLT peer can provide high quality of service, but its recommendations are not trustful.
- LRHT: a LRHT peer can only provide poor quality of service, but it can provide trustful recommendations.
- LRLT: a LRLT peer can only provide poor quality of service, and its recommendations are not trustful.

Considering about the social network in real world, people tend to distrust more than trust when they have no transaction at the beginning. So we assign 0.4 as the initial reputation value and trust value.

We conduct four different experiments, as shown in Table 2. In the first experiment, we assume 30% of the peers provide high quality of service and 70% of peers provide low quality of service, 80% of the peers are trustful peers and 20% of the peers are malicious peers. This configuration simulates a healthy P2P system that only a small portion of peers does not provide genuine information. According to [11], large proportion of the user population, upwards to 70%, enjoys the benefits of the system without contributing too much. In the second and the third experiments, we increase the ratio of malicious nodes to 50% and 80% respectively. These two experiments are used to check the robustness of our reputation model. The fourth experiment simulates a simple reputation model that only direct reputations are used in the calculation of local reputations. In this case, the trust system is disabled because peers do not query reputation values from other peers at all. The purpose of this experiment is to show the effectiveness of our SepRep model in the sense that SepRep model achieves a much faster convergence.

We simulate the behavior of 500 peers with 5000 iteration processes. In a single iteration, each peer executes a transaction with another random peer. In each transaction, peer i asks 20 random peers to get the indirect reputation. Other simulation parameters are shown in Table 3.

Table 1. HRTON Initial Real Value

Peer Type	Value Range
High Reputation (HR)	[0.75, 0.85]
Low Reputation (LR)	[0.15, 0.25]
High Trust (HT)	[0.75, 0.85]
Low Trust (LT)	[0.15, 0.25]

Table 2. Experiment Configuration

Type	Rep. Type	Rep. Ratio	Trust Type	Trust Ratio
1	HR	30%	HT	80%
	LR	70%	LT	20%
2	HR	30%	HT	50%
	LR	70%	LT	50%
3	HR	30%	HT	20%
	LR	70%	LT	80%
4	HR	30%	N.A.	
	LR	70%		

Table 3. Experiment Parameters

Parameters	Value
Peer number	500
Iteration time	5000
β	0.6
$\gamma(t)$	0.4
Neighbor number of a peer	20

4.2 Analysis

We use error sum of squares (SSE) to measure the accuracy of SepRep model. It indicates the reputation discrepancy to the global reputations in each iteration process, as shown in Eq. 11, where a lower SSE error indicated higher accuracy:

$$SSE_{iteration} = \sqrt{\sum_{i=1}^{n}(GR_i - \frac{1}{n-1}\sum_{j \neq i}R_{j->i})^2} \tag{11}$$

where GR_i represents peer i's real global reputation value.

First, we use Experiment 1 to test SepRep's convergence speed and stability with different settings of $\alpha(t)$. For simplicity, we set $\alpha(t)$ as a constant value, α, that does not change with time. We conduct four different simulations, with different values of α: 0.2, 0.4, 0.6 and 0.8. The experimental results are shown in Fig. 3. We can see that the system converges the fastest when α is 0.2. With the increment of α, it takes more and more time for the system to converge. This is reasonable since α determines how important the latest direct transactions are in the calculations of local reputation. But on the other side, if α is too small, history information will not count too much and the local reputation values will be too variant. To achieve a stable and fast convergence, we set α to 0.4 in all the remaining experiments.

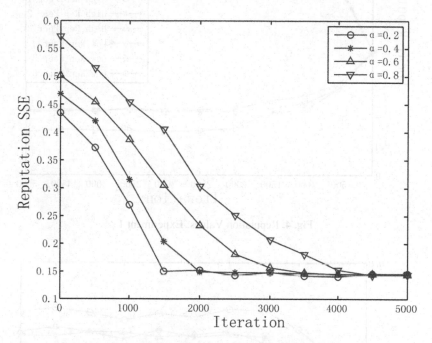

Fig. 3. Reputation SSE with different values of α

Fig. 4, 5, and 6 show changing of reputation values of six random peers, three HR peers and three LR peers, for Experiment 1, 2, and 3 respectively.

Note that Fig. 4 shows the results of a P2P network with 80% creditable peers, Fig. 5 shows the results of a P2P network with 50% creditable peers, and Fig. 6 shows the results of a P2P network with only 20% creditable peers. In all three cases, our SepRep system can distinguish HR peers and LR peers very quickly. The curves in Fig. 5 and 6 are not as smooth as those in Fig. 4. This is because the disturbance caused by malicious peers becomes more and more significant as the ratio of malicious peers increases from 20% to 80%.

Fig. 7 shows the SSE of global reputations for Experiments 1, 2, 3, and 4. Because Experiment 4 does not use reputation propagation, the system takes a very long time to converge. This validates that SepRep model achieves much faster convergence speed. We also observe that the reputation SSE becomes larger with the ratio of malicious nodes increase from 20% to 80%. However, even in the worst situation (Experiment 3), the discrepancy to real value keeps around 0.2, which is still an acceptable level.

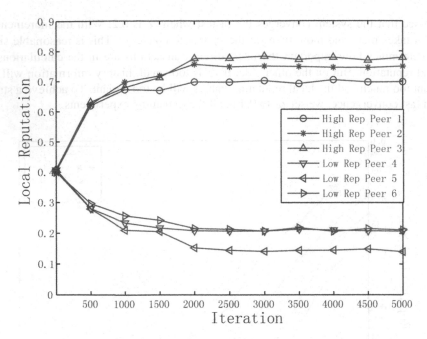

Fig. 4. Reputation Values: Experiment 1

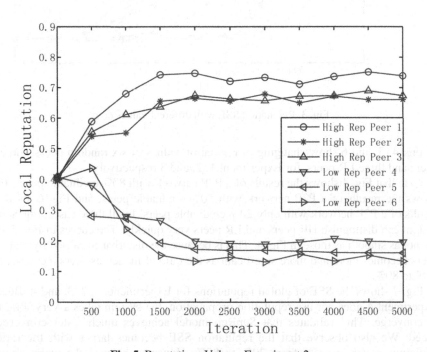

Fig. 5. Reputations Values: Experiment 2

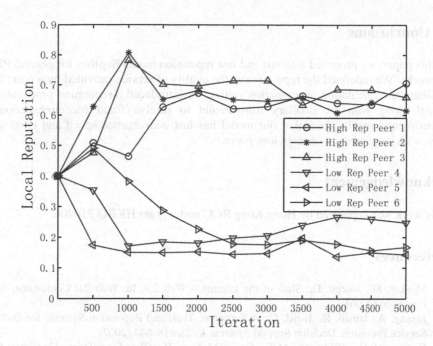

Fig. 6. Reputation Values: Experiment 3

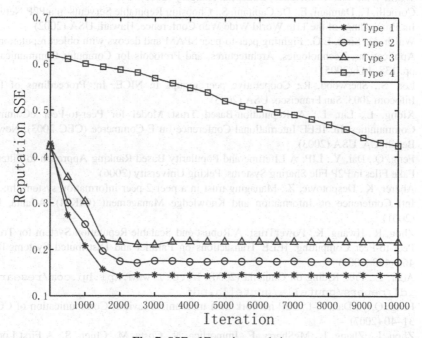

Fig. 7. SSE of Experiments 1-4

5 Conclusions

In this paper, we proposed a robust and fast reputation model SepRep for general P2P networks. We redefined the reputation as the quality of service provided by a peer. To facilitate the calculation of reputation values, we introduced a reputation propagation model along with an auxiliary trust model to resolve fraud recommendations. Experimental results show that our model has fast convergence speed and is robust even with large amount of malicious peers.

Acknowledgement

This work was supported by Hong Kong RGC under grant HKBU 210406.

References

1. Meeker, M., Joseph, D.: State of the Internet – Web 2.0. In: Web 2.0 Conference, San Francisco (2006)
2. Jøsang, A., Ismail, R., Boyd, C.: A Survey of Trust and Reputation Systems for Online Service Provision. Decision Support Systems 43(2), 618–644 (2007)
3. Kamvar, S.D., Schlosser, M.T., Garcia-Molina, H.: The EigenTrust Algorithm for Reputation Management in P2P Networks. In: Proceedings of the Twelfth International World Wide Web Conference, Budapest, Hungary (2003)
4. Cornelli, F., Damiani, E., De Capitani, S.: Choosing Reputable Servents in a P2P Network. In: Proceedings of the 11th World Wide Web Conference, Hawaii, USA (2002)
5. Walsh, K., Sirer, E.G.: Fighting peer-to-peer SPAM and decoys with object reputation. In: Applications, Technologies, Architectures, and Protocols for Computer Communication, pp. 138–143 (2005)
6. Lee, S., Sherwood, R.: Cooperative peer groups in NICE. In: Proceedings of IEEE Infocom 2003, San Francisco, USA (2003)
7. Xiong, L., Liu, L.: A Reputation-Based Trust Model for Peer-to-Peer eCommerce Communities. In: IEEE International Conference on E-Commerce (CEC 2003), Newport Beach, CA, USA (2003)
8. Feng, Q., Dai, Y.: LIP: A LIfetime and Popularity Based Ranking Approach to Filter out Fake Files in P2P File Sharing Systems. Peking University (2006)
9. Aberer, K., Despotovic, Z.: Managing trust in a peer-2-peer information system. In: 10th Intl Conference on Information and Knowledge Management (CIKM), Atlanta, USA (2001)
10. Zhou, R., Hwang, K.: PowerTrust: A Robust and Scalable Reputation System for Trusted Peer-to-Peer Computing. IEEE Transactions on Parallel and Distributed Systems 18(4), 460–473 (2007)
11. Adar, E.: Free Riding on Gnutella (2000), http://www.hpl.hp.com/research/idl/papers/gnutella/gnutella.pdf
12. Feng, Q.-y., Dai, Y.-f.: P2P network trust mechanism review. Communication of CCF 3, 31–40 (2007)
13. Zhou, L., Zhang, L., McSherry, F., Immorlica, N., Costa, M., Chien, S.: A First Look at Peer-to-Peer Worms: Threats and Defenses. In: Castro, M., van Renesse, R. (eds.) IPTPS 2005. LNCS, vol. 3640, Springer, Heidelberg (2005)

14. Christin, N., Weigend, A.S., Chuang, J.: Content availability, pollution and poisoning in file sharing peer-to-peer networks. In: Proceedings of the 6th ACM conference on Electronic commerce (EC 2005), Vancouver, Canada, pp. 68–77 (2005)
15. Liang, J., Naoumov, N., Ross, K.W.: The Index Poisoning Attack in P2P File-Sharing Systems. In: Proceedings of IEEE Infocom 2006, Barcelona, Spain (2006)
16. Wilson, R.: Reputation in games and markets. In: Roth, A. (ed.) Game-theoretic models of bargaining, pp. 65–84. Cambridge University Press, New York (1985)

Off-Line Keyword Guessing Attacks on Recent Public Key Encryption with Keyword Search Schemes*

Wei-Chuen Yau[1], Swee-Huay Heng[2], and Bok-Min Goi[1]

[1] Centre for Cryptography and Information Security (CCIS),
Faculty of Engineering, Multimedia University,
Jalan Multimedia, 63100 Cyberjaya, Selangor Darul Ehsan, Malaysia
{wcyau,bmgoi}@mmu.edu.my
[2] Centre for Cryptography and Information Security (CCIS),
Faculty of Information Science and Technology, Multimedia University,
Jalan Ayer Keroh Lama, 75450 Melaka, Malaysia
shheng@mmu.edu.my

Abstract. The Public Key Encryption with Keyword Search Scheme (PEKS) was first proposed by Boneh et al. in 2004. This scheme solves the problem of searching on data that is encrypted using a public key setting. Recently, Baek et al. proposed a Secure Channel Free Public Key Encryption with Keyword Search (SCF-PEKS) scheme that removes the secure channel for sending trapdoors. They later proposed another improved PEKS scheme that integrates with a public key encryption (PKE) scheme, called PKE/PEKS. In this paper, we present off-line keyword guessing attacks on SCF-PEKS and PKE/PEKS schemes. We demonstrate that outsider adversaries that capture the trapdoors sent in a public channel can reveal encrypted keywords by performing off-line keyword guessing attacks. While, insider adversaries can perform the attacks regardless the trapdoors sent in a public or secure channel.

Keywords: Searching on encrypted data, off-line keyword guessing attack, public key encryption, database security, privacy.

1 Introduction

The Public Key Encryption with Keyword Search Scheme (PEKS) [3] proposed by Boneh et al. is intended to solve the problem of searching on data that is encrypted using a public key setting. Consider an e-mail system that consists of three entities, namely a sender (Bob), a receiver (Alice), and a server (email gateway). Let (pk, sk) be Alice's public and private key pair. Bob sends an encrypted message m to Alice with keyword w in the following format:

$$E(pk, m) \parallel PEKS(pk, w)$$

Alice sends a trapdoor T_w for the keyword w to the email gateway. The PEKS scheme enables the gateway to test whether w is a keyword in the email but learns nothing else about the email.

---

* This research was supported by the Malaysia e-Science Fund (01-02-01-SF0048).

C. Rong et al. (Eds.): ATC 2008, LNCS 5060, pp. 100–105, 2008.

Boneh et al.'s PEKS scheme (BDOP-PEKS) does not support a conjunctive keyword search. For example, Alice may want to search for "Urgent" emails from "Bob" about "Finance". This problem was solved by Park et al. in [6]. They proposed two types Public Key Encryption with Conjunctive Field Keyword Search (PECK) schemes.

One of the limitations of BDOP-PEKS is that the scheme requires secure channel for sending trapdoors. This is to prevent an eavesdropper (Eve) from capturing the trapdoors and thus ensure that only the server has the capability to test emails for certain keywords. In [1], Baek et al. proposed a Secure Channel Free Public Key Encryption with Keyword Search (SCF-PEKS) scheme to solve the problem. In this scheme, the server has to keep its own private and public key pair. The sender creates a PEKS ciphertext using the server's public key as well as the receiver's public key. The testing algorithm requires the server's private key as an input. Since Eve does not have the server's private key, she cannot test emails for certain keywords even she has the trapdoor. Therefore, the trapdoor can be sent over a public channel.

Baek et al. also presented a scheme that combines PKE and PEKS. They proposed a provably secure PKE/PEKS scheme based on ElGamal, BDOP-PEKS and the randomness re-use technique [2]. This scheme is a countermeasure of "swapping attack" where the attacker interchanges PEKS ciphertext so that Alice does not receive the correct message that Bob has sent to her. Also, the scheme can prevent attacker from modifying $E(pk, m) \parallel PEKS(pk, w)$.

Recently, Byun et al. pointed out that BDOP-PEKS [3] and PECK [6] schemes are susceptible to an off-line keyword guessing attack [4]. This attack exploits the low-entropy characteristic of keywords. In general, keywords are chosen from a much smaller space than passwords. This is the fact that users usually choose well-known keywords to search for their documents. For example, a sender may use "Urgent" in the "Title" field as a keyword of an email. In this case, attackers are able to guess some candidate keywords and verify the correctness of their guesses in an off-line manner. This may result the leak of relevant information of encrypted emails as well as the breach of user's privacy.

This research is inspired by the work in [4]. We present off-line keyword guessing attacks on the SCF-PEKS [1] and PKE/PEKS [2] schemes. We demonstrate that outsider adversaries that capture the trapdoors sent in a public channel can reveal encrypted keywords by performing off-line keyword guessing attacks. While, insider adversaries can perform the attacks regardless the trapdoors sent in public or secure channel.

The rest of the paper is organized as follows: In Section 2, we present a brief description of the keyword search scheme proposed in [1], and follow by demonstrating the off-line keyword guessing attack on the scheme. We then briefly review the PKE/PEKS scheme [2] and perform the corresponding off-line keyword guessing attack in Section 3. We compare the consequences of off-line keyword guessing attacks on various PEKS schemes in Section 4. We conclude our paper in Section 5.

2   Attacks on BSS's SCF-PEKS Scheme

Throughout this paper, $(G_1, +)$ and $(G_2, \bullet)$ denote two cyclic groups of prime order q. A bilinear map, $e: G_1 \times G_1 \to G_2$ satisfies the following properties:

1. Bilinearity: For all P, Q, $R \in G_1$, $e(P+Q, R) = e(P, R) e(Q, R)$ and $e(P, Q+R) = e(P, Q) e(P, R)$.
2. Non-degeneracy: There exists P, Q, $R \in G_1$, such that $e(P, Q) \neq 1$.
3. Computability: There is an efficient algorithm to compute $e(P, Q)$ for any P, $Q \in G_1$.

2.1 Review of SCF-PEKS Scheme

Baek et al. proposed a PEKS scheme that does not require a secure channel to send the trapdoor [1]. The secure channel free PEKS (SCF-PEKS) scheme consists of the following algorithms:

- **KeyGen$_{Param}$(k):**
  Take a security parameter k, generate a group $G_1 = <P>$ whose order is prime $q \geq 2^k$.
  Construct a bilinear pairing $e: G_1 \times G_1 \rightarrow G_2$, where G_2 is a group of order q.
  Choose hash functions $H_1 : \{0, 1\}^* \rightarrow G_1^*$ and $H_2 : G_2 \rightarrow \{0, 1\}^k$.
  Output a common parameter $cp = (q, G_1, G_2, e, P, H_1, H_2, d_W)$, where d_W denotes a description of a keyword space.
- **KeyGen$_{Server}$(cp):**
  Select a random $x \in Z_q^*$ and compute $X = xP$.
  Select a random $Q \in G_1^*$.
  Generate the server's public key $pk_S = (cp, Q, X)$ and private key $sk_S = (cp, x)$.
- **KeyGen$_{Receiver}$(cp):**
  Select a random $y \in Z_q^*$ and compute $Y = yP$.
  Output the receiver's public key $pk_R = (pk_S, Y)$ and private key $sk_R = (pk_S, y)$.
- **SCF-PEKS(cp, pk_S, pk_R, w):**
  Select a random $r \in Z_q^*$ and output a PEKS ciphertext $S = (U, V) = (rP, H_2((e(Q, X)e(H_1(w), Y))^r))$.
- **Trapdoor(cp, sk_R, w):**
  Output trapdoor $T_w = yH_1(w)$.
- **Test(cp, T_w, sk_S, S):**
  Check if $H_2(e(xQ + T_w, U)) = V$. If so output 'yes'; if not, output 'no'.

2.2 Off-Line Keyword Guessing Attacks on SCF-PEKS Scheme

An attacker A can perform an off-line keyword attack as follows:

- **Step 1:** A first captures a valid trapdoor $T_w = yH_1(w)$.
- **Step 2:** A guesses an appropriate keyword w', and computes $H_1(w')$.
- **Step 3:** A takes the receiver's public key Y and the hash of the guessed keyword $H_1(w')$, and checks if $e(Y, H_1(w')) = e(P, T_w)$. If so, the guessed keyword is a valid keyword. Otherwise, go to Step 2.
  The equation hold for $w' = w$, i.e., $e(Y, H_1(w')) = e(yP, H_1(w')) = e(P, yH_1(w)) = e(P, T_w)$.

Since a trapdoor is sent without a secure channel, an outsider adversary is able to capture the trapdoor and performs the off-line keyword guessing attack. The attacker may reveal the encrypted keyword w that used by the receiver to search for a document. Similarly, an insider adversary (malicious server) can perform the attack to reveal the keyword in the trapdoor. In addition, the insider adversary can proceed to run the Test algorithm in order to find out which PEKS ciphertext contains the keyword. While, the outsider adversary is unable to distinguish a PEKS ciphertext is the result of encrypting which keyword, as the Test phase requires server's private key.

3 Attacks on BSS's PKE/PEKS Scheme

3.1 Review of PKE/PEKS Scheme

Baek *et al.* proposed an integrated PKE and PEKS scheme that consists of the following algorithms [2]:

- **KeyGen(k):**
  Take a security parameter k, construct a group G_1 of prime order q, generated by $g \in G_1$.
  Construct a bilinear pairing $e: G_1 \times G_1 \rightarrow G_2$, where G_2 is a group of order q.
  Select hash functions $H_1: G_1 \rightarrow \{0, 1\}^{l_1}$; $H_2: \{0, 1\}^* \rightarrow G_1^*$; $H_3: G_2 \rightarrow \{0, 1\}^{l_3}$; $H_4: \{0, 1\}^* \rightarrow \{0, 1\}^{l_4}$, where l_1, l_3 and l_4 are respectively the binary output size of H_1, H_3 and H_4.
  Select a random $x \in Z_q^*$ and compute $X = g^x$.
  Output the public key $pk = (k, q, g, e, G_1, G_2, X)$ and the private key $sk = (pk, x)$.
- **ENC-PKE/PEKS(pk, w, m):**
  Select a random $r \in Z_q^*$ and compute $c_1 = g^r$ and $c_2 = H_1(X^r) \oplus m$
  Compute a PEKS ciphertext $S = H_3(e(H_2(w), X)^r)$
  Compute a tag $\sigma = H_4(X^r, m, c_1, c_2, S)$
  Output (c_1, c_2, S, σ)
- **Trapdoor(sk, w):**
  Output trapdoor $T_w = H_2(w)^x$.
- **Test(T_w, c_1, c_2, S, σ):**
  Check if $H_3(e(T_w, c_1)) = S$. If so, output (c_1, c_2, S, σ); if not, output 'no'.
- **DEC-PKE/PEKS(sk, c_1, c_2, S, σ):**
  Compute $m = H_1(c_1^x) \oplus c_2$.
  Check if $H_4(c_1^x, m, c_1, c_2, S) = \sigma$. If so, output m. Otherwise, output 'reject'.

3.2 Off-Line Keyword Guessing Attacks on PKE/PEKS Scheme

An attacker A can perform an off-line keyword attack as follows:

- **Step 1:** A first captures a valid trapdoor $T_w = H_2(w)^x$.
- **Step 2:** A guesses an appropriate keyword w', and computes $H_2(w')$.
- **Step 3:** A takes the public key X and the hash of guessed keyword $H_2(w')$, and checks if $e(X, H_2(w')) = e(g, T_w)$. If so, the guessed keyword is a valid keyword. Otherwise, go to Step 2.

The equation hold for $w' = w$, i.e., $e(X, H_2(w')) = e(g^x, H_2(w')) = e(g, H_2(w))^x = e(g, H_2(w)^x) = e(g, T_w)$.

In this attack, both insider adversary and outsider adversary may reveal the keyword in the trapdoor. They can then further determine a PEKS ciphertext is the result of encrypting which keyword via Test algorithm. Similarly, this attack works on the two extensions of the PKE/PEKS scheme to the multi-receiver and multi-keyword settings [2].

4 Comparison of Off-Line Keyword Guessing Attacks on Various PEKS Schemes

Table 1 summarizes consequences of off-line keyword guessing attacks on various PEKS schemes. The direct consequence is that the attackers may reveal the keyword that the receiver searches for. In general, all the current off-line keyword guessing attacks on various PEKS schemes need to obtain a trapdoor in the first stage. Since

Table 1. Summary of consequences of off-line keyword guessing attacks

Consequences	Type of Adversary	PEKS Schemes							
		Without Secure Channel				With Secure Channel			
		A	B	C	D	A	B	C	D
Reveal a keyword sent in Trapdoor	Insider	X	X	X	X	X	X	X	X
	Outsider	X	X	X	X				
Determine a PEKS ciphertext is the result of encrypting which keyword via Test phase	Insider	X	X	X	X	X	X	X	X
	Outsider	X	X		X				

A = BDOP-PEKS[3], B = PECK[6], C = SCF-PEKS[1], D = PKE/PEKS[2].

the trapdoor is generated by combining receiver's secret key and the keyword, the attacker can exploit the bilinear property of pairing and relates the combination with the public key using pairing operation. A trivial solution for preventing the attacker from capturing the trapdoor is to provide a secure channel for sending the trapdoor. We argue, however, that the secure channel can only prevent the outsider adversary from performing the attacks. The solution cannot resist attacks by the insider adversary. Therefore, we should take special consideration on the trapdoor generation as well as the bilinear property in designing a PEKS scheme that is secure against off-line keyword guessing attacks.

Once the attacker obtains the correct guessed keyword, he/she can proceed to run the Test algorithm. Consequently, the attacker may determine which PEKS cipher-texts containing the keyword. We note that only SCF-PEKS can avoid such consequence, as the outsider adversary does not have the server's private key to perform the Test algorithm. This, however, does not apply to the insider adversary (malicious server) who possesses the server key.

5 Conclusion

In this paper, we presented off-line keyword guessing attacks on SCF-PEKS and PKE/PEKS schemes. We also pointed out that secure channel is still needed for SCF-PEKS in order to prevent off-line keyword guessing attacks by outsider adversaries. However, even these two schemes apply secure channel they are still susceptible to the attacks by insider adversaries. We observe that most of the current off-line keyword guessing attacks work on public key keyword search encryption schemes based on pairing. In future, we would like to know whether or not public key keyword search schemes that are not based on pairing are susceptible to off-line keyword guessing attacks (e.g., the scheme proposed in [5]). Also, it would be nice to come up with a security model against an off-line keyword guessing attack.

References

1. Baek, J., Safavi-Naini, R., Susilo, W.: Public Key Encryption with Keyword Search Revisited. Cryptology ePrint Archive (2005), http://eprint.iacr.org/2005/191
2. Baek, J., Safavi-Naini, R., Susilo, W.: On the Integration of Public Key Data Encryption and Public Key Encryption with Keyword Search. In: Katsikas, S.K., López, J., Backes, M., Gritzalis, S., Preneel, B. (eds.) ISC 2006. LNCS, vol. 4176, pp. 217–232. Springer, Heidelberg (2006)
3. Boneh, D., Di Crescenzo, G., Ostrovsky, R., Persiano, G.: Public Key Encryption with Keywrod Search. In: Cachin, C., Camenisch, J.L. (eds.) EUROCRYPT 2004. LNCS, vol. 3027, pp. 506–522. Springer, Heidelberg (2004)
4. Byun, J.W., Rhee, H.S., Park, H.-A., Lee, D.H.: Off-Line Keyword Guessing Attacks on Recent Keyword Search Schemes over Encrypted Data. In: Jonker, W., Petković, M. (eds.) SDM 2006. LNCS, vol. 4165, pp. 75–83. Springer, Heidelberg (2006)
5. Khader, D.: Public Key Encryption with Keyword Search Based on K-resilient IBE. In: Gavrilova, M.L., Gervasi, O., Kumar, V., Tan, C.J.K., Taniar, D., Laganá, A., Mun, Y., Choo, H. (eds.) ICCSA 2006. LNCS, vol. 3982, pp. 298–308. Springer, Heidelberg (2006)
6. Park, D.J., Kim, K., Lee, P.J.: Public Key Encryption with Conjunctive Field Keyword Search. In: Lim, C.H., Yung, M. (eds.) WISA 2004. LNCS, vol. 3325, pp. 73–86. Springer, Heidelberg (2005)

An Integrated Solution for Policy Filtering and Traffic Anomaly Detection

Zhijun Wang[1], Hao Che[2], and Jiannong Cao[1]

[1] Department of Computing, The Hong Kong Polytechnic University, Hong Kong
[2] Department of Computer Science and Engineering
The University of Texas at Arlington, Arlington, TX 76019, USA

Abstract. In this paper, we propose a Ternary Content Addressable Memory (TCAM) coprocessor based solution for high speed, integrated policy filtering and TCP flow anomaly detection. In the proposed solution, the TCP flow anomaly is detected through two dimensional (2D) matching. The key features of the solution include: (1) setting flag bits in TCAM action code to support various packet treatments; (2) managing TCP flow state in pair to do 2D matching. The solution's ability for detecting TCP-based flooding attacks based on real-world-trace simulations are conducted. The results show that the proposed solution can match up OC-192 line rate while doing the integrated tasks.

1 Introduction

The future Internet has to address both performance and security issues to survive. On one hand, it is under great stress to meet ever growing/changing application demands while having to sustain multi-gigabit forwarding performance. On the other hand, the Internet becomes more and more vulnerable due to fast spreading malicious attacks.

The fast growing application requirements need the network to provide various types of services. To support differential services, different packets may need to be treated differently based on, e.g., quality-of-service requirements or other policies. To this end, packet classification [2][13][19] based on a set of policy filtering rules must be performed in a router interface to identify the needed treatment of individual packets. Traditional policy filters treat each packet individually, and does not attempt to associate the packet with other packets belonging to the same flow. Flow classification is a stateful packet classification, generally known as packet classification, which tracks the flow state by identifying every packet in every flow. Packet/flow classification has long been identified as the most critical data path function, creating potential bottlenecks for high speed packet forwarding.

One of the major threats to the Internet is Distributed Denial of Service (DDoS) attacks [10]. In DDoS attacks, attackers send a large amount of attacking packets using spoofed source IP addresses to a victim server which eventually runs out of its resources and degrades the performance of legitimate packets. IP traceback [3][5][8][14] [15][16][17][18] is considered as one effective way to defend

C. Rong et al. (Eds.): ATC 2008, LNCS 5060, pp. 106–120, 2008.

against DDoS attacks. Using IP traceback, the attackers can be identified and punished through tracing their physical locations. However, effectively detecting attackers is difficult due to the stateless property of Internet routers/switchs.

The traditional approach to enable security functions is generally separated from the approach that implements typical packet forwarding functions. For example, hash-based IP traceback [17] is generally implemented using dedicated chips for computing hash functions. Packet classification is typically performed as part of the packet forwarding functions in a router interface card, e.g., using a network processor and its associated Ternary Content Addressable Memory (TCAM) coprocessor. Due to its high speed performance, TCAM coprocessor is widely used as packet classifier in industry. However, the separated solutions add the complexity and integration costs to the next-generation Internet design. Hence, it is of both technological and economical importance to develop integrated solutions to enable security functions and high speed forwarding, matching multiple gigabit line rate.

In this paper, we propose a TCAM coprocessor based solution for high speed, integrated policy filtering and TCP traffic anomaly detection. The TCP-based DDoS attacks using spoofed source IP addresses are detected in the edge router through two dimensional (2D) matching [7]. 2D matching means a normal TCP flow generated from one end host to another should have a corresponding flow from the other direction. The key features of the solution are: (1) setting flag bits in TCAM action code to support various packet treatments in the network processor and the local CPU; (2) managing TCP flow state in pair to do 2D matching. In the solution, when a TCP flow has not been matched after a period of time T_{alm}, the flow is considered to have high probability to be an attacking flow. Hence an alarm message composed of the flow identities is sent to the destination server, which in turn can use the information to do IP traceback. Based on the real Internet traffic analysis, the proposed solution requires about 5 Mbits TCAM memory to support OC-192 line rate for the integrated tasks. Such TCAM is available in today's market. We also discuss how to handle TCAM table overflow and analyze the solution's performance in case of table overflow. The simulations based on the real world traffic traces are conducted to evaluate the performance on the detection of TCP-based flooding attacks. The results show that the proposed solution can handle OC-192 line rate.

The rest of the paper is organized as follows: Section II describes the TCP traffic anomaly detection through 2D matching. The details of the integrated solution is presented in Section III. The performance of the proposed solution is evaluated by simulations in Section IV. Section V briefly describes the related work. Finally, Section VI concludes the paper and discusses some future work.

2   Two Dimensional Matching

In this section, we first give the needed definitions and then discuss how to detect anomalous TCP flows through two dimensional (2D) matching.

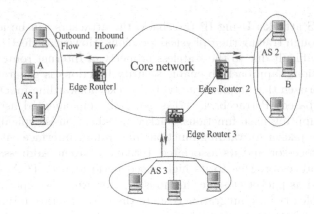

Fig. 1. Internet Architecture

A *flow* is a set of packets which have the same identity. The identity is extracted from the packet header. In this paper, the following five tuples: source IP address (SIP), destination IP address (DIP), source port number (SPN), destination port number (DPN), and protocol (PRO) are used as the *flow identity*. In other words, a flow is uniquely determined by the five tuples <SIP, DIP, SPN, DPN, PRO>.

TCP is a two-way communication protocol. A normal TCP flow generated from one end host (e.g., A) to another (e.g., B) should have a corresponding flow from the other direction (i.e., from B to A). Fig. 1 shows a general Internet architecture. Assume host A in Autonomous System 1 (AS1) sends a SYN packet to host B located in AS2 to initiate a TCP session. After receiving the SYN packet, host B sends a SYN+ACK packet back to host A to establish the session. In this case, the edge router 1 can detect both flows coming from AS1 (called *outbound flow*) and into AS1 (called *inbound flow*). For an outbound flow with flow identity <SIP, DIP, SPN, DPN, PRO>, the corresponding inbound flow identity is <DIP, SIP, DPN, SPN, PRO>. The feature of an outbound flow having a corresponding inbound flow is called two dimensional (2D) matching [7]. An outbound (inbound) flow is called an *unmatched flow* if no corresponding inbound (outbound) flow arrives within a period of time T_{alm}. An inbound (outbound) flow is called the *matching flow* of its outbound (inbound) flow.

2D matching can be effectively applied to detect TCP-based attacks using spoofed IP addresses. For attacking packets using spoofed source IP addresses, the responding packets are routed to the spoofed IP addresses which may be different from the original AS. Thus the edge router at the attackers' AS may only detect the outbound flow, and hence an unmatched flow is detected. Based on these observations, one can do 2D matching at the edge routers for TCP traffic anomaly detection. When an unmatched flow is detected, the router sends an alarm message (e.g., ICMP message) including the flow identity to the destination for possible IP traceback.

The most popular TCP based DDoS attacks are TCP SYN and RESET flooding attacks. In these attacks, the SYN or RESET flag bit is set. To detect these attacks, we only need to maintain all the flows start with SYN and RESET packets. However, there are other types of TCP based attacks [10] which have ACK bit set or no flag bit set. Hence, any TCP packet can be an attack packet. In our solution, if a packet does not belong to any existing flow, the packet is considered to be a new flow and will be monitored in the flow table to allow 2D matching.

Except the attacking packets, unmatched flows may be caused by: (1) the destination server is down; (2) the destination server has changed its IP address, but a cache entry of the old server IP address is still in the domain name server (DNS). In these cases, the destination is unreachable and the flows sent to the destination server can be viewed abnormally.

In the following sections, we will present the details on how to integrate 2D matching and policy filtering using TCAM coprocessors.

3 Integrated Solution of Policy Filtering and Anomaly Detection

This section first gives a brief review of policy filtering using a network processor and its TCAM coprocessor, and then presents the details of the proposed solution.

3.1 TCAM Coprocessor

Packet classification (e.g., policy filtering, IP forwarding table lookup) is one of the most critical data path functions in high speed packet forwarding. TCAM coprocessors are widely used as packet classifiers in today's industry. Fig. 2 shows a system architecture of a network processor using a TCAM coprocessor [20] for packet classification. A TCAM coprocessor stores self-addressable rules which map to different memory addresses in an associated memory (normally an SRAM) containing the corresponding actions.

In particular, a typical rule for policy filtering is composed of 104-bit five-tuple: <SIP, DIP, SPN, DPN, PRO>, same as the flow identity. The rules are usually arranged in an ordered list, with lower memory locations having higher matching priorities. When a packet arrives at the network processor, a search key composed of the same set of five-tuple, extracted from the packet header is passed to the TCAM coprocessor for lookup. The action code in the associated memory corresponding to the matched rule with the highest match priority is returned to the network processor. There is an identical copy of the rule table in the local CPU in charge of rule management. The rule update in TCAM is done through the interface between the TCAM coprocessor and the local CPU. In the proposed solution, when a new flow is detected, its identity serves as a new rule to be added to the rule table, meaning that the rule table for flow classification is combined with the policy filtering table for packet classification. In addition,

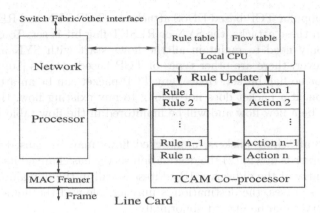

Fig. 2. TCAM coprocessor architecture

a flow table in the local CPU is introduced to store active TCP flow states for 2D matching.

A general rule usually has some wildcarded bits in some tuples, whereas the identity of a specific flow has no wildcarded bits in any tuple. For example, a policy filtering rule may be: <x.x.x.x, x.x.x.x, 128 - 256, 80, 6>. Here 'x' represents a wildcarded byte. A flow identity may be <1.2.3.4, 5.6.7.8, 1028, 80, 6>. A flow identity has higher matching priority than a policy filtering rule. So a flow identify must be located at a lower TCAM memory address than a policy filtering rule.

3.2   Data Structure

The policy filtering rules and the flow identities share the same format. Hence, the integrated approach does not require any modification to the rule table format in TCAM. To support IP traceback, however, the action codes need to be extended to allow flow detection. Before giving the details of the solution, we first present the data structures of the action code and flow table entry.

Fig. 3 (a) shows the format of the action code. The action code is set to 32 bits in length such that the code can be returned in one clock cycle through a 32-bit interface bus. The action code includes one flag bit which indicates if a rule is a policy filtering rule (value 0) or a flow identity (value 1). One forward bit is used to indicate if the action code needs to be passed (value 1) to the local CPU or not (value 0). The following 8 bits indicate the forwarding action associated with the policy filtering, such as the best effort forwarding, dropping the packet and so on. 8 bits can express 256 different actions which are enough to include all possible forwarding actions in today's Internet. The last 22 bits are the flow index which specifies the location of a flow state in the flow table located in the local CPU. 22 bits can represents 4 millions different entries. For a policy filtering rule, all index bits are set to 0. The last two bits are free bits, and always set to zero. In the following, we use a-b-x-y-00 to represent an action

flag	forward	action	flow index	free
1–bit	1–bit	8–bit	22–bit	2–bit

(a) Format of action code

flag	FIN	ACK	Tlocation	Timer
2–bit	1–bit	1–bit	22–bit	32–bit

(b) Format of flow table in local CPU

Fig. 3. Data structures

code. Here a and b represent the binary values of the first two bits, respectively. x the decimal value of the action, and z the decimal value of the flow index. For example, (0-0-5-0-00) represents the action code of a policy filtering rule with action 5; and (1-1-6-234-00) is the action code of a flow identity with action 6, it locates at entry 234 in the flow table, and the forward bit set means the action code needs to be passed to the local CPU.

Fig. 3 (b) gives the data structure of an entry in the flow table. The first 2 bits are flags. The bits 00 indicate an empty entry; 01 an unmatched existing flow; 10 an expected flow; and 11 a matched existing flow. FIN and ACK bits are used to terminate a pair of completed flows. Tlocation is the flow location in the TCAM rule table. Timer is used to trigger an event. There are three timers: T_{alm}, T_{idl} and T_{rmv}. T_{alm} detects an unmatched flow, an alarm message is triggered if a flow has not been matched after T_{alm} time. T_{idl} is used to check if a matched flow is still active. If a pair of flows are not terminated after T_{idl} time, the forward bits corresponding to them are set to check if they are still active. T_{rmv} is used to remove incompletely terminated flows. Similarly, ab-c-d-x-y is used to express a flow entry. a, b, c and d are the binary values of the first four bits, x and y are decimal values of Tlocation and timer, respectively.

To do 2D matching, the flow entries in the flow table are managed in pair. When a new flow arrives, the index is always set to an even number, and the expected matching flow has the index equal to the even number plus one. An index list is used to manage the available indices. The number of entries in the flow table is set to be the number of total TCAM entries allocated for flow identities. Initially, all even indices are on the list. When a new flow is detected, an index on the list is removed and assigned to the new flow. When a pair of flows are finished and removed from the flow table, the corresponding even index is returned to the list.

The rule table in the local CPU is in charge of the TCAM rule table management. It stores the same rules (including both policy filtering rules and flow identities) as those in the TCAM rule table. The management of the two rule tables are the same, hence in the following of the paper, the rule table refers to the rule tables in both local CPU and TCAM.

3.3   Description of the Integrated Solution

In the proposed solution, the local CPU processes packet flows at per flow level while the TCAM coprocessor processes packet flows at per packet level. When a packet arrives at the network processor, the search key composed of five tuples extracted from the packet header is passed to the TCAM coprocessor. The action code (a-b-x-y-00) corresponding to the matched rule with highest matching priority is returned back to the network processor. The network processor forwards the packet based on the action code value. For a non-TCP packet, no extra processing is introduced. For a TCP packet, the action code a-b-x-y-fk is passed to the local CPU for the following three cases: (1) the packet belongs to a new flow (i.e., a=0); (2) the packet belongs to an existing flow but the forward bit is set (i.e., a=1 and b=1); (3) the packet with FIN bit set (i.e., a=1, b=0 and FIN bit=1). The two free bits f and k are set to be the bit values of FIN and ACK bits in the packet, respectively. In the case of the arrival packet belonging to a new flow, the flow identity is also passed to the local CPU for process.

The local CPU is in charge of adding new flows, testing flow activity, removing completed and inactive flows, and triggering unmatched alarms. Now we describe how the local CPU handles different packets and timer timeouts.

Packet in new flow: When a packet belonging to a new flow arrives, if no free entry is available in the rule table, the action code and the flow identity are simply dropped. Otherwise, the new flow (F) and its expected matching flow (E) are added to both the flow and rule tables. In the flow table, suppose the index of F is IN, then the index of E is IN+1. The first two flag bits are 01 at entry IN implying that F is an existing unmatched flow and 10 at entry IN+1 indicating that E is an expected matching flow. The flag bits in the action codes of both flows are set to 1, and the forward bit corresponding to E is set to 1. Hence the action code of the upcoming packet in E will be passed to the local CPU to do 2D matching. The forward bit of F is 0, implying that the upcoming packets in F do not need to be processed in the local CPU. The timer T_{alm} is set for F in the flow table.

Packet in expected flow: If a packet belonging to an expected flow E arrives, the two flag bits in the flow entries for both E and its matching flow F are set to 11 indicating that the two flows are matched. The forward bit in the action code corresponding to E is reset to 0. Then the upcoming packets in the pair of flows will not be processed in the local CPU. Hence a timer T_{idl} is set for both flows E and F. If no FIN bit is detected within T_{idl} time, the forward bits for both flows will be set to test if they are still active.

Packet in matched flow: The forward bits for a pair of matched flows are set after T_{idl} expires. This means that the action codes of the upcoming packets in the pair of flows will be passed to the local CPU. If such a packet arrives, it implies that the pair of flows are still active. Hence the timer T_{idl} is set again for the next check. Then the forward bits in the action codes for the pair of flows are reset to 0.

Packet with FIN and/or ACK bit set: If a packet of F with FIN bit set arrives, the FIN bit for its entry in the flow table is set. The forward bits in the action code for the pair of flows are also set, meaning that the action codes of the upcoming packets in the pair of flows will be processed in the local CPU. If a FIN+ACK packet of F comes, the FIN bit is set for entry F. If its matching flow E has FIN bit set, the packet is an acknowledgement packet of the FIN packet in E, and hence the ACK bit in the entry of E is set. If an ACK packet of E comes after both FIN bits set, this acknowledges FIN packet in F, hence the ACK bit in the flow entry of F is set. If the FIN and ACK bits are set for both flows, this implies that the two flows have been completed and hence to be removed from the flow and rule tables. In order to remove incompletely terminated (without FIN and/or ACK packets) flows, when the FIN bit is set for an entry, timer T_{rmv} is also set for the pair of flows. If no more packet arrives within T_{rmv} time, the flow pair is forced to be removed.

Timer timeout: If the timer T_{alm} times out, it implies that an unmatched flow is detected, an alarm message including the flow identity is generated and sent to the destination server for possible IP traceback. If the timer T_{idl} is triggered, it indicates that no FIN packet in the pair of flows arrives in the past T_{idl} time. However, that does not ensure that the flow pairs are still active, because some flows may be terminated incompletely. Hence it needs to check if they are still active, so the forward bits in their action codes are set, and the timer T_{rmv} is also set. If no packet for the pair of flows arrives within T_{rmv} time, the flows are considered to be inactive and removed from the tables. In this case, if some packets in the removed flows come later, they will be treated as new flows.

3.4   Computational Load on Local CPU

The local CPU processes packet at per flow level. For each flow, the first, FIN and final ACK packets are processed. In addition, 1 packet needs to be processed every T_{idl} time. The real traffic measurement at OC-192 (see Section IV) shows that the average new TCP flows are about 5K per second, and the concurrent active flows are usually less than 50K. That means a flow lasting less than 10 seconds on average. If T_{idl} is set to 5 seconds, then each flow has about 5 packets or 0.2 packets per second to be processed. The local CPU needs to process about 20K packets per second which is not difficult to be handled by a 100MHz CPU.

3.5   Rule Update

The TCAM rule table update is through the interface between the local CPU and the TCAM coprocessor. A consistent rule update algorithm [20] which can update the rule table without interruption of TCAM lookup process is used. A flow identity has higher matching priority than that of policy filtering rules and hence it is added to a TCAM memory location lower than the policy rules. All the flow identities can be stored independently, because a packet cannot match more than one flow identity simultaneously. We keep all the empty entries above the general rules so that for each flow identity addition or deletion, no movement is needed for other rules. Adding one rule takes 5 (a rule plus the action code have $104 + 32$ bits, $(104+32)/32<5$) clock cycles by assuming a 32-bit interface bus. Deleting a rule only takes 1 clock cycle by reset the valid bit of the entry [20]. To update a flow identity, a flow identity is first written and validated in a new location and then the flow identity in the old location is deleted. It takes one rule write and one rule deletion. To process 20K packets, maximum 40K TCAM writes/updates (assume the action code changes before and after the packet being processed) are needed. 40K TCAM writes and deletion only take about 240K clock cycles, this is a very small portion of the processing time for a 100 MHz CPU.

3.6   Table Overflow

There are two critical issues using TCAM for packet/flow classification. One is the TCAM lookup speed, and the other is the memory space. The proposed solution does not introduce any extra TCAM lookups. Hence we only focus on the discussion of TCAM memory space. TCAM coprocessors have limited memory storage. The maximum TCAM memory in today's market is 18 Mbits [4]. A TCAM is usually shared by multiple tables such as longest prefix matching and policy filtering tables. Hence the TCAM memory storage capacity is a critical issue for the proposed solution. A critical concern is that if the TCAM table cannot store all the concurrent active flows, does the solution still work well? In the following, we discuss the performance impacts in case of table overflow.

When the local CPU detects a new flow, it checks if there are a pair of free entries in the TCAM rule table. The flow state is monitored only if a pair of free entries are available. That means an attacking packet may not be monitored immediately in case of table overflow, and hence it may not detect attacks with single attacking packet. But it can still detect the attacks with a large amount attacking packets. In case of table overflow, each coming packet in an un-monitored flow has some probability to be monitored, hence it takes some time to monitor a packet from an attack. The following theorem gives the average time an attack to be monitored.

Theorem I: Assume a TCAM rule table has N entries. There are $n_c > N$ number of concurrent active normal TCP flows, each flow has n_f packets per second, and the TCAM accepts n_s number of new flows per second. Then an attacker sending n_a attacking packets per second can be monitored in $\frac{(n_c-N)n_f-n_s}{n_a n_s}$ time on average.

Proof: The total number of arriving packets per second is $n_c n_f$, among these packets, $N n_f$ packets belong to the flows monitored in the TCAM rule table. The number of packets belonging to the flows which are not monitored is $(n_c - N)n_f$, so each packet has probability $p = \frac{n_s}{(n_c-N)n_f}$ to be monitored. For the attack, each attacking packet has p probability to be monitored, the packet inter arrival time is $1/n_a$. So the average time an attack to be monitored is $t_p = \sum_{k=1}^{\infty}[(1-p)^{k-1}p \times \frac{k-1}{n_a}] = \frac{1-p}{pn_a} = \frac{(n_c-N)n_f-n_s}{n_a n_s}$ $\square$

Theorem I shows that the detection time of an attack is inversely proportional to the attacking rate (i.e., the number of attacking packets per second). The time to be monitored of an attack with 1 packet per second is 10 times of an attack with 10 packets per second on average. This is verified in the simulations (see next Section).

In case of table overflow, every packet in a flow can be the first packet to be monitored. For a pair of TCP flows, if the last packet of these two flows is monitored, the flow will never be matched because both flows are completed. In this case, a normal TCP flow is considered to be an attacking packet, and a false alarm will be generated. The following theorem gives the false alarm probability of a pair of flows with total n number of packets.

Theorem II: Assume there are a total of n packets in a pair of flows, each packet has probability p to be monitored, then the false alarm probability is $p_{false} = (1-p)^{n-1}p$.

Proof: The false alarm happens if the first $n-1$ packets are not monitored and the last one is monitored. So the probability of a false alarm is $p_{false}=(1-p)^{n-1}p$. $\square$

4 Performance Evaluation

This section evaluates the performance of the proposed solution in the case of table overflow. If the TCAM rule table can monitor all the concurrent active TCP flows, the system can detect attacks even with single attacking packet, while the normal TCP flows are not falsely alarmed. In the case of TCAM rule table overflow, it takes some time to monitor an attack; a normal flow may be falsely alarmed; and some packets belonging to un-monitored flows are dropped by the local CPU. These are quantitatively studied by simulations. In the simulations, four performance metrics: the average time (t_m^A) an attack to be monitored, the number (n_{false}) of false alarm flows per second, the number of TCAM writes per second, and the number of un-monitored packets per second are measured. t_m^A is the average time difference between the arrival time of the first attacking packet in an attack and the arrival time of the attacking packet in that attack being monitored. The time an attack to be monitored is zero if the first attacking packet in an attack is monitored.

The simulations are conducted based on the real router traces downloaded from Abilene-IV Trace Data [9]. These traces are captured from OC-192 backbone Abilene router to and from Kansas city. Each trace includes 90-second traffic on both inbound and outbound links. We have tested more than 10 traces, and selected one trace with average statistics (Trace 1) and one with maximum number of packets (Trace 2). Table 1 shows the basic statistics of the two traces. In both traces, the TCP packets account for more than 80% of the total packets. We also note that the number of new TCP flows per second is about 5K, and the number of maximum concurrent active flows is less than 30 K which map to less than 4Mbits TCAM memory (assume each rule takes 128 bits in the

Table 1. Statistics of real traffic trace

	Trace 1	Trace 2
Total number of packet	12,746,894	14,494,880
Number of TCP packets	9,217,812	11,138,762
Average number of new TCP flows per second	4381	5181
Average number of concurrent active flows	19423	24476
Maximum number of concurrent active flows	21030	26718

TCAM rule table). We suggest to use 4 Mbits TCAM rule table to store flow identities to avoid table overflow. Usually there are thousands of policy filtering rules which takes less than 1 Mbits TCAM memory. Hence a TCAM rule table with 5 Mbits memory is enough to do the integrated tasks in OC-192 line rate in today's Internet.

We evaluate the performance of the proposed solution in case of TCAM table overflow by set a small TCAM rule table. In the simulations, the number of entries in the TCAM rule table varies from 5K (640 Kbits) to 25 K (3.2 Mbits). The attacking packets are generated starting at the 15th second. Three attacking rates (R): 20, 100 and 500 packets per second are simulated. In the simulations, a pair of matched flows are tested every 5 seconds ($T_{idl}=5$) to check if they are still active. A pair of flows are removed from all the three tables if they are completely finished or inactive for a time period longer than 5 seconds since it was tested, i.e., $T_{rmv} = 5$. An unmatched flow is considered to be an attacking flow if it exits for a time period longer than 10 second, i.e., $T_{alm} = 10$.

Figs. 4 and 5 show the average time an attack to be monitored (t_m^A) varying with the TCAM rule table size. t_m^A in Trace 1 (2) is within 11 (20) seconds in the

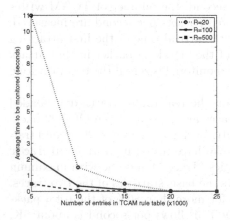

Fig. 4. Average time an attack to be monitored in Trace 1

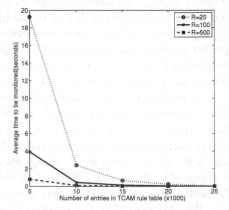

Fig. 5. Average time an attack to be monitored in Trace 2

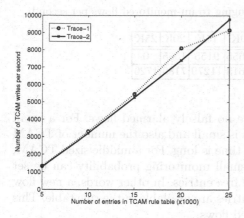

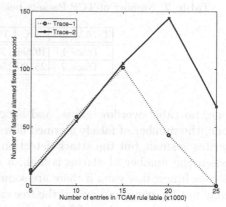

Fig. 6. Number of TCAM writes per second   **Fig. 7.** Number of falsely alarmed flows per second

entire range of rule table sizes. For rule table with 5K entries, t_m^A in trace 1 (2) is about 11 (19.5), 2.2 (4), and 0.4 (0.8) seconds for $R =20$, 100, 500, respectively. t_m^A in Trace 2 is greater than that in Trace 1, because Trace 2 has more new flows per second and more concurrent active flows. From the results, we note that t_m^A is inversely proportional to the attacking rate, verifying Theorem I. So for $R = 1$, t_m^A is about 20 times of that for $R = 20$, i.e., about 220 (400) seconds. t_m^A reduces fast as the number of rule entries increases. This is because the TCAM rule table can accept more rules and hence each packet has higher probability to be monitored. These results show that the proposed solution can quickly detect the attacks even if the attacking rate is low and the TCAM rule table is small.

Fig. 6 shows the number of TCAM writes including adding new flows and update flow entries per second in both traces. The number of writes per second increases from about 1.5K to about 10K as the number of TCAM rule entries increases from 5K to 25K. This is due to the fact that more flows are added to the rule table when the TCAM table size increases. When the number of TCAM entries increases from 20K to 25K, the number of writes per second in Trace 1 increases slowly. This is because almost all TCP flows are monitored in the rule table at 20K, and hence only a few more TCP flows can be added by further increasing the TCAM table size.

The number of false alarm flows per second (n_{false}) is given in Fig. 7. n_{false} increases as the rule table size increases when the table size is small. It then decreases as the table size increases when the table size is over a certain value. The maximum n_{false} in Trace 1 (2) is about 100 (150) at the rule table size 15K (20K). When the number of rule entries is 5K, n_{false} is about 10. As shown in Theorem II, n_{false} depends on the probability (p) of a packet to be monitored. p increases as the rule table size increases, and results in the first increasing and then decreasing behavior.

From these results, we suggest to use either a large (4 Mbits or above) or small (640 Kbits) TCAM rule table to accommodate flow identities. For a large

Table 2. Number of TCP Packets belonging to un-monitored flows per second

TCAM size	5K	10K	15K	20K	25K
Trace 1	19294	13655	9155	1565	0
Trace 2	23160	15613	11279	7189	1726

one, no table overflow exists, and hence no falsely alarmed flows. For a small one, the number of falsely alarmed flows is small and also the number of TCAM writes is small, but the attack detection time is long. For a middle sized TCAM, when the number of alarms is high, a small monitoring probability can be set for each new flow even if there are some free entries. In other words, a new flow may not be monitored even if the free entries are available in the rule table. This can reduce the number of falsely alarmed flows.

The network processor passes the action code of all packets belonging to un-monitored flows to the local CPU. Some of these packets are simply dropped due to lack of free rule entries. Table 2 shows the number of the dropped packets per second at various rule table sizes. The average number of TCP packets per second in trace 1(2) is 102,420 (123,764), the number of packets per second in un-monitored flows are only about 19K (23K) even using a very small TCAM rule table. It reduces quickly as the table size increases.

Through these results, we conclude that the proposed integrated solution can effectively perform the two tasks even using a small TCAM. The proposed solution can be implemented in router/switch which use TCAM coprocessors in its router interface cards.

5   Related Work

The DDoS attacks are the major threat to today's Internet. One effective way to defend against such attacks is to identify and punish the attackers through tracing their physical locations. IP traceback schemes have been extensively studied in the past decade. These schemes includes statistical filtering, hop-by-hop tracing, ICMP messaging based, hash-based and probabilistic packet marking. Statistical filtering [5] [15] drops most likely attacking packets based on the statistics of packet header information such as IP address, port number, protocol type etc.. Hop-by-hop tracing scheme [11] uses a pattern-based scheme to track in progress attacks. ICMP messaging based scheme [3] sends additional ICMP packet to the destination for path reconstruction. Hash-based solution [17] computes and stores a Bloom filter digest of every packet for IP traceback. Probabilistic packet marking solution [8][14] [16][18] marks each packet with partial path information probabilistically. The attacking path is reconstructed using the marking information extracted from a large number of packets.

There are other schemes for DDoS attacks and/or traffic anomaly detection. [12] proposed a general method to diagnose traffic anomaly by measuring traffic volume. [7] designed a bloom filter array for traffic anomaly detection through

2D matching. In [1], a DDoS defense system based on the packet score has been developed. The bad packets with score less than the threshold are discarded.

TCAM has been widely used for longest prefix matching and policy filtering table matching [13][19] in industry. Except the longest prefix matching and policy filtering, another promising application of TCAM coprocessors is high-speed signature matching for intrusion detection [6]. However, there is no application of TCAM coprocessor to enable integrated security and packet classification tasks.

6   Conclusions

In this paper, we propose an integrated solution for TCP-based traffic anomaly detection and policy filtering based on TCAM coprocessors. The DDoS attacks using spoofed source IP address are detected through two-dimensional (2D) matching. The key features of the proposed solution are: (1) setting flag bits in TCAM action code to support various packet treatments; (2) managing TCP flow state in pair to do 2D matching. The performance of the proposed solution has been analyzed and tested by simulation based on the real world traffic traces. The results show that the proposed solution can handle OC-192 line rate.

Acknowledgement

This work is supported by the UGC of Hong Kong under the CERG grant PolyU 5293/06E.

References

1. Ayres, P.E., Sun, H., Chao, H.J.: A High-Speed PacketScore DDoS Defense System. IEEE Journal on Selected Areas in Communications 24(10), 1864–1876 (2006)
2. Baboesu, F., Varghese, G.: Scalable Packet Classification. In: Proceedings of ACM SIGCOMM (2001)
3. Bellovin, S.: ICMP Traceback Messages. Work in Progress, Internet Draft draft-bellovin-itrace-00.txt (2000)
4. Cypress Ayama 10K/20K NSE Series TCAM products, http://www.cypress.com
5. Duan, Z., Yuan, X., Chandrashekar, J.: Constructing Inter-Domain Packet Filters to Control IP Spoofing Based on BGP Updates. In: Proceedings of IEEE INFO-COM (2006)
6. Yu, F., Katz, R.H., Lakshman, T.V.: Gigabit Rate Packet Pattern Matching with TCAM. In: IEEE ICNP (2004)
7. Fan, J., Wu, D., Lu, K., Nucci, A.: Design of Bloom Filter Array for Network Anomaly Detection. In: Proceedings of IEEE GLOBECOM (2006)
8. Goodrich, M.T.: Efficient Packet Marking for Large-Scale IP Traceback. In: Proceedings of ACM Conference on Computer and Communications Security (CCS) (2002)
9. http://pma.nlanr.net/Specical/ips14.html

10. Hussain, A., Heidemann, J., Papadopoulos, C.: A Framework for Classifying Denial of Service Attacks. In: ACM SIGCOMM (2003)
11. Joannidis, J., Bellovin, S.M.: Implementing Pushback: Router-ased Defense Against DDoD Attacks. In: Network and Distributed System Security Symposium (2002)
12. Lakhina, A., Crovella, M., Diot, C.: Diagnosing Network-Wide Traffic Anomalies. In: Proceedings of ACM SIGCOMM (2004)
13. Lakshminarayanan, K., Rangarajan, A., Venkatachary, S.: Algorithms for Advanced Packet Classification with Ternary CAMs. In: Proceedings of ACM SIGCOM (2005)
14. Li, J., Sung, M., Xu, J., Li, L.: Large-Scale IP Traceback in High-Speed Internet: Practical Techniques and Theoretical Foundation. In: Proceedings of IEEE Symposium on Security and Privacy (2004)
15. Li, Q., Chang, E., Chan, M.: On the Effectiveness of DDoS Attacks on Statistical Filtering. In: IEEE INFOCOM (2005)
16. Savage, S., Wetherall, D., Karlin, A., Anderson, T.: Network Support for IP Traceback. IEEE/ACM Transactions on Networkng 9(3), 226–237 (2001)
17. Snoeren, A.C., Partridge, C., Sanchez, L.A., Jones, C.E.: Hash-Based IP Traceback. In: Proceedings of ACM SIGCOMM (2001)
18. Song, D.X., Perrig, A.: Advanced and Authenticated Marking Schemes for IP Traceback. In: Proceedings of IEEE INFOCOM (2001)
19. Spitznagel, E., Taylor, D., Turner, J.: Packet Classification Using Extended TCAMs. In: Proceedings of International Conference of Network Protocol (ICNP) (September 2003)
20. Wang, Z., Che, H., Kumar, M., Das, S.: CoPTUA: Consistent Policy Table Update Algorithm for TCAM Without Locking. IEEE Transactions on Computers 53(12), 1602–1614 (2004)

Secure Safety: Secure Remote Access to Critical Safety Systems in Offshore Installations

Martin Gilje Jaatun[1], Tor Olav Grøtan[2], and Maria B. Line[1]

[1] SINTEF ICT
[2] SINTEF Technology and Society
{Martin.G.Jaatun,tor.o.grotan,maria.b.line}@sintef.no

Abstract. Safety Instrumented Systems (SIS) as defined in IEC 61508 and IEC 61511 are very important for the safety of offshore oil & natural gas installations. SIS typically include the Emergency Shutdown System (ESD) that ensures that process systems return to a safe state in case of undesirable events. Partly as a consequence of the evolving "Integrated Operations" concept, a need is emerging for remote access to such systems from vendors external to the operating company. This access will pass through a number of IP-based networks used for other purposes, including the open Internet. This raises a number of security issues, ultimately threatening the safety integrity of SIS.

In this paper we present a layered network architecture that represents current good practice for a solution to ensure secure remote access to SIS. Also, a method for assessing whether a given solution for remote access to SIS is acceptable is described. The primary objective with the specification of the remote access path is to defend the Safety Integrity Level (SIL) of SIS from security infringements. It also accommodates the special case when security functions have to be implemented within SIS.

Keywords: Process Control, Offshore, Secure remote access, Safety Instrumented Systems.

1 Introduction

The concept of Integrated Operations (IO) is emerging as the preferred way of working in the oil and gas industry. Real-time cooperation between on- and offshore staff is required in order to optimize production, and new technologies and new work processes enable this.

Commercial-off-the-shelf (COTS) hardware and software and Internet connections are among the new technologies introduced, where "new" means that they have not been widely used in the context of process control before. The application area is remote operation, which enables onshore staff to log on to, and perform operations on, process control systems (PCS) and Safety and Automation Systems (SAS) offshore. This opens for a whole new set of threats related to information security that need to be considered.

Safety Instrumented Systems (SIS) are crucial subsystems offshore. According to the IEC 61508/61611 series of standards [1] [2] and the PDS method [3],

C. Rong et al. (Eds.): ATC 2008, LNCS 5060, pp. 121–133, 2008.

they are of paramount importance for the safety of an offshore installation. SIS typically include the Emergency Shutdown System (ESD), which often is the ultimate guarantor for fail-safe properties at such installations.

The use of new technologies must be trusted to not have any negative impact on SIS; i.e. impact that could raise significant doubt on its claimed Safety Integrity Level (SIL) [1]. This means that the communication channels used during remote operations must be technically secure, such that they can not be tampered with, misused or in other ways used to compromise SIS.

Information security is usually defined by the three terms confidentiality, integrity and availability [4]. In this paper the scope is limited to integrity concerns for SIS, which means that the objective of the "good practice for remote access" is to prevent unauthorized changes to SIS.

Industrial safety and information security issues are two related – but still rather different – fields of theory and practice [5]. In some application areas it is useful to seek to combine the two, and process control is an example of such an area. Combination will not be unproblematic, and some problems are already manifest in the mixed vocabulary that needs to be employed when we are addressing safety and security, respectively. Practitioners within both fields are concerned about this challenge. As further discussed in [6], combining these two approaches into a coherent whole is not achieved solely through a technical report, but a modest hope is that this paper may contribute to such a development.

In this paper, a network topology for secure remote access to SIS is presented. The solution includes contractor's network, operator's office network and process control network, and security mechanisms. Also, a method is described that can be used to assess whether a given network solution for remote access to SIS is acceptable. The paper is based on results from the Secure Safety (SeSa) project, funded by the Norwegian Research Council and PDS Forum.

The remainder of this paper is structured as follows: Section 2 refers to related work, and our research method is briefly described in section 3. The good practice network topology is presented in section 4 and section 5. The method for assessing the impact on SIL is described in section 6. We give our conclusion in section 7 and suggest further work in section 8.

2   Related Work

The background and approach for the SeSa project was documented in [7]. Line et al. [5] discuss general challenges in considering both safety and security in a given situation. Schoitsch [8] and Kosmowski et al. [9] explore relationships between traditional "security" assurance and "safety assurance" as exemplified by SIL.

The UK Centre for the Protection of National Infrastructure (formerly NISCC) has published guidelines on security of SCADA systems in general [10], and on firewall deployment in such networks in particular [11]. The US National Institute of Standards and Technology (NIST) has also released a preliminary guide to SCADA security [6]. Naedele [12] presents insights on IEC standardization efforts in industrial IT security, although it does not appear that the IEC today is any closer to a finalized standard.

The Norwegian Oil Industry Association (OLF) has published a set of Information Security Baseline Requirements [13] which all operators on the Norwegian Continental Shelf eventually will have to comply with.

The SeSa project has not significantly extended the good practices mentioned above, but ventures to combine them into a coherent whole for the specific case of secure remote access to SIS.

3   Method

The SeSa project studied a small number of Norwegian offshore operators and contractors, and participated in two sessions of PDS Forum in 2006 [3]. The PDS Forum meetings have a broad participation of experts from the Norwegian process control community.

The interviews and the PDS Forum discussions contributed to the survey on how the communication networks are implemented today within the process control domain. This includes the operator's office network, the contractor's network and their solutions for remote control, the process control systems offshore, and the security mechanisms in use. Possible improvements were then identified, based on state of the art and earlier experiences, regarding structure of the network topology and security mechanisms to be added or modified. The network topology presented in this paper therefore (in similarity with many other "good practice" efforts) represents a synthesis of how it is actually implemented in the offshore industry today and the ideal solution.

4   Structuring the Remote Access Path

A basis for ensuring secure remote operation is that the networks that constitute the remote access path are organized in a manner that adheres to the principle of "defense in depth"[1], and that suitable access control mechanisms are employed.

4.1   The "Onion Model"

The left side of Fig. 1 depicts a layered access model from an operator's point of view. This model is based on two demilitarized zones (DMZ); one serving as a buffer between the operator's network and "the outside world", while the other separates the operator's administrative network (which may span several installations) from the process network (which typically is restricted to a single installation).

All contractors must be considered "external" just like the rest of the Internet, since the operator has no physical control over the contractor's networks (operators may impose contractual restrictions with respect to how and with what equipment contractors are allowed to access the operators' networks, but will have limited means of verifying these arrangements on a continuous basis).

---

[1] This is the opposite of the "Maginot line" principle of relying on a single point of failure.

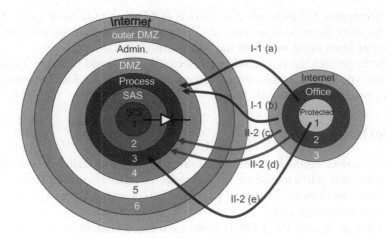

Fig. 1. Layered model with allowed and rejected access attempts

The layered model of Fig. 1 can be argued on several levels. First, the separation of layers 1-3 from the surrounding is based on the requirement for SIS autonomy, as stated in [14]. Furthermore, the separation of the process network from the administrative network is as recommended in the NISCC good practice guide [10]. Finally, the outer DMZ protects against all external actors, with special mechanism to allow authorized contractors to access the appropriate parts of the operator's network.

As the operator has no physical control over the contractors' networks, the latter are likely to differ from installation to installation. By contractual obligations, operators should mandate a minimum layering as illustrated in the right side of Fig. 1, where equipment used to access the operator's network is placed in a zone separated from the general office network. Note that since access in this model conceptually always originates from the contractor, there is no need from our point of view for the contractor to have a DMZ between its office network and the internet - a single barrier (i.e. firewall) is sufficient. This is also illustrated in Fig. 2.

4.2   Threats and Countermeasures

As part of the SeSa method, we have compiled a list of common threats and countermeasures that are applicable to the access model in Fig. 1. This list is based on sources like [15] and [10]. Space does not permit the reproduction of the full list here, but identified threats originating from "the outside" (zone 7) are listed in Table 1. The physical configuration suggestion that is described in the following sections represents a response to the identified threats and necessary countermeasures.

We have as a rule described the threats as originating from an adjoining zone, but the ultimate goal for a given attack may be to traverse all interfaces to affect

Table 1. Threats originating from zone 7

From Zone	To Zone	Threat	Ultimate impact on zone	Countermeasure
7	c1	Attack on contractor's zone 1	1	Configuration control, administrative measures (Specifically: Not allowed to access c1 from c2), Firewalls and c1 tightly configured, hardened
		Malware planted in contractor's "secure zone"	1	Configuration control, administrative measures
7	7	Manipulation of legitimate traffic	1	Encrypt and authenticate
7	6	Attack on firewall A	6	Firewalls must be tightly configured and patched
		Attack on other resource in zone 6	6	Don't have other resources in DMZ, Other resources that have to be in the DMZ must be tightly configured (hardened)
7	6	Attack on DMZ gateway	5	Tight configuration and hardening, Strong authentication, Restrict access to DMZ GW to pre-defined addresses

the innermost zone, e.g. in order to illegitimately shut down an oil installation[2]. Note that no pre-compiled list of threats can ever be considered "complete" for any real networked system; the threats we have identified must be treated as a starting point that as a minimum must be compared with the network to be studied. Threats that are found to be not applicable or irrelevant must be documented as such, and a site-specific analysis must be performed to uncover additional threats.

A conservative threat analysis must adhere to Kerckhoffs' principle [16], and assume that an attacker has access to all pertinent information regarding a system (network topology, configuration) *except* passwords, encryption keys, etc.

4.3 Access Modes

If a substantial part of the need for remote access is to read status information without making any changes, it is strongly recommended to consider a technical solution that offers such "read only" access (see 5.1). A "read-only" solution will in itself be easier to verify than a "full" solution. If read-only and read-write solutions need to coexist, a "double" solution will imply that the entry to the latter solution may be even more restrictive, thus increasing the chance for

---

[2] From a safety point of view, the threat would have been the reverse, i.e., *preventing* a necessary shutdown from taking place.

success in the "1st round" in Fig. 3. Furthermore, a read-only solution may also potentially be reachable from a wider (looser) set of operational contexts on the vendor side, as indicated in Fig. 1.

Hence, for a further reduction of complexity in solutions, we propose that remote access is divided into three coarse categories:

0   No access
I   Read-only access
II Full read/write access to SIS

These can be further refined as shown in Table 2.

Table 2. Access modes

I-1	Snapshots of SIS state (via "information diode" - see section 5.1). In principle, this is the equivalent of a CCTV transmission of the terminal display.
I-2	Real time readout of SIS with possibility of specifying parameters.
II-1	Real time data transmission between installations, e.g. from a Process Station (PS) on one platform to a PS on another. This implies machine-machine communication without user intervention.
II-2	Interactive read/write access to SIS

4.4   Access Examples

The various access options described in section 4.3 can now be mapped to the layered models as illustrated by the arrows in Fig. 1, where it is assumed that "information diode" functionality (see 5.1 for details) is available.

a) Allowed access from contractor's office network to DMZ (e.g. to read historical data from SIS)
b) Allowed access from internet to DMZ
c) Rejected (blocked) access from contractor's office network to process network
d) Rejected (blocked) access from internet to process network
e) Allowed access from contractor's protected network to process network (via broker function in DMZ)

Note that prevention of access from contractor's office network cannot be done reliably by packet filtering alone. Also note that the outer DMZ will have additional access control mechanisms that are not explicitly described here.

4.5   Physical Mapping

An example of how the layered "onion" models presented above may be translated into a physical network configuration is presented in Fig. 2. Note that while the doctrine of "defense in depth" mandates that each of the firewalls A-D should be implemented as separate units, a functionally equivalent configuration using only two units with three interfaces each is possible.

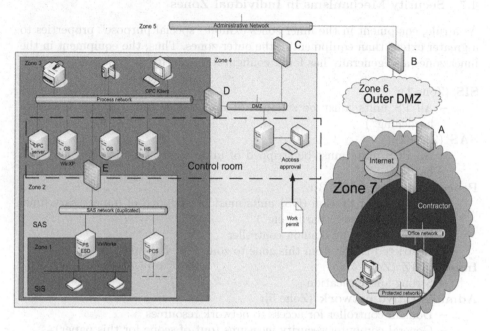

Fig. 2. Case for remote access

We repeat that although not shown explicitly, some sort of access control mechanism is assumed to be placed in the outer DMZ (zone 6).

4.6   Barriers between Zones

Barriers between zones 7-2 are implemented using firewalls A-E. Additionally, there is a manual "access approval" application in the inner DMZ (zone 4), where an operator can grant (or deny) access attempts originating e.g. from onshore contractors. Technically, this may be implemented as part of a terminal server application. Good practice would in this case indicate that all such accesses should be in accordance with a formal work permit.

There is no separate barrier between SAS (Safety and Automation System) and SIS; this implies that the barrier(s) is (are) represented by the command interface offered by the units that straddle the zone boundary, e.g. the ESD. To access the ESD user interface, a remote user must as a minimum authenticate to both the "access approval" application, as well as conventional authentication to log onto the Operator Station.

If the protection against i.e. PCS access to the ESD is insufficient, accessing the PCS is also critical.

Firewall E is shown as a barrier between the process network (zone 3) and SAS (zone 2); it may also serve as a barrier between different SAS segments (if applicable).

4.7 Security Mechanisms in Individual Zones

As a rule, equipment in the inner zones exhibit "special purpose" properties to a greater extent than equipment in the outer zones. Thus, the equipment in the inner zones also generally has fewer configurable security mechanisms.

SIS (Zone 1):
  - All PS units must be stripped of unnecessary functionality ("system hardening")

SAS (Zone 2):
  - All PCS units must be stripped of unnecessary functionality ("system hardening")

Process network (Zone 3):
  - All Operator Station (OS) units must be stripped of unnecessary functionality ("system hardening")
  - Logon verified by domain controller
  - Restricted traffic from this zone to zone 2 by firewall

Inner DMZ (Zone 4):
  - Strong authentication

Administrative network (Zone 5):
  - Domain controller for access to network resources
  - General computer security measures (out of scope for this paper)

Outer DMZ (Zone 6):
  - Access control on various levels;
    • The general public
    • Guests/contractors
    • Own employees

4.8 OPC Communication

A common way of transferring process control information is by the use of the "OLE for Process Control" protocol. OPC was designed for communication over local area networks, which has created a demand for OPC tunnelling solutions when OPC data needs to be transferred from one process network to another. OPC tunnelling is frequently merely a bundling-unbundling operation, in which case it has no added security value as such. Specifically, there is no confidentiality or integrity protection of the tunnelled data.

Based on the dubious security property of OPC, we consider an OPC tunnel between two process networks to be an implicit interconnection of these two networks. Furthermore, it is important that the tunnel is protected against unauthorised modification or disclosure along the transmission path. This implies that the tunnel must be encrypted, and that the plaintext data must have a cryptographically strong message integrity check added before encryption.

Even though newer equipment frequently has incorporated OPC server/client functionality, a configuration that enables a PS to establish OPC communication with any PS in a different installation should be discouraged. This can be regulated using firewall E.

Since it is not known beforehand where an OPC tunnel will go, it must be assumed (as a "worst case") that it also passes through the open internet at some point between the two process networks.

5   Additional Mechanisms

In the previous section, recommendations for structuring the remote access path were described. In certain situations, it may be possible to further mitigate a large number of threats by architectural choices. Two such options are described below.

5.1   Read-Only Status Server

It is possible to configure a read-only status server e.g. by connecting a special device (which we can call "information diode") between the Safety and Automation System and a status server in the inner DMZ. The information diode can be realized by sending UDP data enhanced with extra integrity checksum, ensuring that the receiver has significantly higher bandwidth capacity than the sender, etc. Since UDP does not acknowledge each packet, it is possible to create a device that physically only can transmit information in one direction, e.g. by cutting the "receive" wire on an Unshielded Twisted Pair (UTP) cable[3]. There are also commercially available products (e.g. [17]) that offer this functionality.

The status server is here placed in the inner DMZ based on the premise that the operator will want to retain a certain control over who gets access to this information, and also takes into account that having a single centralized status server for all operations, is likely to introduce too long delays in the system. Having said this, technically there should be nothing to prevent the status server from being placed e.g. in a given installation's administrative network (i.e. on the outside of Firewall D), if this is more in line with the operator's requirements.

Ideally, the status server should receive every conceivable piece of data obtainable in the process/SAS/SIS networks. It must be determined whether this is practically possible, e.g. a new unit may be introduced that is capable of querying every valve, sensor, etc., and push this information through the diode to the status server. The bandwidth requirements must be assessed based on the size of the total data to be monitored.

---

[3] Of course, there are a few more practical problems that must be solved in an implementation of this concept - which also explains why there are commercial alternatives available.

5.2   Inner DMZ Proxy Functionality

In addition to providing a read-only status server, a finer granularity in access control can be achieved by not granting full "remote desktop" access to an Operator Station, but rather having a special-purpose application running in the DMZ (e.g. on the terminal server) which contains options for executing specific operations on SAS (and SIS) devices. Taken to its ultimate conclusion, this idea would imply having a large number of distinct applications to which contractors would be granted time-limited access by use of the work permit access approval regime illustrated in Fig. 2.

It would also be possible to create a single, big "granular access" application, but that would require a separate interface for configuring access rights, and such a large application would be more difficult to verify for correctness.

6   The SeSa Method

Use of the SeSa method on a given case is illustrated in the flow-chart of Fig. 3. In short, the method comprises the following steps:

1. Establish overview of threats and known weaknesses
2. Develop requirements specification of the "security value chain" [7] for the remote access path
3. Determine the impact on SIS/SIL through a HAZOP-oriented analysis
4. If impact cannot be ruled out, try another round based on updated threat/ weakness picture and additional requirements (first round)
5. If impact still cannot be ruled out, identify additional security functions within SIS, and assess through HAZOP whether this will provide sufficient

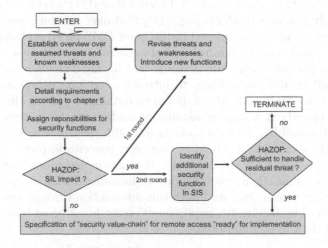

Fig. 3. The SeSa method

protection vs the residual threat (second round). If confidence in security functions within the SIS perimeter is needed according to the previous step, assess whether the assurance level implicitly carried by the specified SIL level, is sufficient

6. If "success" is not achieved after the second round, the proposed solution should be discarded.

The HAZOP (Hazard and Operability Analysis) [18] technique is frequently used and well-established in industrial safety. In the SeSa method we use HAZOP to identify threats and verify whether these threats are mitigated by the proposed design of the remote access path. The SeSa use of HAZOP means that if no "problem" remains after all explicitly known possibilities have been examined exhaustively, the "conclusion" must be that the proposed solution is per definition "secure". However, there will always be a possibility that something is overlooked, or that new threats and vulnerabilities emerge or is revealed at a later time. The SeSa method cannot account for this type of (epistemic) uncertainty. Such potential "flaws" in the judgement must be handled in retrospect, when they are revealed.

It may be difficult to gauge the assurance consequences of adding a COTS component to a system that has a given SIL. Kosmowski et al. [9] argue for a mapping between SIL and Common Criteria Evaluation Assurance Levels (EAL) [19]. However, it should be noted that a given EAL only says something about our assurance that the mechanisms defined in the appropriate Protection Profile have been properly implemented; if these are insufficient to guarantee our desired SIL, a mapping between EAL and SIL is meaningless. On the other hand, if the mechanisms we rely on to provide our given SIL is included in the component's Protection Profile, we believe that the mapping proposed in [9] may be applicable.

7 Conclusion

In this paper, we have presented good practice for secure remote access to Safety Instrumented Systems in an offshore process control system. Furthermore, we have introduced the *SeSa method* for assessing whether a given network solution is acceptable when it comes to ensuring the integrity of SIS.

The network solution presented complies with advice and guidance given by several actors in the industry. This fact contributes to assurance that the solution is acceptable and ensures an appropriate level of security for SIS.

8 Further Work

Further work needs to be done along the following lines:

a) Further trial of the method on "real" cases
b) Extending the scope to broader "SAS" contexts

c) Development of schemes to update "approved" solutions in light of new knowledge of threats and vulnerabilities
d) Operation and implementation of the "value-chain" that is the result of a successful use of the SeSa method.

The latter is considered the most urgent. First, because of the limited scope of the SeSa method presented herein (providing a functional requirement specification), of which implementation and management across organisational borders is not included. Second, because a dynamic environment, both technically and organisationally, is expected to be a central characteristic of the Brave New World of Integrated Operations. The "value-chain" has to be re-constructed and updated rather frequently.

Acknowledgments

This paper has presented results from the SeSa research project funded by the Norwegian Research Council and PDS Forum. We are grateful for the participation of Tor Onshus (NTNU), Knut Øien (SINTEF T&S), Stein Hauge (SINTEF T&S) and all PDS Forum attendees.

Also thanks to Odd Nordland, SINTEF ICT, who made helpful comments on a previous version of this paper.

References

1. Functional safety of E/E/PE safety-related systems, IEC Std. 61 508 (1998)
2. Functional safety - Safety Instrumented systems for the process industry sector, IEC Std. 61 511 (2003)
3. The PDS webpage. Visited, 2007-03-09,
   http://www.sintef.no/static/tl/projects/pds/www/
4. Information technology - Security techniques - Information security management systems - Requirements, ISO/IEC Std. 27 001 (2005)
5. Line, M.B., Nordland, O., Røstad, L., Tøndel, I.A.: Safety vs Security?. In: Proceedings of PSAM 8, New Orleans (2006)
6. Guide to Supervisory Control and Data Acquisition (SCADA) and Industrial Control Systems Security, NIST special publication 800-82 (initial public draft) (September 2006),
   http://csrc.nist.gov/publications/drafts/800-82/Draft-SP800-82.pdf
7. Grøtan, T.O.: Secure Safety in Remote Operations. In: Proceedings of ESREL 2006, Estoril, Portugal (2006)
8. Schoitsch, E.: Design for safety and security of complex embedded systems: A unified approach. In: Cyberspace Security and Defense: Research Issues. NATO Science Series II - Mathematics, Physics and Chemistry, vol. 196 (2006)
9. Kosmowski, K., Sliwinski, M., Barnert, T.: Functional safety and security assessment of the control and protection systems. In: Proceedings of ESREL 2006, Estoril, Portugal (2006)
10. NISCC Good Practice Guide - Process Control and SCADA Security, PA Consulting Group on behalf of NISCC, Tech. Rep. (October 2005),
    http://www.cpni.gov.uk/docs/re-20051025-00940.pdf

11. Byres, E., Karsch, J., Carter, J.: Good Practice Guide - Firewall Deployment for SCADA and Process Control Networks. British Columbia Institute of Technology, on behalf of NISCC, Tech. Rep. (2005), http://www.cpni.gov.uk/docs/re-20050223-00157.pdf

12. Naedele, M.: Standardizing industrial IT security - a first look at the IEC approach. In: Proceedings of 10th IEEE Conference on Emerging Technologies and Factory Automation, vol. 2, p. 7 (2005)

13. OLF Guideline 104: Information Security Baseline Requirements for Process Control, Safety, and Support ICT Systems (2006), http://www.olf.no/?35820.pdf

14. Forskrift om styring i petroleumsvirksomheten (Styringsforskriften), Norwegian Petroleum Directorate, §1 (December 2004)

15. IT Grundschutz Manual. Bundesamt für Sicherheit in der Informationstechnik (2004), http://www.bsi.de/english/gshb/manual/

16. Kerckhoffs, A.: La cryptographie militaire. Journal des sciences militaires IX, 5–38 (1883)

17. Whitepaper: Tenix Interactive Link Data Diode. Tenix America (a subsiduary of Tenix pty). Visited 2007-03-16 (2006), http://www.tenixamerica.com/images/white_papers/TenixIL_DataDiode.pdf

18. Hazard and operability studies (HAZOP studies) - Application guide, IEC Std. 61 882 (2001)

19. Information technology - Security techniques - Evaluation criteria for IT security, ISO/IEC Std. 15 408 (2005), http://www.commoncriteriaportal.org/

SEMAP: Improving Multipath Security Based on Attacking Point in Ad Hoc Networks

Zhengxin Lu[1], Chen Huang[1], Furong Wang[1], and Chunming Rong[2]

[1] Dept. of E. I. E, Huazhong University of Science and Technology, China
luzx@mail.hust.edu.cn, szo094@hotmail.com,
wangfurong@mail.hust.edu.cn
[2] Dept. of E. C. E., University of Stavanger, Norway
chunming.rong@uis.no

Abstract. In hostile Ad hoc network, the possibility of being attacked or attacking others can't be avoided. Most current intrusion detection systems and secure routing protocols only focus on concrete attacking behaviors while neglecting the underlying attacking threat. So it's inevitable to choose malicious nodes during routing establishment. To construct a secure multipath route, we present SEMAP, a secure enhancement mechanism based on Attacking Point (AP) which converts the possibility of security threat to a concrete metric. AP is a description of security status of a node. AP of a node can be easily extended to that of link, path and path set, which provides an important reference in route selection. Our design can exclude the nodes that will be the objects of adversaries from the network before actual routing process. Simulation results show that SEMAP provides an effective security enhancement without compromising the efficiency of original routing protocol.

Keywords: Attack, Possibility, Metric, Multipath, Ad hoc.

1 Introduction

Mobile Ad hoc networks have received tremendous attention in recent years. On one hand, rapid deployment ability, self-organizing configuration and other attracting features make Ad hoc network popular in tactical and military applications; on the other hand, the inherent characteristics of Ad hoc networks, such as open wireless channel, limited computation power and highly dynamic topology also make Ad hoc network vulnerable to malicious attacks.

Constructing a secure route from source to destination is a basic service in Ad hoc networks as well as in any other networks. A secure route should be composed by reliable nodes or the nodes that are not likely to be the objects of adversaries. That's to say, non-reliable nodes and the nodes with hidden trouble should be isolated from the network. Conventionally, Ad hoc network must rely on intrusion detection system (IDS) [1,2] to exclude internal malicious members, and also resort to secure routing protocols [3~7] to make sure that the successful exchange of routing information is among legitimate participants. However, both IDS and secure routing protocol have their limitations: for IDS, as pointed out in [8], adversaries may try to hide their

C. Rong et al. (Eds.): ATC 2008, LNCS 5060, pp. 134–148, 2008.

attacks under protocol-compliant behaviors. For example, it is not easy to distinguish between packet loss caused by normal network congestion and that caused by selfish and malicious behaviors. Additionally, most IDS mechanisms only focus on the discovery of attackers while ignoring the nodes being attacked or the ones that will be the objects of adversaries. These ignored nodes should also be excluded because they may become the weak point of following routing process; for the secure routing protocols, they can't guarantee that they won't select a compromised node as intermediate node during message forwarding, nor do they provide an explicit approach for comparing the security among nodes. IDS and secure routing protocol also have a common short-age that they are lack of prediction for the underlying attacking threat. Before any reaction/recovery mechanism takes effect, the established route may have been disrupted. And route re-construction not only brings significant communication overhead, but also increases end-to-end delay.

From the above analysis, we can get the conclusion that, constructing an absolute secure path is impractical especially in a hostile and unstable environment. Every node has the possibility of attacking others or being attacked. Therefore, designing a flexible secure routing enhancement mechanism which can take the difference of security status of each node into account is crucial. Even when a proportion of nodes suffer from serious security threat, this secure mechanism can make the best choice of path selection to provide a reliable routing service.

(1) Content of this paper
In this paper, we propose a security enhancement mechanism for multipath routing protocols of Ad hoc network, SEMAP, to provide a more reliable end-to-end routing service. SEMAP is compatible with both single path and multipath routing. The fundamental idea of SEMAP is based on a new proposed concept "Attacking Point". Attack Point (AP) is a metric for evaluating the security status of nodes, which is the combination the possibilities of attacking, being attacked and being attacked in the future. Each node will present an abnormal status in its performance while it suffers from attack. But as mentioned above, this status may also a result of the decline of its own capability. No matter which reason causes this phenomenon, this node is not suitable to be a part of routing process in some extent. To concrete this extent, we convert it to AP as a security metric through specific algorithm. AP is the complete evaluation of security status of a node, but a single node only plays a tiny roll in the whole routing process. So after obtaining AP of a single node, we extend it to a path and a path set for obtaining a general security evaluation on an end-to-end connection. By this means, when multiple paths have been established, we have sufficient confidence to choose a suitable path set based on pre-defined AP requirement.

(2) Challenge of SEMAP
We address three major design issues:

   1) How to convert the possibilities of attacking others, being attacked and being attacked in the future to the AP of node;
   2) How to integrate SEMAP to current multipath routing protocol seamlessly;
   3) How to make a decision on selecting a secure communication channel based on AP of a path set developed from that of a node.

(3) Contribution of this paper
SEMAP brings the following improvements on current security mechanisms for Ad hoc networks:

1) Detecting misbehavior and abnormal status of nodes before actual routing establishment;
2) Developing a novel concrete metric for security evaluation in path selection;
3) Integrating AP based security with conventional routing protocols seamlessly with compromising the efficiency.

The following paper is organized as follows: In section 2, we present the related works on multipath routing protocol. In section 3, we provide the details of SEMAP, which includes the three major design issues. Simulation results are given in section 4 and section 5 concludes the whole paper.

2   Related Works

Multipath routing has shown its effectiveness in coping with the frequent topology changes and improving resilience to node/link failures in Ad hoc network [9~12].

Split Multipath Routing (SMR) [9] first establishes a shortest delay route between source and destination. Then it creates a maximum path set whose member path is disjoint from the shortest delay route. SMR relies on RREQ flooding to the entire network to search maximal disjoint paths, which brings considerable communication overhead to the network.

A multipath extension to DSR is proposed in [10]. Source node floods routing request queries to destination node. When intermediate node receives a query, they will duplicate this query and re-broadcasts it. Queries arrive at destination nodes through different paths and only the ones that are disjoint with others will be replied by the destination node.

A multipath extension to AODV (AODVM) [11] is proposed for finding reliable routing paths. Intermediate nodes not only duplicate RREQ during forwarding them, but also preserve these packets. It is obvious that this approach will consume enormous memory and communication overhead.

AOMDV is proposed in [12], which is an extension to AODV for computing multiple loop-free and link disjoint paths. A new concept of "advertised hop count" is introduced to make sure that routing controlling messages won't travel back to original. Intermediate node will guarantee link disjoint when they re-flood routing controlling messages.

3   Security Enhancement Mechanism Based on Attacking Point

3.1   Assumption

(1) Cryptographic method
SEMAP employ asymmetric encryption method. Each node joining the network generates a pair of public and private keys;

(2) Key server
There is a key server in the network. This key server doesn't authenticate any network members, and only provides a storage space for preserving public keys. In our design, this key server is equipped with sufficient storage capability and under strong protection;

(3) Underlying routing protocol
We employ multipath routing protocol AOMDV to establish path set between source and destination. Other protocols are also compatible with SEMAP;

(4) Radio radius and communication channel
The radio radius of node is time-invariant and the wireless channel is bidirectional. The wireless network cards of nodes are all in promiscuous model, which makes neighboring nodes within transmission range can monitor the communication status of each others.

3.2 The Design Details of SEMAP

There are three main components of SEMAP. First of all, an extensible model of AP calculation is the precondition of SEMAP design; the second is the proper integration of AP and underlying routing protocol; finally a path selection policy is set for constructing the most secure path set. This section will provide the details.

3.2.1 The Overview of SEMAP

The concept of "Attacking Point" comes from the observation that, in a hostile and unstable network environment, security threat can't be avoided for any network member. We call this phenomenon as "Pervasive Security Threat". From this concept, possible existing attacks, potential possibility to be attacked and suspicious misbehavior should be all taken into account. Behind the above three security threats, we assume that there exists a "virtual attacker" with a possibility, and we convert this possibility to the new security metric – Attacking Point (AP). Then determining whether a node is suitable for joining routing process or not, can simply compare the value of its AP with pre-defined security requirement.

SEMAP explores the relationship between AP and current multipath routing protocols. As shown in Figure 1. There are four main procedures related with AP: evaluating AP, collecting AP, analyzing AP and monitoring AP. Each procedure can be mapped to corresponding stage of the routing process.

1) Evaluating AP needs the up-to-date operation information of nodes. The period exchange of Hello message can take the responsibility to collect such information, which won't bring additional communication overhead;

2) The first procedure only obtains AP of a single node. To give a security estimate of a whole path, all the AP of nodes along the path should be obtained. Then as routing controlling messages travel along the path, each intermediate node can attach its security evaluation (AP) on its neighboring node on these messages;

3) Based on the analyzing result of AP of each path set, source node will the final decision on path selection;

4) Conventional routing maintenance is based on the availability detection and it can be updated to AP monitoring of neighboring nodes during packet forwarding.

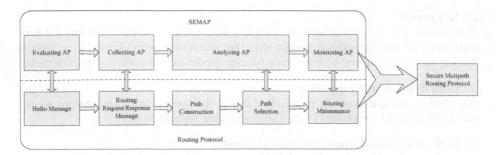

Fig. 1. The Relationship between SEMAP and Routing Protocol

3.2.2 Mathematic Model of Attacking Point

Operation information reflects three kinds of security statuses of node, which include being attacked, being attacked in the future and attacking others. Each status provides a part of reference to form the final AP. So we define three sub-APs to represent their possibilities separately, which are Attacking Influence Point (AIP), Attacking Tempting Point (ATP) and Attacking Launching Point (ALP).

The conversion procedure from the original operation information to the final AP is as follows: collecting the statistic data of performance status in a short time window -> making a contrast between current data with the pre-defined standard data -> estimating the security status from comparison result in the view of possibility -> converting the security status to a concrete value of AP.

(1) Attacking Influence Point (AIP)

The weakness in conventional secure routing protocols is that they seldom consider the influence imposed to network performance from varieties of attack. Node will present diversity in its performance more or less after attack. So a deeper understanding based upon such diversity should be achieved. AIP indicates the possibility of being attacked according to the performance decline and we employ several performance metrics recommended by ITU-T and IETF as follows:

1) IPTD (IP Packet Transfer Delay);
2) IPLR (IP Packet Loss Rate);
3) IPER (IP Packet Error Rate).

It should be pointed out that, the decline of above performance metrics doesn't indicate that node is under attack. For example, the increase of IPTD may be the result of network congestion or shortage of computational power. P_{IPTD}, P_{IPLR} and P_{IPER} are the possibilities of being attacked deduced from each performance decline, as shown in Formula 1~3:

$$P_{IPTD} = \begin{cases} e^{\frac{S_{IPTD} - C_{IPTD}}{S_{IPTD}}} & , C_{IPTD} > S_{IPTD} \\ 0 & , C_{IPTD} \leq S_{IPTD} \end{cases} \qquad (1)$$

$$P_{IPLR} = \begin{cases} e^{\frac{S_{IPLR} - C_{IPLR}}{S_{IPLR}}} & , C_{IPLR} > S_{IPLR} \\ 0 & , C_{IPLR} \leq S_{IPLR} \end{cases} \qquad (2)$$

$$P_{IPER} = \begin{cases} e^{\frac{S_{IPER} - C_{IPER}}{S_{IPER}}} & , \ C_{IPER} > S_{IPER} \\ 0 & , \ C_{IPER} \leq S_{IPER} \end{cases} \tag{3}$$

Where C_{IPTD}, C_{IPLR} and C_{IPER} are the current values of performance metrics; S_{IPTD}, S_{IPLR} and S_{IPER} are the pre-defined standard values of performance metrics. AIP can be calculated with Formula 4:

$$\begin{cases} AIP = \alpha_1 * P_{IPTD} + \alpha_2 * P_{IPLR} + \alpha_3 * P_{IPER} \\ \alpha_1 + \alpha_2 + \alpha_3 = 1 \end{cases} \tag{4}$$

Where α_1, α_2 and α_3 are the influence coefficients of each performance metric in AIP and can be adjusted according to practical requirement. For example, in real-time critical environment, the proportion of IPTD will be increased while that of IPLR and IPER can be reduced.

(2) Attacking Tempting Point (ATP)
Ad hoc network is a completely distributed network in its definition. However the degree of node activity is not uniform across the network in fact. To achieve a maximum damage effect, adversaries will seek for the most desired objects which are the "hop spot" of network, which means that the node has taken part in multiple network activities. For pre-caution, the tempting factors of attack should be extracted to predict the probability of coming threat. We conclude three characteristic tempting factors as follows:

1) NIN (Number of Immediate Neighbors): It reflects the density of an area and the opportunity of being connected with others. Attacking such node will result the destruction of a whole local area;

2) NRP (Number of Routing Process): It is probable that a node belongs to several routing process at the same time, which makes it as the traffic center of network. The failure of such node will result the breakage of multiple paths;

3) LTQ (Length of Task Queue): This indicates the congestion status of node. Node of heavy load intrigues attackers more easily for its failure will bring serious packet loss.

Calculation of the components of ATP employs an experiential model based on segment, as illustrated in Figure 2.

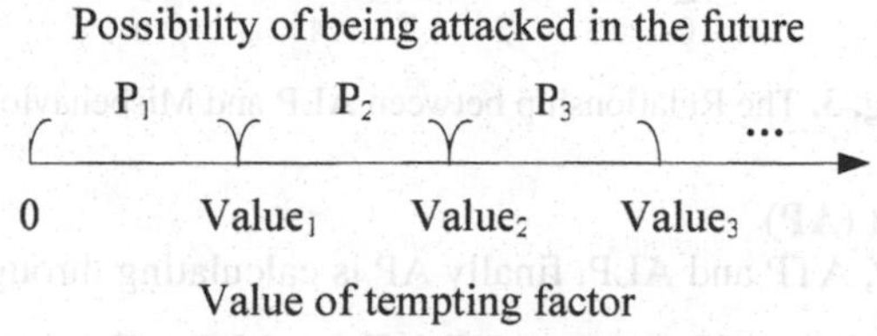

Possibility of being attacked in the future

Fig. 2. A Segment Model for ATP Calculation

For example, the possibility of being attacked in the future deduced from the value of NIN is as follows:

$$P_{NIN} = \begin{cases} P_1, & 0 \le V_{NIN} \le Value_1 \\ P_2, & Value_1 < V_{NIN} \le Value_2 \\ P_3, & Value_2 < V_{NIN} \le Value_3 \\ \dots\dots \end{cases} \tag{5}$$

P_{NRP} and P_{LTQ} can be also obtained through the same model. Then ATP is calculated just as AIP.

$$\begin{cases} ATP = \beta_1 * P_{NIN} + \beta_2 * P_{NRP} + \beta_3 * P_{LTQ} \\ \beta_1 + \beta_2 + \beta_3 = 1 \end{cases} \tag{6}$$

Where β_1, β_2 and β_3 are the proportion of each tempting factor in ATP and can be also adjusted according to security requirement.

(3) Attacking Launching Point (ALP)
An Adversary may possess several misbehaviors simultaneously. The more its misbehaviors, the more threat it will bring to the network. So the calculation of ALP, the possibility of attacking others, is an accumulative model, as shown in Formula 7.

$$ALP = \begin{cases} e^{-k^{-N}}, & N \neq 0 \\ 0 & , N = 0 \end{cases} \tag{7}$$

Where 0<k<1 and N is the number of misbehaviors. The misbehavior list can be seen in [13], which include Unusual Traffic Attraction (UTA), Lack of Error Messages (LEM) and Frequent Route Updates (FRU) and so on. Figure 3 shows that as the increase of misbehaviors, ALP is close to 1.

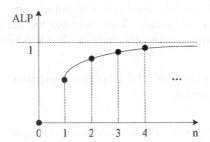

Fig. 3. The Relationship between ALP and Misbehaviors

(4) Attacking Point (AP)
After obtaining AIP, ATP and ALP, finally AP is calculating through Formula 8.

$$\begin{cases} AP = AIP * C_1 + ATP * C_2 + ALP * C_3 \\ C_1 + C_2 + C_3 = 1 \end{cases} \tag{8}$$

C1, C2 and C3 are ratios of AIP, ATP and ALP in AP, which are system parameters. As shown in Figure 4, the mathematic model of AP is extensible and new security related components can be easily added. The only change is internal relationship of the series of α, β and k.

The higher security threat a node has, the higher its AP is. So the goal of SEMAP is to make the routing process away from the nodes with high AP.

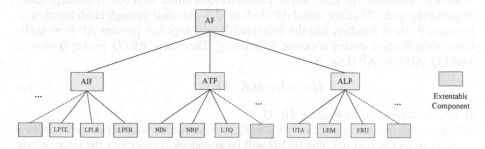

Fig. 4. The Extensible Model of AP

3.2.3 Integration of AP and Routing Protocol

(1) AP evaluation process
Nodes exchange their status information with immediate neighbors periodically and evaluate their AP through the model in 3.3.2. Then as show in Figure 5, nodes classify their neighbors into two categories, suspicious and eligible. Based on the pre-defined AP threshold AP_T, each node maintains an Eligible Neighbor Table (ENT) to record the neighbors whose AP is lower than AP_T for message forwarding.

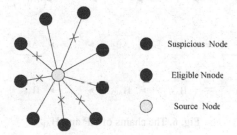

Fig. 5. Node Classifying

(2) Routing controlling message
To integrate AP into current routing protocol, two new fields are added to conventional routing controlling messages such as Routing Request Message (RREQ) and Routing Response Message (RREP): AP List and AP Hash. AP List records AP of nodes along the paths; AP Hash is the Hash value of AP List. Routing controlling messages in SEMAP take the responsibility of colleting AP of nodes along the path.

(3) Routing request procedure
In routing request procedure, RREQ collects AP from source side.

A. Source node generating RREQ
Source node generates a secret random number R and encrypts it with the public key of destination node got from the key server. R_E is the encryption result.

Source node unicasts RREQ to the nodes in its ENT without employing the conventional broadcast. AP List field of each RREQ is filled with AP of corresponding neighboring node. Then the initial AP Hash field is obtained through Hash function as Formula 9. Hash function and the encrypted R will together prevent AP from malicious modification during message forwarding. Then new RREQ packet format is <RREQ, AP List, AP Hash, R_E>.

$$H_{AP} = hash(R, AP) \tag{9}$$

B. Intermediate node forwarding RREQ
When an intermediate node receives RREQ, it first checks whether it comes from a member in its ENT. If not, this RREQ will be abandoned; otherwise the intermediate node extracts AP Hash field from RREQ and calculates new AP Hash based on AP of next hop as Formula 10.

$$H_{AP\_new} = hash(H_{AP\_old}, AP_{nxethop}) \tag{10}$$

AP of next hop and new H_{AP} will be attached after the previous fields of AP List and AP Hash. Then the updated RREQ is re-forwarded to eligible neighbors. As RREQ travels through the network, AP from source side is collected. When RREQ reaches destination node, it will contain a chain of AP and H_{AP}, as shown in Figure 6.

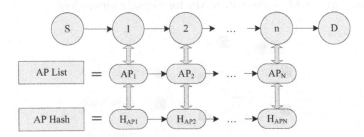

Fig. 6. The chains of AP and H_{AP}

C. Destination node checking RREQ
Intermediate node may secretly decrease its AP value given by its previous hop during message forwarding, which makes it seem more secure. To make sure that AP List is not maliciously modified, destination node will perform the following checking steps:

Step1: Decrypting R_E with its private key and obtaining R;
Step2: Calculating H_{AP}' recursively as Formula 11 and compare each H_{AP}' with H_{AP} in corresponding position of AP Hash chain. If they are not equal, we can deduce that intermediate node in that position is malicious. The path this node belongs to will be discarded.

$$\begin{cases} H_{AP1}' = hash(R, AP_1) \\ H_{AP2}' = hash(H_{AP1}, AP_2) \\ ... \\ H_{APn}' = hash(H_{APn-1}, AP_n) \end{cases} \tag{11}$$

(4) Routing response procedure
In routing response procedure, RREP collects AP from destination side. The basic process of generating and processing the fields of AP List and AP Hash is same as that of routing request procedure, which will not be described again.

A. Destination node generating RREP
In a pre-defined time limit, destination node collects sufficient RREQ from source node and constructs disjoint path sets from the paths that RREQ has transmitted along. Disjoint path set can be denoted as $DisjiontSet = \{Path_1, Path_2, ..., Path_m |$ $\cap_i^m Path_i = \varnothing\}$. The information of disjoint set and AP chain of source side are attached on RREP. RREP will be sent back to source node back along the route RREQ has travelled through.

B. Source node processing RRSP
When source node receives RREP, it obtains AP chain of both source side and destination side, as shown in Figure 7. Then source node can employ the mean value of AP from these two sides as the final and complete security estimation of an intermediate node through Formula 12.

$$AP_{final} = \frac{AP_{sourceside} + AP_{detinationside}}{2} \tag{12}$$

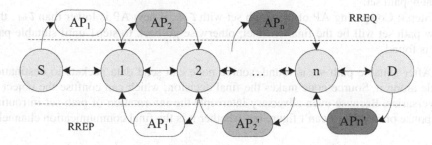

Fig. 7. AP of source side and destination side

3.2.4 Security Analysis Based on AP

(1) The extending concept of AP
When source node gets multiple disjoint paths from destination node, it needs to determine which one is most suitable for final communication channel. To evaluate the security of a path set, we convert AP of a node to AP of a path set. The conversion order is node->link->path->path set.

To estimate path robustness, [14] offers two metrics: the number and the length of disjoint paths. More intermediate nodes and less disjoint paths make end-to-end connection apt to break. From this concept, AP of a path should be higher than that of any intermediate node while AP of a path set should be lower than that of any single path.

AP is the probability that a node is in danger status. So AP is lower than 1. We define AP of a link between node n_i and n_j as

$$AP_{Link} = 1 - (1 - AP_i)(1 - AP_j) = AP_i + AP_j - AP_i AP_j > AP_i \ and \ AP_j$$

We define AP of a path consisting of p links as

$$AP_{path} = 1 - \prod_{m=1}^{p}(1 - AP_{linkm}) < 1 - (1 - AP_{linkm}) = AP_{linkm}$$

We define AP of a path set consisting of q disjoint path as

$$AP_{set} = \prod_{m=1}^{q} AP_{pathm} < AP_{pathm}$$

(2) Further optimization

Source node set a security requirement τ_{set}, and AP of path set should not exceed τ_{set}. There may be two conditions:

1) There are more than one path set satisfying the security requirement. Then source node chooses the path set with the lowest AP as the final channel;

2) There is no path set satisfying the security requirement. Source node will execute the following steps:

Step1: Choosing the path set with the lowest AP;

Step2: Deleting the path with the highest AP from this path set and calculating AP of new path set;

Step3: Comparing AP of new path set with τ_{set}, if new AP is lower than τ_{set}, this new path set will be the final channel; otherwise go back to step1 until suitable path set is found.

After suitable path set is found, source node can send data packets to destination node along it. Source node makes the final decision, which can confuse the object of adversaries. Because even adversary intercepts the information of path set in routing response procedure, it can't figure out whether it is the final communication channel.

4 Simulation

We construct the simulation environment using NS2. The simulation object is to compare the performance of AOMDV with and without SEMAP. As we have pointed out at the beginning of this paper that SEMAP is protocol independent. Then other multipath routing protocols can be also employed in our simulation. We only choose AOMDV as an example. In the simulation, the MAC layer is the IEEE 802.11 protocol with DCF. 200 nodes are placed randomly within a 1000m × 1000m area. The channel capacity is 2Mbps. The maximum node speed is 50m/s and the minimum speed is 1m/s. The simulation time is 600 seconds. We set nodes in high security threat as the nodes whose AP are higher than AP_T. And the ratio of nodes in high security threat can be adjusted according to simulation requirement. Other simulation parameters related with SEMAP is listed in table 1.

Table 1. Simulation Parameters

AP_T	0.3
τ_{set}	0.45
$\alpha_1, \alpha_2, \alpha_3$	0.33
β_1, β_2 and β_3	0.33
k	0.6
C1, C2, C3	0.33

We compare the performance of AOMDV with and without SEMAP at the following three aspects:

1) Packet delivery ratio: The ratio of the amount of packets received by the destination to the total number of packets sent by the source;

2) Average delay: In our simulation, we treat average delay as the average time from the moment of source node sending RREQ to that of destination node receiving the first data packet;

3) Average re-establishment overhead: The average number for source node reestablishing route because of the failure of intermediate nodes.

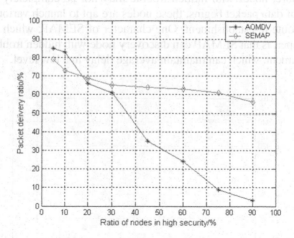

Fig. 8. Comparison on Packet Delivery Ratio

Figure 8 shows that as the increase of the ratio of nodes in high security, packet delivery ratio of AOMDV decreases sharply. When the ratio of nodes in high security reaches 90%, AOMDV nearly loses the routing ability while AOMDV with SEMAP can keep a high packet delivery ratio exceeding 60%. This is because that SEMAP provides a concrete metric for evaluating the security of a node, which can success-fully exclude malicious node from routing establishment process. These malicious nodes may bring continuous damage to the network such as dropping packs silently.

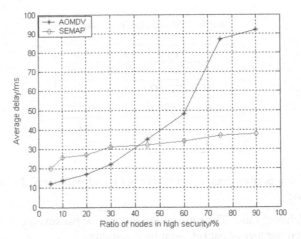

Fig. 9. Comparison on Average Delay

Figure 9 shows that AOMDV with SEMAP also represents a better performance than AOMDV without SEMAP in average delay. The main component of average delay is the time spent in constructing the path. In conventional routing request procedure and routing response procedure, nodes with hidden trouble may not be completely exposed. When the forwarding of data packet begins, these nodes are apt to launch various attacks which bring frequent route re-establishment. One character of SEMAP, which is also a contri-bution of this paper, is that SEMAP can discovery node with hidden trouble before actual routing establishment, which can maintain average delay in a low level.

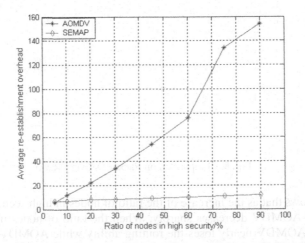

Fig. 10. Comparison on Average Re-establishment Overhead

Figure 10 shows that, there is only a small amount of link breaks in the network employing AOMDV with SEMAP. So communication overhead for route re-establishment can be greatly reduced. As pointed out in the contribution of this paper, SEMAP can be integrated with multipath routing protocol seamlessly, which doesn't any additional message to the network. So SEMAP provides a security enhancement without compromising the efficiency of normal routing protocols.

5 Conclusion

This paper explores the useful information of performance status of nodes in Ad hoc network and presents a secure enhancement mechanism SEMAP which can convert the possibility of security threat to a concrete metric. Then the comparison of security status among nodes is available, which can assist nodes to make the best choice in message forwarding and path selection. Simulation results have proved some attractive features of our mechanism in three aspects: packet delivery ratio, average delay and average route re-establishment overhead. Therefore, autonomic healing cell can be used as a practical solution for securing current multipath routing protocols.

Acknowledgement

This work is supported by National Natural Science Foundation of China under Grant No.60572047 and Program for new Century Excellent Talents in University NCET-06 0642.

References

1. Wei, D.: Research on Intrusion Detection in Ad Hoc Network, PHD thesis, College of Automation ChongQin University, 5 (2006)
2. Zhang, Y., Lee, W., Huang, Y.: Intrusion detection technqiues for mobile wireless networks. ACM Wireless Networks 5, 545–556 (2003)
3. Fei, W., Yijun, M., Benxiong, H.: COSR: Cooperative On-Demand Secure Route Protocol in MANET. In: Proceedings of ISCIT 2006, pp. 890–893 (2006)
4. Guerrero, M.: Securing ad hoc routing protocols. IETF Internet Draft, 06 (2006)
5. Seung, Y., Prasad, N., Robin, K.: Security-aware ad hoc routing for wireless networks. In: Proceedings of MobiHoc 2001, pp. 299–302 (2001)
6. Yih-Chun, H., Adrian, P., Johnson David, B.: Ariadne: A secure on-demand routing protocol for ad hoc networks. Wireless Networks 11(1-2), 21–38 (2005)
7. Papadimitratos, P., Haas, Z.: Secure routing for mobile ad hoc networks. In: Commun. Networks and Distributed Systems Modeling and Simulation Conference (CNDS) (2002)
8. Aad, I., Hubaux, J.-P., Knightly, E.W.: Denial of Service Resilience in Ad Hoc Networks. In: ACM MOBICOM, pp. 202–215 (2004)
9. Lee, S.J., Gerla, M.: Split Multipath Routing with Maximally Disjoint Paths in Ad Hoc Networks. In: Proceedings of the IEEE ICC, pp. 3201–3205 (2001)
10. Nasipuri,, Das, S.R.: On-Demand Multipath Routing for Mobile Ad Hoc Networks. In: Proceedings of IC3N (1999)

11. Ye, Z., Krishnamurthy, S.V., Tripathi, S.K.: A Framework for Reliable Routing in Mobile Ad Hoc Networks. In: IEEE INFOCOM (2003)
12. Marina, M.K., Das, S.R.: On-demand Multipath Distance Vector Routing in Ad Hoc Networks. In: Proceedings of the 9th IEEE International Conference on Network Protocols (ICNP) (2001)
13. Wang, F., Huang, C., Zhao, J., Rong, C.: IDMTM: A Novel Intrusion Detection Mechanism Based on Trust Model for Ad Hoc Networks. In: Proceeding of The IEEE 22nd International Conference on Advanced Information Networking and Applications, AINA 2008 (2008)
14. Goyal., D., Caffery Jr., J.: Partitioning Avoidance in Mobile Ad hoc Networks Using Network Survivability. In: Proceedings ISCC 2002, pp. 553–558 (2002)

Scheduling for Reliable Execution in Autonomic Systems*

Terry Tidwell, Robert Glaubius, Christopher Gill, and William D. Smart

Department of Computer Science and Engineering
Washington University, St. Louis, MO, USA
{ttidwell,rlg1,cdgill,wds}@cse.wustl.edu

Abstract. Scheduling the execution of multiple concurrent tasks on shared resources such as CPUs and network links is essential to ensuring the reliable operation of many autonomic systems. Well known techniques such as rate-monotonic scheduling can offer rigorous timing and preemption guarantees, but only under assumptions (i.e., a fixed set of tasks with well-known execution times and invocation rates) that do not hold in many autonomic systems. New hierarchical scheduling techniques are better suited to enforce the more flexible execution constraints and enforcement mechanisms that are required for autonomic systems, but a rigorous foundation for verifying and enforcing concurrency and timing guarantees is still needed for these approaches. The primary contributions of this paper are: (1) a scheduling policy design technique that can use different decision models across a wide range of systems models, and an example of how a specific (Markov Decision Process) decision model can be applied to a basic multi-threaded system model; (2) novel model checking techniques that can evaluate the behavior of the system model when it is placed under the control of the resulting scheduling policy; and (3) an evaluation of those scheduling policy design and model checking techniques for a simple but representative example of the kinds of execution scenarios that can arise in autonomic systems.

1 Introduction

An autonomic computing system must respond adaptively to varying operating conditions, automatically and without external intervention. The adaptive behaviors that allow such a system to continue to perform under dynamic conditions in turn place varying demands on shared system resources, and the capacities of the system's resources constrain the possible behaviors of the system. Furthermore, to verify that an autonomic computing system can manage its resources both feasibly and adaptively at run-time, checkable models of the interactions among (1) the system's resource management policies and mechanisms, (2) the system's resources, and (3) the adaptive demands that system activities place on the resources, must be developed. How to ensure

* This research was supported in part by NSF grant CNS-0716764 (Cybertrust) titled "CT-ISG: Collaborative Research: Non-bypassable Kernel Services for Execution Security" and NSF grant CCF-0448562 (CAREER), titled "Time and Event Based System Software Construction".

reliable execution of autonomic computing system activities is thus an important and challenging research problem.

Existing approaches to ensuring the verifiably feasible use of system resources online often employ some kind of *reference monitor* [1], which mediates all requests for access to system resources according to specified policies. Although reference monitors have been considered most extensively in the contexts of data security and network security, separation kernels [2,3] for partitioning resource use, and user level sandboxes [4,5,6,7] that intercept system calls made by application programs, illustrate the applicability of resource monitors to managing the execution of system activities.

Limitations of Existing Approaches: As we discuss in further detail in Section 2, while the user level sandbox and separation kernel approaches offer important features for ensuring feasible use of resources by system activities, each of the approaches has important limitations. For the sandbox approach the crucial limitation is in how precisely (especially with reference to timing) the desired execution semantics can be enforced, while for the separation kernel approach the limitation is the burden placed on system developers to encode the nuances of complex system dependences according to strict resource separation semantics.

Real-time schedulers [8] offer what amounts to a kind of (admittedly bypassable) resource monitor by ensuring resource feasibility of a set of system tasks. Although they can offer strong guarantees under non-adversarial conditions, such classical scheduling approaches only apply under very constrained assumptions that do not pertain in many autonomic computing contexts. Hierarchical schedulers [9,10,11,12] offer greater flexibility in enforcing less constrained scheduling policies precisely, and our previous work has shown that integrating hierarchical thread-level scheduling mechanisms within a kernel-level resource monitor is a useful step towards non-bypassable control over the execution of system activities [13,14]. However, rigorous analysis of these more advanced scheduling approaches remains a largely open problem, so that for the most part analytical guarantees of resource feasibility under those policies currently are not available. Furthermore, it is difficult to apply standard verification techniques such as model checking without exploiting knowledge about the specific scheduling policy, which we have also investigated in our prior work [15].

Solution Approach and System Model: To overcome the limitations of existing approaches for ensuring the verifiably feasible use of system resources, we are developing new techniques (1) that are flexible in the policies they can enforce, and (2) within which particular resource monitors can be customized according to their intended use. In this paper, we consider only a very basic and abstract system model in which:

- multiple threads of execution require mutually exclusive use of a single common resource (i.e., a CPU) in order to run;
- whenever a thread is granted the resource, it occupies the resource for a finite and bounded subsequent duration;
- the duration for which a thread occupies the resource may vary from run to run of the same thread but overall obeys a known independent and bounded distribution over any reasonably large sample of runs of that thread;

– a scheduler initially chooses which thread to run according to a given scheduling policy, dispatches that thread, waits until the end of the duration during which the thread occupies the resource, and then repeats that sequence perpetually.

This basic system model serves to illustrate simple but representative examples of the kinds of scheduling enforcement problems that can arise in autonomic systems built atop commonly used operating systems such as Linux or VxWorks. For example in Linux every dispatch of an application thread occupies the CPU for at least a jiffy and the scheduler only preempts threads at jiffy boundaries. Within the Linux kernel, our previous work has considered how hard and soft interrupts also may be threaded and placed under scheduler control [15], with different resulting durations of resource occupation for the different kinds of interrupts.

In Section 3 we present a method for scheduling policy design that can be tailored to specified workloads, which is based on a Markov Decision Process (MDP) approach. The MDP approach is an illustrative example of a more general class of scheduling policy design approaches that could be used in our solution approach, though we defer consideration of other relevant techniques, such as reinforcement learning, to future work. In Section 4 we present a novel model checking approach that makes use of finite execution histories. This approach can be used for exhaustive exploration of possible system traces, to verify properties such as the feasible use of resources under a scheduling policy designed according to the approach in Section 3. In Section 5 we evaluate the application of our approach to a sample system configuration, based on threads being scheduled to maximize adherence to a target utilization for each thread. The results of this evaluation show that these techniques can be practically applied. Finally, in Section 6 we summarize the contributions of this paper, and describe planned future work.

2 Related Work

Reference Monitor Approaches: User-level sandboxes have been used to intercept system call requests and may record, deny, reorder, replace, or dispatch any request. This approach offers significant flexibility because all system calls can be subjected to arbitrary handling by the sandbox. However, sandboxes that do this entirely within user space have difficulty supporting standard features like safe and efficient multithreading [5]. Hybrid interposition architectures [6] therefore move part of the sandbox into the kernel. However, this approach still relies on the kernel's native scheduling policies and mechanisms, which do not offer sufficient control over system components such as interrupts [14], and thus leave system activities vulnerable to accidental or adversarial interference through interaction channels (such as resources shared among threads) that do not pass explicitly through the system call interface.

Separation kernels can provide more stringent enforcement of system policies, but unfortunately existing approaches do so inflexibly, by segregating resources into discrete partitions, and strictly controlling communication and other interactions among different partitions [2,3]. For example, the MILS kernel [3] partitions memory and CPU resources into separate virtual machines on which processes then execute, controlling not only access to resources, but also communication between processes running in

different partitions. Through such strict separation, these approaches allow formal specification and verification [16] of resource isolation between the partitions.

The main limitation of existing separation kernel approaches is that application developers must assign processes to resource partitions correctly, so that independent system activities are isolated, but system activities that have inherent dependences can
still interact appropriately. This obligation places a significant burden on system designers, and examples of non-adversarial interference between activities of complex
autonomous systems, such as the Mars Pathfinder priority inversion problem [17], illustrate that identifying all dependences up front in real-world systems is a daunting task.

Scheduling Policy Design: Many thread scheduling policies have been designed and
analyzed to ensure guaranteed feasibility of resource use in closed real-time systems [8].
Most of those approaches assume that the number of tasks accessing system resources,
and their invocation rates and execution times, are all well characterized. Real-time
systems approaches that allow even such basic extensions such as asynchronous task
arrival must depend on special services (e.g., admission control [18]) to maintain resource feasibility at run-time.

Hierarchical scheduling techniques [9,10,11,12] offer greater flexibility in their
ability to enforce scheduling policies adaptively at run-time, according to multi-faceted
scheduling decision functions that are arranged hierarchically into a single system
scheduling policy. However, there has been little prior work on verification of what
guarantees can be made by such hierarchical scheduling policies. Furthermore, verification of scheduling policies that induce thread preemption and require reasoning
about continuous time may encounter problems with decidability [19], so that special
techniques that exploit knowledge about the structure of the specific scheduling problem [15,20] may be needed before the techniques we are developing can be applied to
systems with more nuanced execution semantics than the basic system model described
in Section 1 (e.g., systems in which an actuator or sensor could be triggered arbitrarily
on a continuous time line).

Dynamic programming has long been used for large-scale scheduling problems, such
as those encountered in large machine shops [21]. A related technique, Reinforcement
Learning (RL) [22] (often called Approximate Dynamic Programming), has been identified as a learning technology that holds great promise for the autonomic computing
community [23]. It has been successfully been applied to several domains, including computer cluster management [24] and network configuration repair [25], and job
scheduling [26]. However, RL algorithms are typically iterative and, in practice provide
an approximation to the optimal solution. This approximation improves over time, as
the algorithm sees more training data but, for realistic problems, convergence to the
optimal is often slow.

3   Scheduling Policy Design

The scheduling decision model consists of sequentially deciding to dispatch one of
n threads whenever the CPU is available. Threads may release the CPU after a non-
deterministic duration, that as we noted in Section 1 falls within a known and bounded
distribution. A dispatched thread always executes for at least one time quantum. The

scheduler's objective is to maintain the relative resource utilization for each thread near some target utilization vector $\mathbf{u}$.

We represent this scheduling decision model as a Markov Decision Process (MDP) [27]. In general, an MDP is a four-tuple (X, A, R, T). X is the set of process states, and A is the set of available actions. The transition function T describes the dynamics of the system as a conditional probability measure $P(y|x, a)$ of transitioning from state x to y on action a. The real-valued reward function $R(x, a, y)$ describes the immediate cost or benefit for transitioning from state x to y on action a. In the discounted reward setting, future rewards are weighted by a factor of $\gamma \in (0, 1]$, which weights rewards by temporal proximity.

A policy π recommends an action in each state. An optimal policy, π^*, maximizes the expected sum of discounted rewards observed as the system executes. Finding π^* reduces to computing the optimal state-action value function Q^*. $Q^*(x, a)$ is exactly the sum of discounted rewards obtainable by taking action a from state x, then executing the optimal policy thereafter. $Q^*(x, a)$ is the solution to the system of Bellman equations

$$Q^*(x, a) = \sum_{y \in X} P(y|x, a) \left[R(x, a, y) + \gamma V^*(y) \right], \tag{1}$$

where $V^*(x) = \max_{a \in A} \{Q^*(x, a)\}$ is the optimal state value function. Given Q^*, $\pi^*(x) = \text{argmax}_{a \in A} \{Q^*(x, a)\}$.

In the scheduling MDP, each action corresponds to the choice to dispatch a particular available thread. The MDP's states are identified by the time quanta utilized by each thread. These are integer-valued vectors $\mathbf{x} = (x_1, \ldots, x_n) \in \mathbb{N}^n$ for a system with n threads. In order to bound the number of states, we introduce a termination time τ, so that the state set $X = \{\mathbf{x} \in \mathbb{N}^n : \|\mathbf{x}\| \leq \tau\}$ where $\|\cdot\|$ denotes the 1-norm. We treat the boundary states $\mathbf{x}$ such that $\|\mathbf{x}\| = \tau$ as *absorbing states*, so that further actions do not change the state of the system. The parameter τ defines the extent to which the scheduler looks into the potential future evolutions of the system's execution state when making a decision.

The MDP's transition function is defined in terms of the run-time distribution for each thread. Let $\Delta_i = (\delta_{i1}, \ldots, \delta_{in})$ be the change in state after thread i executes for a single time quantum; δ_{ij} is the Kronecker delta ($\delta_{ij} = 1$ when $i = j$, otherwise $\delta_{ij} = 0$). The transition probability of the system moving from state $\mathbf{x}$ to state $\mathbf{y}$ after dispatching thread i can be non-zero only when $\mathbf{y}$ and $\mathbf{x}$ differ only in element i, i.e., only when $\mathbf{y} = \mathbf{x} + t\Delta_i$ for some positive integer t. If $\mathbf{y}$ is non-absorbing, the transition probability is exactly $P_i(t)$, the probability that thread i executes for t time quanta. If $\mathbf{y}$ is absorbing, then $P(\mathbf{y}|\mathbf{x}, i)$ is the cumulative probability of executing for t or more time steps, $\sum_{s=t}^{\infty} P_i(s) = 1 - \sum_{i=1}^{t-1} P_i(s)$. To summarize,

$$P(\mathbf{y}|\mathbf{x}, i) = \begin{cases} P_i(t) & \exists t > 0, \ \mathbf{y} = \mathbf{x} + t\Delta_i \text{ and } \|\mathbf{y}\| < \tau \\ 1 - \sum_{s=1}^{t-1} P_i(s) & \exists t > 0, \ \mathbf{y} = \mathbf{x} + t\Delta_i \text{ and } \|\mathbf{y}\| = \tau \\ 0 & \text{otherwise.} \end{cases} \tag{2}$$

We define the reward function $R(\mathbf{x}, i, \mathbf{y})$ in terms of a per-state cost function C. The cost of a state $\mathbf{x}$, $C(\mathbf{x})$, is the squared Euclidean distance between $\mathbf{x}$ and the target utilization at time $\|\mathbf{x}\|$, $\|\mathbf{x}\|\mathbf{u}$:

$$C(\mathbf{x}) = -\sum_{i=1}^{n} (x_i - u_i \|\mathbf{x}\|)^2. \tag{3}$$

Since actions only change one component of the state vector, we define $R(\mathbf{x}, i, \mathbf{y})$ only when $\mathbf{y} = \mathbf{x} + t\Delta_i$ for some t. In order to encourage the scheduling policy to maintain target utilizations while threads execute as well as when decisions are made, we define the reward as the discounted sum of the costs of states from $\mathbf{x}$ to $\mathbf{y}$, excluding $\mathbf{y}$.

$$R(\mathbf{x}, i, \mathbf{y}) = R(\mathbf{x}, i, \mathbf{x} + t\Delta_i) = \sum_{s=0}^{t-1} \gamma^s C(\mathbf{x} + s\Delta_i) \tag{4}$$

Figure 1 depicts the *utilization state space* and its transition function for a problem with two threads and a termination time of three quanta. Each thread in this example has a deterministic run-time of one quantum.

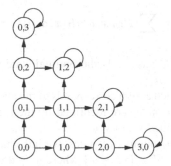

Fig. 1. Transition graph for a scheduling MDP with $\tau = 3$ and two threads. Each thread has a deterministic single quantum run time. Right arrows indicate the change in state as thread 1 runs, up arrows show the state transition when thread 2 runs.

Excluding absorbing states, the scheduling MDP transition graph is acyclic. The future expected rewards of states depend only on states with greater cumulative utilization. This enables us to solve for the value function directly by working backwards from the absorbing states, as long as n and τ are sufficiently small.

We first compute the future expected reward of each absorbing state $\mathbf{x}$. The future expected rewards of these states are the costs of remaining in them forever,

$$V^*(\mathbf{x}) = -\sum_{t=0}^{\infty} \gamma^t C(\mathbf{x}) = -C(\mathbf{x})/(1 - \gamma). \tag{5}$$

Next we iterate over non-absorbing states, working backwards from states with high to low utilization. Let $T = \tau - \|\mathbf{x}\|$ be the number of remaining quanta before termination from one such state. The future expected reward of dispatching thread i in state $\mathbf{x}$ is

$$Q^*(\mathbf{x}, i) = \sum_{s=1}^{T} P(\mathbf{x} + s\Delta_i | \mathbf{x}, i) [R(\mathbf{x}, i, \mathbf{x} + s\Delta_i) + \gamma V^*(\mathbf{x} + s\Delta_i)]. \tag{6}$$

Computing the value function in this case takes $\mathcal{O}(n\tau|X|)$ time. The τ term arises because the future expected reward of a state is the weighted average over possible future states. Computing V^* in the recursion requires maximizing over all n actions from each potential future state. If we know that a thread can only occupy the resource for at most k time steps, then we can replace the τ term with k by restricting the summation in Equation 6 to only the possible run-times. In this paper we consider only problems where n and τ are small enough to allow exact computation of the value function as detailed above. The number of states grows quickly, as $|X| = \sum_{t=0}^{\tau} \binom{n+t-1}{n-1}$, so eventually we would need to approximate the value function as n and τ increase.

4 Verification

Model checking has been applied to the offline verification of a wide range of systems. Model checking verifies systems by first exhaustively enumerating all reachable states and the transitions among them. Specifically, given a transition and a predecessor state, the next state represents the possible values the system variables can take on. To differentiate these states from the *utilization states* in the MDP described in Section 3, we call these states *verification states*. The verification states capture the *possible* evolutions of the system's utilization state.

Safety properties are specified as temporal logic expressions evaluated over the verification state space. A system is verified if, during exhaustive enumeration, no verification state is found where that expression is false. In this paper we do not detail how to evaluate particular temporal logic expressions, but rather describe the strategies for the exhaustive enumeration of the verification state space induced by a particular scheduling policy.

Verification State Representation: When timing constraints must be verified, timed automata are commonly used for modeling systems [28]. Two limitations inherent to timed automata prevent us from using this typical approach for verification of scheduling policies produced by the approach presented in Section 3.

The first limitation is the state representation used by timed automata. Timed automata use continuous clock variables to abstract the passage of time. Verification states are represented as a set of constraints of the form: $c - d < x$, where c and d are clock variables and x is an integer value. Given an arbitrary policy generated by our adaptive approach, there is no guarantee that a particular verification state can be represented using only constraints of this form. In particular, the dividing line between decision regions will most likely parallel the utilization vector. Only in the special case of two threads given equal utilization targets will it be possible to represent the decision boundary as a constraint of this form.

The second limitation precluding the use of of timed automata is the way in which verification states are propagated. Each verification state only captures the relative offset of the individual system clocks, abstracting away total elapsed system time. Timing properties of the system are encoded as guards that govern what conditions must be satisfied for state transitions to occur. These guards are expressed as inequalities between a clock and an integer. Because these inequalities are specified in the model, there is a threshold over which differences between clocks need not be tracked, therefore ensuring the number of possible verification states is finite. This property guarantees state propagation will terminate.

However, in a system that must track utilization, as in the method presented in Section 3, there is no such guarantee. With variables representing a thread's utilization there is no bound on the size of the representation needed to track the changes made by later actions. Total system time and the time spent running any single thread both can grow without bound, and with them the number of bits needed to track utilization by a thread *accurately*.

Therefore, new methods to represent verification state and to perform verification state propagation are needed. We first consider how our scheduling policies will be implemented. One reasonable implementation is to deal with only a manageable finite history when evaluating the next action as the scheduler has finite memory. Based on this observation, the verification state becomes simply a history that encodes the last n actions.

Verification State Propagation: We then must deal with the problem of how to propagate verification states. Given the minimum and maximum execution times for each thread dispatch and a history of the last n actions, we can determine what subsets of utilization states are reachable. A simple decision procedure is then available for verification state propagation: iterate over the current set of utilization states and add the action given by the policy to the set of possible actions. As the results of our evaluation presented in Section 5 demonstrate, significant optimizations to this simple decision procedure may be available for certain scheduling policies.

This representation guarantees coverage of all possible verification states, and also guarantees that verification state space propagation terminates. This follows because the verification state space is finite (there are $\sum_{i=0}^{n} t^i$ possible histories where t is the number of threads and n is the maximum history length).

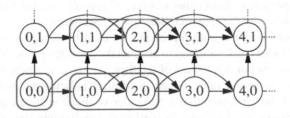

Fig. 2. Example state space exploration

Figure 2 shows the beginning of state space exploration for a simple two thread system. In this example thread one has a deterministic run time of 1 time unit, while thread two runs for either 1 or 2 time units. The variability of thread two's utilization induces (1) multiple possible utilization states in each verification state (except for at the origin), and (2) many utilization states that belong to multiple verification states. The boxes in Figure 2 show how the verification states are overlaid on the set of utilization states from the scheduling policy.

At first the verification state (corresponding to a null history) only includes the origin. However after the first decision, which is to dispatch thread one, the verification state now includes two utilization states, labeled (1,0) and (2,0). After two more decisions the verification state includes three of the underlying utilization states. State exploration continues until no transitions to unexplored verification states can be found.

However, this method is also pessimistic, allowing series of transitions that in practice are not possible. This means that systems positively verified are truly safe, but systems where error states are reachable relative to a given query, are not necessarily unsafe. The pessimism arises because each decision induces constraints on what the possible values of the utilizations are, over the n actions for which the decision was evaluated. As such we can create an increasingly optimistic model by continuously adding another action to the history. However, this leads to more complicated decision procedures. In order to show the applicability of this technique we will use the pessimistic method for full state space enumeration. This gives a good estimate to the relative costs of the search and can provide safety guarantees because of coverage.

5 Evaluation

We demonstrate these techniques on a small example problem with two threads and termination time $\tau = 512$. The resulting MDP has 131,882 states.

The thread run-time distributions are shown in Figure 3. These were generated by sampling Erlang distributions at the integers in the range from 1 to 16 inclusive, then normalizing the results to obtain discrete run-time distributions. The Erlang distribution for thread one has rate $\lambda = 1$ and shape $k = 2$ (mean 2), while the distribution for thread two has $\lambda = 2$ and shape $k = 18$ (mean 9). These distributions illustrate differences we expect to see in real systems, where user threads may be CPU-bound for long but highly variable periods of times while low-level event handlers occupy relatively short, fairly predictable intervals. The scheduling policy must therefore balance the need to maintain temporal predictability (and therefore its bias is toward thread one's smaller mean), with the enforcement of the desired utilization.

The optimal policy for the example problem is shown in Figure 4. The policy recommends dispatching thread one in the dark gray regions, which advances the state

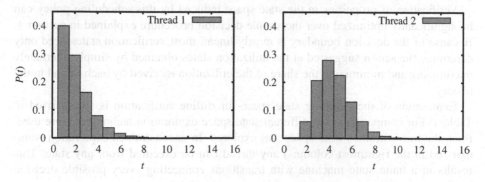

Fig. 3. Example problem run-time distributions

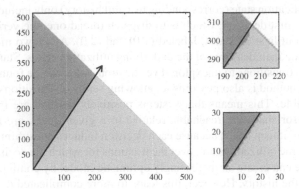

Fig. 4. Left: Optimal policy for this example problem. The ray shown in black shows the target utilization. The policy dispatches thread one (move right) in dark gray states and thread two (move upwards) in light gray states. **Bottom Right:** Close-up at the origin. The decision boundary runs roughly parallel to the target utilization ray. **Top Right:** Close-up at the terminal states near target utilization. Notice the protrusion of dark gray where the policy deviates from parallel.

along the horizontal axis. Thread two is dispatched in light gray states, advancing the state vertically. The target utilization is shown by the black ray. The decision boundary, best seen in the inset figures on the right in Figure 4, is parallel to target utilization, but translated to the right. In this interval it is better to execute thread one even though it is guaranteed to move the system away from target utilization. The alternative is to execute thread two, likely overshooting the target utilization and likely resulting in a net higher cost state because of the longer expected run-time. There is also an edge effect near the decision boundary due to the termination time. In the neighborhood of $\mathbf{x} = (210, 310)$, both actions lead to states that are quite close together because of the proximity of absorbing states. This leads to a short interval where the decision boundary lines up with the target utilization ray. Immediately prior to this interval is a protrusion where it is better to dispatch thread one. Doing so is likely to put the system into a state where dispatching thread two transitions the system directly to a good absorbing state. Due to the relatively small variance of thread one, the system can accurately aim for a good absorbing state a couple of decisions in advance.

Verification of properties in the state space induced by this scheduling policy can be significantly optimized over the simple decision procedure explained in section 4. Because of the decision boundary is mostly linear, most verification states need only determine the action suggested at the utilization states obtained by simply alternately maximizing and minimizing the share of the utilization received by each thread in the history.

Exploration of the resulting state space for offline verification is summarized in Table 1. For comparison, two different state space exploration techniques were used. First, the unconstrained state space was explored. In unconstrained exploration (summarized in the rightmost columns) any thread can be executed from any state. This results in a finite state machine with transitions connecting every possible decision history.

Table 1. Summary of Verification State Space Enumeration with Different History Sizes

History Size	Under Scheduling Policy			Unconstrained		
	States	Transitions	Time	States	Transitions	Time
1	11	12	00:00:00	13	16	00:00:00
2	22	25	00:00:00	29	39	00:00:00
3	45	53	00:00:00	61	76	00:00:00
4	89	108	00:00:00	125	156	00:00:00
5	177	218	00:00:00	253	316	00:00:00
6	353	438	00:00:00	509	636	00:00:00
7	705	878	00:00:00	1021	1276	00:00:00
8	1409	1758	00:00:00	2045	2556	00:00:00
9	2817	3518	00:00:00	4093	5116	00:00:00
10	5633	7038	00:00:00	8189	10236	00:00:00
11	11265	14078	00:00:00	16381	20476	00:00:01
12	22529	28158	00:00:02	32765	40956	00:00:03
13	45057	56318	00:00:09	65533	81916	00:00:13
14	90096	112607	00:00:38	131069	163836	00:00:52
15	180205	225241	00:04:28	262141	327676	00:05:31
16	360420	450509	00:10:20	524285	655356	00:15:04
17	720851	901047	00:38:07	1048573	1310716	00:53:41
18	1441714	1802125	02:36:04	2097149	2621436	03:29:34
19	2883441	3604283	10:47:04	–	–	–

The second state space exploration was informed by the scheduling policy described above. Only a subset of the states reachable in the unconstrained case is reachable in this case, since the policy may be homogeneous over the set of utilization states underlying a particular validation state. Results for the exploration of this state space are summarized in the leftmost columns. As expected, the state space exploration guided by our scheduling policy is smaller and thus faster to compute than the full state space.

6   Conclusions and Future Work

We have described an approach to system verification given a rational scheduler that maximizes a weighted fairness criterion given complete knowledge of distributions of thread execution times. With this knowledge about the system, we are able to derive an optimal policy for each utilization state up to some maximum system termination time. This is a step toward designing verified autonomic systems with specialized scheduling policies.

In practice, the scheduling policies derived from our system model have produced decision surfaces that partition the utilization space into linearly separable segments (up to edge effects). We have empirical evidence suggesting that this is a persistent effect; we are currently attempting to determine formally whether or not this is always the case. If policies are linearly separable, even only in special cases, then in those cases we can apply the simpler decision procedure described in Section 5.

The MDP analysis of the scheduler is a critical component to discovering its behavior at a quantum-by-quantum level. However, this requires explicitly tabulating the possible utilization states of the system, which scales poorly with the number of threads. More importantly, the utilization state space is unbounded, which necessitates the introduction of absorbing states in the model that inadequately express the concerns of the original system that we are modeling. Eliminating termination time from the model is an essential next step towards broadening the applicability of this modeling approach.

It seems possible to eliminate the termination time from the MDP model by taking advantage of the self-similarity of the system dynamics from each utilization state. We can define equivalence classes over utilization states based on the displacement from zero cost states. By establishing a transition function over these equivalence classes we can capture the dynamics of the original system model without relying on some fixed termination time. As time increases the number of equivalence classes also increases, since it is possible to get farther and farther from target utilization. This can be handled by introducing absorbing states. Unlike the absorbing states described in this work, these states would likely be homogeneous with respect to the optimal policy.

One of the key limitations of the verification state spaces presented in this paper is their pessimism. In order to improve upon this, more complicated decision procedures are needed at each step of state propagation in model checking. While general and powerful decision procedures such as those proposed in [29] seem applicable, the resulting increase in the complexity of state propagation may make them intractable in practice.

References

1. Irvine, C.E.: The reference monitor concept as a unifying principle in computer security education, http://citeseer.ist.psu.edu/299300.html
2. ARINC Incorporated Annapolis, Maryland, USA: Document No. 653: Avionics Application Software Standard Inteface (Draft 15) (1997)
3. Vanfleet, W.M., Luke, J.A., Beckwith, R.W., Taylor, C., Calloni, B., Uchenick, G.: MILS: Architecture for High-Assurance Embedded Computing (Crosstalk: the Journal of Defense Software Engineering (August (2005), http://www.stsc.hill.af.mil/crosstalk/2005/08/0508Vanfleet_etal.html
4. Goldberg, I., Wagner, D., Thomas, R., Brewer, E.A.: A secure environment for untrusted helper applications. In: Proceedings of the 6th Usenix Security Symposium, San Jose, CA, USA (1996)
5. Garfinkel, T.: Traps and pitfalls: Practical problems in in system call interposition based security tools. In: Proc. Network and Distributed Systems Security Symposium (2003)
6. Garfinkel, T., Pfaff, B., Rosenblum, M.: Ostia: A delegating architecture for secure system call interposition. In: Proc. Network and Distributed Systems Security Symposium (2004)
7. Provos, N.: Improving host security with system call policies. In: 12th USENIX Security Symposium, Washington, DC (2003)
8. Liu, J.W.S.: Real-time Systems. Prentice Hall, New Jersey (2000)
9. Goyal, Guo, Vin.: A Hierarchical CPU Scheduler for Multimedia Operating Systems. In: 2nd Symposium on Operating Systems Design and Implementation, USENIX (1996)
10. Regehr, Stankovic.: HLS: A Framework for Composing Soft Real-time Schedulers. In: 22nd IEEE Real-time Systems Symposium, London, UK (2001)
11. Regehr, Reid, Webb, Parker, Lepreau.: Evolving Real-time Systems Using Hierarchical Scheduling and Concurrency Analysis. In: 24th IEEE Real-time Systems Symposium, Cancun, Mexico (2003)

12. Aswathanarayana, T., Subramonian, V., Niehaus, D., Gill, C.: Design and performance of configurable endsystem scheduling mechanisms. In: Proceedings of 11th IEEE Real-time and Embedded Technology and Applications Symposium (RTAS) (2005)
13. Migliaccio, A., Tidwell, T., Gill, C., Aswathanarayana, T., Niehaus, D.: Group scheduling in selinux to mitigate cpu-focused denial of service attacks. Technical Report WUCSE-2005-55, Department of Computer Science and Engineering, Washington University, St.Louis (2005)
14. Tidwell, T., Watkins, N., Subramonian, V., Niehaus, D., Gill, C., Migliaccio, A.: The design, modeling, and implementation of group scheduling for isolation of computations from adversarial interference. Technical Report WUCSE-2006-34, Computer Science and Engineering Department, Washington University, St.Louis (2006)
15. Tidwell, T., Gill, C., Subramonian, V.: Scheduling induced bounds and the verification of preemptive real-time systems. Technical Report WUCSE-2007-34, Computer Science and Engineering Department, Washington University, St.Louis (2007)
16. Martin, W., White, P., Taylor, F.S., Goldberg, A.: Formal construction of the mathematically analyzed separation kernel. In: ASE 2000: Proceedings of the 15th IEEE international conference on Automated software engineering, Washington, DC, USA, p. 133. IEEE Computer Society, Los Alamitos (2000)
17. Jones, M.: What really happened on Mars (1997), www.research.microsoft.com/~mbj/Mars_Pathfinder/Mars_Pathfinder.html
18. Zhang, Y., Lu, C., Gill, C., Lardieri, P., Thaker, G.: Middleware support for aperiodic tasks in distributed real-time systems. In: RTAS 2007: Proceedings of the 13th IEEE Real Time on Embedded Technology and Applications Symposium, Washington, DC, USA, pp. 497–506. IEEE Computer Society, Los Alamitos (2007)
19. Kesten, Y., Pnueli, A., Sifakis, J., Yovine, S.: Decidable integration graphs. Information and Computation 150(2), 209–243 (1999)
20. Huang, H.M., Gill, C.: Modeling timed component-based real-time systems. Technical Report WUCSE-2008-1, Computer Science and Engineering Department, Washington University, St.Louis (2008)
21. Held, M., Karp, R.M.: A dynamic programming approach to sequencing problems. Journal of the Society for Industrial and Applied Mathematics 10(1), 196–210 (1962)
22. Sutton, R.S., Barto, A.G.: Reinforcement Learning: An Introduction. MIT Press, Cambridge (1998)
23. Tesauro, G.: Reinforcement learning in autonomic computing: A manifesto and case studies. IEEE Internet Computing 11(1), 22–30 (2007)
24. Tesauro, G., Jong, N.K., Das, R., Bennani, M.N.: On the use of hybrid reinforcement learning for autonomic resource allocation. Cluster Computing 10(3) (2007)
25. Littman, M.L., Ravi, N., Fenson, E., Howard, R.: Reinforcement learning for autonomic network repair. In: Proceedings of the 1st International Conference on Autonomic Computing (ICAC 2004), pp. 284–285 (2004)
26. Whiteson, S., Stone, P.: Adaptive job routing and scheduling. Engineering Applications of Artificial Intelligence 17(7), 855–869 (2004)
27. Puterman, M.L.: Markov Decision Processes: Discrete Stochastic Dynamic Programming. Wiley Interscience, Chichester (1994)
28. Alur, R., Dill, D.L.: A theory of timed automata. Theoretical Computer Science 126(2), 183–235 (1994)
29. Andrei, S., Cheng, A.M.: Verifying Linear Real-Time Logic Specifications. In: 28th IEEE International Real-Time Systems Symposium, Tuscon, AZ (2007)

Measuring and Analyzing Emerging Properties for Autonomic Collaboration Service Adaptation

Christoph Dorn, Hong-Linh Truong, and Schahram Dustdar*

Distributed Systems Group, Vienna University of Technology, Austria
{dorn,truong,dustdar}@infosys.tuwien.ac.at

Abstract. Dynamic collaboration environments in which team member utilize different pervasive collaboration services for their collaborative work pose many challenges for service adaptation. Given a team, the underlying collaboration services must fulfil the team's goal. Thus, it is not enough to adapt collaboration services to the context of an individual. One needs to understand the behavior of the team and the collaboration services in order to adapt these services. Though many research efforts aim at understanding team behavior at the human level, there is no such a framework that focuses on adapting collaboration services for teamwork.

In this paper, we introduce a set of novel metrics that characterizes emergent behavior of teams. We present a team analysis and adaptation framework (TAAF) which monitors diverse collaboration services, analyzes and provides relevant metrics for understanding dynamic teams and for continuous team and service adaptation. This paper also discusses how TAAF can be used to support self-management of collaboration services for collaborative teams.

1 Introduction

Recent advances in pervasive technologies have fostered the collaborative activities of knowledge workers across spatial, organizational, and professional boundaries [1,2]. Those activities are performed in a distributed and dynamic environment comprising of a variety of collaboration services used in different ways. In such an environment, pervasive collaboration services need to continuously adapt to the change of team context which is strongly dependent on the activities of team members. Existing autonomic adaptation approaches, however, concentrate on the adaptation of services to only the context of individuals [3,4]. Given a team of knowledge workers that utilize various collaboration services, a whole new level of complexity emerges when the adaptation needs to incorporate the behavior of the whole team. In this paper, we present a framework enabling adaptation of pervasive collaboration services based on a set of novel team metrics.

1.1 Motivation

Although, each member of a team uses collaboration services in a different way, the underlying services must fulfil the collaborative goal of the team. As a

---

* Part of this work was supported by the EU FP6 project inContext (IST-034718).

C. Rong et al. (Eds.): ATC 2008, LNCS 5060, pp. 162–176, 2008.

result, adapting collaboration services only to the context of an individual is not enough. We need to understand the behavior of the team in order to adapt these services. For example, understanding team execution phases will help reconfiguring service provisioning strategies: a pervasive document management service initially deployed for a small team should adapt its behavior when the team grows. Team resource usage patterns might reveal which services are relevant and should be selected for particular activities. This would significantly enhance current SOA-based approaches — such as in [3] — achieving self-adaptation. In short, if we need to support team-centric self-management of collaboration services, we must be able to understand the complex relations between the team and its utilization of services.

The complexity arising from dynamic teams operating in a heterogenous environment demands for a support framework to aid collaboration services adapting to emerging team behavior. To our best knowledge, there is no such a framework that focuses on adapting collaboration services for teamwork, though many research efforts aim at understanding team behavior at the human level [5]. Current scientific approaches to autonomic service adaptation focus on the system level and limited service consumer context [4,6]. Although research on context-aware systems [7] provides methodologies and frameworks to capture dynamic behavior, previous work consider merely the dynamics of individual humans. This lack of quantitative metrics and framework to provide data on emerging behavior motivates our work in this paper.

To tackle the above-mentioned issues, we apply the autonomic computing paradigm to the adaptation of collaboration services used in teamwork. Our ultimate goal is to develop a supporting software framework for *the adaptation of collaboration services for teamwork*. In our view, this requires a multi-disciplinary research effort where we need to combine research approaches from multiple domains, such as Computer Supported Cooperative Work (CSCW), context-awareness, autonomic computing, and SOA. However, providing such a framework for emergence-based autonomic adaptation is challenging. We need to characterize the behavior of team collaboration in terms of metrics that can be used by software, and to gather information from heterogeneous services and devices by means of monitoring. Based on that we can analyze the behavior of a team and its collaboration services to develop adaptation strategies.

1.2   Contributions

Our salient contributions of this paper are:

- A novel set of metrics characterizing emerging team behavior that can be used for service adaptation.
- An advanced set of analysis techniques for understanding emerging team behaviors in pervasive collaboration environments.
- The design and implementation of a novel framework for measuring and providing team metrics during runtime.

The work presented in this paper results in the *Team Analysis and Adaptation Framework (TAAF)*. To our best knowledge, it is the first attempt to combine delivery of runtime characteristics and context awareness techniques to achieve emergence-based autonomic adaptation. This paper concentrates on the definition, monitoring and analysis of metrics for service adaptation. The subsequent steps of planning and execution to achieve adaptation inside the pervasive collaboration services remain outside the scope of this paper.

Paper Structure: The remainder of this paper is organized as follows. Section 2 discusses team properties and adaptation. Section 3 introduces a set of novel team metrics. The design and implementation of TAAF is detailed in Section 4. We present experiments illustrating TAAF in Section 5. Related work is given in Section 6, followed by the conclusion and future work in Section 7.

2   Team Properties and Adaptation

Our objective is to support autonomic collaboration services. Figure 1 depicts a dynamic collaboration environment in which teams utilize different collaboration services for their collaborative work. Given the complexity of dynamic collaborations among team members, shown in the upper part of Figure 1, pervasive collaboration services (meeting scheduling, notification, document repository, etc.), shown in the lower part of Figure 1, should be adaptive.

Our approach is to define metrics characterizing teams to understand the dynamics services are confronted with. Based on that, we monitor team behavior, capturing the required data to determine and manage team metrics. This is the first step in the autonomic cycle focusing on observable complex relations between team members and their environment. We deliberately do not consider cognitive or psychological properties of the individual team members, as these properties do not constitute emerging team properties. Then, we analyze snapshot metrics and time-series to detect situation requiring adaptation. Threshold analysis, team lifetime phase detection, team comparison, and metric correlation are some supported techniques.

We have to consider several properties of the dynamic collaboration environment to understand how emerging team behavior affects service adaptation.

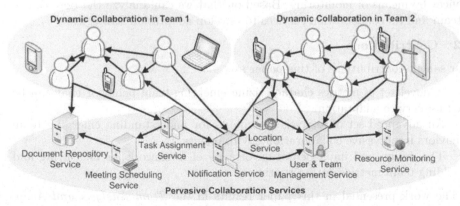

Fig. 1. Dynamic collaboration environment

Location. In dynamic collaboration environments, team members are distributed and mobile. They need to access services and communicate independent of their respective position. Furthermore, services provided by the team members' organizations are equally distributed. Example self adaption strategies benefiting from analyzing the complete set of member movements are content distribution or service replication algorithms.

Organization. Team members originate from various organizations. Monitoring organizational structures and roles as well as dependencies across the whole team will enable the evaluation of the impact of each organization on the services and resources available to the team. For example, scheduling or communication services equipped with self-adaptive behavior can limit the team's dependency on a single organization.

Coordination. Members are coordinated based on goals, tasks, assignments, project-related roles, and skills. Analyzing individual properties is insufficient to understand their relevance in the overall team context. Collaboration services - such as a meeting scheduling service - that monitor coordinative metrics at a team level can self-adapt to select the most relevant meeting participants.

Interaction. Effective communication between distributed team members is vital. Analyzing scope (two members vs. the whole team) or type (synchronous vs. asynchronous) allows selecting the most suitable communication services - email, instant messaging, virtual conferences, mailing lists, or blogs. For example, as the team evolves, monitoring emerging interactions allows a communication recommendation service to continue recommending the most suitable form of communication.

Resources. Team members access a vast number of resources - distributed across a pervasive environment - from a multitude of devices. Rather than analyzing individual resource statistics, focusing on combined resource utilization at team level provides significant potential for adaptation. Example applications are resource monitoring services prioritizing the availability and reliability of the most vital resources.

By studying these properties, we develop and quantify metrics associated with teams. Specifically, we focus on metrics that describe emerging properties, arising from the relation between team members.

Terminologies and Notations: In the scope of this paper, *teamwork* is any work performed by a team to achieve a goal (defined by a Project). A *Team* consists of a set of members (more than one) engaging in teamwork, each *Member* being a human resource. Different members belong to different organizations, while a person can be a member of multiple teams. An *Organization* is a (legal) entity which defines the professional/employment background from which members engage in team work. Organizations can range in size from a single person, a dozen of people, to thousands of people. A *Project* consists of a goal to achieve, work steps specified to a certain degree of formalization, and constraints for achieving the goal. Teamwork consists of a set of *Activities* that describe the work actually performed by members to complete the project. By definition,

Table 1. Notations

Notation	Description
$team_i$	team i
m_i	member i
$size(team_i)$	the number of members assigned to $team_i$
a_i	activity i
$A(team_i)$	the number of activities executed by $team_i$
c_i	interaction i, a subclass of activity
r_i	resource i
org_i	organization i assigning members to a team
$ORG(team_i)$	the list of organizations involved in $team_i$
$l(m_i)$	location of member i
$|X|$	number of elements in list or set X

Interactions are a subclass of activities, having multiple members involved, utilizing resources of type communication service, and being short-lived. A *Resource* is any computing, information, or communication service in pervasive environments that is used by team members in order to fulfil teamwork. Team members use resources to communicate, collaborate, and coordinate teamwork. Table 1 presents notations used in this paper.

3   Team Metrics

From the analysis of team properties we have developed a set of metrics characterizing relations between team members and collaboration services. Table 2 lists main metrics.

Team Location Entropy, TLE($team_k$), describes whether $team_k$ members' movements result in spatial clusters of workers or not, by determining the probability of all members being colocated.

$$\text{TLE}(team_k) = \frac{\sum_{i=1}^{n} \binom{l_i(team_k)}{2}}{\binom{size(team_k)}{2}} \tag{1}$$

where $l_i(team_k)$ is the number of members in $team_k$ at location l_i.

Table 2. Overview of main team metrics

Properties	Metrics
Location	Team Location Entropy TLE($team_k$)
	Team Mobility Entropy TME($team_k$)
Organization	Organization Harmonic Mean OM$_h$($team_k$)
	Organization Arithmetic Mean OM$_a$($team_k$)
	Organization Membership Stability OMS($team_k$)
Coordination	Team Size $size(team_i)$
	Team Stability TS($team_k$)
	Activity Participation Harmonic Mean AP$_h$($team_k$)
	Activity Participation Arithmetic Mean AP$_a$($team_k$)
Interaction	Interaction Participation Harmonic Mean IP$_h$($team_k$)
	Interaction Participation Arithmetic Mean IP$_a$($team_k$)
Resource	Resource Access Harmonic Mean, RA$_h$($team_k$)
	Resource Access Arithmetic Mean, RA$_a$($team_k$)
	Resource Access Distribution, RAD($team_k$)
	Resource Utilization, RU($team_k$)

Team Mobility Entropy, TME($team_k$), describes whether team members of $team_k$ relocate jointly or individually by determining the probability of the whole team being colocated before and after relocation.

$$\text{TME}(team_k) = \frac{\sum_{i=1}^{n} \sum_{j=1}^{n} \text{reloc}_{i,j}(team_k)}{\text{mob}(team_k)} \quad \forall\, i \neq j \qquad (2)$$

where $\text{reloc}_{i,j}(team_k)$ determines the number of members in $team_k$ that have relocating from location l_i to location l_j and $\text{mob}(team_k)$ computes the total number of members in $team_k$ that have moved. Thus, members remaining at their location are not taken into consideration for calculating the TME.

Colocation and joint movements reveal tight interdependencies between members. TME and TLE specifically focus on the spatial relations between team members thus indicate the presence of similar needs and contexts. At the same time colocation and co-mobility reflect the complexity of providing communication and collaboration services. The higher TME and TLE values are, the less effort is required.

The *Organization Harmonic Mean*, $OM_h(team_k)$, is the harmonic mean of member count per organization within $team_k$ and is defined as:

$$OM_h(team_k) = \frac{size(team_k)}{\sum_{i=1}^{|ORG(team_k)|} \frac{1}{|org_i(team_k)|}} \quad \forall\, org_i \in ORG(team_k) \qquad (3)$$

Organization Membership Stability, OMS($team_k$), is derived by observing changes in the number of participating organizations. Each joining or leaving organization, determined by function $changeOrg(org_i)$, results in a change of value 1.

$$\text{OMS}(team_k) = \frac{\sum_{i=1}^{|ORG(team_k)|} (changeOrg(org_i))}{|ORG(team_k)|} \qquad (4)$$

Organization-related metrics provide an indicator of effort to provide services in a uniform manner. Multiple organizations in the same project may have, e.g., conflicting data representations forms or incompatible security policies.

Having an entire organization join or leave or having an unequal distribution of members across organizations has significant impact on the team's performance due to complex coordination and resource provisioning challenges.

Team Stability[1], TS($team_k$), is derived by observing changes in the number of team members. The sum of joining members and leaving members is determined by $changeM_{joint}(team_i)$, respectively $changeM_{left}(team_i)$.

$$\text{TS}(team_k) = \begin{cases} \frac{changeM_{joint}(team_k)}{size(team_k)} & \text{if } changeM_{joint} > changeM_{left} \\ \frac{changeM_{joint}(team_k)}{size(team_k) + changeM_{left}} & \text{if } changeM_{joint} = changeM_{left} \\ \frac{changeM_{left}(team_k)}{size(team_k) + changeM_{left}(team_k)} & \text{if } changeM_{joint} < changeM_{left} \end{cases}$$

---

[1] Answers.com defines team stability as "the degree to which the membership of a team remains the same. Team stability can be defined in terms of length of time that the team members remain together".

Team stability reflects membership dynamics within a team and provides, together with team size, insightful information for determining suitable resource allocation strategies.

Activity Participation Harmonic Mean, $AP_h(team_k)$, specifies the harmonic mean over all activity involvements and is defined by:

$$AP_h(team_k) = \frac{|A_k|}{size(team_k) * \sum_{i=1}^{|A_k|} \frac{1}{inv(a_i)}} \qquad \forall \ a_i \in team_k \qquad (5)$$

where $inv(a_i)$ returns the number of members involved in activity a_i.

Interaction Participation Harmonic Mean, $IP_h(team_k)$, specifies the harmonic mean over the cardinality of all interactions and is defined by:

$$IP_h(team_k) = \frac{|C_k|}{size(team_k) * \sum_{i=1}^{|C_k|} \frac{1}{card(c_i)}} \qquad \forall \ c_i \in team_k \qquad (6)$$

where $card(c_i)$ returns the cardinality (number of participants) of interaction c_i.

Whether interactions tend to include the whole team or just a small subset of members reflects the scope of required interoperability between the employed collaboration and communication services. The same property determines to which extent self-adaptation algorithms will affect the overall team.

Resource Access Harmonic Mean, $RA_h(team_k)$, is the harmonic mean of resource access by members of $team_k$.

$$RA_h(team_k) = \frac{|R_k|}{\sum_{i=1}^{|R_k|} \frac{1}{use(r_i)}} \qquad \forall \ r_i \in team_k \qquad (7)$$

where $usc(r_k)$ returns the amount of times resource r_k is used within $team_k$.

Resource Access Distribution, $RAD(team_k)$, is the average reuse indication how often resources are accessed by different members on average in $team_k$.

$$RAD(team_k) = \frac{DRA(team_k)}{|R_k|} \qquad (8)$$

where the *Distributed Resource Access* $DRA(team_k)$ sums up the total amount of times resources R_k are accessed within $team_k$ by different members m_i. The *Distinct Resource Access*, $DRA(team_k)$, is defined as:

$$DRA(team_k) = \sum_{i=1}^{|R_k|} use_{set}(r_i) \qquad \forall \ r_i \in team_k \qquad (9)$$

where $use_{set}(r_i)$ denotes the count of distinct members having used resource r_i.

In contrast to Resource Access, *Resource Utilization*, $RU(team_k)$ is the reuse indication how long the average resource has been reused.

$$RU(team_k) = \frac{\sum_{s=1}^{|r|} t(r_s)}{t * |r|} \qquad (10)$$

where $t(r)$ indicates the duration in which resource r_s is used within interval t. Resource Access Distribution enables identification of the commonly used resources and services. Subsequently this metric facilitates focusing adaptation efforts on these significant team resources.

The above discussed metrics provide insight into the dynamic properties of teams. These metrics characterize emerging behavior arising from indirect and direct interaction, activity, communication, and resources in teams. While these metrics provide only a snapshot of the team's status at a specific time, temporal analysis of these metrics can detect the effects of preceding adaptation efforts.

4   The Team Analysis and Adaptation Framework

Figure 2 describes TAAF (Team Analysis and Adaptation Framework) which consists of middleware services and tools for monitoring and analyzing team metrics at runtime and utilizing metrics for service adaptations. The *Event Collection* gathers monitoring data related to teams from different collaboration services. Events will be pre-processed to extract the main relevant information which is the input for *Metric Calculation*. Metrics associated with teams are determined during runtime and the resulting metrics are stored into the *Team Data Store*. Based on that, *Metric Provisioning* provides, during runtime, metrics to *Team Analysis* tools and *Service Adaptation* components which require the metrics for adapting collaboration services.

4.1   Monitoring Team Behavior

Our work is focused on analyzing and managing the metrics reflecting properties and changes of teamwork. Thus, we have to cope with the complexity of diverse sources providing data required for team analysis. These data sources are collaboration services deployed on dynamic, heterogeneous hosts in a pervasive environment. In our work, these services are assumed to interact with TAAF

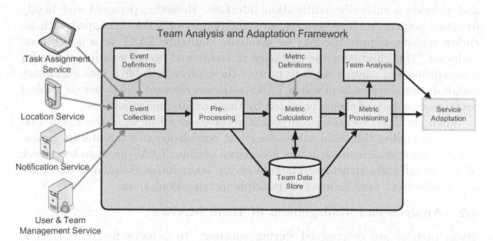

Fig. 2. TAAF architecture and data flow

Table 3. Examples of Event sources

Event Source	Deployment	Event type
Notification Service	Static	Interaction
User & Team Management service	Static	MembershipChangeEvents
Calendar Service	Static	ResourceAccessEvent
Activity & Project Service	Static	ActivityActionEvent
Context Provisioning Service	Mobile/Static	(Re)LocationEvent, InteractionEvent, ResourceAccessEvent
Document Repository Service	Mobile/Static	ResourceAccessEvent
Position Service	Mobile	Location

Table 4. Examples of events encapsulating team data

Events	Description	Frequency
MembershipChange	contains the list of user having joined or left the team	Weekly/Monthly
ResourceAccess	provide details on which member accesses which resource, optionally stating the duration of utilization	Hourly
ActivityAction	inform about members engaging in an activity	Hourly
Interaction	contain tuples of members communicating with each other	Minute/Hourly
Location	hold the current location of members	Minute/Hourly
Relocation	inform about the movement of members from one location to another location	Minute/Hourly

via a well-known interface. Such an assumption can be achieved via Web service standards. To obtain the data, TAAF relies on WS-Notification which is widely supported in pervasive environments, including constraint devices [8].

To describe data that TAAF can process, we have specified an XML schema for describing generic collaboration metadata and specific collaboration data. This schema allows the exchange of data relevant to teams by representing various types of data, such as a team identifier, an event identifer, URI of collaborative services, timestamp, and location information.

TAAF obtains relevant data from collaboration services based on push and publish/subscribe event delivery. Thus, TAAF can support various services with different capabilities. Dedicated collaboration services such as the *User & Team Management service* or the *Notification service* integrate collaboration sensors and provide a subscribe/notification interface. However, personal and highly dynamic sources, such as services on smartphones or PDAs equipped with location sensors, require the user to manually configure TAAF as a notification endpoint. This eliminates the challenge to locate and access volatile sensors for subscription and enables users to protect their privacy. Table 3 lists exemplary collaboration services from which TAAF retrieves relevant data whereas Table 4 presents examples of events provided by these collaboration services.

When the *Pre-Processing* component receives an event from the *Event Collection*, it verifies threshold values for event confidence and timestamp. Subsequently, the overall team structure is updated because TAAF needs to keep track of the overall team structure. The underlying team status is updated only once as a single event may be input to multiple metric calculations.

4.2   Analysis and Management of Team Metrics

Team metrics are determined during runtime. To achieve flexibility, metric calculation is performed within multiple subcomponents that register with the

Pre-Processing component; each subcomponent retrieves pre-processed data according to its subscription. However, in TAAF, tightly connected metrics — such as Team Location Entropy and Team Mobility Entropy — are determined in a joint fashion in order to improve performance. In addition, which metrics should be computed and the schedule of the computation can be defined in advance. Depending on configuration, metrics can be saved in the *Team Data Store*.

To facilitate the exchange of team metrics, we have defined an XML schema for representing metrics associated with teams. This representation can be used to describe various types of information such as metric identifier, and current and previous metric values. Listing 1 gives an excerpt of the metric XML schema.

```
1  <xs:complexType  name="tMetric">
2    <xs:sequence>
3      <xs:element name="URI" type="xs:string" minOccurs="1" maxOccurs="1"/>
4      <xs:element name="CurrentValue" type="tValue" minOccurs="1" maxOccurs="1"/>
5      <xs:element name="History" type="tHistory" minOccurs="0" maxOccurs="1"/>
6    </xs:sequence>
7    <xs:attribute name="enabledHistory" type="xs:boolean"/>
8  </xs:complexType>
9  <xs:complexType name="tTeamSizeValue">
10   <xs:complexContent>
11     <xs:extension base="tValue">
12       <xs:sequence>
13         <xs:element name="Value" type="xs:positiveInteger"/>
14       </xs:sequence>
15     </xs:extension>
16   </xs:complexContent>
17 </xs:complexType>
```

Listing 1. Excerpt of metric specification

Metrics provide the fundamental data required for understanding teams, detecting correlations, and ultimately taking action to counter steer negative tendencies or amplify positive effects. Based on team metrics, we have developed various team analysis features which have been incorporated into a team analysis GUI that allows any user understanding the team metrics and their relevance to subsequent adaptation actions. Self-adaptive collaboration services subscribe at the *Team Analysis* component in order to receive notifications when metric analysis detects relevant metric values.

Threshold Analysis: detects metrics violating a predefined condition over a period of time. This analysis is used together with a notification mechanism to enable runtime reaction in critical situations.

Team Phase Analysis: evaluates general trends in a metric's timeline that indicate several phases, such as project kick-off, execution, and completion phases. Duration and structure of phases provides insightful information for autonomic services making decisions on whether additional or available members and resources should be deployed or reduced.

Multi-team Analysis: compares metric timelines of different teams. With this analysis, we are able to observe teams over time and detect emerging differences. Similar team configurations, such as size and member distribution, can lead to significantly different emergent behavior. Comparing the structure of two teams reveals how the same adaptation decisions — such as deploying or reducing resources — result in different outcomes. In addition, similar patterns in different teams can indicate the occurrence of team transformations.

Correlation Analysis: reveals correlation among multiple metrics. This analyzes relations between metrics, giving more meaning to individual metrics.

4.3 Prototype Implementation

We are currently implementing our framework based on Java. The *Team Data Store* is based on the eXist database[2]. The following collaboration services are currently being integrated with TAAF: *User & Team Management Service, Context Provisioning Service, Calendar Service, Document Repository Service, Notification Service,* and *Activity & Project Service.*

The above-mentioned services are part of the Pervasive Collaboration Service Architecture (PCSA) deployed at multiple sites across Europe, including Vienna, Milan, Genoa, and Aachen, within the inContext[3] project. Inside TAAF, we use OpenJMS[4] to pass events between components. In addition to the existing message header information provided by JMS, we provide extended header fields for storing information on event type, team identifier, activity, user, and source thus enabling efficient intra-framework event selection. Of the metrics described in Section 3 we implemented all except Resource Utilization (RU). We clustered related metrics together such as arithmetic and harmonic mean, or size and stability. For visualizing metrics, we utilize the JFreeChart framework[5]. The user can select the number of desired metrics to be displayed at the same time (see Figure 3). The current prototype uses JMS queues for delivering metric updates. However, we are going to support this kind of update via WS-Notification.

5   Experiments

5.1   Testbed

Section 4.3 introduced the hosting environment for the pervasive collaboration services required for running our experiments; these services are based on the inContext's PCSA. The PCSA is currently being used for project developments only, therefore, we have not been able to obtain enough live data for our experiments. As our main goal is demonstrating how to exploit emerging behavior for autonomic adaptation, we simulate the emerging team behavior arising from a dynamic collaboration environment as depicted in Figure 1 (upper part). We implemented a team simulation based on the concepts introduced in Section 2 to achieve various emerging behavior.

---

[2] http://exist.sourceforge.net/
[3] http://www.in-context.eu/
[4] http://openjms.sourceforge.net/
[5] http://www.jfree.org/jfreechart/

To simulate the team behavior, we adapted the model by Barabási and Albert [5] to create a scale free, directed, acyclical graph (DAG) of interdependent activities which are managed by the *Activity & Project Service*. In this DAG, the vertices represent activities and the edges represent the dependency between two activities. Each activity is associated with the following properties:

- Duration: indicates the amount of time required to complete this activity
- Location: indicates the location at which the activity is performed.
- Cost: specifies the cost associated with an activity.
- Priority: specifies the priority of an activity
- Activity status: is either *pending, available, work in progress*, or *completed*.

The *User & Team Management Service* is then enabled to assign each team member to an organization which provides a set of resources. Initially these resources are available only to members of that organization. *Calendar Service, Document Repository Service* are providing resources in the form of calender entries and documents, respectively. During collaboration, these resources are shared between interacting members. The *Notification Service* provides communication in the form of instant messaging, SMS, and email. Organizations assign new members to a team or withdraw active members from the team. In addition, each member is able to spend a certain amount of time on an activity. Finally, the *Context Provisioning Service* provides details on member mobility.

The data generator then simulates the invocation of our pervasive collaboration services. These collaboration services in turn deliver the actual events. When the simulated project begins, each member selects an *available* activity to work on, that is any activity which has all previous activities *completed*. An activity is *completed* once members have jointly spent enough time/effort to cover the activity's duration.

In each simulation round, we receive the set of collaboration events. Each member's selection results in an activity and location event. Additionally, for members engaging in the same activity at the same time, we receive an interaction event. Finally, interacting members utilize a subset of resources from their combined pool of resources, while members without interaction select resources only from their organization's resource pool. In both cases, services fire respective resource access events.

5.2 Examples for Emergence-Based Adaptation

For the adaptation example in this section, we created an activity graph of 200 nodes with activities spread across 10 different locations. The simulated team consists of 30 members from 4 organizations each providing 5 resources. Figure 3 presents an excerpt of the team analysis GUI visualizing the Activity Participation metric (Left) and Interaction Participation metric (Right) over the team's lifetime. Each graph includes harmonic and arithmetic mean. The meaning of the values are the same for both metrics: a value close to 1 indicates that (almost) all members participate in an activity, respectively an interaction, while a value close to 0 denotes a lack of collaboration as members work mostly alone on different assignments.

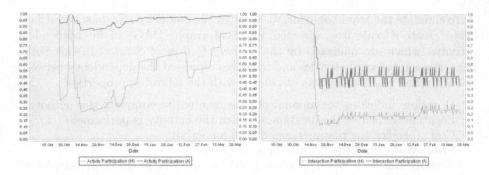

Fig. 3. Team Analysis GUI excerpt: The left graph provides Activity participation metrics while the right graph displays Interaction participation metrics for a team of 30 members working on 200 activities

Threshold analysis is a basic, albeit very useful technique enabling self-adaptive behavior. An exemplary project escalation service can utilize the subscription request in Listing 2 to receive alerts when the Activity Participation metric falls below 0.33. The simulated team crosses this threshold at the end of the kick-off phase (Figure 3 Left).

```
1  <subscription>
2     <type>
3         http://www.vitalab.tuwien.ac.at/projects/taaf/threshold_lowerbound
4     </type>
5     <teamuri>
6         http://www.vitalab.tuwien.ac.at/projects/taaf/teams#demoteam1
7     </teamuri>
8     <metricuri>
9      http://www.vitalab.tuwien.ac.at/projects/taaf#ActivityParticipationHMean
10    </metricuri>
11    <threshold>0.33</threshold>
12    <notificationendpoint>
13       ... [WS-Addressing Endpoint Reference] ...
14    <notificationendpoint>
15 <subscription>
```

Listing 2. Subscribing to threshold analysis

Other examples of potential self-adaptive behavior are:

Threshold Analysis: an autonomic content distribution service can decide to spawn extra distribution nodes when a team features decreasing team location entropy, or reduce the number of nodes when the team becomes more collocated.

Team Phase Analysis: a task scheduling service can ignore team instability at the beginning of a project, but starts to assign backup workers on critical tasks when the team remains instable during its execution phase.

Multi-team Analysis: a recommendation service can compare the effect of selecting the same communication service in different teams to adapt its selection strategy.

Correlation Analysis: Let us assume an inverse correlation of team location entropy and team interaction coverage. In this case, a meeting scheduler can suggest members from all locations to participate in a physical meeting.

6 Related Work

In our previous work, we analyzed teams with respect to impact on service requirements, resulting in a set of team forms and views [9]. Metrics associated with teams, however, have not been defined and quantified.

Scientists have invested great effort in providing concepts and tools for team based adaptation in the scope of context-aware devices and services. Vieira et al. [10] include interaction and organization aspects in their context ontologies but neglect emerging properties. Sterritt et al. [11] make the case for behavioral knowledge from which to compute metrics, but they remain at a general activity-focused level, not considering other teamwork aspects. Work on context gathering prior to these efforts generally focus on individual context neglecting team context altogether.

Current generic autonomic techniques and toolkits such as [4], [6], or [12] do not monitor the context of individual users, respectively limit monitoring to independent user properties such as location or device. De Wolf and Holvoet point out the potential of emergence for autonomic behavior [13] and also discuss the concept of emergence for engineering self-organizing systems [14]. They maintain, however, a pure system-centric view, applying emergent properties only to the autonomic system. In contrast, Bird et al. [15] apply email mining to discover emerging interaction patterns between users, but other major team properties are left aside. In a similar attempt, Valverda and Solé [16] investigate emerging self-organization in large open source social networks based on email repositories. However, such communities feature different characteristics compared to teams. TAAF specifically collects data about emerging properties from a wide range of sources and thus delivers more reliable and expressive data.

TAAF differs from the above-mentioned work in many aspects as it explores emergent team properties for the self-adaptive collaboration services.

7 Conclusion and Future Work

Understanding and detecting emerging behavior, patterns, and transformations in teams ultimately enables team-centric self-adaptation of collaboration services. In this paper, we tackled issues related to team metrics, since runtime information on emerging team properties and team transformations is the key to service adaptation for pervasive collaboration environments. This has not been well addressed until now. We have presented a novel set of team metrics and described TAAF which is a framework for analyzing, managing and providing team metrics for service adaptation during runtime. TAAF can uncover associations between various metrics, notify collaboration services when thresholds are reached, visualize team life-time phases, and compare multiple teams, thus providing necessary features for achieving autonomic collaboration services.

Our future work includes the further development of metric monitoring and analysis parts of TAAF. Furthermore, we will concentrate our work on advanced service adaptation techniques for teamwork in pervasive environments.

References

1. Ferscha, A., Holzmann, C., Oppl, S.: Context awareness for group interaction support. Mobility Management & Wireless Access Protocols, 88–97 (2004)
2. Patterson, D.J., Ding, X., Noack, N.: Location by, for, and of crowds. In: Proceedings of International Workshop on Location- and Context-Awareness (LoCA), pp. 186–203 (2006)
3. Fournier, D., Mokhtar, S.B., Georgantas, N., Issarny, V.: Towards ad hoc contextual services for pervasive computing. In: MW4SOC 2006: Proceedings of the 1st workshop on Middleware for Service Oriented Computing (MW4SOC 2006), pp. 36–41. ACM Press, New York (2006)
4. Sterritt, R., Smyth, B., Bradley, M.: Pact: personal autonomic computing tools. In: EASe Workshop at ECBS 2005, pp. 519–527 (2005)
5. Barabasi, A., Albert, R.: Emergence of scaling in random networks. Science 286, 509–512 (1999)
6. Bigus, J.P., Schlosnagle, D.A., Pilgrim, J.R., Mills, W.N., Diao, Y.: Able: A toolkit for building multiagent autonomic systems. IBM Systems Journal 41(3) (2002)
7. Baldauf, M., Dustdar, S., Rosenberg, F.: A survey on context aware systems. International Journal of Ad Hoc and Ubiquitous Computing 2(4), 263–277 (2007)
8. Aiello, M., Dustdar, S.: Are our homes ready for services? a domotic infrastructure based on the web service stack. Pervasive and Mobile Computing (2008)
9. Dorn, C., Schall, D., Gombotz, R., Dustdar, S.: A view-based analysis of distributed and mobile teams. In: Proceedings of the 5th International Workshop on Distributed and Mobile Collaboration (DMC 2007) at WETICE-2007, IEEE Computer Society, Los Alamitos (2007)
10. Vieira, V., Tedesco, P.A., Salgado, A.C.: Towards an ontology for context representation in groupware. In: Proceedings of the International Workshop on Groupware, CRIWG, pp. 367–375 (2005)
11. Sterritt, R., Mulvenna, M.D., Lawrynowicz, A.: Dynamic and contextualised behavioural knowledge in autonomic communications. In: Proceedings of the 1st Interational Workshop on Autonomic Communication, WAC, pp. 217–228 (2004)
12. IBM: Autonomic computing toolkit: Developer's guide (2004), http://www128.ibm.com/developerworks/autonomic/books/fpy0mst.htm
13. Wolf, T.D., Holvoet, T.: Emergence Versus Self-Organisation: Different Concepts but Promising When Combined. In: Brueckner, S., Di Marzo Serugendo, G., Karageorgos, A., Nagpal, R. (eds.) Engineering Self Organising Systems: Methodologies and Applications (2005)
14. Wolf, T.D., Holvoet, T.: Towards a methodolgy for engineering self-organising emergent systems. In: Proceedings of the Int. Conference on Self-Organization and Adaptation of Multi-agent and Grid Systems, pp. 18–34 (2005)
15. Bird, C., Gourley, A., Devanbu, P., Gertz, M.: Swaminathan, A.: Mining email social networks. In: MSR 2006: Proceedings of the 2006 international workshop on Mining software repositories, pp. 137–143. ACM Press, New York (2006)
16. Valverde, S., Solé, R.V.: Self-organization and hierarchy in open source social networks. Technical report, DELIS - Dynamically Evolving, Large-Scale Information Systems (2006)

Artificial Immune System Based Robot Anomaly Detection Engine for Fault Tolerant Robots

Bojan Jakimovski and Erik Maehle

Institute of Computer Engineering, University Luebeck, Germany
{bojan,maehle}@iti.uni-luebeck.de
www.iti.uni-luebeck.de

Abstract. Robot anomaly detection method described in this paper uses an approach inspired by an immune system for detecting failures within autonomous robot system. The concept is based on self-nonself discrimination and clonal selection principles found within the natural immune system. The approach applies principles of fuzzy logic for representing and processing the information within the artificial immune system. Throughout the paper we explain the working principle of RADE (Robot Anomaly Detection Engine) approach and we show its practical effectiveness through several experimental test cases.

Keywords: Robot anomaly detection, robot fault detection, artificial immune system, clonal selection, self-healing, self-reconfiguration, fault tolerant robot, six legged robot.

1 Introduction

Autonomous mobile robots are complex technical systems which are capable of carrying out predefined tasks without human intervention. In order to fulfil the proposed requirements, they consist of various software and hardware processing units, sensors, actuators. Due to their high complexity, modelling, development and maintenance of such systems is often a tedious and time consuming task.

Declaring them as autonomous means that the robots should operate and complete their tasks under various given scenarios and unforeseen conditions. Additionally they should be reliable and tolerant to system malfunctions such: components failures, parts aging or any other external influences like object collisions. Therefore, they should correctly detect their anomalies and dynamically reconfigure themselves in these situations in order to properly continue executing the predefined mission.

But building a full failure model for robot systems is often an exhaustive process [1]. To overcome this constraint the robots should poses so called self-x properties. These properties, like self-healing, self-reconfiguration, self-learning and the like would aid introducing more robust and reliable robots. In that sense this methodology will directly contribute towards shortening their development and maintenance time.

Biological systems on the other hand have effectively demonstrated to poses the above mentioned self-x features. Such phenomena seen in natural systems have often provided inspiration for their metaphoric implementation in the domain of engineering.

C. Rong et al. (Eds.): ATC 2008, LNCS 5060, pp. 177–190, 2008.
© Springer-Verlag Berlin Heidelberg 2008

Artificial Immune System (AIS) is one of such successfully applied paradigms we have considered for building our RADE (Robot Anomaly Detection Engine) for fault tolerant robots. RADE introduces a robust concept for anomaly detection which aims to decrease the engineering effort in building fault tolerant autonomous robots. Additionally it also opens the possibility for the system through learning to find and resolve errors, which is going to be realized in the next stage of the RADE project. The paper is organized as follows. In section 2 we give a short introduction on AIS as natural immune system inspired paradigm used in RADE. In section 3 we describe RADE and its principle of operation in more detail. In section 4 we discuss several experimental test cases made with RADE on the robot demonstrator.

2   Artificial Immune System

Artificial Immune System (AIS) is directly inspired by the natural immune system as important biological defence mechanism which is able to recognize and defend our organisms from bacteria and viruses.

The natural immune system generally consists of two types of defence mechanisms: innate immune system and the adaptive immune system. Innate immune system is directly involved in providing immediate defence against pathogens and in recognizing them in a generic way. The adaptive immune system defence mechanism instead provides more specific response to the pathogenic antigens. It recognizes and memorises specific antigen signatures so it can rapidly and more effectively react next time it encounters such antigens. The adaptive immune system generally consists of two types of cells: T-cells and B-cells. T-cells are helper cells and are related to activation of the response of the immune system, while B-cells have receptors which detect antigens and are associated with production of antibodies (self) for detecting the antigens (non-self). An important characteristic of the adaptive immune system is the immune response to antigens. This response is well explained through clonal selection theory [2] which states that those cells which are able to recognize the antigenic stimulus will be selected and will proliferate (divide) and differentiate into plasma cells (as antibody secretors) and memory cells. Such process of clonal selection and proliferation is represented on Figure 1.

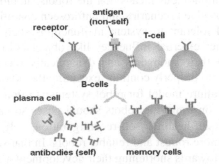

Fig. 1. Clonal selection and proliferation

When memory cells are exposed to a secondary antigenic stimulus, they differentiate into plasma cells and produce high amount of specialized antibodies which bind to the antigens and therefore result in faster secondary response to a particular antigen. Such rapid secondary and subsequent responses are represented on Figure 2. [3].

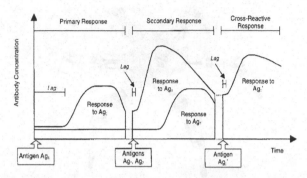

Fig. 2. Secondary and subsequent responses to particular antigen

Similar to the natural immune system, AIS also introduces a metric that allows the system to distinguish between self (correctly functioning system) and non-self (anomaly in the system) and also to memorize and detect specific patterns. Therefore main properties of AIS are: recognition, identification, adaptation, self-organization. It has been successfully applied for various domains: pattern recognition [4], data mining [5], network security [6], robotics [7], [8], [9], [10], [11], and others. There exist several different approaches [12] for AIS. However, the most commonly found in literature are: negative selection [13], positive selection [14], artificial immune networks (AIN) [15] and clonal selection [3].

Negative selection mechanism is based on the ability of the immune system to learn to categorize between non-self and self by providing tolerance for the self. The negative selection consists of generating a set of detectors and evaluation of those detectors. Only the detectors that detect non-self, but do not react to self are considered for further detection. The positive selection, on the other hand, generates, evaluates and enables those detectors that can detect only the non-self. The clonal selection within AIS is based on the proliferation mechanism where self, upon recognizing non-self, starts to proliferate by cloning itself and also memorizing the pattern of the non-self (immune memory), so it has better responsiveness for the next encounter with such a particular non-self pattern.

3 Robot Anomaly Detection Engine (RADE)

For the detection of an anomaly within robot systems different immune system approaches have been considered, like inflammation [9], or usage of negative selection [10]. For our RADE anomaly detection approach we are using the clonal selection method in combination with fuzzy logic for representing the information within the AIS.

Before proceeding further with the discussion on anomaly detection within RADE, we are first going to introduce our experimental hexapod robot OSCAR(Organic Self Configuring and Adapting Robot) [16], [17] shown in Figure 3 on which the RADE experiments are made with.

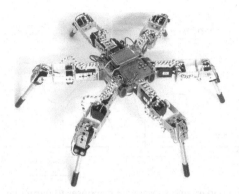

Fig. 3. Experimental hexapod robot OSCAR (Organic Self Reconfiguring and Adapting Robot) has six legs, with three motors per leg. Going from the body – alpha, beta and gamma.

Robot OSCAR has six legs, with three motors per leg, which are named alpha, beta and gamma (going from the body), feet pressure sensors, acceleration sensors and onboard control hardware. With an additional data acquisition setup, we are able to monitor the immediate values of currents and positions of the motors as well as pressure readings from the robot's six foot sensors.

At a given instance of time the robot executes one or several behaviours like walking, standing, going left or right, etc. These behaviours are then related to some movements of actuators within the robot and as result the robot realizes particular behaviour actions. For detecting if an anomaly situation has appeared within the robot system, there are monitor units within the robot control architecture where RADE is situated. Depending on its implementation, within the robot's control model several behaviors (behavior units), several monitors and number of sensors and actuators can be present. This is represented on Figure 4.

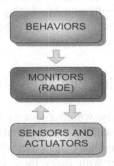

Fig. 4. Monitors (RADE) are related to anomaly detection within the robot control concept

RADE uses fuzzy logic for representing information because an exact recognition is not necessary for triggering of an anomaly response. It is also similar to the way the association is made within the immune system, where given a similar (but not necessarily identical) stimulus, the response can be initiated. In a practical implementation, this would mean for example: if the behavior is walking then the acceleration level should not be low. Or in monitoring the servo's motor status, this can be interpreted as: by normal walking, the servo's current should not be high. In RADE such generalized self / non-self situations can be defined by fuzzy rules which are part of self / non-self sets. The rules in the non-self set detect when there is some anomaly present within the system, and the rules in the self set detect when the situation is not characterised as anomalous. The rules of both sets have the following structure:

```
IF X1&X2&…Xn THEN Anomaly is Y WITH WEIGHT_FACTOR Z
```

The "X1&X2&…Xn" represents the premise part which constitutes of monitored behaviours: walking, standing, etc.; and particular some characteristics like: current, acceleration, etc. The "Y" is the consequence part and can have two types of values: "anomaly is present" or "anomaly is absent". The weight factor "Z" represents the clonal proliferation within AIS, and is in a range from 0.0 to 1.0. The "Z" value will increase for some constant value (for example: 0.1) if the rule has "fired". In parallel to that the weights will decrease in all the rules belonging to the opposite set, just as the concentration of self/non-self drops being influenced by an increased concentration of non-self/self within the immune system. The firing level of each rule is therefore always adjusted, depending on the value of "Z". The weight factor "Z" has also another positive characteristic for the anomaly detection engine. Namely we want to reduce the factor of hand coded elements in RADE, and let the system dynamically adjusts itself to the situation. For example in case we have coded fuzzy rules *without* using weights, depending on the manually pre-designed fuzzy membership sets for the premise parts of the rules, the rules can have an optimal response for some situation and perhaps a not satisfying response for other unforeseen situations. In case the fuzzy rules *have* weights, this would introduce two new features:

- The premise parts of the rules do not require any additional handcrafting and expert designing for their fuzzy membership sets. Therefore they can have some automatically generated "standard" triangular fuzzy membership sets, normally distributed within a valid range for the observed variable. For example such fuzzy membership sets for monitored variable "Current" having values in the range from min 0 to max 3 Amperes can be represented as:

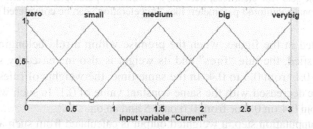

Fig. 5. Fuzzy membership set for monitored variable "Current"

The other membership sets for other monitored variables (for example: acceleration) are going to have the same "standard" triangular fuzzy membership normally distributed for their input range. The nice thing for having such "standard" generated fuzzy membership sets is that they can be part of the learning process, which we plan to introduce in the next step of development of our anomaly detection engine. Having the "standard" fuzzy membership sets for every of the observed parameters, we may build up a rule based learning system which incorporates only new situations since the fuzzy membership sets for the observed parameters are not going to be changed, and so it will be possible to distinguish between what has been already learned and what can be learned.

– The weight factors for such rules having the "standard" generated fuzzy membership sets allow the rule to adapt to the situation even without the rule being optimally pre-designed at start, i.e. having its membership sets optimally pre-designed. Therefore the changes of the weights depend on the particular situation and therefore contribute for the dynamics of overall system.

The previously discussed self and non-self rule sets and the dynamical change of their weights can be visually represented as in Figure 5.

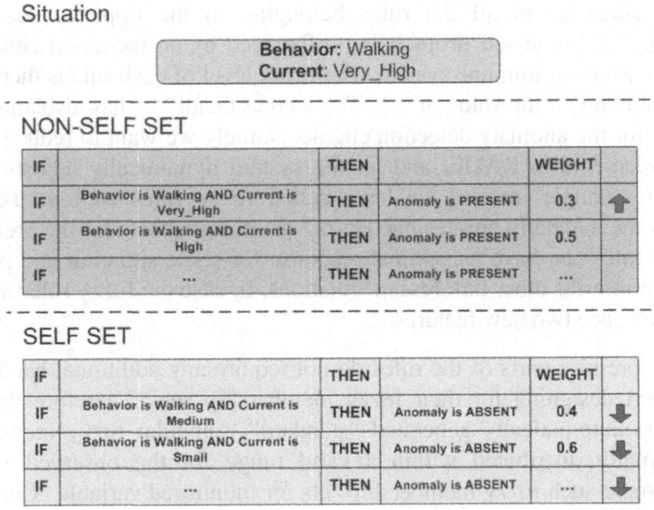

Fig. 6. Functioning principle of RADE and the dynamically changing weights within the self and non-self rule sets (for clearness, here only monitoring parameter "Current" is represented, although additional monitored parameter, like "Acceleration" can be considered as well)

As illustrated in the figure, when the premise within a rule belonging to the non-self set is satisfied, the rule "fires" and its weight is also increased by some constant value, e.g. by 0.1 from 0.3 to 0.4. In the same time, the weights of rules belonging to another set are decreased with the same constant value of 0.1. In such way they lower their value from 0.4 on 0.3 or from 0.6 on 0.5 and so on.

In every computation step, a weighted output is calculated from such a fuzzy system which contains two membership functions: self and non-self. The value is in the range from 0.0 (no anomaly) to 1.0 (full anomaly) and represents the output of the RADE method. The output of RADE is computed in a defuzzification process as a centroid of fuzzy outputs of the "fired" rules. Therefore the output of RADE is influenced by the weight factor of each of the firing rules. The weight factor acts in the similar way as the secondary and subsequent responses within the immune system, i.e. the more the weight is associated to some rules, the more significant will be the response of those rules to the output of RADE in the next moment of their firing.

The change of weights therefore acts as some sort of short memory for events that occurred some moments ago. In such way RADE demonstrates its self-adapting property, where the anomaly output level of RADE depends on its short history and also on actual system's state.

4 Results of Experimental Test Cases

We have made several experiments with RADE on real data acquired from several test cases conducted with our robot demonstrator. The measurements are done considering the following scenarios: normal robot walking (Figures 7a, 7b), obstacle collisions (Figures 8a, 8b), a servo joint motor gets disconnected (Figures 9a, 9b), mechanical problem - a screw on joint is falling off (Figures 10a, 10b).

The output of the fuzzy system has two membership functions: absent and present, which correspondingly represent the absence or presence of anomaly in the system. For the measurement tests we have assumed that the behaviour is walking and we have initialized RADE with several fuzzy rules, which have "standard" triangular membership sets, equally distributed over the valid range for the observed parameters. These rules with their weights factoring can be represented as following:

```
RULE 1:  IF accel IS zero THEN anomaly IS present WEIGHT 0.1;
RULE 2:  IF accel IS small THEN anomaly IS absent WEIGHT 0.1;
RULE 3:  IF accel IS medium THEN anomaly IS absent WEIGHT 0.1;
RULE 4:  IF accel IS big THEN anomaly IS absent WEIGHT 0.1;
RULE 5:  IF accel IS verybig THEN anomaly IS absent WEIGHT 0.1;
RULE 6:  IF scurrent IS zero THEN anomaly IS present WEIGHT 0.1;
RULE 7:  IF scurrent IS small THEN anomaly IS absent WEIGHT 0.1;
RULE 8:  IF scurrent IS medium THEN anomaly IS absent WEIGHT 0.1;
RULE 9:  IF scurrent IS big THEN anomaly IS absent WEIGHT 0.1;
RULE 10: IF scurrent IS verybig THEN anomaly IS present WEIGHT 0.1;
```

The parameter accel in the rules stands for acceleration of the robot and the scurrent stands for the servo current. The weights of the rules are initially set on 0.1 at the start and change dynamically during the runtime of RADE. Such manual pre-initialization of fuzzy rules can be overcome in future with introducing learning within RADE. However the purpose of these tests is to prove the concept by introducing clonal proliferation inspired change of the weights of fuzzy rules and their online adaptation to the situation. The fuzzy rules without weights factoring are the same as mentioned above, but with static weights defined to 0.5.

In Fig. 7 to 10 we are presenting the experimental results. On the horizontal axis we have the time units (seconds). On the vertical axis we can observe the following parameters: servo joint current with values between 0 and 3 Amperes; normalized acceleration level with values between 0 and 1.5 gravity acceleration units; anomaly level with values between 0 and 1, where 0 means no anomaly and 1 is the maximum level of anomaly.

For each scenario, we have conducted experiments with two different types of fuzzy rules:

– fuzzy rules *without* weights factoring (static weights); (case a)
– fuzzy rules *with* weights and clonal proliferation inspired dynamics; (case b)

In order to estimate the effectiveness of our clonal proliferation inspired approach for anomaly detection we have made a comparison between these two types of rules.

The first described scenario is normal walking of the robot.

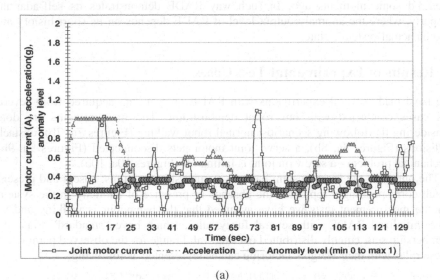

(a)

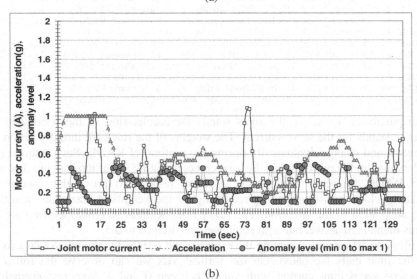

(b)

Fig. 7. (a) Normal robot walking; Fuzzy rules with static weights. (b) Normal robot walking; Fuzzy rules with clonal proliferation dynamics for the weights.

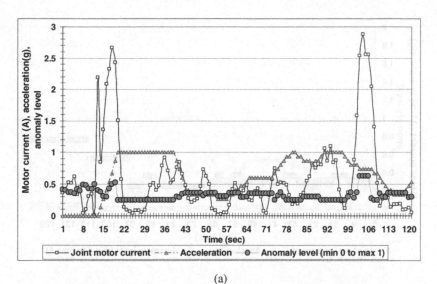

(a)

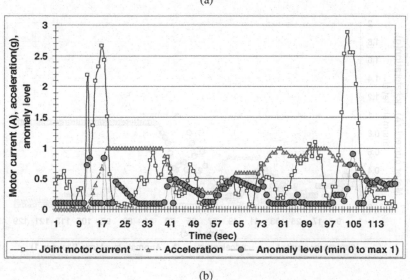

(b)

Fig. 8. (a) Robot hits obstacle with its leg at time moments 12, 18 and 105; Fuzzy rules with static weights. (b) Robot hits obstacle with its leg at time moments 12, 18 and 105; Fuzzy rules with clonal proliferation dynamics for the weights.

For normal walking of robot we observe that the typical level for the anomaly in the both cases is within range of 0.1 and 0.5. In the case where the fuzzy system has static weights the anomaly level does not change much. However, we can observe that for fuzzy rules with dynamic weights, the anomaly level is not that steady in the observed domain from 0.1 up to 0.5, which illustrates how RADE adapts even to the smallest perturbations in the monitored parameters.

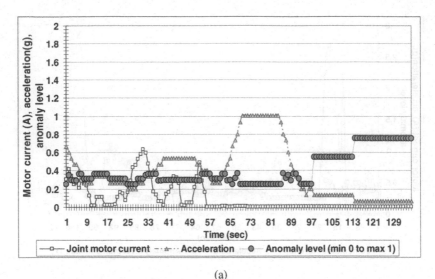

(a)

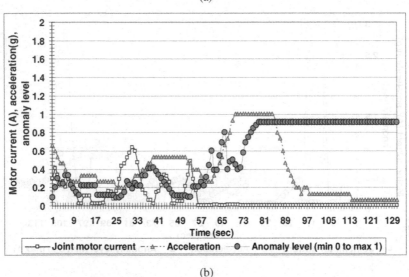

(b)

Fig. 9. (a) Servo joint is switched off at time 56 to simulate some electrical failure; Fuzzy rules with static weights. (b) Servo joint is switched off at time 56 to simulate some electrical failure; Fuzzy rules with clonal proliferation dynamics for the weights.

In Figures 8a, 8b we observe a scenario where the robot hits some obstacles with its parts (legs). We can identify two bigger spikes that represent the current values of a servo joint which appear when the leg hits some obstacle. The comparative differences to the normal walking situation are also recognizable within the values for acceleration level and also in the computed anomaly level, which dynamically rise up in two different time moments. These levels may indicate that some temporal problem has appeared and for example may be an indication for changing the walking gait pattern.

As can be seen from the tests done, within the fuzzy system based on statical weights, when the leg hits the obstacle, the anomaly level rises up in two cases to 0.5 and 0.6 respectively. This may not indicate some particular anomaly in the system which as a consequence may denote that the robot does not properly react to the particular situation. Such an anomaly level computed in the fuzzy logic system using the static weights comes out from the fact that "standard" triangular membership sets may not be best suited for producing optimized reaction for such a situation.

However, in case of fuzzy logic system utilizing the clonal proliferation change of its weights, the anomaly level rises up in three different moments of time to values of 0.85, 0.85 and 0.9 respectively. This clearly indicates that the anomaly detection engine dynamically adapts to the situation even with "standard" triangular membership sets and produces an output correctly recognizing the situation.

On Figures 9a, 9b, a scenario is presented where a servo is switched off in order to simulate some broken contact or similar electrical failure within robot. The servo joint is switched off at time 56, and therefore its current drops to 0 Amperes.

Such a situation where the current value and acceleration level drops very low should result in some anomaly situation. In case of a fuzzy system utilizing static weights only, we can see that the computed anomaly level slowly rises after that moment and at time 98 it goes on level of 0.55 where it persists till time 114, when it goes up to value of 0.75 and stays persistently on that level. This may be not that optimal output for anomaly level in order to detect some severe anomaly. This kind of reaction may be tracked back again to the predefined "standard" triangular membership sets which are perhaps not suited to produce optimal result for every situation.

For the same scenario and input data, we conducted an experiment with fuzzy rules with clonal proliferation dynamics for the weights and same "standard" triangular membership sets as in previous case. We can observe a different output of the anomaly detection method in comparison to the former case with static weights. Namely, after the servo joint gets disconnected at time 56, the anomaly level rises up more rapidly than in the previous experiment with static weights. We can also observe a small disturbance of the anomaly level rising (in time domain 67 to 72), which is due to the acceleration level which rises a bit, as result of the robot's declining on the side on which the servo is disconnected. After that, the anomaly level rises to level of 0.9 where it persists constantly. Such particular reaction would clearly indicate that the robot should reconfigure itself in that case (for example: spatial reconfiguration of the legs). From the comparison of the case with static and with clonal proliferation dynamics for the weights we can observe that the anomaly detection engine in the second case performs much faster and gives a better estimation of the situation.

In Figures 10a, 10b, a scenario is presented where a screw is falling off from a servo joint at time 105 and simulates some sort of mechanical error within the robot. As can be seen from the figures, after the screw has fallen off, the servo joint becomes non-functional and therefore the acceleration of the robot gradually drops down. The level of the servo current in that situation is also very low. As a result from these circumstances, the anomaly level rises up to indicate some anomaly situation.

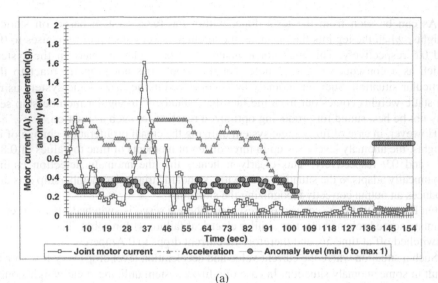

(a)

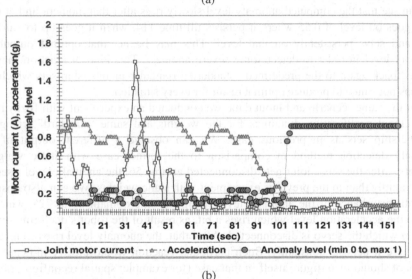

(b)

Fig. 10. (a) Mechanical problem - screw is falling off of one servo joint at time 105; Fuzzy rules with static weights. (b) Mechanical problem - screw is falling off of one servo joint at time 105; Fuzzy rules with clonal proliferation dynamics for the weights.

In case of fuzzy system utilizing static weights we can observe that the anomaly level initially rises up to value of 0.55 till time 138, and then rises again and persists on value 0.75.

In the case of a fuzzy system utilizing clonal proliferation with dynamics for the weights we can observe that the anomaly level rises rather very quickly to value of 0.9 and persists on that value. With such a reaction, the robotic system can clearly better identify the anomaly situation than in the case with static weights and would therefore appropriately reconfigure itself in order to continue its mission.

5 Conclusions

In this paper we have introduced RADE as a new robust concept for anomaly detection for autonomous robots based on Artificial Immune System with clonal proliferation dynamics for the fuzzy rules. Throughout the paper we have explained its characteristics; its principle of functioning and presented results of the experiments done. The test cases demonstrated the practical effectiveness of this approach. Therefore in the next stage of the RADE project we are planning to expand this approach and to introduce a learning feature within the rule based system and to demonstrate its on-line learning potential. In this way RADE will directly contribute towards practical realization of self-healing autonomous robots.

References

1. Haldar, B., Sarkar, N.: Robust fault detection and isolation in mobile robot. In: Proceedings of IFAC, Beijing, China (2006)
2. Forsdyke, D.R.: The Origins of the Clonal Selection theory of Immunity. FASEB. Journal 9, 164–166 (1995)
3. De Castro, L.N., Von Zuben, F.J.: Learning and Optimization using the clonal selection principle. IEEE Transaction on Evolutionary Computation, 239–251 (2002)
4. Cao, Y., Dasgupta, D.: An Immunogenetic Approach in Chemical Spectrum Recognition. In: Ghosh, Tsutsui (eds.) Advances in Evolutionary Computing, Springer, Heidelberg (2003)
5. Nasraoui, O., Cardona, C., Rojas, C.: Using retrieval measures to asses similarity in mining dynamic web clickstreams. In: Proceeding of the eleventh ACM SIGKDD International Conference on Knowledge Discovery in Data Mining KDD (2005)
6. Pagnoni, A., Visconti, A.: An innate immune system for the protection of computer networks. In: Proceedings of the 4th international symposium on information and communication technologies. ACM International Conference Proceeding Series, vol. 92, pp. 63–68 (2005)
7. Michelan, R., Von Zuben, F.J.: Decentralized control system for autonomous navigation based on an evolved artificial immune network. In: CEC apos 2002. Proceedings of the 2002 Congress on Evolutionary Computation, vol. 2, pp. 1021–1026 (2002)
8. Singh, C.T., Nair, S.B.: An Artificial Immune System for a MultiAgent Robotics System. Transactions of Engineering, Computing and Technology 6, 308–311 (2005)
9. Sathyanath, S., Sahin, F.: AISIMAM – An Artificial Immune System Based Intelligent Multi Agent Model and its Application to a Mine Detection Problem. In: 1st International Conference on Artificial Immune Systems, Canterbury, UK (2002)
10. Neal, M., Feyereisl, J., Rascuna, R., Wang, X.: Don't Touch Me, I'm Fine: Robot Autonomy Using an Artificial Innate Immune System. In: 5th International Conference on Artificial Immune Systems, Oeiras, Portugal (2006)
11. Canham, R., Jackson, A.H., Tyrrell, A.: Robot Error Detection Using an Artificial Immune System. In: Proceedings of the 2003 NASA/DoD Conference on Evolvable Hardware (2003)

12. De Castro, L.N., Timmis, J.: Artificial Immune Systems: A New Computational Intelligence Approach, pp. 36–46. Springer, Heidelberg (2002)
13. Forrest, S., Perelson, A.S., Allen, L., Cherukuri, R.: Self-Nonself Discrimination in a Computer. In: Proceedings of the 1994 IEEE Symposium on Research in Security and Privacy, IEEE Computer Society Press, Los Alamitos (1994)
14. Nino, F., Beltran, O.: A change detection software agent based on immune mixed selection. Evolutionary Computation. In: Proceedings of the 2002 Congress on CEC 2002, vol. 1, pp. 693–698 (2002)
15. Galeano, J.C., Veloza-Suan, A., Gonzalez, F.A.: A comparative analysis of artificial immune network models. In: Proceedings of the Conference on Genetic and Evolutionary Computation, Washington DC, USA, pp. 361–368 (2005)
16. El Sayed Auf, A., Mösch, F., Litza, M.: How the six-legged walking machine OSCAR handle leg amputations. In: Workshop on Bio-inspired Cooperative and Adaptive Behaviours in Robots, Rome, Italy (2006)
17. Jakimovski, B., Litza, M., Mösch, F., El Sayed Auf, A.: Development of an organic computing architecture for robot control. In: Informatik 2006 Workshop on Organic Computing - Status and Outlook, Dresden (2006)

Maximising Personal Utility Using Intelligent Strategy in Minority Game

Yingni She and Ho-fung Leung

Department of Computer Science and Engineering
The Chinese University of Hong Kong, Hong Kong
{ynshe,lhf}@cse.cuhk.edu.hk

Abstract. In the traditional minority game, each agent chooses the highest-score strategy at every time step from its initial strategies which are allocated randomly. How can one agent manage to outperform its competitors and maximise its own utility in this competing and dynamic environment? In this paper, we study a version of the minority game in which one privileged agent is allowed to join the game with larger memory size and free to choose any strategy, while the other agents own small number of strategies. Simulations show that the privileged agent using the intelligent strategy outperforms the other agents in the same model and other models proposed in previous work in terms of individual payoff. We also investigate how the number of strategies and the length of memory affect the privileged agent's performance.

Keywords: Minority game, Symmetric phase, Asymmetric phase.

1 Introduction

Inspired by Arthur's 'El Farol Bar' problem [2], the minority game [6] is introduced as a model for adaptive systems of interacting agents. It consists of an odd number of N agents playing the game. At each time step, each of the N agents independently decides to join one of the two groups, labeled 0 or 1. After all agents have made their decisions, those who are on the minority group win, while the other agents belonging to the majority group lose. In the traditional method, each agent makes the decision based on the prediction of a strategy chosen from its S strategies (or predictors), each of which maps the recent M winning history records to a prediction. All agents always use the highest-score strategy to decide their action. They learn and adapt by evaluating the performance of their strategies. A strategy of memory size M is a lookup table consisting of 2^M entries and two columns, 'history' and 'prediction' respectively. Each entry prescribes which group to join in according to the information gathered from the recent winning history of last M time steps, thus there are 2^M entries in each strategy. The prediction at each entry is either 0 or 1, so the total number of strategies is 2^{2^M}. Each agent is randomly assigned S strategies from the 2^{2^M} possible strategies at the beginning of the game. After all agents have made their decisions, traditionally, those who are on the minority group are

C. Rong et al. (Eds.): ATC 2008, LNCS 5060, pp. 191–205, 2008.
© Springer-Verlag Berlin Heidelberg 2008

rewarded one point, while the other agents belonging to the majority group get nothing or lose one point. All strategies which have made the correct prediction are also rewarded one point. All agents keep updating the history dynamically according to the outcome of winning side at every time step.

It has been shown that the fluctuations σ of the attendance size depends on the ratio $\rho = 2^M/N$ between the number 2^M of possible histories and the number N of agents [5]. The length of the possible history is also referred as memory size M. There exists a phase transition of changing direction of σ^2 located at the point ρ_c where σ^2 attains its minimum [3]. When $\rho < \rho_c$, the phase is called the symmetric phase. When $\rho > \rho_c$, the phase is called the asymmetric phase. For small values of M, the strategy space is small and there is much overlap of strategies among agents, hence a crowd of agents behave similarly and decide the same action. This situation is called the 'crowd effect'. Due to limited space, we refer the interested readers to the book of Minority Games [5] for further details.

Because of the 'crowd effect', the winning outcome of an even occurrence of any history is most likely opposite to that of the odd occurrence of this history [20][13] in the case of small ρ. Assuming that every history is equally likely to occur [7], when a particular history occurs for the first time, all agents decide randomly because there is no previous history at the beginning of the game. After the first occurrence of the history, agents learn that the winning outcome is a better choice. In the next occurrence of the same history, a crowd of agents make the same decision as the winning outcome in the last occurrence. This leads to the winning outcome is opposite to that in the last occurrence of the same history. So, at the end of 2×2^M time steps, all the strategies gain the same point on average. For the next occurrence of the same history, the situation is equivalent to a new start of the game, similar to that of the first occurrence. Therefore, the minority game appears the quasi-periodic structure with a periodicity of length 2×2^M in the symmetric phase [13].

In the minority game with the 'crowd effect', how an individual agent can escape from the crowd and maximise its own utility is of great interest. In this paper, we focus on how a privileged agent outperforms its competitors and obtains maximal utility. The only available information for the privileged agent is the history information and its own strategies. We find that the privileged agent with larger memory size than others and all its possible strategies can achieve far larger payoff than the average payoff of the other agents for almost all values of M. In the next section, we introduce some related work in details. In Section 3, firstly, we introduce the inefficient information that the privileged agent can make use of to maximise its own utility. Secondly, we propose an intelligent strategy for the privileged agent. Finally we evaluate the performance of the privileged agent. In Section 4, we further investigate the effects that the parameters M and S have on the privileged agent's payoff and compare the agent's performance using the intelligent strategy with other models'. Then we present an Experience method for the agent using the traditional method with all possible strategies. In the last section, we come up with some conclusions about the paper and suggest some future work.

2   Related Work

For the traditional agents, each of them is assigned S strategies arbitrarily at the beginning of the game and then chooses the highest-score strategy among them at every time step. There exists some similar work focusing on how individual agents outperform their competitors in the minority game. Liu and Liaw [14] consider the gain of a special agent. They propose the 'opposite strategy' for a special agent to maximise its personal gain. It is to use the highest-score strategy among all 2^{2^M} possible strategies when ρ is larger than ρ_c, and use the opposite strategy when ρ is smaller than ρ_c. The opposite strategy is to use the prediction in each entry opposite from that of the highest-score strategy. It is shown that the winning probability of this special agent using the 'opposite strategy' can be larger than 0.5 for almost all values of ρ. The reason that the 'opposite strategy' can enhance the winning probability lies in that it makes use of the quasi-periodic structure of the game: the winning outcome of an even occurrence of any history is most likely opposite to that of the odd occurrence of this history in the case of small ρ.

Yip et al. [19] consider special agents who participate in the game with a probability q per turn. That means these agents have a probability q of joining the game in each turn and a probability of $1 - q$ of staying out of the game in a turn. The other agents participate in the game every turn. For all agents, they choose the highest-score strategies to make the decisions. Besides joining the game only with probability q, the special agents differ from the other agents in that they only assess the performance of their strategies in the turns that they participate. For the turns that the special agents decide not to play, they do not reward or subtract points to their strategies, regardless of the outcome. They find that these special agents with $q < 1$ achieve higher success rate than the average of all other agents when ρ is small. The success rate is the ratio of the number of winning turns to the number of turns the agent has actually participated. Because the special agents do not participate in the game every turn, they can avoid the 'crowd effect'. However, this method is a passive one because the special agents do not participate in the game for all turns. They only enhance their winning probability, but not enhance their overall payoffs.

Sometimes it pays to increase the agent's memory size M. Johnson et al. [9] study a mixed population of adaptive agents with small and large memory sizes, but all agents own the same number of strategies and choose the highest-score one to make decisions. They find that the average success rate of the large-memory agents within a mixed-ability population can be greater than 0.5 by uncovering and exploiting hidden information in the system's recent history. The hidden information is the system's history information which agents can make use of. Challet et al. [4] point out that the special agent with larger memory size can obtain larger gain than all of the other agents in the symmetric phase but the gain cannot be increased further more if the agent increases memory size. Furthermore, in the asymmetric phase the special agent receives a lower payoff than the average payoff of the other agents. Both of these two pieces of work demonstrate the importance of memory size in the minority game, but they ignore the influence of the number of strategies.

Lam and Leung [11] propose an adaptive behavioral strategy for the minority game according to the winning histories h and the net payoff u for choosing side 0 or 1. Each agent has two initial attitudes a_x towards choosing side 0 or 1 and two respective adaptive parameters. At each time step, each agent calculates the attractiveness $(= (1 - a_x) \times h + a_x \times u)$ of side 0 and 1 to make the prediction. If side 0's attractiveness is larger than side 1's, it will choose side 0, and vice versa. At the end of each round, each agent updates its attitudes: if it has chosen side 0 and wins, then its attitude towards side 0 will be increased by the increasing adaptive parameter; if it has chosen side 0 and loses, then its attitude towards side 0 will be decreased by the decreasing adaptive parameter. Effectively, these agents do not use explicit predictors. Simulations show that agents with the adaptive behavioral strategy perform well. However, the performance of the agents with the adaptive behavioral strategy relies on each other because of the limitation of the strategy itself. The strategy can work well only if there are enough agents using it, because the agents update their attitudes according to the winning outcome. The winning outcome need enough agents using the adaptive behaviorial strategy to affect itself so that the agents can update their attitudes in the right way.

3   An Intelligent Strategy

3.1   Motivation

The motivation of the work is that there is a common phenomenon: 'crowd effect' in the minority game when ρ is small $(N \gg 2^M)$. The problem for agents is how to escape from the 'crowd effect' and maximise personal utilities based on the history information and their own strategies. What will happen if the agent is more intelligent, i.e. having larger memory size or more strategies? In previous studies as described in Section 2, [4][19][9][14] propose different methods to escape from the crowd and enhance the winning probability. Based on the previous work that the agent has longer memory [4][9], we anticipate that if a privileged agent has larger memory size M' than the other agents and is free to choose any strategy at every time step while the other agents are using their highest-score strategies drawn randomly from the 2^{2^M} possible strategies, then the privileged agent can also escape from the crowd and hence enhance the success rate. Intuitively, this mechanism can achieve the performance because the privileged agent with longer memory and more strategies is more intelligent than the other agents. The resource allocation problem can be modeled as minority games [8][12]. However, the application of minority games is not included in the domain of this paper.

In order to study the information content of the minority game, we consider $P(1|h_k)$, the conditional probability to have a winning outcome of side 1 immediately following some specific history string h_k of k bits [18][16]. That means when the history string h_k with length of k occurs, the probability of the winning outcome to be side 1 is $P(1|h_k)$. Yip et al. [19] define the inefficiency ε as follows:

$$\varepsilon = \frac{1}{2^M} \sum_{i=0}^{2^M-1} |P(1|i(h_k)) - \frac{1}{2}| \qquad (1)$$

where the sum is over all 2^M possible winning history strings of M bits and $i(h_k)$ is the corresponding integer value of the binary history string h_k of length k. The inefficiency ε measures the information left in the winning history strings that a privileged agent uses to assess its strategies. If $P(1|h_k)$ is larger than 0.5, then the strategies with the prediction of side 1 at that specific history h_k are rewarded more points. If $P(1|h_k)$ is smaller than 0.5, then the strategies with the prediction of side 0 at that specific history h_k are rewarded more points. The agent decides whether to reward points to its strategies based on the winning outcome at the past winning history and chooses the highest-score strategy to make the decision.

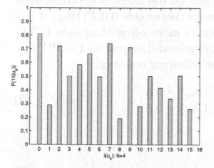

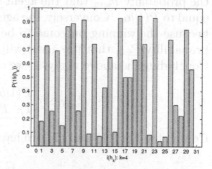

Fig. 1. A histogram of the conditional probability $P(1|i(h_k))$ with $k = 4$ for the game played with $M = 3$

Fig. 2. A histogram of the conditional probability $P(1|i(h_k))$ with $k = 5$ for the game played with $M = 3$

The predictive information is about which will be the minority group at the next time step. Manuca et al. [18][16] have shown that in the symmetric phase of the minority game, the winning history strings with length less than or equal to the memory size contain no predictive information. That means $P(1|h_k) = 0.5$ for any history and hence $\varepsilon = 0$. In Figures 1 and 2, we plot $P(1|i(h_k))$ generated by a game with $N = 101$. One is the privileged agent with larger memory size and all possible strategies and the others have $M = 3$ and $S = 2$. Figure 1 shows the histogram of $P(1|i(h_k))$ for the privileged agent having one longer memory than the memory other agents have, i.e. $k = M + 1 = 4$. Figure 2 shows the histogram of $P(1|i(h_k))$ for the privileged agent having two longer memory than the memory other agents have, i.e. $k = M + 2 = 5$. From the histograms we can see that the distinguished hidden information becomes clearer when having longer memory, because $P(1|i(h_k))$ for $k = 5$ is more approaching to 1 when it is above 0.5 and more approaching to 0 when it is below 0.5. Using the figures in Figures 1 and 2 and Eq. (1), we can get the numerical results of the inefficiency ε: $\varepsilon_1 = 0.154$ for Figure 1 and $\varepsilon_2 = 0.299$ for Figure 2. Obviously, $\varepsilon_2 > \varepsilon_1$.

Thus we are led to the intriguing idea that an individual agent can make good use of this information to maximise its own utility by having longer memory and owning all its possible strategies. At each time step, the side within the highest-score strategy at that specific history is selected to make the decision. After each time step, if the winning outcome is side 1, then the strategy's score with side 1 at that specific history is increased by one. If the winning outcome is side 0, then the strategy's score with side 0 at that specific history is increased by one. The theoretical analysis is as follows: the probability $P(1|h_k) > 0.5$ means that the winning outcome to be side 1 occurs more often than side 0. After some learning steps, the strategy's score with side 1 at that specific history will be greater than the strategy's' score with side 0 at that specific history and this situation lasts through the game. So the agent with longer memory and all possible strategies will always choose side 1 if $P(1|h_k) > 0.5$. This implies that the probability P_{win} that the agent will win through the game is approximately equal to $P(1|h_k)$. Conversely, the agent will always choose side 0 if $P(1|h_k) < 0.5$, because the winning outcome to be side 0 occurs more often than side 1. The probability P_{win} that the agent will win is approximately equal to $1 - P(1|h_k)$. Concluding the above analysis, we can get the following equation:

$$P_{win} \simeq \begin{cases} P(1|h_k) & P(1|h_k) \geq 0.5 \\ 1 - P(1|h_k) & P(1|h_k) < 0.5 \end{cases} \tag{2}$$

Combining Eqs. (1) and (2), we have

$$P_{win} \simeq \frac{1}{2} + \varepsilon \tag{3}$$

Therefore the probability that the privileged agent wins for all occurrences of histories will be greater than 0.5 if $\varepsilon \neq 0$. The larger inefficiency ε is, the larger winning probability is. From these two figures, we can conclude that the privileged agent can lengthen the memory size to get more inefficient information.

3.2   An Intelligent Strategy

In the traditional minority game, all agents keep the same memory size M and the same number of strategies S. As described in Section 1, there is 'crowd effect' in the symmetric phase, all agents behave similarly and obtain similar payoff. So it is hard to distinguish one from others. How can one agent manage to outperform the other agents in terms of individual payoff? Intuitively, the agent should be intelligent enough to avoid the 'crowd effect'. The only available information it can use is the history information and its strategies. So how can the agent make good use of the information to maximise its payoff? Does it need to increase its memory size or the number of strategies it owns?

In the work of Challet et al. [4], they suggest that the payoff of the agent with $M' = M + 1$ and $S' = 2$ cannot be increased furthermore if the agent increases M'. This result is applicable when the agent has the same number of strategies as the other agents but longer memory than the others. However, in addition to having longer memory than the others, if the agent also has greater number of strategies, the situation maybe change.

Inspired by the inefficient information described in Section 3.1, we propose an intelligent strategy for the privileged agent to maximise its own payoff. That is the privileged agent with larger memory size M' than the other agents and free to choose any strategy at each time step. In the present model, we consider a population of N agents in which there is a privileged agent using the intelligent strategy. The other agents have the same memory size M ($M' > M$) and are only assigned S strategies drawn randomly from all the 2^{2^M} possible strategies. For all agents, they choose the highest-score strategies to make the decisions. For tie strategies, the agents make a random choice. After each time step, the winning outcome is announced to the public. Each agent's payoff is increased by one if it makes the accurate decision. All the strategies' score are also updated. If the prediction at the specific history in one strategy is the same as the winning outcome, then the strategy is rewarded one point.

3.3   Experiment Results

In Figure 3 and Figure 4, we plot the payoff of the privileged agent using the intelligent strategy versus the average payoff of the other agents as a function of different memory sizes M. The experiment setting is as follows: the number of total agents is $N = 101$ for Figure 3 and $N = 1001$ for Figure 4, the number of strategies each traditional agent owns is $S = 2$, the range of the memory size M is the integer value between 1 and 15. The memory M' of the privileged agent ranges among $M + 1$, $M + 2$, $M + 3$, $M + 4$, $M + 5$, $M + 7$ and $M + 10$ independently. Note that the memory the privileged agent has is longer than the other agents' memory. All agents are using the highest-score strategy in hands. For each value of M, each data point is the average of 10 independent runs with different initial random distributions of strategies and each runs 10^6 rounds. The purpose for doing so is to cover as many situations as possible because the initial strategies are randomly generated.

From Figure 3 and Figure 4, we can see that the privileged agent with longer memory performs significantly better than the average of the other agents for almost all values of M, no matter whether it is in the symmetric phase ($\rho < \rho_c$) or asymmetric phase ($\rho > \rho_c$). That means the privileged agent can outperform others for almost all values of ρ ($\rho = 2^M/N$). The phase transition occurs at $M_c = 5$ and $M_c = 8$ respectively. Qualitatively, the maximal utility of the privileged agent comes from a successful escape in fully adapting to the history information created by the other agents, and hence it does not become part of

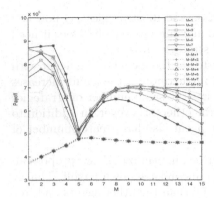 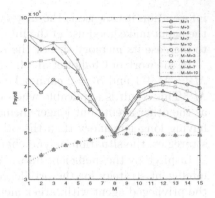

Fig. 3. The privileged agent's payoff with M' and $S' = 2^{2^{M'}}$ versus the average payoff of the other agents with M and $S = 2$ as a function of M. ($N = 101$).

Fig. 4. The privileged agent's payoff with M' and $S' = 2^{2^{M'}}$ versus the average payoff of the other agents with M and $S = 2$ as a function of M. ($N = 1001$).

the crowd. Furthermore, the interesting result is that in the symmetric phase, the agent with longer memory obtains more payoff. As described in Section 3.1, the inefficient information ε is larger for the privileged agent with longer memory. According to Equation (3), the privileged agent's winning probability P_{win} is larger, so it is able to obtain larger payoff. However, in the asymmetric phase, the privileged agent with smaller memory size performs better than the one with larger memory size. In this phase, the memory size M is larger, so the strategy space 2^{2^M} is larger, thus the other agents do not behave similarly. So there is no 'crowd effect' in this phase. The privileged agent cannot make use of any further information by increasing memory size.

Therefore, we can conclude that the privileged agent using the intelligent strategy can maximise its personal utility with larger memory size M' in the symmetric phase and smaller memory size M'' in the asymmetric phase. Both M' and M'' are larger than the others agents'.

4 Discussions and Analysis

4.1 Impact of M and S

In this section, we discuss the impact of M and S on the privileged agent's payoff. In Figure 5, we plot the payoff of two kinds of privileged agents with $M' = M + 1$ versus the average payoff of the other agents with M and $S = 2$ for $N = 101$: the first privileged agent with all the $2^{2^{M'}}$ possible strategies, and the second privileged agent with $S' = 2$. We can see that the first privileged agent always outperforms the second privileged one. The only difference between the two privileged agents is the difference between the number of strategies they

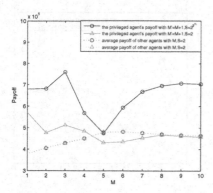

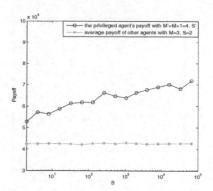

Fig. 5. The privileged agent's payoff with $M' = M+1$ and $S' = 2^{2^{M'}}$ and another one with $M' = M + 1$ and $S' = 2$ versus the average payoff of the other agents with M and $S = 2$ as a function of M. ($N = 101$).

Fig. 6. The privileged agent's payoff $M' = M + 1 = 4$ and S' versus the average payoff of the other agents with $M = 3$, and $S = 2$ as a function of S'. ($N = 101$, S' ranges from 2 to 2^{2^4} and samples 16 values by multiplying 2 every time).

have. So it is the difference of the number of strategies that has caused the first privileged agent to be able to achieve higher payoff. Therefore, we need to do further investigation of the impact of S on the privileged agent's payoff. In Figure 6, we plot the privileged agent's payoff with $M' = M + 1$ and S' versus the average payoff of the other agents with $M = 3$ and $S = 2$ as a function of S' for $N = 101$. We can see that the larger the number of strategies the privileged agent has, the more payoff it obtains. The reason is that if an agent has more strategies, it has more opportunity to explore in the strategy-space and thus predict more accurately. We can also observe that the privileged agent's payoff may decrease as the number of strategies increases. The reason is that the agent behaves based on its strategies, so its payoff is strongly related to the initial distribution of the strategies. If the initially assigned strategies do not predict well, the agent will not perform well. However, this does not affect the principal changing trend: the larger the number of strategies the privileged agent has, the more payoff it obtains.

Next we investigate how the length of memory the privileged agent owns affects its performance. In Figure 7, we plot the privileged agent's payoff with all the $2^{2^{M'}}$ possible strategies and M' ranging among $M + 1$, M, $M - 1$, $M - 2$, and $M - 3$ independently versus the average payoff of the other agents with M and $S = 2$ as a function of M for $N = 101$. For each value of M, the data point is the average of 10 independent runs with different initial random distributions of strategies and each runs 10^6 rounds. From this figure, we can get three results in the symmetric phase. The first one is that the privileged agent with $M' = M$ performs the worst and even achieves less payoff than the average payoff of the other agents. The reason is that the privileged agent has a memory of the same length as the other agents but owns all the possible strategies. That means the

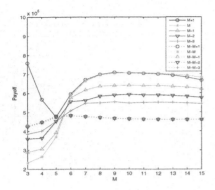
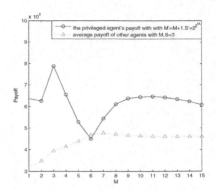

Fig. 7. The privileged agent's payoff with M' and $S' = 2^{2^{M'}}$ versus the average payoff of the other agents with M and $S = 2$ as a function of M. $(N = 101)$.

Fig. 8. The privileged agent's payoff with $M' = M+1$ and $S' = 2^{2^{M'}}$ versus the average payoff of the other agents with M and $S = 3$ as a function of M. $(N = 101)$.

privileged agent will always follow the crowd and become a loser most of the time. The second result is that the payoff of the privileged agent with shorter length of memory than the other agents is smaller than the average payoff. The reason is similar to that of the first one. The third result is that the privileged agent with shorter length of memory than the other agents, such as $M' = M-1$, behaves better than the privileged one with $M' = M$. The reason is that the privileged agent with $M' < M$ does not fully adapt to the history information created by the other agents. So it is able to not be in the crowd sometimes. Thus its payoff is a little larger than the one with $M' = M$. In the asymmetric phase, there is no 'crowd effect'. The agent with $M' < M$ gets less history information about the game than the agent with $M' \geq M$. This is not good for predictions, so it gets less payoff.

Lastly, we investigate the effects that the parameters M and S have on the dynamic phase transition point M_c of such a system with a population with a memory M and one privileged agent with longer memory M' and all its possible strategies. From Figure 3 and Figure 4, we can see that the privileged agent's payoff drops as M increases and reaches a minimum around $M_c = 5$ for $N = 101$ and $M_c = 8$ for $N = 1001$. Then it increases with M again for $M > M_c$. This implies that when N increases, M_c increases. To test whether the dependence of payoff of the privileged agent on M is intrinsic, we carried out simulations for a system with $N = 101$ plotted in Figure 8, in which one privileged agent has $M' = M + 1$ and $S' = 2^{2^{M'}}$ while others have M and $S = 3$. The phase transition for $N = 101, S = 3$ occurs when $M_c = 6$. The result suggests that when S increases, M_c increases. From these two pairs of comparisons, we can conclude that the relationship between M_c and N or S is when N increases or S increases, it leads to increasing M_c.

4.2   Comparisons with Related Work

In this section, we discuss some simulation results using different approaches which all enhance individual agents' utility. These agents all escape from the 'crowd effect'. The model proposed by Yip et al. [19] is a passive way to avoid the overadaptation to the history produced by the collective behavior of the other agents. It assumes that the particular agent decides to whether to participate in the game with a probability q and assesses the performance of its strategies only in the turns that it participates. So, the particular agent's payoff is at most half of the total turns when $q = 0.5$, so the success rate for $q = 0.5$ is at most 0.5. In addition, Yip et al. [19] also show that the enhanced success rate for $q \neq 1$ takes on similar values, so the success rate is at most 0.5 even if q is close to 1. Thus, the payoff is at most half of the number of the total turns for any q. The achievable payoff is not large enough.

In Figure 9, we compare the payoff of the privileged agent using the intelligent strategy with the payoff of another agent using the adaptive behavioral strategy proposed by Lam and Leung [11]. The experiment setting is as follows: the number of total agents is $N = 101$, the number of strategies each of the other agent owns is $S = 2$, the range of the memory size M is the integer values between 1 and 15. The memory M' of the agent using the intelligent strategy is $M + 1$. The agent's initial attitude towards side 0 and 1 and adaptive parameters using the adaptive behavioral strategy are randomly generated at the beginning of the game. The other agents are using the highest-score strategy in hands. For each value of M, the data point is the average of 10 independent runs with different initial random distributions of strategies and each runs 10^6 rounds. This figure illustrates that the privileged agent using the intelligent strategy achieves larger payoff than the agent using the adaptive behavioral strategy for all most values of M. The reason why the agent using the adaptive behavioral strategy does not obtain large enough payoff is as described in Section 2. There is only one agent using the adaptive behavioral strategy in the experiment, so its decision affect little on the winning outcome. So the agent will update its attitudes in the wrong way.

In Figure 10, we compare the payoff of the privileged agent using the intelligent strategy with the payoff of another agent using Liu and Liaw's [14] 'opposite strategy'. The experiment setting is the same as the previous one. The memory M' of the agent using the intelligent strategy is $M + 10$ when $M \leq 5$ and $M + 1$ when $M > 5$. We can see from Figure 3, the agent with $M + 10$ performs better in the symmetric phase and the agent with $M + 1$ performs better in the asymmetric phase. For the agent using the 'opposite strategy', it uses the highest-score strategy when $M > 5$ and uses the opposite strategy when $M \leq 5$. The opposite strategy is the one with the prediction opposite from that of the highest-score strategy at any entry. From this figure, we can see that the agent using the intelligent strategy obtains more payoff than the one using the 'opposite strategy' in the symmetric phase. In the asymmetric phase, the payoff of the agent using the intelligent strategy and the payoff of the agent using the 'opposite strategy' are more or less the same. In fact, as described in Section 1, the winning outcome

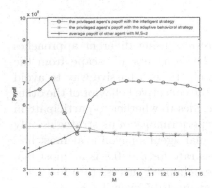

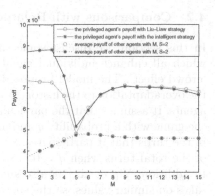

Fig. 9. The privileged agent's payoff with $M' = M + 1$ and $S' = 2^{2^{M'}}$ and the adaptive behavioral agent's payoff versus the average payoff of the other agents with M and $S = 2$ as a function of M. ($N = 101$).

Fig. 10. The privileged agent's payoff with the intelligent strategy and the one with the opposite strategy versus the average payoff of the other agents with M and $S = 2$ as a function of M. ($N = 101$).

of an even occurrence of any history is most likely opposite to that of the odd occurrence of this history [20][13] in the symmetric phase. Since the agent using the 'opposite strategy' use the prediction opposite from that of the highest-score strategy, so it can almost wins for the even occurrence of any history. For the odd occurrence of any history, it has a probability of 0.5 to win. So its winning probability on average will be approximately equal to 0.75. On the other hand, in Section 3.1, statistical results reveal that the inefficient information contained in $M + 2$ is $\varepsilon > 0.25$. Since longer memory can lead to larger inefficient information ε, so the inefficient information ε contained in $M + 10$ is greater than 0.25. Then according to the relationship $P_{win} \simeq \frac{1}{2} + \varepsilon$, the winning probability will be greater than 0.75. Therefore, the agent using the intelligent strategy can obtain more payoff than the agent using the 'opposite strategy'.

From these comparisons, we can conclude that the privileged agent using the intelligent strategy is able to make more accurate decisions with larger memory size in the symmetric phase. However, if the agent does not know when the phase transition will occur, it can just lengthen its memory size by one, i.e. keep longer memory than the other agents' by one, no matter in the symmetric phase or the asymmetric phase. It is because the agent with $M + 1$ performs well for all most values of M. If the agent knows where the phase transition occurs, it can lengthen its memory size more than one in the symmetric phase.

4.3 Equivalence to the Experience Method

Obviously, if an agent owns all 2^{2^M} strategies, the number of strategies will be too large for the agent to handle even when M is moderate. In this section, we present a simple Experience method, and show that agents employing Experience method have the same behavior as agents employing the traditional method with all 2^{2^M} strategies.

The Experience method is as follows. Instead of using any of the 2^{2^M} strategies, an agent simply records, for each immediate past history of length M, the number of times side 0 has won and the number of times side 1 has won. The number of times side 0 or 1 has won is said to be the score of the respective side. To make a decision given an immediate past history of length M, an agent chooses the side with the highest score, and makes random choice at ties.

Let $E_x^i(h)$ denote the score of side x (0 or 1) at time step i for an immediate past history h of length M. Formally, the experience method can be expressed as follows:

$$E_x^i(h) = \begin{cases} 0 & i = 0 \\ E_x^{i-1}(h) & i > 0 \text{ and side } x \text{ loses at time step i} \\ E_x^{i-1}(h) + 1 & i > 0 \text{ and side } x \text{ wins at time step i} \end{cases} \tag{4}$$

At time step i, if the immediate past history is h, an agent chooses side 0 if $E_0^i(h) > E_1^i(h)$, or side 1 if $E_0^i(h) < E_1^i(h)$, or a random choice between 0 and 1 if $E_0^i(h) = E_1^i(h)$. This Experience strategy is intuitively simple and easy to implement. However, the following theorem proves that agents employing such an Experience method are behaviorally equivalent to agents employing the traditional method with all strategies.

Theorem: *The behavior of an agent using the Experience method is equivalent to the behavior of an agent using the traditional method with all possible strategies.*

Proof: Consider an agent using the traditional method, which has all 2^{2^M} strategies. For any strategy P, let $P(h)$ denote the prediction made by strategy P with history h. Choose any two strategies P_1 and P_2. Suppose at time step i with history h, P_1 has the highest score S_1^i and P_2 has the score S_2^i ($S_1^i \geq S_2^i$). Then we have $E_{P_1(h)}^i(h) \geq E_{P_2(h)}^i(h)$ for the following reason. Suppose $E_{P_1(h)}^i(h) < E_{P_2(h)}^i(h)$. As the agent has all possible strategies, there must exist a strategy P_3 with the same prediction in P_2 at the history h ($P_3(h) = P_2(h)$) and with the same predictions in P_1 at all the other histories ($P_3(h') = P_1(h')$ iff $h' \neq h$). So P_3's score $S_3^i = S_1^i - E_{P_1(h)}^i(h) + E_{P_2(h)}^i(h)$. Then $S_3^i > S_1^i$, which contradicts to the fact that S_1^i is the highest score. Therefore, we have $E_{P_1(h)}^i(h) \geq E_{P_2(h)}^i(h)$. In other words, P_1 scores weakly better than any other strategy P_2 for each h.

If both P_1 and P_2 are highest-score strategies at time step i ($S_1^i = S_2^i$), then we have $E_{P_1(h)}^i(h) \geq E_{P_2(h)}^i(h)$ and $E_{P_1(h)}^i(h) \leq E_{P_2(h)}^i(h)$, hence $E_{P_1(h)}^i(h) = E_{P_2(h)}^i(h)$.

In summary, $S_1^i \geq S_2^i$ if and only if $E_{P_1(h)}^i(h) \geq E_{P_2(h)}^i(h)$, and vice versa. Therefore, the agent that uses the Experience method and chooses the side with the highest score at each history is actually using the traditional method with all possible strategies. So their behaviors are equivalent. □

5 Conclusions and Future Work

In this paper, we study the performance of one privileged agent with larger memory size M' and free to choose any possible strategy in a population with a memory M and $S = 2$. We find some significant results. The present results demonstrate that the privileged agent outperforms the other agents for almost all values of M. Moreover, another feature of the results is that in the symmetric phase, the privileged agent with larger memory size can obtain more payoff than the one with smaller memory size but still larger than the others'.

In addition, we compare the payoff the privileged agent using the intelligent strategy with the payoff of another agent using the adaptive behavioral strategy proposed by Lam and Leung[11]. The result shows that the privileged agent can outperform the agent using the adaptive behavioral strategy for all most values of M. We also compare the payoff of the agent using the intelligent strategy with the payoff of another agent using the 'opposite strategy' proposed by Liu and Liaw [14]. The result also shows that the intelligent agent can outperform the agent using the 'opposite strategy' in the symmetric phase. Therefore, the privileged agent using the intelligent strategy we propose outperforms the other agents in the same model and other models proposed in previous work in terms of individual payoff.

We also investigate how the number of strategies and the length of memory affect the privileged agent's performance. We have two conclusions. First, the larger the number of strategies the privileged agent with larger memory size has, the more payoff it obtains. Second, in the symmetric phase, the privileged agent with all strategies and memory size smaller than or equal to the other agents' memory size gets less payoff than the average payoff of the other agents. In the asymmetric phase, the privileged agent with all strategies and memory size smaller than the other agents' memory size gets less payoff than the privileged agent with all strategies and memory size larger than or equal to the other agents'. Finally, we present a simple Experience method for agents with all possible strategies, and prove that agents employing Experience method have the same behavior as agents employing the traditional method with all strategies.

There are some aspects for future work. First, if we allow additional communication between agents or the strategies the agents own is evolutionary [1][10], how will agents make good use of the property to make more accurate decisions? Second, we are interested in applying the intelligent strategy to the resource allocation problem modeled as the extended minority game. There may be not only one resource. The resource capacity may vary over time. Agents may need bundles of resources. So agents do not make a binary decision, but need to predict the resource load to decide which resource to choose. We can also extend the model to more complicated multi-agent systems in real-world environment, such as applications in sensor network [15] and grid computing [17].

Acknowledgments. The work described in this paper was supported by a grant from the Research Grants Council of the Hong Kong Special Administrative Region, China (Project No. 413306).

References

1. Araujo, R.M., Lamb, L.C.: Towards understanding the role of learning models in the dynamics of the minority game. In: Proceedings of the 16th IEEE International Conference on Tools with Artificial Intelligence, pp. 727–731 (2004)
2. Arthur, B.W.: Inductive reasoning and bounded rationality. The American Economic Review 84(2), 406–411 (1994)
3. Challet, D., Marsili, M.: Phase transition and symmetry breaking in the minority game. Physical Review E 60(6), 6271(4) (1999)
4. Challet, D., Marsili, M., Zhang, Y.C.: Modeling market mechanism with minority game. Physica A 276, 284–315 (2000)
5. Challet, D., Marsili, M., Zhang, Y.C.: Minority Games. Oxford University Press, Oxford (2005)
6. Challet, D., Zhang, Y.C.: Emergence of cooperation and organization in an evolutionary game. Physica A 246, 407–418 (1997)
7. D'hulst, R., Rodgers, G.J.: Strategy selection in the minority game. Physica A 278, 579–587 (2000)
8. Galstyan, A., Kolar, S., Lerman, K.: Resource allocation games with changing resource capacities. In: AAMAS 2003: Proceedings of the second international joint conference on Autonomous agents and multiagent systems, pp. 145–152 (2003)
9. Johnson, N.F., Hui, P.M., Zheng, D., Hart, M.: Enhanced winnings in a mixed-ability population playing a minority game. Physica A, 427–431 (1999)
10. Kimura, H., Akiyama, E.: Grand canonical minority games with variable strategy spaces. In: Proceeding of the 19th Workshops of the Japanese Society for Artificial Intelligence, pp. 291–301 (2005)
11. Lam, K.M., Leung, H.F.: An adaptive strategy for minority games. In: AAMAS 2007: Proceedings of the sixth international joint conference on Autonomous agents and multiagent systems, pp. 1176–1178 (2007)
12. Lam, K.M., Leung, H.F.: An adaptive strategy for resource allocation modeled as minority game. In: SASO 2007: Proceedings of the First IEEE International Conference on Self-Adaptive and Self-Organizing Systems, pp. 193–204 (2007)
13. Liaw, S.S., Liu, C.: The quasi-periodic time sequence of the population in minority game. Physica A 351, 571–579 (2005)
14. Liu, C., Liaw, S.S.: Maximize personal gain in the minority game. Physica A 360, 516–524 (2006)
15. Mainland, G., Parkes, D.C., Welsh, M.: Decentralized, adaptive resource allocation for sensor networks. In: NSDI 2005: Proceedings of the 2nd conference on Symposium on Networked Systems Design and Implementation, p. 23 (2005)
16. Manuca, R., Li, Y., Riolo, R., Savit, R.: The structure of adaptive competition in minority games. Physica A 282, 559–608 (2000)
17. Manvi, S.S., Birje, M.N., Prasad, B.: An agent-based resource allocation model for computational grids. Multiagent and Grid System 1(1), 17–27 (2005)
18. Savit, R., Manuca, R., Riolo, R.: Adaptive competition, market efficiency, and phase transitions. Physical Review Letters 82, 2203–2206 (1999)
19. Yip, K.F., Lo, T.S., Hui, P.M., Johnson, N.F.: Enhanced winning in a competing population by random participation. Physical Review E 69(4), 46120(7) (2004)
20. Zheng, D.F., Wang, B.H.: Statistical properties of the attendance time series in the minority game. Physica A 301, 560–566 (2001)

Simulation-Based Optimization Approach for Software Cost Model with Rejuvenation

Hiroyuki Eto[1], Tadashi Dohi[1], and Jianhua Ma[2]

[1] Department of Information Engineering, Graduate School of Engineering
Hiroshima University, 1-4-1 Kagamiyama, Higashi-Hiroshima, 739-8527 Japan
[2] Graduate School of Computer and Information Sciences, Hosei University
3-7-2 Kajino-cho, Koganei, Tokyo, 184-8584 Japan

Abstract. Software rejuvenation is a preventive and proactive maintenance solution that is particularly useful for counteracting the phenomenon of software aging. In this paper we consider an operational software system with multiple degradations and derive the optimal software rejuvenation policy minimizing the expected operation cost per unit time in the steady state, via the dynamic programing approach. Especially, we develop a reinforcement learning algorithm to estimate the optimal rejuvenation schedule adaptively and examine its asymptotic properties through a simulation experiment.

Keywords: Software aging, software rejuvenation, semi-Markov decision process, Q-learning, adaptation, non-parametric statistics, simulation-based optimization.

1   Introduction

When software application is executed continuously for long periods of time, some of the faults cause it to age due to error conditions that accrue with time and/or load. *Software aging* will affect the performance of the application and eventually cause it to fail [2, 7, 9]. Software aging has also been observed in widely-used communication software like Internet Explorer, Netscape and xrn as well as commercial operating system and middleware [9]. A complementary approach to handle software aging and its related transient software failures, called *software rejuvenation*, has been becoming popular [14]. Software rejuvenation is a preventive and proactive solution that is particularly useful for counteracting the phenomenon of software aging. It involves stopping the running software occasionally, cleaning its internal state and restarting it. Cleaning the internal state of a software might involve garbage collection, flushing operating system kernel tables, reinitializing internal data structures, or hardware reboot.

Huang *et al.* [14] considered a degradation phenomenon as a two-step stochastic process in order to represent the uncertain behavior of a telecommunication billing application. From the clean state the software system jumps into a degraded state from which two actions are possible: rejuvenation with return to the clean state or transition to the complete system failure state. They modeled a four-state process as a continuous-time Markov chain (CTMC), and derived the steady-state system availability and the expected operation cost per unit time in

C. Rong et al. (Eds.): ATC 2008, LNCS 5060, pp. 206–218, 2008.

the steady state. Avritzer and Weyuker [3] discussed the aging in a telecommunication switching software where the effect manifests as gradual performance degradation. Garg et al. [11] introduced an idea of periodic rejuvenation (deterministic interval between successive rejuvenations) into the Huang et al.'s model [14] and represented the stochastic behavior by using a Markov regenerative stochastic Petri net. Dohi et al. [8] and Suzuki et al. [19] extended the seminal two-step software degradation models in Huang et al. [14] and Garg et al. [11], respectively, by using semi-Markov processes (SMPs).

As another example, it may be interesting to consider both effects of aging as crash/hang failure, referred to as *hard failure*, and of aging as *soft failure* that can lead to performance degradation. Pfening et al. [17] modeled a performance degradation process by the gradual decrease of the processing rate in a non-stationary Markovian queueing system, and formulated a determination problem of the cost-optimal software rejuvenation schedule by a Markov decision process. Garg et al. [12] analyzed a transaction-based software system, which involves arrival and queueing of jobs, and examined both effects of aging; hard failures that result in an unavailability and soft failures that result in performance degradation. Recently, Eto and Dohi [10] considered the similar but somewhat different multistage degradation models from Pfening et al. [17] via a semi-Markov decision process, by taking account of the presence of system failure. They proved that the control-limit type of software rejuvenation policy should be optimal among all the Markovian stationary policies in a simple multistage degradation model. Bobbio et al. [5] introduced a cumulative process to describe the temporal damage resulted by software aging.

In this paper we consider the same software cost model as Eto and Dohi [10], but focus on a statistical estimation problem. As discussed in Dohi et al. [8] and Suzuki et al. [19], a non-parametric estimation scheme is quite useful to rejuvenate the operational software, because it enables us to trigger the software rejuvenation at the asymptotically optimal timing without specifying the system failure time distribution. Since the approach taken in the references [8, 19] is based on the fixed complete sample that relies on observing system failure times without truncations and its empirical distribution, it would be quite difficult to acquire the complete sample data in an operational phase of software system, and to apply the same technique to an adaptive situation. In other words, for software systems which are long-lived and costly, the luxury of obtaining a sample of complete lifetimes before a rejuvenation policy is implemented may not be available in many cases. Hence, an adaptive non-parametric estimation scheme should be definitely developed to trigger the software rejuvenation in an on-line way. In this paper, a reinforcement learning algorithm, called Q-learning, is used for developing an on-line adaptive algorithm (see [18]). In this estimation framework, it is guaranteed that the optimal software rejuvenation schedule can be estimated adaptively without the complete knowledge on system failure (degradation) time distribution in the operational phase, even if the underlying state transition of software is governed by CTMCs or SMPs. The most attractive point is that the resulting estimator can converge to the real (but unknown) optimal solution almost surely. In that sense, our method can provide an asymptotically optimal software rejuvenation schedule with the incomplete knowledge on the system failure (degradation) time distribution.

The rest part of the paper is organized as follows. In Section 2, we describe the multistage degradation software system by means of CTMC and define the notation and underlying assumptions. The formulation is still valid for an SMP model, where each state transition obeys a non-exponential probability distribution. Section 3 is related to the semi-Markov decision process under the expected operation cost per unit time in the steady state. We formulate the Bellman equation and give the corresponding value iteration algorithm to compute the optimal software rejuvenation timing which minimizes the expected operation cost per unit time. In Section 4, we introduce the Q-learning algorithm as a typical example of reinforcement learning algorithms, and develop a simulation-based adaptive algorithm to trigger the rejuvenation. Since this can guarantee a statistically consistent property, the resulting solution converges to the real optimal solution even if the system failure time distribution is unknown. Section 5 is devoted to given an illustrative example, where we examine the convergence property of the Q-learning algorithm proposed in this paper. Finally, the paper is concluded with some remarks in Section 6.

2   Multistage Degradation Software System

Consider a single use software system which deteriorates with time. State of the software system deteriorates stochastically and changes from i to j $(i, j = 0, 1, \cdots, s + 1, i < j)$, where state 0 and state $s + 1$ are the normal (robust) state and the system down state, respectively. Suppose that the state of software at time t, $\{N(t), t \geq 0\}$, is described by a right-skip free CTMC with state space $I = \{0, 1, \cdots, s + 1\}$ and that the transition rate from i to j is given by $\gamma_{i,j}$ (> 0), where $\sum_{j=i+1}^{s+1} \gamma_{i,j} = \Gamma_i$ for all i $(= 0, 1, \cdots, s)$ (see Fig. 1). When the system failure occurs, then the system is down $(j = s + 1)$ and the recovery operation immediately starts, where the time to complete the recovery operation is an independent and identically distributed (i.i.d.) random variable having the cumulative distribution function (c.d.f.) $H_{s+1}(x)$ and mean $1/\omega_{s+1}(> 0)$.

On the other hand, one makes a decision whether to trigger the software rejuvenation at the time instant when the state of software system changes from i to j $(= i + 1, i + 2, \cdots, s)$. If one decides to continue operation, the state is monitored until the next change of state, otherwise, the software rejuvenation is preventively triggered, where the time to complete the rejuvenation is also an i.i.d. random variable with the c.d.f. $H_i(x)$ and mean $1/\omega_i$ (> 0), depending on the state i $(= 0, 1, \cdots, s)$. Let x_1 (> 0) and x_2 (> 0) be the rejuvenation cost per unit time and the recovery cost per unit time, respectively. In both periods of rejuvenation and recovery operation, the system operation is stopped. Also, it is assumed that the state-dependent cost a_i is incurred per unit operation time for $i = 0, 1, \cdots, s$.

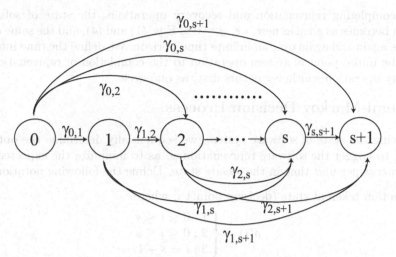

Fig. 1. Semi-Markovian transition diagram of software degradetion level

Note that the system state can be described by only the index j $(0 < j \leq s+1)$. At each time instant when the state changes from i to j, one has an option to choose Action 1 (rejuvenation) or Action 2 (continuation of processing). When the system failure occurs, *i.e.*, the state of system becomes $j = s+1$, the recovery operation (Action 3) is taken. Let $q^{(\delta)}(i,j)$ denote the probability that the state changes from i to j under Action δ $(= 1, 2, 3)$. Then it can be seen that

(i) Case 1 (rejuvenation):

$$q^{(1)}(i,0) = \int_0^\infty dH_i(t) = 1, \quad i = 0, 1, \cdots, s, \tag{1}$$

where the mean rejuvenation time (overhead) is given by

$$h_i = \int_0^\infty t dH_i(t). \tag{2}$$

(ii) Case 2 (continuation of processing):

$$q^{(2)}(i,j) = \gamma_{i,j}/\Gamma_i, \quad i, j = 0, 1, \cdots, s+1, i < j. \tag{3}$$

(iii) Case 3 (recovery from system failure):

$$q^{(3)}(s+1,0) = \int_0^\infty dH_{s+1}(t) = 1, \tag{4}$$

where the mean recovery time (overhead) is given by

$$h_{s+1} = \int_0^\infty t dH_{s+1}(t). \tag{5}$$

After completing rejuvenation and recovery operations, the state of software system becomes as good as new, i.e., $j = 0$ in Eqs. (1) and (4), and the same cycle repeats again and again over an infinite time horizon. We define the time interval from the initial point of system operation to the completion of rejuvenation or recovery operation whichever occurs first, as one cycle.

3   Semi-Markov Decision Process

Observing the state of software system, we sequentially determine the optimal timing to trigger the software rejuvenation so as to minimize the expected operation cost per unit time in the steady state. Define the following notation:

$\delta(i)$: action taken at state (decision point) i, where

$$\delta(i) = \begin{cases} 1 : 0 \leq i \leq s \\ 2 : 0 \leq i \leq s \\ 3 : i = s+1. \end{cases} \tag{6}$$

$G(i, \delta(i))$: mean cost between two successive decision points, when action $\delta(i)$ is taken at state i, i.e.,

$$G(i, \delta(i)) = \begin{cases} x_1 h_i : & \delta(i) = 1 \\ 0 : & \delta(i) = 2 \\ x_2 h_{s+1} : & \delta(i) = 3. \end{cases} \tag{7}$$

$\pi_i(\delta(i))$: expected total time between two successive decision points, when action $\delta(i)$ is taken at state i, i.e.,

$$\pi_i(\delta(i)) = \begin{cases} h_i : & \delta(i) = 1 \\ 1/\Gamma_i : & \delta(i) = 2 \\ h_{s+1} : & \delta(i) = 3. \end{cases} \tag{8}$$

$U(i)$: action space at state i, i.e., $\delta(i) \in U(i)$.
$v(i)$: relative value function in the semi-Markov decision process at state $i \in I$.
$\mathbf{z}_\infty$: expected operation cost per unit time in the steady state, where $\mathbf{z}_\infty^*$ denotes the minimum one.

From the preliminary above, the Bellman equation based on the principle of optimality, is given by

$$v(i) = \min_{\delta \in U(i)} \left[G(i, \delta) - \mathbf{z}_\infty \pi_i(\delta) + \sum_{j=0}^{s+1} q_{i,j}(\delta) v(j) \right]. \tag{9}$$

It is well known that the software rejuvenation policy satisfying Eq. (9) is always optimal among all the Markovian stationary policies [20]. To solve the above functional equation numerically, we can easily develop the well-known value iteration algorithm for the semi-Markov decision process. Define:

$w(i, \delta(i))$: relative value function when action $\delta(i)$ is taken at state i,
$A(n): = \min_{i \in I} \{v^n(i) - v^{n-1}(i)\}$,
$B(n): = \max_{i \in I} \{v^n(i) - v^{n-1}(i)\}$,

ϵ: tolerance level for iterative calculations,

τ: design parameter in the value iteration algorithm which satisfies $0 \le \tau/h_r$, $0 \le \tau\Gamma_i \le 1$ and $0 \le \tau/h_f \le 1$ for all i (see [20]),

where $w^n(i, \delta(i))$ and $v^n(i)$ denote the n-th iteration of the relative value function and its minimum one, respectively. Then the value iteration algorithm for the Bellman equation in Eq. (9) is given in the following:

Value Iteration Algorithm:

Step 1: $n := 0$, $v^0(i) := 0$.
Step 2:

$$w^{n+1}(i, 2) := a_i + \sum_{j=0}^{s+1} \frac{\tau\gamma_{i,j}v^n(j)}{\Gamma_i} + \left(1 - \sum_{j=0}^{s+1} \frac{\tau\gamma_{i,j}}{\Gamma_i}\right)v^n(i),$$

$$w^{n+1}(i, 1) := x_1 + \left(\frac{\tau}{h_i}\right)v^n(0) + \left(1 - \frac{\tau}{h_i}\right)v^n(i),$$

$$v^{n+1}(i) := \min\{w^{n+1}(i, 1), w^{n+1}(i, 2)\},$$

$$v^{n+1}(s+1) := x_2 + \left(\frac{\tau}{h_{s+1}}\right)v^n(0) + \left(1 - \frac{\tau}{h_{s+1}}\right)v^n(s+1),$$

Step 3: If $0 \le B(n) - A(n) \le \epsilon A(n)$, then stop the procedure, otherwise, $n := n + 1$ and go to **Step 1**.

Although we describe the multistage degradation phenomenon of an operational software system by a CTMC, it can be easily extended to an SMP with non-exponential transition rates. Eto and Dohi [10] proved in the somewhat different modeling framework that the control-limit type of software rejuvenation policy is always optimal under mild conditions. Also, they gave an explicit form of the expected operation cost per unit time in the steady state, and provided a simple calculation method without using the value iteration algorithm. However, it is worth mentioning that the analytical approach and/or the value iteration algorithm are effective only for the case where the system failure time distribution is completely known. In addition, when the transition rates are unknown in the CTMC case or the transition probability distributions are unknown in the SMP case, one must spend much time and effort to the statistical estimation and test, in order to validate any parametric model. In the following section, we develop a simulation-based adaptive optimization approach to estimate the optimal software rejuvenation schedule.

4 Reinforcement Learning Algorithm

The reinforcement learning is a simulation-based optimization algorithm, where the optimal value function is approximated with the sample or simulation of observations. In general, the reinforcement learning scheme consists of (i) an environment, (ii) a learning agent with its knowledge base, (iii) a set of different actions taken by the agent and (iv) responses from the environment to different

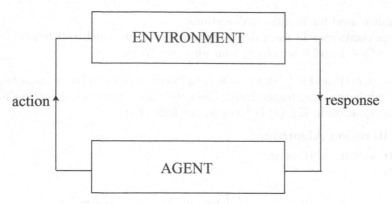

Fig. 2. Configuration of reinforcement learning algorithm

actions in different states (see Fig. 2). That is, the agent learns an interaction from the environment itself. Also, the agent receives the information called reward from the environment, and learns the parameters which govern the environment. In this paper we focus on the representative reinforcement learning, called Q-learning [18], which consists of the following three factors:

Observation of state: Observe the current state,
Selection of actions: Select the best action from possible ones at the current state, where the best action is taken based on an estimate of reward (Q-value),
Learning from environment: Update Q-value with both the current Q-value and the reward earned by the selected action.

The Q-learning has been discussed more specifically within the framework of Markov and/or semi-Markov decision processes. Abounadi *et al.* [1] improved the classical Q-learning algorithm and showed that it can converge to the optimal relative value function in the dynamic programing equation almost surely. Borkar and Meyn [6] and Konda and Bokar [15] proved some convergence properties on the Q-learning based algorithms with the ordinary differential equation (O.D.E.) method and the martingale convergence theorem, respectively. Mahadevan [16] paid his attention to the numerical calculation in the Q-learning. For the good survey on the Q-learning algorithms in Markov/semi-Markov decision processes, see Bertsekas and Tsitsiklis [4] and Gosavi [13].

Define the following notation:

$Q(i, \delta(i))$: estimate of future cumulative cost just after the action $\delta(i)$ is taken in state i,
$t(i, \delta(i), j)$: transition time to state j just after the action $\delta(i)$ is taken in state i,
$r(i, \delta(i), j)$: cost until the state transition to j occurs just after the action $\delta(i)$ is taken in state i,
$REWARD_\infty$: cumulative cost in the steady state, provided that an agent selects the action $\delta(i)$ with smaller Q-value, with probability $1/|U(i)|$,

$TIME_\infty$: cumulative operation time in the steady state, provided that an agent selects the action $\delta(i)$ with smaller Q-value, with probability $1/|U(i)|$,

$REWARD_t$: cumulative cost at each decision point,

$TIME_t$: cumulative operation time at each decision point,

ϕ: design parameter in the Q-learning algorithm,

k: number of iterations,

$\mathbf{z_t}$: transient (instantaneous) operation cost per unit time, *i.e.*,

$$\mathbf{z_t} = REWARD_t/TIME_t, \tag{10}$$

where $\lim_{t\to\infty} \mathbf{z_t} = \mathbf{z_\infty}$.

We derive the Q-factor version of the value iteration algorithm mentioned in Section 3. In the first phase of Q-learning algorithm (Step 1 ~ Step 5 below), the agent learns the Q-value as an estimate of future cumulative cost based on a probabilistic action, and adapts the environment through the update of Q-value. In the second phase (Step 6 ~ Step 9 below), the decision maker (DM) regards the first phase as a simulator, and selects the optimal action based on the updated Q-value by the agent. Although the DM's action at each decision point does not influence neither the agent nor the environment, he or she can behave optimally in the sense of minimization of the Q-value, and can estimate the updated Q-value, say, estimates of the cumulative cost and cumulative total operation time from the history. The estimates in this stage is transient, *i.e.*, they can function to check the convergence.

Q-Learning Algorithm:

Step 1: Agent observes the current state i of software system. Set $k = 0$, $\phi = 1$, $REWARD_\infty = 0$, $TIME_\infty = 0$, $REWARD_t = 0$ and $TIME_t = 0$.

Step 2: For a sufficient large iteration number k_z (*e.g.*, $k_z = 10,000$), if $k \leq k_z$ at each observation point with state i ($= 1, 2, \cdots, s$), then the agent uses a probabilistic strategy, *i.e.*, take an action $\delta(i)$; rejuvenation ($\delta(i) = 1$) or continuation of process ($\delta(i) = 2$) with probability $1/|U(i)|$. Further, if the action taken by the agent minimizes the Q-value, then $\phi = 0$, otherwise $\phi = 1$. On the other hand, if $k \geq k_z$, then the agent takes the optimal action which minimizes the Q-value and stop the procedure.

Step 3: After observing the transition from state i to j, the agent updates the Q-value with the probabilistic strategy δ according to the following formula:

$$Q(i,\delta) \longleftarrow (1-\alpha)Q(i,\delta) + \alpha\Big\{ r(i,\delta,j) - \mathbf{z_\infty} t(i,\delta,j) + \min_{\delta'\in U(j)} Q(j,\delta') \Big\},$$

where $\alpha \in (0,1]$ is the learning rate (free parameter).

Step 4: If $\phi = 0$, then update $REWARD_\infty$ and $TIME_\infty$ as shown below:

$$REWARD_\infty \leftarrow REWARD_\infty + r(i,\delta,j),$$
$$TIME_\infty \leftarrow TIME_\infty + t(i,\delta,j).$$

Step 5: Update the minimum operation cost per unit time in the steady state $\mathbf{z}_\infty$ by

$$\mathbf{z}_\infty \leftarrow REWARD_\infty / TIME_\infty.$$

Step 6: The DM selects the optimal action at state i, minimizing the Q-value updated by

$$\delta(i) = \mathrm{argmin}_{\delta(i)\acute{\in}U(i)} Q(i, \delta(i)).$$

Step 7: Update $REWARD_t$ and $TIME_t$ by

$$REWARD_t \leftarrow REWARD_t + r(i, \delta(i), j),$$
$$TIME_t \leftarrow TIME_t + t(i, \delta(i), j).$$

Step 8: Update $\mathbf{z_t}$ by

$$\mathbf{z_t} \leftarrow REWARD_t / TIME_t.$$

Step 9: Set $k = k + 1$ and $i \leftarrow j$, and go to **Step 2**.

In the actual implementation of the above algorithm, it should be noted that the action whether to trigger the software rejuvenation or not at each decision point is taken in Step 6. Then, an estimate of the expected operation cost per unit time in the steady state is equivalent to that estimated by the agent in Step 5 and is independent of the DM's action. On the other hand, when $\mathbf{z}_\infty \approx \mathbf{z_t}$ at the maximum iteration number k_z, then one can check that the Q-learning algorithm converges and as the result the minimum operation cost per unit time in the steady state can be achieved in the software operation with rejuvenation. In the following section, we give an illustrative example and investigate the convergence properties of the Q-learning algorithm.

5   An Illustrative Example

In this section, we consider the case where the state transition is governed by an SMP. For better understanding the situation, we do not use the notation of transition rate $\gamma_{i,j}(t)$, but, instead, the following one:

$exp(\lambda)$: exponential distribution with mean $1/\lambda$,
$Wei(\eta, m)$: Weibull distribution with scale parameter η and shape paramete m.

Figure 3 depicts the SMP with respective transition probabilities, where $x_1 = 8, x_2 = 15, a_0 = 1, a_1 = 3, a_2 = 5, a_3 = 7, \omega_0 = 0.20, \omega_1 = 0.15, \omega_2 = 0.12, \omega_3 = 0.10, \omega_4 = 0.02$. If one can know all the information on the SMP, it is quite easy to make the so-called *decision table* by solving numerically the value iteration algorithm (see [10]). In this case, the optimal control limit is given by $N^*(t) = 2$ and the corresponding operation cost per unit time in the steady state is $\mathbf{z}_\infty^* = 4.3223$, so that it is optimal to trigger the rejuvenation at the first passage time $\inf\{t \geq 0 : N(t) = 2\}$.

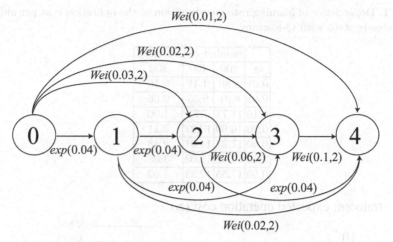

Fig. 3. An example with three degradation levels

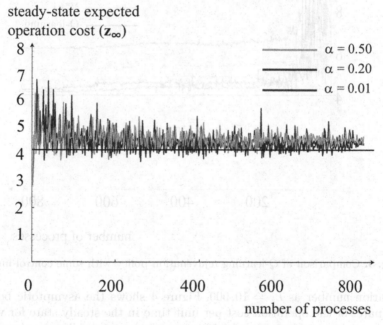

Fig. 4. Asymptotic behavior of operation cost per unit time in the steady state based on Q-learning for varying learning rate

Of our concern is the investigation of convergence properties of the Q-learning algorithm. We perform the Monte Carlo simulation with pseudo random numbers for the exponential and Weibull distributions with the same parameters in Fig.3, and observe realizations of state deterioration time and system failure time. At each decision (observation) point, we behave so as to minimize the Q-value and estimate both $\mathbf{z}_\infty$ and $\mathbf{z}_t$. Throughout this paper, we fix the upper limit

Table 1. Dependence of learning rate on estimation of the operation cost per unit time in the steady state with Q-learning

α	number of processes		
	200	400	800
0.01	6.86	4.41	0.56
0.05	8.91	6.45	0.66
0.10	11.77	7.71	1.00
0.20	16.90	10.27	2.11
0.30	17.33	11.01	2.48
0.40	17.39	11.03	3.08
0.50	17.55	12.32	4.02

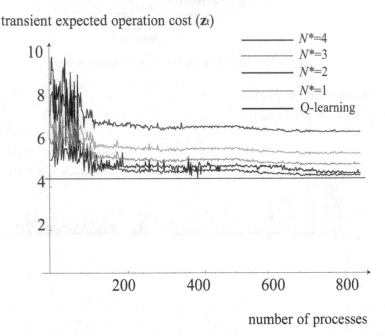

Fig. 5. Comparison of Q-learning rejuvenation policy with some control-limits

of iteration number as $k_z = 10,000$. Figure 4 shows the asymptotic behavior of estimates of the operation cost per unit time in the steady state for varying learning rate, $\alpha = 0.01$, $0,02$ and 0.50, where the horizontal line denotes the real optimal value, $z^*_\infty = 4.3223$. In the figure, we define the unit of a process by the time length of one cycle. From this result, it is seen that estimates of the expected operation cost per unit time in the steady state asymptotically converges to the real optimal value $z^*_\infty = 4.3223$ as the number of processes increases. Hence, the statistically consistent property could be checked numerically.

Note again that this can be achieved with the probabilistic action by the agent. If the learning rate is given by $\alpha = 0.10$ and $\alpha = 0.50$, when the number of processes is fixed as 200, the relative error with respect to z^*_∞ becomes 6.86% and 17.55%, respectively. In general, though the smaller error α leads to much more computation cost, it dose not always guarantee the smaller error. For instance, when the number of processes is 800 with $\alpha = 0.01$, the relative error is given by 0.56%. That is , the careful adjustment of the learning rate would be important to realize the effective estimation. In Table 1, we calculate the estimation errors (%) between estimate and the real optimal value. As the learning rate decreases, the estimation error decreases and afterward the Q-learning tends to underestimate the operation cost per unit time in the steady state.

Next, we examine the asymptotic behavior of the transient cost based on the DM's action. In this example, if the complete information on the system deterioration/failure time distributions is available, as mentioned before, one can know that the optimal threshold level is given by $N^*(t) = 2$. Then, our concern here is to examine the performance of the Q-learning characterized by choosing the minimum Q-value. That is, how close is the estimate of transient expected cost $\mathbf{z}(t)$ to the real optimal solution $\mathbf{z}^*_\infty$? In Fig.5, we carry out the Monte Carlo simulation and compare the Q-learning algorithm with the rejuvenation schedule with fixed threshold level $N(t) = 1, 2, 3, 4$, where $N(t) = 4$ implies no-rejuvenation policy. In this simulation experiment, it can be easily expected that the simulation result with $N^*(t) = 2$ approaches to $\mathbf{z}^*_\infty = 4.3223$. On the other hand, the rejuvenation schedule based on the Q-learning gives the fluctuated results in earlier phase, and latter converges to the real optimal as the number of processes increases. It is evident that the simulation-based optimization algorithm used here can never outperform the really optimal rejuvenation solution with $N^* = 2$ under the incomplete information. However, in the situation where no statistical information on the system deterioration/failure time distributions is available, this non-parametric estimation scheme would be effective.

6   Concluding Remarks

In this paper we have developed an adaptive estimation scheme to trigger the software rejuvenation for operational software systems. The resulting algorithm has several theoretical advantages; non-parametric method without specifying the system failure/degradation mechanism and statistical consistency. As mentioned in Section 1, these seem to be essentially important to construct adaptive preventive maintenance framework for software systems which are long-lived and costly, because the luxury of obtaining the complete sample of system failure times before a rejuvenation policy is implemented may not be available in practice. The algorithm proposed in this paper has been based on a reinforcement learning and been classified into a simulation-based optimization approach.

However, as we have shown the asymptotic behavior of the value function in a numerical example, the convergence speed is never satisfactory, so that we need a number of process executions to achieve the nearly optimal solution. For instance, in our example, over 200 process executions will be needed to get the good performance. This is, of course, a weak point for the reinforcement learning approach under the incomplete knowledge on system failure/degradation mechanism. In the future, the non-parametric adaptive algorithm provided in this paper should be improved in terms of the convergence speed.

References

1. Abounadi, J., Bertsekas, D., Borkar, V.S.: Learning algorithms for Markov decision processes with average cost. SIAM J. Control and Optimization 40, 681–698 (2001)
2. Adams, E.: Optimizing preventive service of the software products. IBM J. Research & Development 28, 2–14 (1984)
3. Avritzer, A., Weyuker, E.J.: Monitoring smoothly degrading system for increased dependabulity. Empirical Software Eng. 2, 59–77 (1997)
4. Bertsekas, D.P., Tsitsiklis, N.J.: Neuro-Dynamic Programming. Atheena Scientific (1996)
5. Bobbio, A., Sereno, M., Anglano, C.: Fine grained software degradation models for optimal rejuvenation policies. Performance Evaluation 46, 45–62 (2001)
6. Borkar, V.S., Meyn, S.P.: The O.D.E method for convergence of stochastic approximation and reinforcement learning. SIAM J. Control and Optimization 38, 447–469 (2000)
7. Castelli, V., Harper, R.E., Heidelberger, P., Hunter, S.W., Trivedi, K.S., Vaidyanathan, K.V., Zeggert, W.P.: Proactive management of software aging. IBM J. Research & Development 45, 311–332 (2001)
8. Dohi, T., Goševa-Popstojanova, K., Trivedi, K.S.: Estimating software rejuvenation schedule in high assurance systems. The Computer Journal 44, 473–485 (2001)
9. Dohi, T., Goševa-Popstojanova, K., Vaidyanathan, K.V., Trivedi, K.S., Osaki, S.: Software rejuvenation modeling and applications. In: Pham, H. (ed.) Handbook of Reliability Engineering, pp. 245–268. Springer, Heidelberg (2003)
10. Eto, H., Dohi, T.: Determining the optimal software rejuvenation schdule via semi-Markov decision process. J. Computer Science 2, 528–534 (2006)
11. Garg, S., Telek, M., Puliafito, A., Trivedi, K.S.: Analysis of software rejuvenation using Markov regenerative stochastic Petri net. In: Proc. 6th Intl Symp. on Software Reliab. Eng., pp. 24–27 (1995)
12. Garg, S., Pfening, S., Puliafito, A., Telek, M., Trivedi, K.S.: Analysis of preventive maintenance in transactions based software systems. IEEE Trans. on Computers 47, 96–107 (1998)
13. Gosavi, A.: Simulation-Based Optimization: Parametric Optimization Techniques and Reinforcement Learning. Kluwer Academic Publishers, Dordrecht (2003)
14. Huang, Y., Kintala, C., Kolettis, N., Fulton, N.D.: Software rejuvenation: analysis, module and applications. In: Proc. 25th Intl Symp. on Fault Tolerant Computing, pp. 381–390 (1995)
15. Konda, V.R., Borkar, V.S.: Actor-critic-type learning algorithms for Markov decision processes. SIAM J. Control and Optimization 38, 94–123 (1999)
16. Mahadevan, S.: Average reward reinforcement learning: foundations, algorithms for Markov decision processes. SIAM J. Control and Optimization 38, 94–123 (2000)
17. Pfening, S., Garg, S., Puliafito, A., Telek, M., Trivedi, K.S.: Optimal rejuvenation for toleranting soft failure. Performance Evaluation 27/28, 491–506 (1996)
18. Sutton, R.S., Barto, A.: Reinforcement Learning. MIT Press, Cambridge (1998)
19. Suzuki, H., Dohi, T., Goševa-Popstojanova, K., Trivedi, K.S.: Analysis of multi step failure models with periodic software rejuvenation. In: Artalejo, J.R., Krishnamoorthy, A. (eds.) Advances in Stochastic Modelling, pp. 85–108. Notable Publications (2002)
20. Tijms, H.C.: Stochastic Models: An Algorithmic Approach. John Wiley & Sons, Chichester (1994)

Organic Control of Traffic Lights

Holger Prothmann[1], Fabian Rochner[2], Sven Tomforde[2],
Jürgen Branke[1], Christian Müller-Schloer[2], and Hartmut Schmeck[1]

[1] Karlsruhe Institute of Technology (KIT)
Univ. Karlsruhe (TH) – Institute AIFB
76128 Karlsruhe, Germany
{prothmann,branke,schmeck}@aifb.uni-karlsruhe.de
[2] Leibniz Univ. Hannover
Institute of Systems Engineering
Appelstr. 4, 30167 Hannover, Germany
{rochner,tomforde,cms}@sra.uni-hannover.de

Abstract. In recent years, Autonomic and Organic Computing have
become areas of active research in the computer science community. Both
initiatives aim at handling the growing complexity in technical systems
by creating systems with adaptation and self-optimisation capabilities.
One application scenario for such "life-like" systems is the control of road
traffic signals in urban areas. This paper presents an organic approach
to traffic light control and analyses its performance by an experimental
validation of the proposed architecture which demonstrates its benefits
compared to classical traffic control.

1 Introduction

In recent years, Autonomic [1] and Organic Computing [2] have become areas
of active research in the computer science community. Both initiatives aim at
handling the growing complexity in today's technical systems. The focus is on
principles that enable the creation of systems with "life-like" properties. Such
systems are capable of adapting to changing environments and handling unforeseen situations. They exhibit *self-x properties* including self-configuration,
self-optimisation, self-protection, or self-healing capabilities. While Autonomic
Computing has a strong focus on server architectures, Organic Computing investigates self-organising technical systems in general.

Urban traffic networks are one promising application domain for Organic
Computing. The traffic volume in cities and on highways is constantly rising
worldwide, leading to serious congestion problems. In many cities, these rising
demands cannot be counteracted by further extending the existing road infrastructure due to the limited space available. Therefore, it is especially important
to use the existing road network efficiently. Traffic lights are a vital factor in
achieving efficient networks since good control strategies are often capable of
improving the network-wide traffic situation (within certain limits). The environmental and economic importance of traffic control systems combined with the

C. Rong et al. (Eds.): ATC 2008, LNCS 5060, pp. 219–233, 2008.

distributed nature of traffic nodes and their constantly changing traffic demands make traffic light control an ideal test case for Organic Computing approaches.

In the remainder of this paper, an organic traffic control (OTC) approach is presented. Section 2 briefly reviews existing control concepts for (isolated) traffic nodes and gives a short introduction to evolutionary techniques relevant for the novel approach proposed in this work. Existing literature on the application of these techniques to traffic control is presented. Section 3 presents an implementation of the generic observer/controller architecture for Organic Computing introduced in [3]. The generic architecture is adopted to create an adaptive, learning node controller. Results comparing a "conventional" system and the organic version including an observer/controller component are presented in Sect. 4 and show the benefits of the OTC approach. Section 5 concludes with a summary of the presented concepts and results and gives an outlook to future work.

2   State of the Art

The approach to traffic control introduced in this paper touches a number of topics of different research disciplines including computer science and civil engineering. The following sections give a brief introduction to the relevant state of the art.

2.1   Traffic Control

Urban areas suffer from increasingly congested road traffic networks. The nodes or intersections are the bottlenecks determining the capacity of the network. Traffic lights are used to allocate the limited resource of space within the intersection needed by conflicting traffic streams by activating the corresponding phase, i. e. switching traffic lights to green. The simplest way to control an intersection – called fixed-time control – is to fix the sequence of phases and their durations. Thus, the actual traffic situation does not influence the behaviour of the controller, but it can be optimised to fit the traffic situation expected on average while the controller is active. This approach can be enhanced by switching between pre-optimised parameter sets at fixed times of day (e. g. to consider different traffic patterns during the morning and afternoon peak periods).

The advantage of fixed-time control is that the hardware needed to run such a controller is very simple and the number of parameters to be tuned is limited: cycle time, split, phase sequence, and offset. The *cycle time* determines how long it takes until all phases have been activated and the cycle is restarted. The *sequence* of all phases to be considered is used to *split* this cycle into fractions of appropriate lengths. Finally, if the intersection should synchronise its operation with neighbouring nodes (to generate a progressive signal system), a global timer is used and the starting point of the cycle is shifted by a certain *offset*. While fixed-time controllers are relatively simple, avoidable delays are induced as the controller does not react on the actual traffic situation (e. g. by cutting short an unused phase).

The performance of a controlled intersection is often measured in terms of the "Level of Service" (LOS) [4], which is in fact the average delay per vehicle passing the intersection, mapped to a discrete scale of six levels labelled A (no delay) to F (heavy congestion). Other measurements like number of stops per vehicle or queue length are sometimes incorporated into a performance index to represent optimisation goals.

To improve performance, sensors can be installed to provide data on the current situation. Inductive loops or infrared sensors are widely used for vehicle detection today and are only slowly replaced by modern video detectors. Traffic-responsive control may use the provided data to determine when to terminate or extend a phase or which phase to activate next. To set up such a controller several parameters for every phase of a node have to be defined. The parameters specify minimum and maximum green times and determine conditions for the traffic-dependent extension of a phase. Synchronisation of such a controller is a dynamic problem, so most controllers run without it.

The significantly enlarged complexity of traffic-responsive control leads to an improved performance, but as the load on the network increases, this advantage decreases. This is due to the fact that traffic-responsive strategies tend to resemble fixed-time controllers when large queues are constantly detected for all intersection approaches. For the SCOOT system (Split Cycle Offset Optimisation Technique, see e. g. [5]), Bretherton reports that at a utilisation of about 80% of the maximum capacity, there is no difference in performance between SCOOT and a fixed-time strategy [6]. The additional complexity gives no advantage in this situation.

In urban areas, it is not sufficient to look at a single node only, but to especially consider the coordination of multiple nodes. The obvious approach to coordination is to establish a single central controller for all intersections. Besides SCOOT, SCATS (Sydney Coordinated Adaptive Traffic System, see e. g. [7]) is a prominent example following this approach. However, such systems are difficult to set up and maintain and demand significant computing power. Therefore, hierarchically structured approaches like "Balance" have been developed [8]. The question whether such coordination is possible using a completely *decentralised* approach remains unanswered, though.

2.2 Evolutionary Computation

Evolutionary computation is a research area in computer science that investigates the application of nature-inspired problem-solving techniques to a wide variety of optimisation and adaptation problems. Evolutionary computation techniques include Evolutionary Algorithms and Learning Classifier Systems.

Evolutionary Algorithms (EA). Are randomised optimisation heuristics that mimic biological evolution to tackle optimisation problems. Their general scheme is simple: Starting with a set (called population) of randomly generated initial solutions, an EA selects solutions with a relatively high quality from its population as parents, which are then combined and locally modified by crossover and mutation operators to form new offspring solutions. Based on their quality, some of the parents and offspring are selected to form the next generation of solutions that replaces the old population. This process is repeated until a stopping criterion (usually a maximum number of generations, a time limit, or some quality level) is reached. Selection, crossover, and mutation are randomised operations, but good solutions have a higher probability to survive and generate offspring. Therefore, the overall quality of solutions is likely to improve over time while the random influence of mutation helps to prevent premature convergence on some local optimum.

Due to their simple working principle and the fact that EAs are black box algorithms that can be applied to any problem where a quality (or fitness) can be assigned to a solution, EAs are widely used in many real world optimisation problems. They also have been applied in the off-line optimisation of traffic light controllers (see Sect. 2.3 for a brief review).

Learning Classifier Systems (LCS). Are closely linked to EA. Their goal is to learn the "right" or "best" response to any stimulus they get. They are applicable to all problems where an action leads to some kind of numerical reward. The core component of an LCS is a rule base, where each rule consists of three parts: condition, action and value. This structure is called a classifier. The selection of an appropriate action is a two-step process. From the rule base of all classifiers a subset called "match set" is built containing all classifiers whose condition matches the current stimulus. For all distinct actions present in the match set the average value of all classifiers advocating that action is computed. The action with the highest value is selected for execution and all classifiers in the match set advocating that action form the "action set". The reward received from the environment is subsequently used to update the value of all classifiers in the action set.

New classifiers are generated in two different ways: Whenever the match set is empty, a classifier consisting of a condition matching the current input, a random action and a default value is inserted into the rule base ("covering"). Furthermore, occasionally, some classifiers are selected to be the "parent individuals" for a reproduction cycle. Genetic operators like crossover and mutation are applied to copies of the parents to form offspring which are inserted into the rule base.

A wide variety of different LCS implementations has been proposed, most of which are based on work done by Wilson [9,10]. While Wilson used a binary coding of the stimuli for these rather simple LCSs, different approaches to represent real-valued input have been examined (e. g. [11,12,13]). The representation and update of the value of a classifier plays a major part in adapting an LCS to a given problem, therefore the emphasis is not always just on maximisation of obtained reward, but in many cases rather on reliability. Most problems investigated in LCS research involved conditions of only limited size and a limited number of actions to choose from.

2.3   Evolutionary Computation in Traffic Control

Both Evolutionary Algorithms and Learning Classifier Systems have been applied to problems related to traffic control. This section presents and discusses relevant work in this area.

EAs in traffic control. The first work that used EAs for signal timing determination known to the authors was published in 1992 by Foy et al. in [14]. In a simulated Manhattan-type network of four simple two-phase intersections, cycle length and green time splits were optimised for a fixed traffic situation. The minimisation of the resulting delays served as the objective. According to Foy et al. their EA found near-optimal solutions which proved the feasibility of EAs for the task.

In the following years, other authors applied EAs to traffic control problems. The considerable number of publications on the topic can be grouped with respect to the following criteria:

- *Fixed-time vs. traffic-responsive controllers:* In general, the optimisation of traffic-responsive controllers is more complex due to the larger number of available parameters. Therefore, publications dealing with fixed-time controllers should be distinguished from those optimising traffic-responsive controllers.
- *Isolated intersections vs. networks:* While some publications focus on single intersections, others consider networks. In general, the optimisation of networks is more complex, since the necessary coordination among the network's intersections induces additional parameters.
- *Single- vs. multi-objective optimisation:* While in single-objective optimisation only one criterion is considered for optimisation, multi-objective approaches deal with several (usually contradicting) objectives. The goal is to find optimal trade-off solutions (called Pareto-optima), i. e. solutions that cannot be improved in any objective without worsening at least one other objective. In traffic control, delay times and the resulting number of stops induced by a signal program are often used as contradicting objectives since delay minimisation leads to shorter cycles while the minimisation of stops tends to increase the cycle length.

The remainder of this section presents selected publications, starting with the recent work of Stevanovic et al. [15] who focus on the optimisation of traffic networks:

Their test case was an arterial road of twelve intersections in Park City, USA. They optimised cycle length, offsets, phase sequences, and green splits of the networks' intersections, trying to minimise their performance index that combines delay and the resulting number of stops into a single objective. The controller considered in their work was a traffic-responsive NEMA controller that is common in the US. Solutions discovered by this approach outperformed timing plans found by SYNCHRO – a traditional optimisation tool – by at least 8%.

Multi-objective approaches are discussed by Sun et al. and Branke et al. among others: Sun et al. investigated the use of NSGA-II – a multi-objective EA – for signal timing optimisation in [16]. Delay times and the resulting number of stops were minimised for a two-phase isolated intersection controlled by a fixed-time controller. Approximation formulas by Webster and Akçelik served as objective functions in their experiments.

Branke et al. used NSGA-II for the optimisation of an isolated intersection at Karlsruhe, Germany, that was equipped with a traffic-responsive controller [17]. Again, delay time and number of stops served as objectives, but controller settings were evaluated with the help of a microscopic traffic simulation software. Solutions found by NSGA-II outperformed a reference solution provided by a traffic-engineer with respect to the considered objectives.

In the references mentioned above, EAs have been used for the off-line optimisation of traffic light controller settings, i.e. the controller parameters are optimised before they are applied, but no further on-line optimisations take place when the parameters are used in the traffic system. Therefore, the parameters' quality runs the risk of being decreased over time due to changing traffic demands (an effect called "ageing" for fixed-time controllers). To avoid this problem, parameters can be adapted on-line, but the on-line usage of EAs is challenging due to their run-time requirements.

LCS in traffic control. Although LCSs are on-line learning systems, the authors are aware of only few recent publications discussing the application of LCSs to traffic control [18,19]. These publications investigate the use of an LCS as an intersection controller in small networks of two-phased intersections. An LCS is used to adapt the phase durations at each intersection based on detected queues, but the investigated intersection model is fairly simple. The approaches should not be applicable to a real intersection without major extensions.

The OTC approach presented here uses an EA for off-line parameter optimisation but combines it with an LCS that selects and evaluates parameters on-line. Details are presented in Sect. 3.

3   Architecture

This section presents the OTC architecture for the control of signalled intersections. An industry-standard traffic light controller (TLC) – the *System under Observation and Control* (SuOC) in terms of Organic Computing – is extended by an observer/controller component that reconfigures the TLC depending on current traffic conditions. The architecture – which is an implementation of the generic observer/controller architecture presented in [3] – is depicted in Fig. 1. The resulting traffic control system is self-configuring and self-optimising.

3.1   Overview

The SuOC consists of a parametrisable TLC responsible for physically setting the intersection's traffic lights. Different industry-standard TLCs may be
implemented in the SuOC, the only precondition being that the controller is
parametrisable, i.e. that its behaviour can be specified by a set of parameters
which can be varied by the observer/controller. Possible controllers include simple fixed-time controllers (FTC) or more complex traffic-responsive variants like
VS-Plus [20] or NEMA controllers [21]. A good setup of the TLC's parameters
that matches the current traffic conditions has an important influence on the
resulting delay times and number of stops for these systems.

The TLC's parameters are adapted by
an additional observer/controller component introduced with the OTC architecture. In Fig. 1, this component is split
into two separate layers according to the
different tasks performed by the observ-
er/controller. Layer 1 is responsible for
the on-line selection of TLC parameters
depending on local traffic conditions. An
observer component monitors the traffic
flows crossing the intersection, combines
the determined flow values into a vector representing the local traffic situation,
and provides this information regularly to
a modified real-valued LCS. The LCS selects appropriate parameters from its rule
base. New classifiers for unforeseen traffic conditions are created on Layer 2 by
off-line optimisation. Here, an EA evolves

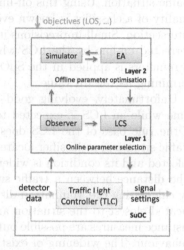

Fig. 1. The OTC architecture for traffic light control

TLC parameters for a specified traffic situation and evaluates the parameters'
quality using a simulation component. Important architectural aspects are discussed in the remainder of this section, further details can be found in [3,22].

3.2   On-Line Selection of TLC Parameters

The traffic-dependent selection of TLC parameters is performed by a modified
real-valued LCS. For an intersection with n turnings, the system input consists
of an n-dimensional real-valued vector containing the traffic flows measured in
vehicles per hour (veh/h) for each of the intersection's turnings. The condition
part of the classifiers accordingly consists of n interval predicates forming an
n-dimensional hyperrectangle containing all inputs matched by the classifier,
while the action part contains a TLC parameter set. For a given input, the LCS
determines all matching classifiers. One of the TLC parameter sets present in
this match set is selected as with standard LCS (see Sect. 2.2 for details) and
used to configure the TLC of the intersection.

Although LCSs are evolutionary on-line learning systems, some modifications are necessary before using them for the control task. Existing systems like XCS – which is used as a basis for the modified version presented here – create classifiers in a stochastic process and evaluate their quality by applying their actions directly in the environment. For the task of traffic control, these systems would test and evaluate arbitrary TLC parameters directly at the controlled intersection. Since the use of inappropriate parameters leads to long average delays and a large number of stops, this approach is infeasible.

In the OTC architecture, new classifiers – or more precisely their action parts containing the TLC parameters – are evolved by an EA that uses a traffic simulation software to evaluate the parameters' quality with respect to a specific traffic situation. Using this off-line simulation-based approach, an approximate quality of a classifier is known even if it has not been previously applied at the intersection. Small imprecisions induced by the simulation-based evaluation are corrected on-line by the LCS when the classifier's action containing the TLC parameters is applied in the SuOC and its impact is evaluated later on by determining its reward value.

Unfortunately, evolving good parameters based on simulations takes some time while an LCS is expected to react on new traffic situations immediately. If the rule base of the LCS does not contain classifiers matching an observed traffic situation, a classifier located most "closely" to the unmatched situation is selected and its condition is widened as far as necessary to match the situation. The distance between a traffic situation and a classifier condition is measured by calculating the Manhattan distance between the point of the hyperrectangle located closest to the situation and the point representing the situation. Other distance measures are possible but should not significantly influence the system's behaviour. The widening of existing classifiers that are located close to an unmatched situation enables an immediate response of the LCS while on the other hand the situation-dependent quality of TLC parameters remains (somewhat) predictable.

In test runs, the modifications described in the previous paragraphs resulted in a weak competition among existing classifiers: In many cases an extensively widened classifier A matches a situation while a more specific but not matching classifier B is located close by. In these cases, the parameters proposed by classifier A are used in the SuOC although the parameters advocated by B would often exhibit a better performance since they were originally created for a situation closer to the current input. The problem is illustrated in Fig. 2 for the 2-dimensional case.

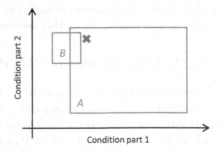

Fig. 2. A situation is matched by a widened classifier A, but not by a more specific classifier B

To improve the performance of the LCS, the match set creation has been modified further: If the set of classifiers matching a situation does not contain at least d distinct TLC parameter sets, widened copies of not matching classifiers in the proximity of the situation are included in the match set (but not yet in the rule base) until the required number of d distinct parameter sets is reached or no more classifiers are available. Based on this match set, the action set is formed and TLC parameters for the SuOC are returned. If the action set contains a widened copy of an originally not matching classifier it is included in the rule base. The overall process is shown in Fig. 3.

Reconsidering the constellation depicted in Fig. 2, both classifiers A and B will now be included in the match set, and depending on their quality, B's parameters might be used in the SuOC. In the performed test runs, this modified selection process resulted in significantly better performance of the controlled intersection.

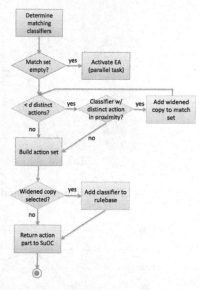

Fig. 3. Overview of the modified match set creation process

4   Results

The OTC architecture presented in the previous section has been evaluated for different three- and four-armed traffic nodes. This section provides details of the experimental setup and presents the obtained results.

4.1   Experimental Setup

To perform the experiments, simulation models of existing traffic nodes have been built using the microscopic traffic simulator Aimsun [23]. The models (called K3 and K7) are based on maps of intersections located at Hamburg, Germany. They are depicted in Fig. 4. While K7 is a three-armed intersection allowing six turning manoeuvres, K3 is four-armed and consists of eleven turnings.

For both nodes a fixed-time signal program used in reality was available and is used as a reference controller in the evaluation. Traffic demands are modelled according to data taken from a traffic census. In the census, cars and trucks passing the intersection were counted and documented for each turning with a time resolution of 15 minutes.

Experiments were conducted for a simulated period of six hours starting at 6 a. m. This period was chosen because it starts with a phase of low traffic density that is quickly replaced by the morning peak hour (lasting approximately from

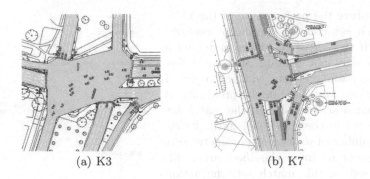

(a) K3   (b) K7

Fig. 4. Simulation models of the intersections K3 and K7

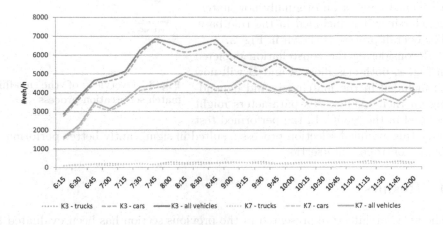

...... K3 - trucks   --- K3 - cars   ——K3 - all vehicles   ...... K7 - trucks   --- K7 - cars   ——K7 - all vehicles

Fig. 5. Traffic demands for K3 and K7

7.30 a.m. to 8.30 a.m.) with high traffic demands. Till noon, traffic settles down to a medium level. The total number of vehicles passing K3 and K7 are depicted in Fig. 5.

To compare the performance of different traffic light controllers, the intersection's average delay is used. It is defined as

$$\frac{\sum_{t \in T} f_t \cdot d_t}{\sum_{t \in T} f_t},$$

where T is a set containing all turnings of the intersection. The variables f_t and d_t denote the flow and the average delay for a turning $t \in T$. The intersection's average delay is the basis for the established Level of Service classification (see Sect. 2.1) and should be minimised by a traffic light controller. Delays have been measured using the microscopic traffic simulator Aimsun (version 5.1), which was used to simulate the SuOC and to provide a fitness evaluator for the EA on Layer 2 of the OTC architecture.

The OTC approach was evaluated in three consecutive experiments (labelled Day 1, Day 2, and Day 3). At the beginning of Day 1, the rule base of the LCS was empty. For Day 2 and Day 3 the rule base that evolved on the previous day(s) was used. Simulations of each day have been repeated at least three times using different random seeds. The EA optimised cycle length and phase splits for the intersections while using the phase sequence from the reference TLC.

After some preliminary testing, the configuration listed in Table 1 was used in the experiments. Most parameters are standard for LCSs and EAs, respectively, but some need explanation: For the LCS, no *rule base size limit* has been implemented to avoid bad system performance due to a limited rule base capacity. No subsumption or deletion of classifiers has been performed. The *interval width for new classifiers* defines the initial width of the intervals used in the condition of new classifiers created by Layer 2. While the initial width should be preferably small to keep the EAs quality prediction accurate, larger intervals can reduce the number of EA activations especially on the first day of simulation. The *number d of distinct actions needed in the match set* has been introduced in Sect. 3.2.

For the EA, the parameters *warm-up* and *simulation duration* define the simulated duration of evaluation runs used to determine the quality of TLC parameters. While the traffic can build up during the warm-up period of an evaluation, delay statistics are only gathered for the simulation duration. Shorter simulations allow for a faster evaluation of TLC parameters, but longer simulations reduce the variance of the quality estimates. For the selected durations, an optimisation run takes about 4 to 6 minutes on a recent standard processor, depending on the simulated node and traffic demands.

Table 1. Configuration used for the experiments

Layer 1 (LCS)		Layer 2 (EA)	
rule base size limit N	none	population size	10
learning rate β	0.2	# generations	10
initial prediction error ε_I and fitness F_I	50, 0.01	# offspring	5
accuracy determination param. α, ε_0, ν	0.1, 1.5, 5	warm-up duration	900 sec.
interval width for new classifiers	120	simulation duration	3600 sec.
# d of distinct actions in match set	3		

4.2   Simulation Results

This section presents results of the simulation study, comparing the average vehicle delay resulting from the reference solution and the OTC approach. Furthermore, some statistics on the development of the LCS rule base are included.

Results for K7. Results of the experiments for K7 are depicted in Fig. 6. For Day 1, the OTC approach can quickly improve the average vehicle delay compared to the reference solution for the low traffic period preceding the morning peak. In this period, TLCs found by the EA can easily outperform the reference solution that was designed to suit higher traffic volumes. During the morning peak, the OTC approach performs slightly better than the reference solution. Due to the quickly rising traffic demand at the intersection, Layer 2 is heavily used during this period and existing classifiers need to be widened frequently since the initially empty rule base does not contain appropriate classifiers. After the morning peak, the OTC approach leads to smaller delays than the reference solution. Overall, the average improvement for Day 1 with respect to the reference solution is about 10 %.

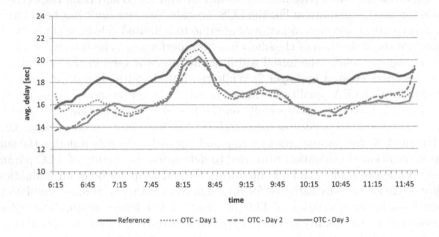

Fig. 6. Comparison of OTC approach and reference solution for K7

For Day 2 and 3, the OTC approach can outperform the reference solution for the whole simulation period. The system has learned appropriate TLC parameters for most traffic situations recognised by the observer, therefore appropriate TLC parameters are often available instantly or existing classifiers need to be widened only to a small extent. The average improvement with respect to the reference solution is about 12 %.

Results for K3. Results obtained for intersection K3 are depicted in Fig. 7. The results resemble the simulations for K7 presented above: For Day 1, an improvement of about 6 % could be obtained in comparison to the reference controller despite the initially empty LCS rule base. For Days 2 and 3, the system profits from is populated rule base, handling especially the morning peak better than on Day 1. This results in an average delay reduced by 8 % compared to the reference solution for both days.

The presented results for K3 and K7 indicate that the OTC approach is capable of autonomously improving the performance of signalised intersections. The system's self-optimisation capabilities allow the continuous on-line adaptation to changing traffic demands, thereby easing the job of a traffic engineer. Since the OTC architecture represents a novel approach, further improvements of its optimisation and adaptation capabilities can be expected in the future.

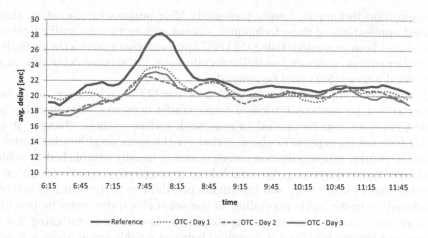

Fig. 7. Comparison of OTC approach and reference solution for K3

LCS statistics. For both intersections, statistics on the number of classifiers, the number of classifiers with distinct TLC parameters, and the number of optimisations performed by Layer 2 were gathered. The average of these measures for the repetitions of each simulated day are shown in Table 2.

Table 2. LCS statistics

	K3			K7		
	Day 1	Day 2	Day 3	Day 1	Day 2	Day 3
# classifiers in rule base	230	415	577	248	424	574
# optimisations	120	77	65	123	69	53
# distinct TLC parameters in rule base	97	142	174	105	152	187

For both nodes, several new classifiers are created each day by widening operations or EA optimisations. While the new classifiers initially lead to a rapidly growing rule base, more and more typical traffic situations are covered by classifiers, resulting in a smaller number of optimisations and a reduced rule base growth on subsequent days. Accordingly, the number of distinct TLC parameters is rising slowly after a large number of parameters has been created on Day 1. Their absolute number is relatively large since even slightly different parameter sets are counted separately.

5   Summary and Outlook

This paper presented traffic control as an interesting application for Organic Computing. A brief introduction into existing traffic control systems was given and Evolutionary Algorithms and Learning Classifier Systems – two Evolutionary

Computation techniques – were presented. After summarising existing traffic-related applications of these techniques, a novel architecture for traffic light controllers has been presented. Using the OTC approach that extends the traffic light controller with an observer/controller architecture, the average delay time at the controlled intersection could be reduced.

Future work focuses on the extension of the OTC architecture to make it better suited for the application in larger traffic networks. Although the presented approach can be applied in a network setting without changes, it currently includes no explicit mechanism that synchronises neighbouring nodes. In urban networks, synchronisation among nodes is usually established to achieve smoother traffic flows (e. g. by establishing a progressive signal system on an arterial road). Future work will investigate possibilities to dynamically establish synchronised traffic lights depending on the network's traffic flows by providing a communication mechanism among the nodes. It will be investigated if a decentralised approach of local interactions between neighbouring nodes is feasible to establish useful synchronisations or if an additional coordination component is needed to perform this task.

Acknowledgement

We gratefully acknowledge the financial support by the German Research Foundation (DFG) within the priority programme 1183 "Organic Computing".

References

1. Kephart, J.O., Chess, D.M.: The vision of Autonomic Computing. IEEE Computer 36(1), 41–50 (2003)
2. Schmeck, H.: Organic Computing – A new vision for distributed embedded systems. In: Proceedings of the 8th IEEE International Symposium on Object-Oriented Real-Time Distributed Computing (ISORC 2005), pp. 201–203 (2005)
3. Branke, J., Mnif, M., Müller-Schloer, C., Prothmann, H., Richter, U., Rochner, F., Schmeck, H.: Organic Computing – Addressing complexity by controlled self-organization. In: Margaria, T., Philippou, A., Steffen, B. (eds.) Proceedings of the 2nd International Symposium on Leveraging Applications of Formal Methods, Verification and Validation (ISoLA 2006), pp. 200–206 (2006)
4. Transportation Research Board Washington, D.C.: Highway Capacity Manual (2000)
5. Robertson, D.I., Bretherton, R.D.: Optimizing networks of traffic signals in real time – the SCOOT method. IEEE Transactions on Vehicular Technology 40(1), 11–15 (1991)
6. Bretherton, R.D., Rai, G.I.: The use of SCOOT in low flow conditions. Traffic Engineering & Control 23(12), 574–576 (1982)
7. Sims, A.G., Dobinson, K.W.: The Sydney Coordinated Adaptive Traffic (SCAT) System – Philosophy and Benefits. Proceedings of the International Symposium on Traffic Control Systems 29(2), 19–41 (1980)

8. Friedrich, B.: Ein verkehrsadaptives Verfahren zur Steuerung von Lichtsignalanlagen. Veröffentlichung des Fachgebiets Verkehrstechnik und Verkehrsplanung. Technische Universität München (1999)
9. Wilson, S.W.: ZCS: A zeroth level classifier system. Evolutionary Computation 2(1), 1–18 (1994)
10. Wilson, S.W.: Classifier fitness based on accuracy. Evolutionary Computation 3(2), 149–175 (1995)
11. Wilson, S.W.: Get real! XCS with continuous-valued inputs. In: Lanzi, P.L., Stolzmann, W., Wilson, S.W. (eds.) IWLCS 1999. LNCS (LNAI), vol. 1813, pp. 209–219. Springer, Heidelberg (2000)
12. Dam, H.H., Abbass, H.A., Lokan, C.: Be real! XCS with continuous-valued inputs. In: Rothlauf, F., et al. (eds.) Proceedings of the 2005 Workshops on Genetic and Evolutionary Computation (GECCO 2005), pp. 85–87 (2005)
13. Stone, C., Bull, L.: For real! XCS with continuous-valued inputs. Evolutionary Computation 11(3), 299–336 (2003)
14. Foy, M.D., Benekohal, R.F., Goldberg, D.E.: Signal timing determination using genetic algorithms. In: Transportation Research Record No. 1365, Transportation Research Board, pp. 108–115 (1992)
15. Stevanovic, A., Martin, P.T., Stevanovic, J.: VISGAOST: VISSIM-based genetic algorithm optimization of signal timings. In: Proceedings of the 86th Transportation Research Board Meeting (2007)
16. Sun, D., Benekohal, R.F., Waller, S.T.: Multi-objective traffic signal timing optimization using non-dominated sorting genetic algorithm. In: Proceedings of the IEE Intelligent Vehicles Symposium, pp. 198–203 (2003)
17. Branke, J., Goldate, P., Prothmann, H.: Actuated traffic signal optimization using evolutionary algorithms. In: Proceedings of the 6th European Congress and Exhibition on Intelligent Transport Systems and Services (ITS 2007) (2007)
18. Cao, Y.J., Ireson, N., Bull, L., Miles, R.: Distributed learning control of traffic signals. In: Oates, M.J., Lanzi, P.L., Li, Y., Cagnoni, S., Corne, D.W., Fogarty, T.C., Poli, R., Smith, G.D. (eds.) EvoIASP 2000, EvoWorkshops 2000, EvoFlight 2000, EvoSCONDI 2000, EvoSTIM 2000, EvoTEL 2000, and EvoROB/EvoRobot 2000. LNCS, vol. 1803, pp. 117–126. Springer, Heidelberg (2000)
19. Bull, L., Sha'Aban, J., Tomlinson, A., Addison, J.D., Heydecker, B.: Towards distributed adaptive control for road traffic junction signals using learning classifier systems. In: Bull, L. (ed.) Applications of Learning Classifier Systems, pp. 276–299. Springer, Heidelberg (2004)
20. Swiss Verkehrs-Systeme AG: VS-Plus webpage, http://www.vs-plus.de
21. National Electrical Manufacturers Association: NEMA Standards Publication TS 2-2003 v02.06 – Traffic Controller Assemblies with NTCIP Requirements (2003)
22. Rochner, F., Prothmann, H., Branke, J., Müller-Schloer, C., Schmeck, H.: An organic architecture for traffic light controllers. In: Hochberger, C., Liskowsky, R. (eds.) Informatik 2006 – Informatik für Menschen. LNI, vol. P-93, pp. 120–127. Köllen Verlag (2006)
23. TSS Transport Simulation Systems: Aimsun webpage, http://www.aimsun.com

Concepts for Autonomous Control Flow Checking for Embedded CPUs*

Daniel Ziener and Jürgen Teich

Hardware/Software Co-Design
Department of Computer Science
University of Erlangen-Nuremberg, Germany
{daniel.ziener,teich}@cs.fau.de

Abstract. In this paper, we introduce new concepts and methods for checking the correctness of control flow instructions during the execution of programs in embedded CPUs. Detecting and avoiding the execution of faulty control flow instructions is a problem of growing importance w.r.t. reliability and security. On the other hand, hardware cost overheads and an easy integration into the design flow are of utmost important for cost sensitive embedded systems. Our proposed methodology is able to monitor all direct jumps and branches as well as calls and returns form subroutines autonomously during program execution. Furthermore, we propose and evaluate an implementation of an *autonomous checker unit* which is closely coupled to the processor and can detect and even avoid the execution of a faulty control flow instruction. Upon detection of a faulty instruction, we propose a method to refetch and reexecute the incorrect jump or branch instruction. Other benefits of this novel approach are that the application code must not be changed or augmented by signatures or additional instructions, and that there is no measurable performance impact in terms of execution latency. From the user point of view, our approach is completely transparent to a program developer.

1   Introduction

Modern electronic systems are integrated more and more together with communication devices. In the past, aero planes were steered by cables, axes and hydro pneumatic systems. Now, planes become fitted with "fly-by-wire" systems without any direct mechanical coupling between the pilot's control elements and the actuators. Clearly, such systems require a very high standard of reliability. The Airbus A380, for instance, has reached a new dimension on integration of wire-based and wireless communication components [1].

Thus, from the researcher's point of view, the focus is constantly shifting from the integration of new technologies to the effort to increase the reliability and security of existing systems.

---

* This work has been supported by BMBF project 01 M 3083 "Autonome Integrierte Systeme."

C. Rong et al. (Eds.): ATC 2008, LNCS 5060, pp. 234–248, 2008.

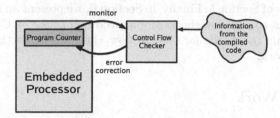

Fig. 1. Concepts of autonomously interacting control flow checker that can monitor the program counter and detect false jumps or branches based on information of the compiled code. Moreover, the checker should also be able to correct false jumps or branches.

Robustness, reliability and security are essential requirements of todays SoCs (Systems on Chips). Modules and their integration in the system have to be designed to be still operational also in difficult and inference-prone areas as well as insecure environments.

In this paper, our goal is to investigate methods to recognize, analyze, and correct sporadic and/or permanent errors occurring in the control paths of embedded RISC-CPUs. Our vision thereby is to define autonomously behaving elements to resolve functional errors of a RISC-CPU-Core locally inside the core.

These autonomous elements called *control flow checkers* are supposed to recognize, evaluate, and correct errors during the program execution of the processor. In particular, soft errors [2] as well as malign security attacks [3] are in the focus of this paper.

In the following, we propose such concepts and an implementation of a corresponding control flow checker hardware (see Figure 1). The main task of the control logic in a CPU is to control the program flow. The actual state of execution of a program is, in general, given by the value of the program counter and the CPU registers. Usually, the next instruction to fetch is given by an increment of the program counter, but also branches and jumps may occur.

Sources of errors that we want to autonomously detect and correct include accidental sporadic, permanent, or intended errors caused by local attacks that try to manipulate the program execution. These errors can effect a wrong program counter value. Errors may also be caused by pure software means such as buffer overflows. Here, a wrong jump destination or a wrong return address from a subroutine might cause an execution of infiltrated code. If an error is detected, the control flow checker should be able to initiate the reexecution of the control flow instruction.

Definition 1. *Control flow checking denotes the task to test whether a sequence of program counter values is correct with respect to a given program specification.*

The paper is structured as follows: In Section 2, a general overview of related work is given. In Section 3, we present a classification of control flow instructions. Subsequently, in Section 4, two different methodological concepts for control flow checking are introduced. Architectural concepts for implementing these ideas present the focus of Section 5. Finally, in Section 6, we present an implementation of an autonomous control flow checker for a given real *Leon3* [4] CPU and analyze the corresponding overheads for control flow checking in Section 7. Section 8 concludes the work.

2   Related Work

Error detection and correction methods have important roots in the area of fault-tolerance. Here, one of the most familiar method for error detection is the duplication of a given processor core with subsequent comparison of the results [5]. Duplication of processing units is, however, too cost-intensive and thus often prohibitive due to cost (area) and power consumption. Hence, these approaches are only used in safety-critical systems with a high demand on reliability.

In the following, we first define relevant criteria when comparing different methodologies for control flow checking quantitatively. Here, the following criteria will be used: *Error coverage* denotes the degree of faults that can be detected by a method. For example, some methods for control flow checking discussed in the following can only detect a certain type of control flow instructions (e.g., direct branches and jumps). Some may detect not 100% of all control flow errors. Another criterion for comparison is the *detection latency*. The detection latency denotes the time between occurrence of a fault and its detection. This time is important to prevent a system failure. Only if an error is detected with a low latency, the error handling can react to transfer the system into a secure state or to trigger error correction measures. On the other hand, the following overheads may be caused: *execution time overheads* (CPU time), *memory overheads* and *area overheads* (hardware cost overheads).

Related work on control flow checking can be divided into approaches using an additional hardware checker unit or a watchdog processor [6,7,8,9,10], and approaches which are completely software-based [11]. In these approaches, the program code is first structured into basic blocks[1].

Control Flow Checking using Assertions (CCA) [11] denotes a software-based approach. After creating a basic block graph, a sequence of special control instructions is inserted into the program code at the beginning as well as at the end of each basic block. These additional instructions verify that only legal branch or jump destinations according to the specification, given by the basic block graph is taken. The advantage is that no additional hardware (area overhead) is required, but this approach has an obvious impact on the performance of the program code (execution time overhead). Undesired jumps caused by faults occurring on instructions inside a basic block cannot be detected at all.

---

[1] A basic block is a sequence of code which is executed successively without any jumps or branches except at the end. The basic block can only be left at the end of a block and can only be entered at the beginning. Only the last instruction can be a jump or branch and only the first instruction can be a jump or branch destination (see Section 4.1).

A good overview over software methods for control flow checking for security and fault tolerance is given in [12].

To check all types of instructions, a signature (hash or a CRC value) of all instructions of a basic block can be calculated offline (at compile time). At runtime, a hardware checker can calculate the signature of the executed instruction in a basic block. When leaving a basic block, the signatures can be compared and errors inside the basic block can be found. Signature methods can be divided into two groups, namely *Embedded Signature Monitoring* (ESM) [6,7,8] and *Autonomous Signature Monitoring* (ASM) [9,10].

In the ESM methods, the offline calculated signature (golden signature) is stored in the program code with additionally inserted instructions at the end of each basic block. These instructions read out the calculated signature of the executed instructions from the checker unit and compare it to the golden signature. The advantage of these methods is that all types of instructions can be checked and a new program contains already the corresponding signature. The disadvantages are a significant performance impact (execution time overhead) and that a fault can only be detected at the end of a basic block which may be too late to prevent a system failure (detection latency). Also, a single event upset during the execution of the additionally inserted instruction can lead to a false detection or spoofing of an error.

In the ASM methods, the golden signature is stored in a separate memory belonging to the checker unit. Also, the comparator for the golden and the calculated signature is implemented in hardware. The information of the basic block graph is mapped into microinstructions, located inside the instruction memory of the checker. Jumps and branch destinations can thus also be checked. The advantages are that the program code must not be altered and that there is no performance impact. Also, all types of instructions can be monitored. The disadvantages are that an extra memory for the checker unit is required (memory overhead) and that synchronization between the CPU and the checker unit is difficult. So, interrupts, multi threading, and indirect jumps cannot be completely covered.

An ASM approach for security applications is described in [10]. The *Intra-Procedural Control Flow Checking* is similar to our method. The advantages of our methods however is, that we are a) more flexible in using memories to store the control flow (instruction) graph instead of a finite state machine in logic. Moreover, we have b) no performance impact in the error free case, and c) our checker unit is simpler and thus requires less resources.

Finally, the Diva approach [13] describes a pipeline which accepts only checked results for the further processing after the commit phase. A redundant second pipeline is a simple rudimentary pipeline, where the results of arithmetic functions are recalculated with a separate checker, and memory items are refetched. The weakness is that the second pipeline is assumed to be fault-free, which might not be the reality in today's deep submicron designs. The area overhead of Diva is lower than in the case of fully redundant units, but also performance reduction exists due to a longer pipeline.

3   Branches and Jumps

Control flow instructions (CFI) can be categorized into conditional branches and unconditional jumps. Conditional branches depend on the result of a logical or arithmetic operation.

Both groups of control flow instructions can be subdivided into direct (static) and indirect (dynamic) jumps or branches. The destination of direct branches or jumps is fixed at compile time and is encoded into the jump or branch instruction in an absolute or relative address. For indirect jumps or branches, the destination address is determined during program execution. The destination address is given by either a register value or as the result of an operation with registers or the result of an operation with a register and a constant value which is encoded into the instruction. Absolute or relative addressing modes can be used there.

Summarizing, four types of control flow instructions exist: *(Unconditional) direct jumps* (e.g., `call`, `goto`), *(Conditional) direct branches* (e.g., if .. then .. else), *(Unconditional) indirect jumps* (e.g., `return` from subroutine), and *(Conditional) indirect branches*.

Furthermore, the class of unconditional indirect jumps can be subdivided into *returns from subroutine, register indirect calls* and *other jumps*. A return from subroutine is an example of an indirect jump, because the program counter jumps to the address where the routine is called from, and this address is only known at runtime. Register indirect calls are calls where the address of called subroutine is determined at runtime.

Finally, also jumps which are not triggered by an instruction can occur such as *interrupts* and *traps*. The destinations of interrupts are typically given by the start address of the main interrupt service routine, and so, interrupts are direct jumps. Traps occur on exception conditions (like divide by zero). Here, the program jumps to the address of an exception handler, and so, traps can be treated as direct jumps.

Table 1 presents an analysis of the occurrence rates of these different types of branches and jumps on the SPARC architecture for the SPEC CINT2000

Table 1. Accumulated number of control flow instructions of benchmarks of the SPEC CINT2000 test suite [14] when compiled to the SPARC [15] architecture

SPEC	direct		indirect		
program	branches	jumps	returns	calls	other jumps
gzip	1426	599	111	4	0
gcc	54676	22340	2188	140	273
vpr	2810	2065	248	2	7
mcf	288	82	26	0	0
crafty	4544	3848	77	0	11
parser	3189	1703	320	0	2
gap	18733	4158	828	1262	5
vortex	12537	8491	913	15	21
bzip2	748	380	73	0	0
twolf	5701	2060	189	0	2

benchmark [14] for a given list of programs. As been seen, indirect calls and jumps occur relatively rarely as opposed to direct branches and jumps.

4 Methods for Autonomous Control Flow Checking

In SoCs, a CPU often executes only a few specified programs over lifetime. This holds true particularly for embedded applications where the system is often only programmed once, and the code is never changed during the lifetime of the product, except for the update of the SoC with a new firmware and software. Furthermore, it is well known that in many computational intensive problems, most of the execution time is spent in only few subroutines. So, it is beneficial to analyze these subroutines for branches and jumps statically.

If we assume that only direct jumps and branches exists in a given code segment, we are able to check the control flow of this code by verifying the correct execution of each direct control flow instruction as well as the (successively) linear execution of all the other instructions (the program counter value is incremented by one word address after each instruction).

To check the correct execution of control flow instructions, we need to check the correct address of the control flow instruction and the correct target address. The program counter value before and after the execution of a control flow instruction can be compared to these addresses. If there is a mismatch, an error signal may be raised.

In the following, we propose two alternative methods to obtain the correct addresses of control flow instructions of a given machine program and the corresponding targets.

The first method is called *basic block* or *control flow method* (CF). The second method is called *control flow instruction method* (CFI).

4.1 Control Flow (CF) Method

First, a given compiled machine code is separated into a set of basic blocks BB. The following instructions define the begin of a basic block: a) the first instruction in a program or segment, b) the instruction following a control flow instruction, c) instructions which are destinations of control flow instructions.

From this information, the control flow graph $CFG(BB,T)$ is built: Each node $BB_i \in BB$ of the control flow graph represents a basic block. The nodes are sorted with increasing start address of the corresponding basic block in ascending address order. Each edge $t \in T$ represents a transition of the control flow from one basic block to another. If the last instruction of a basic block BB_i is a direct branch instruction, the basic block has two successors. One is the basic block next in the list BB_{i+1} (if the branch is not taken), and to a basic block where the first instruction is the branch destination (if the branch is taken). Jumps have only one successor, and if the last instruction is not a control flow instruction, the successor basic block is always the next basic block BB_{i+1}. An example program is shown in Figure 2 which is separated into basic blocks. Also, the corresponding CFG is shown.

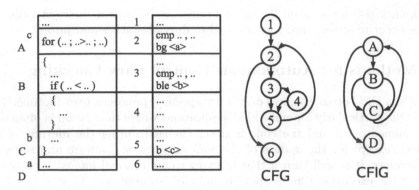

Fig. 2. An example program code is given on the left side with the corresponding assembler code. The CFIs are denoted A to C, and the CFI destinations with a to c. D denotes the end of the program or segment to be checked. Furthermore, the code is divided into basic blocks, denoted with 1 to 6. In the middle, the corresponding CFG and on the right side, the corresponding CFIG are shown.

With the given CFG, we have all information to check a sequence of program counter values for correctness as follows: The information of the CFG can be either used to directly define a *finite state machine* (FSM) to check the correctness of control flow instructions. Alternatively, an implementation using microinstructions of a microprogrammed circuit can be deducted from the CFG.

For an implementation of a microprogrammed circuit, the information of the CFG can be stored inside memories. We need for each basic block, the start and the end address and also the successors basic blocks indexes. The start address of a basic block is the end address of the previous basic block incremented by one. To minimize the memory overhead, we need only the end address and a global start address. Also, we need to store only one successor of the basic block for branches because if the branch is not taken, always the basic block with the next index (BB_{i+1}) is the successor.

The correct control flow instruction address may directly be stored inside the memory (basic block end address). The corresponding target address is the start address of the successor basic block, given by its index. To get this address, the end address of the basic block with the previous index is fetched and the address is incremented $(BB_{i-1} + 1)$. Having both addresses, the control flow instruction can be verified.

For example, [10] describes a CF method, where the CFG is implemented in a FSM and the lookup table for resolving the control flow instruction addresses and indexes is implemented in memories.

4.2   Control Flow Instruction (CFI) Method

In case of direct branches and jumps, the start and target address is known at compile time. So, it is possible to extract this information from the binary or the disassembled program code by decoding the instructions. The control flow instructions are then sorted by increasing addresses in ascending address order.

Then, the *control flow instruction graph* $(CFIG(CFI, T))$ is built: Here, each control flow instruction in the code which should be checked represents a node $(CFI_i \in CFI)$. The edges of the CFIG denote transitions $t \in T$ to the following control flow instruction.

Like in a CFG, each node can have a maximum of two successors: two for a branch instruction and one in case of a jump instruction. For a branch instruction CFI_i, one successor is CFI_{i+1} (branch is not taken). The other successor of a direct branch and jump instruction is CFI_n which is the next control flow instruction in the program code after the branch destination (branch is taken). The CFIG from the example program code is shown on the right side in Fig. 2.

Like in the CF method, the information of the CFIG can be used as a specification of a control flow checker unit and implemented either directly by a FSM or as microinstructions of a microprogrammed circuit. For the microprogrammed circuit, we store for each CFI the start and the target address in memory. Also the index of the successor CFI must be stored inside this memory. For direct branches, we store the successor CFI for taken branches. If the branch is not taken, the successor CFI is CFI_{i+1}.

4.3 Methods Conclusions

Both introduced methods can only check direct branches and jumps, where start and destination address can be extracted from the compiled code. For indirect control flow instructions, we will present extensions for both methods. Some of these extensions are discussed later.

The advantage of the CF method is that in the most cases, fewer additional memory resources are needed than the CFI method. Furthermore, we can extend this method to check the integrity of all types of instruction sequence inside a basic block with a CRC or hash value. This value can be run time calculated from the executed instructions and can be compared at the end of a basic block with a precalculated value [9].

The disadvantage of the CF method is that we need two times access to the memory for each control flow instruction. One access for the end address of the basic block and one for the start address of the successor basic block. To ensure that on a branch or jump the correct start and destination address is available, we can preread both values. But this preread can only be done if the basic block has more than one instruction. If a basic block consists only of one instruction, we must stall the processor pipeline to verify the control flow instruction.

The advantages of the CFI method are that the checker unit is very simple and uses only few logic resources. Also we have no performance impact, because the correct control flow instruction address and target address may be loaded from the memory in a single clock cycle. The disadvantages are that usually more memory resources are needed as for CF method, and that we are not able to check the integrity of non-control flow instructions.

5 An Architecture for Lightweight Control Flow Checking

In the following, we introduce an architecture of a lightweight control flow checker to monitor and to correct the executed control flow instructions of a RISC CPU. Our approach can monitor direct jumps and branches as well as call and returns from subroutine. To achieve a correction of a corrupt program, a detected incorrect jump or branch can be reexecuted. Our checker is called lightweight, because with little area overhead, we can detect and correct many though not all errors. Our architecture concept is modular in the sense that coverage aspects can be treaded off with implementation overheads.

5.1 Handling of Direct Jumps/Branches

We are using the CFI method described in Section 4.2 to check direct jumps and branches where the CFIG is implemented in a dedicated memory. The checker must know the instruction's program address and the address of the next instruction to execute. Since most CPU architectures today are pipelined, these addresses can easily be taken from successive pipeline stages of the program counter.

If no jump or branch instruction occurs, the next instruction address PC_{n+1} is typically one instruction word higher than the value of the current program counter PC_n. So, an incremented instruction address can be compared to the address after the instruction (see comparator a in Figure 3). If the current instruction is a direct jump or branch instruction, the next program counter is the jump destination, or, in the case of a branch the branch destination, or, if the branch is not taken, the next address in the program code.

Each pair of control flow instruction address and target address is stored in two RAMs of the checker unit, one for the start and one for the target address (see Figure 3). The addresses of the branch or jump instructions are stored successively in the start address RAM ($sAdrRam$) and the corresponding targets in the jump address RAM ($jAdrRam$). Also, a checker unit program counter ($CUPC$) is needed which points in these RAMs to the cell, where the address of the next direct branch or jump is stored. This start address is compared to the current program counter to determine when the branch or jump instruction is executed (comparator b). In this case, the following program counter value is compared to the address of the jump address RAM to verify the correct execution of the branch or the jump (comparator c). Now, the $CUPC$ must point to the next branch or jump address. This can be achieved by introducing a third RAM ($ctrlRam$) where the next $CUPC$ is stored for each branch or jump. In the case of a branch, it must also be determined if the branch is taken or not. If the branch is taken, the next $CUPC$ has the value which is stored in the $ctrlRam$. If the branch is not taken, then the $CUPC$ can be incremented. The $CUPC$ and the $ctrlRam$ presents a microprogrammed architecture which implements the CFIG. The $CUPC$ can be compared with the index of the CFI. The transitions of the CFIG are stored in the $ctrlRam$.

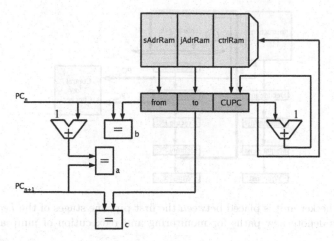

Fig. 3. Architecture for control path checker with the three Rams and comparators. Also, the control unit program counter ($CUPC$) is shown.

Also, control flags are stored in the *ctrlRam*. So, the checker unit can distinguish between jumps or branches or can activate or deactivate the checker unit based on specific program addresses. This can be done by storing the checking start or end address in the *sAdrRam* and setting the checking start or end flag in the corresponding cell in the *ctrlRam*. If the program flow reaches the starting address, the checker unit will be activated, or, if the checking end address is reached, the checker unit deactivates itself. Finally, parts of the program flow, e.g., non-critical sections or sections which can not be checked due to not supported indirect jumps, might be excluded from the checking process by setting the checking start and end flags.

5.2 Handling of Calls and Returns

The most frequent use of indirect jumps occur in the form of returns from subroutine. By executing a *return from subroutine instruction*, the program counter jumps to the next address after the instruction from where the subroutine was called from. The return address is typically stored in a CPU register, so the return instruction is a special indirect jump. Returns can be verified also in our approach by introducing an additional *hardware stack*. Upon a call (direct or indirect), the return address is stored in the stack and when the return instruction is executed, the target address can be verified.

5.3 Correction by Reexecution

If a faulty jump or branch instruction occurs, this instruction will be reexecuted as follows: The error can be detected fast enough to ensure that the state of the CPU is not altered by the faulty instruction execution. To guarantee this, the

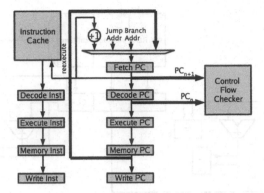

Fig. 4. The checker unit is placed between the first pipeline stages of the *Leon* core [4]. All bold lines denote new paths for monitoring and reexecution of jump and branch instructions.

checker must monitor the program counter in the first pipeline stage of a CPU. Unfortunately, in most architectures, the jump or branch instructions need more than one cycle to execute. So, until the error is detected, some other instructions after the jump might be executed. After error detection, the program counter is reset to a value previous the error occurs by looping back the program counter value from a subsequent pipeline step. The details of the reexecution process depends highly on the processor architecture and design.

The SPARC architecture allows to execute one instruction after a branch instruction or two instructions after a jump instruction before the branch or jump is performed (see [15]). If an error is detected and the jump or branch instruction must be reexecuted, also these following instructions must be reexecuted. It must also be ensured that these instruction cannot alter the state (e.g., register content or memory operations) of the CPU before reexecution (see Section 6).

6   Implementation

We implemented and analyzed our methods of lightweight control flow checking for the open source SPARC CPU *Leon3* from Gaisler Research [4] in a *Virtex 4* FPGA from Xilinx. The checker can monitor direct branches, jumps and calls as well as indirect returns and has also the possibility to reexecute a corrupted jump or branch instruction by fetching it again from the memory. Other features of the checker are the support of the activate and deactivate procedures described in Section 5.1. The complete methodology for control flow checking consists of the concept of checking of direct jumps and branches (Section 5.1), the return stack (Section 5.2) and the repair mechanism (Section 5.3). To minimize the resource overhead, some features can be disabled (see Section 7). Indirect jumps which are not returns, are not supported so far, but many application programs or routines in embedded systems have none of these instructions.

The checker is placed between the first pipeline stages of the *Leon3* core (see Figure 4). The current program counter for the checker is the program counter in the decode pipeline step and the next program counter is the program counter of the fetch pipeline step. For reexecuting a jump or branch, the program counter of the memory step is looped back to the program counter generation (a step prior to the fetch step), and the instructions are annulled after the memory step, so the incorrect instructions are not executed and no registers or memories are written. Because of the loop back, the jump is executed again, and if this execution is correct, the program is continued normally.

To prepare an application, the compiled code is analyzed by a program which decodes the instructions and searches for jumps, branches, calls and returns (see Figure 5). The addresses of these instructions are stored in the *sAdrRam* initialization file and the destination address, except for the return instruction, is stored in *jAdrRam* initialization file. Also, the initialization file for the control Ram (*ctrlRam*) is generated, and the activate and deactivate instructions for the checker unit are inserted. The original program of the application remains completely unchanged.

The memory initialization files can be used for the synthesis of the checker unit, or the content of the rams can be initialized directly in the bitfile of the FPGA with the Xilinx tool *"data2mem"*. For future FPGA and ASIC versions of the checker, the memories could be initialized also at runtime over a memory bus or the processor.

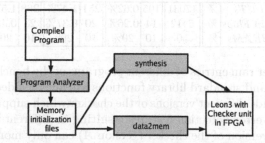

Fig. 5. From the compiled code, the program analyzer extracts all branches, calls, and returns and generates the memory initialization files for the *sAdrRam*, *jAdrRam*, and *ctrlRam*. The checker rams can be initialized during the synthesis or later in the bitfile with the *data2mem* tool.

7   Overhead Analysis

Next, we analyze the number of entries of the checker rams (*sAdrRam*, *jAdrRam*, and *ctrlRam*) and the area overhead of the checker for different supported features. Furthermore, the verification process of the checker unit is described in this section.

We analyze the number of required entries of the checker ram for the SPEC CINT2000 benchmark [14] compiled to the *Leon* processor. Table 2 shows the

Table 2. Number of required entries in the checker rams for different programs of the SPEC CINT2000 benchmark [14]

SPEC program	gzip	gcc	vpr	mcf	crafty	parser	gap	vortex	bzip2	twolf
checker ram entries	2138	79206	5125	398	8471	5214	23721	21943	1203	7952

Table 3. Area overheads of different checker unit versions for a *Leon3* core without PCI and Ethernet. The area and memory overhead of the full version C and the reduced versions (A and B) and for different checker ram sizes are shown.

Overhead		Leon3	Version A		Version B		Version C	
checker rams with 512 entries								
LUTs	%	17031	106	0.62%	242	1.42%	259	1.52%
Flip Flops	%	5412	11	0.20%	17	0.31%	20	0.37%
BRAMs	%	50	3	6%	3	6%	3	6%
checker rams with 1024 entries								
LUTs	%	17031	111	0.65%	248	1.46%	265	1.56%
Flip Flops	%	5412	12	0.22%	18	0.33%	21	0.39%
BRAMs	%	50	5	10%	5	10%	5	10%
checker rams with 2048 entries								
LUTs	%	17031	112	0.66%	250	1.47%	267	1.57%
Flip Flops	%	5412	13	0.24%	19	0.35%	22	0.41%
BRAMs	%	50	8	16%	8	16%	8	16%
checker rams with 4096 entries								
LUTs	%	17031	105	0.62%	251	1.47%	268	1.57%
Flip Flops	%	5412	14	0.26%	20	0.37%	23	0.42%
BRAMs	%	50	10	20%	10	20%	10	20%

number of checker ram entries of different programs of the benchmark. Operating system routines and standard library functions are not included in this analysis.

Next, we provide different versions of the checker which support different jump instructions and error detection features resulting in different area overheads.

The smallest version of the checker (version A) can only monitor direct jumps or branches. All indirect jumps are not supported and not allowed in the code, but it is allowed that indirect jumps can occur in the unchecked code. This includes also returns from subroutine, so this technique can only be used for a single procedure or function. But many of these procedures and functions can be checked if the checker unit is deactivated at calls and returns, and activated inside the function.

The second version (version B) is version A with an additional 32 entry return stack. With this version, we can also monitor calls and returns, so the most application programs can be fully monitored.

The last version (version C) has the additional capability of repeating an incorrect jump or branch instruction as described in Section 5.3 and Section 6.

Table 3 shows the overhead of different versions, synthesized and implemented on a *Virtex 4* with ISE 8.2 with different checker ram sizes. The results show that the area overhead for logic (lookup tables and Flip Flops) is very small. If more control flow instructions shall be monitored and more checker ram entries are needed, only the overhead of the block rams increases. A qualitatively comparison of the overhead to other approaches is difficult due to different target architectures.

The verification of the checker has been performed by simulation and the Leon in-circuit debugger. Instruction faults are simulated between the instruction cache and the integer unit by an XOR with an error mask, read in from a file. With the in-circuit debugger, control flow instructions can be altered inside the memory (for example the jump destination encoded inside the instruction). With these techniques, the checker and the correction of incorrect jump instruction has been verified.

8   Conclusions and Future Work

We introduced a systematic methodology for autonomous control flow checking for embedded RISC CPUs which can monitor direct jump and branches as well as returns from subroutine. Experimental results show that the additional hardware overhead is small. In particular, lookup tables and Flip Flops overhead amount to an overhead of less than 2% in all cases. So, the only overhead results from the additional memory needed to monitor the control flow instructions. A modular concept for generation of checker units has been proposed, so the area overhead can be further reduced, by removing some functions. The detection of faults is very fast, so we have the possibility to react immediately during the execution of a faulty instruction and are able to prevent incorrect instructions from being executed. Furthermore, an incorrect jump or branch instruction can be refetched and reexecuted. With this technique, we therefore have no performance impact on the CPU and the compiled program code remains unchanged.

We introduced a second independent program counter $CUPC$ with its own state machine and own microcode with own microinstructions ($ctrlRam$). The checker program code is based on the extracted branch and jump instructions from the program code at compile time. This reduced code covers only direct branches or jumps without the instructions between two branch points. With this technique, we enhanced the CPU with a reduced second independent program counter and instruction unit at minimum additional hardware cost and full control of the program flow.

Further extensions can be the support of indirect jumps, multi threading, and the check of the conditionals of branches. Also, an interface to the OS could be usefully to count the errors and to report the reliability of the CPU.

Finally, if the checker unit has a bus interface, the contents or part of the content of the checker rams may be stored in the system memory. Only the content for checking the current part of program (e.g. the current function or a set of functions which are current in use) may be hold in the local checker rams. If the checker needs informations which are not stored inside the local checker rams, the checker can generate a page-fault-like event to signal the operating system to reload the checker rams with the needed contents. This concept of caching can reduce the the among of memory overhead significantly.

References

1. Ziegler, B.B.P.: Fliegendes Rechnernetz. In: CT, Heise Verlag (2005)
2. Lee, K., Shrivastava, A., Issenin, I., Dutt, N., Venkatasubramanian, N.: Mitigating soft error failures for multimedia applications by selective data protection. In: CASES 2006: Proceedings of the 2006 International Conference on Compilers, Architecture and Synthesis for Embedded Systems, pp. 411–420. ACM, New York (2006)
3. US-CERT: Vulnerability notes database CERT Coordination Center, http://www.kb.cert.org/vuls/
4. Gaisler Research: LEON3 SPARC V8 Processor core, http://www.gaisler.com
5. Mueller, M., et al.: RAS strategy for IBM S/390 G5 and G6. IBM J. RES. DEVELOP 43(5/6) (1999)
6. Lu, D.J.: Watchdog processors and structural integrity checking. IEEE Trans. Computers 31(7), 681–685 (1982)
7. Schuette, M.A., Shen, J.P.: Processor control flow monitoring using signatured instruction streams. IEEE Trans. Comput. 36(3), 264–277 (1987)
8. Majzik, I., Pataricza, A., Cin, M.D., Hohl, W., Honig, J., Sieh, V.: Hierarchical checking of multiprocessors using watchdog processors. In: European Dependable Computing Conference, pp. 386–403 (1994)
9. Michel, T., Leveugle, R., Saucier, G.: A new approach to control flow checking without program modification. In: FTCS, pp. 334–343 (1991)
10. Arora, D., Ravi, S., Raghunathan, A., Jha, N.K.: Hardware-assisted run-time monitoring for secure program execution on embedded processors. In: IEEE Transactions on VLSI Systems, Washington, DC, USA. IEEE Computer Society, Los Alamitos (2006)
11. Goloubeva, O., Rebaudengo, M., Reorda, M.S., Violante, M.: Soft-error detection using control flow assertions. In: DFT 2003: Proceedings of the 18th IEEE International Symposium on Defect and Fault Tolerance in VLSI Systems, Washington, DC, USA, p. 581. IEEE Computer Society, Los Alamitos (2003)
12. Abadi, M., Budiu, M., Erlingsson, Ú., Ligatti, J.: Control-flow integrity. In: CCS 2005: Proceedings of the 12th ACM Conference on Computer and Communications Security, pp. 340–353. ACM Press, New York (2005)
13. Austin, T.M.: DIVA: A reliable substrate for deep submicron microarchitecture design. In: International Symposium on Microarchitecture, pp. 196–207 (1999)
14. Standard Performance Evaluation Corporation (SPEC): SPEC CPU, V1.3. (2000), http://www.spec.org
15. SPARC: The SPARC Architecture Manual V8, http://www.sparc.com/standards/V8.pdf

Autonomous Querying for Knowledge Networks

Kieran Greer[1], Matthias Baumgarten[1], Chris Nugent[1], Maurice Mulvenna[1],
and Kevin Curran[2]

[1] School of Computing and Mathematics and Computer Science Research Institute,
University of Ulster, Northern Ireland, UK
[2] School of Computing and Intelligent Systems and Computer Science Research
Institute, University of Ulster, Northern Ireland, UK

Abstract. A knowledge network is a construct that will organise knowledge in a way that allows it to be efficiently retrieved and used. While an Internet-based network is the obvious application area, the system would also be suitable for pervasive sensorised environments. Key elements thereof are its lightweight, reference-based structure and its autonomous nature. This paper is concerned with describing the querying process that will be used to retrieve information from the network. For this process, the network metadata will act as a lightweight and distributed ontology, where the hierarchical structures of the network will describe the main relationships and guide the search. Then, using autonomous querying, the ontology can be updated with personal references between sources, allowing for semantically unrelated concepts to also be linked together. A novel linking mechanism is described that is shown to be effective, dynamic and adaptive, and could be particularly useful in tomorrow's Semantic Web environment.

Keywords: Autonomous, Knowledge, Query, Network, Stigmergy.

1 Introduction

A knowledge network is a generic structure that organises distributed knowledge of any format into a system that will allow it to be retrieved efficiently. The rationale of the knowledge network is to act as a middle layer that connects to a multitude of sources, organises them based on various concepts and finally provides well-structured, pre-organised knowledge to individual services and applications. Baumgarten et al. 2006 and Mulvenna et al. 2006 have described the initial philosophy behind this network concept in their earlier works. The term 'knowledge network' has nonetheless been used by different researchers; see for example Lee et al. 2004. For the context of this paper, a knowledge network could be understood to be a network that organises information sources through the use of ontologies and intelligent links, to provide some sort of meaning to the associations. By meaningful it is meant that the associations will be understood by the user of the network. The network can also be loaded with any number of services that can intelligently process or reason over the stored information. This

C. Rong et al. (Eds.): ATC 2008, LNCS 5060, pp. 249–263, 2008.

sounds a lot like the Web 3.0 and is a reasonably good generic definition. However, this work would extend the definition to also accommodate the pervasive sensorised environments. The sensors would act as data sources, providing information to a more intelligent system that could combine such information with heterogeneous data sources found on the Internet, for example. Thus dynamic and real-time aspects of an environment can also be used to answer queries and can also be combined with existing knowledge sources.

The knowledge can be represented by understanding the context in which each node is used. For example, the metadata describing a node can be used to compare and link the node with other nodes. However, this cannot provide a complete organisation, as in a dynamic environment everything cannot be known beforehand. There is also the problem of distriminating between several nodes of the same type. Thus temporary overlay views are required to further optimise and these can dynamically change over time to reflect the use of the system. The mechanism that is used to optimise and generate these views is by stigmergically linking sources that are related through the querying process. If we consider the ant colony optimisation algorithm (ACO) (Dorigo and Di Caro, 1999), then with this algorithm, pheromone trails between nodes in a network can be strengthened or weakened to define a route through them. A similar strengthening/weakening mechanism is used to link the sources related to each other through the queries.

The semantically related organisation (see Fig. 1 in section 4) and reasoning is new work on the system that is being presented in this paper. The main focus however is the query process that will be used to query the knowledge. It is possible to use the querying mechanism as an additional part of the knowledge organisation mechanism, to autonomously create the temporary views that reflect the use of the system. The challenges faced for querying this knowledge can therefore be identified as follows:

1. Ontologies are typically used to represent knowledge as they allow for a richer set of querying operations, but the knowledge needs to be represented in a relatively lightweight way.
2. The querying construct should also be lightweight. However, complex sources are allowed, when they would also need to be queried.
3. The querying is distributed, retrieving information from several sources. This requires the query to be constructed dynamically from partial results as it is executed.
4. The knowledge organisation must be autonomous and does not assume any prior knowledge of the environment. The system is to be generic, dynamic and self-organising.
5. The potential size of the network could be huge, therefore some query optimisation, directing the search to the most relevant sources, would make a querying process more practical.

The rest of the paper is organised as follows: Section 2 describes related work. Section 3 describes the problems faced in querying the network and introduces a proposed solution. Section 4 describes the query process in more detail. Section 5 describes details of the implemented system, while section 6 discusses the paper's findings and presents the conclusions of the work.

2   Related Work

In this section some related methods for representing and storing knowledge are discussed, as well as some related work on autonomous querying.

2.1   Knowledge Representation

This section describes the usage of some XML-based knowledge representation methods used in distributed network environments. There is a strong emphasis on Semantic Web technologies in this area, where knowledge representation is an important topic. Knowledge representation generally deals with using ontologies. There are different definitions of what an ontology is depending on what subject area you are dealing with. Gruber 1993 gives the following definition for the area of 'AI and knowledge representation', which is suitable for this work:

'An ontology is an explicit specification of a conceptualisation. The term is borrowed from philosophy, where an ontology is a systematic account of Existence. For knowledge-based systems, what 'exists' is exactly that which can be represented. When the knowledge of a domain is represented in a declarative formalism, the set of objects that can be represented is called the universe of discourse. This set of objects, and the describable relationships among them, are reflected in the representational vocabulary with which a knowledge-based program represents knowledge. Thus, we can describe the ontology of a program by defining a set of representational terms. In such an ontology, definitions associate the names of entities in the universe of discourse (e.g., classes, relations, functions, or other objects) with human-readable text describing what the names are meant to denote, and formal axioms that constrain the interpretation and well-formed use of these terms.'

With the Semantic Web, the relations between concepts need to be deduced automatically. This can be achieved by semantic mapping, or it can also be achieved by examining the context in which different elements are used. This could be compared to knowledge or experience-based approaches. Due to the large amount of literature on knowledge representation and management, this topic is only briefly mentioned here, however RDF 2008 and languages derived from it such as OWL 2008 are popular standards for representing the knowledge.

Cuzzocrea 2005 addresses the issue of peer-to-peer processing of knowledge. He suggests a knowledge representation model in the form of a Semantic Relationship Matrix (SRM). The SRM for a peer is a 2-D matrix, having as rows the neighbouring peers and as columns the set of neighbouring concepts. This adds semantics to a p2p IS (peer-to-peer information system), giving a peer the knowledge it needs to query its neighbours. Sartiani et al. 2004 have also worked in the area of p2p systems. They suggest a p2p system called XPeer that contains super-peers that aggregate or organise other peers. The super-peers also combine the schema of the other peers automatically, allowing the system to be queried without the need for human administration. Dragan et al. 2005 also use the super-peer system. They allow peers to become super-peers if they continually reroute queries. The network structure described in this paper is essentially the same, with aggregated nodes referenced by other nodes and a lightweight linking mechanism based on flat or nested hashtable structures. This structure will be described in more detail in later sections.

2.2 Autonomous Querying

There has not been a lot of work presented on autonomous querying and published research seems to be different to the stigmergic linking methodology proposed in this paper. Mano et al. 2006 discuss the main mechanisms used in this paper for 'linking' (stigmergy, self-organisation, reinforcement). Stigmergy has now been used widely to self-organise in distributed mobile or ad-hoc networks (MANETs). These networks are highly dynamic and need a flexible and robust mechanism that can adapt and allow them to self-organise. As these systems can be on a massive scale, some centralised controlling mechanism may not be practical. Babaoglu et al. 2006 and Breukner and Parunak 2004 are papers that discuss this problem. Dragan et al. 2005 is also relevant, as the dynamic linking of sources will also in effect reroute queries. Another example can be found in Raschid et al. 2006. They apply linking to the problem of optimising routes through Web resources in the area of Life Sciences. In this set of resources, there are known to be different routes to different resources that may answer the same query and so one route can be more optimal than another. An example of linking based purely on the query experiences includes Koloniari et al. 2005. They try to cluster nodes in a p2p network based on query workloads. They try to cluster nodes with similar workloads together, which will maximise the number of relevant nodes that can be visited in a time period to answer a particular query, by having them just a few links apart. They describe that the mechanism for calculating the workload value is still an open issue and could be based on a node storing statistics on the queries that pass through it.

There are also several self-organising systems of other types. Construct (Stevenson et al., 2006), for example, is a self-aggregating system, where information from sources can be aggregated to provide higher levels of abstraction as required by the application. Construct is a service-based context-aggregation system that is self-organising. Pitoura et al. 2003 describe a service-oriented data management system that also queries massively distributed and autonomous p2p systems. They use ontologies to organise metadata describing the services and use filters to route the queries to the appropriate services. They also create user profiles that describe the user's use of the system. De Meo et al. 2003 and Marrow and Koubarakis 2005 also self-organise based on user profiles. The system to be described in this paper does not organise users, although it does globally organise the results of the users' requests. Hence the results are available to anyone who uses the network and not only to the specific users that performed the queries. This has advantages and disadvantages depending on what the individual users' want. A user new to the network may find the results of previous users to be helpful, whereas an experienced user with specific criteria may find this generalisation less useful. Nevertheless, the system does not prevent user profiles from also being used, for example, local views of the network can also be generated using the same linking mechanism and could be tailored to each individual user.

3 The Querying Problem

To retrieve the information that is contained in the knowledge network requires an efficient querying mechanism. This query mechanism should take maximum advantage of the relations already built by the knowledge network, but also, it should not alter them for each request. Therefore, the scope of the querying system is to build a temporary view of individual components without altering the structure of the underlying network. The architecture is intended to be generic allowing any type of source and any size of network. The knowledge represented by the network will be stored in XML format, where RDF or XML only will be allowed at the sources.

The ontology information can be distributed over the whole network, when the subclass or more obvious relations can be represented at each node. This provides a more lightweight structure than a large centralised repository. Then through the experience of the query results, other less obvious relations in the knowledge can be discovered that will be used to direct the search process more efficiently. These links are temporary and can complement the permanent organisation provided by the hierarchical network structure and help to create the views of the request layer. As will be explained in section 4, these links are created in a stigmergic way. Stigmergy uses changes in the environment rather than some knowledge-based approach to derive information and so tends to be more lightweight. Fig. 1 is an example of a hierarchical network related to weather and clothes concepts. The hierarchy associates concepts with sub-concepts, ending with instances of particular leaf concepts. The semantics or keywords that describe each node can thus be used as a lightweight ontology. In the figure, the solid arrows are semantically-based organisation, while the dashed lines are stigmergic links between specific source nodes.

4 The Query Process

To try and keep the network as lightweight as possible there will be two initial phases to the querying. The first phase is a search through the network to find the most suitable sources. This can also be used by itself as a search engine. The second phase is then to actually query those sources. The query search and execution is performed through the network structure itself. This is in keeping with a distributed system. The two phase approach, retrieving only source addresses in the first phase, also means that these addresses can be stored locally and the sources queried at any later time to retrieve information that might dynamically change. Thus the system can cope with more dynamic information

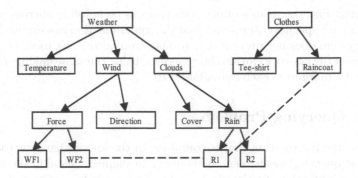

Fig. 1. Hierarchical network with experience-based linking

as well. There can then be a third phase that autonomously updates the knowledge based on the query process. The nodes in the network used for navigation (the higher level aggregating nodes) will store and process metadata, in RDF format, for example. There are then a set of source nodes at the leaf positions that access the sources directly. These do not perform any extra navigation but rather query a source to retrieve some information. These nodes do not have to process RDF but can be heterogeneous with respect to the query language and so should store a query engine suitable to the source. If there is a complex XML document, then the query engine might be something like XQuery (Chamberlin, 2002) or Xcerpt 2008. If there is a simple sensor, then an RDF query engine could be stored. A Query Mediator can convert the query request into the form suitable for the source. The source can then executes the query and returns the result to the mediator, which converts it back and combines it with all the other replies.

The following scenario will describe what this heterogeneous approach would allow: Consider the case where there are a number of distributed weather sensors and there is an XML document with knowledge on the clothes that people wear in different weather conditions. The query is 'retrieve what to wear when temperature and wind sensors indicate good conditions'. The query in the form of a typical 'select-from-where' statement may look like:

Select clothes.what_to_wear, From clothes, weather_station Where (clothes. weather Equals weather_station.conditions) and (weather_station.temperature_ sensor Equals hot) and (weather_station.wind_force_sensor Equals light)

Thus both sensors and knowledge sources can be used and combined to answer a dynamic query based on current conditions.

4.1 Autonomic Knowledge Updating

So the user submits a query and initiates a query process. The nodes visited to answer the query are recorded, which can be defined by the paths through the network. These nodes can then be informed of the query parts that they answered and form links between each other. This will in effect create temporary views to reflect the current network use. If the network use changes, then so will these views. Weighted values can be updated for links between sources that consistently answer the same types of query. If the weight values reach a certain threshold then the use of the system suggests that these sources are now related. This has the advantage of linking separate sources and not whole groups of sources. For example, if we have 100 temperature sensors and only 1 is used as part of a query, then only that single sensor could be linked to another part of the network while the other sensors are not included. This may also help to group nodes in a situational sense, as particular areas of the network may typically answer the same query. In Fig. 1 for example, when the Raincoat node is queried again with relation to Rain and Wind, the query engine can look at just the nodes R1 and WF2, omitting R2 and WF1. The linked paths are shown by the dashed lines and this would achieve some degree of optimisation.

This kind of linking is in line with the lightweight approach the knowledge network wishes to adopt. The nodes used to answer the query are informed and they strengthen their related links. If other sources are not used, their links may be weakened, until they are removed altogether. In this system, the exact node that should be visited to answer the first part of the query will not be indicated by the linking mechanism, however, local views of the whole network structure can also be constructed that will indicate nodes most commonly visited by the local application. This can be constructed using the same linking mechanism and will reduce the search to the first node type visited. The aim is then to indicate the other nodes for the rest of the query through related links, to try to reduce query time and improve the quality of service (or answer). For example, if the following query is executed:

Select budget.available, clothes.cost, clothes.what_to_buy, From budget, clothes, weather_station Where (budget.available Greater_Than clothes.cost) and (clothes. weather Equals weather_station.conditions)

Then the first part of the query that is solved is 'clothes.weather Equals weather_station.conditions'. The weather stations to look at could be indicated by a local view and resolved with clothes sources through comparisons or related links. Then, only these selected clothes sources are used to answer the second part of the query 'budget.available Greater_Than clothes.cost', which would also retrieve links to any related budget sources.

This is like the ACO method, where relations (pheromone trails) between nodes are strengthened/weakened. Because this weight updating is calculated through changes in the environment (nodes visited) and not by any knowledge-based process, it can be called stigmergic. It is also possible to include learning algorithms or fix and redistribute the total amount of allowed memory, ensuring that the structure stays lightweight. Work has also revealed levels of reasoning that can be obtained from the linking mechanism, by aggregating values based on the links (Greer et al., 2007b). For example, several linked source values could be averaged to give a 'best' value. Thus the knowledge of the users of the system (who create the links) can be used to perform some levels of reasoning over the contained information.

4.2   Test Results

A substantial amount of testing has demonstrated that the linking mechanism is indeed very effective. Tests have been conducted to try and determine the amount of variability that the linking mechanism will be able to cope with. For example, if all queries are the same then it should be easy to link the appropriate sources, while if they are always different then the linking mechanism will not work. To investigate these concepts further, random networks and queries were generated, with the queries being skewed towards certain types. The data generated was of the numerical type and so a metric could try to maximise the sum total for the answer to determine what the best answer would be. It is only important to specify in some way that one source is better than another. Then the linking mechanism must try to learn this relation.

The skewing was performed by placing source or value types into probability bands and then selecting from a band depending on a random number. For example, a 90:10 split would place certain source or value types in a 90% probability band with the rest in the 10% probability band. When retrieving a source or value type, the 90% band would be visited much more often, skewing the queries towards the types in that band. Statistics are compared between a full search that is guided only by the hierarchy and a linked search that also uses links between the source nodes. Node count and quality of answer are measured. The full search has access to all source nodes and so will always return the best answer. The linked search will not visit all source nodes. If the linking is correct however, linking the appropriate sources, it will still return a good answer. If it is not correct, then it will return a poorer answer. Greer et al. 2007a 2007b gives some more information on the testing procedure and potential for the linking mechanism. Greer et al. 2007a showed the result that the querying mechanism needed to be supervised as too many links could in fact be added. When this happened the linking mechanism would need to be adapted to improve performance again. So as well as self-organisation through the linking mechanism, self-supervision would also be necessary. The values for this evaluation were for a split of 90:10 and one would expect to obtain an effective performance from the linking mechanism with this amount of variability. However, down to a 70:30 split could also be effective. Table 1 gives some indication of performance levels for the linked search compared to a full search for different levels of skewing.

For these tests, the random network was constructed from the following parameters: There were a total of 10 different source types and 5 different value types. For the skewing, the source types were split 3:7, while the value types were split 2:3. Each value type was assigned a random value in the range 1 to

Table 1. Example of possible search reduction with related loss of QoS values for different query skewing

	70:30 - EO	80:20 - EO	90:10 - EO	70:30 - AC	80:20 - AC	90:10 - AC
Search Reduction	89%	86%	87%	92%	92%	94%
Loss of QoS	11%	9%	5%	13%	11%	7%

10. For the random network there were 30 instances of each source type and thus 300 sources nodes with 315 nodes in total. Thus a 70:30 skew indicates 3 source types and 2 value types in the 70% band, with the other 7 source types and 3 value types in the 30% band. Queries that used the equivalence only (EO) comparison or used all comparison (AC) operators were tested and the results are an average over 3 test runs. The results show that while the search reduction remains relatively constant for each query type, the greater skewing significantly improves the quality of answer. The equivalence only queries also have an improved quality of answer over the all comparison queries, as you would expect, due to the smaller variability in possible query types.

5 System Details

The knowledge network concepts have been implemented as an integral component of a larger system. This system includes a communication package, the knowledge network components and an admin/user application. The communication package is a separate package designed on the XML-RPC mechanism. This package has been given the name 'licas' (lightweight communication for autonomic services). The packages allow for networks of nested services to be built and stored on distributed servers. The licas package also contains the linking package used to dynamically link the different services (or nodes) based on the query feedback. This server-side p2p framework is then extended by the knowledge network components themselves, which are used to build the actual network. Data is provided by an internal structure in each source node that stores XML values, although some sensors have also been accessed by the software[1]. The knowledge network package also contains the functionality to generate random networks and queries, the ability to test these and also measure statistics based on the querying process. Thus a reliable evaluation of the linking mechanism can be obtained. The client side consists of an admin/user application. This acts both as an admin gui and also as a practical application with which to query the network.

All queries are of the 'select-from-where' type, while the data is in XML format. Currently the query engine can perform either a search or a full evaluation of source nodes. All of the metadata used to describe the services is retrieved when a network is loaded and so when using the search engine, this can then be used to identify which services to access. For example, if considering Fig. 1, the user could ask for nodes (or services) relating to Raincoat or Wind, etc. Then addresses to the relevant nodes can be found and returned, together with some metadata describing the service. If the queries specify specific values for specific nodes, then an evaluation of the node values is also performed and the resulting best value returned as the answer. Depending on what sort of query is being executed, some amount of query re-writing is performed to provide a standard 'select-from-where' format to process. All of the main functionality is held in different services that are loaded as and when needed. For example, a statistics

---

[1] Nicola Bicocchi, University of Modena and Reggio Emilia.

service will store statistics for each node, or a linking service will store and update the linking structure. The main focus of the work to date has been on the autonomic and stigmergic aspects, but now work is also focusing on semantic evaluations. A metadata service already exists that is used to process the query request by matching it to the metadata held at each node. While the system is very much a prototype, the metadata service even allows pattern matching of XML fragments, as you would expect in an XML-based query language. Now also, RDF schema can be parsed and the network structure constructed from the schema contents.

The RDF parser can also read SWRL rules and use them to answer queries not directly answerable by the network semantics. The RDF parser has read an OWL ontology called 'myfamily.rdf' (this can be found at http://www.agnbi.de/research/swrlengine/#why%20additional%20rules) and constructed the network from that. This ontology also contains a number of rules that describe relations between the different family members. Fig. 2 shows the admin/user application after a reasoning query has been performed. This is a new query process recently added to the system. The reasoning process shows how the stigmergic links and the semantics can be combined to answer queries that each could not answer individually. The links can be entered manually for testing, but would occur naturally through the use of the system in a real environment. An example of a link can be seen in the top half of the Knowledge Network window. The links represent the relations built up between the network components by the users of the system. The semantics then represent the knowledge that is already known about the network. The query being executed is asking if a child called 'Charlie' has an uncle. For testing purposes concepts can be removed from the network construction, so that they have to be answered using rules. The rule used to answer this links the concepts 'Child' with 'hasParent' and 'hasParent' with 'hasBrother'. The query can be constructed as shown in the Query Client window. A standard 'select-from-where' query is constructed, but the question is added to the front of the query. The standard query is processed and this returns an answer, finding a child source with a value of 'Charlie'. The source used to answer this is taken to be the starting point to process the rule. The rule states that you have an uncle if you have a parent and your parent has a brother. The rule looks for stigmergic links from the starting source to the related sources to determine if a path exists that will satisfy the question. All rules can be parsed and only the ones that contain the appropriate concepts need to be traced. In this case a path does exist and the name of the uncle is 'Jack'. You could imagine nested select statements with additional questions, where the select clause would provide the starting point for a rule search that would provide further starting points for further select clause queries, etc. This could provide quite a powerful reasoning engine. The knowledge network that is constructed can be seen in the bottom right panel of the Knowledge Network window. The structure is to have a flat repository of sources and then to create the hierarchy through referencing the different source types. The values are single XML elements. The bottom left panel shows the results of a reasoning query.

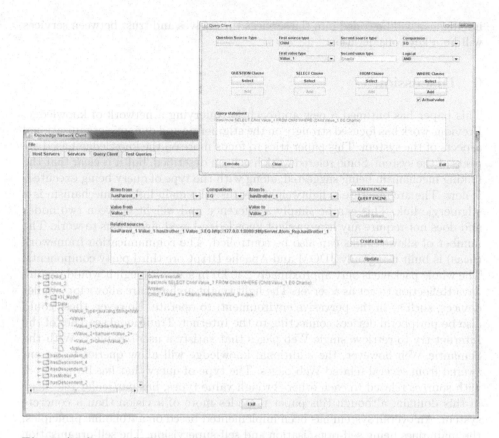

Fig. 2. Application GUI showing the result of a reasoning query. The network is constructed from the 'myfamily.rdf' schema.

5.1 Autonomic Aspects

The developed system shows several autonomic features. The querying process has already been described. This is related to dynamic/adaptive systems, emergence and self-organisation. It is autonomic because it can self-organise based on the feedback from the query process. The links are dynamic and can change over time, thus it is the system itself, based on its use, that determines what links are constructed. Self-supervision based on measuring the linking performance is also possible (Greer et al. 2007a). The licas system has security features in the form of password protection. Nevertheless it is also expected that the individual services will negotiate with each other to determine if they can use each other. Specific functionality for this is not in place and it would be very much application dependent. Method skeletons exist however for agent-like communication, when a service can also decide to give its password based on a description of the asking service. The system is completely open. Once a password has been given any service is free to call any other service. Thus it is expected that intelligence will be coded into the services themselves and trust between services will be a key consideration.

6 Discussion

This paper has outlined a new approach for querying a network of knowledge. Previous work has focused strongly on the stigmergic and dynamic organisational aspects of the system. This paper tries to focus more on the knowledge-based aspects of the system. Some related work has been described, but it is clear that the linking mechanism being suggested, along with the type of query being executed, is new. The architecture is lightweight because the main linking mechanism is a stigmergic link. This can be simply a reference and weight between two nodes and does not require any heavyweight knowledge-based algorithms to work. The number of allowed links can also be controlled. The communication framework (licas) is built using only JDOM and Apache HttpCore third party components. The whole package is only approximaely 240 kb in size, although it would require Java Reflection to act as a server. The lightweight architecture allows for smaller devices, such as in the pervasive environment, to operate. However, these could also be peripheral devices connecting to the Internet. Traditional searches of the Internet try to retrieve single Web pages that satisfy a user's request. With the Semantic Web however, the additional knowledge will allow queries to be answered from several related Web pages. The type of query that has been tested, with sources related to each other through value types, has particular relevance in this domain, although this paper provides more of a vision than a concrete system. An overall system has been implemented based on autonomic principles, the main ones being self-organisation and self-supervision. The self-organisation is controlled by the linking mechanism and will emerge through the results of the query requests. The ontology information may be integrated into the network itself, making use of the elements that already exist.

The licas package is generic, but the knowledge network and client packages rely on the knowledge network components. However, there is nothing special about the organisational structure or type of data that is stored and so the basic organisation and querying principles are also generic and could be applied to many different systems. The organisation could be obtained from an algorithm, or thorugh reading XML schemas. Previously constructed schemas should, in theory, provide a correct hierarchical organisation of the knowledge. Because the potential size of the network can be huge, the stigmergic links can then prune most of the nodes from the search process, making querying of larger networks more practical. The architecture is one of distributed networks that talk to each other, but the query process has a certain amount of sequential processing that would slow down the query process. This is due to comparisons between specific values of specific nodes. Thus while the node count can be shown to be dramatically reduced, no claims about overall search time are being made. However, the same process without the stigmergic linking would be much slower.

The querying process suggests two initial stages - one to traverse the network and one to query the sources. The search will be largely guided by the hierarchical structure, which is permanent. Given that the main navigation is accounted for, the query process can try to improve the network performance in an experience based way by directly linking semantically unrelated sources for certain query types. Thus if many source instances of the same type exist, optimisation can indicate only specific ones to look at. This is performed in a stigmergic and autonomic manner and will allow temporal and situational factors to be included. Tests have then shown that the query performance can be improved further through supervising it to adapt the linking mechanism when performance begins to drop again. It is also clear that a complete organisation of the network requires both semantics and experience-based techniques and so semantic processing is now also being looked at.

The problems that needed to be solved at the end of the Introduction section can now be addressed as follows:

1. Ontologies - the hierarchical structure, together with the metadata stored at each node, represents sufficient ontology information to allow for a search through the network. The network acts like an indexing system and for the search the essential relation would be the subclass relation. This is provided by the hierarchical links.
2. Lightweight - the main architecture is lightweight, but it is also flexible, allowing for more heavyweight components/services if required.
3. Distributed querying - the query process is a 2-stage process to answer the query and a third stage to update the linking structures. The search is performed in a distributed manner, through the individual nodes. Also, any evaluation that can be executed locally at a source is performed there. For example, a value type compared to an actual value will be evaluated at the source and the source address returned only if the evaluation is true. Comparing different source types must be performed sequentially, however, as we need all sources first to make the comparison. The rest of the query evaluation then also requires the related linked nodes from the previous parts before it can be performed.
4. Knowledge organisation - the static organisation is not dynamic but permanent based on semantics. The stigmergic linking however is autonomous and dynamic, providing temporary overlay views. This allows the knowledge organisation to adapt to the changing use of the system.
5. Query optimisation - both the hierarchical structure and the stigmergic links will provide for optimisation of the search process. The hierarchy provides clear paths to the source nodes while the links can select individual source nodes of the same type. Tests have shown that the stigmergic linking can improve search over using just the hierarchy by 80 - 90%, while the hierarchy will obviously improve over searching the whole network by a very large amount.

Acknowledgements

This work has been carried out in the project CASCADAS (IST-027807), which is supported by the European Framework VI FET Proactive Initiative IST-2004-2.3.4 programme of the European Commission.

References

Babaoglu, O., Canright, G., Deutsch, A., Di Caro, G.A., Ducatelle, F., Gambardella, L.M., Ganguly, N., Jelasity, M., Montemanni, R., Montresor, A., Urnes, T.: Design Patterns from Biology for Distributed Computing. ACM Transactions on Autonomous and Adaptive Systems 1(1), 26–66 (2006)

Baumgarten, M., Bicocchi, N., Curran, K., Mamei, M., Mulvenna, M., Nugent, C., Zambonelli, F.: Towards Self-Organizing Knowledge Networks for Smart World Infrastructures. In: Invited Session on Service Development and Provisioning through Situated and Autonomic Communications at International Conference on Self-Organization and Autonomous Systems in Computing and Communications (SOAS 2006), September 18-21, 2006, Erfurt, Germany (2006)

Breukner, S.A., Van Dyke Parunak, H.: Self-Organising MANET Management. In: Di Marzo Serugendo, G., et al. (eds.) AAMAS 2003 Ws ESOA. LNCS (LNAI), vol. 2977, pp. 20–35. Springer, Heidelberg (2004)

Chamberlin, D.: X Query: An XML query language. IMB Systems Journal 41(4), 597–615 (2002)

Cuzzocrea, A.: Towards a Semantics-based Framework for KD- and IR-style Resource Querying on XML-based P2P Information Systems. In: Proceedings of the 2005 IEEE/WIC/ACM International Conference on Web Intelligence (WI 2005) (2005)

De Meo, P., Mbale, J., Terracina, G., Ursino, D.: An XML-based multi-agent system for the user-oriented management of QoS in telecommunications networks. In: 2003. IAT 2003. IEEE/WIC International Conference on Intelligent Agent Technology, October 13-16, 2003, pp. 96–102 (2003)

Dorigo, M., Di Caro, G.: Ant colony optimization: a new meta-heuristic, Evolutionary Computation 2. In: Proceedings of the 1999 Congress on CEC 1999, p. 1477 (1999)

Dragan, F., Gardarin, G., Yeh, L.: MediaPeer: a safe, scalable P2P architecture for XML query processing. In: Proceedings, Sixteenth International Workshop on Database and Expert Systems Applications, August 22-26, 2005, pp. 368–373 (2005)

Greer, K., Baumgarten, M., Mulvenna, M., Curran, K., Nugent, C.: Autonomic Supervision of Stigmergic Self-Organisation for Distributed Information Retrieval. In: Workshop on Technologies for Situated and Autonomic Communications (SAC), at 2nd International Conference on Bio-Inspired Models of Network, Information, and Computing Systems, BIONETICS 2007, Budapest, Hungary, December 10-13 (2007)

Greer, K., Baumgarten, M., Mulvenna, M., Nugent, C., Curran, K.: Knowledge-Based Reasoning through Stigmergic Linking. In: Hutchison, D., Katz, R.H. (eds.) IWSOS 2007. LNCS, vol. 4725, pp. 240–254. Springer, Heidelberg (2007)

Gruber, T.: A translation approach to portable ontology specifications. Knowledge Acquisition 5, 199–220 (1993)

Koloniari, G., Petrakis, Y., Pitoura, E., Tsotsos, T.: Query workload-aware overlay construction using histograms. In: Proceedings of the 14th ACM International Conference on Information and Knowledge Management, pp. 640–647 (2005)

Karvounarakis, G., Christophides, V., Plexousakis, D., Alexaki, S.: Querying community web portals, Technical Report, Institute of Computer Science, FORTH, Heraklion, Greece (2000)

Lee, M., Stanley, Y., Su, W., Lam, H.: Event and rule services for achieving a Web-based knowledge network. Knowledge-Based Systems 17, 179–188 (2004)

Mano, J.-P., Bourjot, C., Lopardo, G., Glize, P.: Bio-inspired Mechanisms for Artificial Self-organised Systems. Informatica 30, 55–62 (2006)

Marrow, P., Koubarakis, M.: Self-organising Applications Using Lightweight Agents. Engineering Self-Organising Systems, 120–129 (2005)

Mulvenna, M.D., Zambonelli, F., Curran, K., Nugent, C.D.: Knowledge Networks. In: Stavrakakis, I., Smirnov, M. (eds.) LPAR 2005. LNCS (LNAI), vol. 3835, pp. 99–114. Springer, Heidelberg (2005)

OWL, Web Ontology Language Reference (last accessed on 10/1/08), http://www.w3.org/TR/owl-ref/

Pitoura, E., Abiteboul, S., Pfoser, D., Samaras, G., Vazirgiannis, M.: DBGlobe: a service-oriented P2P system for global computing. ACM SIGMOD Record 32:3, SPECIAL ISSUE: Special topic section on peer to peer data management, 77–82 (2003)

Raschid, L., Wu, Y., Lee, W.-J., Vidal, M.-E., Tsaparas, P., Srinivasan, P., Sehgal, A.K.: Ranking Target Objects of Navigational Queries. In: 8th ACM International Workshop on Web Information and Data Management WIDM 2006, pp. 27–34 (2006)

RDF, Resource Description Framework (RDF) (last accessed on 10/1/08), http://www.w3.org/RDF/

Sartiani, C., Manghi, P., Ghelli, G., Conforti, G.: XPeer: A Self-organising XML p2p Database System (last accessed on 10/1/08), http://www.di.unipi.it/~ghelli/papers/SarManGhe04-p2pdb.pdf

Stevenson, G., Nixon, P., Dobson, S.: Towards a reliable wide-area infrastructure for context-based self-management of communications. In: Stavrakakis, I., Smirnov, M. (eds.) WAC 2005. LNCS, vol. 3854, pp. 115–128. Springer, Heidelberg (2006)

Xcerpt, Xcerpt - Rule-Based Querying and Reasoning on the (Semantic) Web (last accessed on 10/1/08), http://www.xcerpt.org/

Discovery of Useful Patterns from Tree-Structured Documents with Label-Projected Database*

Juryon Paik[1], Junghyun Nam[2], Hee Yong Youn[1], and Ung Mo Kim[1]

[1] Dept. of Computer Engineering, Sungkyunkwan University, Republic of Korea
quasa277@gmail.com, youn@ece.skku.ac.kr, umkim@ece.skku.ac.kr
[2] Dept. of Computer Science, Konkuk University, Republic of Korea
jhnam@kku.ac.kr

Abstract. Due to its highly flexible tree structure, XML data is used to capture most kinds of data and provides a substrate in which almost any other data structure may be presented. With the continuous growth of XML tree data in electronic environments, the discovery of useful knowledge from them has been a main research area in the information retrieval community. The mostly used approach to this task is to extract frequently occurring subtree patterns from a set of trees. However, because the number of frequent subtrees grows exponentially with the size of trees, a more practical and scalable alternative is required, which is the discovery of maximal frequent subtrees. The maximal frequent subtrees hold all the useful information, though, the number of them is much smaller than that of frequent subtrees. Handling the maximal frequent subtrees is an interesting challenge, and represents the core of this paper. As far as we know, this is one of the first studies to directly discover maximal frequent subtrees without any candidate sets generations as well as eliminating the process of useless subtree pruning. To this end, we define and use a new type of projected database to represent XML tree data efficiently. It significantly improves the entire process of mining maximal frequent subtree patterns. We study the performance and the scalability of the proposed approach through experiments based on synthetic datasets.

1 Introduction

With the ever-increasing amount of XML data in electronic environments, the ability to extract valuable knowledge from them becomes increasingly important and desirable, because a data-rich environment does not mean an information-rich environment. This caused that the data mining community has been challenged to come up with an efficient and scalable method for uncovering useful

---

* This work was supported in part by the Ubiquitous Autonomic Computing and Network Project, 21st Century Frontier R&D Program, and by the ITRC(Information Technology Research Center) support program supervised by the IITA(Institute of Information Technology Advancement) (IITA-2008-C1090-0801-0028), both funded by the MKE(Ministry of Knowledge Economy), Korea.

C. Rong et al. (Eds.): ATC 2008, LNCS 5060, pp. 264–278, 2008.

information from a large collection of XML data, where the problem of finding information from XML data has not been very well studied, in spite of its applicability to a broad variety of problems in XML world. Since XML has tree structure, traditional extraction methods which are typically applied to flat structure cannot be used directly to XML data. Even though XML data can be flattened out into a set, this may result in loss of significant structural information. It is not trivial work to discover useful information from XML trees. With increasing demands, however, it is necessary to develop new extraction methods or adjusting the existing ones for the data of XML. Various works have been proposed.

The most common approaches are *apriori* [2]-based and frequent-pattern-growth(FP) [5]-based techniques. The apriori-based algorithms extract frequent subtrees by the well known anti-monotone property, *every non empty subtree of a frequent tree is also frequent*, for candidate-generate-and-test. Since it provides significant reduction of the number of candidate sets and leads to good performance gain, various techniques, such as mining of path, enumeration tree, prefix subtree, scope of nodes, least general generalization, have been issued [11,1,14,4,9].

However, apriori-based algorithms suffer from two high computational costs: generating a huge number of candidate subtrees and scanning a same database repeatedly for the frequency counting of candidate sets. To solve such problems, FP-growth is extended to mine tree patterns. The algorithms [10,15] which base on the FP-growth avoid candidate sets generation. Instead, they construct a concise in-memory data structure that preserves all necessary information related to the frequent subtrees, recursively partition an original database into several conditional databases and search for local frequent subtrees to assemble larger global frequent subtrees, which is that the strategy of divide-and-conquer. A potential problem with this approach, however, is that the recursive projection may again lead to a lot of pointer chasing and poor cache behavior.

The goal of all the mentioned approaches above is to discover frequent subtrees from a database of trees. However, as observed in Chi et al's papers [4], the number of frequent subtrees usually grows exponentially with the size of trees due to the combinatorial explosion in candidate subtrees generation. This causes severe problems with the completion time of mining algorithm and the huge amount of potentially uninteresting patterns. Therefore, finding all frequent subtrees becomes infeasible for a large number of trees.

The more practical and scalable alternative is to mine maximal frequent subtrees, which was presented by Xiao et al. [12] and Chi et al. [4]. A maximal frequent subtree is a frequent subtree for which none of its proper supertrees are frequent, and the number of them is much smaller than that of frequent subtrees. However, finding maximal frequent subtrees is still in the immature stage and needs to be further researched, compared to the substantial achievements in finding frequent subtrees. Handling the maximal frequent subtrees is an interesting challenge, thought, and represents the core of this paper.

As a step toward this direction, from the perspective of the design of knowledge extraction algorithm, we consider the challenging problem of efficient reduction of subtree generation for finding maximal frequent subtrees. The proposed solution relies on a newly introduced concept of label-projected database, and it leverages the properties of the proposed approach that is inherently list-based as opposed to tree-based. The proposed method not only gets rid of the process for infrequent tree pruning, but also totally eliminates the problem of generating candidate subtrees. Hence, it significantly improves the whole mining process. To the best of our knowledge, the algorithm proposed in this paper is the first one directly discovering maximal frequent subtrees without any subtree generation.

2   Problem Definition

XML represents data as *trees*, and makes no requirement that the trees be balanced. Indeed, XML is remarkably free-form, with the only requirements being that it has to be rooted and labeled.

General tree concepts. A *rooted tree* is directed acyclic graph satisfying (1) there is a special node called the <u>root</u> that has no entering edges, (2) every other node has exactly one entering edge, and (3) there is a unique path from the root to each node. A tree is a *labeled tree* if there exists a labeling function that assigns a label to each node of a tree. Let $T = (r, N, E, \mathcal{L})$ be a rooted labeled tree, where $r \in N$ is the root node, N is a set of nodes, E is a set of edges, and $\mathcal{L}$ is a labeling function for nodes in the tree; for any node $v \in N$, $\mathcal{L}(v)$ assigns the label of v. Any node u on the unique path from r to v is called an ancestor of v. If u is an ancestor of v, then v is a descendant of u. If u is an immediate ancestor of v, then u is called the parent of v, and v is the child of u. Each node v has only one parent while a node u can have one or more children. Nodes that share the same parent are siblings. A node with no children is a leaf node; otherwise, it is an internal node. For brevity, in the remaining of this paper, unless otherwise specified, we call a rooted labeled tree as simply a tree.

Tree inclusion has been suggested as an important primitive for expressing queries on structured document databases [6]. A structured document database is considered as a collection of trees. The tree inclusion is used as a means of retrieving information from them [3]. The general tree inclusion problem given a pattern tree S and a target tree T is to *find the subtrees* of T that are instances of S. The subtree is said to *occur* or *match* at the root of the trees that are instances of the pattern. The subtree discovery from a set of trees, however, is not trivial because of the hierarchy of tree.

Embedded subtrees. Given a tree $T = (r, N, E, \mathcal{L})$, we say that a labeled rooted tree $S = (r', N_S, E_S, \mathcal{L}')$ is included as an *embedded subtree* of T, denoted $S \preceq T$, iff (1) $N_S \subseteq N$, (2) for all edges $(u, v) \in E_S$ such that u is the parent of v, u is an ancestor of v in T, (3) the label of any node $v \in N_S$, $\mathcal{L}'(v) = \mathcal{L}(v)$. The tree T must preserve ancestor relation but not necessarily parent relation for nodes in S.

The primary goal of finding valuable knowledge from some set of data is to provide information often occurred in the dataset. Roughly speaking, often occurred information means some data patterns which are frequently used by various users or applications. However, it is not straightforward in the case for trees unlike the case for traditional item data.

Support and frequent subtree. Let $\mathcal{D} = \{T_1, T_2, \ldots, T_i\}$ be a set of trees and $|\mathcal{D}|$ be the number of trees in $\mathcal{D}$, where $0 < i \leq |\mathcal{D}|$. Given a tree S, the *frequency* of S with respect to $\mathcal{D}$, $freq_{\mathcal{D}}(S)$, is defined as $\Sigma_{T_i \in \mathcal{D}} freq_{T_i}(S)$, where $freq_{T_i}(S)$ is 1 if S is a subtree of T_i and 0, otherwise. The *support* of S with respect to $\mathcal{D}$, $sup_{\mathcal{D}}(S)$, is the fraction of the trees in $\mathcal{D}$ that have S as a subtree. That is, $sup_{\mathcal{D}}(S) = \frac{freq_{\mathcal{D}}(S)}{|\mathcal{D}|}$. A subtree is called *frequent* if its support is greater than or equal to a minimum value of support specified by users or applications. This user-specified minimum value is often called the *minimum support* (*minsup or* σ). The problem of mining frequent subtrees is defined as to uncover all pattern trees S, such that $sup_{\mathcal{D}}(S) = \frac{\Sigma_{T_i \in \mathcal{D}} freq_{T_i}(S)}{|\mathcal{D}|} \geq minsup$.

The discovery of frequent subtrees appearing in a large set of trees, however, is not easy task to do. As explained in the earlier pages, to get frequent subtrees are generated first candidate subtrees by repeatedly joining nodes. The combinatorial time for subtree generation becomes an inherent bottleneck of frequent subtree extraction and it causes that finding all frequent subtrees is impossible. The maximal frequent subtree is one of frequent subtrees which none of its proper supertrees are frequent. Thus, there are fewer maximal frequent subtrees than the number of frequent subtrees. In addition, by uncovering only maximal frequent subtrees, we do not lose other frequent information by the fact that the set of maximal ones subsumes all frequent subtrees.

3 Scheme of SEAMSON

In this section, we introduce a new algorithm SEAMSON (Scalable and Efficient Algorithm for Maximal frequent Subtrees extractiON) appropriate for use as the core of discovering valuable information from a database of rooted labeled trees, where data not only exhibit heterogeneity but also are distributed. The suggested approach is inspired by the mining algorithms, such as FP-Tree mining [5], FST-Forest [12], and EXiT-B [7,8]. Especially, SEAMSON mainly adopts the fundamental idea of FP-tree, which is to devise a compact database that preserves all necessary information.

3.1 Label-Projected Database

Given a tree database $\mathcal{D}$, trees are originally stored based on their relating documents; each document is treated as a transaction. The database is organized as a set of rows, with each row representing a tree in terms of the nodes that are labeled with rich set of labels in a tree. The data layout is document-driven. Finding frequently occurred subtrees is actually to discover the subtrees whose nodes are assigned by the frequently occurring labels. In order to check a label is frequent or not, the frequency of a given label has to be computed. In document-driven layout, the entire trees are scanned whenever frequency of a label is computed. This work computationally requires $O(|\mathcal{D}||N||L|)$ time complexity to get frequencies of the whole labels. It is not serious problem if the total number of trees ($|\mathcal{D}|$) and number of nodes of a tree ($|N|$) are small. However, it becomes infeasible to compute the frequency of labels efficiently, because both are usually large in real world.

What if the database was organized in a label-driven layout? That means each label plays a key role which has been generally taken by tree indexes or transaction indexes. All the tree information in $\mathcal{D}$ are rearranged according to labels. During scan of the trees in $\mathcal{D}$, all nodes with the same label are grouped together. The nodes composed of the same tree form a member of the group and the number of members actually determines the frequency of the given label; the maximum number of members is a number of trees in $\mathcal{D}$, which is called **label-projection**. After all labels are projected, the document-driven layout is changed into label-driven layout in which the time complexity to check labels' frequency requires at most $O(|L||\mathcal{D}|)$. If hash-based search is used, the complexity is reduced up to $O(|\mathcal{D}|)$. Apparently, the label-driven layout shows much less computational cost than that of document-driven layout in obtaining the label frequency. SEAMSON applies the concept of label-projection for storing original input trees in a new compact database in space efficient way and easy to manipulate need to be constructed. The database will also need to handle the structural semantic information inherent in tree data. List representation is one of the simple empirical ways of representing tree. With the practical union of the list representation and the concept of label-projection, we build a collection of list-based units from a set of trees, and make the units store crucial and quantitative information for potentially maximal frequent subtrees.

Starting from the organization of a label-projected database, SEAMSON consists of 3 main phases: (1) Construction phase – a label-projections are performed and a set of list-based structures is constructed. (2) Refinement phase— frequently used labels and its related information, such as nodes indexes, parent nodes, and trees indexes, are remained in the lists. (3) Derivation phase— maximal frequent subtrees are discovered.

3.2   Construction Phase

Construction phase is initiated by scanning a trees database, $\mathcal{D}$, and results in generating a label-projected database within the memory. We refer to this new database as a dictionary, more specifically *label-dictionary*, and denote *L-dictionary*. The dictionary is composed of several linked list-like structures. For each one of the lists, followings are mainly stored: a projected label, node indexes, and tree indexes.

Definition 1 (label list). Let l be a label in L. During pre-ordered scanning trees, tree indexes and node indexes which are projected by l construct a single linked list. It is called a *label list* of the label l and is denoted ℓ_l-list.

The ℓ-list provides some perspectives on the appropriate uses of the list, especially when each ℓ-list is required to be distinguished apart from other ℓ-lists and to access all the relevant information about a given label. According to different requirement of the different perspectives, the structure of ℓ-list contains two separate divisions.

Definition 2 (head & body). A part whose purpose is to clearly identify each ℓ-list leads the ℓ-list, thus, it is called *head of ℓ-list*, notated ℓ-*list.h*. The other part concerns about how many times the projected label is occurred and where the nodes assigned by the label are placed in original tree structures. Since this part directly follows its corresponding head part, it is called *body of ℓ-list*, notated ℓ-*list.b*.

With regards to the intended purposes, the head and body parts have different kinds of data. A head is composed with one key field, one satellite data of the key, and one link field, which are a projected label, node indexes being mapped the label, and a link pointing to its body[1], respectively. The purpose of head part, identification of ℓ-list, is envisaged by the labels in key fields because there is no duplicated label-projection in more specifically *label-dictionary*, and denote *L-dictionary*. Node indexes in the satellite data field are those nodes whose labels in trees are exactly same as the label in the key field.

The body of ℓ-list follows its head immediately. The main concerns of the body is to evaluate how many trees have the same label in its pairing head and to remember parents indexes of the nodes in the head. The former is for dealing with the frequencies of each label, while the latter is for handling the hierarchical information of the label. To achieve such intentions the structure of body is a sequence of elements which is arranged in a linear order. Each element is an object with a key field, one link field pointing to the next element, and one satellite data field. One tree index number is stored in as a key of an element and this indicates that the projected label in its corresponding head is used in the tree. Because only the trees which assign the projected label to their nodes are eligible to create the element, the total number of elements in a body is the number of trees that contains the label in the head. During pre-ordered scanning trees, the element is generated and inserted into the bodies of ℓ-lists. The newly inserted element is added to the end of a proper body and the link field of its previous element points this new element.

Definition 3 (size of ℓ-list). The body of ℓ-list provides the method we can judge how many trees have the projected label, and this is supported by a number of elements. We define the number of elements as *size of ℓ-list* because it determines the occurrence number of each label-projection. For a given label l, its size is notated $|\ell_l\text{-list}|$. The size of each ℓ-list mainly used to determine if a current ℓ-list is frequent or not.

The satellite data used in an element is related to the node indexes in head because it is the positions of their parent nodes in the tree whose index is the

---

[1] More accurately, it points to the first element of a body.

key of the element. Since a same label can be assigned to several different nodes within a same tree, there definitely exist several parent nodes. By storing parent node indexes in elements, it is feasible to induce the relations between nodes without tree structure. Note that we use a special node index 0 to represent zero parent node because of the root node. Even more, based on such information, we can eliminate the burdensome candidate subtrees generation. It will be discussed later in this paper how the time consuming subtree generation has been removed from our approach and what the alternative way is.

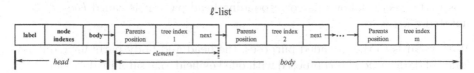

Fig. 1. Structure of a single ℓ-list

The structure of a ℓ-list is illustrated in Fig. 1. Compared to the original linked list structure, the role of head has been extended to deal with the identification of ℓ-lists. As shown in the picture, a number of trees which include the projected label of this ℓ-list is m, because $|\ell\text{-}list|$ is same as the number of elements, m. Fig. 2 shows a depicted example of how $L\text{-}dictionary$ and its ℓ-lists are constructed and managed from the database $\mathcal{D}$. Each alphabet represents the projected labels. As explained in the previous pages, the bodies of ℓ-lists decide the frequencies of corresponding labels. For instance, the label A is only occurred one time, while the other labels are occurred three times. Consequently, the label A does not satisfy the given minimum value which is set $\frac{2}{3}$.

3.3   Refinement Phase

The complete $L\text{-}dictionary$ produced by the construction phase contains less than or equal to $|L|$, because the purpose of the first phase is just to convert the whole tree structured data in $\mathcal{D}$ into a label projected database according to the distinct labels which are used by nodes. Therefore, the firstly obtained $L\text{-}dictionary$ contains all the ℓ-lists whose labels appeared in trees at least one time. It will not cause any problem for us to manage the current $L\text{-}dictionary$ only if a given minimum support is $\frac{1}{|\ell-\text{list}|_{max}}$; $|\ell-\text{list}|_{max}$ is that the maximum number of elements which a ℓ-list can have is $|\mathcal{D}|$. Since in such case the maximum number of trees being frequent is 1, every label is eligible to be frequent.

In most cases, however, the minimum number of occurrence is more than 1. Therefore, ℓ-lists of the projected labels in $L\text{-}dictionary$ have to be verified if they are frequent or not, because some labels may be frequent but some are not. This procedure is seemed to be analogous that if the first step in apriori-based techniques. Because the initial $L\text{-}dictionary$ is similar to the set of single-node trees, those ℓ-lists whose sizes do not confirm the condition of being frequent

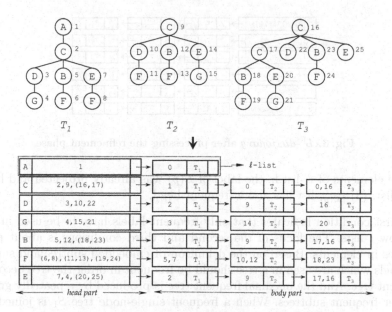

Fig. 2. *L-dictionary* after the construction phase

have to be eliminated from the dictionary. Furthermore, every ℓ-*list itself in L-dictionary should be frequent* (we will describe the meaning of frequent ℓ-list in the following paragraph) to extract maximal frequent subtrees. This is the purpose of the refinement phase and it will explained how this second phase works.

Definition 4 (frequent head). Given a minimum support σ, a ℓ_l-list is said to have a *frequent-head* iff $|\ell_l-\text{list}|$ is greater than or equal to $|\ell-\text{list}|_{max} \times \sigma$. Otherwise, it is said to have an infrequent-head.

The ℓ-lists contained in the initial *L-dictionary* are required to verify if they have a frequent-head. If a ℓ-list has an infrequent-head, it is filtered out from the *L-dictionary*. Such pruned ℓ-lists organize some table by themselves in order to support another pruning process. The detailed explanation will be given later. After every ℓ-list in *L-dictionary* is checked for its frequent head, only the ℓ-lists which have frequent heads are left in *L-dictionary*. The state of *L-dictionary* is changed from having all ℓ-lists to having all the ℓ-lists with frequent heads. Because the ℓ-lists with infrequent heads are filtered out from the initial *L-dictionary*, we denote the current state of *L-dictionary* simply L_F-*dictionary*, and the ℓ-lists in L^F-*dictionary* can be parallel to the frequent single-node subtrees in which their nodes are labeled by the projected labels of frequent heads.

Definition 5 (frequent ℓ-list). Given an arbitrary label list ℓ_l-list in L^F-*dictionary* is said to be a *frequent ℓ-list* iff it satisfies the following conditions: (1) the list ℓ_l-list has a frequent-head. (2) For every parent index p in

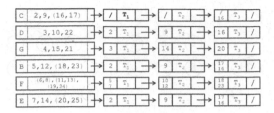

Fig. 3. L^R-*dictionary* after processing the refinement phase

all the elements of ℓ_l-list.h, the label of $\mathcal{L}(p)$ was already projected and has its $\ell_{\mathcal{L}(p)}$-list. (3) $\ell_{\mathcal{L}(p)}$-list has also a frequent-head.

The first condition indicates that only frequent labels have to be used in order to grow ℓ-lists. The focus of the second and third conditions is about parent indexes in elements. Based on the definition of embedded subtree and support, all labels which are used in a tree should be frequent in order the tree becomes a frequent tree. And the maximal frequent tree is produced by repeatedly growing smaller frequent subtrees. When a frequent single-node tree S_1 is joined by a node n, the label of n should be frequent if let the grown tree S_2 want to be frequent.

Within a single ℓ-list are actually contained several subtrees whose sizes are $k = 2$ where k is a number of nodes. Due to the structure of ℓ-list's body, especially parent indexes in elements, a ℓ-list implicitly includes subtrees as many as the number of parent indexes in it. With regards to a current L^F-*dictionary*, it is guaranteed that the node indexes in ℓ-list.h have frequent labels, however, it is not in case of the parent indexes in ℓ-list.b. In spite of the fact that a parent index is a member of the ℓ-list which has a frequent-head, it is uncertain whether the label of that parent index forms a corresponding ℓ-list which also has frequent-head. Because L^F-*dictionary* has been produced by considering the frequency of labels, only the heads part were concerned. The label of parent node p has to be frequent in order that a subtree made by joining p is qualified for being frequent. To resolve the mentioned problem we refine every parent node p in L^F-*dictionary* by following procedures: (1) a parent index p in elements is tested by means of a candidate_hash_table [2] to determine a given node index has a frequent label or not. If its label is found in the table, it means that the label is infrequent, because it is not in L^F-*dictionary*. (2) If $\mathcal{L}(p)$ is found in the table, p is marked by 'replace' and its record is retrieved to search an alternative node index which has a frequent label. (3) Step(1) and (2) continue until the alternative node index is found. (4) p is replaced by the found node index which is actually an ancestor node index of p. (5) Through step(1) to (3), thought, if the alternative node index is not found, p is replaced by 0.

After the replacement according to the procedure, finally all the ℓ-lists in L^F-*dictionary* satisfy the conditions of Definition 5. The ℓ-lists in L^F-*dictionary*

---

[2] This table is constructed with the ℓ-lists which could not included in the L^F-*dictionary*.

are all frequent label lists and this makes the state of current L^F-*dictionary* is different from that of L^F-*dictionary* which is the one before refining. Thus, we denote the refined L^F-*dictionary* as L^R-*dictionary*. Fig. 3 presents L^R-*dictionary* obtained from the L^F-*dictionary* on Fig. 2 which has all the ℓ-lists except ℓ_A-list.

Parent nodes in a same element may have different labels, or share a same label. As an example, we compare the indexes in ℓ_F-list's first element and those in the third element. The former is in case of having different labels, $\mathcal{L}(5) = B$ and $\mathcal{L}(7) = E$. The latter is, however, in case of having the same labels, $\mathcal{L}(18) = \mathcal{L}(18) = B$. It is waste of memory to store several nodes having a same label in the same tree. Hence, all nodes in an element which are assigned by the same label are removed from the element except only one node which is a representative of the label. The final outcome of the end of the refinement phase is shown on Fig. 4. Note that a dummy list is inserted to L^R-*dictionary*, which is the special label list of the symbolic label $/$. It is for representing and setting the root of some tree including the goal of this paper.

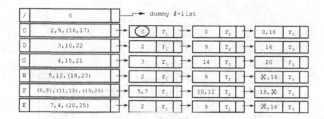

Fig. 4. L^R-*dictionary* after removal of the parent node indexes having same label

3.4 Derivation Phase

The last state of L^R-*dictionary* contains all ℓ-lists whose projected labels are frequently occurred and all paths which could possibly be frequent in original trees. It is, however, not guaranteed that paths are always frequent, even though all nodes of the paths are labeled by the frequent labels. This stems from the fact that a path is a sequence of edges, $p = e_1 e_2 \ldots e_i$, and an edge is a line segment joining two nodes in a tree, $e = (a, b)$. Therefore, two nodes composing an edge should have frequent labels and appear together as many as $\sigma \cdot |\mathcal{D}|$ if the edge wants to be frequent, and all edges composing a path should be frequent and they also appear together as many as $\sigma \cdot |\mathcal{D}|$ if the path wants to be frequent. Even though a and b are labeled by the frequent labels, the edge cannot be frequent if both a and b do not occur together. This causes a path cannot be frequent if all edges are not frequent.

To verify paths frequencies, explicit edges between any two nodes have to be unveiled from L^R-*dictionary*. During the read of ℓ-lists, edges are formed by joining symbolic nodes whose labels are the projected labels of ℓ-lists and symbolic nodes of parent indexes in ℓ_l-list.b. Unveiling edges totally relies on every frequent label lists because the symbolic nodes of parent indexes' labels have also their frequent label lists. The hidden paths between ℓ-list and other label lists are discovered by extending the node of label in ℓ-list.h with the nodes of the labels in other ℓ-lists.

Definition 6 (label list extension). Given L^R-*dictionary*, let a frequent label list be ℓ_l-list and p be one of parent indexes in its elements. For ℓ_l-list, firstly a symbolic node whose label is l is set and the node is prepared to join with its parent. The second symbolic node is set from the parent index p. Its label is easily obtained by $\mathcal{L}(p)$ and the corresponding $\ell_{\mathcal{L}(p)}$-list is in L^R-*dictionary* due to the definition 5. Consequently, the node labeled by l is joined to the node labeled by $\mathcal{L}(p)$. We call this operation *label list extension* and denote $\ell \leftarrow \mathcal{L}(p)$ where '$\leftarrow$' indicates the direction of parent to child.

Note that the extension is performed with labels not the node indexes in ℓ-lists. The node index is used to just get label or its corresponding ℓ-list. A symbolic node is created whenever a label requires it. The fundamental method is actually to extend labels, thus, we say label list extension is essentially performed by label extension.

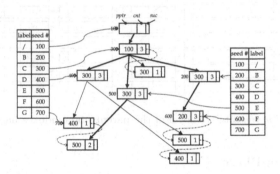

Fig. 5. The derived PMP-tree from L^R-*dictionary*

The label list extension is committed to each label list in L^R-*dictionary*. After completing the work of extension, the projected labels of frequent ℓ-lists are joined together via symbolic nodes. The structure of the result is a tree whose root is labeled by /. This tree contains all of potentially maximal frequent subtrees and thus is named Potentially Maximal Pattern tree (PMP-tree in short). The tree[3] is actually derived from L^R-*dictionary*, where each edge has its own count to keep how many often it is occurred in the derived tree (TreeHeaderTable supports to build the tree; the detailed explanation is omitted due to the space). Based on those counts, the edges whose counts are less than a given $\sigma \cdot |\mathcal{D}|$ are cleared off from PMP-tree. After deleting such edges and rearranging the tree, the goal of this paper is produced. The final result from L^R-*dictionary* in Fig. 5 is shown in the following illustration.

---

[3] We duplicate the nodes shared by different parents/ancestors to avoid deriving a graph. The duplicated nodes are marked with dotted bold lines.

Theorem 1. After pruning infrequent edges and theirs entering nodes, the number of children of PMP-tree's root is the same as the one of maximal frequent subtrees.

Proof. Let ℓ_α-list, ℓ_β-list, ℓ_γ-list be the arbitrary frequent label lists in L^R-*dictionary*. Let $|\ell_\alpha\text{-}list| = |\ell_\beta\text{-}list| = 2$, $|\ell_\gamma\text{-}list| = 4$, and the given $\sigma \cdot |\mathcal{D}| = 2$. We assume each element of them has only one parent index, for the sake of simplicity. The elements of ℓ_α-list and ℓ_β-list have the parent index 0, which means the actual parent indexes are empty and they have the symbolic labels $/$. Let the parent indexes in elements of ℓ_γ-list be p_1, p_2, p_3, and p_4. Then, we can consider the following three cases:

- **Case I.** ($\mathcal{L}(p_1) = \mathcal{L}(p_2) = \alpha$ and $\mathcal{L}(p_3) = \mathcal{L}(p_4) = \beta$) : **Two** nodes labeled by α and β are direct children of the root, because both edge frequencies satisfy 2. The node labeled by γ is clones to prevent being a graph since both edge frequencies of different parents also satisfy 2. Therefore, total *two* maximal frequent subtrees, one is $(\alpha, \{\alpha, \gamma\}, \{(\alpha, \gamma)\}, \mathcal{L})^4$ and the other $(\beta, \{\beta, \gamma\}, \{(\beta, \gamma)\}, \mathcal{L})$, are obtained.
- **Case II.** ($\mathcal{L}(p_1) = \mathcal{L}(p_2) = \mathcal{L}(p_3) = \alpha$ and $\mathcal{L}(p_4) = \beta$) : The number of children of the root is same as the one of case I, which is two. The edge (α, γ) satisfies the threshold as 3, but the edge (β, γ) is not. Therefore, the actual maximal frequent subtrees are $(\alpha, \{\alpha, \gamma\}, \{(\alpha, \gamma)\}, \mathcal{L})$ and $(\beta, \{\beta\}, \{\phi\}, \mathcal{L})$, which is total **two**.
- **Case III.** ($\mathcal{L}(p_1) = \mathcal{L}(p_2) = /$ and $\mathcal{L}(p_3) = \mathcal{L}(p_4) = \alpha$ or β) : The root has total three children whose labels are α, β, and γ. By the second condition, $\alpha\|^5\beta$ is joined with γ. Therefore, the maximal frequent subtrees are $(\alpha/\beta, \{\alpha/\beta\}, \{\phi\}, \mathcal{L})$, $(\alpha/\beta, \{\alpha/\beta, \gamma\}, \{(\alpha/\beta, \gamma)\}, \mathcal{L})$, and $(\gamma, \{\gamma\}, \{\phi\}, \mathcal{L})$, total **three**.

In each case, the number of maximal frequent subtrees are exactly same as the total number of children of the root of PMP-tree.

4   Experimental Evaluation

We performed several experiments to evaluate the performance of SEAMSON algorithm using synthetic datasets. All experiments were done on a 2.2GHz AMD Athlon 64 3500+ PC with 1GB main memory, running Windows XP operating system. All algorithms were implemented by Java.

The synthetic datasets are generated by the tree generation program whose underlying ideas are inspired by Termier [9] and Zaki [14]. The generator constructs a set of trees, $\mathcal{D}$, based on some parameters supplied by the user: $\mathcal{T}$: the number of trees in $\mathcal{D}$, L : the set of labels, f : the maximum branching factor of a node, d : the maximum depth of a tree, ρ : the random probability of one node in the tree to generate children or not, η : the average number of nodes in each

---

[4] $T = (r, N, E, \mathcal{L})$.
[5] or.

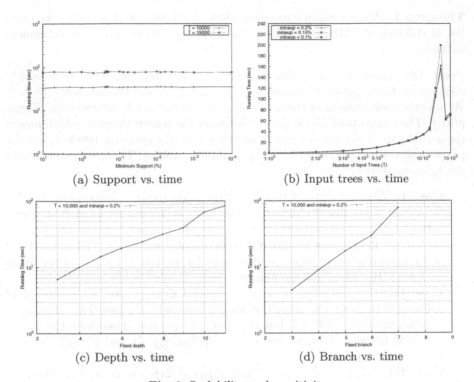

(a) Support vs. time

(b) Input trees vs. time

(c) Depth vs. time

(d) Branch vs. time

Fig. 6. Scalability and sensitivity

tree in $\mathcal{D}$. We used the following default values for the parameters: the number of trees $\mathcal{T} = 10,000$, the number of labels $L = 100$, the maximal branch factor $f = 5$, and the maximum depth $d = 5$.

In the following experiment, we want to evaluate the scalability of our algorithm with varying minimum support and the number of trees $\mathcal{T}$, while other parameters are fixed as: $L = 100, f = 5, d = 5, \rho = 20\%, \eta = 13.8$ and 20.5 (when $\mathcal{T} = 10,000$ and $15,000$, respectively). Fig. 6 shows several results, where the minimum support is set from $\sigma = 10\%$ to $\sigma = 0.0001\%$. In this figure, both X- and Y-axis are drawn on a logarithmic scale for the convenience of observation.

From Fig. 6(a), we can find that the running time increases when the number of trees $\mathcal{T}$ increases, however, both running times are rarely affected by the decrease of the minimum support. With the σ becoming smaller, there is no big difference in execution time for both datasets. This is because SEAMSON relies on the number of labels not the number of nodes. Thus it is very efficient for datasets with varying and growing tree sizes. Then, Fig. 6(b) shows the scalability with size of dataset – the number of input trees. The parameter $\mathcal{T}$ varies from 1,000 to 15,000 with $\eta = 20$. We evaluated three different minimum support, 0.2%, 0.15%, and 0.1%. The corresponding graphs show considerable similarity which slowly increases until $\mathcal{T} = 11,000$ and suddenly go up between $\mathcal{T} = 11,000$ and $\mathcal{T} = 13,000$. Afterwards, the graphs are started to rapidly deteriorate. Our understanding of this phenomena is that the sizes of L^R-*dictionary* and its ℓ-lists are maximized with 100 distinct node labels when the number of input trees reaches at 12,000 and 13,000.

Next, we want to check how sensitive the running time is to the depth and the branching factors of the dataset. We generated a set of databases with the same number ($\mathcal{T} = 10,000$) of trees embedded. With $L = 100, \rho = 50\%, \eta = 15, minsup = 0.2\%$, we changed two factors that determine the depth of each tree and the fanout of each node. In Fig. 6(c), we only vary d from 3 to 10. The trend of the graph gradually increases until $d = 9$ and goes up quickly from 9 to 10. Afterwards, it gently slopes. In Fig. 6(d), the performance of the different branching factors is similar to the case of depths, except that the slope of the graph is more steep than that of the graph in Fig. 6(c).

5   Conclusion

We presented a new and simple lists and labels based approach to extract maximal frequent subtrees from a database of trees. Unlike the traditional approaches, the proposed method did not perform any candidate subtree generation. To this end, we devised both a special database *L-dictionary* which introduced the concept of label-projected database, and its basic unit ℓ-list which preserved all necessary information to discover maximal frequent subtrees.

The beneficial effect of our method is that it not only got rid of the process for infrequent tree pruning, but also eliminated totally the problem of candidate subtrees generation. Hence, we significantly improved the whole mining process, especially when the minimum supports are small and dynamic, which made SEAMSON be L-dependent not σ-dependent.

References

1. Asai, T., Abe, K., Kawasoe, S., Arimura, H., Satamoto, H., Arikawa, S.: Efficient Substructure Discovery from Large Semi-Strucutured Data. In: Proceedings of the 2nd SIAM International Conference on Data Mining, pp. 158–174 (2002)
2. Agrawal, R., Srikant, R.: Fast Algorithms for Mining Association Rules in Large Databases. In: Proceedings of the 20th International Conference on Very Large Databases (VLDB 1994), pp. 487–499 (1994)
3. Chen, Y., Chen, Y.: A New Tree Inclusion Algorithm. Information Processing Letters 98, 253–262 (2006)
4. Chi, Y., Yang, Y., Muntz, R.R.: Canonical Forms for Labeled Trees and Their Applications in Frequent Subtree Mining. Knowledge and Information Systems 8(2), 203–234 (2005)
5. Han, J., Pei, J., Yin, Y.: Mining Frequent Patterns without Candidate Generation. In: Proceedings of 2000 ACM SIGMOD International Conference on Management of Data (ICMD 2000), pp. 1–12 (2000)
6. Mannila, H., Raiha, K.-J.: On Query Languages for the P-String Data Model. In: Information Modelling and Knowledge Bases, pp. 469–482. IOS Press, Amsterdam (1990)

7. Paik, J., Shin, D.R., Kim, U.M.: EFoX: a Scalable Method for Extracting Frequent Subtrees. In: Sunderam, V.S., van Albada, G.D., Sloot, P.M.A., Dongarra, J. (eds.) ICCS 2005. LNCS, vol. 3516, pp. 813–817. Springer, Heidelberg (2005)
8. Paik, J., Won, D., Fotouhi, F., Kim, U.M.: EXiT-B: a New Approch for Extracting Maximal Frequent Subtrees from XML Data. In: Gallagher, M., Hogan, J.P., Maire, F. (eds.) IDEAL 2005. LNCS, vol. 3578, pp. 1–8. Springer, Heidelberg (2005)
9. Termier, A., Rousset, M.-C., Sebag, M.: TreeFinder: a First Step towards XML Data Mining. In: Proceedings of IEEE International Conference on Data Mining (ICDM 2002), pp. 450–457 (2002)
10. Wang, C., Hong, M., Pei, H., Zhou, H., Wang, W., Shi, B.: Efficient Pattern-Growth Methods for Frequent Tree Pattern Mining. In: Dai, H., Srikant, R., Zhang, C. (eds.) PAKDD 2004. LNCS (LNAI), vol. 3056, pp. 441–451. Springer, Heidelberg (2004)
11. Wang, K., Liu, H.: Schema Discovery for Semistructured Data. In: Proceedings of the 3rd International Conference on Knowledge Discovery and Data Mining (KDD 1997), pp. 271–274 (1997)
12. Xiao, Y., Yao, J.-F., Li, Z., Dunham, M.H.: Efficient Data Mining for Maximal Frequent Subtrees. In: Proceedings of IEEE International Conference on Data Mining (ICDM 2003), pp. 379–386 (2003)
13. Zaki, M.J.: Scalable Algorithms for Association Mining. IEEE Transactions on Knowledge and Data Engineering 12(3), 290–372 (2000)
14. Zaki, M.J.: Efficiently Mining Frequent Trees in a Forest: Algorithms and Applications. IEEE Transactions on Knowledge and Data Engineering 17(8), 1021–1035 (2005)
15. Zou, L., Lu, Y., Zhang, H.: Mining Frequent Induced Subtrees by Prefix-Tree-Projected Pattern Growth. In: Yu, J.X., Kitsuregawa, M., Leong, H.-V. (eds.) WAIM 2006. LNCS, vol. 4016, pp. 18–25. Springer, Heidelberg (2006)

Using Multiple Detectors to Detect the Backoff Time of the Selfish Node in Wireless Mesh Network*

Furong Wang[1], Yipeng Qu[1], Baoming Bai[2], Fan Zhang[1], and Chen Huang[1]

[1] Dept. of E. I. E, Huazhong Univ. of Sci. & Tech., Wuhan, Hubei, China
[2] State Key Lab. of ISN, Xidian University, Xi'an, Shaanxi, China
wangfurong@mail.hust.edu.cn, cathyqyp@163.com,
bmbai@mail.xidian.edu.cn
zhangview@163.com, szo094@hotmail.com

Abstract. The security of wireless mesh network has been more and more important these days. Although many works have been done to analyze the MAC layer misbehavior such as the selfish node which changes its backoff time to make itself more profits in 802.11 DCF mechanisms, most of them are under the assumption that the backoff time of the sender can be correctly detected. However because of the hidden node problem, misdiagnosing occurs frequently. In this paper, we propose a method to detect the backoff time of the sender using multiple detectors. It can avoid the misdiagnosing due to the hidden node problem. We also propose an algorithm to calculate the detection results using weighting parameters get by the probability that the detect nodes will suffer from the hidden node problems. The simulation result shows that the proposed method has a better performance in detecting the backoff time.

Keywords: Wireless mesh network, MAC layer, selfish node, multiple detectors.

1 Introduction

Recently, much work has been done to improve the security of wireless mesh networks. Due to the lack of routing infrastructure, cooperation of both routers and terminals becomes an important part in maintaining the reliable communication in mesh networks. In the Medium Access Control (MAC) layer, 802.11 based wireless mesh networks use distributed coordination function (DCF) for sharing the wireless channel[1]. The DCF mechanism is based on fully cooperation and trust between each node. However, in real world networks, not all of the nodes can be trusted and some nodes may misbehave by deviating from the mechanism.

There are two kinds of misbehaviors, one is selfish misbehavior and the other is malicious misbehavior. The selfish nodes aim at improving there own preferment

---
* This work was supported by National Natural Science Foundation of China under Grant No.60572047, Program for new Century Excellent Talents in University NCET-06-0642, and the National High-Tech Research and Development Program ("863"Program) of China under Grants No.2006AA01Z267 and No. 2007AA01Z215.

such as to gain more chance to access the channel, more bandwidth and more throughput. On the other side, the malicious nodes aim at disrupting the normal functions of the network.

In DCF, the sender should wait for a random chosen backoff before the competition for the channel. The backoff time is randomly chosen in a range [0, CW-1], where CW is the contention window size. After an unsuccessful approaching to the channel, the contention window size is doubled until it reaches the upper bound CW_{max}. A selfish sending node, who wants to improve its own performance, however may not follow the DCF mechanism honestly. It always chooses smaller backoffs than the honest nodes instead of randomly choose the backoffs, or simply do not double the contention widow size after the failure. By doing these, the selfish nodes would have more chance to access the channel and get more throughput or bandwidth, but the performance of the performance of the honest nodes and the equality of the network would be severely degraded.

On the other side, malicious nodes, they focus on destroy the normal functions of the networks [2]. The malicious nodes may refuse to forward the packets from other nodes in order to destroy the routing of the network or continuously send data to the other nodes causing the power exhaust. This attack would cause a denial of service (DoS) and so degrade the performance of the whole networks. A new type of vulnerabilities was raised in [3], time out attack, that a node can change the SIFS value in 802.11 to cause the data transmission to be time out.

In this paper we only focus on the detection of the selfish nodes.

2 Related Work

For the selfish nodes, what they want is to improve their own performance to the maximum extend. They only interested in their own throughput, latency, energy and so on. They don't especially focus on degrade other nodes' performance. Up on this, Game-theoretic techniques have been used to consider the problem [4][5][6]. The protocol developed from the Game-theoretic are designed to reach a fair equilibrium called "Nash equilibrium" that the selfish nodes can not get more advantage than the well-behaved nods. But the assumption in the Game-theoretic protocols that all the nodes can observe all others' actions can not always be reached. So it can not solve the selfish misbehavior problems.

Since the aim of the selfish nodes is known, direct methods to detect the misbehaving nodes is raised. In [7], A. Cardenas and S. Radosavac have raised a method to detect it. The method is to direct test the backoff time for the nodes each time. There are two algorithms: one is to test for the change in the mean, the other is to estimate the entropy of the backoff time. Since the selfish nodes always have smaller mean backoff times so that they can access the channel more easily. And the entropy is one of the most used measures of randomness. For the nodes those are smart who knows the test threshold, they can choose specific backoff windows to avoid be detected.

In order to eliminate the selfish senders, the method that the receivers choose backoff time was introduced [7][8]. After finding a node may be a misbehavior node, some extra time can be added in the backoff time. This can mitigate some bad impact of the selfish node if the node does not want to be detected. However, this is based on that the receivers are well behaved nodes. But in the real mesh networks any node can be a receiving node, so not all of the receivers can be trusted.

Lei Guang and Chadi Assi have raised another method to mitigate the selfish misbehavior in MAC layer[9]. It is called Predictable Random Backoff (PRB) algorithm. The idea of it is to get a lower limit for the backoff time, so that a node can not always choose a small backoff time.

3 Problem Statement

In all of the diagnosis methods, the real backoff time that the sender takes should be detected. Most of the researchers does not focus on how to get the exact backoff time and always simply assume that it can be easily detected. However it is not the truth.

Most of the algorithms use the receiver to detect the backoff time of the sender. After sensed the channel to be idle the receiver starts its timer. The time between the start of the timer and the receiving of the RTS sent by the sender is the estimation of the backoff time of the sender. But whether the times of the two nodes are synchronized is the problem.

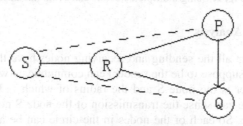

Fig. 1. Occurrence of misdiagnosis

Consider the following case. As shown in figure 1, the nodes P and Q are continuous sending data. The node S wants to access the channel to communicate with the node R. For the sending node S, it is out side of the transmission range of the nodes P and Q, so it can not sense the transmission of between them and it will judge that the channel is idle, and starts its timer. But for the receiving node, it is near the nodes P and Q, and it can sense the channel are occupied by them, so it will not start its timer until the transmission between them is end. So the two timers are not synchronized well. This leads to the wrong estimation of the backoff time. This is the problem of hidden terminals.

4 Multiple Detectors Approach

Since the hidden terminal problem makes the starting time of the sender and observer's clocks start at a different time. The method that uses multiple detectors is raised.

As shown in figure 2, we add two nodes, node M and node N, to help detect the backoff time of the sender. Both nodes M and N can sense the transmission of the sending node S, but neither of them is near enough to the nodes P and Q. So both of the nodes M and N would sense the channel to be idle at the same time as the sender S does. With the help of nodes M and N, the estimation of the senders' backoff time would be more accurate.

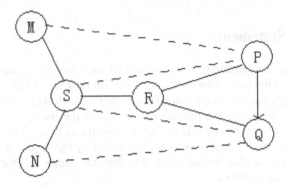

Fig. 2. Using multiple detectors can avoid misdiagnosis

4.1 Mathematic Analysis

Firstly suppose that all the sending and receiving nodes have the same sensing range Rm. So a node S (suppose to be the sender) can communicate with all the nodes in the circle whose center is the node S and the radius of which is Rm. And all the other nodes in that circle can sense the transmission of the node S no matter which node is the receiving node. So each of the nodes in the circle can be a detector to detect the backoff time of the sender S. And for one of the detectors, for example the receiving node, it has the same radius of its sensing region. If there are any nodes in its sensing region are in transmission, the node would judge that the channel is occupied by the others. But the sensing regions of the sender and the receiver are not the same. It leads to the diverse of the sensing result.

4.1.1 Hidden Nodes Probability

As shown in figure 3, node S is the sending node, it wants to communicate with the node R. The circle I denotes the sensing range of node S and circle II denotes the sensing range of node R. The distance between node S and R can be any value between 0 and the sensing radius Rm. All the nodes in region I can be used to detect the backoff time of the node S, such as node R and node N. Take node R as an example. Region III is the region that in the circle II but not in the circle I, which means that the transmission of nodes in region III can only be detected by node R but not node S. Suppose that there is a node H in region in transmission, and no other nodes in region I is currently in transmission. Then nodes S would find that the channel is idle and begin to decrease its timer from the backoff time to zero and send the RTS to node R. But node R has sensed that the channel is in occupied by node H, and it would not begin to decrease its timer. So when node R receives the RTS sent by

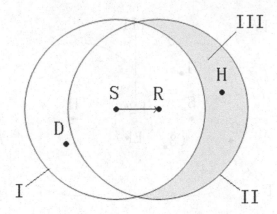

Fig. 3. The area that a hidden node can be found

S, the backoff timer of node R is not time out and R would judge that the sending node S misbehaved.

The probability of misjudging is proportional to the area of region III. Since the nodes are randomly and uniformly distribution in the whole area, the larger region III is, the more hidden nodes in the region.

Let the distance between node S and R is X meters, then the area of region III can be expressed as the function of X.

Area of III (Hidden nodes occurring range):

$$A_H = \pi \times Rm^2 - 4[\frac{\theta \times Rm^2}{2} - \frac{1}{2} \times \frac{X}{2} \times \sqrt{Rm^2 - \frac{X^2}{4}}]$$

$$= (\pi - 2\theta) \times Rm^2 + X \times \sqrt{Rm^2 - \frac{X^2}{4}} \qquad (1)$$

In (1), $\theta = \arccos\frac{X}{2Rm}$, X is in the range of 0~Rm

Since the nodes are randomly and uniformly distributed in the whole area, the probability of the occurrence of a hidden node is the ratio between the area of III and the whole area:

$$P_H = A_H / \pi Rm^2. \qquad (2)$$

With the increase of the distance between the sender and the receiver, the probability of hidden nodes occurring increases too. The range of hidden nodes may occur also increase as the radius of the sensing range.

4.1.2 Using of Multiple Detectors

When a hidden node H exists, as shown in figure 4, we can use multiple detectors to decrease the probability of misdetection. H is any node that in the shaded area of figure 3.

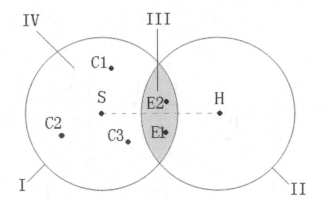

Fig. 4. Scenario where multiple detectors are used

In figure 4, circle I denote the communication range of the send node S, which means that all the nodes in circle I can detect the node S and compute its backoff time as well. The circle II is the communication range of node H, and all the nodes can sense the channel to be busy when H holds the channel. Circle II divides the inter area of circle I into two parts, region III and region IV. In region III, the nodes can both sense node S and node H. When H is in transmission, they would not judge the channel to be idle as the node S does. So they would make error detect of the backoff time of node S. But for the nodes in region IV, they don't sense the node H as well as node S, so they sense the same channel condition as node S, and would get the true length of the backoff time of node S.

In the figure, nodes E1 and E2 would make mistake when detecting the backoff time of S with the influence of H, but nodes C1, C2 and C3 would not.

When using multiple detectors, the number of correct detection and error detection are also related to the area of the two ranges.

Let node S and H are apart in the distance of K, the radius of the sensing range are still be Rm, then the two area can be denoted as follows:

Area of region III, error range:

$$A_E = 4 \times \left[\frac{\theta Rm^2}{2} - \frac{1}{2} \times \frac{K}{2} \times \sqrt{Rm^2 - \frac{K^2}{4}} \right]$$

$$= 2\theta Rm^2 - K \times \sqrt{Rm^2 - \frac{K^2}{4}} \tag{3}$$

Area of region IV, correct range:

$$A_C = \pi Rm^2 - 4 \times \left[\frac{\theta Rm^2}{2} - \frac{1}{2} \times \frac{K}{2} \times \sqrt{Rm^2 - \frac{K^2}{4}} \right]$$

$$= (\pi - 2\theta) Rm^2 + K \times \sqrt{Rm^2 - \frac{K^2}{4}} \tag{4}$$

In (3) and (4), $\theta = \arccos \dfrac{K}{2Rm}$, and K is in the range of Rm~2Rm.

If we only use one detector, the error rate of detection is $A_E / \pi Rm^2$, that is the ratio between the shade area of figure IV and the area of the circle. Denote the one detector error rate is:

$$P_1(K) = A_E / \pi Rm^2 . \tag{5}$$

Then when multiple detector are used, the probability that all the node are in the error region is $P_1(K)^n$.

4.2 Algorithm Analysis

Suppose that we use 1, 2, 3…n detectors to detect the backoff time of the sender S. Each of the detectors gets a result denoted as T(k), k=1, 2, 3…n
The total result of the backoff time can be calculated as:

$$\overline{T} = \frac{T(1) + T(2) + \cdots + T(n)}{n} = \frac{1}{n} \sum_{k=1}^{n} T(k) . \tag{6}$$

This is Average method. Consider two extreme conditions: if all the detectors are in the correct region (region IV in figure 4), the estimation of backoff time should be equal to the real time T; and if all the detectors are in the error region (region III in figure 4), the result should be the same as we only use one detector and it gets the wrong result. For most of the conditions the result would be between the two extreme values.

Our aim is to make the estimate result more and more approach to the real backoff time. In equation (6), whether the result is approach to the real value depend only on the position of the detectors. As the hidden nodes goes more and more near the sending nodes, more and more detectors would gets the wrong value and the final result would be farer away from the real value. The detector's position only be categories into two types, in error region or outside of the error region, and the other position information does not make any sense in it. So we propose a new algorithm using the position information of the detectors to improve the accuracy of the estimation result.

Then we propose a weighted method. We use it to get a weight for the result get by each detector. The equation (6) can be written as

$$\tilde{T} = w_1 T(1) + w_2 T(2) + \cdots + w_n T(n) = \sum_{k=1}^{n} w_k T(k) . \tag{7}$$

The detection results gotten by the detectors who would get less probability of influence by the hidden node should get larger weight. The following equation is based on this idea.

$$w_k = \frac{1-P_{Hk}}{(1-P_{H1})+(1-P_{H2})+\cdots+(1-P_{Hn})} = \frac{1-P_{Hk}}{n-\sum\limits_{i=1}^{n}P_{Hi}}. \tag{8}$$

Look back to equation (2), P_H is related to the distance between the sender and the detector. For each specific detector, it has its own distance to the sender, and it has its own weight parameter.

P_H is the probability that a detector node would be influenced by the hidden node problem. Then $1-P_H$ is the probability that the detector would not be influenced by a hidden node. The node that have larger $1-P_H$, which means it would be less influenced by the hidden node problem, will have larger weight.

5 Simulation Scenario

We use Matlab to test the performance of the two algorithms.

The scenario is a 400m * 200m region. And all the sender and detectors have the same sensing range Rm=100m. The sending node is fixed at the coordinate (100,100). The hidden node is lies in the line y = 100, and x in the range 200 to 300. And the other detector nodes, is randomly and uniformly distributed in the left square 100m * 100m area.

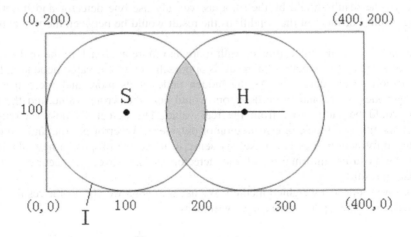

Fig. 5. Simulation scenario

6 Simulation Results

In the simulation we have test the two methods, average method and weighted method in two aspects. First we make the assumption that the true value of the backoff time chosen by the sender is 2, and the detectors would detect the value to be 1 if they have been influenced by the hidden node, otherwise they will get the correct result.

We first test the impact of the number of the detectors on the detection result. Figure 6 shows that no matter how many nodes are used to detect the sender's backoff time, the weighted algorithm will always have better performance. And more detectors provide a more similar approach to the optimize value. In this scenario the hidden node is fixed at the coordinate (250,100).

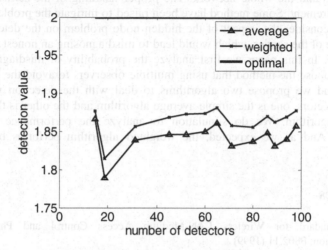

Fig. 6. Impact of number of detectors on the result

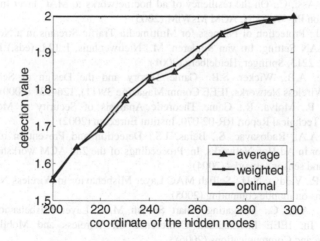

Fig. 7. Impact of the position of the hidden node on the result

Then we test the impact of the position of the hidden node on the result. When the hidden node is moving away from the sender, the percentage of the nodes that would decrease, then the result would be more and more close to the true value. Also the weighted algorithm always has better performance than the average method. Both of the trends are as we expected. The number of detectors in this scenario is about 70.

7 Conclusion

The selfish in wireless mesh network would degrade the performance of the other honest nodes and the whole network. The proper handling of the selfish nodes is a crucial requirement. Some method have been raised to mitigate the problem, however they didn't consider the impact of the hidden node problem on the detection of the backoff time of the sender, which would lead to misdiagnosing an honest node to be a selfish node. In this paper we first analyze the probability of misdiagnose occurs. Then we propose the method that using multiple observers to avoid the hidden node problem. And we propose two algorithms to deal with the detection value of the multiple detectors, one is the simple average algorithm and the other is the improved weighted algorithm. We do simulation to analyze the performance of the two algorithms. And as we expected, the weighted algorithm performs better in the simulation.

References

1. IEEE standard for Wireless LAN-Medium Access Control and Physical Layer Specification, P802.11 (1999)
2. Guang, L., Assi, C.: Vulnerabilities of ad hoc network routing protocols to MAC misbehavior. In: IEEE/ACM Wimob (2005)
3. Guang, L., Assi, C.: On the resiliency of ad hoc networks to MAC layer misbehavior. In: Workshop on PE-WASUN, ACM MsWiM (2005)
4. Konorski, J.: Protection of Fairness for Multimedia Traffic Streams in a Non-Cooperative Wireless LAN Setting. In: van Sinderen, M., Nieuwenhuis, L.J.M. (eds.) PROMS 2001. LNCS, vol. 2213, Springer, Heidelberg (2001)
5. MacKenzie, A.B., Wicker, S.B.: Game Theory and the Design of Self-Configuring, Adaptive Wireless Networks. IEEE Comm.Magazine 39(11), 126–131 (2000)
6. Michiardi, P., Molva, R.: Game Theoretic Analysis of Security in Mobile Ad Hoc Networks. Technical Report RR-02-070, Institut Eurecom (2002)
7. Cardenas, A.A., Radosavac, S., Baras, J.S.: Detection and Prevention of MAC Layer Misbehavior in Ad Hoc Networks. In: Proceedings of the 2nd ACM workshop on Security of ad hoc and sensor networks (2004)
8. Kyasanur, P., Vaidya, N.H.: Selfish MAC Layer Misbehavior in Wireless Networks. IEEE Transactions on mobile computing (2005)
9. Guang, L., Assi, C.: Mitigating Smart Selfish MAC Layer Misbehavior in Ad Hoc Networks. In: IEEE International Conference on Wireless and Mobile Computing, Networking and Communications (2006)

Self-reconfiguration in Highly Available Pervasive Computing Systems

Hadi Hemmati[1] and Rasool Jalili[2]

[1] Simula Research Laboratory, P.O. Box 134, NO-1325 Lysaker, Norway
hemmati@simula.no
[2] Department of Computer Engineering, Sharif University of Technology, Tehran, Iran
jalili@sharif.edu

Abstract. High availability of software systems is an essential requirement for pervasive computing environments. In such systems self-adaptation, using dynamic reconfiguration is also a key feature. However, dynamic reconfiguration potentially decreases the system availability by making parts of the system temporary frozen, especially during incomplete or faulty execution of the reconfiguration process. In this paper, we propose Assured Dynamic Reconfiguration Framework (ADRF), consisting of run-time analysis phases, assuring the desired correctness and completeness of dynamic reconfiguration process. We also specify factors that affect availability of reconfigurable software in pervasive computing systems. Observing the effects of these factors, we present availability improvement of our method in comparison to the other reconfiguration mechanisms.

Keywords: Dynamic Reconfiguration, Pervasive Computing, Autonomic Systems, Availability.

1 Introduction

Pervasive Computing Systems (PCSs) are going to change the focus of software systems from information and services to users. In such user-centric PCSs, availability and adaptability are parts of the software development fundamentals [1]. High availability of services in PCSs forces such systems to be self-adaptive. Self-adaptation or adaptability is the software ability to change its architecture behavior in the execution time whenever it is needed [2]. Changing software architecture in run-time without shutting the system down is called dynamic reconfiguration [3].

Our perception of dynamic reconfiguration covers all kinds of run-time changes on application in the level of software architecture such as upgrading, updating, bug fixing, and adapting to a new situation. Mainly, dynamic reconfiguration is performed to adapt a system to the new situation to improve system performance and software qualities. One of the most important quality attributes, which is necessary in distributed systems and much more in PCSs, is system availability. This is due to the facts that unavailable systems can not (1) be invisible from users for a long time (2) respond to user intent sufficiently (3) be trusted as secure systems and (4) be

C. Rong et al. (Eds.): ATC 2008, LNCS 5060, pp. 289–301, 2008.
© Springer-Verlag Berlin Heidelberg 2008

considered as dependable systems to be used anytime, anywhere, and from any device. Reconfigurable software in PCSs has the following features [4]:

- PCS software potentially has the ability to perform many reconfigurations in their life-time because of systems adaptiveness and reconfigurations context-awareness.
- In ordinary systems, reconfigurations are usually simple such as upgrading a component. But in PCSs, reconfigurations usually consist of several operations to adapt the system to completely new situations. Reconfigurations with several operations are called complex reconfiguration.
- Most of PCSs do not have any external administrator. This fact forces them to be self-managed. From this point of view, PCSs are similar to autonomic systems which need self-reconfigurablity.
- Wireless communication, device mobility, limited power, and other limited resources make pervasive computing environments error-prone. Therefore, the risk of failure during reconfiguration process in such environments is very high.

Hence, if there is not any mechanism for correct execution of reconfiguration process, dynamic reconfiguration decreases the system availability in the case of reconfiguration failure.

Although adaptability in PCSs has been discussed in many papers, the problem of run-time assurance for reconfiguration process has not been considered properly. Most of current run-time monitoring, validation, and verification techniques are at the code level [5, 6]. There exists some tools such as ArchStudio [7] and Mae [8] which manage dynamic reconfiguration but they do not have enough run-time analysis. In [9] replicated components have been used during reconfiguration, and after completion of reconfiguration process. This solution suffers from having an extensive overhead for changing all replicas of a component after a reconfiguration. In addition, the replicated component can not be used, when the old version is functionally wrong or not applicable.

To achieve the assured reconfiguration, we need some assurance analyses in the specification time and run-time. As the main focus of this paper is run-time analysis, we assume that all reconfiguration specifications are correct. Having a verified reconfiguration specification is not enough because of unexpected run-time errors and unsuitable reconfiguration starting time [10]. In this paper, we propose a run-time monitoring method in ADRF to ensure correct and complete execution of dynamic reconfiguration in PCSs. Also, we demonstrate how much the PCS availability can be improved by performing reconfiguration under ADRF supervision.

Section 2 introduces ADRF with its architecture and process. In sections 3 monitoring and analysis of reconfiguration in ADRF is demonstrated. Section 4 discusses some availability issues in ADRF, and section 5 evaluates ADRF in terms of system availability.

2   Assured Dynamic Reconfiguration Framework

Assured Dynamic Reconfiguration Framework (ADRF) is aimed to provide correct and complete reconfiguration in PCSs [11]. In addition, ADRF improves system availability through reducing the risk of incomplete and faulty reconfigurations. In this section ADRF architecture and its reconfiguration process are explained.

2.1 ADRF Architecture

ADRF, illustrated in Figure 1, is located between the middleware and the user interface. It surrounds the application and monitors it in the reconfiguration period. ADRF rules can be updated through the user interface. Utilizing the middleware distribution facilities, ADRF can support distributed applications, which is out of the scope of this paper. Inside ADRF, there are three main components for providing assured reconfiguration process: A context-manager (CM), a reconfiguration-manager (RM), and a service-manager (SM). CM is responsible for triggering RM and the application when a related context changes. RM is responsible for performing assured reconfigurations when preconditions are triggered by CM. SM is responsible for preparing components and software for reconfiguring in a suitable manner by freezing and unfreezing some components.

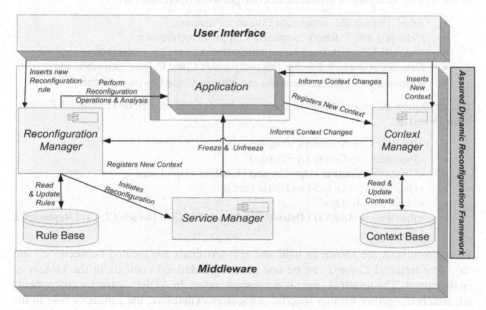

Fig. 1. The Architecture of ADRF

2.2 Reconfiguration Process in ARDF

In the ADRF component model, components are interconnected through messages and messages are buffered in the source and destination components. Therefore, connectors are just some pointers and do not have significant role in our view of the software architecture. A UML-like state-chart is used for specifying component behavior. Software configuration in ADRF is represented by a graph of components. The system behavior is characterized using the components behavior in addition to its architectural configuration. The reconfiguration process in ADRF consists of four steps:

1. Detecting the need for a reconfiguration (or reconfiguration initiation)
2. Selecting a reconfiguration map
3. Performing the reconfiguration map
4. Analyzing the architecture after reconfiguration

The first step starts when a change in the system or environment occurs which satisfies a reconfiguration's pre-conditions. These pre-conditions in PCSs are context-aware. It means that they are triggered by changes in the system, user, or environmental contexts. In fact, system designers or architects use these pre-conditions to define situations where system needs reconfiguring its architecture. The followings are some examples of these situations in PCSs: the need for tolerating faults, using new services, adapting to existing resources, automatic evolution, and supporting change in user intents.

In the second step the corresponding map for the pre-condition is fired. A reconfiguration map is a set of reconfiguration operations which should be performed sequentially. Each reconfiguration has a rule, which contain preconditions and corresponding map. In ADRF, reconfiguration rules are specified in the design time by the system designer or architect. Reconfiguration operations are:

- $Add(C_i)$ which adds component C_i to an architecture,
- $Delete(C_i)$ which deletes component C_i from an architecture,
- $Attach(C_i, C_j)$ which attaches two components C_i and C_j to each other,
- $Detach(C_i, C_j)$ which detaches two components C_i and C_j from each other, and
- $Replace(C_i, C_j)$ which replaces two components C_i and C_j with each other.

The definition of reconfiguration rules can be defined in EBNF (Extended Backus-Naur Form) as:

- <RecRule> ::= <Precond>, <Map>
- <Precond> ::= <Cond> {Λ <Cond>}*
- <Cond> ::= **Context** <Op> **Context** I **Context** <Op> **Const**
- <Op> ::= < I > I <= I => I == I ≠ I in I not in
- <Map> ::= <RecOp>$^+$
- <RecOP> ::= **Add(Ci)** I **Delete(Ci)** I **Attach(Ci, Cj)** I **Detach(Ci, Cj)** I **Replace(Ci, Cj)**

Where terminals are shown in bold and non-terminals are located between "<" and ">". The terminal *Context* can be one of the pre-defined contexts in the system or environment. The terminal *const* is a constant value. In ADRF, software components are attached together without specific connectors. Therefore, the connector role in the reconfiguration operations is omitted.

In the third step of the reconfiguration process, the reconfiguration map is performed by sequentially executing its reconfiguration operations on the software. Executing these operations, it is necessary to block (freeze) some parts of the software which are participated in the reconfiguration. It is due to the fact that in most cases components can not be reconfigured, when they are being executed through a running process. During freezing period, services which are provided by frozen components are not available. Freezing has two problems which should be solved in the reconfiguration process: finding the best time to freeze, and finding the minimum components which should be frozen.

After freezing, the reconfiguration operations are performed and then the frozen components are unfrozen. In the fourth step, some run-time analyses are carried out before unfreezing the modified software architecture to check its conformance with the architect anticipation.

3 Monitoring and Analysis of Reconfiguration Process in ARDF

Run-time assurance analysis in ADRF is performed in three phases: before, during, and after reconfiguration. In the initialization phase of ADRF, the context-aware application and each reconfiguration rule register themselves in CM. Each rule may include some contexts in its pre-condition. Such pre-conditions are registered in CM in the initialization phase as well as new rules insertion time. If all preconditions of a reconfiguration are satisfied, CM will trigger RM to fire the reconfiguration. In the following sub-sections, we explain the details of the three reconfiguration analysis phases.

3.1 Freezing the Affected Area

The first phase of analyzing a reconfiguration, which is done before reconfiguration execution, is freezing the affected area by SM. Affected area in a specific reconfiguration, is the set of components affected by the reconfiguration. It consists of all components which have been given as parameters to the reconfiguration operations. For example, if a reconfiguration attempts to replace c1 with c2; c1 should be frozen and added to the affected area of this reconfiguration. Unfrozen components continue their execution regardless of the frozen part. If a running component sends a message to one of the frozen components, the message will remain in the destination component buffer, until the component is unfrozen.

After recognizing the affected area, SM should find the best time to freeze. When components of the affected area are in their Safe Reconfiguration Points (SRPs) is the best time. SRPs are states in the component state-chart where the component state can be correctly transferred. In fact, components that are not in SRP states can not be reconfigured. Recognizing SRPs in the state-chart can not be done completely automatic due to the lack of some semantic information which should be given by the architect. In ADRF we assume that the architect specifies SRPs in the component state-chart. SRPs are defined per component without taking into account the difference between reconfigurations. Therefore, we need additional restriction on SRPs to find allowed starting states per reconfiguration. In ADRF this is done by a Transfer Function, which corresponds some SRPs of the component to new states after a specific reconfiguration. Transfer Function of a reconfiguration is given in a table called T-Table. This table is a list of following pair states <Permissible SRP from the reconfiguration point of view, Corresponding state after reconfiguration>.

In ADRF, each component is executed in a separate execution process and each user instantiates the component in a separate execution thread. A reconfiguration execution reaches to a break-point when all its threads are in their permissible SRPs regarding T-Table. When the freeze instruction is invoked, execution threads will be stopped by SM in the first break-point. If the affected area components can not reach to a break-point in a defined time, the reconfiguration is regarded as unsafe and ADRF will reject it.

3.2 Structural Analysis

The second assurance analysis is structural correctness checking after performing the reconfiguration. In ADRF this analysis is done by Assurance Automata. The automaton is created during reconfiguration to model the intermediate architectures, from the initial to the expected target architecture. In Assurance Automata, each state represents the anticipated architectures during reconfiguration. ADRF continually monitors current system configuration and compares it with the states of Assurance Automata. There are some techniques and methods for capturing the current system architecture such as [12]. Assurance Automata is defined more formally as $(S, S', \delta, F, \Sigma)$ where:

Σ is the automaton alphabet and includes reconfiguration operations:

$\Sigma = \{Add(C_i), Delete(C_i), Attach(C_i, C_j), Detach(C_i, C_j), Replace(C_i, C_j)\} \cup \{Er, Hld\}$, Where Er indicates the incorrect execution and Hld shows the unexecuted operation.

S_i represents a configuration (valid or invalid) of an architecure. The configuration is shown by G(V,E). G is a directed graph, where its nodes are the architecture components and its edges are connectores (links between attached components).
δ is the transition function defined by either correct execution of an operation (destination: the *next* state) or incorrect execution in the case of run-time errors (destination: *other* states or one *trap* state in online and offline methods respectively) or unexecution, for any reason (destination: the *current* state).

S' is the initial state, equivalent to the system architecture just before reconfiguration.

F is the final state, equivalent to the target architecture.

Structural analysis by Assurance Automata can be done in offline or online methods:

Offline Method: In the offline method, a snapshot of the system is captured and then reconfiguration starts. After a predefined time, which depends on the number of reconfiguration operations, RM compares the system state (current configuration) with the target state in Assurance Automata. The reconfiguration execution is structurally correct if those states match. Otherwise, the system state is compared to the all intermediate states in Assurance Automata in the reverse order, until finding an equal state. Afterward, the reconfiguration is re-executed from the discovered state with remained operations. If none of the states are equal to the system state, the system is in a *trap* state and it should be recovered from *initial* state, which is stored in the captured snapshot, and then the reconfiguration is re-executed.

In this method, besides the timeout, the number of executed operations is another stopping criterion for reconfiguration process. RM restricts the number of performed operations to the number specified in the map.

Online Method: In the online method, when the expected time to execute an operation is passed, RM compares the current system state with the expected state in Assurance Automata. The expected states represent correct execution of each reconfiguration operations. If the system state is equal to the *next* state of the automaton, the execution has been performed correctly. If the system state is not equal to the *next* state, but equal to the "before transition" (*current*) state, the last operation must be re-executed. If the system state is not equal to either the *next* or *current* state, system has gone to the *other* state. In this case, system must be recovered from the *current* state and then the last operation should be re-executed.

The main advantage of this monitoring and control mechanism is online error detection that is suitable when some repair mechanism is available.

3.3 Behavioral Analysis

The behavioral analysis is the third phase in assurance analysis which is performed at the end of the reconfiguration process and before unfreezing the affected area. RM checks component states which should match with the T-Table information. If Assurance Automata passes the reconfiguration but a component is found in the affected area which is not in its expected state, the behavioral assurance is not satisfied and the state transfer should be repeated. In ADRF, the current state transfer algorithm is simple but can be replaced without any change in the core of the framework.

Finally, if the three assurance analysis phases are passed successfully, the reconfiguration process is regarded as assured and SM can unfreeze the affected area.

4 Availability Issues of Reconfigurable Software in PCSs

The term availability is defined as the ratio of the total time a functional unit is capable of being used during a given interval to the length of the interval. The most simple representation for availability is as a ratio of the expected value of the uptime of a system to the aggregate of the expected values of up and down time, or *MTTF/(MTTF+MTTR)*. Where MTTF is the mean time to failure and MTTR declares the mean time to repair.

Although a successful reconfiguration can improve system availability by 1) replacing faulty components with the debugged version and 2) adding extra components to reply requests of overloaded components, but it has the possibility of freezing some components at run-time, causing them to be unavailable for a while. Replication of components seems to be a solution. However, it has problems such as the overhead of reconfiguration of all replicas. In addition, in cases where the new component functionality is not valid anymore, replicated components are inapplicable. ADRF tries to minimize the mentioned unavailability time of the affected area components.

4.1 Availability Definition in Reconfigurable Software

To define the system availability in ADRF, we assume the importance of all services in the system is the same and freezing a component results in unavailability of only that component services. Accordingly, we can define the system availability as the simple average (instead of weighted) of its services or components availability. The availability of each component itself is the average of all its instances availability.

Component instances are instantiated from a base component for each user session where the component is invoked. Reconfiguration process is performed on the base components. By reconfiguring a base component all its instances should also be reconfigured accordingly. When all instances of a component are frozen, the component is frozen and ready to be reconfigured.

Putting all together, the system availability is the average availability of all system component instances. Let call j^{th} instance of ith component, C_{ij}, so in a system having n components and m_i instances for each component C_i, the system availability is defined as equation 1.a.

The availability of a component instance is equivalent to its up time (CIUT) divided by its life time (CILT). CILT is the time between the instantiation of an instance and its destruction. With respect to the reconfiguration process, CIUT is a part of CILT that the component instance is not frozen, multiply by α . α is the component's normal availability without considering the reconfiguration process. The freeze time of a component instance depends on the number of reconfigurations performed on the instance during its life time (p) and the instance freeze time during each reconfiguration (CIFT(R_k)). CIUT is obtained by subtracting the sum of all freeze times of an instance from the instance life time, multiplying by α . The system availability is obtained by the average value of Availability(C_{ij}) for all component instances in the system (replacing Availability(C_{ij}) in equation 1.a by Availability(C_{ij}) from equation 1.b).

$$\text{a) Availability(system)} = \frac{\sum_{i=1}^{n} \sum_{j=1}^{m_i} \text{Availability}(C_{ij})}{\sum_{i=1}^{n} m_i} \tag{1}$$

$$\text{b) Availability}(C_{ij}) = \frac{\text{CIUT}}{\text{CILT}} = \frac{\alpha * (\text{CILT} - \sum_{k=1}^{p} \text{CIFT}(R_k))}{\text{CILT}}$$

4.2 Availability Factors for Reconfigurable Software in PCSs

We extracted factors that affect the system availability based on the above discussion. The effective factors are defined as follows (concentrating on the reconfiguration effects on availability, we assume that CILT and α are constants):

- **Number of reconfigurations:** As the number of reconfigurations is increased, the component freeze time is increased. Therefore, the component availability and consequently the system availability are decreased.
- **Number of involved components:** Since all involved components should be frozen during reconfiguration, the more components involved in a reconfiguration the less system availability. If a component instance does not participate in any reconfiguration during its life time, its availability has the

maximum value (α). For each participation, an unavailability time (CIFT) is added to the components down time and so decreases the system availability.

- **Number of users:** If the number of system users is increased, the number of component instances involved in the reconfiguration is increased. Therefore, available instances and the system availability will be decreased.
- **Number of reconfiguration operations:** The number of reconfiguration operations directly affects the total execution time of the reconfiguration process. Accordingly, long reconfigurations (including many operations) decrease system availability.
- **Error Rate:** The more errors occurrence the more validity checks and recovery done.

5 Availability Evaluation in ADRF

In our study, a simple PCS simulator was implemented to fill the absence of a real pervasive system. The simulator takes an XML file describing a context-aware application through its architectural component-diagram plus the state-chart of each component. Contexts can be changed randomly in the simulator. A sample of context is location and its change demonstrates the user mobility. Application execution is simulated by transferring messages among components. A prototype of ADRF has also been embedded in the PCS simulator implementation in order to manage reconfiguring the applications running in the simulator.

To evaluate ADRF and its impacts on availability, a smart library case study has been studied. Smart library provides a map-based guidance to books and collections on a Smart Digital Assistants. Main components in the system architecture which are distributed in the environment servers, gadgets, and user mobile devices are User Profile Manager, User Interface, Library Books Manager, Search Engine, Positioning Engine, Location Manager, Path Finder, and Map Manager. The reconfiguration which is used here is replacing Location Manager (LM) component with a new location manager (ULM) which supports updating the user current position while he is walking towards a selected rack. The study focuses on comparing availability of the system when using one of the following reconfiguration mechanisms:

- **BASE:** This mechanism ignores occurrence of errors. The system administrator is responsible for recovering the system and re-executing the reconfiguration. Involving the external human administrator in the reconfiguration process makes this mechanism unsuitable for PCSs. Evaluating this mechanism, the average recovery time by the external administrator is added to the unavailability time of all involved instances in the unsuccessful reconfiguration.
- **OPTIMISTIC:** This mechanism uses offline method of ADRF for structurally analyzing the reconfiguration process. If the system falls into an error state, it is automatically recovered after reconfiguration process and repeats the reconfiguration with the hope of correct execution. In this approach, capturing the system snapshot is done in the background while the system is available, but automatic recovery time is considered as a part of component's downtime.

- **ADRF:** This mechanism uses online method of ADRF in the structural analysis phase. The check and repair time for each operation, is important in the online method. In ADRF, each reconfiguration operation should be performed correctly. In the case of any error in the operation execution, it should be detected and repaired on-line. The smaller check and repair time, the quicker reconfiguration process and more available systems.

Our first observation is the effect of *number of users* on system availability. The number of library users in this case varies from 1 to 36. As shown in Figure 2.a, the availability in BASE mechanism is decreased more rapidly due to its long external recovery time. While the system availability in ADRF and OPTIMISTIC mechanisms are close to each other, ADRF provides more availability as the number of users increases. The reason is dependence between the number of users and the number of component instances. Therefore, OPTIMISTIC mechanism makes systems with many users more unavailable.

The next experiment focuses on the number of reconfigurations. In this case, another reconfiguration which replaces ULM with LM is defined. These two reconfigurations are applied repeatedly on the software architecture by required context changes. Figure 2.b depicts the effect of varying the number of reconfigurations on the system availability. As shown, decline of the system availability in the BASE mechanism is very sharp, because of the huge external overhead per reconfiguration. As the number of reconfigurations increases, the re-execution overhead in the OPTIMISTIC mechanism results in less availability in comparison to the ADRF mechanism. This experiment recommends ADRF for adaptive context-aware systems which have many reconfigurations during their life-cycle.

The effect of the number of reconfiguration operations on the system availability is evaluated, as the next experiment. We increase the number of operations by replacing more components and adding new components. As depicted in Figure 2.c, by increasing the number of reconfiguration operations, the availability of ADRF against BASE and OPTIMISTIC mechanism is less decreased. The BASE mechanism is the worst, because of the higher chance of failure (when the number of operations increases) as well as the high external recovery time. For long reconfigurations OPTIMISTIC approach decreases the system availability more than ADRF, because of re-executing the reconfiguration process from the beginning.

Our concentration in Figure 2.d, is the effect of error rate on availability. Generally, when a fault happens it means that an error has happened before. This error could be in communication links, computation, storage, or anywhere else. We assume no difference between errors. Therefore, error rate is assumed as the rate of fault occurrence. By changing the average error rate between 0.05 and 0.5, the difference among availabilities gained in the three mechanisms is specified in error-prone environments. As expected, the OPTIMISTIC mechanism is not suitable in such environments even worse than the BASE mechanism because of its optimistic view on error occurrence and its huge re-execution overhead. According to Figure 2.d, when the risk of falling into error states in each operation execution is high, online detection and repair in ADRF is the best.

Based on the level of decline on availability, the number of reconfigurations is the most effective factor. Therefore, the mechanism tolerating this effect is more suitable for PCSs. Our above-mentioned evaluations determined that ADRF is an appropriate framework for reconfiguration in PCSs especially when the environment is error-prone, the software is complex, context-aware, very adaptive with long reconfigurations, and lots of users. This is because of ADRF assurance mechanism which provides not only the correct and complete reconfiguration but also a highly available reconfiguration process, in comparison to performing reconfigurations without any assurance checks or simple offline optimistic validation mechanisms. Additionally, ADRF demonstrates itself scalable in terms of the number of users, reconfiguration operations, and the error rate.

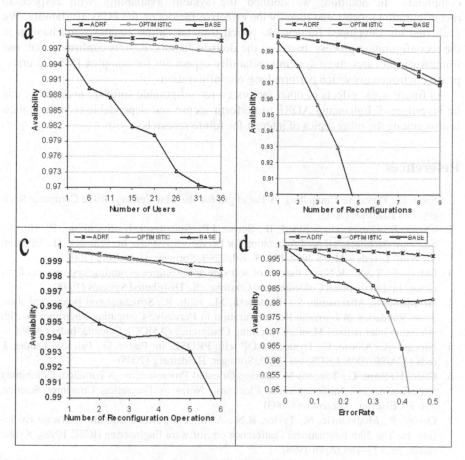

Fig. 2. The Effect of a) Number of Users, b) Number of Reconfigurations, c) Number of Reconfiguration Operations, and d) Error Rate on system availability

6 Conclusions and Future Work

Software reconfiguration will play an important role in the future computing environments. Most research on this domain and especially on the reconfiguration in PCSs are restricted to finding the best change strategies. However, applying these reconfiguration strategies in a running system has problems such as reconfiguration failure which affects service availability. Without monitoring and validating the reconfiguration process at run-time, system invisibility and adaptability can be damaged.

In this paper, we proposed an Assured Dynamic Reconfiguration Framework, ADRF, capable of performing run-time reconfiguration on PCSs. Achieving three assurance analysis phases (before, during, and after reconfiguration process), ADRF ensures architect that his defined reconfigurations will be performed correctly and completely. In addition, we defined the system availability with respect to reconfiguration process and identify the effective factors on the PCSs availability. We evaluated our developed framework, which uses an online assurance mechanism in the reconfiguration process, based on the defined factors. Results confirmed that, our framework provides more system availability especially for complex PCSs in error-prone environments which perform long reconfigurations.

As future work, effects of other factors on reconfigurable software availability can be investigated. Enhancing ADRF to perform secure and dependable reconfiguration is also among the other topics of interest for future research.

References

1. Saha, D.: Pervasive Computing: A Paradigm for the 21st Century. IEEE Computer Society, Los Alamitos (2003)
2. Cheng, S., Garlan, D., Schmerl, B., Sousa, J.P., Spitznagel, B., Steenkiste, P., Hu, N.: Software Architecture-based Adaptation for Pervasive Systems. In: Schmeck, H., Ungerer, T., Wolf, L. (eds.) ARCS 2002. LNCS, vol. 2299, Springer, Heidelberg (2002)
3. Oreizy, P., Taylor, R.N.: on the role of software architectures in runtime system reconfiguration. In: International Conference on Configurable Distributed Systems (1998)
4. Hemmati, H., Aliakbarian, S., Niamanesh, M., Jalili, R.: Structural and Behavioral Run-Time Validation of Dynamic Reconfiguration in Pervasive Computing Environments. In: 4th Asian International Mobile Computing Conference (AMOC), Calcutta, India (2006)
5. Nicoara, A., Alonso, G.: Dynamic AOP with PROSE. In: Pastor, Ó., Falcão e Cunha, J. (eds.) CAiSE 2005. LNCS, vol. 3520, Springer, Heidelberg (2005)
6. Chen, F., Rosu, G.: Towards Monitoring-Oriented Programming: A Paradigm Combining Specification and Implementation. Electronic Notes in Theoretical Computer Science, vol. 89. Elsevier, Amsterdam (2003)
7. Oreizy, P., Medvidovic, N., Taylor, R.N.: Architecture-Based Runtime Software Evolution. In: The 20th International Conference on Software Engineering (ICSE 1998), Kyoto, Japan, pp. 177–186 (April 1998)
8. Roshandel, R., Hoek, A.V., Mikic, M., Medvidovic, N.: Mae – A System Model and Environment for Managing Architectural Evaluation. ACM Transactions on Software Engineering and Methodology (April 2004)
9. Diaconescu, A., Murphy, J.: A Framework for Using Component Redundancy for self-Optimising and self-Healing Component Based Systems. In: ICSE 2003 Workshop on Software Architectures for Dependable Systems, Portland, Oregon, USA (May 3 2003)
10. Niamanesh, M., Jalili, R.: A Dynamic-Reconfigurable Architecture for Protocol Stacks of Networked Systems. In: 31st Annual International Computer Software and Applications Conference, Beijing, China (July 2007)

11. Hemmati, H., Niamanesh, M., Jalili, R.: A Framework to Support Run-Time Assured Dynamic Reconfiguration for Pervasive Computing Environments. In: The first IEEE International symposium on wireless pervasive computing ISWPC, Thailand (2006)
12. Hamou-Lhadj, A., Braun, E., Amyot, D., Lethbridge, T.: Recovering Behavioral Design Models from Execution Traces. In: Ninth European Conference on Software Maintenance and Reengineering (CSMR 2005), pp. 112–121 (2005)

Modeling Modern Social-Network-Based Epidemics: A Case Study of Rose*

Sirui Yang, Hai Jin, Xiaofei Liao, and Sanmin Liu

Services Computing Technology and System Lab
Cluster and Grid Computing Lab
School of Computer Science and Technology
Huazhong University of Science and Technology, Wuhan, 430074, China
hjin@mail.hust.edu.cn

Abstract. The social-network-based epidemics, such as email-based ones, have been long studied. However, few have noticed some newly emerging epidemics which especially based on portable devices. In this paper, we think of such viruses and take a representative, the *Rose* epidemic, for case study. We build a model with a system of differential equations and closed-form solutions for three propagation scenes correspondingly. With both theoretical and numerical analysis, we find out that (1) Rose is able to infect hosts as exponentially as the Internet-based worms do;(2) In the Internet cafe scene, it is difficult to contain Rose even with reactive recovery measures; (3) the most influential factors for Rose's propagation are the amount of hosts and portable devices and the lifetime of Internet cafe machines, while the arrival rate of clients and the proportion of immune machines only affect in the print service office scene.

Keywords: Social Network, Portable Device, Rose Epidemic, Modeling.

1 Introduction

Information security has been challenged by Internet epidemics for decades [1][2]. These epidemics, such as worms, Trojans and malware, are able to self propagate by taking advantage of vulnerabilities on online hosts. For instance, the random scanning worms [3] will examine a random series of Internet hosts, and compromise vulnerable ones rapidly. Researchers have proposed plentiful measures against both known and potential Internet based epidemics. For example, a simple and traditional solution is the reactive immunization [4][5].

Social network: There have already been extensive researches on social network [6][9]. Similar to the World Wide Web (WWW), the web of human sexual contacts, or criminal networks, which often do not have an engineered architecture but instead are self-organized by the actions of a large number of individuals, social network can

---

* This work is supported by National Science Foundation of China (NSFC) under grants No.60433040 and No.60731160630, the Research Fund for the Doctoral Program of Higher Education under grant No.20050487040.

C. Rong et al. (Eds.): ATC 2008, LNCS 5060, pp. 302–315, 2008.

emerge as small-world properties or scale-free degree distributions [13]. Traditionally, it is believed that the junk email is one of the most important security issues in social network. However, with modern techniques, we believe there are more complicated epidemics taking advantage of social network.

Modern social network based epidemics: The traditional social network based epidemics can be concluded as *acquaintance-based*, e.g., the junk emails, rumor dissemination. However, modern epidemics have the characteristics that do no need contacts to know each other. They simply need a certain form of *medium*. For instance, an epidemic called *Rose* [7] has been prevalent in China since April, 2006. It never takes advantage of Internet but *portable devices* only. An infected device will harm vulnerable hosts as well as other devices through social networks. Further, if such a feature is integrated with Internet techniques, the harm can be much strong. For example, *Panda* [8] which relies on portable devices and some vulnerable websites even infects millions of hosts and leads to a great deal of loss from December, 2006 to April, 2007.

Intuitively, Internet is much more clustering and fast-speed than social network. However, due to the power-law principles in the free-scale networks, epidemics based on social network are still fast propagating. Besides, many offline epidemics are not taken into account in existing virus database of major anti-virus companies' products. This greatly increases the prevalence of offline epidemics and raises the difficulty to clean such viruses.

As introduced, the typical propagation measure for modern social network based epidemics is to make use of portable devices, especially *flash drives*. As Rose is a purely portable device based epidemic, our further analysis is based on Rose.

In this paper, we study the social network based epidemics especially aiming at portable devices. Specifically, we bring forward Rose's three typical propagation scenes and establish corresponding differential equations, as well as closed-form solutions. The specific contributions of this paper are as follows:

(1) To the best of our knowledge, we are the first to explore the portable device based social network epidemics. We build a system of differential equations to model the Rose epidemic. The model contains the cases both with and without recovery mechanisms. We propose the closed-form solutions for these equations. Our methodology is meaningful that the models without and with recovery are suitable for the propagating phase and the eliminating phase, respectively. The model indicates that Rose can propagate exponentially as most Internet based epidemics do.

(2) We conduct numerical experiments of this model, and the results show that Internet cafe scene is the most important one where Rose can not be eliminated even with recovery mechanisms.

(3) The most influential factors in the dissemination of Rose are the amount of hosts and portable devices and the lifetime of Internet cafe machines. In the print service office scene, the arrival rate of clients and the percentage of immune machines also have some influence.

The rest of this paper is organized as follows: in section 2, we introduce the destruction and mechanism of Rose, as well as its three propagation scenes. In section 3, we model Rose for each of the scenes respectively, both with and without defense. In Section 4, the numerical experiments and results are shown. In Section 5, we introduce the related work. In Section 6, the conclusion is drawn and the future work is presented.

2 The Rose Epidemic

Portable device technique has been rapidly developed recently. Among all portable devices, portable storages (e.g., flash drives) are most popular. It allows users to connect a storage disk to a computer and use it immediately. The flash drives are prevalent because of their convenience and mobility. However, these features also provide viruses yet another manner to propagate. Once a virus compromises a flash drive, it will automatically propagate itself to any vulnerable machines to which the storage is plugged-in. Rose is such a virus that purely takes advantage of portable storages.

2.1 The Mechanism of Rose

Rose first appeared in the central China in April, 2006 which infected Windows systems. Once a computer is compromised, there will be two virus producing files called *rose.exe* and *autorun.inf* in all drives. When double clicking the drive icon, the drive can not be open. However, the virus is auto-propagating at background. The harms of the Rose virus are high resource occupation rate and possible system crash.

As we mentioned, the propagation of Rose epidemic is based on portable devices. Once a virus-containing portable device is connected to a susceptible computer, it will automatically copy the virus files onto all other drives. A susceptible computer is a machine that allows flash drives to auto run if there is an *autorun.inf* file on the exact drive. As this function is enabled by default in Windows, a large proportion of computers are susceptible. If other clean portable devices are connected to this infected computer, they will also be compromised recursively. Besides, not until the auto run system function is disabled, simply deleting virus files can not immune the machine.

The propagation mechanism of Rose seems simple and weak. However, such epidemics have become rampant for a long period. Most anti-virus software have not provided corresponding virus database for Rose currently. We estimate it is because of two reasons: (1) such epidemic is not significant at the beginning because they do not transfer through Internet, so the virus database is not updated in time. (2) Considering that the *autorun.inf* file is a normal text file, which is used for the auto run function in legal manner, it is rude to simply disabling the function and remove such a file.

2.2 Three Propagation Scenes

To our knowledge, there are mainly three places where Rose is significantly propagated.

Print Service Office (PSO): The print service offices help clients print sheets, such as papers, documents, images. In each office, there are several computers where clients can freely use their flash drives to upload files for print. As the service providers are mostly unprofessional in system security administration, many machines in PSOs are susceptible to Rose. Once a client uses an infected flash drive on the machine, it is compromised and can further infect following clients' portable devices.

Internet Cafe (IC): The Internet cafe is a place where net surfers pay for Internet service. Clients are also allowed to use flash drives freely. In this case, the IC scene is same to the PSO scene. However, we concentrate on a specific kind of IC, i.e., the one where the *storage protection cards* are used. A storage protection card, also called *system reset card*, is a piece of hardware used to recover the disk content and system configuration on the boot of the machine. It is usually a PCI device and takes effect before the operating system is loaded. Thus, the virus files will be removed automatically at any reboot of the machine. As many ICs provide service in the all-day manner, a machine will then be restarted only by the clients' operation, e.g., when the system is down.

Friendship Network (FN): In many cases, friends will share (i.e., borrow and lend) portable storages when needed. For instance, a person attended a party and will use the photographer's portable storage to copy some pictures. In this way, the virus can also be propagated. Friendship network is totally a traditional social network as we mentioned.

In the following sections, we will explain the details of these scenes, and study each of them to build the model.

3   Epidemic Modeling

Now we analyze Rose virus and establish a model of it. We will consider the occasions both with and without recovery mechanisms. We assume only computers can be immunized, while portable storages can not be immunized but cleaned by the immune machines. The case when the storages are set read-only to immunize themselves is not taken into account. We also suppose a client owns one and only one portable device. The sum of the clients (also portable storages) is very large but limited, which is practical for describing Rose epidemic in a specified region (e.g., a college or a city).

3.1   Modeling Print Service Office Scene

For simplicity, we make following assumptions in this subsection: (1) Clients visit each printing service computer with the same arrival rate; (2) There are two kinds of machines in PSO, the infected ones and the immune ones. An immune machine is a computer having auto run function disabled and cleanup software installed. Thus, a clean portable storage will only be contaminated when connecting to an infected machine. On opposite, a virus containing flash drive will be cleaned on connecting to an immune machine. The infected machines are propagated by outside environment and all flash drives are clean at the beginning.

The frequently used notations are list in Table 1. As a flash drive is either clean (susceptible) or infected, we have $x+y=W$.

Without Recovery. In this subsection, we study the case when there are no recovery mechanisms. Namely, $M=0$. Suppose the probability for a client to visit an infected machine is p, then:

Table 1. Frequently used notations in the model

M	# of immune machines
N	# of susceptible machines
μ	Client arrival rate for each machine
W	# of total clients
x	# of clean flash drives
y	# of infected flash drives
p	probability to visit an infected machine
C_i	Constants in formal solutions

$$p = \frac{N}{M+N}$$ (1)

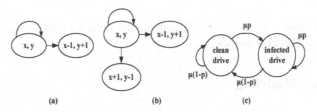

(a)   (b)   (c)

Fig. 1. State transition diagram in PSO scene: (a) Markov process without recovery (b) Markov process with recovery (c) transition probability

Considering the tuple (x, y), it is a Markov process. Figure 1(a) shows the state transitions for this process. From the state (x, y) the system can go to the state:

- $(x-1, y+1)$: when a clean client visits an infected machine;
- (x, y): otherwise.

Let $y=y(t)$, i.e., the number of infected clients at time t. Thus, we have:

$$\dot{y} = \frac{x}{x+y} \cdot \mu \cdot p = \frac{W-y}{W} \cdot \mu \cdot p = (1-\frac{y}{W}) \cdot \mu \cdot p$$ (2)

This differential equation has the formal solution:

$$y = y(t) = W - C_1 e^{-\frac{\mu \cdot p}{W} t}, t \geq 0$$ (3)

Consider the boundary condition that $y(0)=0$, we can get $C_1=W$. Then, the closed-form solution is:

$$y(t) = W - W \cdot e^{-\frac{\mu \cdot p}{W} t}, t \geq 0$$ (4)

With Recovery. In this subsection, we take into account that there are some passive solutions such as vaccination. Then, the Markov process (x, y) and the state transitions are shown in Figure 1(b). Then the system at state (x, y) can jump to the state:

- $(x-1, y+1)$: when a clean client visits an infected machine;
- (x, y): when an infected client visits an infected machine, or a clean client visits an immune machine;
- $(x+1, y-1)$: when an infected client visits an immune machine.

Therefore, we also get a differential equation for $y(t)$ in this case:

$$\dot{y} = \frac{x}{x+y} \cdot \mu \cdot p - \frac{y}{x+y} \cdot \mu \cdot (1-p) = \mu \cdot p + \frac{\mu \cdot y}{W} \tag{5}$$

with the closed-form solution that:

$$y(t) = pW(1 - e^{-\frac{\mu}{W}t}), t \geq 0 \tag{6}$$

3.2 Modeling Internet Cafe Scene

As introduced, a computer in the IC scene will receive arriving clients and keeps working until it is rebooted. The period between two reboots is called the *lifetime* of the computer. It will be infected at a random time during its lifetime when an infective client uses his flash drive on it. So different from PSO scene, the flash drive in IC scene is possible to infect a computer and flash drives arriving in the remaining of this lifetime.

Also, we make some assumptions for simplicity: (1) Clients visit each Internet service computer with the same arrival rate; (2) An infective client may arrive at a random time during this period; (3) Compared with the long investigation time, the lifetime is assumed much shorter, and all machines are regarded synchronously working.

The length of the lifetime is denoted as T. We assume the lifetime yields exponential distribution with the parameter λ. Then, $T=1/\lambda$. We use y_0 for the initial number of infected flash drives in IC scene, which is determined by outside environment.

Without Recovery. In this case, still $M=0$. We denote the time point for a clean machine to receive an infected client during one lifetime as $1-q$, i.e., the machine is clean in $[0, 1-q]$ and it is infected in $[q, 1]$. For one machine, we can get the differential equation of the number of the newly infected clients during its lifetime:

$$\dot{y} = \frac{x}{x+y} \cdot \mu \cdot q \cdot p, 0 \leq t \leq T \tag{7}$$

The formal solution of this equation is:

$$y = W - C_2 e^{-\frac{\mu \cdot q \cdot p}{W}t}, 0 \leq t \leq T \tag{8}$$

As $y(0)=y_0=0$, then $C_2=W$. We integrate Formula (8) over $[0, T]$ and get the number of newly infected clients that:

$$y(T) = W(1 - e^{-\frac{\mu \cdot q \cdot p}{W}T}) \tag{9}$$

Further, if the arrival rate for rebooted machines and normal machines are same, i.e., $q=1/\mu$, and $T=1/\lambda$, we can derive Formula (9) into:

$$y(T) = W(1 - e^{-\frac{1}{\lambda p W}}) \tag{10}$$

Then, in each period of lifetime, there are $y(T)$ machines to be infected. As supposed, T is much more transient compared with the long observation time. Namely, the infecting rate $\lambda_T = dy/dT = y(T)$. Further, we can build the differential equation for the whole observation that:

$$\dot{y} = \frac{x}{x+y} \cdot \lambda_T = \frac{W-y}{W} \cdot \lambda_T = (1 - \frac{y}{W}) \cdot \lambda_T \tag{11}$$

The solution is:

$$y = W - (W - y_0) \cdot e^{-\frac{y(T)}{W}t} = W - (W - y_0) \exp(-(1 - e^{-\frac{1}{\lambda p W}}) \cdot t), \, t \geq 0 \tag{12}$$

With Recovery. The Markov process for Rose propagation with recovery in IC scene is shown in Figure 2.

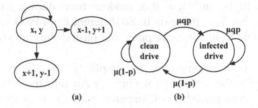

Fig. 2. State transition diagram in IC scene: (a) Markov process with recovery (b) transition probability

Then Formula (8) should be adjusted to:

$$\dot{y} = \frac{x}{x+y} \cdot \mu \cdot q \cdot p_2 - \frac{y}{x+y} \cdot \mu \cdot p_2, \, 0 \leq t \leq T \tag{13}$$

The solution is:

$$y = \frac{Wq}{1+q}(1 - e^{-\frac{\mu p_2 (1+q)}{W}t}), \, 0 \leq t \leq T \tag{14}$$

By replacing $t=T$, $q=1/\mu$, and $T=1/\lambda$ into this solution, we can get:

$$y(T) = \frac{Wq}{1+q}(1 - e^{-\frac{\mu p_2 (1+q)}{W}T}) = \frac{W}{(1+\mu)}(1 - e^{-\frac{p_2(1+\mu)}{\lambda W}}) \tag{15}$$

Similar to *Without Recovery* case, we get the propagation process during the whole observation that:

$$y = W - (W - y_0) \exp(-t \cdot (1 - e^{-\frac{p_2(1+\mu)}{\lambda W}})/(1+\mu)), \, t \geq 0 \tag{16}$$

3.3 Modeling Friendship Network

According to the theory of social network, the friendship network is a scale-free (SF) network [12][13][14]. Since such networks and corresponding epidemics (as shown in Figure 3) have been extensively studied, we simply present the results in the FN scene. The propagation manner is shown in Figure 3.

In this scene, we suppose the friendship network is composed by *individuals* who own personal machines, some of which have flash drives and others not. The one who has no flash drives will borrow others' and use them on his machine. Then the infected flash drives propagate Rose epidemic among these machines and drives. An *infected individual* is the one with either an infected machine or an infected flash drive. Otherwise, it is a *clean individual*. During each step, each susceptible (clean) individual is infected with rate v if it is connected to one or more infected nodes. Meanwhile, infected nodes are cured and become again susceptible with rate δ, defining an effective spreading rate $\lambda_f = v/\delta$.

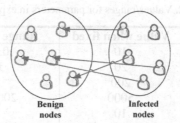

Benign   Infected
nodes   nodes

Fig. 3. Infected nodes and epidemics in social networks

It is known that the probability of an individual to have k friends is $k^{-\gamma}$ ($\gamma=3$ is used in most computations) [12]. Further, in the scale-free model, the connectivity distribution of all the individuals yields $P(k)=2m^2/k^{-3}$. Then, the percentage of infected individuals (ρ) yields [13]:

$$\rho \cong 2e^{-\frac{1}{m\lambda_f}} \qquad (17)$$

Notice that Formula (17) is the case with recovery. While, in cases without recovery, $\lambda_f=v$.

For coherency purpose, we use y to denote the number of infected individuals, and the number of individuals is still W, thus

$$y = \rho \cdot W \cong 2We^{-\frac{1}{m\lambda_f}} \qquad (18)$$

4   Analysis and Implications of Parameters

We have obtained a system of differential equations and closed-form solutions to model the propagation of Rose epidemic in three scenes. In this section, we analyze the parameters' effects and implications. The following analysis is based on Formula (6) and (16), i.e., the cases with recovery. When investigating one parameter, the others are fixed and the investigated one is varied within a range. The values and ranges for the parameters are listed in Table 2.

Arrival rate: First, we investigate the influence of the arrival rate of clients in the PSO and IC scenes, i.e., parameter μ. The results for PSO model and IC model are shown in Figure 4.

In the PSO scene, the arrival rate has shown significant influence. When $\mu=100$, the curve is a fast increasing exponential one and about *10%* clients have been compromised within *250* time units. When μ is reduced to *10*, the progress is milder and *10%* clients have been infected within about *2000* time units. When μ reaches *1* or below, the curves are almost linear and the propagation is much slowly evolving. This result is intuitive to the real world that if PSO receives a flurry of clients when epidemics take place, the epidemic is able to disseminate rapidly. Also, we can see from Figure 4 that with recovery, there are no more than *10%* clients infected.

Table 2. Values/ranges for parameters in experiments

Parameter	Value when fixed	Range when varied
μ	10	0.1~1000
M	20	10~200
N (fixed)	200	N/A
W	5000	2000~50000
y_0	10	1~100
λ	0.01	0.001~1

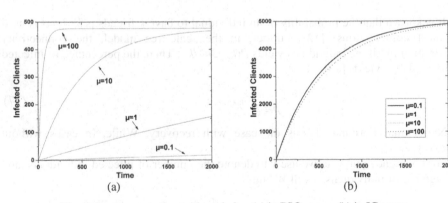

Fig. 4. Rose propagation with varied μ: (a) in PSO scene; (b) in IC scene

However, Figure 4(b) indicates that the arrival rate influences unnoticeably in the IC scene. This is because the machines in the IC scene will reboot every *100* time units (i.e., $\lambda=0.01$). This period is short compared with our observation period (about *2000* time unit as shown in the figure). Besides, the first arrival of an infective client after the reboot is random. Therefore, the affect of parameter μ is much neutralized. The result implies that it is fortunate that with the help of storage protection card, the arrival rate of clients in IC scene is ignorable.

Immune machine percentage: In Figure 5, we show the results of the propagation with different immune machines in PSO and IC scenes.

The infected client number in the PSO scene is bounded to about *470* when *M=10*, which is decreased to *250* when *M=200*. The effect of the immune machine percentage in IC scene is also perceivable but a bit weaker than in PSO scene. It is promising that we can limit the epidemic to affect less than *10%* clients by inducing *5%* immune machines (i.e., *M=10* while *N=200*) in the PSO scene. However, the case in the IC scene is not acceptable, e.g., even if *M=200* the limitation reaches to *4500* (i.e., *90%*). Moreover, we also notice that the decrement of infected client boundary is inverse exponential to the increment of immune machines. This suggests that to simply increase the immune machines is not a sufficient solution to eliminate Rose epidemic.

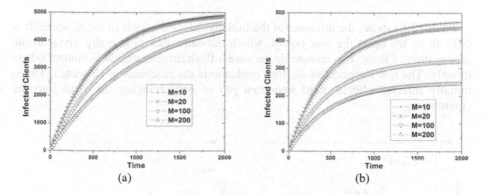

Fig. 5. Rose propagation with varied *M*: (a) in PSO scene; (b) in IC scene

Client amount: As we suppose the epidemic is disseminated within a limited but large scale, we study the influence of the sum of clients and the results are shown in Figure 6. It is intuitive that in both the PSO and IC scenes, the growth of infected client number is much slower with *W* getting larger. Unlike the former two experiments, the influences of the client amount are totally homogeneous in both the two scenes. Notice that the threshold of infected clients is still less than *10%* in the PSO scene but nearly *100%* in the IC scene.

Machine lifetime and initially infected clients: Now we study the particular parameters in IC scene, i.e., the lifetime and the initially infected clients.

The effect of lifetime in the IC scene is presented in Figure 7(a). With longer lifetime, the propagation is much sharper. That is because the IC machine stays infective once it receives a virus containing client; and the longer its lifetime is, the more it will compromise following clients. When *λ=0.001* (i.e., the lifetime of a machine reaches *1000* time unit which is half of our observation period), which means the IC machines are nearly always-on, the whole clients are infected very soon (in about *300* time units).

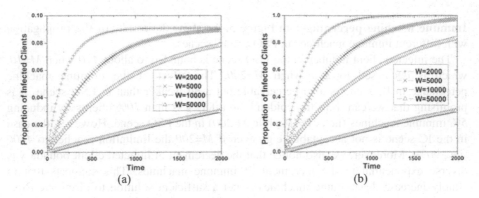

Fig. 6. Rose propagation with varied W: (a) in PSO scene; (b) in IC scene

Figure 7(b) shows the influence of the initially infected clients in the IC scene. It is difficult to tell apart the four curves, which indicates that y_0 is really trivial to the propagation of Rose. It is reasonable because a flash drive is unable to contact others directly. The real intermediate of Rose epidemic is the machines in all scenes. The y_0 initially infected clients' most important *job* is only bringing the virus into the community.

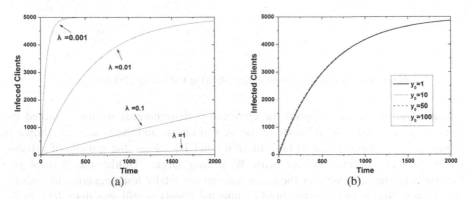

Fig. 7. Particular parameters in IC scene: (a) with varied λ; (b) with varied y_0

Recovery existence: The models without recovery are able to describe the propagating phase of Rose epidemic, while the models with recovery can be used to represent the eliminating phase. Now we examine the difference between the two kinds of models. Our current analysis is based on Formula (4), (6), (12) and (16).

Figure 8 shows the respective results in PSO and IC scenes. In Figure 8(a), the recovery mechanism can greatly reduce the number of infected clients (limited to about *10%* of the values when recovery is absent). It means in the PSO scene, the Rose epidemic tends to be under control with sufficient recovery measures, e.g., the immunization. Nevertheless, the result in Figure 8(b) indicates that it is difficult to recover from Rose in the IC scene. The curves show that even with common

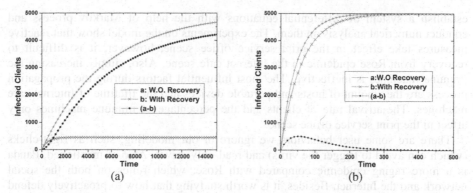

Fig. 8. Model comparison in without and with recovery cases: (a) in PSO scene; (b) in IC scene

immunization solutions, the epidemic can be disseminated quickly and widely. The recovery mechanism is nearly of no use (the bottom curve in the figure). It implies that in IC scene a passive recovery is quite insufficient against Rose.

5 Related Work

Many researchers have studied sorts of security issues in Internet, such as random scanning worms [3]. Especially, they build some models which can introduce the epidemics well. However, some researches have been transferring into epidemics in social network, which happens in an offline manner. A most common concern among these researches is the junk email issue.

Levi et al. [15] pointed out there are some risks in using emails, such as the bogus email with someone else's email name and address when SMTP servers do not check sender authenticity. They proposed a digital signature and globally-known trustworthy certification authority solution.

Newman et al. [16] proposed that the emails can compose a network to propagate computer viruses. The network is formed in the way that viruses make use of computer users' email address books as a source for email addresses of new victims. Further, they investigated empirically the structure of this network using data drawn from a large computer installation, and discussed the implications of this structure for the understanding and prevention of computer virus epidemics.

There are more studies on filtering junk emails [17][18]. However, as we introduced above, a new security issue has emerged in the form of leveraging portable devices. The representation of this kind of epidemics is Rose [7] and Panda [8]. In these epidemics, people share machines and portable devices, thus form a social network and facilitate the propagation of the epidemics.

6 Conclusion and Future Work

In this paper, we explore a kind of modern social network based epidemics which leverages portable devices and Windows OS vulnerabilities. We take Rose epidemic as a case study and analyze the models in three scenes of Rose's propagation. We establish a system of differential equations with the help of Markov process and conduct numerical analysis on them. The experiments on the model show that reactive measures take effect in the print service office scene, however, it is difficult to recovery from Rose epidemic in the Internet cafe scene. Also, simply increasing the immune machines is ineffective. The most influential factors during the propagation process are the amount of hosts and portable devices and the lifetime of Internet cafe machines. The arrival rate of clients and the percentage of immune machines only affect in the print service office scene.

There are some user behaviors we ignore in our modeling, such as right-clicks (which can avoid to trigger the virus) and read-only drives. Also as mentioned, Panda is a more raging epidemic compared with Rose, which relies on both the social network and the Internet. Besides, it is worth studying that how to proactively defend the non-Internet epidemics, since it is shown reactive solutions take little effect. We leave them as our future work.

References

1. Blaster Worms, CERT Advisory CA-2003-20 W32/Blaster Worm,
   http://www.cert.org/advisories/CA-2003-20.html
2. Code Red Worms, CAIDA Analysis of Code-Red,
   http://www.caida.org/analysis/security/code-red/
3. Weaver, N., Staniford, S., Paxson, V.: Very fast containment of scanning worms. In: Proc. of the 13th USENIX Security Symposium (2004)
4. Cohen, R., Havlin, S., Ben-Avraham, D.: Efficient Immunization Strategies for Computer Networks and Populations. Physical Review Letters 91(24), 247–901 (2003)
5. Yang, S., Jin, H., Liao, X., Yao, H.: OnRipple: A Distributed Overlay Framework for Targeted Immunization in Large-Scale Networks. In: Proc. of ACIS SNPD 2007, Qingdao, China, July 30-August 2 (2007)
6. Scott, J.: Social Network Analysis: A Handbook, 2nd edn. Sage, London (2000)
7. Rose Epidemic, Rose Virus and Solution (in Chinese),
   http://grid.hust.edu.cn/cgcl/rose.htm
8. Nimaya Worm, Worm.Nimaya (Panda) and Special Cleanup Tools (in Chinese),
   http://it.rising.com.cn/Channels/Service/2006-
   11/1163505486d38734.shtml
9. Ebel, H., Davidsen, J., Bornholdt, S.: Dynamics of Social Networks. Complexity 8(2), 24–27 (2002)
10. Newman, M.E.J.: The Structure and Function of Complex Networks. SIAM Review 45(2), 167–256 (2003)
11. Pasteor-Satorras, R., Vespignani, A.: Epidemics and Immunization in Scale-Free Networks. In: Handbook of Graphs and Networks: From the Genome to the Internet, Wiley-VCH (2003)
12. Grabowskia, A., Kosiński, R.A.: The SIS Model of Epidemic Spreading in a Hierarchical Social Network. Acta. Phys. Polon. B 36, 1579–1593 (2005)
13. Pastor-Satorras, R., Vespignani, A.: Epidemic Spreading in Scale-Free Networks. Physical Review Letters 86(14), 3200 (2001)
14. Liu, Z., Hu, B.: Epidemic spreading in community networks. Europhys. Lett. 72(2), 315 (2005)

15. Levi, A., Koc, C.K.: Risks in Email Security. Communications of the ACM 44(8), 112–112 (2001)
16. Newman, M.E.J., Forrest, S., Balthrop, J.: Email networks and the spread of computer viruses. Phys. Rev. E 66(035101) (2002)
17. Takahashi, K., Abe, T., Kawashima, M.: Stopping Junk Email by Using Conditional ID Technology: privango. NTT Technical Review 3(3), 52–56 (2005)
18. Oda, T., White, T.: Immunity from spam: an analysis of an artificial immune system for junk email detection. In: Proc. of 4th International Conference on Artificial Immune Systems, pp. 276–289 (2005)

An Evaluation Study of the Effectiveness of Modeling NASA Swarm-Based Exploration Missions with ASSL

Mike Hinchey[1] and Emil Vassev[2]

[1] Lero–the Irish Software Engineering Research Center, University of Limerick, Ireland
mike.hinchey@lero.ie
[2] Concordia University, Montreal, Quebec, H3G 1M8, Canada
i_vassev@cse.concordia.ca

Abstract. We assess the effectiveness of using the Autonomic System Specification Language (ASSL) to model ANTS (Autonomous Nano-Technology Swarm), a NASA concept swarm-based exploration mission. In this study, we draw upon our preliminary results of modeling some of the autonomic features of ANTS, to discuss and evaluate the advantages and shortcomings of this approach. Moreover, this paper, which documents the results of that study, identifies challenges and aspects of ANTS that cannot be modeled with ASSL. Therefore, an important contribution of this study is a critical analysis of ASSL as a specification language designed specifically for autonomic systems.

Keywords: Autonomic computing, system modeling, specification language.

1 Introduction

Autonomic Computing (AC) [5] is an emerging field for developing complex large-scale systems by transforming them into self-managing autonomic systems (ASs), which are intrinsically intended to reduce complexity through automation. However, the very complexity inherent in many systems that lend themselves well to AC can often cause difficulty in designing that same AS. All of this emphasizes the need for a specification language that allows for modeling and validation of such systems. ASSL is a formal framework for modeling ASs that reveals a new specification style, going far beyond the initial specifications pertaining to functional and interfacing issues [1].

NASA exploration missions increasingly rely on the concepts of AC, exploiting these to increase the survivability of remote missions, particularly when human tending is not feasible. NASA swarm-based exploration missions [2, 3, 4] represent a new class of concept missions based on swarm intelligence attained through collective, cooperative interactions of nodes at all levels of the system. One such mission is the concept Autonomous Nano-Technology Swarm (ANTS), in which "a thousand picospacecraft, each weighing less than three pounds, will work cooperatively to explore the asteroid belt" [2]. ANTS provides self-management to meet the requirements of changing configurations and harsh external conditions.

C. Rong et al. (Eds.): ATC 2008, LNCS 5060, pp. 316–330, 2008.

Research Problem. In general, ANTS must afford autonomous operation without intervention from Earth, while operating under harsh conditions in space. ANTS poses many challenges related to its heterogeneous architecture, the need of continuous re-planning, re-configuration, and re-optimization. Thus, considering the hostile environment in which it must survive, we need to design and implement ANTS as a system able to perform an arbitrary number of in-space exploration tasks over multiple years and also able to autonomously manage itself, by integrating at least the baseline AC self-management policies: self-configuring, self-healing, self-optimizing and self-protecting [5].

Therefore, the need for prototyping, and formal modeling, which will aid in the design and implementation ANTS, are becoming increasingly necessary and important as the urgent need for high levels of assurance regarding correctness and autonomic behavior persists in the ANTS requirements [2, 3, 4]. Moreover, an evaluation of the effectiveness of the approach under consideration should be performed in the context of a comprehensive study about ANTS, thus including architecture, objectives, and operational environment.

Our Approach. In this research, we place emphasis on modeling ANTS's autonomic properties with ASSL and build a set of specification models for ANTS. Having completed our initial steps of modeling ANTS with ASSL, we are able to evaluate the effectiveness of our preliminary results, before further research will be undertaken. The result of this evaluation study will allow us to improve the current specification models and continue specifying incrementally. The latter also includes relating the current specification models together into a whole and more-complete specification model that will allow us to generate Java code, which will be the base for a functional prototype of ANTS. The latter could be extremely useful when undertaking further investigation based on practical results and will help to test the autonomic behavior under simulated conditions. The goals of this paper can be stated as following:

1) to give a brief survey of the current ASSL specification models for ANTS; and
2) to present a thorough and critical analysis of the models under consideration.

The rest of this paper is organized as follows. In Section 2, we review related work on the current formal approaches to ANTS and AC formal specification platforms. As a background to the remaining sections, Section 3 provides a brief description of ANTS, and Section 4 introduces the ASSL framework. Section 5 presents an overview of the current and prospective ASSL specification models for ANTS. In section 6, we provide an evaluation of using ASSL with the ANTS concept mission. Our conclusions and future work directions are outlined in Section 7.

2 Related Work

A NASA developed formal approach, named R2D2C (Requirements to Design to Code) is described in [9]. In this approach, system designers may write specifications as scenarios in constrained (domain-specific) natural language, or in a range of other notations (including UML use cases). These scenarios are then used to derive a formal model that fulfills the requirements stated at the outset, and which is subsequently used as a basis for code generation. R2D2C relies on a variety of formal methods to express the formal model under consideration. The latter can be used for various types of analysis and investigation, and as the basis for fully formal implementations as well as for use in automated test case generation.

IBM has developed a framework called Policy Management for AC (PMAC) [10] that provides a standard model for the definition of policies and an environment for the development of software objects that hold and evaluate policies. For writing and storing policies, PMAC uses a declarative XML-based language called AC Policy Language (ACPL) [10, 11]. A policy written in ACPL provides an XML specification defining the following elements:

- condition — when a policy is to be applied;
- decision — observable behavior or desired outcome of a policy;
- result — a set of named and typed data values;
- action — invokes an operation;
- configuration profile — unifies result and action;
- business value — the relative priority of a policy;
- scope — the subject of the policy.

The basis of ACPL is the AC Expression Language (ACEL) [10, 11]. ACEL is an XML-based language developed to describe conditions when a policy should be applied to a managed system.

3 ANTS

The Autonomous Nano-Technology Swarm (ANTS) concept sub-mission PAM (Prospecting Asteroids Mission) is a novel approach to asteroid belt resource exploration. ANTS necessitates extremely high levels of autonomy, minimal communication requirements with Earth, and a set of very small explorers with a few consumables [2, 3]. These explorers forming the swarm are pico-class, low-power, and low-weight spacecraft units, yet capable of operating as fully autonomous and adaptable agents. The units in a swarm are able to interact with each other and self-organize based on the emergent behavior of the simple interactions.

Fig. 1 depicts the ANTS concept mission. A transport spacecraft launched from Earth toward the asteroid belt carries a laboratory that assembles the tiny spacecraft. Once it reaches a certain point in space, where gravity forces are balanced, termed a Lagrangian, the transport ship releases the assembled swarm, which will head for the asteroid belt. Each spacecraft is equipped with a solar sail, thus it relies primarily on power from the sun, using only tiny thrusters to navigate independently. Moreover, each spacecraft also has onboard computation, artificial intelligence, and heuristics systems for control at the individual and team levels.

As Fig. 1 shows, there are three classes of spacecraft — *rulers, messengers* and *workers*. They form teams that explore particular asteroids in an ant colony analogy. ANTS exhibits self-organization since there is no external force directing its behavior and no single spacecraft unit has a global view of the intended macroscopic behavior.

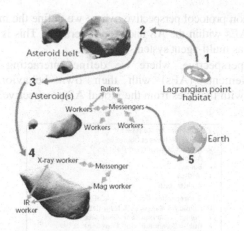

Fig. 1. ANTS Mission Concept [2]

In general, a swarm consists of several sub-swarms, which are temporal groups organized to perform a particular task. Each swarm group has a group leader (*ruler*), one or more *messengers*, and a number of *workers* carrying a specialized instrument. The messengers are needed to connect the team members when they cannot connect directly, due to a long distance or a barrier.

4 ASSL

The Autonomic System Specification Language (ASSL) [1] is a framework that provides a multi-tier structure for specifying ASs and targets at the generation of an operational framework instance from the ASSL specification. In general, the framework helps to design and generate an AC wrapper that embeds the components of existing systems; i.e., it allows non-intrusive addition of self-management features to existing systems. Moreover, the framework allows a top-down development approach to ASs, where the generated framework instance will guide the designers to the required components, and their interfaces, of the system under consideration.

ASSL Rationale. By its virtue, ASSL is generic and expressive enough to describe a variety of ASs [6, 7]. The ASSL framework is defined through formalization tiers. Over these tiers, ASSL provides a multi-tier specification model that is designed to be scalable and exposes a judicious selection and configuration of infrastructure elements and mechanisms needed by an AS. Thus, ASSL defines the latter with its interaction protocol and AEs, where the ASSL tiers and their sub-tiers describe different aspects of the AS under consideration. Fig. 2 depicts the ASSL specification model, which decomposes an AS in two directions — first into levels of functional abstraction, and second into functionally related sub-tiers. The first decomposition presents the system from three different perspectives, three major tiers:

- a general and global AS perspective, where we define the general system rules, architecture and global actions, events, and metrics applied in these rules;

- a communication protocol perspective, where we define the means of communication between AEs within the AS under consideration. This is crucial, since ASSL considers ASs as multi-agent systems;
- a unit-level perspective, where we define interacting sets of individual computing elements (AEs) with their own behavior, which must be synchronized with the rules from the global AS perspective.

Fig. 2. ASSL Tiers [1]

With the second decomposition, we decompose the major tiers into functionally related sub-tiers, where new AS properties emerge at each sub-tier. This allows a very flexible approach to specification. For example, we can start with a global understanding of the system by specifying the service-level objectives and digging down to find the needed metrics at the very detailed-level, or we can start working at the detailed levels and build our system bottom-up, or we can work on both abstract and detailed-level sides by constantly synchronizing their specification.

ASSL Tiers. The AS Tier specifies an AS in terms of service-level objectives (AS SLO), self-management policies, actions, events, metrics, and architecture. The AS SLO is a high-level form of behavioral specification that establishes system objectives such as performance. The self-management policies could be the four self-management policies (the so-called self-CHOP) of an AS: self-configuring, self-healing, self-optimizing and self-protecting, or they could be others. The metrics constitute a set of parameters and observables controllable by the AEs.

At the AS Interaction Protocol tier, the ASSL framework specifies an AS-level interaction protocol (ASIP). ASIP is a public communication interface, expressed as communication channels, communication functions and messages.

At the AE Tier, the ASSL formal model considers AEs to be analogous to software agents able to manage their own behavior and their relationships with other AEs. At this tier level, ASSL describes the individual AEs of an AS.

5 ASSL Specification Models for ANTS

In order to evaluate the effectiveness of modeling ANTS with ASSL, in the course of this evaluation study, we partially specified some of the ANTS concept mission autonomic properties. The following subsections present a critical analysis of the current specification models together with prospective ASSL models for ANTS.

5.1 Current ASSL Models for ANTS

In our endeavor to specify ANTS with ASSL, we emphasized modeling ANTS self-management policies of self-configuring, self-healing and self-scheduling. In addition, we propose a specification model for the ANTS safety requirements. In general, a complete specification of these autonomic properties requires a two-level approach. They need to be specified at the individual spacecraft level (AE tier) and at the level of the entire swarm (AS tier). To specify the ANTS safety requirements we use the ASSL SLO structures (cf. Section 4). Moreover, to specify the self-management policies we used four base ASSL elements:

- *a self-management policy structure* — which describes the self-management policy under consideration. We use a set of *fluents* and *mappings* to specify this policy [1]. With *fluents* we express specific situations, in which the policy is interested, and with *mappings* we map those situations to actions. A fluent has a timed duration, for example a state like "there is a lack of idle x-ray workers". When the system gets into that condition, the fluent is initiated.
- *actions* — a set of actions that can be undertaken by ANTS in response to certain conditions, and according to that policy.
- *events* — a set of events that initiate fluents and are prompted by the actions according to the policies.
- *metrics* — a set of metrics [1] needed by the events and actions.

Note that the specifications presented here are partial, because some of the aspects that must be specified, or have been specified, are left out, due to space limitations.

5.1.1 Self-configuring

ANTS must support concurrent exploration and examination of hundreds of asteroids. Thus, in order to coordinate science operations while simultaneously maximizing resource utilization, ANTS should allow team formation "on the fly", where the ANTS resources must be configured at both the swarm and team (sub-swarm) levels.

Fig. 3 presents a partial specification of the self-configuring behavior of ANTS when a new asteroid has been detected [6]. This policy specifies the "on the fly" configuration of different teams of ANTS spacecraft units for asteroid exploration.

Shortcomings and Improvements. The model shown in Fig. 3 prompts reconfiguration immediately after a new asteroid has been discovered. ANTS will explore the asteroid belt where hundreds of thousands of asteroids are currently known, and the total number ranges in the millions or more. Thus, while working on some asteroids, ANTS should discover many new asteroids in a steady fashion, thus causing a constant reconfiguration that will block the entire swarm. A possible solution is to add more *guards* to the

```
AS ANTS {
    ASSELF_MANAGEMENT {
        SELF_CONFIGURING {
            FLUENT inANTSReconfigurationForNewAsteroid {
                INITIATED_BY { newAsteroidDetected } TERMINATED_BY { reconfigurationForNewAsteroidDone } }
            MAPPING { // force ANTS reconfiguration
                CONDITIONS { inANTSReconfigurationForNewAsteroid }
                DO_ACTIONS { ACTIONS.reconfigureANTS } } } } // ASSELF_MANAGEMENT
    METRICS {
        METRIC numberOfAsteroids {
            METRIC_TYPE { RESOURCE }
            DESCRIPTION { "# of detected asteroids for the ANTS lifecycle." }
            THRESHOLD_CLASS { Decimal [min, max] } } }
    ACTIONS {
        ACTION reconfigureANTS {
            GUARDS { EVENTS.newAsteroidDetected }
            ENSURES { EVENTS.reconfigurationForNewAsteroidDone }
            DOES { call IMPL ReconfigurationForNewAsteroid }
            ONERR_TRIGGERS { reconfigurationForNewAsteroidDenied } } } // ACTIONS
    EVENTS { // these events are used in the fluents' specification
        EVENT newAsteroidDetected { changed AS.METRICS.numberOfAsteroids }
        EVENT reconfigurationForNewAsteroidDone { }
        EVENT reconfigurationForNewAsteroidDenied { } } // EVENTS
} // AS ANTS
```

Fig. 3. ANTS Self-Configuration

reconfigureANTS action to ensure that reconfiguration will take place only when there is a sufficient number of idle workers and rulers to form a team that will explore the newly discovered asteroid. This requires metrics to track the number of idle workers and rulers in the swarm.

The proposed specification model specifies only the AS-level self-configuration. For completeness, we need to specify the self-configuring policy for each ruler. This will allow rulers to release idle workers, which then can participate in the formation of new teams. A major deficiency here is the lack of support for cooperation among the rulers to achieve better self-configuring. A possible solution will be to specify a negotiation protocol [1] to allow negotiation among the rulers for idle workers.

The biggest challenge in this model is the reconfiguration of ANTS on the fly. Our temporary solution is to delegate this task to further implementation. The ASSL **IMPL** clause states for "further implementation" [1], which means that the ASSL framework will generate an empty routine and its content should be implemented manually. To solve this problem, we must investigate possible self-configuring mechanisms for group formation and scheduling in accordance with the ANTS and environmental conditions, and then specify the **IMPL** routine (cf. Fig. 3) with ASSL.

Self-configuring may also be required as the result of a failure or anomaly of some sort. For example, a worker may be lost due to collision with an asteroid, failure of its communication devices, or hardware failure. The loss of a worker may result in the role of that worker being performed by another. Therefore, a great improvement of this model will be the specification of self-configuration due to the loss of a worker.

5.1.2 Self-healing

In Fig. 4, we present a partial specification of the self-healing policy. In our approach, we assume that each worker sends, on a regular basis, *heartbeat messages* to the ruler [6]. The latter uses these messages to determine when a worker is not able to continue its operation, due to a crash or malfunction in its communication device or instrument (cf. Fig. 4).

Fig. 4 shows only fluents and mappings, these forming the specification model for the self-healing policy. The key features of the proposed model are:

- an *inCollision* fluent that takes place when the worker crashes into an asteroid or into another spacecraft, but it is still able to do self-checking operations;
- an *inInstrumentBroken* fluent that takes place when the self-checking operation reports that the instrument is not operational anymore;
- an *inHeartbeatNotification* fluent that is initiated on a regular basis by a timed event to send the *heartbeat* message to the ruler;
- a *checkANTInstrument* action that performs operational checking on the carried instrument.
- a *distanceToNearestObject* metric that measures the distance to the nearest object in space.

```
AE ANT_Worker {....
  AESELF_MANAGEMENT {
    SELF_HEALING {
      FLUENT inCollision {
        INITIATED_BY { EVENTS.collisionHappen } TERMINATED_BY { EVENTS.instrumentChecked } }
      FLUENT inInstrumentBroken {
        INITIATED_BY { EVENTS.instrumentBroken } TERMINATED_BY { EVENTS.msgInstrumentBrokenSent } }
      FLUENT inHeartbeatNotification {
        INITIATED_BY { EVENTS.timeToSendHeartbeatMsg } TERMINATED_BY { EVENTS.msgHeartbeatSent } }
      MAPPING { // if collision then check if the instrument is still operational
        CONDITIONS { inCollision } DO_ACTIONS { ACTIONS.checkANTInstrument } }
      MAPPING { // if the instrument is broken then notify the group leader
        CONDITIONS { inInstrumentBroken } DO_ACTIONS { ACTIONS.notifyForBrokenInstrument } }
      MAPPING { // time to send a heartbeat message has come
        CONDITIONS { inHeartbeatNotification } DO_ACTIONS { ACTIONS.notifyForHeartbeat } } }
  } // AESELF_MANAGEMENT
  .....
  ACTIONS { .....
    ACTION checkANTInstrument {
      GUARDS { collisionHappen }
      ENSURES { instrumentChecked }
      VAR Boolean canOperate;
      DOES { canOperate = call CheckInstrument }
      TRIGGERS { IF not canOperate THEN instrumentBroken END } }
  } // ACTIONS
}
```

Fig. 4. ANTS Self-Healing

Shortcomings and Improvements. In our current model, we specify the self-healing policy only from the worker's viewpoint. For a complete specification, we need to specify this policy also on the ruler's side and for the entire swarm (AS tier). Moreover, the instrument checking operation should check also for the instrument's performance; i.e., the instrument can be still operational but its performance can be degraded. This will allow self-optimization, where low performing workers will be replaced with high performing ones. In addition, in order to complete the model, we also need to specify self-checking on the worker's navigation and communication systems, and self-testing of the worker's computational unit.

Part of the self-healing process could be assigning a new worker with an identical instrument to the team when a malfunctioning worker has been discovered. This will prompt self-configuration. Moreover, as is stated in [2], a worker with a malfunctioning instrument can be transformed into a ruler. This can be specified in the self-healing policy as an increase in the total number of rulers and as a decrease in the total number of workers. This can be handled by metrics conscious of the number of rulers and the number of workers in the entire swarm and for each team.

Another shortcoming here is that the self-healing model does not take into consideration recovery from mistakes, e.g., position displacement. A better specification shall include all the possible mistakes per spacecraft and their appropriate recovery actions or intrinsically specified recovery protocol [1].

5.1.3 Self-scheduling
In the course of this research, we documented a formal approach to the self-scheduling mechanism in ANTS and specified this mechanism as a self-management policy from both the ruler's and worker's sides [7]. Because some of the tasks in ANTS are time-constrained, in our approach we employed fault tolerance measures to both value and timing violations. We used ASSL to model self-scheduling in ANTS by capturing the timing and schedulability requirements, and by modeling scheduling at group and individual level.

Modeling self-scheduling for ANTS [7] was the most complex exercise in the course of this project. We specified self-scheduling as a distinct self-management policy. Note, that ASSL allows specification of distinct self-management policies that can be classified as neither one of the four self-CHOP policies [5]. We specified self-scheduling as any regular policy - with a set of related fluents, events, actions, and metrics. For more information on this model, the reader is asked to consult [7].

Some of the key fluents and actions used in this model are:

- *inPlanning* is a fluent that takes place when a request to the team to perform a new task has been issued. The fluent is initiated when a new asteroid had been discovered and terminated when the planning task had been done or when the system had rejected the planning task.
- *inScheduling* is a fluent that resists until the ruler has successfully scheduled the instrument tasks generated by a task planning action. The latter will perform while there are enough idle workers in the system.
- *inMonitoring* is a fluent that performs monitoring over the workers, which perform the instrument tasks, these generated by the *inScheduling* fluent.
- *PlanTask* is an **IMPL** routine [1] that plans the team task as a sequence of instrument tasks.
- *EvaluateWorkerPerformance* is an **IMPL** routine that evaluates worker performance and computes the same as a real number. The worker performance is needed by the ruler to do load balancing and task scheduling.

Shortcomings and Improvements. A possible improvement could be the ASSL specification of the *planning* task. In our current solution, we delegate this task for further implementation (the *PlanTask* **IMPL** routine). To solve this problem, we must investigate possible expressions of ANTS states, because the proposed model needs the initial state and the goal state of the system.

A shortcoming is that the current model does not provide a full specification of the *heartbeat* message. The latter is sent by the workers to notify the associated ruler about their status. An improvement to this model will be a complete specification of this message as a composite structure including the worker's health status (damage in %), the worker's operational status (% of complete work) and its coordinates.

Moreover, the *EvaluateWorkerPerformance* **IMPL** routine can be specified with ASSL. In the current model, we present performance as a real number, but it could be specified with the ASSL structures. Any performance improvement initiative begins with an analysis of the factors affecting performance. These possible factors can be divided into two major groups: external and internal. Almost anything that affects worker's performance in any activity will fall into one of the above classifications. Some possible external factors are space (environmental conditions), teammates, and communication. Some possible internal factors are knowledge, instrument capacity, health status etc. Although this will help to specify all the performance related factors, we still need to figure out how to express the correlation between these factors, and hence their impact on each other, thus resulting into a more precise estimation of their global impact on worker's performance. In addition, it is difficult to express the environmental conditions and worker's health and operational statuses, which are needed for the computation of the worker's performance. A possible solution is to express them at two levels: first as composite data structures, and second as quality or resource metrics derived from these structures.

Another shortcoming is the missing specification of how rulers and workers learn about asteroids, and how they exchange information related to their learning.

5.1.4 Safety

In our approach, the system's safety properties are defined in terms of SLO (service-level objectives). In the course of this research, we formulated the ANTS safety service-level objectives (Safety SLO) to ensure that both ANTS AS and ANTS AEs contribute to the achievement of the ANTS global safety strategy [6].

NASA uses two software safety standards [12]. These standards define four qualitative hazard severity levels: *catastrophic, critical, marginal,* and *negligible.* In addition, four qualitative hazard probability levels are defined: *probable, occasional, remote,* and *improbable.* We applied these standards to define the following hazards:

- a collision with the other spacecraft units or asteroids — we considered this as catastrophic and probable (index 1);
- high-density magnetic fields — critical and occasional (index 2);
- high radiation-marginal and remote (index 4);
- a high energy level due to a solar eruption — critical and occasional (index 2);
- a loss of the communication with other units — critical and probable (index 1).

Fig. 5 shows the safety SLO specification for the ANTS AS, based on the hazard model above. The *Safety_RiskGroup1* SLO corresponds to the hazards with the risk index 1, and the two other groups correspond to the risk index 2 and the risk index 4 respectively. The *Safety_RiskGroup1* SLO has the highest priority and they must be held in order to proceed to the *Safety_RiskGroup2* and the *Safety_RiskGroup4* SLO.

```
ASSLO {
  SLO Safety_RiskGroup1 {
    foreach AE in AS { not AE.EVENTS.collisionHappen }
    foreach AE in AS {
      IF AE is ANT_Worker THEN not AE.EVENTS.communicationRullerLost; END;
      IF AE is ANT_Ruler THEN not AE.EVENTS.communicatgionMessangerLost; END;
      IF AE is ANT_Messanger THEN not AE.EVENTS.communicatgionLost; END } }
  SLO Safety_RiskGroup2 {
    IF Safety_RiskGroup1 THEN
      foreach AE in AS { not AE.EVENTS.highDensityMagneticField AND not AE.EVENTS.highSolarEnergyLevel }
    END }
  SLO Safety_RiskGroup4 {
    IF Safety_RiskGroup1 AND Safety_RiskGroup2 THEN
      foreach AE in AS {not AE.EVENTS.highRadiationLevel }
    END }
}
```

Fig. 5. ANTS Safety SLO Specification

Shortcomings and Improvements. The proposed model does not specify the safety SLO at the AE level. The latter are AE SLO (cf. Section 4.4) and could be expressed as a sequence of AE-level Boolean expressions. A possibility is to express them with the worker's (AE-level) metrics and events. Therefore, for a complete ANTS safety specification, we should specify these events and metrics at the AE tier and map them to appropriate actions. Moreover, the events must be attached to the metrics under consideration, which should detect hazard parameters such as the distance between the ANTS spacecraft and another near space objects, the magnetic field density, the radiation level, the solar energy level, the presence of a communication link, and the bandwidth of the communication link.

5.2 Prospective ASSL Models for ANTS

5.2.1 Self-optimizing

Optimization of ANTS [2, 3] should be specified at both individual and swarm levels. The former will be specified at the AS tier and the latter at the AE-tier, where we should specify the self-optimization policy for *rulers*, *workers*, and *messengers*.

Self-optimization for *rulers* could be specified as a process of learning. For example, rulers should learn about asteroids by collecting data on different types of asteroids, thus allowing them to better determine the characteristics of different asteroids that are of interest and perhaps asteroids that are difficult to orbit or get data from, for example, an asteroid with a fast rotation that is difficult to focus on.

Self-optimization for *messengers* could be specified as a process of positioning to balance the communications between the rulers and workers and perhaps adjusting its position so it can send data back to Earth.

Self-optimization for *workers* could be specified as a process of learning about the asteroids. This will allow workers to gain experience. Therefore, more experienced workers should be able to automatically skip over asteroids that are not of interest, thus saving time and optimizing the entire exploration process.

5.2.2 Self-protecting

The self-protecting policy should be specified to back up the safety SLO (cf. Section 5.1.4) again at both individual and swarm levels. Thus, the self-protecting behavior of the team will be interrelated with the self-protecting behavior of the individual members. The anticipated hazards will be the same as those used in the specification of safety SLO. Therefore, appropriate actions and events should be specified to avoid the safety hazards, e.g., actions that will prevent collisions or actions that will protect against solar storms.

6 Overall Evaluation of ASSL

We consider ASSL as a highly expressive specification language, this being supported by the multi-tier specification model (Section 4) and the constituted hierarchical approach to specifying ASs where the low-level tiers express high-level detail structures of AEs, and the high-level tiers express a general architectural view of an AS. The ASSL specification models presented in Section 5.1 intrinsically inherit all the advantages coming with the ASSL specification model.

The following sections describe some remarkable pros and cons common to all the ASSL specification models for ANTS and ASSL in general.

6.1 Pros

Self-management Policies. The ASSL specification models for ANTS exposes the self-management policies as a sort of state-transition machine where the states are described as fluents, and the transitions are triggered by events. The advantages are that the designers can see how the system will behave, and the specification is expressed in a form that can be easily verified.

IMPL Routines. The IMPL routines (cf. Section 5.1.1 and Section 5.1.3) are a kind of abstract actions, which require a complex ASSL specification, or which we do not need to specify at all. The IMPL routines are a way of referring to the further implementation; i.e., they are sort of specification stubs needed to complete the specification model under consideration. In general, by using IMPL routines we simplify that model. Note, that the IMPL routines still have to be specified with their guards, ensures, and trigger clauses, which makes their utilization safe for the model. Moreover, by using IMPL routines we simplify the specification model.

Metrics. The proposed models use metrics widely. Metrics in ASSL have a dual role. First, they are observables that measure specific system quantities and can be controlled by the AEs, and second, they give the software developer assurance that a given set of values is sufficiently sensitive to track range errors [1]. A great advantage of using ASSL metrics is that they are adaptive and can take into account the SLO.

Actions. The actions in the proposed models are specified following the el "design by contract" principle [8] elaborated by ASSL. Therefore, the ASSL models for ANTS benefit from the following advantages:

- a better understanding of the "pre-" and postconditions on the models' actions and, more generally, of the self-management policies construction;
- a systematic approach to specifying bug-free actions;
- a technique for dealing with abnormal cases, leading to a safe and effective ASSL construct for exception handling (cf. Fig. 3).

Communication Protocol. Some of the ASSL models for ANTS benefit from the specification of a dedicated communication protocol. For example, for the self-scheduling model we specify at the ASIP tier (cf. Section 4) a communication protocol needed by the ruler and the workers to communicate and transfer data for the needs of the self-scheduling policy. Thus, the models take advantages of special communication functions, messages and channels.

Model Consistency. We are currently developing a Model Consistency Checker (MCC) tool as part of the ASSL framework. MCC is a tool for automatic verification and analysis of ASSL specification models. The consistency of the latter is checked at two levels: consistency among the different system views (the major tiers AS, ASIP and AE) and internal consistency among the sub-tiers. The ASSL models for ANTS will be checked for consistency based on the ASSL grammar rules, on the ASSL type system, and on a set of embedded in the models constraints.

Multilevel SLO. As shown in the ANTS safety SLO specification, ASSL allows the existence of more sophisticated SLO, i.e. SLO with multiple levels.

Code Generation. With ASSL, we are aiming at code generation. Hence, once completed and consistent, the ASSL specification models will be translated to Java code, which will form the skeleton of the ANTS autonomic prototype. The latter can be used for further investigation and verification based on practical results.

Partial Specification. When formal methods are applied to a project for the first time, experience has shown that it may be advisable to use them on a smaller scale, other than the entire project. ASSL exposes a multi-tier specification model that allows designers to specify partially the system under consideration. This allows designers to evaluate their system design at the early stages of system development and better understand what parts of the system will most benefit from modeling with ASSL.

Convenient Coding Style. Writing specifications with ASSL is analogous to writing programs in a conventional programming language.

There are also other intrinsically pros like the ASSL logic-centric specification style (in contrast to the data-centric specification style), inheritance (we used AECLASS structures in the self-scheduling specification [7]), specifications written in ASSL — an easy to read and cope with formal language [1], etc.

6.2 Cons

System State. The system states in ASSL are specified with fluents, these connecting events and actions. A shortcoming in this approach is the lack of data presentation in the fluents. Thus, our ASSL specification models cannot easily describe states related to possible configurations of ANTS data. Instead, we need to use events related to metrics that observe specific data, and which events initiate specific fluents.

Metrics. ASSL expresses the metrics with a set of metric threshold classes. A threshold class determines ranges for valid/invalid metric values. Although this approach may work well for a small number of metrics, it has two disadvantages. First, many performance-related metrics are mutually dependent. Therefore, dependencies among their threshold classes may likely exist as well. Second, some metrics are of minor importance for self-management, but ASSL does not provide a straightforward mechanism for grading them by importance. The major problem stemming from these two factors is multicolinearity; i.e., it will be difficult to assess the effect of the independent metric on the dependent one, due to the mutual dependency among the metrics and due to the different level of importance. This implies that introducing additional metrics into the model under consideration should be done with great caution.

Modeling Managed Systems. ASSL helps to design and generate AC (autonomic computing) wrappers in the form of ASs that embed the components of non-AC systems. The latter are considered as managed systems (managed resources), those controlled by the AS under consideration [1]. ASSL places emphasis on the AC functionality and AS architecture, but not on the managed system functionality and architecture. ASSL specifies only the interface needed to control the managed system and does not provide any means for software design of that system.

Therefore, the proposed ASSL specification models for ANTS are an AC wrapper that embeds ANTS and where each AE embeds an ANTS spacecraft unit. To complete these models we need to specify, for each AE, the managed interface that controls the associated ANTS spacecraft unit (worker, ruler, or messenger), but with ASSL we cannot design this unit. Although, this could be considered as a shortcoming, the clear distinction between the AC and non-AC parts of an AS allows for much better understanding and handling of the system's AC features.

Modeling Large-Scale Systems. Large-scale ASs can easily have over a hundred thousand AEs. Specifying such ASs may require a very complex and labor-intensive modeling process, because the self-management policies may require a complete specification for each AE. Fortunately, ASSL provides class structures and inheritance, which can help when specifying a group of similar AEs. For example, ANTS consists of thousands of pico-spacecraft units, which requires the specification of thousands of AEs, but the latter can be grouped by the instrument they are carrying.

Tool Support. The current tool support for ASSL (developed and under development) is limited to editing and consistency checking. Moreover, we consider as a shortcoming the lack of answers to the following questions, which require more investigation and additional tool support allowing model checking:

- What is the quality of the proposed ASSL models?
- How can this quality be assessed and assured?

7 Conclusion and Future Work

This paper has described our evaluation study on the effectiveness of modeling ANTS — a concept NASA swarm-based exploration mission, with ASSL. In the course of this evaluation study, we have evaluated the current ASSL specification models for ANTS's self-configuring, self-healing, and self-scheduling policies, and for the ANTS's safety service-level objectives. This study has revealed the shortcomings of and has made key recommendations to these models, thus to make them more effective and complete. In addition, we have outlined two prospective ASSL models for ANTS—self-optimizing and self-protecting, which together with the recommended modifications in the currently existing models will help us to specify ANTS as a whole system, and then successfully generate the code for the future functional prototype of ANTS. Moreover, this study has helped us to define and present some important common pros and cons of modeling ANTS (and autonomic systems in general) with ASSL.

With this evaluation study, we have aimed at investigating the effectiveness of ASSL when modeling complex autonomic systems like ANTS. Although far from a thorough evaluation, we consider that the ASSL specification models for ANTS are worthy of expanding and developing further. Despite the shortcomings presented here, these models provide didactic evidence that ASSL is an appropriate means for specifying AS, particularly ANTS. Moreover, the possibility to improve the specification models demonstrates the high expressiveness of ASSL.

Future research is concerned with further ANTS modeling with ASSL, this including specification of the perspective models and applying in the current models the recommended by the evaluation study modifications. Next will be code generation and supplementary implementation of the functional prototype.

References

1. Vassev, E., Paquet, J.: ASSL — Autonomic System Specification Language. In: 31st Annual IEEE/NASA Software Engineering Workshop (SEW-31), pp. 300–309. IEEE Press, Baltimore (2007)
2. Truszkowski, W., Hinchey, M., Rash, J., Rouff, C.: NASA's swarm missions: The challenge of building autonomous software. IT Professional 6(5), 47–52 (2004)
3. Hinchey, M., Rash, J., Truszkowski, W., Rouff, C., Sterritt, R.: Autonomous and Autonomic Swarms. In: 8th Biennial Conference on Real Time in Sweden (RTiS), SNART (reprinted with permission from SERP 2005), Skövde, pp. 65–73 (2005)
4. Hinchey, M., Dai, Y., Rash, J., Truszkowski, W., Madhusoodan, M.: Bionic autonomic nervous system and self-healing for NASA ANTS-like missions. In: The 2007 ACM Symposium on Applied Computing (SAC 2007), pp. 90–96. ACM Press, Seoul (2007)
5. IBM Corporation: An architectural blueprint for autonomic computing, 4th edn. White paper (2006)
6. Vassev, E., Hinchey, M., Paquet, J.: Towards an ASSL Specification Model for NASA Swarm-Based Exploration Missions. In: 23rd Annual ACM Symposium on Applied Computing (SAC 2008) – AC Track. ACM Press, Fortaleza (2008)
7. Vassev, E., Hinchey, M., Paquet, J.: A Self-Scheduling Model for NASA Swarm-Based Exploration Missions using ASSL. In: 5th IEEE International Workshop on Engineering of Autonomic and Autonomous Systems (EASe 2008), IEEE Computer Press, Belfast (2008)
8. Leavens, G.T., Cheon, Y.: Design by contract with JML. Technical report, Formal Systems Laboratory (FSL) at UIUC (2006)
9. Hinchey, M.G., Rash, J.L., Rouff, C.A.: Requirements to design to code: Towards a fully formal approach to automatic code generation. Technical Report TM-, -212774, NASA Goddard Space Flight Center, Greenbelt (2005)
10. IBM Tivoli: Autonomic Computing Policy Language.Tutorial, IBM Corp. (2005)
11. Agrawal, D., et al.: Autonomic Computing Expressing Language. Tutorial, IBM Corp. (2005)
12. NASA-STD-8719.13A: Software Safety. NASA Technical Standard (1997)

Distributed Performance Control in Organic Embedded Systems

Steffen Stein and Rolf Ernst

Institute of Computer and Communication Network Engineering
Technical University of Braunschweig, Germany
{stein,ernst}@ida.ing.tu-bs.de

Abstract. This paper introduces compositional performance analysis into evolving organic systems. It presents a layered distributed framework that can follow the platform and system evolution, continuously monitoring the effect of changes in the application on real-time constraints. For that purpose, an existing methodology based on iterative compositional performance analysis was adapted to a distributed algorithm. A buffering strategy is introduced to improve the algorithm convergence to the same order as the existing centralized offline algorithm. The effects are demonstrated in experiments.

1 Introduction

Organic Computing [10] has recently emerged as a new challenge in computer science. As ubiquitous and embedded computing systems become increasingly powerful, the development paradigms shift from implementing the technically possible to building robust and easily usable systems. Organic computing systems tackle this challenge by introducing adaptation, learning and self-configuration into complex computer systems. Initiatives as IBM's Autonomic Computing Initiative [8] or Intel's Proactive Computing [14] show that this is not only an academic endeavour.

Real-time systems constitute a notable share of todays embedded computers that needs special attention. The Design of robust and fault-tolerant real-time systems is a highly active research area, that has produced numerous approaches for evaluating and increasing system robustness against selected fault scenarios. Existing approaches use offline sensitivity analysis to optimize for robustness, meaning low sensitivity [6]. These methodologies can be applied throughout the design process of an embedded system and yield systems that are highly robust against a selected set of disturbances in the field.

Future embedded systems however, will undergo an evolution in both hard- and software configuration during their lifetime. In the automotive industry, it is already common to update or add software components during the lifetime of a product, producing a variety of software configurations in the field. To ensure functional and temporal correctness of all possible configurations, OEMs have to maintain a complex versioning database and perform exhaustive testing to cover the whole configuration landscape. This already constitutes a problem today, which will grow into a major challenge in the future. Designing embedded systems robust and fault-tolerant will not ultimately solve

C. Rong et al. (Eds.): ATC 2008, LNCS 5060, pp. 331–342, 2008.

this problem, as the evolution an embedded systems goes through during its lifetime cannot be foreseen at design time.

Introducing self-*-properties into embedded system will enhance them by flexibility for future updates in hard- or software, thus enabling evolution during their lifetime. Key properties of evolving (embedded) systems are the ability to assess its current situation (self-awareness) and to reconfigure themselves (self-configuration) in order to adapt to new situations as may be implied by software updates. For hard real-time systems, the challenge of implementing self-configuration and adaptation is not only to ensure functional, but also temporal correctness of a system.

This paper will introduce on a concise problem statement, highlighting the timing-related problems and challenges caused by the evolution of embedded real-time systems. It will then present a control framework building on formal methods for performance analysis capable of managing evolution while still ensuring temporal correctness of a system utilizing established methodologies from literature. It will close with an experimental examination of a prototype implementation the formal analysis engine.

The remainder of this paper is organized as follows. In the next section, we will introduce related work to then go into detail on the challenges to be addressed by our approach. The fourth section discusses the architecture of a performance control framework, where the fifth section goes into detail on the analysis methodology used by our framework. Before we conclude the paper, experimental results are presented.

2   Related Work

Designing adaptive, self-organizing real-time systems touches two highly active fields of current research. For once, we need to consider current development in the field of adaptive and fault-tolerant system design, but we also need to have a closer look into research concerning the analysis of timing properties of a given real-time system.

Currently, fault-tolerant and resilient systems are built by introducing explicit redundancy on a per computer level, such as TMR in avionics.

Later research has introduced redundancy not on a per computer, but on a per task level. The RecoNets project [7] has designed a prototype system consisting of multiple microcontrollers running a driver assistance application. It can survive failure of one or more board, since each task is shadowed on another microcontroller. Checkpointing techniques allow to seamlessly migrate execution of tasks from one microcontroller to another in case a failure is detected. This approach, however does not take global system timing issues into account when spawning shadow tasks at different points in the system.

Recently, also design of robust and fault tolerant systems taking into account timing properties has been tackled. In the AiS project [5] for example, common fault scenarios are identified and analysed for their possible impact on system performance. For selected scenarios, compensation mechanisms are implemented in the system, making it robust against these faults.

In the context of the "Organic Computing" priority program of the German DFG [10], many projects aim at building adaptive and self-configuring systems. This is usually achieved by extending the system by a control loop that observes the current system state, evaluates it and performs control operations based on a knowledge base that may be constructed using reinforcement learning techniques such as Learning Classifier Systems [1]. These architectures are referred to as Observer/Controller Architectures; a general discussion of which can be found in [4].

In addition to current research in fault-tolerant and resilient systems, research in formal performance analysis of real-time systems has to be considered. In the past years, several approaches to system level timing analysis have been proposed by different research groups (i.e. [11,2,15,12]). System level timing analysis requires task-level worst-case execution times as input data. Recent research has produced formal approaches to derive these from a given task description [16].

For the purpose of this paper, we can divide the approaches to system level performance analysis in two classes. Holistic approaches that try to use as much information as possible in order to perform a tight analysis of the real-time behaviour of a given system and compositional approaches that are capable of making abstractions at intermediate analysis steps.

The first class of techniques yields tightly bounded results on the timing properties of a given system at the prize of high computational complexity. Current approaches use different semantics to describe their systems ranging from dataflow graphs [11] to timed automata [9].

The second class, like the approaches proposed in [15] or [12] trade analysis accuracy for computational complexity. Here, local analysis techniques are composed using load descriptions of intermediate event streams.

Dynamic scheduling algorithms (i.e. [3]) adapt the scheduling parameters to a change in load conditions. Global schedulers can cover several processors, but only following a coherent homogeneous scheduling approach. In this sense, they are comparable to holistic analysis approaches. Global scheduling algorithms also do not easily adapt to changing hardware topologies and timing constraint types. Furthermore, they do not take system properties such as end-to-end latencies into account.

3 Problem Formulation

For the means of this paper, we focus on loosely coupled distributed real-time systems as can be found i.e. in cars. A real-time system can generally be described as a set of processing units (processor, PU) interconnected by busses, onto which a set of timing constrained applications is mapped. On each processor, a scheduling policy is applied, if multiple tasks are mapped onto it.

In order to give a precise problem formulation, we will first present a terminology.

We consider a set of processors interconnected by buses (or other communication channels) the system *architecture* or *(hardware) platform*. Onto this platform, a set of *applications* is to be executed, each consisting of a set of *tasks*, whose relationships are defined by a *task graph*. Furthermore, applications may be temporally constrained. In this case, we speak of *real-time applications*. We consider an architecture together with a set of (real-time) applications a *(real-time) system*. In order to completely describe running real-time systems, a set of design *parameters*, such as task mappings, scheduling parameters (i.e. priorities), or clock rates also need to be defined. We consider a real-time system together with a complete set of parameters a *system configuration*. A given configuration has a set of *properties*, such as application end-to-end latencies.

Note that in each design stage, a different set of system parameters is available to the designer. These will be referred to as *available parameters*. For the sake of simplicity, we will use the term *parameter* equivalent to *available parameter* and account the parameters that are not available in the current design step to the set of *properties*. We consider a given system configuration *feasible*, if all applications adhere to their timing constraints.

The challenge addressed in this paper is to find a methodology for designing adaptive systems that not only ensure functional correctness, but also adhere to system-wide temporal constraints such as end-to-end latencies. With respect to the terminology introduced above, this means finding a methodology that enables a system to verify that its current configuration is feasible, protect itself against transitions into infeasible configurations and ultimately to reconfigure itself to reenter a feasible state. To achieve the latter, the system must perform self-optimization using available parameters during run-time. For our purposes, we assume scheduling parameters, such as priorization or execution sequences to be available as is the case in most real-time kernels. Other parameters, such as task mapping can also be made available by implementing adequate techniques from literature.

From the problem statement, one can deduce the necessary components of such a framework. One needs a feasibility evaluator for a given system configuration, a sensor component, that monitors the current system properties to be fed into the feasibility evaluator, an optimization component in order to generate alternate configurations, as well as an actuator component, that transitions the system from one configuration into another. Furthermore, a framework for the interactions of these components must be put into place.

The feasibility evaluator is the key component in the setup outlined above. It is desirable to use an evaluator, that can not only decide on feasibility, but is also able to compute fitness values for a given system configuration, so that it can also be used by the optimization component.

Furthermore, since we are targeting hard real-time systems and want to give guarantees on real-time performance, the evaluator must use a formal approach to computing the current system properties. As stated in the related work section, current approaches solve this problem in diverse ways. In distributed organic real-time systems, non-centralized solutions to fitness evaluation of a current system configuration that adapt to the system's evolution are preferred over centralized ones, that introduce single points of failure. Thus, only distributable approaches to performance verification are considered for a suitable fitness evaluator.

The next sections will go into detail on the feasibility evaluator and give a closer description of a framework capable of online performance control of an evolving real-time system.

4   Performance Control Framework

We chose the methodology described in [12] as a driving technology for the evaluator for several reasons. The compositional approach is strongly decoupled by efficiently parameterized event models and a distributed analysis algorithm following the approach has already been presented in [13]. Furthermore, the computational load implied by

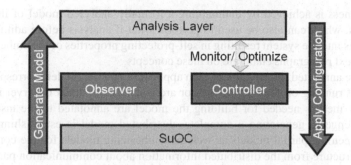

Fig. 1. Framework Architecture

the analysis engine can easily be scaled by applying more or less sophisticated local scheduling analysis techniques. For static priority scheduling this could mean taking inter-event-correlations into account or simply performing a context-blind schedulability analysis. Both approaches yield conservative results for local worst-case response times, but with different accuracy. This opens the possibility to trade analysis accuracy for computational load.

In order to build a system model compliant with the analysis approach, for each task, a worst-case execution time, the activation scheme described by a standard event model ([12]), its communication partners, as well as the maximum communication volume with each partner must be known. The same is true for scheduling policies on each shared resource. We assume that these values are annotated to the task set, although we do not go into detail on how these values are found. Possibilities range from formal analysis [16], to extensive offline simulation and tracing. These methods are already successfully applied for design-time system timing analysis by early adaptors of formal methods e.g. in the automotive industry. In case of real-time constrained applications, we assume that the applicable constraints are also annotated to the task set.

In order to enable adaptation in evolving real time systems, the feasibility evaluator must be embedded in a framework for online real-time control. We divide the structure of the control framework into three major parts, an observer, a controller and an analysis layer (see figure 1). The actual real-time systems is depicted as SuOC - the "System under Observation and Control" [4]. An Observer continuously monitors the systems behaviour to build and maintain an analysable model of the current configuration ("monitor component"). This model is analysed by the formal analysis layer. The results of the analysis are in turn used by a Controller to monitor whether the system complies with all temporal constraints. Thus, the analysis engine, together with part of the Controller form the "feasibility evaluator". For continuous self-optimization, the controller can use the analysis layer to perform optimizations based on the current system model. If optimization results in a new (better) configuration, it is also the Controllers task to inject the new configuration into the system ("actuator component").

Using this framework, one can implement self-awareness and self-protection with respect to timing properties of the current system configuration in an embedded system.

Self-awareness is achieved by maintaining a formally analysed model of the system at all times, which can also be used to perform what-if analysis before admitting new applications into the system resulting in self-protecting properties of the embedded system. The next paragraphs elaborate on these concepts.

From the annotated information of each application, partial models corresponding to the task set running on the local processor are generated by local observer instances. As the key metrics needed for building the model are annotated to the task set, the main challenge in generating a complete, distributed model is establishing connectivity between the partial models as well as synthesizing models for the communication infrastructure from the distributed information about communication partners and volumes.

Before an application is accepted to be mapped on the platform, the current system model is extended by the application and tested for feasibility. If no constraints are violated in the model, the application may execute and is guaranteed to meet its constraints, as long as no application in the system violates its timing properties as annotated. We consider this construct a *service contract* between the system and the applications. This construct ensures that the system will only transition from one provenly save configuration into the next provenly save configuration, thus introducing self-protection into evolving real-time systems.

To ensure compliance with the service contracts, we propose to implement local watchdogs monitoring execution times and communication volumes as well as activation frequencies. The observed values will continuously be compared with the information forming the service contracts of the individual applications. In case a violation of a service contract of an application is detected, a controller is notified, in order to take immediate action. Possibilities range from shaping the load implied by the application to the load defined in the service contract (thus achieving isolation from the other applications), to stopping the application.

At the same time, the current system model is updated to reflect the newly observed configuration. If the resulting system still complies with all given constraints, the application may be readmitted into the system with an adapted service contract. Otherwise, optimization algorithms may be used to find a feasible configuration.

As violations of service contracts may not only be caused by faulty application annotations, but also by component failures or degradation, the above techniques also constitute a self-healing technique efficiently using slack present in the system to cope with component faults and failures. The efficiency of this technique directly scales with the power of the system optimization algorithms put into place.

Figure 2 shows a more detailed view on the architecture of the performance control framework. Distributed observer instances generate partial models of their local environment that are communicated to local analysis engines. These engines, in turn cooperate to perform a distributed system-wide performance analysis of the currently observed system configuration as described in [13]. Clearly, actuator components also need to be distributed over the whole system, in order to efficiently perform system configuration transitions, thus, the controller must also be implemented distributedly. The cooperating observers, controllers and analysis engines form a global performance control plane.

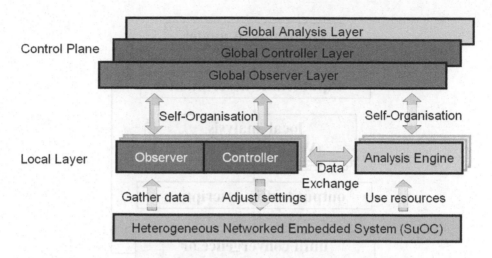

Fig. 2. Control Framework

5   Analysis Methodology

We use the analysis technique proposed by Richter et al [12] to form the global analysis and evaluator plane. A general approach to distributed performance analysis using this technique has been proposed in [13]. As this approach is discussed in the experimental section, we give a short overview on the approach to distributed performance analysis in the next paragraphs. First, the SymTA/S approach is introduced shortly, then the extensions for distributed computation are outlined.

The compositional performance analysis methodology used for this project, solves the global system-level performance verification problem by decomposing the system into independently investigated components.

Each Processor or Bus is modeled as a component (*computation, communication resource*) that may contain tasks. The possible I/O timing between the tasks (*event streams*) is captured with event models that can efficiently be described by a small set of parameters.

Input event models capture event patterns leading to task activations. These are used to perform a local scheduling analysis of a resource to derive the local response times as well as *output event models*.

These output event models are propagated to subsequent resources where they are used, in turn, as input event models. In setups with cyclic dependencies the assumed event streams become increasingly more generic. This procedure either converges (and provides a conservative estimation of system properties such as jitter and latencies which can be checked against given constraints), or the system's schedulability can not be guaranteed. Figure 5 shows the structure of the analysis loop as implemented in the tool.

The analysis of a SymTA/S model can easily be distributed over multiple analysis engines, as local scheduling analysis runs are strongly decoupled by event streams. A method to connect partial models managed by multiple analysis engines has been

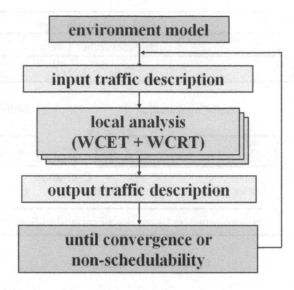

Fig. 3. Analysis Loop

proposed in [13]. Here, it is proposed to tunnel event stream information between multiple analysis engines using existing communication infrastructure. Distributed analysis control performs a local scheduling analysis on a resource as soon as an input event stream changes. As a major advantage, this scheme is naturally adapted to the underlying platform topology and can follow its evolution, as communication with other analysis engines is only necessary, if mapped applications communicate over an existing link. Thus, if communication between analysis engines is necessary, suitable infrastructure must be present.

6   Experimental Study

In this section, we take a closer look at the expected computational load an embedded SymTA/S analysis engine will impose on an embedded system. To do this, we implemented the distributed control algorithm as proposed in [13] by extending the offline tool. Performing schedulability analysis is the compute intensive part of the iteration loop. Thus, the load imposed by an analysis engine scales with the number of schedulability analysis runs needed to analyse a given system and the load imposed by a single schedulability analysis run. Here, we want to assess the quality of distributed algorithm steering the iteration. As a quality measure for a given analysis control algorithm, we propose the convergence speed of the system wide performance analysis, as measured by the number of schedulability analysis runs needed to analyse the properties of this system. We consider a control algorithm optimal for a given problem, if it solves the global fix-point iteration with a minimal number of schedulability analysis runs. This also implies that an optimal control algorithm imposes the minimal load for a given system and schedulability analysis algorithm implementation.

For testing, we used an in-house system generator tool to generate analysable system models. The generated systems contain a configurable amount of connected tasks an resources. For testing purposes, we generated systems, scaling them in the number of tasks, resources and length of task chains. To benchmark the distributed analysis control mechanism, we analysed these systems using the distributed approach as well as the centralized approach implemented in the tool. We assume that the centralized approach performs close to optimal.

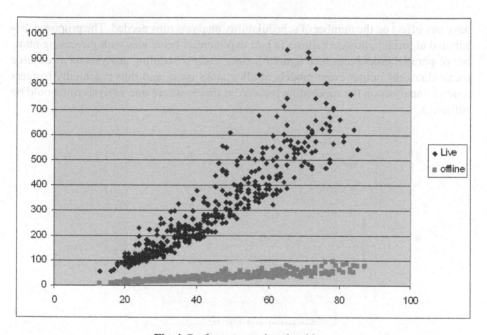

Fig. 4. Performance naive algorithm

The result of a first test can be seen in figure 4. It shows the number of schedulability analysis runs needed for a complete system analysis over increasing system size. The upper point cloud shows the performance of the naive algorithm as proposed in [13], the lower one shows the performance of the offline algorithm as implemented in the tool SymTA/S.

The distributed approach shows weak performance w.r.t. schedulability analysis runs needed to analyse big systems. A closer look at possible causes reveals a system configuration that requires an exponentially growing number of schedulability runs to be analysed if using the distributed performance analysis control algorithm, where theoretically a linear relationship suffices: Suppose a system consisting of a series of resources that host a number of independent task chains as depicted in figure 5(a). The system can be scaled in two dimensions - the number of resources and the number of parallel task chains. The minimum number of schedulability analysis runs that is needed scales linearly with the number of resources in the system, as each resource only needs to be analysed once (from left to right). Increasing the number of parallel chains does not

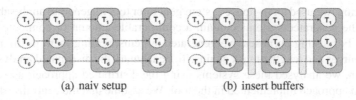

(a) naiv setup   (b) insert buffers

Fig. 5. Chained System

have any effect on the number of schedulability analysis runs needed. The proposed distributed algorithm, however shows in part exponential behaviour with increasing number of parallel task chains (see figure 6), since each scheduling analysis on a resource recalculates the output event models of all n tasks on it, and thus potentially triggers renewed analysis on the succeeding resource n times, where one analysis run would be sufficient.

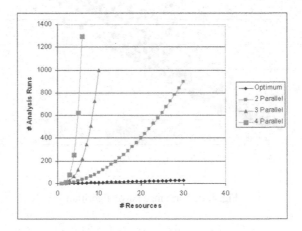

Fig. 6. Performance in number of analysis runs

A solution to this problem is to introduce buffers between successing resources as shown in figure 5(b) that collect the changes of incoming event streams resulting from one schedulability analysis on a preceeding resource and release them in as on event reducing the number of reanalysis events for the succeeding resource to one. This approach reduces the number of analysis runs needed to the theoretical minimum for this class of systems.

We implemented the buffering scheme in our offline prototype and redid the experiments outlined above. The results as shown in figure 7 show that this improvement to the distributed analysis control already yields convergence speeds comparable to those of the offline tool for the class of systems produced by our system generator. Interestingly, the distributed control algorithm sometimes even outperforms the centralized algorithm. This is due to the fact that the centralized algorithm does not exploit all

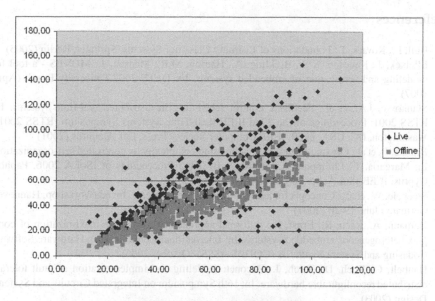

Fig. 7. Performance with buffering

knowledge about the system model to precompute an optimal sequence of schedulability analysis runs. This would imply computing a topological sort on the resource graph. Thus the distributed algorithm can outperform the centralized one, if the activation scheme coincidentally follows a topological sort of the graph. The fact that the experiments contained many of these cases may be due to the regular structure of the generated system models.

Further improvements to both, the offline and the distributed control algorithms can be made by first performing a topological sort of the resources in the system model, that can be used to determine an order of local scheduling analysis runs, yielding an optimal control algorithm.

7 Conclusion

In this paper, we introduced a framework that enables the implementation of organic real-time systems. It is sensitive to changes in the hardware architecture as well as software configuration of the system.

It is based on a layered architecture of observers and controllers and a distributed analysis layer that evaluates the local analysis results and event model parameters. Experiments with a prototype implementation of the analysis methodology to be used have shown, that the computational load implied remains small.

The presented approach is suitable for implementing evolving hard real-time that are capable of self-protection against transitions into non-feasible system states w.r.t. timing properties.

References

1. Bull, L., Kovacs, T.: Foundations of Learning Classifier Systems. Springer, Berlin (2005)
2. Ellebæk, J., Knudsen, K.S., Brekling, A., Hansen, M.R., Madsen, J.: MOVES - a tool for modeling and verification of embedded systems. In: DATE 2007 University Booth (April 2007)
3. Stankovic, J.A., et al.: Feedback control scheduling in distributed real-time systems. In: RTSS 2001: Proceedings of the 22nd IEEE Real-Time Systems Symposium (RTSS 2001), Washington, DC, USA, p. 59. IEEE Computer Society Press, Los Alamitos (2001)
4. Branke, J., et al.: Organic computing - addressing complexity by controlled self-organization. In: Margaria, T., Philippou, A., Steffen, a.B. (eds.) Proceedings of ISoLA 2006, Paphos, Cyprus. IEEE-ISoLA, pp. 200–206 (November 2006)
5. Stechele, W., et al.: Concepts for autonomic integrated systems. In: edaWorkshop, Hannover, Germany, June 19-20 (2007)
6. Hamann, A., Racu, R., Ernst, R.: A formal approach to robustness maximization of complex heterogeneous embedded systems. In: International Conference on Hardware/Software Codesing and System Synthesis (CODES+ISSS) (October 2006)
7. Haubelt, C., Koch, D., Teich, J.: Reconet: modeling and implementation of fault tolerant distributed reconfigurable hardware. In: 16th Symposium on Integrated Circuits and Systems Design (2003)
8. Horn, P.: Autonomic computing: Ibm's perspective on the state of information technology (October 2001), http://www.research.ibm.com/autonomic/manifesto/autonomic_computing.pdf
9. Larsen, K.G., Pettersson, P., Yi, W.: Uppaal in a nutshell. International Journal on Software Tools for Technology Transfer (STTT) 1, 134–152 (1997)
10. Mueller-Schloer, C.: Organic computing - on the feasibility of controlled emergence. In: IEEE/ACM/IFIP International Conference on Hardware/Software Codesing and System Synthesis (CODES + ISSS 2004) (2004)
11. Poplavko, P., Basten, T., Bekooij, M., van Meerbergen, J., Mesman, B.: Task-level timing models for guaranteed performance in multiprocessor networks-on-chip. In: CASES 2003: Proceedings of the 2003 international conference on Compilers, architecture and synthesis for embedded systems, pp. 63–72. ACM Press, New York (2003)
12. Richter, K.: Compositional Scheduling Analysis Using Standard Event Models. PhD thesis, Technical University of Braunschweig, Department of Electrical Engineering and Information Technology (2004)
13. Stein, S., Hamann, A., Ernst, R.: Real-time property verification in organic computing systems. In: 2nd IEEE International Symposium on Leveraging Applications of Formal Methods, Verification and Validation (ISoLA) (November 2006)
14. Tennenhouse, D.: Proactive computing. Commun. ACM 43(5), 43–50 (2000)
15. Thiele, L., Chakraborty, S., Naedele, M.: Real-time calculus for scheduling hard real-time systems. In: International Symposiumon Circuits and Systems (ISCAS) (2000)
16. Wilhelm, R., et al.: The worst-case execution time problem — overview of methods and survey of tools. Technical report, Malardalen Real-Time Research Centre, Malardalen University (March 2007)

An Operating System Architecture for Organic Computing in Embedded Real-Time Systems

Florian Kluge, Jörg Mische, Sascha Uhrig, and Theo Ungerer

Department of Computer Science - University of Augsburg
86159 Augsburg, Germany
{kluge,mische,uhrig,ungerer}@informatik.uni-augsburg.de

Abstract. To overcome the rising complexity of computing systems, the paradigms of Autonomic Computing and Organic Computing have been introduced. By using an observer/controller architecture, Organic Computing aims to make embedded systems more life-like by providing them with so-called Self-X properties. Embedded real-time systems can also gain great benefit from these techniques. In this paper, we show what new requirements arise when introducing Autonomic/Organic Computing into the area of real-time applications. These requirements flow into the architecture of the real-time operating system CAROS. CAROS combines several concepts to provide a solid base for the implementation of Self-X techniques in embedded real-time systems. We show the practicability of our concepts with a prototypical implementation on the multithreaded CarCore microcontroller.

1 Introduction

Today, embedded systems are constantly growing, and establishing whole networks of *Embedded Control Units* (ECUs). For example, a car can contain over 70 ECUs fulfilling most different duties. With increasing size these networks become harder if not impossible to manage. The paradigms of Autonomic and Organic Computing promise to handle this topic.

In 2001 IBM introduced *Autonomic Computing* (AC) [1, 2] to overcome the problem of increasing complexity of computing systems. AC focuses on self-management of large server systems by implementing the so-called Self-X properties of self-configuration, self-healing, self-optimisation and self-protection (also referred to as "Self-CHOP"). To implement such self-management techniques, Autonomic Managers are proposed that control the system at runtime by a closed control loop of Monitoring, Analysis, Planning, and Execution (MAPE cycle).

A few years later, *Organic Computing* (OC) [3] took up the Self-X concepts, focusing on distributed embedded systems. In general, AC/OC aspire to the development of robust, flexible and highly adaptive computing systems. To support the Self-X properties, Richter et al. [4] developed a generic observer/controller architecture similar to the MAPE cycle. A *System under Observation/Control* (SuOC) is embedded into the control loop of an observer/controller. The observer monitors relevant system parameters and analyses these data. It can also

C. Rong et al. (Eds.): ATC 2008, LNCS 5060, pp. 343–357, 2008.

deduce predictions of possible future behaviour by comparing current observations with past ones. The controller uses this information to infer appropriate actions. This derivation is influenced by user-defined objectives and uses simulation and adaptation models. Execution of the derived actions closes the control loop.

Whereas the SuOC is able to run for itself, the surrounding control loop will improve its operation by means of the Self-X properties. Thereby, the observer/controller can run both in a centralised or distributed way, depending on the system it is applied to.

Throughout this paper we will use the term *Organic Manager* to subsume the observer/controller architecture of Organic Computing respectively the MAPE control cycle of Autonomic Computing.

Operating system requirements that arise from AC/OC are (1) the extensive monitoring of system parameters and running application threads and (2) a concept to implement the Organic Manager without disturbing application thread execution. Self-healing and self-optimisation require (3) the ability to move tasks between different control units. Most of these functionalities can be implemented by means of helper threads, which run in parallel to the real-time applications. Thereby, they support the operation of the real-time applications without disturbing their timing behaviour.

There is also another point where operation of automotive networks can be improved. In the traditional way of implementation, a manufacturer supplies a device with its microcontroller and software in-a-box, with nearly no possibilities for changes due to warranty reasons. Especially safety-critical and real-time devices are affected. Microcontrollers in such devices usually have free processing time, which cannot be utilised.

With our approach we want to provide a solution to make the free processing time available to other applications without influencing the safety-critical or hard real-time tasks. Thereby, it can happen that two or more hard real-time tasks need to be executed on one device. Additionally, these tasks could be developed by different manufacturers. Hence, we need a system, hardware and software, that allows hard real-time threads to run in full isolation from each other and potential non real-time threads like helper threads.

But, hard real-time systems must not miss any deadline. Therefore, the analysability and predictability of the timing behaviour of all real-time tasks within one system is an essential requirement. This point concerns not only the application itself but also the operating system services it is using.

In this paper we present the architecture of the real-time operating system CAROS (Connective Autonomic Realtime Operating System). CAROS is aimed to combine the requirements of hard real-time systems and the potentials of AC/OC. Therefore, we design CAROS itself as a System under Observation/Control [4]. CAROS extends operating system techniques for the use in an "organic environment". Additionally, CAROS targets networked high-performance embedded microcontrollers.

CAROS supports extensive and non-intrusive monitoring, an Organic Manager implementation by helper threads, and task migration concepts. All these capabilities can be implemented without disturbing the timing behaviour of hard real-time application threads running in parallel.

This paper is organised as follows: Section 2 gives an overview of work related to real-time operating systems and Autonomic/Organic Computing (AC/OC). In section 3 we state the requirements arising from the Organic Computing paradigm for a real-time operating system. Section 4 presents the architecture we developed to accomplish these requirements. In section 5 we describe a prototypical implementation on the CarCore Processor. In section 6, we show how AC/OC implementations will benefit from the proposed operating system architecture and section 7 concludes the paper.

2 Related Work

Over the last years, research in the area of Organic Computing was mainly promoted within the German Science Foundation Priority Program "Organic Computing" [5]. Projects here focus on systems of small networked components like sensor networks. Although, real-time systems currently only play an underpart within this program. The project DoDOrg [6] investigates a *digital organism* for real-time applications. This project aims at the use of reconfigurable hardware to implement virtual organs that can handle specific tasks.

The work of Rammig et al. [7] tends at the development of a distributed OS for real-time applications. It implements techniques for self-optimisation and self-configuration. The latter is also performed with the help of reconfigurable hardware.

These projects have similar aims as the CAROS architecture. However, the mentioned approaches differ strongly from our concept, as they make use of reconfigurable hardware, whereas we aim at high-performance embedded microcontrollers.

In the area of commercial real-time operating systems, the concepts of Organic Computing, when regarded at all, are currently only addressed marginally. An example would be QNX Neutrino [8], which provides a micro-kernel-based implementation of the POSIX standard (IEEE Std. 1003.1, [9]). The current version includes an instrumented kernel and support for self-healing systems, but does not further address the ideas of Organic Computing.

Helper threads have been proposed for future high-end multithreaded processors by rapidly spawning threads that are executed simultaneously to the main thread thus helping the processor to speed up the execution of the single main thread. Such helper threads are proposed for tasks like branch prediction [10], prediction of accessed memory addresses [11, 12, 13], exception handling [14, 15] and accelerated execution of loops [16]. In the embedded Java microcontrollers Komodo [17] and jamuth [18] helper threads are also used for a real-time capable garbage collection and the dynamic preloading of software updates of running hard real-time threads [19]. Also, a helper thread can be used to accelerate task switching in the embedded multithreaded Infineon TriCore 2 microcontroller [20].

The design of CAROS extends the helper-thread concept by another application. Helper threads, running in the "timing shadow" of real-time applications, here will be used as containers for Organic Management functionalities.

3   Requirements

In this section, we state the minimum requirements for a real-time operating system, and show how these must be extended for the support of the observer/controller architecture of Organic Computing.

A *Real-Time* Operating System (RTOS) typically fulfils the following properties [21]:

1. A RTOS is multi-threaded and preemptible.
2. The notion of thread priority exists.
3. The OS supports predictable thread synchronisation mechanisms. These include means to prevent priority inversion and/or deadlocks.
4. The OS behaviour should be known, esp. interrupt latencies, maximum execution time of system calls (must be bounded, predictable, and independent of objects in the system)

These requirements are fulfilled by most current RTOS implementations. However, the introduction of AC/OC by means of helper threads imposes some further requirements. Our concept extends requirement 2:

2'. The OS allows to run additional applications in fully temporal isolation from the hard real-time threads.

Furthermore, the observer/controller architecture needs the following requirements to be fulfilled:

5. Monitoring of system parameters and running threads is required to provide detailed runtime information.
6. The OS provides points to intervene into the operation of the system.
7. A concept for mobile code allows the migration of applications between nodes.
8. Safety and security measures ensure the proper operation of the remaining system, even if a failure occurs in one application.

Figure 1 summarises the requirements and how they are classified into the domains of Real-Time and Autonomic/Organic Computing. On this basis, we are now able to propose an OS architecture that fulfils all the afore mentioned requirements.

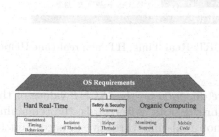

Fig. 1. Requirements for an Organic Real-Time Operating System

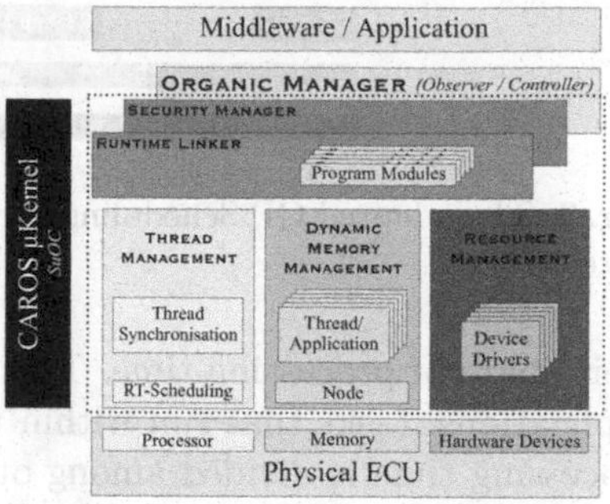

Fig. 2. Architecture of CAROS

4   Architectural Design

4.1   Overview

The design of the CAROS architecture follows the microkernel principles. The OS kernel comprises only the most necessary functionalities, like the scheduler, resource management etc., whereas all additional functions run outside the kernel as separate components, using only a predefined kernel interface. Thus, such modules can be exchanged without impairing other parts of the system. Also, a failure within one module leads not necessarily to the failure of the complete system. Figure 2 gives an overview of the proposed architecture.

Two of the core functionalities are the *Thread Management* and the *Resource Management*, like in any other RTOS. To permit code migration required by self-optimisation and self-healing techniques, the kernel is extended by a *Dynamic Memory Management* and a *Runtime Linker*. To ensure real-time operation of applications, CAROS strongly utilises pre-allocation techniques. Resources are allocated to a new application as far as possible before it starts real-time operation. A concept for *Security Management* completes the architecture. Monitoring points are available throughout all OS modules. The Organic Manager itself is not part of the operating system, but its implementation by helper threads is supported by CAROS (see below). The next sections will describe the five individual kernel parts in more detail.

4.2   Thread Management

Scheduler. The Scheduler is the most important part of the Thread Management. It implements a real-time capable scheduling scheme. However, this scheduling scheme must allow to run non real-time threads in parallel to real-time application(s). Hence, we propose the adoption of the Guaranteed Percentage (GP) scheduling [22], where each thread is guaranteed a constant fraction of processing time during a repeating interval. Figure 3 illustrates the proposed scheduling scheme. During one scheduling period, first the real-time threads get

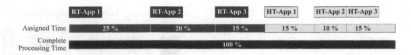

Fig. 3. The adapted GP Scheduling Scheme (RT: Real-Time; HT: non real-time Helper Thread)

their share of processing time. This share depends on the WCET values of the applications' tasks that run within the thread slots. Afterwards, the remaining processing time is divided among other non real-time threads e.g. accordant to a weighted round robin scheme.

As CAROS must be able to accept new applications at runtime whose timing constraints are known just then, the scheduler must provide information about the current load of the processor. Using the adopted GP scheduling, the scheduler can easily provide this information. Thus the Thread Management can decide whether it is possible to start a new application on the node. This information can also be used as monitoring data for an Organic Manager that runs as a helper thread in the "timing shadow" of the real-time application(s).

Helper Threads. Helper threads are not allowed to disturb the timing behaviour of the running hard real-time threads. On a sequential processor they may run in the idle times of the hard real-time threads, but must be preempted with fixed overhead as soon as a hard real-time thread is triggered. Thus, they do not run concurrent to a hard real-time thread and cannot interrupt the observed threads. On a multithreaded processor, helper threads can be executed in own thread slots concurrent to the hard real-time thread, provided that a hardware-based real-time scheduler is available. Helper threads can also run in separate cores of a multicore processor.

Synchronisation. Components for thread synchronisation are provided by the Thread Management module. As the synchronisation mechanisms usually must intervene deeply into the threads, they are directly managed by the Thread Management. The employed mechanisms are apt for the use in real-time environments.

4.3 Resource Management

Features. Management of hardware resources is also an important task of an operating system. Because of the microkernel concept, the CAROS kernel only manages the most essential system resources directly, i.e. processing time and memory. Other resources, especially peripheral devices are managed through a dedicated *Resource Management.* Access to these resources is done through device drivers. Following the microkernel principles, these drivers must not be executed within the kernel, but in userspace. This concerns the generic `read`/`write` operations as well as driver-specific I/O operations. However, access to the device (`open`/`close` operations) and configuration of the driver (`ioctl` operation) is granted by the security manager running within the kernel.

The problem of concurrent use of devices can be reduced to thread synchronisation for which the Thread Manager already provides solutions. However, the Resource Management may extend these mechanisms or implement more apt solutions.

The device drivers need not be linked statically to the kernel, instead they can be loaded at bootup or runtime using the Runtime Linker (see 4.5 below). With this concept, it is also possible to exchange or update a device driver during runtime.

Following these criteria, the Resource Manager forms an important base for Self-Configuration techniques. The ability to exchange drivers at runtime allows a high and flexible adaptation of the system through an organic manager.

The drivers themselves must provide at least rudimentary status information for the operating system about the functional state of the corresponding devices. For the support of an organic management, the drivers may implement more sophisticated monitors.

Real-Time Considerations. Generally, there is no limitation on the number of drivers supported by the resource manager. However, this leads inevitably to the use of dynamic data structures within the manager, which cannot guarantee a bounded timing behaviour for device accesses. For the use in real-time applications, the resource management must also provide constant-time-handlers. The number of devices an application uses is limited and known in advance. So the handlers for these devices can be arranged during the preparation of the application's execution environment during bootup (for statically deployed applications) respectively subsequent to the linking process (for dynamically loaded application). Thus, device accesses can be performed in constant time. The device access for non-real-time applications can still be done over a dynamic name resolution or similar.

4.4   Dynamic Memory Management

The memory management must allow a separation of the running threads. At the same time it should enhance the possibilities for real-time applications, and therefore must be real-time capable itself. We suggest the introduction of a two-layered memory management, and the use of memory pre-allocation. On the first layer, the *Node Memory Management* allocates large blocks of memory for the individual threads. As this allocation must be guarded by locks to keep the overall state of the memory consistent, here blocking of threads can occur. However, this allocation is usually only done before the relating thread is started, so influences on the real-time behaviour will not occur. Also, the impacts of this blocking are reduced through the real-time capable synchronisation techniques of the thread management. On the second layer, the *Thread Memory Management* allocates memory to the program running in the specific thread. This can be done without locking, as the memory is taken from the blocks allocated in the first stage exclusively for the thread.

Another advantage of such a two-layered architecture can be seen in figure 4. When working with several threads, it is necessary to keep track which memory block belongs to which thread. As shown in 4(a), this usually would be done by putting these blocks into a linked list, using the list pointer (LP) fields. Using the conventional (one-layered) allocation scheme, each block must have such a pointer. Thus, management overhead will be increased strongly. When using the proposed two-layered architecture, the list pointers need only be added to the large blocks allocated on node stage, as shown in 4(b). As can be seen, even in this rather simple example some memory is saved. Thus, the higher expenses for keeping two layers of management data will be weighed up.

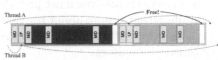

(a) Conventional memory management; the memory blocks of threads A and B are highly mixed

(b) Two-stage memory management, the outer boxes display the blocks of the global memory management; the threads' memory is kept separated

Fig. 4. Example layout of used memory with two threads; MD: Management data of the memory allocator, LP: List Pointers to keep track of thread's memory

The two-layered architecture also facilitates cleaning up after a thread termination, as only few large blocks need to be deallocated by the node management. There is no need to take care of the internal structure of these blocks. In the single-layered case, instead, each small block would need its own deallocation call, prolonging the time until the memory could be reused.

On the thread level, the possibility to use various implementations of memory allocators unfolds. If a real-time application requires the flexibility of dynamic storage allocation, a real-time capable allocator with bounded execution time can be used. For non-real-time applications, efficiency of memory usage can be improved by a best-fit allocator. The thread level allocation runs in userspace. This saves time especially during the real-time allocation by avoiding costly system calls.

A high locality of dynamic memory allocation will be gained by the two-layered architecture. Especially the node memory management can be further improved if the underlying hardware provides a memory management unit. The availability of a memory protection system would raise the security of the whole system, because it would allow nearly a full isolation of threads on the memory level.

By adding specialised monitors to the two stages of storage allocation, the proposed two-layer architecture allows a very fine-grained monitoring of memory usage and fragmentation. Thus, an Organic Manager is enabled to detect memory contention very early and to react in time.

4.5   Runtime Linker

A Runtime Linker represents the premise for loading program modules at runtime. It is also utilised by the Resource Management to load device drivers. Therefore, it must provide a framework for module and driver development. The compiled code of such modules usually contains symbolic references to functions of the operating system or of other modules. These references are resolved by the runtime linker when loading the module on a specific node.

Due to these symbolic references, the linking process itself is not real-time capable. Instead, the time for linking a module depends strongly on the number and kind of symbolic references it contains and the data structures used for resolution. But the linker can still be used to improve real-time operation of a system by running a linking process as a helper thread [19].

For reasons of safety and security, the operating system must support a concept of namespaces. Symbols provided by modules must not be available to all applications on the host. Instead, access to these symbols is restricted to the application that loaded the module in the first place. However, the application is allowed to grant access to the module to other, selected applications.

Furthermore, the runtime linker has to provide a way to remove modules from a running system again (module unloading). Particularly, if a module is replaced by an updated version, the memory of the old version should be freed. Also, if an application is migrated to another ECU, not only its runtime memory must be freed, but also the process image usually has to be removed. The runtime linker hereby must ensure consistency of the loaded module. This is notably critical, if a module is to be removed that does not represent an application, but is rather used as a library to support other modules.

The placement of the runtime linker inside the kernelspace may not seem obvious in the first place. But as it has high responsibility regarding the migration of applications, it must strongly interact with the Thread Management in some places and is also important for the Resource Management for loading device drivers.

4.6   Security Management

Especially the uncontrolled start of new applications on an ECU can have heavy impact on the system's behaviour. The same applies for an excessive or uncontrolled use of system memory.

To prevent such situations, a *Security Management* provides several stages of privileges. If an operating system service is invoked, the OS first checks the calling application's privileges before executing the service. The Security Manager also provides a coherent scheme for propagation of privileges, e.g. if an application starts another one.

Another point of security and safety regards the communication with other nodes. The kernel itself does not provide a communication module. Thus, it also cannot directly support secure communication with other ECUs. However, it is possible to build in support for communication and security modules loaded by the runtime linker. Furthermore, a Security Manager can provide its own encryption functions, which can be regarded as "trusted" functions in contrast to dynamically loaded modules from unknown sources.

5   Prototypical Implementation

A first prototypical implementation of CAROS was performed on the simultaneous multithreaded (SMT) CarCore processor. SMT allows to run helper threads concurrently to real-time threads in temporal isolation guaranteed by the hardware-based real-time scheduler of the CarCore. In the following sections, we describe shortly the architecture of the CarCore, and present our experiences with CAROS.

5.1   The CarCore Processor

The CarCore (see fig. 5) is the SMT processor core of the CAR-SoC[1] [23]. It is binary compatible to the Infineon TriCore architecture [24]. Its back-end is similar to the TriCore, consisting of two pipelines each with *Decode*, *Execute*, and *Write Back* stages. The preceding front-end stages (*Instruction Fetch* and *Schedule*) are shared between both pipelines. Scheduling of threads is separated into two layers, namely the *Schedule* stage within the pipeline, and a dedicated *Thread Manager* (not to be confused with CAROS' Thread Management).

Instructions are issued in-order and two instructions of a thread can be issued in parallel, if an integer instruction is directly followed by an address instruction. Otherwise, the other pipeline is filled by an instruction of another thread.

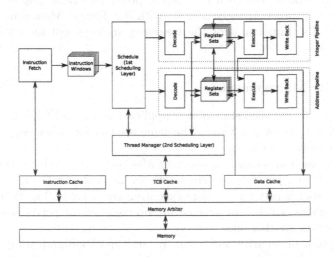

Fig. 5. Architecture of the CarCore Processor

---

[1] **C**onnective **A**utonomic **R**eal-time **S**ystem-**o**n-**C**hip.

The Schedule stage implements the First Scheduling Layer. It predecodes the instructions depending on the priority of the thread slots and assigns them to the appropriate pipelines. In case of latencies, instructions of the next prior thread are selected. The priorities of the thread slots are assigned by an external signal from the hardware Thread Manager, which implements the Second Scheduling Layer. The Thread Manager allows to run an arbitrary number of threads managed completely by hardware, thus reducing software overhead. It implements a Guaranteed IPC Scheduling, which works similar to the Guaranteed Percentage Scheduling (see section 4.2). Here, one or more real-time threads are guaranteed a specific IPC rate within a predefined period each. The remaining processing time in each period is distributed among non real-time threads (e.g. helper threads). This scheduling technique is real-time capable. It is described in more detail in [25]. The multithreaded hardware architecture and the special scheduling technique enable us to have non real-time threads running in parallel to hard real-time threads, but without influencing their real-time behaviour.

The binary compatibility to the Infineon TriCore architecture enables us to use COTS development tools, like the TriCore GCC from HighTec [26], instead of having to write our own compiler.

5.2   Implementation of CAROS

As mentioned, the CarCore provides a hardware-based, real-time capable thread scheduler. On OS level, scheduling functionality is reduced to managing the hardware thread slots and ensuring consistency of all scheduling parameters. Especially the helper thread concept can be implemented very easily. However, to ensure the real-time behaviour, we limited the number of real-time threads as described in 4.2. The Thread Manager supports dependency models for applications. Hence, it is possible to prepare a real-time application from a helper thread, and pre-allocate all needed resources. So when the application starts running, real-time behaviour can be guaranteed for all resource accesses.

Thread synchronisation is achieved by the conventional mechanisms of lock and conditional variables. To overcome the problem of priority inversion, a priority inheritance mechanism as described in [27] is used.

Dynamic memory management on the node level is currently performed by an allocator based on Lea's allocator [28] (DLAlloc). On the thread level, the user can choose between DLAlloc again, and the real-time capable TLSF [29]. Both stages are equipped with extensive monitoring functions, to measure memory usage and fragmentation. Unfortunately, the CarCore currently provides no memory protection system, so we can not yet guarantee a total isolation of the separate threads on the memory level. However, the node level of the dynamic memory management is ready to manage multiple types of memory in parallel. Thus, we are able to provide a kind of *Quality of Service* on the memory level.

The runtime linker is able to use the GCC-generated object files (.o). The development framework ensures that these object files have a certain format and contain the information that is necessary for the integration of modules or drivers into a running system.

The implementation of the resource management is geared to the POSIX standard [9]. For handling of devices, it provides `open/close` and `read/write` operations. Configuration of the device drivers is done using the `ioctl` operation. These operations are called through the kernel, which must grant the access using the Security Manager. However, the device access by the driver is executed in userspace again. Thus, the kernel can not be affected by malfunction of the driver.

The Security Management is mostly implemented in a distributed fashion. The only central point, the assignment and manipulation of privileges, is integrated into the thread management. The checks whether an application is allowed to perform a specific operation or not are performed within the operation, because usually only few privileges must be checked. Due to the implementation of the privileges as bit sets, these checks can be done with very low overhead.

6   Benefits for Organic Computing

The following section shows, how Autonomic and Organic Computing will benefit from the CAROS architecture. Thereby, special attention is paid to the targeted area of networks of embedded high-performance microcontrollers.

As a result of the presented architecture, the OS kernel can provide very detailed runtime information about its state to an Organic Manager running on top of the OS. This fine-grained architecture enables the integration of equally fine-grained actuators, to influence the runtime behaviour of the system. Thus, the CAROS architecture provides good support for the MAPE resp. the observer/controller architecture for AC/OC. Depending on the application and system architecture, the management components can run in one or more helper threads, or even distributed over multiple nodes of a network.

The dynamic capabilities of the CAROS architecture enable the implementation of sophisticated Self-X techniques. The following points will expose in more detail, how the specific Self-X properties profit from CAROS.

6.1   Self-configuration

The possibility to load device drivers and program modules even at runtime enables flexible reactions to environmental changes. Necessary re-configuration can be performed in the background using helper threads, while the main application is still working. When re-configuration is finished, execution of the main application is switched to the new code [19].

The reconfiguration itself is not real-time capable, but isolation of the helper thread from other running threads guarantees hard real-time behaviour for the running application threads, while a helper thread loads the new code.

6.2   Self-healing

The isolation on the memory level allows a strict segregation of applications. If malfunction (e.g. through deadlocks or infinite loops) of an application is detected, its initial state can be recovered and the application be restarted. Due to the two-layered memory management architecture, this can be performed in a very efficient way.

Self-Healing is also supported on the network level. If here an ECU drops out, the applications that were running on it can be restarted on another ECU. This only demands the availability of further code images of the applications in the network.

6.3 Self-optimisation

On a single ECU, the timing information of the Thread Manager can be used to optimise the share of processing time a real-time thread gets without missing its deadline. Thus, more processing time is available for non real-time threads.

On the level of a network, the processing load of the ECUs can be optimised by migrating applications from ECUs with high load to such ones with a low processing load. It is even possible to have backup ECUs with no dedicated application. Instead, jobs are assigned to them at runtime due to dynamically arising requirements.

6.4 Self-protection

The security manager limits access especially to system functions. Applications can be prevented from manipulating e.g. the scheduling parameters of other applications and thus endangering the real-time behaviour of the system.

The memory isolation induced by the two-layered memory management and supported by a hardware memory protection system prevents malicious applications from changing other application's code or data.

Many of the presented techniques make use of a communication network connecting several ECUs. To be real-time capable, the network device drivers must implement special protocols, like the OSEK Fault-Tolerant Communication [30] or FTT-CAN [31].

7   Conclusion and Future Work

We have presented the CAROS architecture, proposing a real-time operating system with inherent support for Autonomic/Organic Computing. Through the integration of dynamic features, like a runtime linker, the potentials for implementing Self-X techniques are increased. The stated requirements of the kernel architecture consider especially the observer/controller architecture proposed in [4] by ensuring extensive monitoring information. A prototypical implementation on the multithreaded CarCore processor shows the feasibility of our concepts. Thereby, the special hardware scheduler of the CarCore brings a great ease to the implementation.

In the future, we will develop an Organic Management system that implements the Self-X techniques based on the CAROS architecture. Thereby, special consideration will go into real-time aspects, and as well in the generality of the developed concepts.

For better comparability, an implementation of CAROS on a recent single-threaded processor is targeted. The use of memory protection concepts is another point, that will be investigated in more depth.

References

[1] Horn, P.: Autonomic Computing: IBM's Perspective on the State of Information Technology. IBM Manifesto, IBM Corporation (October 2001)
[2] Kephart, J.O., Chess, D.M.: The vision of autonomic computing. Computer 36(1), 41–50 (2003)
[3] Müller-Schloer, C.: Organic computing: on the feasibility of controlled emergence. In: CODES+ISSS 2004: Proceedings of the 2nd IEEE/ACM/IFIP international conference on Hardware/software codesign and system synthesis, pp. 2–5. ACM Press, New York (2004)
[4] Richter, U., Mnif, M., Branke, J., Müller-Schloer, C., Schmeck, H.: Towards a generic observer/controller architecture for organic computing. In: Hochberger, C., Liskowsky, R. (eds.) GI Jahrestagung (1). LNI, GI, vol. 93, pp. 112–119 (2006)
[5] : DFG Priority Program 1183 Organic Computing visited (April 2008), http://www.organic-computing.de/SPP
[6] Becker, J., Brändle, K., Brinkschulte, U., Henkel, J., Karl, W., Köster, T., Wenz, M., Wörn, H.: Digital on-demand computing organism for real-time systems. In: Karl, W., Becker, J., Großpietsch, K.E., Hochberger, C., Maehle, E. (eds.) ARCS Workshops, LNI, GI, vol. 81, pp. 230–245 (2006)
[7] Rammig, F.J., Götz, M., Heimfarth, T., Janacik, P., Oberthür, S.: Real-time operating systems for self-coordinating embedded systems. In: Proceedings of the Dagstuhl Seminar MBEES: Modellbasierte Entwicklung eingebetteter Systeme II, Wadern, Germany (2006)
[8] : QNX Software Systems , http://www.qnx.com/
[9] : IEEE Std 1003.1, 2004 Edition. The Open Group Base Specifications Issue 6 (2004)
[10] Chappell, R.S., Stark, J., Kim, S.P., Reinhardt, S.K., Patt, Y.N.: Simultaneous subordinate microthreading (ssmt). In: ISCA, pp. 186–195 (1999)
[11] Collins, J.D., Wang, H., Tullsen, D.M., Hughes, C.J., Lee, Y.F., Lavery, D.M., Shen, J.P.: Speculative precomputation: long-range prefetching of delinquent loads. In: ISCA, pp. 14–25 (2001)
[12] Luk, C.K.: Tolerating memory latency through software-controlled pre-execution in simultaneous multithreading processors. In: ISCA, pp. 40–51 (2001)
[13] Zilles, C.B., Sohi, G.S.: Execution-based prediction using speculative slices. In: ISCA, pp. 2–13 (2001)
[14] Keckler, S.W., Chang, A., Lee, W.S., Chatterjee, S., Dally, W.J.: Concurrent event handling through multithreading. IEEE Trans. Computers 48(9), 903–916 (1999)
[15] Zilles, C.B., Emer, J.S., Sohi, G.S.: The use of multithreading for exception handling. In: MICRO, pp. 219–229 (1999)
[16] Marcuello, P., González, A., Tubella, J.: Speculative multithreaded processors. In: International Conference on Supercomputing, pp. 77–84 (1998)
[17] Pfeffer, M., Ungerer, T., Fuhrmann, S., Kreuzinger, J., Brinkschulte, U.: Real-time garbage collection for a multithreaded java microcontroller. Real-Time Systems 26(1), 89–106 (2004)

[18] Uhrig, S., Wiese, J.: jamuth – an ip processor core for embedded java real-time systems. In: Proceedings of the 5th International Workshop on Java Technologies for Real-time and Embedded Systems (JTRES) (2007)

[19] Pfeffer, M., Ungerer, T.: Dynamic real-time reconfiguration on a multithreaded java-microcontroller. In: ISORC, pp. 86–92. IEEE Computer Society, Los Alamitos (2004)

[20] Kluge, F., Mische, J., Uhrig, S., Ungerer, T., Zalman, R.: Use of helper threads for os support in the multithreaded embedded tricore 2 processor. In: Lu, C. (ed.) Proceedings Work-In-Progress-Session of the 13th IEEE Real-Time and Embedded Technology and Applications Symposium, pp. 25–27 (2007)

[21] : FAQ of comp.realtime (1998), visited April 2008,
http://www.faqs.org/faqs/realtime-computing/faq/

[22] Kreuzinger, J., Schulz, A., Pfeffer, M., Ungerer, T., Brinkschulte, U., Krakowski, C.: Real-time scheduling on multithreaded processors. In: RTCSA, pp. 155–159. IEEE Computer Society, Los Alamitos (2000)

[23] Uhrig, S., Maier, S., Ungerer, T.: Toward a processor core for real-time capable autonomic systems. In: Proceedings of the Fifth IEEE International Symposium on Signal Processing and Information Technology (2005)

[24] Infineon Technologies AG: Tricore^{TM}1 Core Architecture. 1.3 edn. (2005)

[25] Kluge, F., Mische, J., Metzlaff, S., Uhrig, S., Ungerer, T.: Integration of Hard Real-Time and Organic Computing. In: ACACES 2007 Poster Abstracts, L'Aquila, Italy, Academia Press, Ghent (Belgium) (2007)

[26] : HighTec EDV-Systeme GmbH, http://www.hightec-rt.com/

[27] Sha, L., Rajkumar, R., Lehoczky, J.P.: Priority inheritance protocols: An approach to real-time synchronization. IEEE Trans. Comput. 39(9), 1175–1185 (1990)

[28] Lea, D.: A memory allocator. Unix/Mail 6/96 (1996)

[29] Masmano, M., Ripoll, I., Crespo, A., Real, J.: TLSF: A New Dynamic Memory Allocator for Real-Time Systems. In: ECRTS 2004: Proceedings of the 16th Euromicro Conference on Real-Time Systems (ECRTS 2004), Washington, DC, USA, pp. 79–86. IEEE Computer Society, Los Alamitos (2004)

[30] OSEK/VDX Fault-Tolerant Communication, Version 1.0 (2001)

[31] Almeida, L., Fonseca, J.: FTT-CAN: a Network-Centric Approach for CAN based Distributed Systems. In: 4th IFAC Symposium on Intelligent Components and Instruments for Control Applications (SICICA 2000) (2000)

Towards an Autonomic Peer-to-Peer Middleware for Wireless Sensor Networks

Reinhard Mörgenthaler, Markus Zeller, and Josef Jiru

Fraunhofer Institute for Communication Systems ESK, Munich, Germany
{reinhard.moergenthaler,markus.zeller,josef.jiru}@esk.fraunhofer.de
http://www.esk.fraunhofer.de
Hansastr. 32, 80686 Munich, Germany

Abstract. In this paper we present an approach for the design of a wireless sensor network (WSN) architecture and the corresponding middleware. The middleware, with the main functions service discovery and task management, interacts with the WSN and allows an efficient collaboration of the services on top. Design criteria for a WSN architecture and the middleware are scalability, fault-tolerance and self-organization. To meet these requirements it is necessary to minimize the need for communication of a single sensor node and to distribute the functionality of a node with respect to its properties autonomously. Therefore, our system approach envisions a four layer model for the sensor network and its middleware: Two layers of sensor nodes, one layer of gateway peers and one layer of process peers. The middleware's communication model is based on a peer-to-peer approach to reduce communication complexity. Important aspects of the system are already implemented and evaluated with respect to energy consumption and message complexity.

1 Introduction

A WSN is a wireless network of autonomous devices using sensors or actuators to observe physical or environmental conditions or to interact with the environment.

Römer et al. [16] introduced a design space for wireless sensor networks to show the various characteristics that influence the design of WSNs. Here, we will focus on the main aspects of the design of a wireless sensor network - scalability, energy efficiency, message efficiency, optimal resource management and hence management of heterogeneous nodes.

Currently, there are a number of applications that indicate the usefulness of WSNs like vital sign monitoring [2], power consumption [12] and grape monitoring [3].

Another typical example is Roves [11], an implementation of a self-organizing network to link and control electronic lock cylinders (Figure 1). After activation, each cylinder autonomously associates and authenticates itself with the most suitable gateway in range. This gateway announces the cylinder's presence to the administration. Then, the administration is capable of controlling the cylinder. If a gateway fails, a cylinder will automatically associate itself to another gateway in range.

C. Rong et al. (Eds.): ATC 2008, LNCS 5060, pp. 358–372, 2008.

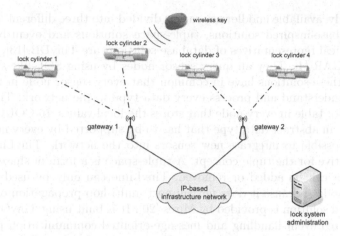

Fig. 1. Roves system architecture

To handle the data delivered by sensor nodes and to manage them a middleware on top of the WSN is necessary. Requirements for such a middleware are defined in [15] and [14]. Again, scalability is an important issue along with expandability, inherent dynamism and aspects of self-organization such as self-management, self-configuration, self-healing and self-protection.

In this paper we want to present a novel approach for a system architecture and middleware for wireless sensor networks. We want to provide functions similar to UPnP to discover and control sensor nodes and build a middleware following the peer-to-peer paradigm on top to compensate the disadvantages of UPnP that would make it ineffective to use with low power sensor nodes. Therefore the focus of our interest is divided into two areas – (i) development of an integrated network structure for WSNs and the corresponding middleware and (ii) development of the middleware that interacts with the WSN.

Naturally, the network structure has to satisfy the above-mentioned requirements for WSNs. The middleware relies on peer-to-peer technology to provide scalability, fault-tolerance and self-organization.

The rest of this paper is structured as follows. Section 2 references related work in the relevant areas. Section 3 explains the requirements for sensor networks and the middleware and explains the aspects of self-organization that are required. Section 4 takes a closer look at the system architecture. In Section 5 some implementation details of Roves and results of the middleware's implementation are presented. In Section 6 we present our conclusion and some aspects for future work.

2   Related Work

In this section we discuss work in the research areas relevant to this paper. These are sensor operating systems, methods of service discovery, peer-to-peer technology and sensor middleware with aspects of autonomous and organic computing.

Currently, available middleware can be divided into three different approaches [9] – database-inspired solutions, tuple-space solutions and event-based solutions. Typical representatives of database solutions are TinyDB [13], SINA [19] and COUGAR [4]. They all query sensor nodes by using SQL-like statements. However, these solutions have in common that every sensor node in the system needs to understand and process every data type in the network. TinyDB creates a sensor table in every node that stores the local values. In COUGAR every sensor has an abstract data type that has to be supported by every node. Thus, it is not possible to integrate new sensors into the network. TinyLime [5] is a representative for the tuple concept. A tuple-space is a form of shared memory where data can be added or removed. TinyLime can only be used for querying local nodes because it does not support multi-hop propagation of data. An event-based solution is provided by Mires [20]. It is built using TinyOS and uses its integrated event-handling and message-oriented communication paradigms. Mires allows sensor nodes to advertise the type of sensor data they provide, lets client applications subscribe to advertised services and publishes sensor data to clients that subscribe to it.

Sensor middleware is mostly built on top of sensor operating systems (OS). However, the separation between sensor OSs and middleware is not very clear as OSs usually include aspects of middleware systems. Nowadays, a lot of operating systems are available. Some examples are TinyOS [10], SOS [8], Contiki [6] and Nano-RK [7]. Most operating systems support some kind of task management which brings along some overhead during system execution. Additionally, they are usually only supported by a small number of sensor node models, which narrows their applicability in highly heterogeneous environments. As this paper's concern is mostly about middleware for sensor networks we will not discuss sensor operating systems any further.

Automated device and service discovery can be found in UPnP networks. After a device is activated it advertises its services by multicasting discovery messages. A device searching for other UPnP devices also multicasts its request. However, for resource-constrained sensor nodes, the continuous transmission and reception of these broadcast messages consumes a lot of energy. After discovering a device, interested clients (called control points) can request a description of each service and device. These descriptions contain information on how to control a service, what events a client can subscribe to and how to monitor the service. A sensor node describing itself to every interested client and interacting with everyone would require a large number of messages. This is very energy consuming and should be avoided in a sensor network.

Effective message routing can be achieved via structured peer-to-peer networks like Chord[21], Pastry[17] or Tapestry[25]. Peers use a dynamic hash table (DHT) to map keys (e.g. IP addresses) to values. A key is stored on a peer that has an ID (also a key) closest to the key. A peers routing table contains only a fraction of peers in the network and a key is always routed to the peer with the closest ID in the routing table. This mechanism assures that only O(log n) messages are necessary to locate a key.

Peers in peer-to-peer networks are usually considered uniform in resources. So, to deal with heterogeneous peers, a "super peer" based approach was introduced [26]. Each super peer acts as a central server to a group of peers. These peers send their search requests to the responsible super peer that at first uses the super peer overlay network to process the request. Only if a key cannot be located, the regular peer-to-peer network will be used. The "super peer approach" reduces the required bandwidth and completes requests faster.

A peer-to-peer event-notification architecture called Scribe, following the publish-subscribe approach, was introduced in [18]. A peer can create topics which any peer can subscribe to. To efficiently disseminate events to the subscribers over the network a multicast tree for every topic is created.

An example for a peer-to-peer middleware that autonomously manages service distribution and relocation in a ubiquitous environment is AMUN [23]. This system is based on JXTA, an open-source peer-to-peer framework.

3 Requirements

The requirements to fulfill our goal can be classified as requirements for a wireless sensor network which can partially be met through the design of our middleware and the requirements for the middleware itself.

3.1 Sensor Network

In [16] a design space for wireless sensor networks was proposed. Here, we only want to define the requirements we intend to meet with the proposed middleware. These requirements are: energy efficiency, message efficiency, optimised resource management, scalability and the management of heterogeneous nodes.

A sensor node should possibly last several years. Therefore, efficient energy management is required. To optimize power consumption it is also necessary to optimize message transmissions. The number of messages used to control a node or to notify events should be limited as far as possible. Furthermore, other resources in a sensor network, such as processing power and available memory, are also very restricted and need to be used efficiently. Scalability ensures proper functionality even as the number of nodes in a network amounts to tens of thousands. Like in Roves, devices in a network can be very heterogeneous in terms of their capabilities. So, in order to optimize their efficiency, different devices need to be configured differently.

3.2 Middleware

A middleware is the interface between a wireless sensor network and the applications using it. Its main purpose is to manage the WSN, to enable applications to inject queries into the WSN without knowing implementation details and to execute these queries.

A middleware has to manage a large number of nodes. Hence, it should be highly scalable. For example, locating a particular piece of data needs to be done efficiently without querying every available device (as might happen in a worst case scenario) because in an environment with tens of thousands of nodes this would be impossible to achieve in a reasonable amount of time. Scalability also includes self-configuration and self-maintenance issues because an approach requiring human interaction would not scale well enough.

Expandability addresses the ability of the middleware to integrate and distribute new program components at runtime. The support of new sensor nodes or sensors, new tasks or a new communication medium are examples.

Inherent dynamism deals with the fluctuating state of the network. Sensor nodes can change position, lose connection or fail because of power outages at irregular intervals. Even middleware peers can join or leave the network at any time. It is necessary to develop a system which is capable of dealing with these challenges and which detects nodes, peers or services when they (re-)appear or disappear.

Additionally, there are some functional requirements we consider most important in a middleware. These are: service discovery and task management.

Service discovery will be used to discover new sensor nodes and sensors in the network and to make their services available to the user and other services. A similar approach is implemented in the UPnP protocol [24] but needs to be adapted to satisfy the requirements and properties of a sensor network. Using task management functions, tasks submitted to the middleware will be executed on devices that offer enough resources to handle them.

3.3 Overall Requirements

Traditionally, computer networks have an administrator who is responsible for creating and managing the network. Because of the potentially large numbers of sensor nodes and middleware devices, this approach is not suitable in our context. An autonomous system like AMUN [23] has the capability to configure, manage and optimize itself and thus offers the basis to maintain large and highly dynamic networks.

Furthermore, it is crucial to the WSN as well as to the middleware's network to reduce network traffic as much as possible. To achieve that, it is necessary to avoid broadcast messages and to access the WSN as little as possible.

4   System Architecture

This section takes a closer look at the system architecture. First, a four layered network structure is introduced and then other aspects of the system's design are discussed.

4.1   Network Structure

Considering Roves, we divided the structure of the sensor network and its middleware into four layers (Figure 3). The layers are ordered from bottom to top with

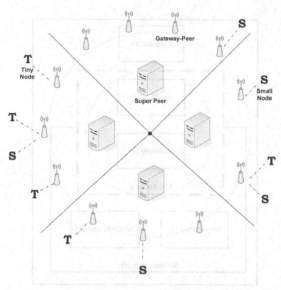

Fig. 2. System Architecture

increasing functionality but a device in any layer can always possess the capabilities of lower layers. Figure 2 shows a descriptive illustration of the network structure.

Tiny-Node Layer. The lowest layer consists of small battery-powered sensor nodes with minimal processing power and maximal life time. Their only purpose is to collect sensor data but they do not process data in any way. Each node associates itself to a peer in the Gateway Layer. This peer then acts as a "man in the middle" and is responsible to forward all messages intended for this sensor node. Tiny nodes do not communicate with each other. Each node possesses a configurable low-power radio transceiver to communicate. For security reasons communication messages may also be encrypted. An example for a tiny node is the Roves wireless key.

Small-Node Layer. Nodes in the Small-Node Layer provide the same functions as tiny nodes with some additional features. They do not only possess sensors to deliver data, they can also have actuators like the Roves lock cylinder. Additionally, battery power is not that restricted as in the Tiny-Node Layer. If a node is not in range of a gateway peer, it can establish a multi-hop connection to a gateway by relaying messages through other nodes of the Small-Node Layer. Furthermore, sensor data cannot be only collected, it is also possible to perform further calculations with it.

Gateway Layer. The actual middleware begins with the Gateway Layer. However, Gateway Layer devices belong to the sensor network as well as to the middleware. All devices are organized in a peer-to-peer network. Typically, a

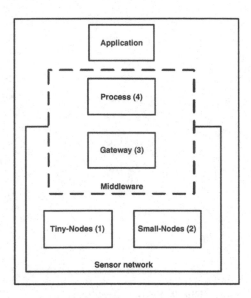

Fig. 3. Four Layer Schema

gateway peer has two means of communication, a low-power radio transceiver to communicate with tiny/small-nodes and a device to enable IP communication. Tiny and small nodes associate themselves to a gateway that publishes the node and its services over the middleware's peer-to-peer network. Any gateway peer can be assigned a task, like collecting sensor data from locally associated sensors. It can also store histories of collected data. Additionally, all clients submitting tasks to the middleware or waiting for events join the peer-to-peer network at least temporarily. These client peers will be treated as gateway peers without associated sensor nodes.

The gateway peers will be disseminated in a way that every sensor node can find at least one peer. This avoids the need for multi-hop communication. The hardware platform for a gateway peer is a WLAN Router with MIPS architecture that has been extended with a low-power radio transceiver and uses the uCLinux operating system.

Process Layer. Process layer peers act as super peers in the middleware's peer-to-peer network. Basically, super peers are gateway peers that possess the most capabilities to handle requests made by clients. They receive new tasks, divide them into sub-tasks that can then be partially carried out by gateway peers. These peers are the only ones that have complete system knowledge.

4.2 Medium Access Control of WSN Nodes

In order to provide reliable, low-power communication between sensor nodes and gateway peers, a CSMA/CA based medium access control (MAC) layer was developed to manage communication over the radio transceiver. In addition, the MAC layer makes it possible to configure the response time of a sensor node according to the middleware's needs or to consume less power. The MAC layer was developed for the Chipcon 1100 low-power radio transceiver [22]. The transceiver supports "wake-on-radio" (WOR) that makes it possible for a sensor node's microcontroller unit (MCU) to sleep until a message is received. This provides a simple way to significantly reduce current consumption.

WOR basically works as follows: The transceiver sleeps for a specified amount of time, e.g. 1000 ms. Then it wakes up and switches to receive (RX) mode for some time large enough to receive the Sync Word of two subsequent messages. In this case messages need to be repeated by the transmitter for a minimum of 1000 ms to make sure one message has fallen into the receiver's RX slot. Every message will be acknowledged by the receiver to let the transmitter know that the message was successfully delivered.

Before sending a message, the transmitter performs a clear channel assessment (CCA) for a predetermined time. Only then a message will be sent. For example, when using the 1000 ms WOR cycle and a 3.91 ms RX time a sensor node can perform WOR for about 1000 days, if batteries delivering 1700 mAh are used.

4.3 Sensor Association and Description

Once a sensor node has been activated, it starts an association process to make itself accessible through the middleware. Therefore, the node selects an appropriate gateway peer in range. Additionally, a node autonomously starts a new association process if the selected gateway peer fails or if the link quality has fallen below a specified threshold. Furthermore, there is the possiblity to perform mutual authentification between sensor node and gateway peer. During the association the gateway peer checks if the sensor node is already known in the system. If this is not the case, the peer requests a description of the node that will be sent to the peer after the association has been completed. This description will be stored in the peer-to-peer system and is accessible in the future which enables the sensor node to skip the description process in the future. After completion of association and if neccessary description, a node periodically sends alive messages to the associated gateway peer to indicate that it is still online.

4.4 Gateway Layer Peer-to-Peer

The peer-to-peer system will be a structured peer-to-peer network using a DHT to route messages. This provides an easy way to locate information with only O(log n) messages.

The peer-to-peer mechanism ensures an even distribution of the key/value entries between all peers. However, a peer storing the above-mentioned data is not necessarily the same peer where a sensor node is associated to or a task is running. Typical information items in our network are a list of active and known nodes, a list of available services, running tasks, etc. If a peer joins or leaves the network, the storage of a key may change but not the peer executing a task or keeping the connection to a sensor node. As described in [21] a new key will be inserted in (r) carefully chosen nodes to achieve the desired degree of redundancy (r) in case a node fails.

Typically, gateway layer peers are either small embedded devices acting as a gateway to the sensor nodes or clients submitting a query to the middleware. A client can only become a super peer, if there is a high probability that it stays in the network for some time, e.g. when it subscribes to an event that continuously sends messages to the client for a time longer than a specified threshold.

4.5   Super Peers in Process Layer

A common unstructured peer-to-peer network considers all peers uniform in resources like CPU speed, bandwidth and storage capabilities. In reality, this is usually not the case. This is the reason why our middleware uses gateway and process layer peers. Super Peers are responsible for task execution. Furthermore, the process layer peers are the only ones that can have complete knowledge about the system's state, e.g. which sensors are online, which services are available or which tasks are currently executed. Consequently, a client joining the network only needs to query its responsible super peer for information about available sensor nodes, services, etc. Following the peer-to-peer principle the failure of a super peer does not result in the loss of information of the system's state because all relevant information is stored redundantly on several super peers. The amount of super peers in the system will be adjusted based on the number of super peers necessary to efficiently execute every query and task. If there are no tasks to be executed, there are only enough super peers neccessary to maintain the required amount of redundancy. The number of super peers must be large enough that a new task can always find a peer that is capable of handling it.

4.6   Tasks

Any authorized client can submit queries into the middleware. A query will be implemented in a way similar to TinyDB [13]. A super peer will be responsible for processing it. Basically, this means finding the peers, the sensor nodes are associated with and sending them subqueries concerning their nodes. These peers are responsible to forward the query to the sensor node if necessary.

Usually, executing a query follows an event-based approach. The client submitting the query will receive periodic updates on the sensor readings. Additionally, the super peer can monitor these update messages, record them and hence create a history for later use.

4.7   Self-organization

Using the design explained in this section the system's self-organization aspects can be shown.

- Self-configuration: The sensor nodes and peers automatically join the network without the need of user interaction.

- Self-optimization: The distribution of tasks occurs based on the workload and available resources of the peers.
- Self-healing: Peers can dynamically join or leave the system without compromising its integrity [21]. Due to distributed and redundant storage of data items, no data will be lost.
- Self-protection: Before a sensor node or peer joins the system it needs to authenticate itself. Furthermore, messages can be encrypted to ensure privacy.
- Self-description: New sensor nodes and services describe themselves to the middleware.

5   Results

At this point, we want to describe some features already implemented in Roves and how the super peer selection will be done. Then, we want to take a closer look at how our approach improves message efficiency.

5.1   Energy Consumption

Using our first implementation as an example, an estimation of a sensor node's lifetime can be provided. Our reference design uses the CC1100 together with an Atmel ATMega64L microcontroller [1] running at 3 volts. The lifetime estimation is based on the power delivered by a common battery with 1700 mAh. The transceiver's output power was set to 0 dbm. With this settings and having a one second WOR cycle with 3.91 ms RX time per second the energy consumption is around 0.21 mJ. This enables the sensor node to perform WOR for approximately 1000 days. Furthermore, energy consumption for a successful transmission of 61 bytes is 0.5 mJ. The lifetime of a sensor node is around 970 days if it is in WOR mode and sending one alive message every minute. Ideally, sensor association needs to be done only once therefore its energy consumption can be neglected. Additionally, when sending one data message every minute the sensor node's lifetime further reduces to 937 days.

5.2   Association and Authentication

To include a sensor node into the network it needs to be associated to a gateway peer. This process is similar to a three-way handshake and includes a challenge/response procedure to mutually authenticate both devices (Fig. 4).

A sensor node broadcasts an "Associate Broadcast Request" message. This message contains the node's unique associate ID and a random number as first challenge. Any peer receiving this request responds with an "Associate Broadcast Response" message. The payload of the response message contains (i) the sensor node's unique associate ID, (ii) the ID of the responding peer, (iii) the number of the currently associated nodes at the peer and (iv) a second random number created by the responding peer. Additionally, the sensor node calculates the received signal strength indication (RSSI) value for each receiving message.

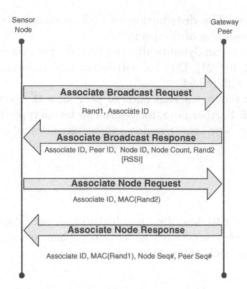

Fig. 4. Association of a Sensor Node

Per definition, the node waits for a predefined number of responding peers and decides which peer to choose based on a peer's currently associated nodes and the RSSI value of the "Associate Broadcast Response" message. An "Associate Node Request" message containing the message authentication code (MAC) for the second random number will then be sent to this peer. After confirming the sensor node's identity by comparing the received MAC with the locally calculated one, the node is authenticated by the peer which immediately responds with an "Associate Node Response" message. This message also contains the MAC for the first random number and two randomly generated sequence numbers. These sequence numbers are basically session IDs for incoming and outgoing messages, which will be increased by one for every outgoing respectively incoming message to ensure tamper-proof encrypted communication. However, if no encryption is necessary, the sequence numbers can be omitted. Furthermore, we want to mention that only the "Associate Broadcast Request" message is a real broadcast message. However, its message header contains a randomly generated temporary node ID that defines the destination address for the response message. By activating the radio's hardware address filter, the response will only be processed by devices using the same hardware filter address. If, by any chance, there is another device with the same hardware filter address, the message will be ignored at a later point.

5.3 Selection of Super Peers

Initially, after joining the peer-to-peer network a device is treated as a gateway peer with no associated sensor nodes. The selection of a new super peer takes place only if the necessity arises. This occurs if the resources available on the current super peers are too low to execute another task. Each peer monitors its own workload and informs its associated super peer about the available resources. Furthermore, each super peer knows about the workload of every other super peer. If one of them decides that a new super peer is necessary, a super peer selection process is started and the peer offering the most resources will be selected as new super peer. This selection process only involves process layer peers because the state of all other peers is already known within the process layer.

5.4   Evaluation of Network Traffic

As mentioned before, our system uses functions similar to UPnP to discover and interact with sensor nodes. However, UPnP contains a few disadvantages that made a redesign neccessary. Device and service discovery and description has to be done for every client that searches for UPnP devices and has to be redone if a client was shut down and later reactivated. In addition, every client subscribes directly to particular services on the devices and therefore a sensor node has to send a number of event messages linear to the number of subscribed clients. Also, UPnP is based on the http protocol and the size of messages is of no concern. In contrast the maximum payload of radio messages is 64 bytes and therefore the message size and the energy neccessary to transmit a message is very important.

Using our system's peer-to-peer properties these deficiencies can be overcome. Figure 5 shows the basic approach. During association the capabilities of a sensor node are submitted to the middleware. This needs to be done only once because the information will be stored redundantly in the peer-to-peer network and is therefore always available in the future. Furthermore, when a client joins the network and asks for information there is no need to query sensor nodes because the neccessary data is already known. In addition, if possible a client can search for tasks already running and simply subscribe for event messages from the same task. This can be done without querying any sensor node. Table 1 shows

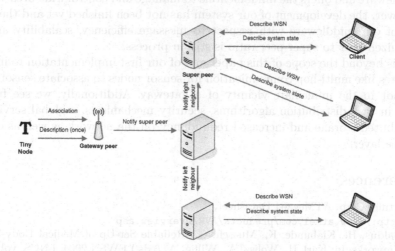

Fig. 5. Discovery by middleware

Table 1. Comparison of Messages

Task	UPnP	Middleware
Association/Discovery	per Client	per System
Description	per Client	once per System
Event	per Client	one to gateway, distribution via Scribe to subscribers

the differences of the message complexity. However, if the required data is not already available, e.g. the sample rate of a sensor data item is too low, it sends a query to the nodes in question. When this query arrives at the responsible gateway peer, the peer instructs the sensor node to update the data item's sample rate to the higher rate, ideally in a way that satisfies the old task and the new one with one event message. The distribution of the event messages to the interested clients follows the Scribe[18] approach to achieve effectiveness and scalability.

As mentioned in Section 5.1 a sensor node's lifetime is approximately 937 days if one client receives an event message every minute. Using the UPnP approach and having ten clients that want to receive the same event message the lifetime reduces to approximately 724 days. In contrast, with our approach the sensor node only sends one message to the gateway peer regardless of the number of clients that subscribed to this event. Therefore, the lifetime does not depend on the number of interested clients and stays at 937 days.

6 Conclusion and Future Work

The development of a middleware for WSNs is an extensive research topic with many different approaches. We believe that the design of a peer-to-peer middleware for wireless sensor networks is a promising approach to create an autonomic middleware and offers the fundamentals to manage and control wide-area WSNs. However, the development of our system has not been finished yet and the analysis of our middleware with respect to message efficiency, scalability and an optimized peer to super peer ratio is still in process.

It is beyond the scope of this paper and of our first implementation to include features like multi-hop communication for sensor nodes to associate sensors that are not in the immediate vicinity of a gateway. Additionally, we see further work in task distribution algorithms, security mechanisms, a global service for distributed storage and increased redundancy on the network as well as on the service layer.

References

1. Atmel Corp. ATMega64 Datasheet,
   http://www.atmel.com/products/AVR/overview.asp
2. Baldus, H., Klabunde, K., Muesch, G.: Reliable Set-Up of Medical Body-Sensor Networks. In: Karl, H., Wolisz, A., Willig, A. (eds.) EWSN 2004. LNCS, vol. 2920, Springer, Heidelberg (2004)

3. Beckwith, R., Teibel, D., Bowen, P.: Pervasive Computing and Proactive Agriculture. In: Ferscha, A., Mattern, F. (eds.) PERVASIVE 2004. LNCS, vol. 3001, Springer, Heidelberg (2004)
4. Bonnet, P., Gehrke, J., Seshadri, P.: Towards Sensor Database Systems. Mobile Data Management (2001)
5. Curino, C., Giani, M., Giorgetta, M., Giusti, A., Murphy, A.L., Picco, G.P.: TINYLIME: Bridging Mobile and Sensor Networks through Middleware. In: Proc. of the 3IEEE Int. Conf. on Pervasive Computing and Communications (PerCom), pp. 61–72 (2005)
6. Dunkels, A., Gronvall, B., Voigt, T.: Contiki - a Lightweight and Flexible Operating System for Tiny Networked Sensors. In: First IEEE Workshop on Embedded Networked Sensors (2004)
7. Eswaran, A., Rowe, A., Rajkumar, R.: Nano-RK: An Energy-Aware Resource-Centric Operating System for Sensor Networks. In: IEEE Real-Time Systems Symposium (2005)
8. Han, C.-C., Kumar, R., Shea, R., Kohler, E., Srivastava, M.: A dynamic operating system for sensor nodes. In: MobiSys 2005: Proc. of the 3rd international conference on Mobile systems, applications, and services, pp. 163–176 (2005)
9. Henrickson, K., Robinson, R.: A survey of middleware for sensor networks: state-of-the-art and future directions. In: Proc. of the international workshop of Middleware for sensor networks, Melbourne, Australia, pp. 60–65 (2006)
10. Hill, J., Szewczyk, R., Woo, A., Culler, D., Hollar, S., Pister, K.: System architecture directions for networked sensors. In: Proc. of ASPLOS (2000)
11. Augel, M., Jiru, J., Mörgenthaler, R.: Selbstorganisierendes Schließanlagensystem und Verfahren zum Organisieren eines derartigen Systems. German Patent Application, 10 2006 047 939.4-31 (2006)
12. Kappler, C., Riegel, G.: A Real-World, Simple Wireless Sensor Network for Monitoring Electrical Energy Consumption. In: Karl, H., Wolisz, A., Willig, A. (eds.) EWSN 2004. LNCS, vol. 2920, Springer, Heidelberg (2004)
13. Madden, S.R., Franklin, M.J., Hellerstein, J.M., Hong, W.: TinyDB: an acquisitional query processing system for sensor networks. ACM Trans. Database Syst. 30(1), 122–173 (2005)
14. Modukuri, K., Hariri, S., Chalfoun, N.V., Yousif, M.: Autonomous middleware framework for sensor networks. Perser 0, 17–26 (2005)
15. Römer, K., Kasten, O., Mattern, F.: Middleware Challenges for Wireless Sensor Networks. MC2R 6(2) (2002)
16. Römer, K., Mattern, F.: The Design Space of Wireless Sensor Networks. IEEE Wireless Communications 11(6), 54–61 (2004)
17. Rowstron, A., Druschel, P.: Pastry: Scalable Distributed Object Location and Routing for Large-Scale Peer-to-Peer Systems. In: Proceedings of IFIP/ACM Middleware 2001 (2001)
18. Rowstron, A., Kermarrec, A.-M., Castro, M., Druschel, P.: SCRIBE: The design of a large-scale event notification infrastructure. In: Crowcroft, J., Hofmann, M. (eds.) NGC 2001. LNCS, vol. 2233, Springer, Heidelberg (2001)
19. Shen, C., Srisathapornphat, C., Jaikaeo, C.: Sensor Information Networking Architecture and Applications. IEEE Personal Communications (2001)
20. Souto, E., Guimarães, G., Vasconcelos, G., Vieira, M., Rosa, N., Ferraz, C., Kelner, J.: Mires: a publish/subscribe middleware for sensor networks. Personal and Ubiquitous Computing 10(1), 37–44 (2006)

21. Stoica, I., Morris, R., Karger, D., Kaashoek, F., Balakrishnan, H.: Chord: A scalable peer-to-peer lookup service for internet applications. In: Proc. ACM SIGCOMM, San Diego (2001)
22. Texas Instruments, Datasheet for Chipcon CC1100, Revision SWRS038B, http://focus.ti.com/lit/ds/symlink/cc1100.pdf
23. Trumler, W., Petzold, J., Bagci, F., Ungerer, T.: AMUN: an autonomic middleware for the Smart Doorplate Project. Personal and Ubiquitous Computing 10(1), 7–11 (2006)
24. UPnP Device Architecture 1.0, http://www.upnp.org
25. Zhao, B.Y., Kubiatowicz, J.D., Joseph, A.D.: Tapestry: An infrastructure for fault-tolerant wide-area location and routing, UC Berkeley (2001)
26. Zhu, Y., Wang, H., Hu, Y.: A Super-Peer Based Lookup in Structured Peer-to-Peer Systems. In: ISCA PDCS, pp. 465–470 (2003)

Embedding Dynamic Behaviour into a Self-configuring Software System

Paul Ward, Mariusz Pelc, James Hawthorne, and Richard Anthony

Dept. Computer Science,The University of Greenwich, Park Row, Greenwich, London, UK
{P.A.Ward,M.Pelc,J.Hawthorne,R.J.Anthony}@gre.ac.uk

Abstract. This paper describes a methodology for embedding dynamic behaviour into software components. The implications and system architecture requirements to support this adaptivity are discussed. This work is part of a European Commission funded and industry supported project to produce a reconfigurable middleware for use in automotive systems. Such systems must be trustable against illegal internal behaviour and activity with external origins, additional devices for example. Policy-based computing is used here as an example of embedded logic. A key contribution of this work is the way in which static and dynamic aspects of the system are interfaced, such that the behaviour can be changed very flexibly (even during run-time), without modification, recompilation or redeployment of the embedded application code. An implementation of these concepts is presented, focussing on achieving trust in the use of dynamic behaviour.

Keywords: Dynamic embedded systems, Policy-based computing, Automotive control systems, Fault-tolerance in autonomics.

1 Introduction

This paper presents a methodology for embedding decision making capability into software components. The target system is a distributed middleware for automotive systems with a mixture of mandatory and optional software components located at each processing node. A component may perform a single function or service for either the system or directly to fulfill an application requirement. In a self-managing system such components may need to be aware of information from within and around the system (the environment). This context-awareness allows the system to make decisions in order to adapt to changing conditions during run-time.

We propose an approach for embedded systems with self-configuration logic embedded into many individual components rather than a centralised node or service, with the goal of improving flexibility and extensibility. Each of the components will have specific tasks and contain modules that can be replaced at run-time. This allows the behaviour of the system to be altered, making the system very dynamic.

The development of an embedded architecture is a requirement of the DySCAS project [1]. This project deals with the dynamic configuration and use of Electronic Control Units (ECUs) within the architecture of an automobile. Additional devices and services may be added during run-time such as a mobile phone or an internet connection when the vehicle is in a hotspot area. Device detachment or ECU failure

C. Rong et al. (Eds.): ATC 2008, LNCS 5060, pp. 373–387, 2008.

during run-time will require a reconfiguration. Other challenges include the use of heterogeneous ECUs, some of which are very resource-constrained; use cases which involve field upgrades of functionality; and flexible dynamic reconfiguration to optimise resource usage and to mask some types of failure. These challenges have brought on the necessity for a dynamic and reconfigurable architecture for embedded systems. A static architecture simply would not be appropriate for this frequently changing environment. See [1, 2, 3] for more on the DySCAS project.

Automotive systems developers face a dilemma in that they need to continuously add new desirable features to maintain market share, whilst keeping the behaviour of vehicles completely safe. Autonomic techniques are an attractive means by which 'smart' context-aware behaviour can be embedded into vehicles. However, the acceptance of autonomics concepts into the automotive area is highly dependent on the trustability of the developed mechanisms, and of the underlying development methodologies used. If changes in the system behaviour are to be allowed, the vehicle manufacturer must be certain that the new configuration is safe and will not cause any illegal or potentially dangerous behaviour. The important issue of trust impacts on this project in two distinct ways: the system behaviour must itself be trustable and the system must automatically make trust decisions concerning externally connected devices (and data transmitted from such devices), as well as making trust decisions concerning software patches and upgrades transmitted to the vehicle. The automotive domain is challenging for the implementation of autonomics, having requirements of real-time performance and very high robustness.

Embedded systems traditionally have fixed functionality. Whilst this approach remains valid for systems with a very narrow and fixed purpose, such as a washing machine controller for example, it is generally not applicable to embedded systems with greater functionality, or that operate in more variable environments. Certainly this is not true in the case of DySCAS in which the configuration and behaviour of the system is context sensitive. More complex embedded systems will often need the capability to change behaviour to meet changing higher level requirements, for example an event which was previously dealt with in a particular way, will now be required to be handled in a completely different way. A static architecture would require recompilation and re-deployment of the executable code to bring the new functionality into effect. A dynamically reconfigurable architecture would not need the system to be halted while making the change. In some cases, halting of the system may even be undesirable or unsafe.

The dynamic nature of the architecture means unavoidable greater complexity over a static system, adding a requirement on validation and verification procedures. Our strategy is to validate as much as possible at design time, such as verifying the correctness of replaceable decision modules before deployment. Due to resource constraints in embedded automotive systems, it is favourable to minimise the validation tasks at run-time.

Inspiration for our methodology comes from policy-based computing where a system's actions are specified by both the compiled code and some policies. Depending on the scheme, a policy can be anything from a simple template containing some pre-determined constants to a decision system with various rules and complex functions. At a particular point in a running process, a policy is evaluated and the result is used to influence the system behaviour. Policy evaluation is carried out by a specialised library that is able to interpret the policy file and produce the correct result. This means that by loading and evaluating a new policy the system can act in a different way. Such policy changes can occur, post-deployment, as frequently as required and even without having to halt or restart the system. This form of updating a computing system is simpler, quicker and less costly than rebuilding and reinstalling whole software components or even a whole system image.

There is also a very real danger here of creating a system which is increasingly complex in implementing the required dynamic behaviour, and in doing so, it becomes more challenging to implement this than it is to implement the main system. Anthony refers to this in [4] as *'complexity tail-chasing'*. The work with AGILE is focused on the use of policies within autonomic systems. One of the advantages of AGILE policies is that they are capable of creating a wide range of self-configuring logic whilst remaining flexible to use and requiring low levels of run-time system resources to evaluate. For other types of policy language see [5, 6].

2 Related Work

A promising approach to achieving autonomic computing is through context-aware run-time adaptation and dynamic reconfiguration. This may, in general, be achieved in two ways. Firstly, by embedding the context-awareness into the application or middleware and providing individual system software components (objects, services, etc.) with common centralised supervision. This method makes the whole system context-aware. However, in the case of more complex systems that manage more system components, this may lead to an increase in communication and computation effort, therefore reducing system performance. The central supervisor may have its own detailed implementation which is separate from methods employed by the rest of the system. The second method (the one advocated in this paper) is to distribute the context-aware functionality by placing it into the system software components directly. This should lead to a reduction of the system load related to the self-adaptation decision making process. Most significantly, overall complexity is reduced, as the need for a monolithic supervisor component is avoided, and flexibility is increased as each component can potentially use a different self-configuration technique. Configuration decisions are localised within each component, reducing communication costs and adaptation latency.

An example of centralised configuration decision making is found in [7]. Entire system configurations are stored and switched between as required. For a complex system, each configuration can be large, complex and would likely require system restart to enact a configuration change. This 'mode' based operation best suits critical systems with a small number of required configurations. The standard configurations are pre-validated, the run-time adaptation is limited to selecting between 'modes'. However the approach generally suffers limitations of scalability and flexibility.

[8] Presents a specific CORBA-compliant middleware that assures system context-awareness. To assure this feature, a context-sensitive application object structure equipped with context-sensitive interfaces is proposed. In this case context-sensitivity is built-in to the component directly, but context analysis is external from this component which has a negative impact on communication intensity and also

decision-making latency. Decisions made by adaptive object containers using context information, activate or deactivate selected object methods, altering the behaviour.

In [9] the ability of a system to perform dynamic reconfiguration in response to context changes is facilitated by a middleware supporting modularized customisable key services. These services achieve reconfiguration by dynamically instantiating and destroying static and non-context-aware components to achieve the appropriate system behaviour. The functionalities that components provide are visible through a set of corresponding fixed interfaces. An advanced middleware layer provides communication between services and applications. The instantiation and destruction of components requires complicated dependency and resource availability analysis each time a change is required. Consequently this technique is of limited suitability for real-time and embedded systems.

Reconfigurable hardware and embedded system software which is partitioned into autonomous units of execution (called intelligent hardware agents) interacting with the environment in an intelligent manner is described in [10]. Three models of reconfiguration are discussed: static, non-buffered dynamic and buffered. Intelligent hardware agents: make use of domain specific knowledge; are able to learn from the environment; and are able to adapt themselves to environmental changes.

A layered architecture of context-aware software infrastructure as well as layered structure of context information management is proposed in [11]. This work also presents commonly used context modelling and context abstraction techniques that support the decision making process involved in mapping of context information to appropriate application behaviours. The adaptation layer uses three repositories: situation, preference, and trigger, which dynamically provide the application layer with appropriate services from the lower layers.

The concept of Service-Oriented Context-Aware Middleware (SOCAM) as well as formal context models used to address issues including context reasoning, context classification, and dependency are presented in [12]. This architecture aims to provide an efficient infrastructure to support building context-aware services that are assumed to make use of different levels of context and adapt the way they behave according to the current situation. In this approach a special Context Reasoner service interacts with context-aware services using for example rule-based reasoning. Different inference rules can be created in a predefined format and then preloaded into the Context Reasoner. This approach centralises decision making. In a system with many context-aware components interacting, this centralisation may lead to a reduction of the system performance and excludes this solution from real-time embedded systems.

An architectural approach towards embedded reconfiguration is undertaken in [13]. This work describes a structure of components with dynamically defined interfaces. External events are bound to ports on the software component; these bindings can be changed to alter the system structure. Using events as external interfaces enables components to be integrated into the system with minimal coupling. This approach focuses on the reconfiguration mechanism, and does not specify the decision making system to perform the reconfiguration.

An approach to verifying the design of adaptive embedded systems is presented in [14]. Design time modelling and formal specification are used to verify the behaviour before the system is implemented and deployed. The use of software tools to aid this process is discussed. The adaptive behaviour itself is formed of several possible configurations for each service which can be enabled if a condition is met. The main disadvantage of this solution lies in the finite number of possible reconfigurations that are predetermined at design time.

In [15] policy engines are decomposed into components. According to this paper, the main disadvantage of such an approach is the use of pre-built policy engines that support particular, usually fixed, languages based on text, GUI, or programming interfaces for "plugging in" custom policy logic usually constructed from scratch. This can represent reduced flexibility and thus usefulness in real-world applications. In contrast, our approach does not assume any pre-defined decision engine. This means that, for example, the AGILE policy library [4, 16] or a neural network reasoning engine can be used, as appropriate to the type of decision making required.

Aspect Oriented Programming (AOP) and reflection could be used and combined as described in [17, 18] to implement runtime adaptable system changes as an alternative to using policies. Reflection however allows the rules of encapsulation to be broken, possibly leading to an un-maintainable system. The problem with AOP is that a dynamic compiler and/or weaver need to be developed and used to enable runtime changes to be possible.

In [19] a dependable self-adaptive software system is described called the Architectural Run-time Configuration Management (ARCM). This approach is similar to our own, in that changes to the system can be rolled back if required. However, they say that to increase the trust in any dynamic changes made requires visual feedback in order for a system administrator to detect and correct problems. This goes against the concept of autonomics whereby tedious activities such as this should be dealt with by the system and not require human intervention.

In [20] it is suggested that trust of a component could be increased by testing it several times before use. The problem here is that it is generally not possible to capture (or even know) all possible system configurations during the testing phase.

The approach advocated in this paper is differentiated from the current state of practice as described above by its key characteristics which include: distributed decision points local to the required point of adaptation; independent operation of decision points within components thus avoiding any synchronisation requirement and permitting independent updates to occur; The ability to change policies at runtime; and a dynamic wrapper which automatically and silently handles errors that may occur in the evaluation of a decision point. These characteristics are described and evaluated in the remainder of the paper.

3 Self-managing System Overview

In our scheme (in contrast to those systems discussed in the previous section) decisions about the reconfiguration are embedded within the software system itself, instead of outside. The decision making process is distributed throughout many software components as shown in figure 1. Two types of components are shown, those that contain embedded decision making and those that do not. If a component is enabled with embedded decision making its behaviour can be changed during runtime by altering the configuration module currently loaded into its decision points. A regular component will behave as a deterministic functional block that is fixed once the system is deployed. The nature of the context information is determined by the application area and comprises of all of the information that is available. Output from the system will have an affect on the environment and thus the context. This creates the feedback loop through the application specific outputs and ensuing consequences.

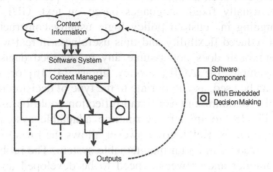

Fig. 1. Simplified system-centred view of a context-aware software system with self-configuration decision making embedded inside components

Context information arriving at the system must be correctly delivered to the software components. In the diagram a conceptual "Context Manager" is shown to provide this functionality; in practice how this operates is specific to the implementation. However, it is clear that communication is required between all components using this context information and the context manager. We suggest that a service oriented approach is taken whereby components register with the context manager to be updated about certain items of context. This would allow an event driven pattern or time-dependant operation with components notified regularly of the context that they are interested in. It is quite conceivable that the context manager could contain some embedded decision making that could be loaded at instantiation and/or altered during run-time. This flexibility provides the ability for different modes of operation depending on the current context. During the lifetime of this system the context information may change, for example if new hardware devices or resources become available. Such new information should be made available to the software components by the context manager.

An important distinction of this approach over an externally supervised system is improved scalability. As a system with embedded decision making increases in size, the number of components also increases. Management of the required resources to operate such a system is relatively trivial, a main advantage being that even though there are numerous distributed decision points, the complexity of each can be very low. However, if the decision making process were centralised, any additions to the software system would require an equivalent change to the decision system. Further difficulties can be caused by a communication bottleneck between the controlling and controlled system.

4   Embedding into Software Components

The described system can be said to be dynamically reconfigurable because its behaviour can be changed during run-time by altering the embedded decision making of one or more software components. The component architecture, shown in figure 2, is designed specifically to allow this. The component developer will leave one or more open decision points that will later be filled with a decision making process, effectively dividing the functionality into basic, fixed, functional blocks and flexible decision points. Software design techniques appropriate for this type of component will require further investigation.

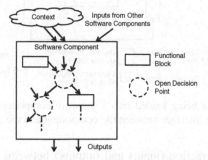

Fig. 2. A single software component with open decision points left by the designer for embedding decision making modules

Any open decision points left in the component must later be filled using some type of decision system, producing a result when inputs are applied. The type of technology used here is flexible; in section 5 policy-based computing is presented as implemented in the DySCAS project. Two stages are required to fill such a decision point, a Decision Evaluation Module (DEM) and a Decision Configuration Module (DCM). The type of evaluation module is matched to the configuration module; together they define the behaviour of this decision point. A DEM is compiled offline and is able to process the inputs together with a DCM and return the appropriate result. While the functionality of a DEM is generally fixed; there may be many versions of a DCM destined for the same component. The behaviour of a component changes depending on which of these variants are currently loaded. Also, different DCMs may require different context information to enact their desired function. The DEM should be ready before the software component is required to run, for example, by compiling into the component or be loaded at run-time for example.

The DCM is essentially a collection of data items that configure the DEM to produce decision making behaviour. For example, a DEM could be a neural network with a DCM containing a set of weights. Therefore, by loading a different DCM, the network weights are changed and component behaviour altered.

Changes in the DCM used in a component can occur without the need to halt the system. This loading process is shown in figure 3. A storage area is assumed to be available to persist various DCMs, along with access to all software components. The DCM is then transmitted to the software component using a predefined standardised interface. Inside the component there is an open decision point with a DEM already installed, the DCM is passed to this and loaded.

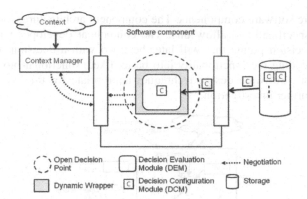

Fig. 3. A decision module being loaded into a software component during run-time and the negotiation of the dynamic interface between the component and the context manager

To facilitate the interaction (inputs and outputs) between the component and the open decision point we introduce a dynamic wrapper concept. This provides an interface to allow inputs to enter the decision point from the component and ensures a legal result is returned. The component can then take the result and use it to inform further processing as required. To maximise flexibility, we allow each DCM to have individual requirements for context information, thus the interface between the component and decision point is not fixed during the component's design. The interface is negotiated at the point of loading a DCM into a decision point at run-time, therefore the dynamic wrapper will vary with every new DCM.

The negotiation of the wrapper takes the following steps (as shown in figure 3):

1. A DCM is loaded into the DEM.
2. The DEM reads the DCM to gain the list of required context information and outputs produced.
3. The DEM passes the list of required context and decision outputs to the dynamic wrapper.
4. The dynamic wrapper compares the decision outputs with those expected by the component.
5. If the decision outputs correspond correctly, the required context list is forwarded to the context manager, via the component interface.
6. The context manager checks if the context required is available and responds with the result.
7. If all context information is available, the load is complete and the component is ready to operate.
8. If the required context is not currently available or the decision outputs do not match between the component and DCM, the DCM is unloaded.

The DEM is responsible for checking DCM validity, for example parsing a configuration file, with an invalid DCM causing a load failure. A decision point without a functioning DEM and correctly loaded DCM will not be able to be evaluated normally. In this case there are several possibilities to ensure the robustness of the system, which of these is chosen is dependant on the specific component. The simplest option is for a safe default outcome to be supplied for each decision point and given as the decision result when an error occurs. Alternatively, the previous working or a default DCM for this decision point could be loaded. Whichever strategy is chosen, the default (safe) behaviour is defined for each decision point by the component developer at design-time. This approach minimises the amount of run-time error handling required while at the same time maximising safety. Further investigation of validation and verification techniques for this system is required.

Figure 3 also shows an interface between the component and the context manger. It is important to manage the communication and to allow for multiple open decision points within a single component, via some implementation specific addressing mechanism. A common data structure is needed to allow a flexible amount of context information to flow between the context manager, component interface and dynamic wrapper. The format should be of variable length and be able to convey the type, name and value of each context item.

Using a general dynamic interface will allow any embedded technology to be used (e.g.: policies, neural network weights, etc) provided a component has the correct evaluator for this type of technology. The type of embedded technology a component uses could even be changed at run-time, by the loading and unloading of evaluation modules stored in the system. In the first instance it may be sensible to use only one technology for the DEM in all components in a single system. This approach is used in the DySCAS project with policy-based computing. However, if the dynamic wrapper concept is implemented in a general way, several technologies could be used in the same system. An even more flexible system would allow the DEM in a single decision point to be changed during run-time by unloading and loading of modules.

In this description it is assumed that loading of a DCM is triggered by some event from within the system. The concept does not restrict the possible implementation of this in any way. For example, the component itself could request a new DCM, perhaps as the result of a configuration decision. Alternatively, a DCM load could result from a special interrupt, whereby a new DCM is pushed onto the component. This continues the theme of making the architecture as flexible as possible.

5 Implementation in the DySCAS Project

The overall goal of the DySCAS project is to develop a middleware that supports self-management within automotive systems. The increased demands on configuration flexibility and scalability of such systems results in the necessity to implement knowledge-based autonomics within the system middleware in order to make this system aware of the dynamically changing environment.

Policy-based computing is one of the techniques that supports autonomic decision making and is one of the most suitable solutions to be applied in the resource constrained context-aware environments. Policies written using defined semantics are usually held externally to the complied embedded code and may be changed at run-time, enabling post-deployment changes in system functionality.

In this context one of the specific technologies that can be used for expressing dynamic behaviour is AGILE, a general policy description language [16, 21]. Main features of this language include support for dynamic reconfiguration and self-stabilisation. The variety of constructs available in AGILE make this a very efficient tool for the implementation of policy-based configurations.

The AGILE library is written for the .NET environment and supports AGILE policy language syntax and semantics and provides set of tools and interfaces for writing policy-based context-aware applications. Because this library wasn't designed to satisfy typical embedded systems resource constraints, a more efficient and resource conscious version of this library, called AGILE-Lite, has been developed. Main features of the AGILE and AGILE-Lite [21] libraries are compared in figure 4.

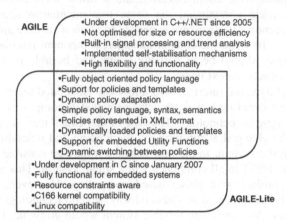

Fig. 4. Comparison of features of the AGILE and AGILE-Lite libraries

DySCAS specifies a set of use-case scenarios to be supported. These serve to both define functional requirements the DySCAS middleware must provide and showcase some novel aspects of this project. Use-case scenarios are categorised into four so-called Generic Use-Cases (GUC) and a subset of Specific Use-Cases (SUC) within each GUC. DySCAS Generic Use-Cases are the following:

- GUC1 - New device attached to the vehicle;
  - o   exemplary SUC2: Negotiating and contracting of functionalities.
- GUC2 - Integrating new software functionality;
  - o   exemplary SUC1: Selecting software packages to be installed.
- GUC3 - Closed reconfiguration;
  - o   exemplary SUC6: Planning new system configuration.
- GUC4 - Resource optimization;
  - o   exemplary SUC1: Optimisation intelligence.

All of the mentioned use-case scenarios must be supported by the DySCAS middleware, which makes the middleware architecture design a very challenging issue. This middleware will contain numerous services (such as device discovery service, security service, prioritisation service, resource management and mapping service, etc.), that can each be policy-configurable and in this way context-aware. For each decision point the policy is loaded at the system initiation stage or later, in run-time, depending on the current environment context. The whole policy life-cycle, presented in figure 5, has to be supported by the middleware.

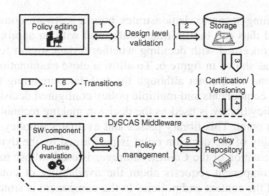

Fig. 5. The life-cycle of policies in the DySCAS project

The policy life-cycle begins with policy editing by the use of software tools. During this process the policy is validated (transition 1) in order to detect any semantic or logic errors. After the policy is validated, it is placed (transition 2) into storage (hard drive, memory key, etc.). Uploading the policy consists of certification/versioning (transition 3) to ensure integrity and the storage of the policy into the correct location in the repository (transition 4). In response to the context changes (for example a user-made or event-based decision) the policy update process is triggered. The policy manager has to find the appropriate policy version in the repository and store the decision point's currently used policy (transition 5) for rollback purposes. Finally, the new policy is transferred to the component (transition 6). This procedure allows the AGILE-Lite library to perform embedded run-time evaluation process on the newly loaded policy when a decision point is evaluated.

In reference to the architecture presented in sections 3 and 4, DySCAS uses policy based computing to implement embedded decision making. The Decision Evaluation Module (DEM) being the AGILE-Lite library and the Decision Configuration Module (DCM) is a policy file. In this implementation policy loading can be triggered by user interaction, new device connection or servicing of a vehicle by the manufacturer, for example. To aid the use of these technologies policy creation tools are under development and validation and verification methods are being investigated.

5.1 Automated Trust Decisions in DySCAS

The DySCAS project has identified a number of advanced use cases to illustrate the applicability and versatility of the dynamic adaptation scheme. A mix of simulations and demonstrator implementations are being prepared for validation and dissemination purposes. This section describes one such demonstrator which focuses on an infotainment-oriented use case involving data streaming from an external attached device such as an MP3 player or Personal Data Assistant carried by an occupant of the vehicle. Several of the mechanisms discussed above are demonstrated, including the decision point implementation with a dynamic wrapper. Due to the large variability in portable devices and media encoding schemes it is expected that during the vehicle lifetime many changes will occur. A major aim of DySCAS is to allow the vehicle's computer system to be updated throughout its lifecycle to keep up with such changes. The application also shows how robustness issues are incorporated into the methodology.

The data streaming scenario demonstrates how a software component embeds a decision point, and thus can be run-time configured with an appropriate policy. The decision point is concerned with deciding whether a data stream feed to the vehicle should be trusted, as shown in figure 6. To allow a close examination of the concepts we focus on just one component although the full data streaming use-case involves several interacting components and multiple policy configured decision points.

The AGILE policy library is used as the decision making technology and is linked inside the decision point. This library parses and evaluates a policy file as requested; all other functionality of the decision point is performed by the dynamic wrapper. A simplified implementation of the *Context Manager* is used, whose main responsibility is to respond to component requests about the availability of context information. Communication of the context and policies to the component is simulated as assumed to be operative. For diagnostic and dissemination purposes this example has been implemented in a high-level programming environment designed to run on a desktop computer and provide a view into the working of the concepts. A parallel implementation is occurring, designed to run on typical vehicle embedded hardware.

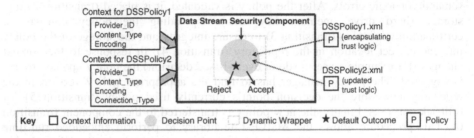

Fig. 6. A typical use of the methodology in a data stream security component

Figure 6 shows two sets of context information, which are required for evaluation of the policies "DSSPolicy1.xml" and DSSPolicy2.xml". These context requirements are specified inside the policy and are used during the wrapper negotiation process described previously. The following excerpt from "DSSPolicy1.xml" shows the specification of context requirements, ("Environment Variables" in the AGILE grammar.

```
<EnvironmentVariables>
  <EVariable Name="Provider_ID" Type="string"/>
  <EVariable Name="Content_Type" Type="string"/>
  <EVariable Name="Encoding" Type="string"/>
</EnvironmentVariables>
```

The decision point and wrapper mechanisms make it very easy for the software component developer to insert open decision points into code at any place where it is necessary to defer decision-making logic. The specification of each decision point includes the decision point identifier, the default outcome and any other possible outcomes. Output from the decision point will always be consistent with this specification. In our example, the decision point will return 0 for "Reject" or 1 for "Accept", this is assured by the wrapper which is transparent to the developer. The following C# code is used to create this decision point.

```
DecisionPoint d = new AGILEDecisionPoint("DP","0","1");
addDecisionPoint(d);
```

Here the decision point is created to operate with the AGILE library, however if other decision making technology is available a different type of decision point can be placed here. At the point in the component code where the decision point should be evaluated the following line is placed.

```
string result = evaluateDecisionPoint("DP");
```

Along with the evaluation result, the decision point also provides access to other information such as, was the default outcome used and other diagnostics. In figure 7 diagnostic traces are presented to illustrate the fault tolerance features provided by the dynamic wrapper, such as policy load errors and default behaviour.

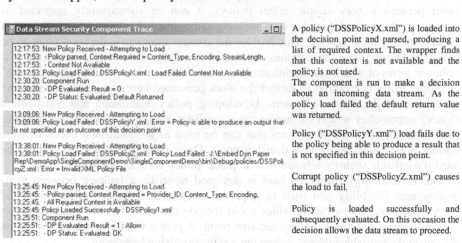

Data Stream Security Component Trace

12:17:53: New Policy Received - Attempting to Load
12:17:53: - Policy parsed, Context Required = Content_Type, Encoding, StreamLength,
12:17:53: - Context Not Avaliable
12:17:53: Policy Load Failed : DSSPolicyX.xml : Load Failed: Context Not Avaliable
12:30:20: Component Run
12:30:20: - DP Evaluated: Result = 0
12:30:20: - DP Status: Evaluated: Default Returned
13:09:06: New Policy Received - Attempting to Load
13:09:06: Policy Load Failed : DSSPolicyY.xml : Error = Policy is able to produce an output that is not specified as an outcome of this decision point
13:38:01: New Policy Received - Attempting to Load
13:38:01: Policy parsed, Policy Load Failed : J:\Embed Dyn Paper Rep\DemoApp\SingleComponentDemo\SingleComponentDemo\bin\Debug/policies/DSSPolicyZ.xml : Error = Invalid XML Policy File
13:25:45: New Policy Received - Attempting to Load
13:25:45: - Policy parsed, Context Required = Provider_ID, Content_Type, Encoding,
13:25:45: - All Required Context is Available
13:25:45: Policy Loaded Successfully : DSSPolicy1.xml
13:25:51: Component Run
13:25:51: - DP Evaluated: Result = 1 : Allow
13:25:51: - DP Status: Evaluated: OK

A policy ("DSSPolicyX.xml") is loaded into the decision point and parsed, producing a list of required context. The wrapper finds that this context is not available and the policy is not used.
The component is run to make a decision about an incoming data stream. As the policy load failed the default return value was returned.

Policy ("DSSPolicyY.xml") load fails due to the policy being able to produce a result that is not specified in this decision point.

Corrupt policy ("DSSPolicyZ.xml") causes the load to fail.

Policy is loaded successfully and subsequently evaluated. On this occasion the decision allows the data stream to proceed.

Fig. 7. Annotated diagnostic traces of the Data Stream Security Component

These traces show three occasions that a policy is not loaded correctly into the decision point. Notice how subsequent evaluation of the decision point does not result in an error, or illegal behaviour, instead the default 'safe' result is given. This feature, handled by the transparent wrapper, is at no cost to the developer and increases trust in the robustness of the methodology. An example of successful policy load and evaluation is also included. The interested reader is invited to obtain this application and investigate its functionality [22].

6 Conclusions and Future Work

In this paper we described a methodology for a dynamic embedded system where the system logic is componentised. The behaviour of these components can be altered by replacing or changing the embedded decision making module. There is a growing need for this type of dynamic architecture in embedded systems, which this work goes some way to addressing. This is made quite scalable with the use of individual localised decision points rather than a centralised controlling component. A specialised component architecture is presented to allow context-aware behaviour and run-time replaceable decision modules. A more detailed and descriptive specification of the context manager is needed to fully realise the potential of this approach.

A partial demonstration of one of the automotive use-cases has been presented, which illustrates the way in which run-time configuration can be achieved using the methodology and implementation mechanisms described. A challenging use-case was used to illustrate the need for the deferment of configuration and decision making logic. The way in which trust decisions are made will evolve over the lifetime of an artefact such as a vehicle and thus there needs to be a way to easily update the decision logic without having to replace or upgrade the embedded software mechanisms. Trust logic may also be implemented differently by different vehicle manufactures, and in some scenarios (such as fleet transport) it may be necessary to support customisation by vehicle owner or driver. As shown in this paper, once a decision point has been inserted (with perhaps a very simple initial policy), it can be subsequently upgraded as necessary. The methodology for implementing autonomic behaviour also incorporates a context management service. This enables the context inputs of a decision point to be configured during run-time, and thus not placing any design-time restrictions on the new policy in terms of which context information is available inside a particular component.

Future effort is required to further the work presented here concerning trust in the robustness of the dynamic system. Developing policy Validation and Verification (V&V) approaches would further increase confidence and acceptance. We propose that metadata be added to policies that can be used as an additional check that the correct policy is loaded into a decision point. Design time (offline) V&V could be used if a suitable security scheme were in place; policy certification for example.

The methodology presented here is designed to strike a balance between post-deployment flexibility and trust to improve acceptance. Future exploration of the autonomic possibilities this provides could include the use of a set of policies, with various context requirements, per decision point. A policy would be selected based on the currently available context, achieving a self-optimising behaviour.

Acknowledgements and DySCAS project information. The DySCAS project is funded within the 6th framework program "Information Society Technologies" of the European Commission. Project number: FP6-IST-2006-034904.

The partners are: Volvo Technology AB (the project coordinator), DaimlerChrysler AG, Enea Services AB, Robert Bosch GmbH, The University of Greenwich, The University of Paderborn, The Royal Institute of Technology (KTH), Systemite AB, and Movimento. The project started in June 2006 and runs until November 2008. Further details are available at the project website [1].

References

1. DySCAS project website: http://www.DySCAS.org
2. Anthony, R., Ekelin, C.: Policy-driven self-management for an automotive middleware. In: 1st Intl. Workshop on Policy-Based Autonomic Computing (PBAC) at 4th IEEE Intl. Conf. Autonomic Computing, pp. 55–64 (2007)
3. Anthony, R., Rettberg, A., Jahnich, I., Törngren, M., Chen, D., Ekelin, C.: Towards a Dynamically Reconfigurable Automotive Control System Architecture, Embedded System Design: Topics, Techniques and Trends, IFIP, pp. 71–84. Springer, Heidelberg (2007)

4. Anthony, R.: Policy-centric Integration and Dynamic Composition of Autonomic Computing Techniques. In: 4th International Conference on Autonomic Computing (ICAC 2006), IEEE Computer Society, Washington (2007)
5. IBM Research, Policy technologies,
   http://www.research.ibm.com/policytechnologies/
6. Lobo, J., Bhatia, R., Naqvi, S.: A policy description language. In: Proc. AAAI, pp. 291–298 (1999)
7. Kramer, J., Magee, J.: Self-Managed Systems: an Architectural Challenge. In: Proceedings of the 2007 Future of Software Engineering, pp. 259–268. IEEE Computer Society, Washington (2007)
8. Yau, S.S., Karim, F.: An Adaptive Middleware for Context-Sensitive Communications for Real-Time Applications in Ubiquitous Computing Environments. Real-Time Syst. 26(1), 29–61 (2004)
9. Costa, P., Coulson, G., Mascolo, C., Mottola, L., Picco, G.P., Zachariadis, S.: Reconfigurable Component-based Middleware for Networked Embedded Systems. International Journal of Wireless Information Networks 14(2), 149–162 (2007)
10. Naji, H.R., Wells, B.E., Etzkorn, L.: Creating an adaptive embedded system by applying multi-agent techniques to reconfigurable hardware. Future Gen. Comput. Syst. 20(6), 1055–1081 (2004)
11. Henricksen, K., Indulska, J.: Developing context-aware pervasive computing applications: Models and approach. Pervasive and Mobile Computing 2(1), 37–64 (2006)
12. Gu, T., Pung, H.K., Zhang, D.Q.: A service-oriented middleware for building context-aware services. J. Netw. Comput. Appl. 28(1), 1–18 (2005)
13. Wang, S., Shin, K.G.: An architecture for embedded software integration using reusable components. In: Proc. 2000 Intl. Conf. Compilers, Architecture, and Synthesis for Embedded Systems, pp. 110–118. ACM Press, New York (2000)
14. Schneider, K., Schuele, T., Trapp, M.: Verifying the Adaptation Behavior of Embedded Systems. In: 2006 International Workshop on Self-Adaptation and Self-Managing Systems (SEAMS 2006), pp. 16–22. ACM Press, New York (2006)
15. Beznosov, K.: On the Benefits of Decomposing Policy Engines into Components. In: ACM Intl. Conf. Proceeding Series, vol. 80 (2004)
16. Anthony, R.: The AGILE Policy Expression Language for Autonomic Systems. Intl. Trans. on Systems Science and Applications 1(4), 381–397 (2006)
17. McKinley, P.K., Sadjadi, S.M., Kasten, E.P., Cheng, B.H.: Composing adaptive software. IEEE Computer 37(7), 56–64 (2004)
18. Gilani, W., Naqvi, N.H., Spinczyk, O.: On adaptable middleware product lines. In: Proc. 3rd Workshop on Adaptive and Reflective Middleware, pp. 207–213. ACM, New York (2004)
19. Georgas, J.C., van der Hoek, A., Taylor, R.N.: Architectural runtime configuration management in support of dependable self-adaptive software. In: Proc. 2005 Workshop on Architecting Dependable Systems (WADS 2005), pp. 1–6. ACM, New York (2005)
20. Elfatatry, A.: Dealing with change: components versus services. Commun. ACM 50(8), 35–39 (2007)
21. Pelc, M., Anthony, R.: Towards Policy-Based Self-Configuration of Embedded Systems. System and Information Sciences Notes 2(1), 20–26 (2007)
22. Policy Autonomics website, demonstration application, http://staffweb.cms.gre.ac.uk/~ar26/Research/PolicyAutonomics/publications_development/embedbehavior

Service Discovery of IP Cameras Using SIP and Zeroconf Protocols

Yi-Chih Tung[1], Chien-Min Ou[2], Wen-Jyi Hwang[1,*], and Wei-De Wu[1]

[1] Department of Computer Science and Information Engineering,
National Taiwan Normal University, Taipei, 117, Taiwan
{g94470041,whwang,g95470103}@csie.ntnu.edu.tw
[2] Department of Electronics Engineering, Ching-Yun University,
Chungli, 320, Taiwan
cmou@cyu.edu.tw

Abstract. This paper presents a novel framework for remote access of IP cameras with minimum pr-configuration cost. Although the usual service discovery protocols such as Zeroconf can be adopted for simplifying the pre-configuration procedures, the protocols are limited only for local services. The proposed protocol, termed STDP (Service Trader Discovery Protocol), is able to provide remote IP camera services while requiring minimum configuration complexity. The STDP is a hybrid combination of Zeroconf and SIP (session initial protocol). The Zeroconf is adopted for the discovery and/or publication of local services; whereas, the SIP is used for the delivery of local services to the remote nodes. With simple plug-and-play pre-configuration, services provided by IP cameras are then remotely available. This protocol is well-suited for high mobility applications where the fast deployment and low administration efforts of IP cameras are desired.

1 Introduction

An IP camera (IP CAM) is a video camera that contains a hardware video encoder and an embedded processor with a TCP/IP interface. It is a stand alone unit that can be directly connected to the internet without the need for a separate computer. It also has a built-in web server, which provides the ability for accessing digital images and configuring the camera. Its digital output allows the camera easily integrated with a wide range of applications, including e-surveillance, web attractions and remote monitoring. In these applications, IP CAMs are usually deployed in the environments with dynamic locations. Without a static IP address information, accessing the web server associated with the IP CAMs is difficult. In addition, for a service consumer, it is not possible to always have a complete overview over these applications and their availability. The dynamics of recent networks make this process even more complex.

One way to solve the problem is by the employment of service discovery protocols, such as SLP (Service Location Protocol) [3], Jini [10], UPnP (Universal

---

* To whom all correspondence should be sent.

C. Rong et al. (Eds.): ATC 2008, LNCS 5060, pp. 388–402, 2008.

Plug-and-Play) [5], and Zeroconf [2], [4]. In the service discovery environment, IP CAMs and other devices advertise themselves, supplying details about their capabilities and the information one must know to access the service (e.g., the IP address). Nevertheless, existing service discovery protocols are limited only to local area networks (LANs). For many IP CAM applications, remote access is required. An effective protocol for remote service of IP CAMs is therefore desired for these applications.

This paper proposed a novel SIP (Session Initiation Protocol)-based framework, termed STDP (Service Trader Discovery Protocol), for the remote accesses of IP CAMs. SIP [9] is a protocol developed by IETF to assist in providing advanced telephony services across the internet. Basically it is a signaling protocol used for establishing sessions in an IP network. In the SIP, location of clients are maintained and updated in the registrar server. The IP address of the target node can be obtained by a query to the server. Although a direct deployment of SIP to an IP CAM is possible for accessing digital images, a number of modifications are desired. For many home network applications, costly manual pre-configurations should be avoided. However, the deployment of SIP requires the assignment of an unique pair of SIP URI and password to each IP CAM. This may result in a high manual pre-configuration cost when the number of IP CAM is large. On the contrary, there is no pre-configuration cost for the existing service discovery protocols permitting accesses only to LAN. The goal of STDP therefore is to simplify/eliminate the administration efforts associated with the remote access protocols for IP CAM applications.

The proposed STDP protocol is a hybrid combination of the Zeroconf and SIP protocols. The Zeroconf protocol is a light weight protocol supporting service discovery in a LAN. As compared with other service discovery protocols, it imposes minimal implementation cost for an embedded system. IP CAMs using the Zeroconf protocol can be deployed with simple plug-and-play. Consequently, the hybrid combination allows the remote accesses of IP CAM while enjoying low pre-configuration cost.

To implement the STDP, the SIP is required to be deployed only on a single node, termed trader, in the LAN. This assures the minimal pre-configuration cost for the system. The trader is responsible for collecting the service information provided by all the other nodes in LAN via the Zeroconf protocol. A remote access to any IP CAM in the LAN can be accomplished by first retrieving the service information from the trader using the SIP. Based on the information, the IP address of any IP CAM in the LAN can be found. A remote node can then access the web server associated with the target IP CAM based on the retrieved service information. The proposed STDP protocol has been implemented in a dynamic network environment. Physical tests reveal that the IP CAMs supporting only simple Zeroconf protocols can be easily accessed by a remote host. The proposed STDP protocol is therefore beneficial for a wide range of IP CAM applications requiring dynamic deployment.

2   Preliminaries

The proposed STDP is a hybrid combination of SIP and Zeroconf. Therefore, in this section, we give a brief description of these two protocols. The independent applications of these two protocols for accessing IP CAMs are also discussed.

2.1   SIP

SIP is a signaling protocol used for establishing sessions in an IP network. The user agents and servers are the major components of the protocol. A user agent is a end-user device. A user agent client (UAC) issues a request and a user agent server (UAS) responds to the request. When the SIP is applied for the remote access of a IPCAM, in the simplest form the UAC is a viewer and the UAS is the IP-CAM, as shown in Figure 1. In this case, the location of the IP-CAM should be fixed, and should be known to the viewer.

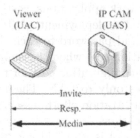

Fig. 1. Basic application of SIP for IP CAM

To support the mobility for the IP CAM, the employment of SIP servers are necessary. Commonly used SIP servers include the registrar and proxy server. A SIP registrar handles registration messages. It is associated with a databases (termed location server) containing user agent locations. A SIP proxy server can be viewed as the router in the SIP level that forward SIP requests and responses. In addition, it provides functions for authentication and authorization.

Figure 2 shows a simple example, which uses proxy, registrar and location servers with the INVITE message for session establishment. As shown in the figure, an IP CAM first registers its location in the location server. A SIP proxy server then accepts an INVITE request made by a UAC and queries location server to find UAS location. Based on the address received from the server, the proxy server forwards the INVITE message to the UAS. The session will then be established after the acknowledgements from UAS are received. It can be observed from the example that the viewer does not have to know the IP CAM location prior to a connection establishment. In addition, the UAS is allowed to change its location without informing the UAC. Only a registration request to the registrar server for location updating is required.

In addition to supporting the user mobility, the SIP offers the event notification framework [7], [8], which uses SUBSCRIBE/NOTIFY messages for subscribing to, and receiving notifications of, SIP-related events within SIP networks.

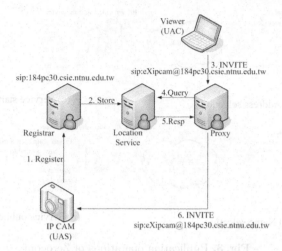

Fig. 2. A simple SIP-based framework for remotely accessing IP CAM

The ability to request asynchronous notification of events proves useful in many services for which cooperation between devices is required. Examples of such services for IP phone applications include automatic callback services (based on terminal state events), buddy lists (based on user presence events) and message waiting indications (based on mailbox state change events).

The SIP allows the remote access of IP CAM with mobility support and event notification. To use the SIP, however, each IP CAM should be associated with a pair of SIP URI and password. The high manual pre-configuration cost and administration efforts for the deployment of IP CAMs are therefore necessary. This is undesirable for many IP CAM applications.

2.2 Zeroconf

Zeroconf is a protocol for discovering services available in a local network. A Zeroconf network is one that can exist without a central control component, and works without any kind of manual pre-configuration.

Zeroconf can directly be adopted for discovering IP CAM in the LAN. It involves address assignment, name translation and service discovery without central servers. The address assignment for a node in Zeroconf network can simply be accomplished by randomly selecting an address in the range of 169.254.1.0 to 169.254.254.255. The node then does an ARP probe for the address. If there are any responses, the node chooses another IP address at random, and tries the ARP probe again.

The name translation in Zeroconf network is solved by the multicast DNS (mDNS) standard, which eliminates the requirement for DNS server. In the standard, all the nodes in the LAN listens to a specific IP multicast address. A node wish to publish a name will broadcast the selected name to this multicast address. Other nodes having the same name then reply to the requesting node. The name translation can be accomplished in a similar fashion. Instead of using

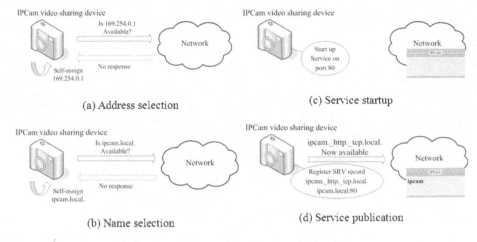

(a) Address selection

(c) Service startup

(b) Name selection

(d) Service publication

Fig. 3. Publication operations of Zeroconf

fully qualified domain name (FQDN), a node name in the .local name space is used for mDNS.

Another standard, termed DNS Service Discovery (DNS-SD) can be used for the service discovery in Zeroconf. DNS-SD works particularly well with mDNS, since it also uses DNS records. Three basic operations are included in the DNS-SD: publication, discovery and resolution. The goal of publication is to advertise a service. The discovery operation is used to browse for available service. Based on the results of discovery operation, the resolution operation is adopted for translating service names to addresses and port numbers.

Figures 3, 4 and 5 show a simple example of these DNS-SD operations for a local network consisting of an IP CAM. The publication operations of Zeroconf are shown in Figure 3, which consists of address selection (Figure 3.(a)), name selection (Figure 3.(b)), service start up (Figure 3.(c)) and service broadcast (Figure 3.(d)). In Figure 3.(a), the IP CAM randomly selects the IP address 169.254.0.1, and announces it to the network. Because no devices respond to the announcement, the IP CAM takes the address as its own. In Figure 3.(b), it starts up its own multicast DNS responder, requests the host name ipcam.local., verifies its availability, and takes the name as its own. In Figure 3.(c), the IP CAM starts up a video service on TCP port 80. Finally, in Figure 3.(d), it publishes the service instance, of type _http._tcp, under the name ipcam, in the .local domain. It should be noted that the service type (i.e., _http._tcp) contains two fields: the first field (i.e., _http) is service dependent, and the second field (i.e., _tcp) indicates the transportation protocol used by the service. The service type will be used for service browsing and discovery. The instance name (i.e., ipcam) is device dependent. That is, devices sharing the same service type will have different instance names. The service instance therefore can be used for the query of port and IP address of a device.

Figure 4 depicts the service query and discovery in the Zeroconf network. In this example, the service type queried by the viewer shown in Figure 4.(a)

(a) Query by service type   (b) Response

Fig. 4. Service query and discovery in Zeroconf

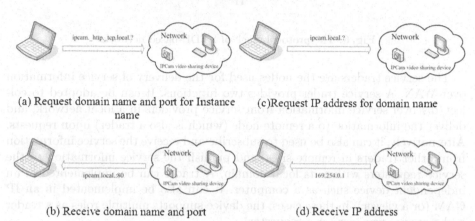

(a) Request domain name and port for Instance   (c)Request IP address for domain name
name

(b) Receive domain name and port   (d) Receive IP address

Fig. 5. The query for domain name, port and IP address in Zeroconf

is _http._tcp. The service instance discovered from the network is ip-cam._http._tcp.local, which represents an IP CAM. Based on the service instance, the viewer can further query for the port, domain name and IP address of the IP CAM using resolution operation, as shown in Figure 5.

Although Zeroconf requires no pre-configuration cost, it has the major drawback that the protocol can only be used in a local network. For IP CAM applications, however, remote accesses are usually desired.

3   STDP

The goal of STDP is to eliminate the drawbacks of accessing IP CAMs based only on SIP or Zeroconf protocols. It provides remote access of IP CAM with minimal pre-configuration cost. As shown in Figure 6, the STDP is an application layer control protocol that utilizes both SIP and Zeroconf. A STDP-based network contains three basic components: service provider, service requester, and service trader. In our design, the service provider and requester are an IP CAM and a viewer, respectively. Although the primary goal of the STDP is for the design of IP CAM systems, the STDP apply equally well to the broader group, where the service provider and service requester can be any networked appliances demanding low pre-configuration cost and efficient remote access.

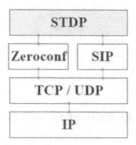

Fig. 6. The protocol stack of STDP-based networks

The service traders are the nodes used for the delivery of service information over WAN. A service trader provides two functions. It can be adopted to collect/discover service information from service providers in a local network, and deliver the information to a remote node (which is also a trader) upon requests. Alternatively, it can also be used to subscribe and receive the service information from other traders in remote sites, and publish the service information to the service requesters within its local domain. A trader can be implemented in an independent device such as a computer. It can also be implemented in an IP CAM (or a viewer). In these cases, the device supports multiple roles as a trader and a service provider (or a requester).

The communications between two service traders are based on SIP protocol, as shown in Figure 7. Each trader can be an UAC and/or an UAS. Each local network needs only one service trader. Each of the service providers and requesters talk to its trader in the same LAN for the delivery of local service information. From Figure 7, we observe that the Zeroconf is adopted for the communication between a trader and a service requester (or a provider). Therefore, in our design, the service provider and requester need to support Zeroconf protocol.

To obtain information from a service provider to a service requester, both the SIP and Zeroconf protocols are used. The STDP provides a mechanism for the service information exchange between the SIP and Zeroconf. Based on the acquired service information, the viewer then can access the IP CAM using the HTTP protocol.

To discuss the STDP protocol in more detail, we divide the protocol into three parts, as depicted in Figure 8. The first part concerns with the communication between a trader and a service provider. It can be observed from Figure 8.(a) that the trader will receive service information published by an IP CAM. The trader can also actively discover the service provided by an IP CAM. All the publish and discovery operations are based on Zeroconf protocol, which are illustrated in Figures 3-5.

However, it should be noted that the address assignment scheme shown in Figure 3.(a) is not adopted in our design. This is because the address selected by Zeroconf is valid only for local access. Our design allows any address assignment scheme for acquiring an IP address for global access, including the dynamic address assignment using the DHCP.

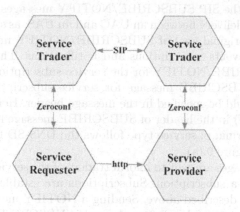

Fig. 7. STDP topology

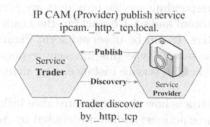

(a) Communication between Trader and Provider

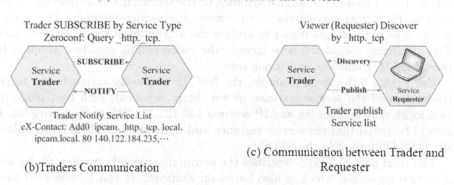

(b)Traders Communication

(c) Communication between Trader and Requester

Fig. 8. STDP protocol messages

The second part of the STDP protocol focuses on the interactions between traders. This part of the protocol is based on the SIP. Service traders accompanied by service providers are the UASs in the SIP. An UAS discovers/collects local services available, and delivers the service information to other UACs upon request. An UAC is the service traders accompanied by service requesters. It sends subscription requests to UASs for acquiring the service information. Once the UAC obtains service notifications from UASs, it publishes the service information to its own service requesters.

In the STDP, the SIP SUBSCRIBE/NOTIFY messages are used for the service information delivery between an UAC and an UAS, as shown in Figure 8.(b). In the SIP, the original goal of SUBSCRIBE/NOTIFY messages is to provide the SIP related events subscriptions and notifications. The STDP extends the usage of SUBSCRIBE/NOTIFY for the service subscription and notification.

To use the SUBSCRIBE message for service subscription, the type of services desired should be specified in the message header. Here we augment a field (termed Zeroconf) in the header of SUBSCRIBE message for specifying the service type. The format of service type follows the DNS-SD format as _http._tcp, as depicted in Figure 9.(a).

NOTIFY messages are sent to inform traders of the service available for which the traders have a subscription. Subscriptions are established using the SUBSCRIBE method described above. Sending a NOTIFY message does not terminate the corresponding subscription. A single SUBSCRIBE request may trigger several NOTIFY messages. In each NOTIFY message, the list of services and the IP address of the corresponding service providers are carried. We also augment two fields (termed Zeroconf and eX-Contact) in the header of NOTIFY message to achieve this objective. It can be observed form Figure 9.(b) that the Zeroconf field indicates the service type this message response to. The eX-Contact field contains 5 items: action, service instance, host name, port number and IP address.

The action item instructs how the service instance included in field should be handled. There are three actions: addition (denoted by Add), deletion (denoted by Del), and updating (denoted by Upd). The addition action instructs the target service trader to add the service instance to the service list. The deletion action informs the target service trader to remove the service instance. The update action directs the target trader to update the attributes of the service instance. The attributes considered here include the video coding standard adopted by the IP CAM, frame size and frame rate.

Use Figure 9.(b) as an example, the NOTIFY message instructs the target trader to add the service instance ipcam._http._tcp.local, with host name ipcam.local, port number 80, and IP address 140.122.184.235, to its service list. It should be noted that the service instance and domain name should also follows the DNS-DS format in the STDP.

The final part of STDP describes the communications between a trader and a service requester, which is also based on Zeroconf. It can be observed from Figure 8.(c) that the trader will then publish the service information collected from other traders to the service requester. The service requester may also actively discover the service information from the trader.

Three parts of the STDP protocol depicted in Fig.8 may operate independently. That is, the SIP and Zeroconf protocols are not required to operate at a pre-specified order in the STDP. Figure 10 shows two examples of STDP message flows. For the sake of brevity, only two LANs are considered in each example. Nevertheless, the message flows can easily be extended to the scenarios containing large number of LANs. As shown in Figure 10, LAN A in each example

SUBSCRIBE SIP URI of Trader A
From: SIP URI of Trader B
To: SIP URI of Trader A
Contact: SIP URI of Trader B
Call-ID: call identifier
CSeq: sequence number SUBSCRIBE
Event: presence
Expires: seconds until SUBSCRIBE expires
Allow-Events: presence, refer
Zeroconf: Query _http._tcp
Content-Length: 0

(a) SUBSCRIBE message for service subscription

NOTIFY SIP URI of Trader B
From: SIP URI of Trader A
To: SIP URI of Trader B
Contact: SIP URI of Trader A
Call-ID: call identifier
CSeq: sequence number NOTIFY
Event: presence
Subscription-State: active;expires= seconds until SUBSCRIBE expires
Allow-Events: presence, refer
Zeroconf: Response _http._tcp
eX-Contact: Add0 ipcam._http._tcp.local. ipcam.local. 80 140.122.184.235,
Content-Length: ...

(SDP not show)

(b) NOTIFY message for service notification.

Fig. 9. Extensions of SUBSCRIBE/NOTIFY messages for STDP service subscription and notification

contains a service requester and a trader (termed Trader 1). LAN B consists of two service providers (termed Service Provider 1 and Service Provider 2) and a service trader (termed Trader 2).

Figure 10.(a) illustrates the scenario, in which Trader 1 and Trader 2 first find their own service requester and service providers via PUBLISH/DISCOVERY messages. The service information of the service providers is then delivered from LAN B to LAN A via SUBSCRIBE/NOTIFY messages. After receiving the service information, Trader 1 then publishes this information to the Service Requester. As shown in Figure 10.(a), after the Service Requester received the service information, it selects the Service Provider 2 as its target device. The Service Requester then issues directly a service request via HTTP protocol to Service Provider 2. Direct video delivery from Service Provider 2 to Service Requester then follows.

For the scenario shown in Figure 10.(b), it is assumed that the Service Requester and Service Providers are not online at the beginning. The communication between Traders 1 and 2 is first established. This is then followed by a

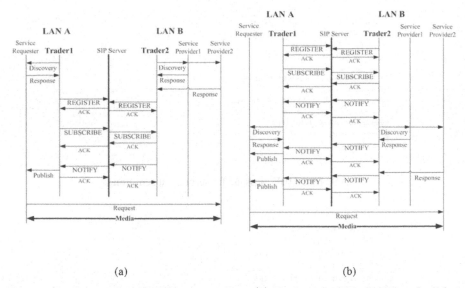

(a)   (b)

Fig. 10. Two examples of STDP message flow: (a) Trader 1 and Trader 2 first find their own service requester and service providers via PUBLISH/DISCOVERY messages. (b) Trader 1 and Trader 2 first establish their connection via SUBSCRIBE/NOTIFY messages.

series of service information updating/notification when service providers and service requester become available. Similar to the case shown in Figure 10.(a), the Service Requester finally selects the Service Provider 2 as its target device for the IP CAM service.

As shown in Figure 7, the service trader plays a major role in STDP. It connects different local networks, and operates in back-to-back mode. It acts as a SIP user agent on one side, and as a Zeroconf end device on the other side. A trader has 4 operations. To further elaborate these operations, Figure 11 depicts their flowchart in detail. The first operation is to send Discovery or Publish messages. In this operation, the trader acts as a Zeroconf end device searching or publishing the services available. In the second operation, the trader acts as a SIP UAC, and send SUBSCRIBE message for triggering the SIP event notification mechanism. After sending the SUBSCRIBE message, the trader will then waits and receives one or more NOTIFY messages for updating the service list. The trader behaves as a SIP UAS in the third operation, which receives the SIP SUBSCRIBE message. The trader will then send one or more NOTIFY messages to the subscribing node. The fourth operation receives the Discovery or Publish messages, where the trader functions again as a Zeroconf end device. This operation and the first operation are essential for a trader to acquire the service available from the service provider, or deliver the service to the service requester.

Note that the SIP is required to be installed in the service traders because of the operations of SUBSCRIBE/NOTIFY. Only one node in a local network needs

Fig. 11. Operation flowchart of a trader

to be the service trader. For the other nodes, only the implementation of Zeroconf is necessary. The employment of Zeroconf protocol can effectively reduce the pre-configuration efforts, because the protocol allows the simple plug-and-play. By contrast, the SIP devices require the assignments of SIP URI and password. For the stand alone embedded systems such as IP CAMs, the assignments may require considerable efforts especially when the number of IP CAMs is large. The STDP therefore provides an effective approach for lowering pre-configuration cost and providing remote access.

4   Experimental Results

The STDP protocol has been implemented in a test-bed that realizes the scenario proposed in Figure 12. Similar to Fig.10, The scenario consists of two local networks (termed LAN A and LAN B in the figure). LAN A consists of a number of laser printers, one IE browser and 4 IP CAMs. LAN B contains a number of laser printers, one personal computer and one IE browser. As shown in the figure, an IP CAM and a personal computer serve as the service trader in the LAN A and LAN B, respectively. The IE browser in each local network is the service requester in that local network.

All the IP CAMs and laser printers in both LANs are the service providers. They are all of the type _http._tcp. Their IP addresses are dynamically assigned by a DHCP server. Each IP CAM obtains its own hostname following the procedure shown in Figure 3.(b). Consequently, no manual pre-configuration is necessary for the IP CAMs serving only as the service provider. Only the IP CAM functioning both as trader and service provider requires the manual pre-configuration, because the assignments of SIP URI and password are necessary.

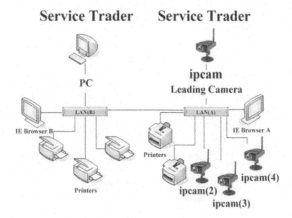

Fig. 12. The scenario for our experiment

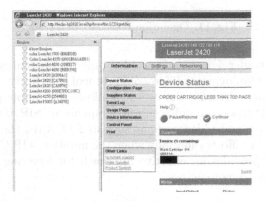

Fig. 13. All the services of type _http._tcp discovered in LAN B without the employment of STDP

Note that, in addition to the IP CAMs, the laser printers are included in this scenario. Since the laser printers supports Zeroconf, detecting the service provided by the laser printers in different local networks demonstrates the fact that the proposed protocol can be adopted for the discovery of services provided by various Zeroconf-based devices.

In our experiment, a reference design kit (RDK) based on a 200-MHz ARM 920 CPU and an MPEG4 encoder ASIC is used for the IP CAM design. The employment of MPEG4 ASIC allows the source video sequence to be encoded in real-time. Both the wired and wireless LAN interfaces (i.e., 802.3 and 802.11) are also available in the IP CAMs. The operating system of the IP CAMs is Linux. The Bonjour software development kit (SDK) [1] is adopted for the Zeroconf implementation in the IP CAM. In addition, the PJSIP library [6] is used for the SIP UAC and UAS implementations of the IP CAM functioning as a trader (i.e., the IP CAM with host name ipcam in Figure 12).

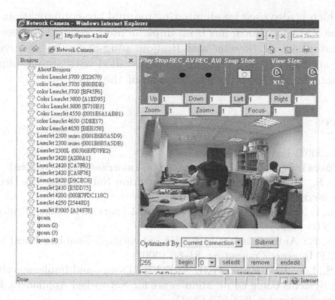

Fig. 14. All the services of type _http._tcp discovered in LAN B with the employment of STDP

Since the IE browser is used as the service requester in each LAN, it is necessary for the browser to support the Zeroconf. In our implementation, the Bonjour plug-in is adopted, which is able to discover the services of type _http._tcp. Figure 13 shows all the services of type _http._tcp discovered by the IE browser in LAN B without the employment of STDP. It can be observed from the figure that these services are actually the services provided by the laser printers in LAN B. This is consistent with our scenario presented in Figure 12. Figure 14 depicts the search results by the same IE browser with the employment of STDP. In the figure, it can be found that all the services of type _http._tcp available in LAN A and LAN B can be identified. In particular, all the IP CAMs in LAN A can be discovered by the IE browser in LAN B. Moreover, the web page and source video of each IP CAM can be easily accessed by clicking the host name of that IP CAM in the browser, as shown in Figure 14 for accessing the IP CAM with host name ipcam(4). Based on the experiments, it can then be concluded that the STDP provides an effective approach for the remote access of IP CAMs, while requiring minimal pre-configuration cost and administration efforts.

5   Conclusion Remarks

The proposed STDP protocol has been found to be effective for IP CAM applications. It allows both remote access and dynamic deployment of IP CAMs without the need of manual pre-configuration. In the STDP, the service lists from remote hosts are obtained by SIP SUBSCRIBE/NOTIFY event notification mechanism. The service discovery and publish in a local network are then based on Zeroconf protocol, which is also used for eliminating manual pre-configuration. A test-bed verifying the STDP protocol has been implemented. From the experiment, it is observed that a basic IE browser with Bonjour plug-in can be effectively used for the remote access of IP CAMs, which are installed with simple plug-and-play. All these facts demonstrate the effectiveness of the STDP.

References

1. Bonjour (2007) lasted visited,
   http://developer.apple.com/opensource/internet/bonjour.html
2. Cheshire, S., Steinberg, D.H.: Zero Configuration Networking: The Definite Guide. O'Reilly Media, Inc, Sebastopol (2005)
3. Guttman, E., Perkins, C., Veizades, J., Day, M.: Service Location Protocol, Version 2, RFC 2608 (1999)
4. Guttman, E.: Autoconfiguration for IP Networking: Enabling Local Communication. IEEE Internet Computing, 81–86 (2001)
5. Kim, D.S., Lee, J.M., Kwon, W.H., Yuh, I.K.: Design and Implementation of Home Network Systems Using UPnP Middleware for Networked Appliances. IEEE Trans. Consumer Electronics, 963–972 (2002)
6. PJSIP.ORG last visited (2007), http://www.pjsip.org/
7. Rahman, M., Braun, D., Bushmitch, D.: A framework to access networked appliances in wide area networks. In: Proc. IEEE Consumer Communications and Networking Conference, pp. 261–266 (2005)
8. Roach, A.: Session Initiation Protocol (SIP)-Specific Event Notification, RFC 3265 (2002)
9. Rosenberg, J., Schulzrinne, H., Camarillo, G., Johnston, A., Peterson, J., Sparks, R., Handley, M.: SIP: Session Initiation Protocol, RFC 3261 (2002)
10. Waldo, J.: The Jini Specifications, 2nd edn. Addison-Wesley, Reading (2000)

Adaptability of the TRSIM Model to Some Changes in Agents Behaviour*

Alberto Caballero, Juan A. Botia, and Antonio Gómez-Skarmeta

Universidad de Murcia, Campus Espinardo, Murcia, España
{acaballero,juanbot,skarmeta}@um.es

Abstract. Trust and reputation models are very useful tools to assist decision making process within agents. They can help to represent and to approximately predict the behaviour of the agents in a system. Trust and reputation values can be used to recognize the agents with a good-expected performance. This way, trust and reputation models offer an adaptive mechanism to guide interactions between agents. In this paper we study the behaviour of TRSIM model when it is applied to consumer-provider scenario. We present several experimental evidences related with the stability of the model for different types of requirements of the consumer, and recognition of different types of providers. Also, we study the ability of the model to adapt to behavioural changes of provider agents.

1 Introduction

To mitigate the absence of information or the existence of incomplete or inaccurate information about the behaviour of the agents into a system, we need some mechanisms to reduce the risks produced by choosing eventually inappropriate agents to interact with them.

Each agent in a multi-agent system can show very different behaviour given the situation defined by its environment and the user requirements. For instance, in a consumer - provider scenario, consumer agents prefer to interact (to negotiate, to cooperate, etc.) with high-performance providers. In a number of these environments, there is not a central entity capable to provide information about the behaviour of others. For that, each agent must create and update their own information model about the performance of others. This way, it can decide whom interacts to solve a particular problem, given a certain situation.

Trust and reputation models offer good solutions to represent and to predict the behaviour of agents in a system [7,11,9,5,11,4,6,8,10,3]. Trust and reputation values can be used as a criterion to identify agents who are expected to show good behaviour. In other words, those who are able to offer a high-quality solution for a given problem. Thus, a trust and reputation model can provide adaptive

* This paper is supported by a Fundación Carolina scholarship and also by the Spanish Ministry of Education and Science in the scope of the Research Project TIN-2005-08501-C03-02 and by the Project "Análisis, Estudio y Desarrollo de Sistemas Inteligentes y Servicios Telemáticos" through the Fundación Séneca within the Program "Generación del Conocimiento Científico de Excelencia".

C. Rong et al. (Eds.): ATC 2008, LNCS 5060, pp. 403–417, 2008.

mechanisms to guide the interactions. The models can use trust and reputation information to recognize the quality of the solution that agents offer.

A robust trust and reputation model can be capable to adapt to the changes that take place in the behaviour of agents. In each moment, the models need to adjust the trust and reputation values in order to give an updated and real estimate about the performance of other agents. For instance, when a given agent decreases the quality of the responses that offers, the models must be capable to reduce the trust in him. In the same way, when some agent improves the quality of his responses, trust in him must be increased.

This paper shows some experimental evidence about the behaviour of the TRSIM model, from different points of view, when is applied to a consumer - provider environment. This work studies the way that TRSIM reaches a stable status for different types of consumer requirements, the ability of the model to recognize the type of providers given the quality of the responses that they offer, and the ability to adapt to behavioural changes of provider agents.

The paper is structured as follows. Section 2 talks about previous studies and the relationship with other works. Section 3 introduces structure, main characteristics and general functionality of the model. Section 4 defines the experimental conditions and simulation algorithm used in these studies. In section 5 we present a set of experiments where the quality of solutions that agents have do not change in the simulation. In this case, we study when and how the model stability is reached for different consumer requirements, and, how the model is capable to recognize the quality of solutions that agents have using trust and reputation information. In other hand, section 6 offers experimental results related to the ability of the model to adapt to some changes in the behaviour of provider agents. Finally, in section 7 some conclusions are given.

2   Motivation and Related Work

In previous works we define a trust and reputation model in a MAS to propose a suitable response for a consumer requirement in a P2P environment where agents can be consumer or provider of resources [1]. This model considers trust and reputation as emergent properties of direct interactions between agents, based on multiple interactions between two parties. In this model, trust is a belief an agent has about the performance of the other party to solve a given task, according to its own knowledge. Moreover, reputation is related to the same belief but based on the opinions of other agents in the community.

Contrary to other models [9,5,11], where trust and reputation values are obtained as global values only associated to a peer, our model associates trust and reputation to the specification of the task that agents need to delegate by contracting. The performance of a given agent can be very different, according to the specification of the task that it executes or the requirements of the user that it represents. Some models consider that trust or reputation are associated to the user requirements or a particular dimension [7,4,6,8]. Griffiths [4] proposes a experience-based mechanism to model the trustworthiness of agents according to various criteria. He presents the notion of multi-dimensional trust to manage several facets of trust and combine them into a unique value, according to the preferences of the agent. Wang and Vassileva propose a P2P model to compute trust and reputation from different dimensions and combines them using Bayesian networks [10]. Ramchurn *et al.* [6] combine trust and reputation from different informational sources using a weighted average, where each weight represent the importance of each source.

In other previous work, we study some experimental results related with the refinement process of our model in order to identify the suitable structure, functions and parameters to correctly manage trust and reputation [2]. Now, we study the stability and adaptability of the model analyzing some metrics such as satisfaction degree, error in recommending the suitable response, and trust for a given agent. In this way, we take into account the criterion of stability used by Carbó *et al.* [3]. They consider that model reaches the stability when the variations of error do not exceed a given threshold.

3 Model Structure

Basically, the model is structured and operates following the schema given in the figure 1. TRSIM model is composed by a set of information bases that each agent stores about the behaviour of the others and a set of functions to operate with these bases. Following a distributed approach imposed by P2P environments, each agent manages its own bases of experiences. Functions appearing in the figure produces values to guide the interactions between agents, based on trust and reputation concepts.

From the point of view of an agent, that needs to solve a given task, the model has two bases of experiences to obtain trust and reputation values for

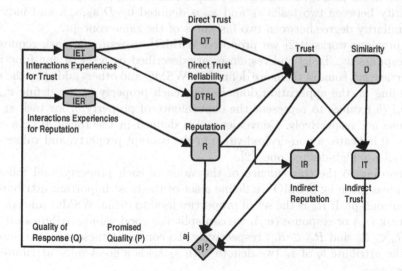

Fig. 1. Relationship between different parts of the model

this task: base of experiences for trust (IET) and for reputation (IER). Trust and reputation values are produced by means of the right combination of some functions, and information interchanged between agents. (The way to combine informational sources is based on the ideas given by ReGreT [7]). First, by introspection of the bases of experiences, the model calculates direct trust (DT), reputation (R) and reliability of DT $(DTRL)$, and combines them to produce a unique value of global trust, using the function (T). The value, aggregated from direct trust DT, its reliability $DTRL$ and reputation R, is used to select the partners in the interaction, to ask about the solution or about others.

If the bases of experiences do not have available information about the previous experiences for a given task, the model obtains the values of trust (by means of function DT) and reputation (by means of function R) for a similar task and combines these values with the similarity degree between two tasks, given by function D. For that, the model uses functions IT and IR to select the partners in the interaction for both purposes.

Initiator agent interacts with the recommended agent and solves its task with the response offered by the selected partner. In this moment, the initiator agent produces information related with the interaction that it may use to update its own bases of experiences. For that, our model gives two functions: fulfillment of the promised satisfaction (P) and quality of the response (Q).

3.1   Domain-Dependent Functions: Quality and Similarity

There are two important functions in the model whose definition depends on the representations of tasks and responses: quality of the solution given the task that it solves, and similarity between two tasks. The quality of the solution, denoted by $Q(w_j, s_k)$, indicates how much the response w_j satisfies the requirements specified in the task s_k, based on the comparison of both concepts. In other hand, similarity between two tasks s_k and s_p is denoted by $D(s_k, s_p)$, and indicates the similarity degree between two instances of the same concept.

In previous works [1,2] we proposed WSMO[1] to represent task request s_k and response w_j. Tasks and responses are described by a set of non-functional properties (b_i), some of them are defined by WSMO and others added by the user, depending on the application domain. For each property b_i, we define $v_{s_k}(b_i)$ and $v_{w_j}(b_i)$ values to represent the convenience of property b_i for task s_k and response w_j, respectively. Convenience are defined in the range $[0,1]$, a value near to 0 indicates a non-desired value in the concept property, and values near to 1 indicate high-desired ones [2].

According to the convenience of the value of each property, and following some ideas given by WSMO we define a set of the most important attributes of a given concept. If R_u is the set of properties used to define WSMO concepts, for each task (s_k) or response (w_j), we can split the good-value attributes into the sets $R_g \subset R_u$ and $R_w \subset R_u$, respectively. To construct these sets, we consider that the attribute b_i of s_k (we denote with $s_k.b_i$) is a good-value attribute and

---

[1] Web Service Modeling Ontology. http://www.w3.org/Submission/WSMO/

hence $b_i \in R_g$ if $s_k.b_i \geq \lambda_i$ (λ_i is a domain-dependent threshold value). In the same way, an attribute b_i of w_j is a good-value and $b_i \in R_w$ if $w_j.b_i \geq \lambda_i$.

Using the sets of the most prominent attributes, defined above, and considering how many task attributes are satisfied by response, the function to compute the quality of the solution is written as follows:

$$Q(w_j, s_k) = \sin\left(\frac{\pi}{2} \cdot \frac{|Q'_{w_j,s_k}|}{|R_u|}\right)$$

where R_u is the set of all properties of tasks and responses, $Q'_{w_j,s_k} \subset R_u$ is the set of these properties such that its values in the task s_k are less restrictive than the values in the response w_j:

$$Q'_{w_j,s_k} = \{b_i | b_i \in R_u, v_{s_k}(b_i) \leq v_{w_j}(b_i)\}$$

Satisfaction degree function is like a ratio between the satisfied s_k attributes and the total number of attributes R_u of any task or response. The maximum satisfaction degree is obtained when all (not only good-value) attributes desired in task s_k are satisfied by response w_j. On the contrary, the worst satisfaction is obtained when any attribute of task s_k is satisfied by attributes of response w_j.

In other hand, similarity between two tasks is defined in the following way:

$$D(s_k, s_p) = 1 - \frac{1}{n} \cdot \sum_{i=1}^{n} |v_{s_k}(b_i) - v_{s_p}(b_i)|$$

considering the same elements defined above related with the description of tasks using WSMO.

4 Experiments Scenario

All experiments we are presented have been developed considering the same simulation scenario, defined from a unified set of experimental conditions. This scenario summarizes, in a simple way, some common characteristics of a wide range of distributed systems (such as Grid, P2P systems, MAS, etc.).

The frame of experiments is defined from a scenario based on the interactions among agents. Agents play two roles: provider or consumer of resources. All agents play the provider role, but for each round only one agent acts as consumer, according to the requirements of the user randomly assigned at the beginning of the round.

At the beginning of the simulation, the set of tasks S and the set of responses W are defined. These sets consist of 6 tasks and 10 responses, respectively. The 1/3 of the tasks belong to *High-demanding* tasks, the 1/3 to *Medium-demanding* tasks, and 1/3 to *Low-demanding* tasks.

The degree of demand of a given task indicates how much difficult is to satisfy this task using the set of the solutions that agents may offers. In the definition of the scenario of simulation, we consider that the demand of a task is given by the values of its non-functional attributes. Comparing two tasks, the degree of demand of a task is greater than other when it has higher values for its non-functional attributes.

One solution (or response), from the set of solutions W, is assigned to each agent when it acts as provider, defining three types of agents. The 30% of agents have *High-quality* responses, the 40% have *Medium-quality* responses, and 30% have *Low-quality* responses. At the beginning of each replica of the simulation, only one consumer agent is assigned to represent the requirements of the users, randomly obtained from the set of task specifications S.

A round is a minimal unit of time considered in the simulation. It begins when the requirements of initiator agent are established, by means of the task specification selected, and finalizes when the bases of experiences are updates. 400 rounds carry out in each simulation.

The algorithm of the simulation is offered in figure 2. However, the way to assign responses from W to each agent from N determines different experimental situations. For this reason, the experiments analyze the following cases:

- task assigned to initiator agent is randomly selected from the set of tasks;
- always a *High-demanding* task is assigned to initiator agent;
- always a *Medium-demanding* task is assigned to initiator agent; and
- always a *Low-demanding* task is assigned to initiator agent;

The experimental evidences, that we comment in the following sections, are the result from the simulation of TRSIM functionalities using our own implementation in Java. The values, shown in each figure, are the mean of the values obtained from 20 replicas of the experiments.

- to create the set of agents N, responses W, tasks S
- to assign one response from W to each agent of N
- to select one agent a_i from N
- **for all** (round t)
  - to select one task s_k from S as requirements of a_i
  - to select the agent(s) a_j to ask solutions for s_k
  - $InteractionResults := (t, a_i, a_j, s_k, q = Q)$ ...to evaluate the interaction
  - $updateBases(InteractionResults)$ ...to update the bases of experiences, taking into account the solution w_j given by a_j
- **end for**

Fig. 2. General algorithm of the simulation

Each figure studies the evolution of some metrics about the behaviour of the model: satisfaction degree with the recommended solution, and error in recommending it. These metrics show how suitable is the recommendation of the model. The error in recommending is defined as the difference between the quality of the recommended solution and the optimum quality (it means, the value of the quality of the best of all solutions in the system). We consider that model reaches stability when variations in error do not exceed 0.01.

Given that the main objective of the trust and reputation model is to assist the selection of the best solutions, some experiments also study the trust evolution for each type of agent. The three types of agents are defined from the quality of the solutions that they offer.

5   Bootstrapping the Model

Here, we present a set of experiments where the quality of the solutions that agents give does not change in the entire simulation. The first of them, presented in section 5.1, studies how the model reaches an stable condition, particularized for different types of tasks. The second one, in section 5.2, analyzes the ability of the model to recognize different types of agents using trust and reputation.

5.1   Stability of the Model

This experiment is devoted to analyze the behaviour of the model for different requirement degrees of the task in each round. For that, figure 3 compares the error evolution for different ways to select the tasks that initiator agent must solve. This figure shows that the behaviour of the model, for each type of tasks, is stabilized after a relative small number of rounds.

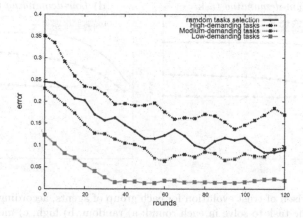

Fig. 3. Comparison of error in recommending the suitable response, according to the degree of demand of the task in each round: a) random, b) high, c) medium, d) low

Figure 3 shows how the error decreases for each alternative. These values depend on the demand of the task to be resolved in each moment. When demanding of the task is lower, the error decrease is bigger and the error reaches lower values. This means that, the stability of the model is reached before, when the requirements of the task is lower. This is a desired behaviour of the model: it is easier to satisfy *Low-demanding* tasks. The same response guaranties higher satisfaction values for a *Low-demanding* task that for a *High-demanding* one.

5.2   Recognition of Types of Agents Using Trust and Reputation

Following, we study the evolution of trust that initiator agent has in the rest of agents, according to the quality of the responses that agents offer. We analyze the ability of the model to classify the agents according to the quality of the responses that they offer, using trust and reputation information.

Figure 4 shows the evolution of trust that initiator agent has in the rest, grouping by the degree of demand of the task that agent needs to solve in each round.

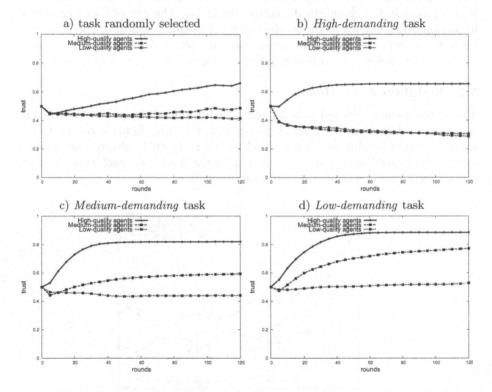

Fig. 4. Comparison of trust evolution for each group of agents, according to the degree of demand of the task to solve in each round: a) random, b) high, c) medium, d) low

We conclude that, independently of the type of the task, the model is capable to recognize the quality of the agent solutions, using trust and reputation information. In general way, the trust in *High-quality* agents grows. For instance, we observe that, for random selection of tasks (Figure 4.a), trust in *High-quality* agents is greater than trust in *Medium-quality* and *Low-quality* agents. At the same time, trust in *Low-quality* agents decreases slightly, and in *Medium-quality* agents keeps around average values between *High-quality* and *Low-quality* values. A similar behaviour is shown when the type of the task is fixed at the beginning:

High-demanding tasks (Figure 4.b), *Medium-demanding* tasks (Figure 4.c) or *Low-demanding* tasks (Figure 4.d).

However, the model is incapable to differentiate *Medium-quality* from *Low-quality* to solve *High-demanding* tasks (Figure 4.b). Given the high demand of the tasks that initiator agent needs to solve in this case, model only increases the trust in the *High-quality*. Only *High-quality* agents are suitable to solve *High-demanding* tasks. Neither the *Medium-quality* agents nor the *Low-quality* are adequate to solve these tasks, and them, the trust for these two types of agents decreases in the same way. This is a desired behaviour of the model. In other cases, when initiator agent solves a not *High-demanding* task, model shows different evolutions for trust in *Medium-quality* and *Low-quality* agents (Figures 4.c and 4.d).

6 Adaptability of the Model to Changes on the Behaviour of Provider Agents

The set of experiments shown in this section, is devoted to study the ability of the model to adapt to changes on the behaviour of provider agents. This type of experiments is interesting to find out how capable is the model to recover an stable status, and when the stabilization is reached, taking into account some specific variations in the behaviour of provider agents. For that, after the stabilization of the model, we induce some changes in the quality of the response of the provider agents and analyze how the model reacts in from these changes. The main experiments are related with the following situations: (1) behaviour of a single agent degrades and then improves, and (2) behaviour of a single agent improves and then degrades.

Each experiment shows the degree of satisfaction with the recommended solution in the cases when provider agents change their behaviour, comparing with the cases when agents keep stationary. Each figure shows in a separate way the evolution for *High-* and *Medium-demanding* tasks. We do not consider *Low-demanding* tasks because the previous experiments (presented in section 5) show that *High-* and *Medium-demanding* tasks are the unique cases in which the model is really useful. *Low-demanding* tasks can be satisfied efficiently for any type of tasks. For *Low-demanding* tasks, similar high satisfaction values (very near to 1) can be obtained by randomly-selected responses. In other words, any solutions in the system can guarantee high satisfaction values for a *Low-demanding* task.

Also, figures bring out trust evolution for behaviour-changed agents to study the ability of the model to capture the changes produced in the quality of its solutions.

6.1 Simulation of Changes in the Behaviour of Provider Agents

Behaviour of agents depend on the values of attributes which describe responses to requests of tasks. Hence, simulating changes in the behaviour of provider agents implies modifying these values.

We consider that behavioural changes are produced gradually, during 20 rounds of the simulation, and they take place once the model reaches a stable condition. Changes begin on the round $t = 200$. All figures, offered to analyze the ability of the model to adapt to changes, show the metrics related to the model performance, from the round $t = 190$ to the round $t = 250$.

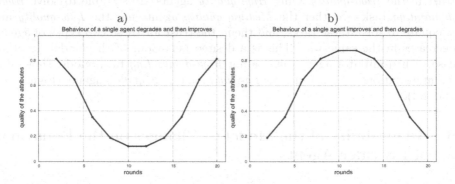

Fig. 5. Types of changes in the behaviour of agents: a) behaviour of a single agent degrades and then improves, b) behaviour of a single agent improves and then degrades

Figure 5 defines the variations produced in the attributes of the responses, given by agents that modify its behaviour during several rounds. Figure 5.a shows the worsening and recovery of attributes of a given response: the value of each attribute is gradually decreased during 10 rounds and then recovers it original value, in the same gradual way. In other hand, figure 5.b shows the improvement and worsening of attributes of a given response: the value of each attribute is gradually improved during 10 rounds and then decreased to its initial value.

Each figure is related with the behavioural changes that we study in the experimental simulations presented below.

6.2   A *High-Quality* Agent Degrades Their Behaviour and Returns to Improve

Figure 6 shows the evolution of the satisfaction degree with the recommended solution when a *High-quality* agent degrades their behaviour and then improves it, compared with the case that the agent does not change. We analyze the cases when the initiator agent solves *High-demanding* and *Medium-demanding* tasks.

For both types of tasks, figure 6 shows that the model is effectively capable to adapt to this type of changes in solutions given by a *High-quality* agent. During the change, the satisfaction degree with the recommended solution and trust in the agent that gives it, are decreased and returned to improve in the same way that the quality of the agent solution changes. The satisfaction degree is decreased after its quality becomes worse, and then it is gradually increased when its quality is recovered. The differences in this metric between both situations are higher for *High-demanding* tasks than *Medium-demanding* one.

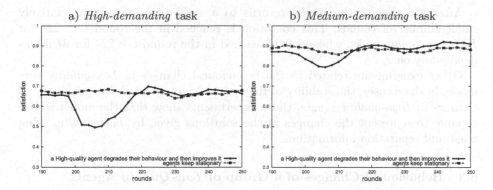

Fig. 6. Comparison of satisfaction degree with the recommended solution, according to the type of the task to solve in each round (a) *High-demanding*, b) *Medium-demanding*), when the agents do not change during the simulation and when a *High-quality* agent degrades their behaviour and then improves it

Figure 7 shows the variations in the trust in the *High-quality* agent that degrades their behaviour and then improves it, according to the type of the task to solve in each round. It compares the cases when agents keep stationary during the simulation and when a *High-quality* agent degrades their behaviour and then improves it. This figure makes clear that the model is capable to represent, using trust values, this type of behavioural changes of agents. In this case, the model decreases the trust when agent makes worse (during the first part of the change). But, when agent recovers it quality, trust is increased reaching similar values that it has at the beginning of the change.

Similarly to other metrics, the variations of the trust in the agent that changes the quality of the responses is lower for *Medium-demanding* tasks.

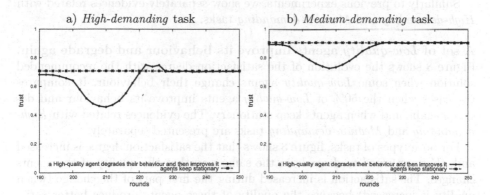

Fig. 7. Comparison of trust evolution in the *High-quality* agent degrades their behaviour and then improves it, according to the type of the task to solve in each round (a) *High-demanding*, b) *Medium-demanding*)

After the change, the model returns to a stable condition in a relatively small number of rounds. This condition is reached in the round $t = 228$ for *High-demanding* tasks, whereas it is reached in the round $t = 224$ for *Medium-demanding* ones.

Other experiments related to the behavioural changes in *Low-quality* were made. In these cases, the stability of the system is not affected. But, similarly to changes in *High-quality* agents, these experiments show that the model is also capable to represent the changes in the solutions given by *Low-quality*, using trust and reputation information.

6.3   Behavioural Changes of a Group of *Low-Quality* Agents

Here, we offer experimental results related with the performance of the model in situations where the behaviour of *Low-quality* agents changes. There is not variation in the stability of the model, when a *Low-quality* agent changes individually. There are not significant variations in the main metrics (degree of satisfaction with the recommended solution, error in recommending the suitable response, trust in the recommended agent).

These measures do not change because there are a lot of *High-quality* agents in the set of agents with high trust and reputation values. These *High-quality* agents are selected during the change, offering the same satisfaction degree, error and trust in the recommended solution. The variations in the *Low-quality* agents do not affect the system performance.

In this experiment we consider that there is not any *High-quality* agent. This way, we study the performance of the model when several *Low-quality* agents change their behaviour in absence of *High-quality* ones. This experiment take into account that the 50% of *Low-quality* agents improve its behaviour and degrade again, when the population of agents in the simulation consist of 60% of *Low-quality* agents and 40% *Medium-quality* ones. The rest of experimental conditions are the same that the previous experiments shown in section 6.2.

Similarly to previous experiments, we show separately evidences related with *High-demanding* and *Medium-demanding* tasks.

A set of *Low-quality* agents improve its behaviour and degrade again. Figure 8 shows the evolution of the satisfaction degree with the recommended solution when some *Low-quality* agents change their behaviour. It compares the cases when the 50% of *Low-quality* agents improve its behaviour and degrade again, and when agents keep stationary. The evidences related with *High-demanding* and *Medium-demanding* tasks are presented separately.

For both types of tasks, figure 8 shows that the satisfaction degree is increased and, then, returned to degrade in the same way that the quality of the agents changes. The satisfaction is increased during the first part of the change (when quality is increased) because the quality of these agents produce better satisfaction degrees that *Medium-quality*. (Before the change, the *Medium-quality* agents produced the best satisfaction values.) After that, satisfaction values are decreased until similar values at the beginning of the change. The differences of

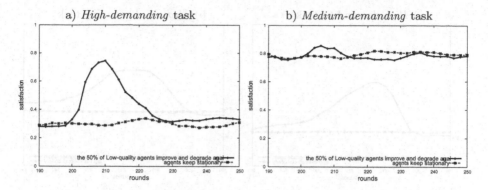

a) *High-demanding* task   b) *Medium-demanding* task

Fig. 8. Comparison of satisfaction degree with the recommended solution, according to the type of the task to solve in each round (a) *High-demanding*, b) *Medium-demanding*), when the agents do not change during the simulation and when the 50% of *Low-quality* improve their behaviour and then degrade again

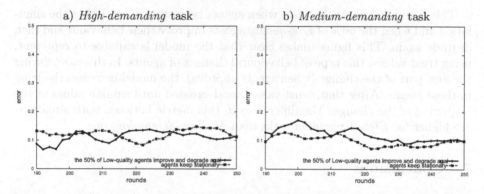

a) *High-demanding* task   b) *Medium-demanding* task

Fig. 9. Comparison of error in recommending the suitable response, according to the type of the task to solve in each round (a) *High-demanding*, b) *Medium-demanding*), when the agents do not change during the simulation and when the 50% of *Low-quality* improve their behaviour and then degrade again

this metric between both situations are higher for *High-demanding* tasks than *Medium-demanding* one.

Despite the different values of satisfaction, the model does not show significant variations in the evolution of error recommending the suitable response (Figure 9). The evolution of error values points out the ability of the model to recommend the most suitable solution using trust information, in every round. The little variation in error means that trust model is capable to identify the agent to offers the best solution in every moment. In other words, the model keeps a stable status when the 50% of *Low-quality* agents change its behaviour.

Figure 10 shows the mean of the variations in the trust in the *Low-quality* agents that change, according to the type of the task to solve in each round.

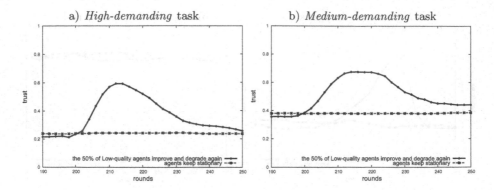

Fig. 10. Comparison of trust evolution in the *Low-quality* agents that change their behaviour, according to the type of the task to solve in each round (a) *High-demanding*, b) *Medium-demanding*), when the agents do not change during the simulation and when the 50% of *Low-quality* improve their behaviour and then degrade again

This figure compares the cases when agents keep stationary during the simulation and when the 50% of *Low-quality* agents improve their behaviour and then degrade again. This figure makes clear that the model is capable to represent, using trust values, this type of behavioural changes of agents. In this case, during the first part of the change (when agents improve), the model increases the trust in these agents. After that, trust values are decreased until similar values at the beginning of the change. The differences in this metric between both situations are higher for *High-demanding* tasks than *Medium-demanding* one.

7   Conclusions

The performance of TRSIM is studied taking into account an experimental consumer-provider scenario, where the requirements of consumers and responses of providers are represented using WSMO.

Two set of experiments are presented. One of them is related to the performance of the model where agents do not change their behaviour. In this group we study the stability of the model and the ability to recognize the agents according to the quality of responses. TRSIM reaches a stable status for each type of consumer requirement. The stability is reached before when the degree of demand of the requirement is lower. Also, the model is capable to show different behaviours for each type of agent for all types of provider demanding. Generally, trust values in high-quality agents are increased, values in low-quality agents are decreased, and values in medium-quality agents are kept around average values.

The second group of experiments analyzes the behaviour of the model when the quality of the responses that agents give changes. We offer experimental results related with some situations where an agent or a group of agents change their behaviour. In all situations, the model is capable to represent the behavioural changes of agents using trust and reputation values. In the cases where the stability of the model is affected, the model reaches a new stable state after a small number of rounds.

References

1. Caballero, A., Botía, J., Skarmeta, A.: A New Model for Trust and Reputation Management with an Ontology Based Approach for Similarity Between Tasks. In: Fischer, K., Timm, I.J., André, E., Zhong, N. (eds.) MATES 2006. LNCS (LNAI), vol. 4196, Springer, Heidelberg (2006)
2. Caballero, A., Botía, J., Skarmeta, A.: On the Behaviour of the TRSIM Model for Trust and Reputation. In: Petta, P., Müller, J.P., Klusch, M., Georgeff, M. (eds.) MATES 2007. LNCS (LNAI), vol. 4687, pp. 182–193. Springer, Heidelberg (2007)
3. Carbó, J., Molina, J.M., Dávila, J.: Trust Management Through Fuzzy Reputation. Int. Journal of Cooperative Information Systems 12(1), 135–155 (2003)
4. Griffiths, N.: Enhancing peer-to-peer collaboration using trust. Expert Systems with Applications 31(4), 849–858 (2006)
5. Huynh, T.D., Jennings, N.R., Shadbolt, N.R.: An Integrated Trust and Reputation Model for Open Multi-Agent Systems. Journal of Autonomous Agents and Multi-Agent Systems 13(2), 119–154 (2006)
6. Ramchurn, S.D., Jennings, N.R., Sierra, C., Godo, L.: A computational Trust Model for Multi-Agent Interactions based on Confidence and Reputation. In: Falcone, L.K.M.S.R., Barber, S. (eds.) Proceedings of the 6th International Workshop on Trust, Privacy, Deception and Fraud in Agent Systems (AAMAS 2003), vol. 3, pp. 69–75 (July 2003)
7. Sabater, J., Sierra, C.: Social ReGreT, a reputation model based on social relations. ACM SIGecom Exchanges 3(1), 44–56 (2002)
8. Sierra, C., Debenham, J.: Trust and honour in information-based agency. In: AAMAS 2006: Proceedings of the fifth international joint conference on Autonomous agents and multiagent systems, pp. 1225–1232 (2006)
9. Wang, Y., Singh, M.P.: Formal Trust Model for Multiagent Systems. In: Proc. of IJCAI 2007, pp. 1551–1556 (2007)
10. Wang, Y., Vassileva, J.: Trust-Based Community Formation in Peer-to-Peer File Sharing Networks. wi 00, 341–348 (2004)
11. Yu, B., Singh, M.P.: Distributed reputation management for electronic commerce. Computational Intelligence 18(4), 535–549 (2002)

Trusting Groups in Coalition Formation Using Social Distance

Peter Shaw, Paul Sage, and Peter Milligan

School of Electronics, Electrical Engineering and Computer Science,
Queen's University, Belfast, Northern Ireland
Tel.: +44 (0)28 9097 4873; Fax: +44 (0)28 9097 5666
{pshaw05,p.sage,p.milligan}@qub.ac.uk

Abstract. In environments where distributed team formation is key, and defections are possible, the use of trust as social capital allows social norms to be defined and compared. An agent can use this information, when invited to join a group or coalition, to decide whether or not its utility will be increased by joining. In this work a social network approach is used to define and reason about the relationships contained in the agent community. Previous baseline work is extended with two decision making mechanisms. These are compared by simulating an abstract grid-like network, and preliminary results are reported.

1 Introduction

In environments such as sensor networks, supply networks and virtual organisations, distributed team formation is an increasingly important factor in the success of any application [1]. When autonomous agents need to make decisions in the face of uncertainty, some model or representation of trust is used, and where agents are unreliable, either intentionally or otherwise, trust serves an important role in decision making [2].

Trust metric research has often overlooked the impact of groups, as gregarious networks have been uncommon, while the use of trust in decision making and group formation implies social division [3]. Peer to peer computing (P2P) and Grid computing are starting to converge [4], therefore, the implication of trusting relationships in the formation of coalitions and virtual organisations is an area requiring further research.

The contribution of this paper is an investigation into the effect of the social position of an agent in a network relative to established groups as a critical factor in the subjective application of trust metrics in coalition formation and delegation in open systems, within the context of P2P and Grid computing.

Social capital refers to the level of investment in the network of relationships in a society. If the relationships are strong, then more reliable results will be achieved. The algorithms proposed in this paper allow agents to use knowledge of trust relationships to determine the degree of social capital locally, and to use this information to modify their behaviour to maximise their own utility. Two preliminary experiments have been conducted, and the results are presented and analysed.

C. Rong et al. (Eds.): ATC 2008, LNCS 5060, pp. 418–428, 2008.

2   Related Work

Griffiths and Luck [2] use trust to decide which agents are most likely to be good group members, and use what is known about the agents' motivations to decide whether or not to join the group.

Alternatively, Khambatti et al. [5] use the degree of expertise and group centrality in a specific "role based" domain to imply trust values. "Regret" [6], another interpersonal trust metric, builds up a trust metric using personal experience, the experience of colleagues, and the experiences of the agent's colleagues. However, neither of these approaches measure a group's trustworthiness.

Tackling the issue of social capital directly, [7] proposes observability in a network as a method to reduce a class of malicious behaviours on peer to peer style networks. However, they do not apply the idea of social capital to group formation protocols.

Bulka et al [8] presented an adaptive learning algorithm that outperformed a random algorithm for the effective formation of distributed groups. In this work, the agents were considered to be 'reliable' and therefore did not defect.

In summary, these approaches have not used trust to reason about a group's trustworthiness in the presence of unreliable group members, and using that information, to decide whether or not to join such a group.

3   Trust as Social Capital

Intuitively there is a relationship between the relative position of agents in a community and their trust relationships. For example, one can suppose that a stranger trying to enter an established group would have to prove that they are trustworthy, much more than an established group member would to be accepted in a group project. Equivalently, the power that is provided to the members of a group by having pre-existing relationships can be demonstrated in raising the entry requirements for those "on the outside, looking in".

It would be useful perhaps to define what is meant by the "group", and so define who is in and who is outside the group. The definition may well depend on the application. At one end of the spectrum is an organisational boundary providing a definite list of who is in the group and who is not. At the other end of this spectrum there are groups that are defined by a loose cluster of relationships, for example where a series of preferential relationships over time provide a defacto group. Therefore, some general mechanism is needed to define the boundary of any group. We take a social network view [9] to describe the relationships and properties of the society.

This paper assumes that there is a mechanism for acquiring the directional trust value between any two agents in the society [10], and so the level of "trust" between any two agents will be used as the relationship that defines the network. In this way trust becomes a measure of the social capital between any two agents.

Assuming there is a "boundary", providing a means to say who is in the group, and who is not, this boundary indicates a social norm. This paper investigates the use of these social norms when deciding whether to join a group or not.

This paper recognises that there are two seperate processes or roles involved in group formation. The first process is that of selecting the most appropriate agents to invite to join the group. By avoiding agents that are likely to defect, the coordinator can maximise the efficiency of the formation process. The second process is that of deciding to join a group, that is, to accept an invitation. In order to simplify the analysis, this paper will look at accepting invitations and a future paper will address the offering of invitations.

4   Team Formation Environment

As with the work of Bulka et al. [8], a random coalition is formed through the agent relationships within the society. A network of directional relationships is established in an initialisation phase, and while the value of each relationship may vary, the relationship connections are held constant for each simulation. Tasks require agents with particular skills, and are advertised for a particular duration. If sufficient agents have not formed the group by this advertising deadline, the task does not run, and the agents are released from their committment. If there are enough committed agents at the deadline, the task runs for a particular duration. Tasks are advertised globally, and one task is added at each time step.

As these agents are self interested, it may be reasonable for an agent to quit one task, to join another that has a higher utility. Therefore, this paper extends the approach of Bulka et al. by allowing a committed agent to remove itself from that task. In other words, these agents may defect.

Bulka et al. [8] provided a basic coalition formation algorithm, which is reused here. An agent is eligible to work on the task if they are not currently committed to a task, have a direct relationship with someone already in the group, and have a skill that is required by the task. At each timestep, eligible agents are asked in a random order to join the group, until the group is completed and the task starts, or the advertising deadline is reached and the group is disbanded. Within that context two new coalition-joining heuristics are presented, simulated and analysed.

5   Previous Work

As each eligible agent (the "deciding agent") is asked whether it wishes to join a particular group, it must decide whether its utility is increased by doing so at this timestep. To make this decision, four group joining heuristics were defined and are used as a baseline for the current work.

The first heuristic is referred to as 'Trust your neighbours'. A "Group" refers to the agents already committed to the task, and in this case, the group was joined if the average trust from the agent to the group was greater than the average trust from the agent to its immediate neighbours. ie The group was joined if $TrustInGroup > TrustInNeighbours$.

Definition 1. *The set of all tasks:* $T = \{t_1, t_2, \ldots t_{numOfTasks}\}$

Definition 2. *The set of all resources:* $R = \{r_1, r_2, \ldots r_{numOfResources}\}$

Definition 3. *The set of all edges:* $E = \{e_{ij}\} \forall i, j$ *such that* $\exists$ *a directed trust relationship from* r_i *to* r_j

Definition 4. *The trust values:* $V = v(e_{ij})$ *where* $v(e_{ij})$ *is the discounted history of previous direct interactions between* r_i *and* r_j

Definition 5. *The set of all task groups:* $G = \{G_{t_1}, G_{t_2}, \ldots G_{t_{numOfTasks}}\}$

Definition 6. *The set of immediate neighbours:* $N_{r_i} = \{r_j\}$ *iff* $\exists e_{ij} \in E$

$$TrustInNeighbours(r_i) = \frac{\sum v(e_{ij})}{sizeof(N_{r_i})} \forall j, e_{ij} \in E \qquad (1)$$

$$TrustInGroup(r_i, G_{t_k}) = \frac{\sum v(r_{ij})}{sizeof(G_{t_k})} \forall j, e_{ij} \in G_{t_k} \qquad (2)$$

The second method looks at where the 'Group meets the Cluster'. Here "Cluster" refers to the set of agents connected by trusting relationships from the deciding agent. Currently this cluster is "hollow", meaning that it is discovered using a depth first search in the trust network, and only the leaves of the search are included in the resulting cluster. The probability of accepting an offer is proportional to the size of the intersection between the cluster and the group. ie The group was joined with probability $\propto TrustInGroupMeetsCluster$.

$$Cluster(r_i, d, threshold) = \qquad (3)$$
$$d \leq 0 \rightarrow \{\}$$
$$d > 0 \rightarrow \{r_j\} + Cluster(r_j, d - 1, threshold) \forall j, v(e_{ij}) > threshold$$
$$ClusterBoundary(r_i) \equiv CB(r_i) = \qquad (4)$$
$$\{r_j\} \forall j, e_{ij} \in cluster(r_i, d, threshold), v(e_{jk}) \leq threshold$$
$$TrustInGroupMeetsCluster(r_{ij}, G_{t_k}, d, threshold) = \qquad (5)$$
$$\frac{sizeof(G_{t_k}) \bigcap CB(r_i, d, threshold)}{sizeof(G_{t_k})}$$

The third method uses 'Social Norms'. The social norm of the group is taken to be the average of all trusting relationships within the group (Equation 6), while the social norm of the deciding agent is taken to be the average of its neighbours trustworthiness (Equation 7). If the social norm of the group is greater than the social norm of the deciding agent, the group is joined.

$$TrustInGroupSocialNorms(G_{t_k}) = \qquad (6)$$
$$\frac{\sum v(e_{ij})}{sizeof(e_{ij})} \forall i, j, suchthat r_i, r_j \in G_{t_k}$$
$$TrustInAgentsSocialNorm(r_i) = \qquad (7)$$
$$\frac{\sum v(e_{ij})}{sizeof(e_{ij})} \forall e_{ij} \in E$$

These three decision strategies were then compared against accepting invitations at 'Random'. Under the 'Random' approach the group was joined with a probability inversely proportional to the number of advertised tasks.

6   Baseline Results

The agents were modelled as nodes in a graph, with directed edges representing the valued trust from one agent toward another. Each simulation run had a graph with 100 nodes, and 800 randomly selected edges. An agent's behaviour was set during initialisation phase and was taken at random from a flat distribution ranging from 0, always defect, to 1, never defect. The initial trust values (edge weights) were randomly generated and were then refined through a discounted history of direct interactions.

For this experiment, 1000 tasks were introduced, one at each timestep. Only one skill was introduced to the system, so that all agents were suitable for all tasks. Each task required 10 identical agents, was advertised for 10 timesteps, and subsequently "executed" for 10 timesteps.

Two aspects of agent behaviour were analysed: to what extent did the decision making method effect the society's overall performance, and conversely, what effect did the method have on the individual performance of the agents.

The "Social Utility" graph (Figure 1), measures the global success of the various methods under investigation. All decision methods plateau after 500 timesteps, this coincides with the stability of the learnt trust values (not shown).

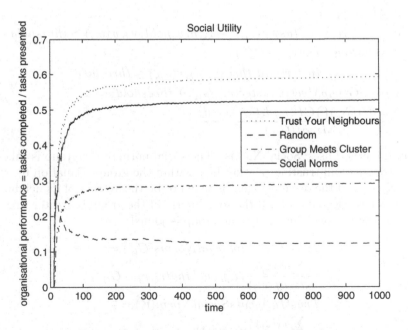

Fig. 1. Organisational performance against time

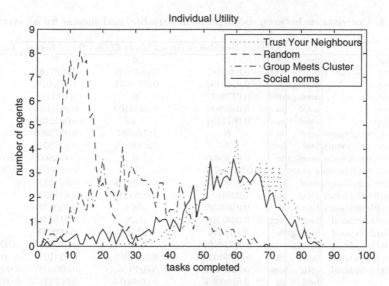

Fig. 2. Agents with the same number of successful tasks

In the presence of defections the "random" method performed poorly, with aproximately 12% of all tasks completed. The best social outcome is found when an agent prefers the most trustworthy immediate neighbours. When the society is composed of "trust your neighbours" agents, aproximately 60% of the tasks are completed.

The "Individual Utility" graph (Figure 2) presents a breakdown of the breadth of successful outcomes within the society. Literally it shows the number of agents succeeding, and the number of agents at each level of success. As a fully deployed agent can process a total of 100 tasks in 1000 timesteps, the graph represents a distribution of the work achieved by the individual agents in the community.

In the presence of defections the "random" method provides a small set of agents with minor success, while all the other agents are excluded from successful outcomes. Comparing the social norms of the group and the immediate neighbourhood allows the broadest participation within the society. "Trust your neighbours" and "social norms" allow some of the agents to complete almost 90% of their potential, while still permitting broad participation within the community.

7   Correlations and Social Distance

The four heuristics were analysed to discover any correlations between the social position of the agent making the decision to accept an offer, and the number of successful outcomes.

Various measurements of the graph structure were used to characterise the agents position in the social network. As the graph used directional edges, measurements were taken for both "inward" and "outward" edges. The edge weight

Table 1. Correlations between social position variables and success for all strategies

Variable			Trust	Neighbours Group Meets Cluster	Social Norms	Random
this agent	best	in	0	0	0	0
this agent	best	out	0.0429387	0.0652026	0.0267161	0
this agent	average	in	0.0200308	0.0398571	0.038015	0
this agent	average	out	0.0479077	0	0.033328	0
this agent	total	in	0.0407946	0.0454109	0.0735013	0
this agent	total	out	0.0671361	NaN	0.0612176	0
immediate neighbours	best	in	0	0.106637	0.0572399	0
immediate neighbours	best	out	0	0.0509812	0.0261016	0
immediate neighbours	average	in	0.0249456	0	0.00829533	-0.0431845
immediate neighbours	average	out	0.00429786	0	0.0631625	0.0152801
immediate neighbours	total	in	0.00348265	0.0249011	0.0211221	0
immediate neighbours	total	out	0.0391652	0.0233749	0.0455316	0
local neighbourhood	best	in	0.0169605	NaN	0.0305721	0
local neighbourhood	best	out	0.0267395	NaN	0.0146344	0
local neighbourhood	average	in	0.015614	0.049149	0.028678	0
local neighbourhood	average	out	0.00776662	0	0.0166917	0.0288254
local neighbourhood	total	in	0.00751014	0.0411369	0.0341038	-0.00151335
local neighbourhood	total	out	0.0147399	0.0279165	0.0703052	0.00034982
group	best	in	0.0130603	0.0369075	0.0671317	0.00189634
group	best	out	0.0372578	0.0302561	0.281333	0.0232269
group	average	in	0.0335759	NaN	0.237916	0.0238936
group	average	out	0.257363	0	0.0891814	0.00609973
group	total	in	0.137826	0.06194	0.143565	-0.00180655
group	total	in	0.146905	0.0593814	**0.802156**	0.00197573
cluster	best	in	0.0907392	0.432135	**0.817632**	0
cluster	best	out	**0.798045**	0.386057	0.033961	0
cluster	average	in	0	0	0	0
cluster	average	out	0	0	0	0
cluster	total	in	**0.798904**	0.0996071	0.0341785	0.00809271
cluster	total	out	0.00836592	NaN	NaN	-0.00592662

represented the trust value. Therefore the best trust value, the average trust value and the total of all trust relationships in the same direction were recorded. These were recorded seperately for both inward and outward edges. These values were measured relative to five different foci: the agent itelf, the agent's immediate neighbours (one hop away), the agent's local neighbourhood (up to two hops away, to maintain some "local" identity), the group associated with the task, and the cluster starting at this agent, giving 30 variables in all.

Simulations with 1000 tasks were completed 10 times, and the measures listed above were recorded for each task success or failure. All the results for each strategy were appended and correlations were calculated on the whole data set for that strategy. Due to aproximation errors in recording the measurement data, NaN values were introduced, and have been subsequently treated as non-correlations.

The correlations are set out in the table below (Table 1). A value of +1 indicates the strongest possible positive correlation between the measurement and the success of that strategy. A value of 0 indicates no correlation, while -1 indicates the strongest negative correlation.

The most significant correlations were found to relate to group and cluster variables, and their values are in bold on the table. The two social position variables "out edge total trust for the group" and "in edge best trust for the cluster" were both most succesful with the "social norms" strategy. The "out edge best trust for the cluster" and the "in edge total trust for the cluster" were associated with the "trust neighbours" strategy.

Concentrating on these four correlations a hybrid strategy was designed that allowed each agent to adopt the most successful strategy for its current social position.

$$a : GroupTotalOutEdgesNormed = \tag{8}$$

$$\frac{\sum v(e_{ij})}{4.sizeof(\{e_{ij}\})} \forall r_i \in G_{t_k}, \forall e_{ij} \in E$$

$$b : ClusterTotalInEdges(r_i) = \tag{9}$$

$$\frac{\sum v(e_{ji})}{4.sizeof(\{e_{ij}\})} \forall r_i \in cluster(r_i, d, threshold), \forall e_{ij} \in E$$

$$c : ClusterBestInEdge(r_i) = \tag{10}$$

$$max\{v(e_{kj})\} \forall r_j \in cluster(r_i, d, threshold), \forall e_{kj} \in E$$

$$d : ClusterBestOutEdge(r_i) = \tag{11}$$

$$max\{v(e_{jk})\} \forall r_j \in cluster(r_i, d, threshold), \forall e_{jk} \in E$$

$$\tag{12}$$

Definition 7. $X = \{a,\ b,\ c,\ d\}$

$$TrustUsingCorrelations(r_i, G_{t_k}) = \tag{13}$$

$$max(X) = a|c \rightarrow TrustInSocialNorms,$$

$$max(X) = b|d \rightarrow TrustInNeighbours,$$

This was compared to a "social distance" heuristic. "Social distance" refers to the distance from a cluster boundary. A cluster boundary is a set of boundary agents: where an agent has out edges that leave the set of agents forming the cluster. If an agent forms part of the cluster boundary it has a social distance of zero. If it is inside the cluster, and is therefore surrounded by boundary agents, it has a negative social distance. If it is outside the cluster it has a positive social distance. The heuristic uses this social distance to weight the decision to accept a group offer or not.

$$TrustInSocialDistance(r_i) = \tag{14}$$

$$r_i \in Cluster(r_i, d, threshold) \rightarrow 0 - shortestPath(r_i, CB(r_i, d, threshold))$$

$$r_i \neg \in Cluster(r_i, d, threshold) \rightarrow shortestPath(r_i, CB(r_i, d, threshold))$$

Currently this heuristic takes no account of the group. If the social distance is zero, it accepts offers with probability 0.5. If the social distance is negative, this probability drops to 0.0 at some maximum distance, while at the other end, the probability rises to 1.0 at maximum positive distance.

8   Preliminary Results

These two heuristics are compared Figures 3 and 4.

The two methods reached their final values around the 500 timestep mark, which coincides with the trust values stabilising (not shown). "Using correlations" had a final social utility of aproximately 60% and "social distance" a social utility of aproximately 59%. Compared to the baseline results, the social utility of "using correlations" and using "social distance" is as good as the previously most successful strategy.

As expected, the individual utility of "using correlations" was largely similar to the results on which it was based. However "social distance" produced a very different result. While the two distributions of successful tasks in Figure 4 have similar means, at around 62 successful tasks, which represents 62% of maximum capacity for any individual agent, the tighter distribution of social distance may imply that only well positioned agents are successful. However there may be enough of these agents to produce aproximately the same profit as when using correlations (confer Figure 3).

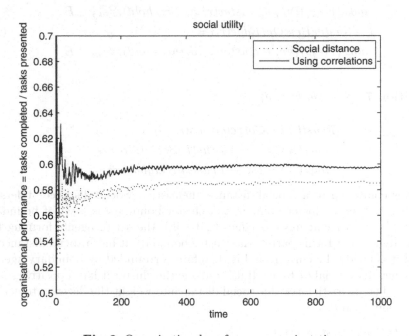

Fig. 3. Organisational performance against time

Using correlations has a much broader distribution, describing a society where many more agents are able to participate in coalition formation, and while some agents do not participate in many successful tasks, some agents out-perform social distance to a point where they are almost at maximum capacity.

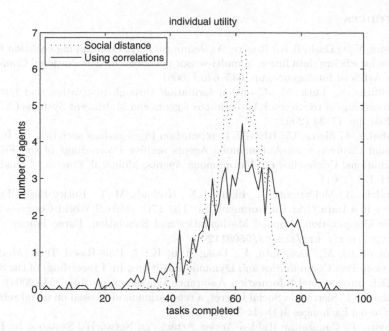

Fig. 4. Agents with the same number of successful tasks

9   Conclusion

The effect of an agent's social position during coalition formation has been investigated in a static network of directional relationships. Several heuristics for deciding whether or not a coalition should be joined have been implemented and compared by simulation. The results show that the social position of an agent can greatly effect the performance of the individual and of the society as a whole during coalition formation.

The use of social distance appears to be an interesting heuristic and forms questions for the ongoing research.

These include:

- Can social distance (and the other algorithms) be implemented effectively using only local knowledge?
- How accurate does the information need to be to make accurate decisions?
- In social distance, are the groups constantly changing or are the groups repeating?
- Can these areas of the graph be categorised?
- Is it one cluster? or several clusters joined with boundary spanners?
- How does this relate to finding replacements and subsequent task success/ failure?
- What is the average social distance? are most people on the boundary??
- Does the performance of these heuristics change when the number of available agents decrease?

References

[1]   Dang, V.D., Dash, R.K., Rogers, A., Jennings, N.R.: Overlapping coalition formation for efficient data fusion in multi-sensor networks. In: 21st National Conference on Artificial Intelligence, pp. 635–640 (2006)

[2]   Griffiths, N., Luck, M.: Coalition formation through motivation and trust. In: Proceedings of the Second Autonomous Agents and Multiagent Systems (AAMAS 2003), pp. 17–24 (2003)

[3]   Sabater, J., Sierra, C.: REGRET: reputation in gregarious societies. In: International Conference on Autonomous Agents archive Proceedings of the Fifth International Conference on Autonomous Agents, Montreal, Quebec, Canada, pp. 194–195 (2001)

[4]   Hudzia, B., McDermott, L., Illahi, T.N., Kechadi, M.-T.: Entity Based Peer-to-Peer in a Data Grid Environment. In: The 17th IMACS World Congress Scientific Computation, Applied Mathematics and Simulation, Paris, France (2005), http://arxiv.org/abs/cs/0608112

[5]   Khambatti, M., Dasgupta, P., Dong Ryu, K.: A Role-Based Trust Model for Peer-to-Peer Communities and Dynamic Coalitions. In: Proceedings of the Second IEEE International Information Assurance Workshop, pp. 141–154 (2004)

[6]   Sabater, J., Sierra, C.: Social Regret, a reputation model based on social relations. SIGecom Exchanges 3(1), 44–56 (2002)

[7]   Moore, T.: Countering Hidden-Action Attacks on Networked Systems. In: Fourth Workshop on the Economics of Information Security, Cambridge, MA (2005), www.infosecon.net/workshop/pdf/18.pdf

[8]   Bulka, B., Gaston, M.: desJardins: Local Strategy Learning in Networked Multi-Agent Team Formation. In: Journal of Autonomous Agents and Multi-Agent Systems (JAAMAS), vol. 15(1), pp. 29–45. Kluwer, Dordrecht (2006)

[9]   Wasserman, S., Faust, K.: Social Network Analysis. Cambridge University Press, Cambridge (1994)

[10] Xiong, L., Liu, L.: PeerTrust: Supporting Reputation-Based Trust for Peer-to-Peer Electronic Communities. IEEE Transactions On Knowledge And Data Engineering 16(7), 843–856 (2004)

Adjustable Trust Model for Access Control

Maryna Komarova and Michel Riguidel

Ecole Nationale Supérieure des Télécommunications,
46 rue Barrault, Paris 13, France
{komarova,riguidel}enst.fr

Abstract. The purpose of this work is to give a service provider or a resource holder the opportunity to evaluate the trustworthiness of each potential client, react to the client's activity by adapting access policies to the actual risk level, and derive user's access rights from his previous behavior, recommendations from third party and the actual circumstances. It is supposed that the system is able to observe and to log the activity of each client and use this information to estimate correspondent trust values.

Keywords: Trust values, Trust evolution, Access Control.

1 Introduction

In the modern virtual world the concept of trust plays a significant role. Trust and reputation models are widely used in electronic commerce systems, social networks and peer-to-peer communications. The traditional trust models implemented for access control are static and reflect relations between the truster and trustee only at the time the agreement is established. Traditional access control mechanisms are not suitable to the ubiquitous environment where all interacting entities are potentially unknown and, therefore, untrusted. The number of users is extremely large and their behavior is difficult to predict, and risks for service providers change dramatically in such circumstances. It becomes impossible for an administrator to analyze system's logs and fit security policies to the actual situation. Thus, a mechanism should be developed to provide access control to resources and to automated management of access policies. The concept of trust represents a promising basis for such a mechanism. The access network provider should be motivated to implement a dynamic trust model to manage the access rights of all clients. The use of such a model facilitates restricting access to services for suspicious users and provides more privileges to users who have demonstrated good behavior. Fair users are also motivated to participate in the trust construction because a good reputation allows them to have access to a larger set of services.

Formalization of the human understanding of trust may serve to treat user behavior history better in order to estimate a risk that serving this user represents to a network, to restrict access for potentially malicious users, and to favor good users.

C. Rong et al. (Eds.): ATC 2008, LNCS 5060, pp. 429–443, 2008.

The proposed trust-based access control mechanism provides a response to the challenges presented by the ubiquitous environment in the following way. We add a dynamic aspect to trust relationships management between entities providing services. If roaming agreements are established between two providers, each of them is able to construct trust with another one, based on the observation of activity of recommended clients. Access policies modification, in order to enforce resource protection, is carried out in an automated and autonomic manner. We provide a trust formalization model with clear dependency between access policies and the obtained trust value. The observation-based trust calculation permits dealing with a long-term history of interactions with each user and restricting or prohibiting access to malicious users.

The proposed model operates in three stages: in the first stage, the client authenticates to the service provider; in the second stage, the service provider calculates the trust value for the authenticated client; and, finally, the obtained trust value is matched against service access policies to determine access rights of the user.

2   Concepts and Notions

2.1   Our Understanding of Trust

Trust has been defined in different ways in different works depending on purposes and usage scenarios for which the trust concept is implemented [1], [2], [3]. To formalize the reason for collaboration between two entities, in the literature both trust and reputation models are discussed.

People will not completely trust somebody based only on his reputation. We distinguish notions of trust and reputation in the following manner. Trust represents an active and decisive concept: if one entity trusts another entity, the latter is allowed a determined set of actions. Reputation may serve as a source of trust; however, it does not directly define allowed actions. Trust is subjective, while reputation is also subjective but is not based on personal observations. Trust always has a clear reason: one entity trusts another via some information or experience. Reputation usually comes from an external universe and it does not reflect personal experience of the interested party. In our understanding, reputation is one reason for establishing trust. We define the mechanism for establishing the relationship between reputation and trust.

Our trust model is designed to assure more secure interaction between two entities. One of these entities provides various services and another entity requests and consumes services; for that reason, we consider a client-server collaboration model. We define trust in the context of our model as follows. One entity has a certain degree of trust for another entity and therefore allows it to execute certain actions and to access some resources because the trustee has collaborated with the truster in the past and the latter was satisfied by the result of this collaboration, or a trusted third party has recommended the trustee. So, the truster supposes that the trustee will behave satisfactory during the interaction.

We distinguish degrees of trust as follows. An entity may be *non-trusted*, which means that the trust is not formed yet. Over time and after several interactions an entity becomes *trusted* with a correspondent trust value and, finally it may become *completely trusted, distrusted* or *completely distrusted*. If the entity is completely trusted, it is allowed to perform all actions associated with the given type of entities. The difference between distrusted and completely distrusted states is that a distrusted entity potentially may regain trust while a completely distrusted one may not.

2.2   The Agents

In our trust model we consider two types of agents: a service provider and a service consumer. There may be contractual relationships established between service providers, and one service provider may recommend his subscribers to his partner service provider. Actions performed by a service provider may include, for example, providing network connectivity, allowing access to data storage or providing different kinds of information. The user may perform a wider and less defined range of actions. The action provided by the user is considered positive if it does not conflict with the service provider's security policies. Otherwise it is considered to be negative. An agent is characterized by a role and history of previous interactions. This role changes in different situations. The agent providing services may be a home authority or a visited authority for the user served. The user may be a subscriber, a recommended user or a well-known user for the serving agent.

2.3   Sources of Trust

Two main sources of trust are considered in this work.

Personal observations. This is the most trustworthy source of trust. The value of trust is based on the history of the past behavior of a particular user. If services provided by the access network are located in another network belonging to the same security domain, feedback from these networks is considered a personal observation.

Recommendations are the opinions of trusted authorities on a particular agent. In our approach, recommendation expresses the positive opinion and means that the recommended user is considered trustworthy by the recommender. This information is very important if the truster deals with an unknown user. In this case there is a single source of trust. Otherwise this source of trust has less influence on decision making about the trustworthiness of the user. The situation in which the recommender is not fair or is not aware of the behavior of the recommended user is also possible. That is why it is necessary to estimate the trustworthiness of each partner that might recommend users.

3   Requirements, Assumptions and Limitations

We have designed the trust-based access control model to address the problem of trust establishment and trust management between previously unknown agents in an open and dynamic environment. Considered usage scenarios include interactions between peers in an overlay network, interactions between the user and web services, and interactions between a mobile user and a non-home access network. In our model it is assumed that the value of trust to the user is calculated after authentication between the entities that are going to communicate. We also assume that one agent is able to recognize another agent's identity and the service provider has means to observe, record and analyze a user's activity. The proposed mechanism should define a way whereby the service provider can mitigate attacks denying access to potentially dangerous users while protecting fair users.

We assume that each service provider has its own access policies. These policies define sets of services that a user with a particular trust level can access. There should be a clear match between access policies and the parameters of a trust model. The formalized model should translate access policies into trust in a simple and visible manner. Just as in the world of human interaction, in the digital world it may take a long time to establish trust, but a relatively short time to lose it. In such a way, it should be possible to retain long-term history of interactions between agents to avoid the situation in which malicious agents lose trust yet after a short time are able to regain trust and recommence malicious activity. The trust value attributed to the user should depend on the entire past experience.

The deployment of any model imposes resource-related limitations. The memory of every system has a limited size; therefore, a long history of interactions between agents should be summarized and retained in an efficient manner. To save on resources (time, battery life, and computing power), the trust model must be simple and must not be computationally heavy.

4   Model for Service Access Control

Depending upon the services provided, trust for a user may have many levels, as well as just two levels (trust/do not trust). An unknown user is considered as non-trusted and may be granted a basic non-privileged set of services that may include limited bandwidth and limited possibility of accessing or downloading information. If this user visits the service provider frequently and manifests good behavior, it becomes firstly near-trusted and then a trusted client. As the trust level increases the client's access rights also increase. The "bad" or malicious client is considered distrusted and is prohibited from accessing the serving network. Two thresholds define each trust level: the lower and the upper thresholds.

Authorities that are trusted by the provider are combined into *Contractual groups (CG)*. Each contractual group has a set of agreed services. A user unknown to the serving network is given access to the service set corresponding to the Contractual group to which the recommender belongs. Over time the service set available for a user is either extended or reduced, according to the actual trust value. The reputation of each authority also evolves as a function of the behavior of recommended clients and of payment for consumed services. In this model we consider only the behavioral component of this function.

We define the following sets of services provided by the access network: $S(T)$ - service set for each trust level T, $S(CG)$ - service set for a contractual group CG. Table 1 provides an example of mapping between trust values and service access policies.

Table 1. Example of service sets and correspondent trust levels

Trust levels	Groups of services	Description
Trusted	$S(T3)$	Access to specific services
Near-trusted	$S(T2)$	Internet access, higher speed, higher limit for download
Unknown	$S(T1)$	Internet access, limited speed, limited download
Distrusted	$S(T0)$	Access denied

The user u has a recommendation from the authority m and it tries to join the target service provider s. To fix the appropriate service set the access network uses the algorithm:

if $S(T_s(u)) \cap S(CG_m) \neq \emptyset$
    then $S' = S(T_s(u)) \cup S(CG_m)$ **else** $S' = S(T_s(u))$

If the service provider offers chargeable service, the presence of a Recommendation is mandatory, because the reference for a payment source is required. Definition of payment schemes is outside the scope of this work.

5 Trust: Generalized Model

We develop a centralized trust model in which the entity providing services does not completely trust its partners and relies on its personal observation rather than on feedback or recommendation from third parties.

In our model, trust is calculated based on experience the network has with each user, recommendations on the user (e.g. certificates) and the reputation of the entity that has recommended the user. Services may be located both in the network managed by the service provider and in its partner network. Based on the evaluated trust value, one of two possible solutions is selected: allow or block the access to services for a particular user. The proposed trust evaluation approach allows decisions to be made about the user's trustworthiness, taking into account developing trust and a dynamically changing environment. The trust evaluation and definition of the available service set are performed automatically. These procedures are transparent to the user and do not require the intervention of a system administrator.

When a user requests access to services, the server provider generates parameters for trust calculation based on the interaction history with this user, information concerning the agent recommending this user, and current access policies. Updated parameters are used to calculate the observation-based trust value that is used in construction of a general trust value. The obtained trust value is mapped with access levels defined in advance and, as a result of this mapping, the service provider makes a decision to serve or not the user making the request. The activity of an accepted user is observed, analyzed and recorded in the history both of the user and the agent (partner) that has recommended this user.

5.1   Computing General Trust

Trust relations are always bilateral and are not symmetric. The fact that one agent s trusts another one u is denoted as $T_s(u)$. Trust values continuously change in the interval [0,1]. Hence, one agent completely trusts another one if $T_s(u) = 1$ and it completely distrusts him if $T_s(u) = 0$. We present a formalized model for trust calculation based on analysis and the reasoning provided above. Trust relationships between two agents may be established only if at least one source of trust is available at the time of collaboration. We consider that the full trust value to the user is formed from values of experience $T_O(u)$ with the agent u, reputation $R(m)$ of a recommender m and recommendation (advice) giving by the recommender m on the agent u $A(m)$ as follows (Eq.1). Meaning of weight β is explained in Section 5.2.

$$T_s(u) = \beta \cdot T_O(u) + (1 - \beta) \cdot A(m) \cdot R(m),$$
$$T_O(u) \in [0,1], A(m) \in 0,1, R(m) \in [0,1] \tag{1}$$

Experience (Observation-based trust) expresses the result of the interaction with the particular user u in the past. This value is calculated by the service provider itself and takes on real values from zero to one.

Reputation generally shows the common opinion about the trustworthiness of an agent. It may be based on feedbacks from other agents. In the proposed model, reputation is used to construct trust for an unknown user and it represents the reputation of the agent that has recommended this user. In the formula for trust calculation, reputation serves as a trustworthiness weight for recommendation. The reputation of the recommender changes over time and it depends on results of interactions with recommended users. Reputation takes on real values from zero to one. We do not consider negative values because there is no interest to collaborate with an agent with a negative reputation and it is useless to keep and manage exact information about such an agent.

For each of its partners the service provider keeps the number of interactions performed with users recommended by this partner N and the number of interactions considered as successful or positive n_{pos}. After each interaction with a recommended user the rate of positive recommendation is renewed using the new values of the number of interactions N' and the number of positive experiences n'_{pos}. It may remain the same in a case when there were no negative interactions performed in the past and it may increase or decrease. In the two latter cases the rate of positive recommendation should have an effect on the reputation value. This functional dependence is defined as follows (Eq.2):

$$R(m) = R(m) + \left(\frac{n'_{pos}}{N'} - \frac{n_{pos}}{N} \right) \tag{2}$$

In the proposed model, reputation already reflects the degree of trust for each recommender.

Recommendation means some direct statement concerning the particular user presented to a potential service provider by a trusted authority. A digital certificate may be viewed as an example of the recommendation information. The way in which a user provides recommendations is outside the scope of this work.

An agent may recommend a user to another agent who in this situation is playing the role of a service provider by, for example, a digital certificate or by the user's identity confirmation in the authentication process between a user and a service provider. Recommendation in our model takes on two values: "0", which means the absence of a recommendation, and "1" in case of the presence of a recommendation. The trust value for an unknown user is computed on the basis of the reputation of the recommender. If the unknown user has no recommendation, it is then considered as untrusted and is refused to access resources provided by the truster.

5.2   Trust Development

In our model, the influence of different sources of trust on the final trust value develops over time. When dealing with an unknown user, the service provider has insufficient information to estimate the trustworthiness of this user. That is why the trust calculation relies mostly on recommendations received form trusted partners and depends on their reputation calculated by the service holder authority. In time a number of interactions may take place between the previously unknown user and the network providing it with information about the user's behavior. When the trust value for a user with a certain interaction history is calculated, the influence of the personal observation on the final trust value increases and, finally, trust is calculated based on personal observations rather than on the reputation of recommenders.

In Eq.1 the influence of each trust source on the final trust value is expressed by weight β for observation-based trust and $1 - \beta$ for reputation of recommenders. At the beginning of interaction between two agents unknown to each other, the service provider collaborates only with users recommended by its partners. Then, during the period called the *learning time* (tl) the allowed service set is determined both by the user's reputation and by the presence of a recommendation for him. Finally, the trust to a well-known user depends only on his pas behaviour. The value of the weight for trust calculation is obtained for each session, using the following equation (Eq.3):

$$\beta = \begin{cases} \frac{n_{vis}}{tl}, & \text{if } \frac{n_{vis}}{tl} \leq 1, \\ 1, & \text{otherwise.} \end{cases} \tag{3}$$

where n_{vis} is the number of interactions (sessions) performed between the service provider and the user. Interactions performed during the *learning time* period

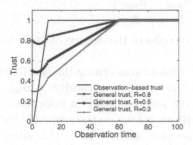
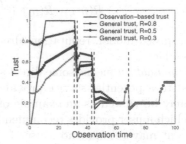

Fig. 1. Effect of observation-based trust and recommender's reputation on general trust value

serve to construct the behavior pattern of the user. We include the number of visits in (Eq.3) in order to distinguish users that frequently visit the network and, thus, the latter is able to collect statistic on their behaivior, from those who perform few interactions during the *learning time* and, so, cannot be served without recommendation.

Fig. 1 provides two examples of trust earning by a user. Each example depicts both the observation-based and the general trust. In the first case (Fig. 1) the user shows only positive behavior. Trust gaining rapidity is determined only by the reputation of the recommender. In the second case (Fig. 1), several interactions with the user are considered as negative. During the learning period the resulting general trust value may be higher than the value of observation-based trust if the user's recommender has good reputation.

6   Observation-Based Trust

6.1   Model Description

The proposed model is designed for automated decision making about the trustworthiness of each particular user based on recorded past experience and service access policies. Trust evolves over time and users considered as non-trustworthy in the past may be forgiven, based upon the access policies.

The unknown user is presumed not to be malicious and it is granted the minimal trust value sufficient to access the network and is able to attain the maximum possible trust value and access the maximum provided service set. If this user frequents the network and demonstrates good behavior, it becomes a trusted one. Trust takes on only positive values varying between 0 and 1. Negative values of trust are useful in distributed trust and reputation models [4], [5], [6] when trust calculation is based on feedbacks from other agents concerning an agent's activity. In the proposed model the user is considered to be distrusted and the service provider does not serve him if the correspondent trust value is equal to or less than zero. In this situation the exact negative trust value has no importance and does not influence decision-making about trustworthiness of this user. Trust calculation is based on parameters derived from network/service access policies, number of trust levels and user-related information. *Network/service access policies* used for trust computing are:

1. The user u becomes completely trusted ($T_O = 1$) after continuous $n_{begtrust}$ visits with observed good behavior.
2. The user u becomes distrusted ($T_O = 0$) after $n_{stoptrust}$ visits with observed bad behavior.
3. The distrusted user is forgiven with a loss of one trust level after $t_{forgive}$ days.
4. There are m trust levels, each level has an upper threshold Tu:
   Level 0: distrusted ($T_O = 0$);
   Level 1: ($T_O \in (0, Tu_1]$) ...
   Level i: ($T_O \in (Tu_{i-1}, Tu_i]$)...
   Level m-1: ($T_O \in (Tu_{m-2}, 1]$);
5. The service provider makes access policies stricter if the rate of negative behavior across all users is more than or equal to N_{max}. Making access policies stricter means that the value of the parameter $n_{begtrust}$ is increased and the value of the parameter $n_{stoptrust}$ is decreased.

To obtain an accurate trust evaluation of the user, the service provider retains the following *user-related information*:

1. The number of positive experiences with the user n_{pos}.
2. The number of negative experiences in collaboration with the user n_{neg};
3. The number of times the user was distrusted $n_{distrust}$;
4. The time label indicating the distrust lifetime, corresponding to the moment when the user may be forgiven $t_{forgive}$.
5. Boolean variable f that indicates whether the user can be forgiven ($f = 1$) or whether the client is completely distrusted ($f = 0$).

To update user-related information, a very simple procedure is used. If the user has displayed good behavior during a visit, this visit is considered as a positive experience and the number of positive experiences n_{pos} is incremented. Otherwise this visit is considered as a negative experience and the number of negative experiences n_{neg} is incremented.

6.2   Trust Formula

Upon an access request from the user, the service provider calculates the updated value of trust according to Eq.4. To formalize the development of trust for the user the linear model was chosen. All parameters of the proposed linear model are defined by access policies and past experience with the particular user. For a "good" user the value of trust grows linearly with an increasing number of visits and reaches the maximum value equal to one. In order to calculate the trust value for the user a discrete formula is defined as follows (Eq.4):

$$T_O = \begin{cases} \alpha \cdot n_{pos}, & \text{if } T_O \leq k, \\ k, & \text{otherwise.} \end{cases} \tag{4}$$

Where T_O denotes the observation-based trust for a user at a particular moment, α is a parameter of a model called "optimism", and another parameter k, "tendency", expresses the maximum trust possible to earn for the user with the given history and with respect to current access policies. Trust for the same user may change if access policy changes.

6.3   Optimism and Tendency

The number of positive and negative experiences defines the trust value for the user, the optimism parameter α and the tendency parameter k. The former expresses the rate of trust earning and the latter corresponds to the maximum value that user trust can actually reach.

The *optimism* parameter expresses the speed of trust earning by the user and it is represented by the tangent of the angle between the line corresponding to trust evolution and the time axis. The upper threshold of the trust level Tu is the maximum trust that can be reached by the user. Optimism is defined by the number of positive interactions $n_{begtrust}$ needed to be initiated and performed by the user in order to reach the maximum trust and the number of negative experiences gathered by the service provider during working with this user (Eq.5):

$$\alpha = \frac{Tu}{n_{begtrust} + n_{neg}} \tag{5}$$

The *tendency* parameter k is introduced in order to regulate the maximum trust value that can be achieved by the user (Eq.6):

$$k = Tu \cdot (1 - \frac{n_{neg}}{n_{stoptrust}}) \tag{6}$$

An example of trust variation for a user that reveals different behavior during interaction with the service provider is shown in Fig. 2. A user loses trust depending on the number of negative experiences, and after several positive experiences it regains trust, however, the new trust value is limited by the tendency parameter. Each negative experience decreases the maximum achievable trust value.

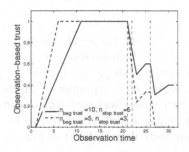

Fig. 2. Effect of negative experiences and policies on the trust value

The number of positive experiences is not included in calculation of parameters to prevent attacks by strategic users (as described in Section 3).

7 The Memory Model and Forgiving

The appropriate model for retaining the interaction history between two agents should be designed taking into account the limitation of memory size dedicated to store history-related data and the timing factor. The timing factor is very important because more recent events must have more influence on the decision about the trustworthiness of the user, however, the information about past behavior should be also taken into account. Generally the history is represented by a more or less long sequence of single events [7], [8]. The number of events to retain remains the question. A very long history allows more accurate trust estimation but it requires more processing time and more storage space. A short history lets past bad experiences be forgotten, with malicious users thereby quickly regaining a high trust level. Another problem related to this type of history organization is the aggregation of events in order to compute the actual trust value. In order to represent the varying relevance of events that occurred at different times for the actual trustworthiness of an agent, various solutions are proposed in the literature.

The main implementation difficulty related to trust models proposed earlier [1], [7], [4] consists in the necessity for model parameters selection. These parameters are not directly defined by access policies. Fig. 3 illustrates the trust evaluation in the Beta Reputation System [4], Giang's trust model [7] and our model on a simple example. These models were chosen for comparaison because thay are designed to be implemented in the same scenario as we consider. We evaluated trust to a user that performed 100 interactions with the studied network. Interactions from 49 to 52 were negative and all the rest were positive. Parameters for the referenced models were set in order to allow a user to gain the trust value of "1" and to be penalized for negative experiences.

In the Giang's model the malicious user regains a high level of trust just after stopping to behave maliciously, while in the Beta Reputation System more time is required to achieve the highest trust value. After negative interactions trust

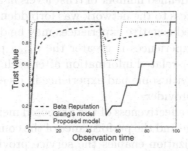

Fig. 3. Trust development in different models

to the user was not significantly degraded due to the previous good experience that the system had with this user. In this experiment a long memory window containing 100 interaction was chosen for referenced models.

Instead of using memory windows, fading memory or forgetting factors proposed in [4], [5], [9], we keep the history of interactions in scalar variables. The number of negative and positive experiences changes over time due to the dynamic behavior of users and to the system forgetting old experience. However, old experience does not mean obsolete and useless experience. The proposed memory model allows retaining information for long-term observation history and performing more accurate trust evaluation.

In our model we implement different forgetting models for positive and negative experiences. It is necessary to distinguish between the user that was distrusted in the past and a user that was newer distrusted. Trust models proposed earlier do not permit this kind of distinction.

With the proposed trust model the user becomes distrusted after several visits when negative behavior has been displayed. We define a mechanism for forgiving distrusted users in our trust model. The distrusted user may be forgiven after a certain period of time $t_{forgive}$, defined by the administrator of the system. The forgiving period is defined by the actual values of access control policies, the risk level and the number of times the user has been deemed distrusted.

For example, the service provider has defined four levels of trust with corresponding threshold trust values for each level *unknown (0, 0.37], near trusted (0.37, 0.63], trusted (0.63, 0.8] and completely trusted (0.8, 1]*. For a user that has never been considered distrusted the maximum reachable trust value is *1*; for one that has been penalized once the maximum reachable trust value is *0.8*; if it has been penalized twice, the maximum reachable trust value is *0.63*, and after the third penalty the user cannot be forgiven. After having been forgiven, the user loses one trust level. For instance, if the maximum potentially reachable trust value before the trust lost was *"trusted"*, then the maximum reachable trust value will be set to *"near trusted"* for the forgiven user.

The system "forgets" the number of positive and negative experiences with the forgiven user but retains the number of times this user was distrusted. If the forgiven user behaves well, the trust value grows with less optimism for him than for a user that was never considered a distrusted agent. The maximum achievable trust value Tu depends on the defined number of trust levels m and the number of fatal errors $n_{distrust}$, when access to the network was forbidden to it.

The number of recorded negative experiences may be decreased if the number of consequent positive experiences is greater the n_{visit} parameter. The service provider updates the user-related information after each completed interaction. Fig. 4 shows how a user with some bad experience in its early history can regain the trust of the service provider.

We have evaluated the effectiveness of the proposed memory model in terms of interaction history storage and the performance of the computational model. The proposed memory organization enables the service provider to keep long-term history for each user in only five variables, and operations performed for updating

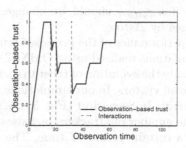

Fig. 4. Regaining trust by a user. The number of interactions with a positive result is set to 10.

history are linear. Access rights attributed to each user change automatically with policy changes.

8   Adapting Access Policies

In the proposed trust model we use the concept of risk to adapt the server provider's access policies to a changing environment. At each moment, the *risk value* is defined as the ratio of the number of recorded negative experiences calculated for all users that are allowed to access services compared to the overall number of sessions with these users. The parameters involved in the trust calculation depend on access policies that may change according to the actual risk level. Increasing the number of positive experiences needed to achieve the maximum trust value enforces protection against early bad users, and thus they are able to damage a limited set of resources. Nevertheless, under these circumstances strategic bad users are still able to gain maximum trust from the service provider, and thereby privileged access to critical resources.

To decrease the negative impact that these users' actions can have on the service provider, the policy corresponding to the number of negative interactions with a user needed to lose trust should be decreased. To manage access policies the service provider defines several negative rate thresholds $thrrate_i$ and correspondent values Δbeg_i and $\Delta stop_i$ by which the policies will change if the actual negative rate exceeds the given negative rate threshold. When the policy changes, the user either loses or acquires a higher trust level. The tendency parameter and the maximum achievable trust Tu changes accordingly. Access policies ($n_{begtrust}$ and $n_{stoptrust}$) change according to the following rules:

> **if** $rate_{neg} < thrrate_1$
> **then** $n_{begtrust}$=initial value, $n_{stoptrust}$=initial value;
> **if** $thrrate_2 > rate_{neg} > thrrate_1$
> **then** $n_{begtrust} = n_{begtrust} + \Delta beg_1$, $n_{stoptrust} = n_{stoptrust} - \Delta stop_1$;
> ...
> **if** $rateneg > thrrate_p$
> **then** $n_{begtrust} = n_{begtrust} + \Delta beg_p$, $n_{stoptrust} = 1$.

The risk value defines if $n_{begtrust}$ should be changed by the Δbeg_i and if $n_{stoptrust}$ should be changed by $\Delta stop_i$.

We have evaluated the performance of the proposed trust-based access control method via a series of simulations realized using OMNeT++ simulator. The aim of the simulation was to study the evolution of trust to each user in a network as a function of the behavior of all visitors. In our simulations we considered different scenarios of bad user's activity. In Scenario 1 (Fig. 5) the system is attacked at a particular moment and the number of attackers increases gradually, all involved attackers stay active for a certain period of time. The situation, where users started to misbehave keep malicious activity, is figured in Scenario 2 (Fig. 5).

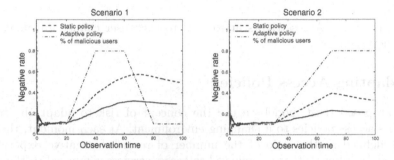

Fig. 5. Effect of policies adaptation on the rate of user's negative behavior

We simulated a service provider's network interactions with 200 clients. Initial values for $n_{begtrust}$ and $n_{stoptrust}$ were set to 10 and 5 correspondently. For illustration purposes only one negative rate threshold was set. If negative rate exceeds the value 0.1 then the value of $n_{begtrust}$ is increased by 5 and the value if $n_{stoptrust}$ is decreased by 4. It can be seen that policy adapting helps to better mitigate attacks as compared with the model with static policies.

9   Conclusions

The proposed trust model may be implemented to improve access control in open environments such as wireless networks of Internet Service Providers that serve a large number of users. This model is also suitable for peer-to-peer environments such as grids or file sharing systems. The generalized formalization of notions of trust, behavior and risk allows the model to be suitable for different deployment scenarios. In this work we consider the aspect of trust evolution over time rather than different aspects of trust propagation. The main improvement made in this work consists in using a direct and clear relationship between network access policies and trust model parameters. The proposed memory model aims to reduce the space necessary to store long-term user behavioral history in a set of discrete variables, rather than using a time series or description language, as has been proposed in related publications. A linear trust model provides better performance when compared with non-linear models described in the literature. In the proposed model, the originality is the use of different sources of trust, the possibility of dynamic adaptation to the changing environment and the ability to work with long-term user history.

References

1. Marsh, S.: Trust and Reliance in Multi-Agent Systems: A Preliminary Report. In: MAA-MAW 1992, 4th European Workshop on Modeling Autonomous Agents in a Multi-Agent World, Rome (1992)
2. Yahalom, R., Klein, B., Th., B.: Trust Relationships in Secure Systems - a Distributed Authentication Perspective. In: IEEE Symposium on Security and privacy (1993)
3. Th, B., Borcherding, M., Klein, B.: Valuation of trust in open networks. In: ES-CORICS 1994, Brighton, UK (November 1994)
4. Jøsang, A., Ismail, R.: The Beta Reputation System. In: Proceedings of the 15th Bled Conference on Electronic Commerce (2002)
5. Ravichandran, A., Yoon, J.: Trust management with delegation in grouped peer-to-peer communities. In: Proceedings of SACMAT 2006, USA (2006)
6. Tchepnda, Ch., Riguidel, M.: Distributed Trust Infrastructure and Trust-Security Articulation: Application to Heterogeneous Networks. In: AINA, pp. 33–38 (2006)
7. Giang, P.D., Hung, L.X., Lee, S., Lee, Y.-K., Lee, H.: A Flexible Trust-Based Access Control Mechanism for Security and Privacy Enhancement in Ubi-quitous Systems. In: IEEE MUE (2007)
8. Chakraborty, S., Ray, I.: TrustBAC - Integrating Trust Relationships into the RBAC Model for Access Control in Open Systems. In: Proceedings of the eleventh ACM symposium on Access control models and technologies, pp. 49–58 (2006)
9. Krukow, K., Nielsen, M., Sassone, V.: A Framework for Concrete reputation systems with Applications to History-Based Access Control. In: CCS 2005 (2005)

Towards Trustworthiness Establishment: A D-S Evidence Theory Based Scorer Reliability Tuned Method for Dishonest Feedback Filtering*

Chunmei Gui, Quanyuan Wu, Huaimin Wang, and Jian Qiang

School of Computer Science
National University of Defense Technology
410073, Changsha, China
plantsperfume@yahoo.com.cn

Abstract. Trust is an important character in next generation Internet. Entity's reputation aims at embodying trustworthy interaction information in history and constructing anticipation in future. Spurious reputation threatens to cause latent cheat and leakage in reputation mechanism, which is an exigent problem to be considered in wide distributed, dynamic domain. Based on D-S evidence theory, tuned by scorer reliability, the proposed approach evaluates entities' ratings on multi-facet and filters out dishonest feedbacks and malicious referrers. Importing self-adaptation mechanism, the status of reputation can be adaptively formed, updated, used and evolved in dynamic real-time environment. Compared with other methods, this approach accords with human filtering psychology naturally, is especially instructive in application.

1 Introduction

The guarantee of high trustworthiness holds the balance for secure sharing and efficient collaboration among entities in wide distributed, dynamic domain. Recently, most papers elaborate on architectures or mechanisms for designing reputation service and resource selection. The presence of inaccurate testimonies and malicious referrers is necessary to be considered. There are two main researches on trust for entity, one is based on accreditation and the other is based on evidence. accreditation-based research validates consistence through security accreditation collection, request, and security policy issued by the third-party. Trust relation is acquired through accreditation or accreditation chains, which is relative fixed, no risk or uncertainty consideration. Evidence-based research measure entity's trust degree through historical interacting results and recommending information, which dynamically reflects the natural attributes in forming, using, evolving and adaptation. Based on reputation, the credibility and reliability of decision-making are significantly improved, which drives efficient resource sharing into benign circle with broad prospect.

---

* This work is supported by the National 973 Basic Research Program of China under the Grants No. 2005CB321804.

C. Rong et al. (Eds.): ATC 2008, LNCS 5060, pp. 444–454, 2008.

However, rating and recommending on entities' reputation are not completely trustworthy. Attack often occurs because of dishonesty feedback, collusive deceiving, and malicious testimonies. They achieve their purpose through biding up or debasing the reputation of entity. Therefore, unfair rating filtering, as a fundamental step, is important to guard the efficiency of reputation system. Most of current work [1-7] draw conclusion by directly composing historical rating information, which is not sufficient for grasping the essence of trust and is easy to form the leak of reputation mechanism. The reputation of entity aims at embodying historical interaction status and providing anticipation for user in future. Filtering out malicious evaluation, respecting species' rating habits, entity's genuine reputation level can be constructed.

A D-S evidence theory based unfair rating filtering approach is presented in this paper. D-S evidence theory supports a considerable accurate depiction for unknown or uncertainty, which holds advantage on situation when difference of character is not sufficient to distinguish honesty or not. Learning ideas from psychology, integrating information of multiple features, the approach takes rating habits and partiality into consideration. Self-adaptive mechanism enhances the universal usage of system and experiment shows the validity of detecting unfair rating. It provides prominent support to trustworthy reputation evidence erecting, trustworthy resource selection, and trust architecture constructing.

The rest of this paper is structured as follows: in Section 2, Dempster-Shafer evidence theory is introduced. In Section 3, A D-S evidence theory based scorer reliability tuned unfair rating filtering approach is introduced. In Section 4, experiment and results are presented. Related work is briefed and compared in Section 5. Finally in Section 6, we summarize future work and conclude the whole paper.

2 The Dempster-Shafer Evidence Theory

The Dempster-Shafer evidence theory [8], based on probability and composing rules, is a set of mathematical reasoning theory. Importing different precision depiction for unknown and uncertainty, adopting reliability function as measurement, using decision-making to eliminate uncertainty in information, it ascertains the impersonal differentiation. The D-S evidence theory presents composition formula for evidence composition, and after composition, the character of basic probability in evidence will be satisfied. As an important uncertainty reasoning method, the D-S evidence theory has been applied in fields as target detection, classification and identification, risk analysis, and multi-rule decision.

D-S evidence theory is constituted on discerning frame Θ. Deeming that all probability in a problem are denoted as set $\Theta \{\theta_1, \theta_2, \cdots, \theta_n\}$, then any proposition corresponds to a subset of Θ, i.e. one element in power set $P(\Theta)$. If $\Theta = \{\theta_1, \theta_2\}$, then the power set of Θ is $2^\Theta = \{\phi, \Theta, \{\theta_1\}, \{\theta_2\}\}$. D-S evidence theory defines a probability function to support a system status about an evidence, named basic probability assignment (shorten form is BPA).

Definition 1. Deem that Θ is discernment frame, if set function $m : P(\Theta) \rightarrow [0,1]$ satisfies: $m(\phi) = 0$, $\sum_{A \subset \Theta} m(A) = 1$, then m is called the basic probability assignment on frame Θ; $\forall A \subset \Theta$, $m(A)$ is called basic reliability of A.

Definition 2. Deem that Θ is discerning frame, $m : P(\Theta) \rightarrow [0,1]$ is basic probability assignment on frame Θ, then the $Bel(A) = \sum_{B \subset A} m(B)(\forall A \subset \Theta)$ defined function: $Bel : P(\Theta) \rightarrow [0,1]$ is the belief function on Θ.

Definition 3. Dempster rules formalizes composition rule multi-evidence as: Deem that $Bel_1, \cdots Bel_n$ are belief functions on the same discerning frame Θ, $m_1, \cdots m_n$ are corresponding basic probability assignment, if $Bel_1 \oplus \cdots \oplus Bel_n$ exists and basic probability assignment is m, then $\forall A \subset \Theta, A \neq \phi, A_1, \cdots A_n \subset \Theta$,

$$m(A) = K^{-1} \sum_{\substack{A_1, \cdots, A_n \subset \Theta \\ A_1 \cap \cdots \cap A_n = A}} m_1(A_1) \cdots m_n(A_n), \tag{1}$$

where K is normalization factor, $K = \sum_{\substack{A_1, \cdots A_n \subset \Theta \\ A_1 \cap \cdots \cap A_n \neq \phi}} m_1(A_1) \cdots m_n(A_n)$.

3 The D-S Evidence Theory Based Unfair Rating Filtering Approach

Rating on reputation includes genuine rating and unfair rating. Genuine rating is founded on normal rating psychology and rating ability, sincerely reflects status of entities, and should belong to entities' honesty reputation evidence. Unfair rating bids up or debases entities' value, influences and even imperils the whole reputation system. As unfair rating often behaves unconventionally, according to observing information, this paper draws integrated aggregation and distinguishes between truth and false.

3.1 The Model of Reputation Evidence

During the process of collaboration, entities evaluate each other on their behavior, whose value is within the scope of 0 to 100. Here, we denote the first-hand rating e_i given to e_j at the time of t as $R_{\langle t, e_i, e_j \rangle}$. The bigger $R_{\langle t, e_i, e_j \rangle}$ is , the higher satisfaction degree is given to e_j. The assess is also given to each feature item, which is described as $\{R_{c_1}, R_{c_2}, \cdots, R_{c_k}, \cdots R_{c_n}\}_{\langle t, e_i, e_j \rangle}$, i.e., at the time of t, the rating e_i given to e_j on feature C_k is R_{c_k}.

Trustworthy ratings are brought into entity's trustworthy set of reputation evidence, and form entity's reputation norm after learning and maintenance. The norm embodies the impersonal reputation situation of an entity. Subsequent detection can be done on the basis of norm. The norm is required to be fresh and righteous ,the group-scale should be suitable, and the distribution is requested to be even. Similarly, it is denoted as $\{R_{c_1}, R_{c_2}, \cdots, R_{c_k}, \cdots R_{c_n}\}_{\langle t, n_p, e_j \rangle}$, i.e., at the time of t, the rating of norm n_p given to e_j on featureC_k is R_{c_k}.

3.2   Detecting Architecture of Reputation Evidence

Unfair rating filtering can be summed as discriminating the genuineness or dishonesty of evaluation. In this paper, representative feature items of rating are firstly selected, which should be distinguishable and reflect the whole condition. Meanwhile, profiles which represent the conditions of reputation norm are always learned and updated. The probability assignment is calculated according to the deviation between current rating and norm profile. Based on Dempster rules, integrating probability assignment of multi-features, respecting rating habits, the paper gives the last result about unfair rating filtering. In figure 1, the D-S evidence theory based system framework is given.

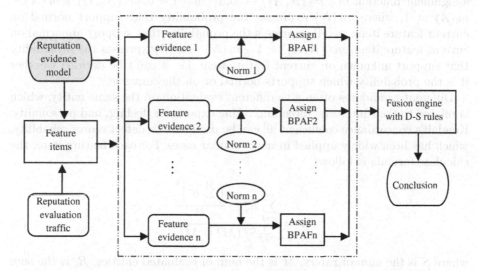

Fig. 1. D-S evidence theory based detecting architecture of reputation evidence

3.3   Selecting Features of Reputation Evidence

Resource sharing is an essential character in internet. For the large scale and the high strangeness, reputation evidence often comes from the third party. The amount of evaluation diverse among species due to the distributing phenomena of power law [13], and their own reputation should be considered.

It is not especially restricted to choose feature items in this paper. Only that the environment evaluating occurs and the form rating shows should be respected, which represent certain psychology characters and society characters. The chosen features of reputation evaluating should be impersonal, accurate, timing, and embodying expectation.

Concretely speaking, we can detect the rationality of rating on key item. For example, deceiving or not, obviously different from promise, uncompleted service, service complete but overtime, filch user's personal information etc. As to consumer, for example, executing malicious code or not, laying trojan horse, occupying overtime, pay in time, no rubbish files left behind. Sum up, the evaluation features can be integrated as performance, security level, expectation degree etc.

3.4   The D-S Evidence Theory Based Unfair Rating Filtering Engine

In this paper, all the candidates' ratings are objects to-be-detected. According to D-S evidence theory, the frame $\Theta = \{N, A\}$ is defined, where N expresses normal and genuine, A expresses abnormal and dishonesty, and $N \cap A = \phi$. Then, nonempty subset of 2^Θ includes $\{N\}, \{A\}, \{N, A\}$. Define the probability assignment function $m : P(\{N, A\}) \rightarrow [0, 1], m(\phi) = 0, m(\{N, A\}) + m(N) + m(A) = 1$, where, $m(N)$ expresses the probability that support normal on current feature item, $m(A)$ expresses the probability that support abnormal on current feature item, $m(\{N, A\}) = 1 - m(N) - m(A)$ expresses the probability that support unknown on current feature item, i.e. it can't be decided whether it is the probability which supports normal or on the converse.

Different candidates often give different evaluation on the same entity, which is related to their interests' direction, rating experience, feeling, and personality. Kendall's concordance coefficient [9] can be used here to detect scorer reliability, which has been widely applied in many similar cases. For each feature item, the calculate formula is follow:

$$W = \frac{\sum_{i=1}^{M} R_i^2 - \frac{\left(\sum_{i=1}^{M} R_i\right)^2}{M}}{\frac{1}{12}S^2(M^3 - M)},\tag{2}$$

where S is the num of raters, M is the num of evaluated entities, R_i is the sum of ratings an entity gains.

Considering the design principle of probability assignment function: when candidate is quite consistent with norm in rating probability, it shows candidate's rating is in a relative normal scope, so its probability supporting normal should be relatively high and the probability supporting abnormal should be relatively low; Along with the depressing of rating consistence, the probability which supports normal will reduce and the probability which supports dishonesty will gradually heighten. Based on scorer reliability, we can get the probability assignment function of formula (3) on the kth feature item, named $BPAFk$:

$$\begin{aligned}
m_k(\{N\}) &= W \times (1 - \alpha_k), \\
m_k(\{A\}) &= (1 - W) \times (1 - \alpha_k), \\
m_k(\{N, A\}) &= \alpha_k.
\end{aligned}\tag{3}$$

Where, $\alpha_k \in S, S = \{\alpha_1, \alpha_2, \cdots \alpha_n\}$ is the set of uncertainty degree on features, the value is given according to experience and importance.

Pseudo code for the algorithm of D-S based unfair rating filtering is follow:

```
Algorithm URF          (*Unfair Rating Filtering*)
Input: (1) Collection of Candidates C={ c₁,c₂,...,c_l }
       (2) Collection of Norms N={n₁,n₂,...,n_s}
       (3) Collection of Entities E={ e₁,e₂,...,e_m }
       (4) Collection of Features F={ F₁,F₂,...,F_n }
       (5) Collection of Uncertainty Degree S= {α₁,α₂,...,α_n}
Output: Candidates' Probability Assignment Table CPAT
Begin
1.   Construct the Entities' Reputation Rating Table ERRT
2.   for i=1 to l do
3.       MNAᵢ ← φ
4.   for each Feature Item Rₐ ∈ F in ERRT do
5.       for i=1 to l do
6.           for j=1 to m do
7.               Rⱼ= ∑ₙₚ∈N R₍ₙₚ,ₑ,⟩ + R₍ₐ,ₑⱼ,⟩
8.               W=Formular2(s+1, m, {Rⱼ, for all j=1...m)})
9.           (mᵢ({N}), mᵢ({A}), mᵢ({N, A}))=Formular3(W, αₖ)
10.          MNAᵢ ← MNAᵢ ∪ {(mᵢ({N}), mᵢ({A}), mᵢ({N, A}))}
11.  CPAT ← φ
12.  for i=1 to l do
13.      (m({N}), m{A}), m({N, A}))=Formular1(MNAᵢ)
14.      CPAT ← CPAT ∪ {(m({N}), m{A}), m({N, A}))}
15.  return CPAT
End
```

Fig. 2. Pseudo code for algorithm URF

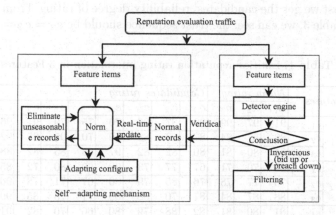

Fig. 3. Self-adaptation mechanism

3.5 Adaptive Mechanism

The status of entities' reputation is time-dependent, it could be even, ascending and descending. It is necessary to import self-adaptive mechanism for reputation norm. In the beginning, current evaluation is served as entities' original reputation norm, and then, the next on-line ratings will be detected. Current norm profile is learned and updated, which is provided for the next use.

The detecting system can be deployed easily in real environment. Importing self-adaptive mechanism, system operates well after a short-time adaptive training, which provides fundamental basis for the whole reputation architecture.

4 Experiment and Result

Based on eBay's business trace, the first-hand evaluating data of reputation is scored from 0 to 100 in table 1, which is the to-be-evaluated information system. $n_1 \sim n_3$ stand for 3 norm evaluators, which are trustworthy and may come from history detection or experts; $c_{.1} \sim c_{.8}$ stand for 8 candidates whose rating are to be detected; $e_1 \sim e_3$ are 3 entities to be rated on service performance F_1 (for example: arriving within 3 days, pay within 24 hours, and service consistent with promise etc.), security level F_2 (for example: no inaccurate testimonies deviated from real, no malicious cancellation, and no rubbish files left etc.), and optimal anticipation F_3 (for example: entity performance increase in advance, service update effectively, and ratio of performance to price is increasing etc.). 11 entities' rating tendency on 3 feature items is depicted in figure 4.

Using uncertainty coefficient α_1=0.05 for service performance, $\alpha_2$0.03 for security level, and $\alpha_3 = 0.10$ for optimal anticipation, according to the algorithm, probability assignment of normal, dishonesty, and unknown on features can be calculated in table 2. To further comparison, probability assignment supporting normal of 8 candidates on 3 features are depicted in figure 5.

According to the algorithm, integrating the probability assignment on 3 features, at last we get the candidates' reliability degree of rating. From the results shown in table 3, we can see: the trust sequence should be $c_{.1} = c_{.3} = c_{.5} = c_{.8} \approx$

Table 1. Entities' reputation rating information in 3 Features

Features		Norm rating			Candidates rating							
		n_1	n_2	n_3	$c_{.1}$	$c_{.2}$	$c_{.3}$	$c_{.4}$	$c_{.5}$	$c_{.6}$	$c_{.7}$	$c_{.8}$
R_{c_1}	e_1	91	97	99	90	87	96	70	75	79	91	96
	e_2	88	87	84	87	93	88	80	70	95	85	92
	e_3	81	80	81	80	82	82	97	65	85	82	88
R_{c_2}	e_1	69	70	71	67	77	73	98	60	80	72	85
	e_2	75	77	78	76	85	79	80	67	71	78	90
	e_3	88	87	84	87	70	88	65	71	76	85	99
R_{c_3}	e_1	81	80	81	82	88	79	80	66	70	82	91
	e_2	89	88	87	89	76	89	65	70	75	90	98
	e_3	75	77	78	77	83	76	89	61	80	78	85

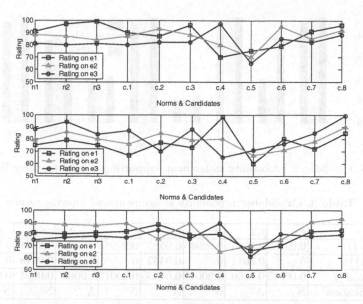

Fig. 4. Rating behaviors on three features (a) rating behaviors in service performance; (b) rating behaviors in security level; (c) rating behaviors in anticipation about optimization

Table 2. Candidates' probability assignment on features

BPA		Candidates							
		$c_{.1}$	$c_{.2}$	$c_{.3}$	$c_{.4}$	$c_{.5}$	$c_{.6}$	$c_{.7}$	$c_{.8}$
F_{1_1}	$m_1(\{N\})$	0.95	0.772	0.95	0.238	0.95	0.416	0.416	0.95
	$m_1(\{A\})$	0.00	0.178	0.00	0.712	0.00	0.534	0.534	0.00
	$m_1(\{N, A\})$	0.05	0.05	0.05	0.05	0.05	0.05	0.05	0.05
F_{2_1}	$m_2(\{N\})$	0.97	0.424	0.97	0.242	0.97	0.424	0.788	0.97
	$m_2(\{A\})$	0.00	0.546	0.00	0.728	0.00	0.546	0.182	0.00
	$m_2(\{N, A\})$	0.03	0.03	0.03	0.03	0.03	0.03	0.03	0.03
F_{3_1}	$m_3(\{N\})$	0.90	0.394	0.90	0.225	0.90	0.394	0.731	0.90
	$m_3(\{A\})$	0.00	0.506	0.00	0.675	0.00	0.506	0.169	0.00
	$m_3(\{N, A\})$	0.10	0.10	0.10	0.10	0.10	0.10	0.10	0.10

$c_{.7} \succ c_{.2} \succ c_{.6} \succ c_{.4}$; $c_{.4}$ must be filtered out because it is dishonesty feedback and $c_{.6}$ should be filtered out too; filtering out $c_{.2}$ or not can be considered by system decider according to their application requirement; although first-hand ratings from $c_{.5}$ are generally low, the result shows whose probability assignment of normal supporting is high, which means ratings from $c_{.5}$ should be reserved and $c_{.5}$ might be strict; at the same time, although first-hand ratings from $c_{.8}$ are generally high, the result shows whose probability assignment of normal supporting is high, which means ratings from $c_{.8}$ should be reserved and $c_{.8}$ might be lenient; of course, $c_{.1}$ and $c_{.7}$ should be reserved and it seems consistent with their first-hand ratings status.

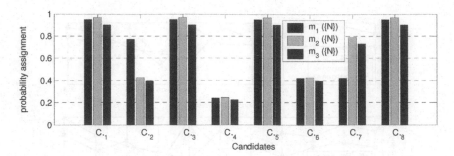

Fig. 5. Candidates' probability assignment supporting normal on three features

Table 3. Candidates' probability assignment and filtering results

BPA	$c_{.1}$	$c_{.2}$	$c_{.3}$	$c_{.4}$	$c_{.5}$	$c_{.6}$	$c_{.7}$	$c_{.8}$
$m(\{N\})$	0.99985	0.6983	0.99985	0.0535	0.99985	0.3386	0.9048	0.99985
$m(\{A\})$	0	0.3011	0	0.9462	0	0.6609	0.0948	0
$m(\{N, A\})$	0.00015	0.0006	0.00015	0.0003	0.00015	0.0005	0.0004	0.00015
Justification	N	A	N	A	N	A	N	N

4.1 Related Work

Undoubtedly, reputation is not only of great helpful to humanities, but also important as a formalizing computational concept in scientific computing field. Recently, reputation is widely adopted in most popular ecommerce website such as eBay, Amazon and is introduced to multi-agent systems, semantic web, P2P systems and Grid systems [1-7].

Generally speaking, most of these papers elaborate on architectures or mechanisms for designing reputation service and resource selection. In [4], a trust modeling is presented which aims at providing resources security protection in grid through trust updating, diffusing and integrating among entities. In [5], Grid Eigen Trust, a framework used to compute entity's reputation in grid. In [6], "personalized similarity" is adopted to evaluate an entity's credibility. In [7], "the propagation of distrust", an interesting idea, which allows the proactive dissemination of some malicious entity's bad reputation and maintains positive trust values for peers at the meanwhile.

However, the presence of inaccurate testimonies and malicious referrers is necessary to be considered. As to dishonest feedback filtering, to the best of our knowledge, we find the small number of work: In [10], controlled anonymity is used to avoid unfairly low ratings and negative discrimination and cluster filtering techniques based on value and frequency are used to reduce the effect of unfairly high ratings and positive discrimination. Such filtering method does not take an entity's rating habit into consideration and might filter out ratings from lenient raters. In [11], a statistical filtering technique is described for excluding unfair ratings. By comparing the overall reputation score of a given agent with the probability distribution of the ratings on that agent from each rater, this scheme dynamically determines an upper and lower threshold for which raters should be judged unfair and thereby excluded. The work is efficient in mitigating the influence of individual inaccurate testimonies. Meanwhile, it is vulnerable to the presence of collusive inaccurate testimonies and malicious referrers. It is infeasible in open Internet environment that it assumes the existence of cumulative rating vectors for each rater. In [12], based on the idea of Weighted Majority Algorithm, the work modifies recommenders' reputation, which is some extent effective to punish malicious referrer. However, Influence has been spread before the punishment that reputation system might have cost so much.

4.2   Conclusions and Future Work

The guarantee of high trustworthiness holds the balance for secure sharing and efficient collaboration among entities in wide distributed, dynamic domain. The work offers fundamental step towards trust establishment for further research. There are 4 main features: 1) Dishonest feedbacks and malicious referrers can be filtered out whatever they are single or collusive, no doubt it is necessary when reputation mechanism is intensive used. 2) Respecting entity's rating habits, for example, some raters are lenient while some are strict and they are distinctly different from inaccurateness, rating habits and abundant rating connotation are unified considered in this paper. 3) Integrating D-S evidence theory and relative psychology method, importing adaptive mechanism, the work effectively embodies the nature characters of reputation in forming, updating, using and evolving. 4) The cost of calculation is low, which is apt to be deployed in open environment and will be effective after short time of training.

This paper is helpful for trustworthy resource selection, reputation constructing, and more reputation related research work. Next, we suggest that mechanism of punishment and promoting should be taken into consideration.

References

1. Sepandar, D.K., Mario, T.S., Hector, G.M.: The EigenTrust Algorithm for Reputation Management in P2P Networks. In: Proceedings of the Twelfth International World Wide Web Conference, Budapest, Hungary (May 20-24, 2003)
2. Massa, P., Bhattacharjee, B.: Using Trust in Recommender Systems: an Experimental Analysis. In: Jensen, C., Poslad, S., Dimitrakos, T. (eds.) iTrust 2004. LNCS, vol. 2995, pp. 221–235. Springer, Heidelberg (2004)
3. Griffiths, N., Chao, K.-M.: Experience-based trust: Enabling effective resource selection in a grid environment. In: Herrmann, P., Issarny, V., Shiu, S.C.K. (eds.) iTrust 2005. LNCS, vol. 3477, pp. 240–255. Springer, Heidelberg (2005)
4. Song, S., Hwang, K., Macwan, M.: Fuzzy Trust Integration for Security Enforcement in Grid Computing. In: Jin, H., Gao, G.R., Xu, Z., Chen, H. (eds.) NPC 2004. LNCS, vol. 3222. Springer, Heidelberg (2004)
5. Alunkal, B.K.: Grid EigenTrust: A Framework for Computing Reputation in Grids. MS thesis, Department of Computer Science, Illinois Institute of Technology (November 2003)

6. Xiong, L., Liu, L.: PeerTrust: Supporting Reputation-Based Trust in Peerto-Peer Communities. IEEE Transactions on Knowledge and Data Engineering, Special Issue on Peer-to-Peer Based Data Management 16(7) (July 2004)
7. Guha, R., et al.: Propagation of Trust and Distrust. In: Proc. ACM World Wide Web Conference (WWW 2004), pp. 403–412. ACM Press, New York (2004)
8. Dempster, A.: Upper and lower probabilities induced by multivalued mapping. Annals of Mathematical Statistics 38(2), 325–339 (1967)
9. Cronbach, L.J.: Essentials of Psychological Testing, 5th edn. Happer & Row, publishers, N.Y (1996)
10. Dellarocas, C.: Immunizing Online Reputation Reporting Systems Against Unfair Ratings and Discriminatory Behavior. In: Proceedings of the 2nd ACM Conference on Electronic Commerce, Minneapolis, MN (October 17-20, 2000)
11. Whitby, A., Jsang, A., Indulska, J.: Filtering out unfair ratings in bayesian reputation systems. In: Proceedings of the Workshop on Trust in Agent Societies, at the 3rd Int. Conf. on Autonomous Agents & Multi Agent Systems (2004)
12. Weng, J., Miao, C., Goh, A.: A Robust Reputation System for the Grid (2006), http://www.cais.ntu.edu.sg/~wengjs/cgi-bin/schlabo/dl.pl?file=TR&get=1
13. Barabási, A.-L., Bonabeau, E.: Scientific American, vol. 288, p. 50 (2003)

A User Behavior Based Trust Model
for Mobile Applications

Zheng Yan[1], Valtteri Niemi[1], Yan Dong[2], and Guoliang Yu[2]

[1] Nokia Research Center, Helsinki, Finland
{zheng.z.yan,valtteri.niemi}@nokia.com
[2] Institute of Psychology, Renmin University of China, China
dongpsy@ruc.edu.cn, yugllxl@sina.com

Abstract. A mobile application is a software package that can be installed and executed in a mobile device. Which mobile application is more trustworthy for a user to purchase or install becomes a crucial issue that impacts its final success. This paper proposes a trust model based on users' behaviors, which assists the evaluation and management of the mobile application's trust with user friendliness. We achieve our model through exploratory factor analysis, reliability analysis and correlation analysis based on the data collected from a questionnaire survey. It is indicated that a user's trust behavior is a multidimensional construct composed of four aspects: usage behavior, reflection behavior, correlation behavior and management behavior. Particularly, the practical significance of our work towards usable trust management, the limitations of current empirical study and future work are also discussed.

1 Introduction

A mobile application is a software package that can be installed and executed in a mobile device (e.g. a mobile phone), for example, a mobile email client to access emails. Generally, this software package developed by various vendors can be downloaded from a web site or received from another device for installation. Which mobile application is more trustworthy for a user to purchase or install becomes a crucial issue that impacts its final success.

Trust is a multidimensional, multidisciplinary and multifaceted concept. The concept of trust has been studied in disciplines ranging from economics to psychology, from sociology to medicine, and to information science. We can find various definitions of trust in the literature. Common to these definitions are the notions of confidence, belief, faith, hope, expectation, dependence, and reliance on the goodness, strength, reliability, integrity, ability, or character of a person or thing [1]. Generally, a trust relationship involves at least two parties: a trustor and a trustee. The trustor (i.e. a trusting subject) is the person or entity who holds confidence, etc. on the reliability, integrity, ability, etc. of another person or thing, which is the object of trust - the trustee (i.e. a trusting object).

A user's trust in a mobile application is, being highly subjective, inherently hard to measure. Furthermore, trust is built up over time and changes with the use of the application due to the influence of many factors. As it is an internal 'state' of the user,

C. Rong et al. (Eds.): ATC 2008, LNCS 5060, pp. 455–469, 2008.
© Springer-Verlag Berlin Heidelberg 2008

there is no way of measuring it directly. Fully supporting trust evaluation and management on mobile applications requires a number of usability studies regarding extracting user's trust criteria/standards in different contexts, user's experience or feedback dissemination and user's decision about trust or distrust. This may introduce a lot of efforts in order to achieve feasible usability and perhaps the system designed based on the existing literature solutions cannot be finally accepted by the end users due to heavy user-device interaction, complexity and misunderstanding.

Marsh reasoned that it might prove more suitable to model trust behavior rather than trust itself, removing the need to adhere to specific definitions [17]. This paper attempts to develop a user behavior based trust model for mobile applications. Thus, through auto-monitoring users' behaviors via user-device interactions, we can extract useful information for evaluating and managing trust of mobile applications in an autonomic and user-friendly measure. With this way, it is also possible to avoid heavy interactions that may be required by some existing trust management solutions, e.g. [2]. Developing such a trust model is significant for a mobile device to provide trust information to its user in order to encourage usage. It also benefits a mobile application provider that could offer its user suggestions for selecting a valuable mobile application.

The rest of the paper is organized as follows. Section 2 gives a brief overview of the literature. Section 3 proposes hypotheses regarding a user behavior based trust model. Section 4 designs a measurement scale to prove the hypotheses followed by data analysis. In section 5, we report our experimental results and the achieved model. Furthermore, we discuss the limitations of our empirical study, and the practical significance of developing this trust model in Section 6. Finally, conclusions and future work are presented in the last section.

2 Background and Related Work

2.1 Trust Model (From a Psychological View Towards an Engineering View)

Current trust models have been developed based on specific security issues and also solely on knowledge, experience, practices, and performance history [3]. Much of the prior research in trust of automation has focused primarily on the psychological aspect [4]. But prior research lacks an integral understanding of both the psychological and engineering aspects of trust, which is essential for developing an appropriate trust model towards a trustworthy system that is easily accepted by the users.

Many proposals have been presented to link some of the psychological aspects of trust with engineering issues. For example, attempts have been made to map psychological aspects of trust (e.g. reliability, dependability, and integrity) to human-machine trust clusters associated with engineering trust issues such as reliability and security [5]. Lance, et al. studied trust from a number of influencing factors from the engineering and psychological points of view and tried to combine these factors in order to provide a comprehensive model [6]. Most of existing work follows the research steps that, what is trust referent, what are factors or aspects related to trust, and evaluate or assess trust based on those factors and aspects and try to manage trust accordingly [1]. But it is actually hard to computationally model some influencing factors, such as usability and a user's subjective factors. Since trust is a subjective concept, assessing trust need to understand the trustor's trust criteria regarding each factor or aspect, even for different contexts. This may raise a lot of interaction requirements in order to get the trustor's criteria in various situations or contexts. In most digital information systems, the trustor is a user and the trustee is a device or a device application. This will increase interactions between the user and device, and thus cause a usability issue that requires more efforts to overcome.

Initial trust refers to trust in an unfamiliar trustee, a relationship in which the actors do not yet have credible, meaningful information about, or affective bonds with, each other [8]. McKnight et al. proposed and validated measures for a multidisciplinary and multidimensional model of initial trust in e-commerce [9]. The model includes four high-level constructs: disposition to trust, institution-based trust, trusting beliefs, and trusting intentions, which are further delineated into sixteen measurable, literature-grounded sub-constructs. The cross-disciplinary nature of the trust typology in this study highlights the multiple, interrelated dimensions of e-commerce trust.

The technology trust formation model (TTFM), is a comprehensive model of initial trust formation used to explain and predict people's trust towards a specific information system [10]. The above two models used the framework of the TRA to explain how people form trust, and both integrated important trusting antecedents into their frameworks in order to effectively predict people's trust [9, 11]. Since the objective of TTFM model was to predict initial trust (trusting intention) before any actual interaction with the trusting object, trust-related behavior (i.e. trust behavior: a trusting subject's actions to depend on, or make her/him vulnerable to a trusting object) was excluded from this model. McKnight model did not study the trust behavior either.

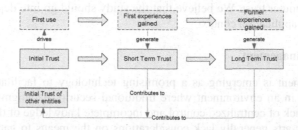

Fig. 1. Relationships among initial trust, short term trust and long term trust

On the other hand, *short-term trust* is built up over the first interactions with a system and *long-term trust* is developed with the continuous use of a system over a longer period of time. *On-going trust* appeared in [9] concerns the short-term trust and the long-term trust. In our study, we mainly focus on the on-going trust evaluation based on the user's behaviors. The relationship among initial trust, short term trust and long term trust are described in Fig.1. In particular, the on-going trust could contribute to the trustee's reputation and thus greatly help other entities building up their initial trust.

2.2 Human-Computer Trust

Trust is firstly a social phenomenon. With the rapid growth of computer and networking technology, human – computer trust has been paid attention to.

One issue that contributes to whether the users purchase a new product (e.g. a mobile application) is how much they trust the technology. Muir is one of the first researchers to look at a decision process between supervisors and automated systems. She verifies the hypothesis proposed by Sheridan et al. that the supervisor's intervention behavior is based upon his/her trust in automation [12]. The relationship between trust and interaction behavior is obvious. Her work provides a basic guideline to design a trust model regarding human-computer interaction.

Muir tested her theory in two studies [4, 13]. The first study supported the "progression of trust" aspect of her theory, and the second study found a positive correlation between trust and use. Lee and Moray [14] found that trust in a system partially explained system use, but other factors (such as the user's own ability to provide manual control) also influenced the system use. These three studies have provided some support for Muir's theory, but additional research is needed to evaluate her hypotheses in more depth, especially in other domains. All above work plays as the foundation of our study: a user's trust in mobile applications can be evaluated based on the user-device interaction behavior.

However, the above study focused on human's trust in an automation and intelligent machine. Little work has been conducted regarding mobile application's user trust although this study is crucial. Prior arts also lacked study on the influence of recommendations and usability with regard to human-computer trust. With the rapid development of mobile computing technology, a mobile device becomes a multi-application system for multi-purpose and multi-usage. It always has a network connection. It is also an open platform that allows deploying new or upgraded applications at anytime and anywhere. Therefore, such a dynamically changed system introduces new challenges for human-computer trust. We believe that the study should go into depth in the newly thrived mobile application context.

2.3 Trust Management

Trust management is emerging as a promising technology to facilitate collaboration among entities in an environment where traditional security paradigms cannot be enforced due to lack of centralized control and incomplete knowledge of the environment. However, prior arts generally lack considerations on the means to gather experiential evidences for effective trust evaluation. Many systems rely on a user to provide feedback [15]. Sometimes, it may not be appropriate or convenient to require him/her to provide feedback because it could cause many usability problems. This introduces a requirement for experiential feedbacks to be largely automated. Our work aims to support automatic evidence collection for trust evaluation and management with user friendliness.

English and Terzis presented an interaction monitor that enables automated collection of detailed interaction evidence based on interaction modeling [16]. The monitor is a prototype implementation of a generic interaction monitoring architecture that applied a well-understood rule engine and an event management technology. However, this study and our previous work presented in [2] focused on monitoring the trustee's behavior, not the trustor's trust behavior, which could provide a more direct channel to achieve trust information.

3 Hypotheses

Our research question is what interaction behaviors are related to the user's trust in a mobile application. We hypothesize that the user's trust in a mobile application can be studied through the user's behaviors, which can be monitored via the user-device interaction during the application usage. The concrete hypotheses about trust behaviors are listed in Table 1. All four types of behaviors comprise the user's trust behavior in a mobile application. They contribute to the calculation of the device's confidence on the user's trust in the mobile application.

Table 1. Hypotheses on Trust Behaviors

Behavior Type	Hypotheses	Remarks
§1 Usage Behavior	§1.1 The user trusts a mobile application more, if he/she has more time, times and frequency of usage; §1.2 Trust in a mobile application could influence the user's behavior regarding high risk and high importance tasks; §1.3 The user becomes more professional in using a mobile application if he/she has experienced more features of the mobile application.	The user's expertise could influence his/her usage, thus indirectly influence his/her trust in a specific mobile application.
§2 Reflection Behavior (behaviors after confronting application problems or having good/bad experiences)	§2.1 Trust impacts the user's behavior, the usage after experiencing error, failure or bad performance implies more trust; after application error usage implies more trust, otherwise, distrust due to bad experience; §2.2 Good/bad application performance and usage experience of a mobile application could increase/decrease the user's trust; §2.3 Good/bad application performance or usage experience could influence the user's behavior on high risk and high importance tasks.	Notably, the difference of the reflection behavior and the usage behavior lies in the fact that the first one is a type of event-related behavior while the second one is about general usage statistics. Their contributions to trust could be different.
§3 Correlation Behavior (behaviors correlated to similar functioned applications)	§3.1 For two similar functioned applications, higher usage rate (i.e. usage time, usage times, usage frequency, and experienced features) of one application means more trust in it; §3.2 Trust in a mobile application influences the behaviors of recommendations and comments.	
§4 Management Behavior (behaviors related to application management)	§4.1 Trust in a mobile application influences the behaviors of application management, such as application installation, deletion and replacement, etc.	

4 Methods

We applied a psychometric method to examine our hypotheses. We designed a questionnaire (see Appendix), taking Short Message Service (SMS) as a concrete example of mobile application. Each item in the questionnaire is a statement for which the participants need to indicate their level of agreement. The questionnaire is anchored using a seven-point Likert scale ranging from "strongly disagree" to "strongly agree".

4.1 Scale Development

There are four basic parts in the scale. As shown in the Appendix, for the usage behavior (UB), we designed a list of items about a) normal using behaviors (NUB), (item 1-3 for testing hypothesis §1.1); b) usage behaviors about application features (UBAF), (item 7, 8 for testing hypothesis §1.3); c) usage behaviors related to trust (UBT) (item 9, 10 for testing hypothesis §1.1); and d) usage behaviors related to risk and context (UBRC) (item 5, 6 for testing hypothesis §1.2). Regarding the reflection behavior (RB), we designed a number of items about a) good performance reflection behaviors (GPRB) (item 4, 13, 14 for testing hypothesis §2.2); b) bad performance reflection behaviors (BPRB) (item 11, 12, 15, 16 for testing hypotheses §2.1 and §2.2); c) experience reflection behaviors (ERB) (item 17, 18 for testing hypotheses §2.1 and §2.2); and d) experience reflection behaviors related to risk and context (ERBRC) (item 19, 20 for testing hypothesis §2.3). In the part about the correlation behavior (CB), we design items about a) comparison of behaviors regarding similar applications (CBSA) (item 21-25 for testing hypothesis §3.1); and b) recommendation behaviors (REB) (item 26, 30-33 for testing hypothesis §3.2). Finally, we designed items about the application management behavior (MB) such as replacing, deleting, installing and rejecting a mobile application (item 27-29 for testing hypothesis §4.1).

4.2 Data Collection

An experiment was conducted by three psychologists. The questionnaire was administered to undergraduate students enrolled in a psychology class in a university. In the beginning, the participants were arranged to answer the questionnaire in a big auditorium. Then, the questionnaires were collected and each participant was offered a small gift. Almost all participants had past experience of answering a questionnaire survey. They are familiar with the basic rules for this kind of experiment. Meanwhile, the conductors explained the basic concepts appeared in the questionnaire before the participants answered the questionnaire. The average questionnaire response time was about 15 minutes.

The participants were composed of 318 undergraduate students, among whom, 151(47.5%) were women and 167 (52.5%) were men; 11 participants were below 18 years and others were between 19-29 years. 229 (72%) participants major in science or technology, while 89 (38%) in arts. Table 2 provides the information about the participants' experience on mobile application usage. According to the survey, 153 (48.1%) participants had experiences of using the internet accessed applications (e.g. a mobile internet browser), 274 (86.2%) had experiences of using the mobile network accessed applications (e.g. SMS and Contacts) and 262 (82.4%) had that of non-network accessed applications (e.g. Profile).

Table 2. Participants' Experience on Mobile Application Usage

The experience on mobile applications		Number of participants	Percent (%)
Time of phone usage	Below 0.5 hour/day	31	9.7
	0.5-1 hour/day	85	26.7
	1-5 hours/day	104	32.7
	More than 5 hours/day	97	30.5
	Missing	1	.3
	Total	318	100.0
Times of SMS usage	Below 3 times/day	15	4.7
	3-10 times/day	106	33.3
	More than 10times /day	195	61.3
	Missing	2	.6
	Total	318	100.0

4.3 Data Processing and Analysis

SPSS 11.5 was adopted to process the data collected from the questionnaire survey. In the first phase, exploratory, principal components, factor analysis was conducted in order to explore the basic constructs of trust model (i.e. the principle factors that determine trust). The purpose of using principle components analysis (PCA) was to cull out the items that did not load on the appropriate high-level construct. Kaiser's criterion was applied in the PCA, which considers factors with an eigenvalue greater than one as common factors [18]. The PCA was performed using both orthogonal and oblique rotation. McKnight et al. argued if the trust constructs form a model of causally linked variables (which implies positive correlations), oblique rotation should be applied in the PCA [7]. While, the orthogonal rotation assumes that constructs are not correlated. Since no theory was found to support obvious correlations among different types of trust behaviors, and the correlations among extracted factors are not high as shown in Section 5.3, we applied a rotation strategy named Quartimax to conduct the orthogonal rotation. We also applied the oblique rotation with Promax method (with default *Kappa=4*). The results based on the oblique rotation are similar to those achieved based on the orthogonal rotation. So in the next section, we report our results of the PCA based on the orthogonal rotation. In addition, we also conducted reliability analysis and correlation analysis in order to further prove our hypotheses and the further achieved model.

5 Results

5.1 Principle Components Analysis

Factor loadings illustrate correlations between items and factors. Based on PCA, eleven factors were marked by high loadings (i.e. more than 0.4) with total items, in which four factors (i.e. NUB, UBAF, UBT, and UBRC) were formed for the usage behavior, with no cross-loadings above 0.4. A second analysis using the items only designed to measure the usage behavior was also conducted. We obtained the same four factors. The results of PCA relating to the usage behavior are shown in Table 3 and Table 4, respectively. As presented, all item loadings were greater than 0.5, and the four factors had explained 65.266% of the usage behavior. It is important to note that the sums of squared loadings of variance corresponding to a factor reflect the percentage that can be explained by the factor regarding the total variance of all items (e.g. the variance of the usage behavior).

Table 3. Eigenvalues and Sums of Squared Loadings of Variance of Usage Behavior

Factors	Eigenvalues	Sums of squared loadings of variance (%)	Sums of squared loadings of cumulative variance (%)
NUB	2.088	18.557	18.557
UBAF	1.539	16.108	34.666
UBRC	1.229	15.473	50.139
UBT	1.018	15.128	65.266

Table 4. Rotated Component Matrix of Usage Behavior

Variable	Factor Loadings			
	NUB	UBAF	UBRC	UBT
Item 3	.807			
Item 2	.803			
Item 1	.541			
Item 8		.816		
Item 7		.744		
Item 6			.848	
Item 5			.764	
Item 10				.795
Item 9				.787

Four factors (i.e. GPRB, BPRB, ERB and ERBRC) were obtained in terms of the reflection behavior. The PCA results of the sole reflection behavior based on its items were presented in Table 5 and Table 6, respectively. All the item loadings were over 0.5 and the four factors had explained 63.031% of the reflection behavior.

Table 5. Eigenvalues and Sums of Squared Loadings of Variance of Reflection Behavior

Factors	Eigen-values	Sums of squared loadings of variance (%)	Sums of squared loadings of cu-mulative variance (%)
BPRB	3.412	21.847	21.847
GPRB	1.510	16.188	38.035
ERBRC	1.408	13.541	51.576
ERB	1.233	11.454	63.031

Table 6. Rotated Component Matrix of Reflection Behavior

Variable	Factor Loadings			
	BPRB	GPRB	ERBRC	ERB
Item 15	.778			
Item 16	.769			
Item 12	.748			
Item 11	.646			
Item 31	.539			
Item 13		.884		
Item 14		.833		
Item 4		.562		
Item 19			.839	
Item 20			.795	
Item 17				.840
Item 18				.753

There are two factors formed for the correlation behavior, but item 26's loading was below 0.4 and one item's cross-loading was above 0.4. It was found that the latter item was originally designed to measure the reflection behavior; therefore, it should be placed in the reflection behavior. Then, a second analysis was performed after we deleted these two items. We obtained the same two factors (i.e. CBSA and REB), but there was another item (24) enjoying a cross-loading of 0.4. However, this item was finally retained because the value of cross loading was lower than the loading. More-over, the reliability analysis showed that dropping this item reduced the alpha for the correlation behavior from 0.78 to 0.73. Important to note that alpha is a reliability co-efficient, which is an index to retain an item. The results of PCA for the adjusted items of the correlation behavior are presented in Table 7 and Table 8, respectively. The loading for each item was greater than 0.5 and the two factors had explained 57.873% of the reflection behavior.

Table 7. Eigenvalues and Sums of Squared Loadings of Variance of Correlation Behavior

Factors	Eigenvalues	Sums of squared loadings of variance (%)	Sums of squared loadings of cumulative variance (%)
CBSA	3.312	37.317	37.317
REB	1.317	20.556	57.873

Table 8. Rotated Component Matrix of Correlation Behavior

Variables	Factor Loadings	
	CBSA	REB
Item 22	.896	
Item 21	.860	
Item 23	.849	
Item 25	.598	
Item 24	.570	
Item 32		.742
Item 33		.700
Item 30		.523

With respect to the management behavior, one factor was obtained (i.e. MB), with no cross-loadings above 0.4. Likewise, a second analysis was performed using the items just designed to measure the management behavior. We got the same one factor, including the user's behavior of rejecting, deleting and replacing a mobile application. The results for the management behavior were presented in Table 9 and Table 10, respectively. As depicted, the factor had explained 56.089% of the management behavior and all item loadings were greater than 0.5.

Table 9. Eigenvalues and Sums of Squared Loadings of Variance of Management Behavior

Factors	Eigenvalues	Sums of squared loadings of variance (%)	Sums of squared loadings of cumulative variance (%)
MB	1.68	56.089	56.089

Table 10. Component Matrix of Management Behavior

Variable	Factor Loadings
	MB
Item 28	.844
Item 29	.827
Item 27	.535

5.2 Reliability Analysis

Reliability is a value between 0 and 1 with a larger value indicating better reliability [5]. We also conducted internal consistency reliability analysis using Cronbach's alphas [5], as shown in Table 11. The reliabilities of the usage behavior and the management behavior were not high enough. We plan to revise or add new items in the questionnaire to improve them in the future work. Notably, low Alpha value reflects that the items' consistency is not so good. But it does not mean the construct is bad, which has been examined by the PCA.

Table 11. Reliability Analysis

Type of Behavior	No. of Cases	No. of Items	Alpha
Reflection behavior	318	12	0.76
Usage behavior	318	9	0.57
Manage behavior	318	3	0.60
Correlation behavior	318	8	0.78
Total trust behavior	318	32	0.82

5.3 Achieved Model and Correlations

According to the aforementioned results, a 32-item scale was created that measures the usage behavior, the reflection behavior, the correlation behavior and the management behavior of the trust behaviors (as in Appendix). A graphic and linguistic trust model of mobile applications based on the users' behavior can also be achieved, as shown in Fig. 2. In summary, the reflection behavior, the usage behavior, the management behavior and the correlation behavior represent the user's trust behaviors. The PCA and reliability analysis showed that the questionnaire has positive psychometric properties with respect to construct validity and reliability. Thus, the proposed trust model built upon our hypotheses is reasonable.

In addition, the relationships of different components in Fig.2 are set based on the correlations of four types of trust behaviors. We found that all of them had significant correlation with the trust behavior at the 0.01 level, which indicates that these four types of behaviors can represent the trust behavior. We also found that these four factors had lower correlations with each other than their correlations with the trust behavior. This indicates that the four factors can measure not only the general aspects but also the specific aspects of the trust behavior. Particularly, the results show that the management behavior and the correlation behavior had no significant correlation, which suggests that the two behaviors have no influence with each other. Other behaviors have more significant correlations, which indicate that those behaviors have influence or impact with each other.

Furthermore, we illustrate the internal relationships of the usage behavior, the reflection behavior and the correlation behavior based on the factor correlations in Fig. 3., Fig. 4., and Fig. 5., respectively. As can be seen from the figures, the correlation between each internal factor (e.g. GPRB) and its corresponding principle behavior type (e.g. RB) is higher than the correlations among the factors. This indicates that the

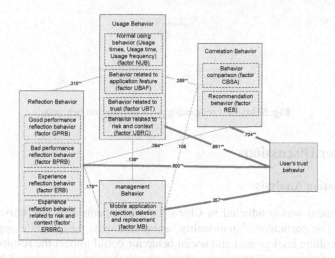

Fig. 2. The trust model of mobile applications based on users' behavior[1]

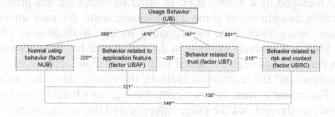

Fig. 3. Internal relationships of usage behavior[1]

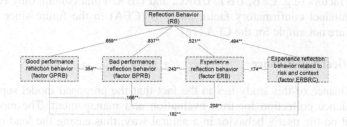

Fig. 4. Internal relationships of reflection behavior[1]

factors belonging to a concrete type of trust behavior can measure not only the general aspects but also the specific aspects of this type of trust behavior. Therefore, our results are pretty sound.

---

[1] * Correlation is significant at the 0.05 level (2-tailed).
   ** Correlation is significant at the 0.01 level (2-tailed).

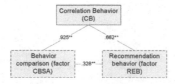

Fig. 5. Internal relationships of correlation behavior[1]

6 Further Discussions

6.1 Limitation Analysis

The experiment was conducted in China. Its participants are only university under-graduates. The participants' nationality, ages, interests, past mobile application experiences, culture background and social behavior could impact the results.

In the experiment, all the items about trust behavior are designed based on the SMS. However, the trust behavior is related to many facets, some of which could be hard to reflect through SMS. For example, SMS is a system default application. It could not be managed by a normal user. In order to overcome this problem, we provided a situation assumption in some questionnaire items for easy understanding in the experiment. Since SMS is the most popular mobile application in China, we believe taking SMS as a concrete example in the experiment has its special advantages.

Although the scale has been examined with the principle components analysis, the reliability analysis and the correlation analysis, the results show that improvement is still needed. For example, there are two items having cross loading on two factors; the reliability analysis showed that the usage behavior and the management behavior have comparatively low reliability coefficients. So we plan to add or revise the items in order to improve the expression of them. In addition, new items should be introduced into some factors (e.g. ERB, UBT, UBRC, and UBAF) that contain only two items in order to conduct confirmatory factor analysis (CFA) in the future since containing two items are not ample for the CFA [18].

6.2 Practical Significance

The significance of this study lies in the fact that the proposed model supports automatic evidence collection for trust evaluation and management. The model studies trust based on the user's behavior in a natural way, thus easing the load of extra human computer interaction towards usable trust management. This is because the trust behavior is possible to be monitored through auto-observation mechanism located at the mobile device. There is no much extra usability study needed if deploying a trust management solution based on our model.

Since trust is a multifaceted concept, it is influenced by many factors and the influencing rates could be different for different persons in different contexts. In many situations, it is hard to have a comprehensive consideration on all factors, not to mention that getting information of some factors requests interaction to extract the trustor's preference (e.g. the considerations of different influencing factors, user's emotion and intension/motivation to trust, etc.). Obviously, some information is hard to be achieved and quantified, and thus it is impossible to be aggregated with other factors in a digital measure. All of these introduce additional challenges to manage trust with sound usability, especially for mobile devices with limited user interface. In our model, the user's trust in mobile applications is investigated through trust behaviors. This greatly helps us overcome the challenges caused by those trust influencing factors hard to be extracted, monitored, calculated and aggregated.

In addition, this model is examined through user study. Therefore, it is easy to be accepted by the end user. This model based trust explanation mechanism could be easy for the user to understand. Meanwhile, a recommendation from one user or a user agent can be further assessed and explained with this trust model in order to help other users selecting a trustworthy mobile application.

More importantly, we could further design a computational trust metric on the basis of the achieved model towards calculating a user's trust in a mobile application based on the trust behaviors. We will report our future results in another paper.

7 Conclusions and Future Work

User-application trust is becoming more and more important for developing and facilitating mobile applications and mobile internet based services. Studying the trust behavior helps greatly in explaining trust status because real behavior based explanation is more convinced. In this paper, we proposed a trust model for mobile applications based on users' behaviors and examined it using the principle components analysis, reliability analysis and correlation analysis. Based on the results achieved, we got the main factors and construct of trust behavior that contribute to the calculation of the user's trust in a mobile application. Concretely, the PCA, reliability and correlation analysis showed that far from being unitary, the trust behavior has multiple dimensions. We explored four dimensions: the usage behavior, the reflection behavior, the correlation behavior and the management behavior; and figured out their internal constructs. Meanwhile, we tested and analyzed the measurement scale's feasibility and reliability for studying and validating the proposed trust model. Based on the results we proved that the proposed model is feasible and reasonable in most aspects. The experiment proved our hypotheses and provided us a number of hints for further optimizing the initial scale.

Regarding the future work, we will further improve the scale in order to conduct a formal experiment with larger number of participants for confirmatory factor analysis in order to achieve causal relations among different types of behaviors. Another target is to digitalize the model and apply it into a mobile reputation system for managing trust of mobile applications with context-awareness support.

Acknowledgments

We would like to express our special thanks to Dr. Rong Yan for his help in arranging the experiment and proof reading the paper manuscript.

References

[1] Yan, Z., Holtmanns, S.: Trust Modeling and Management: from Social Trust to Digital Trust. Book chapter of Computer Security, Privacy and Politics: Current Issues, Challenges and Solutions. IGI Global (2007)

[2] Yan, Z., Prehofer, C.: An Adaptive Trust Control Model for a Trustworthy Component Software Platform. In: Xiao, B., Yang, L.T., Ma, J., Muller-Schloer, C., Hua, Y. (eds.) ATC 2007. LNCS, vol. 4610, Springer, Heidelberg (2007)

[3] Daignault, M., Marche, S.: Enabling Trust Online. In: Proceedings of the Third International Symposium on Electronic Commerce (October 2002)

[4] Muir, B.M.: Trust in Automation: Part I. Theoretical Issues in the Study of Trust and Human Intervention in Automated Systems. Ergonomics 37(11), 1905–1922 (1994)

[5] Crocker, L., Algina, J.: Introduction to Classical and Modern Test Theory. Thomson Leaning (1986)

[6] Lance, J., Hoffman, L.J., Kim, L.J., Blum, J.: Trust Beyond Security: an Expanded Trust Model. Communications of the ACM 49(7) (July 2006)

[7] McKnight, D.H., Cummings, L.L., Chervany, N.L.: Initial Trust Formation in New Organizational Relationships. Acad. Management Rev. 23(3), 473–490 (1998)

[8] Bigley, G.A., Pearce, J.L.: Straining for Shared Meaning in Organization Science: Problems of Trust and Distrust. Acad. Management Rev. 23(3), 405–421 (1998)

[9] McKnight, D.H., Choudhury, V., Kacmar, C.: Developing and Validating Trust Measures for E-Commerce: an Integrative Typology. Information Systems Research 13(3), 334–359 (2002)

[10] Li, X., Valacich, J.S., Hess, T.J.: Predicting User Trust in Information Systems: a Comparison of Competing Trust Models. In: Proc. of 37th Annual Hawaii International Conference on System Sciences, p. 10 (January 2004)

[11] Fishbein, M., Ajzen, I.: Beliefs, Attitude, Intention and Behavior: an Introduction to Theory and Research. Addison-Wesley, Reading (1975)

[12] Sheridan, T.: Computer Control and Human Alienation. Technology Review, 61–73 (1980)

[13] Muir, B.M.: Trust in Automation Part II: Experimental Studies of Trust and Human Intervention in a Process Control Simulation. Ergonomics 39(3), 429–469 (1996)

[14] Lee, J., Moray, N.: Trust, Control Strategies and Allocation of Function in Human-Machine Systems. Ergonomics 35(10), 1243–1270 (1992)

[15] Xiong, L., Liu, L.: A Reputation-Based Trust Model for Peer-to-Peer Ecommerce Communities. In: Proceedings of the 4th ACM conference on Electronic commerce, pp. 228–229 (2003)

[16] English, C., Terzis, S.: Gathering Experience in Trust-Based Interactions. In: The 4th International Conference on Trust Management (2006)

[17] Marsh, S.: Formalising Trust as a Computational Concept. Ph.D. Thesis, Univ. Stirling (1994)

[18] Nunnally, J.C.: Psychometric Theory, 2nd edn. McGraw-Hill, New York (1978)

APPENDIX: Measures

1. Sending a message again (especially after the first try) means that you satisfy previous experiences in average.
2. More times of using the messaging means you trust it more.
3. More frequency of using the messaging means you trust it more.
4. You trust the messaging more if you spent more time on it.
5. You do more important tasks through the messaging if you trust it more.
6. You do higher risk tasks through the messaging if you trust it more.
7. You try more features of the messaging if you trust it more.
8. After trying more features of the messaging, you become more expertise on it.
9. If you distrust the messaging, you do not use it.
10. You don't use the messaging any more after the first try because you distrust it.
11. You use the messaging less after meeting an error or a failure.
12. You use the messaging less frequently after meeting an error or a failure.
13. You increase the time/times of using the messaging because of good performance.
14. You increase the frequency of using the messaging because of good performance.
15. You decrease the time/times of using the messaging because of bad performance.
16. You decrease the frequency of using the messaging because of bad performance.
17. After a very bad experience of using the messaging, you stop using it.
18. After a very bad experience of using the messaging, you will use it less.
19. After a very bad experience of using the messaging, you will use it to do less risky task.
20. After a very bad experience of using the messaging, you will use it to do less important task.
21. Using the messaging more times than another similar functioned mobile application means you trust it more.
22. Using the messaging more frequently than another similar functioned mobile application means you trust it more.
23. Spending more time in using the messaging than another similar functioned mobile application means you trust it more.
24. Using the messaging to fulfill a more important task than another similar functioned mobile application means you trust it more.
25. Using the messaging to fulfill a more risky task than another similar functioned mobile application means you trust it more.
26. You recommend the messaging to your friends because you trust it. (This item is removed because its loading is below 0.4.)
27. You replace the messaging application with a new one because you trust the new one more.
28. You delete the messaging because you don't trust it any more.
29. You reject installing a messaging application because you distrust it.
30. You would like to provide good or bad comments about the messaging when you trust or distrust it.
31. After experienced a bad performance of the messaging, you generally don't use it as trust as before.
32. If you have a very good experience using the messaging, you generally would like to recommend it.
33. For two similar functioned mobile applications, you trust more in the one you would like to recommend.

Managing Contracts in Pleiades Using Trust Management

Christoffer Norvik[1], John P. Morrison[1], Dan C. Marinescu[2], Chen Yu[2],
Gabriela M. Marinescu[2], and Howard Jay Siegel[3]

[1] Dept. of Computer Science
University College Cork, Cork, Ireland
{c.norvik,j.morrison}@cs.ucc.ie
[2] School of Electrical Engineering and Computer Science
University of Central Florida, Orlando, Fl, 32816
{dcm,yuchen,magda}@cs.ucf.edu
[3] Dept. of Electrical and Computer Engineering
and Dept. of Computer Science
Colorado State University, Fort Collins, CO 80523-1373
hj@colostate.edu

Abstract. The advent of multicore technologies is set to significantly increase
the average compute power per machine. Effective and efficient exploitation of
this power poses unprecedented challenges and opportunities. The Pleiades system, currently under development in UCF, CSU and UCC [1], proposes the construction of a distributed, heterogeneous, and secure marketplace for trading and
administer these resources whose owners sign up to various quality of service
(QoS) contracts, in return for financial and in-kind payment. This paper presents
a very important part of the Pleiades system: addressing the role of Trust Management (TM) in the generation and enforcement of these contracts. The approach
taken significantly reduces the overhead that is traditionally assumed with cryptographic solutions, by the dynamic and a priory creation of a secure environment
in which these expensive checks associated with cryptographic solutions, are not
required.

1 Introduction

As far back as 1989, Intel researchers suggested that multicore technology could be
used to meet ever increasing compute requirements [2]. Today, two to eight core processors are standard, and microprocessors containing 10-100 cores together with crucial advances in memory technology, throughput and latency are imminent [3]. It is
clear that multicore technology will be available in all standard machines sold in the
near future at no appreciable cost increase. Even though the motivation for constructing
these machines is to satisfy the compute requirements of more and more sophisticated
applications, history tells us that large user communities will not immediately avail of
this increase in power. To appreciate this point, one needs only to look at current usage profiles, in which many machines still spend much of their time doing nothing.
In these communities, increased power will translate into greater wastage of compute

C. Rong et al. (Eds.): ATC 2008, LNCS 5060, pp. 470–480, 2008.

resources. At the same time, other user communities seem to have insatiable compute requirements and can absorb any and all technological advances [4] [5].

The general user community is partitioned into those who have more than enough resources to meet their needs and those who never have enough. As technology advances, the disparity between these groups will widen, and the opportunity for the creation of a market economy based on the buying and selling of compute resources becomes more and more attractive. In addition to the supply and demand outlined above, social, economic, and security considerations must be successfully implemented for such a market authority to succeed. The Pleiades system grapples with these issues in concert for the creation of an effective market authority. Pleiades encourages users to join together to form organisations, to enable resource sharing. These organisations adopt necessary components, provided by Pleiades, to facilitate resource sharing. These components are governed by policies, enabling organisations to tailor these, in order to meet their demand of fault-tolerance, quality of service and security. Adopting this approach allows organisations and users to self organise into existing organisations and joining old organisations to form new ones, by simply changing their policies.

This paper addresses a specific component of the Pleiades system, namely the secure and reliable trading of resources through the creation and management of Quality of Service contracts based on Trust Management.

Primary motivation for this paper is to demonstrate how the KeyNote Trust Management System can be flexibly used in the dynamic management of contracts. The flexibility of the system, allows users to tailor their contracts to meet their own needs, and to adopt to new contracts schemes when collaborating with different organisations and users.

Section 2 discussed related work using virtualization and trust management as a basis for leasing spare resources. An introduction to Trust Management is given in Section 3. Section 4 introduces the proposed tools needed to sell and consume resources. Section 5 explains how contracts are created and issued. Section 6 shows how we use contracts to establish virtual machines to take advantage of leased resources, and briefly outlines steps to reimburse providers for their services. Finally, Section 7 draws some conclusions and looks forward to incorporating the work into the overall Pleiades system.

2   Related Work

Extensive research and work has gone into enabling virtual machines to work in a distributed and Grid environment. Reference [6] proposes an architecture to support trust management contracts, to establish virtual machines to trade resources. All though exploring similar ideas, the implementation uses a specifically developed trust management system, to create contracts for resource consumers and providers.

TrustCoM [7] is a project to develop a framework enabling dynamically evolving Virtual Organisations [8] to manage trust, security and contracts. This will allow VOs to share their resources and make use of secure, collaborative, business processing [9].

Reference [10] proposes similar usage of KeyNote credentials in order to support payments in a distributed environment, these payments are defined on the level of graph and graph nodes to be computed. This requires prior knowledge to the compute time of the graph and nodes, though this information is not always known.

Our contribution is in using an established application, KeyNote, to allow each MA to tailor the construction of contracts to meet their requirements. Subsequently, allowing contracts to be used between different MAs, with different contract specifications, and the establishment of virtual organizations [11], to share resources amongst themselves, using a subset of the information in contracts.

We are not required to have prior knowledge to the compute requirements needed by the resource consumers, nor are we concerned to what extent these requirements are. The expressiveness of KeyNote and in the manner in which it is supported here, ensures that our approach is extensive enough to support a secure and viable economy.

3   Trust Management

Combinations of Access Control Lists (ACL), and X.509 public key infrastructure is argued to be less suitable for authorization and authentication schemes in distributed systems [12]. ACL involves verifying if a user is valid, e.g., providing authentication. If the user is deemed to be valid, the requested actions must be checked to determind if the authenticated user is authorized to perform the requested actions. To summarize, one can ask the following question, "is the user with the following username a valid user, and if so, is the user allowed to perform the requested actions?" The complexity of keeping ACLs up to date and the necessary steps to perform authentication and authorization will increase the complexity of maintaining the current and future users (generally referred to as *principals* within the system), thus effecting the scalability of the system.

Scalability issues can be addressed by introducing the concept of trust management [12]. Trust management binds the names of principals to public keys, and their authorized actions to security policies. This solution achieves authorization and authentication in one step instead of two. Thus, the question becomes "is the holder of this key allowed to perform the requested actions?" KeyNote [13] is a trust management application that allows for writing of signed and non-signed security policies, called *assertions*. These assertions allow principals to delegate trust and authorized actions to others in a flexible and expressive language. The unsigned security policy acts as a root policy, from which trust is delegated. When a principal wishes to delegate actions, the principal will write a policy describing which principals are allowed to do those actions, and signs it with the private key. This policy is now referred to as a *credential*. The signer can send the credential to a recipient over an unsecured connection. The recipient cannot tamper with the credential in an attempt to gain additional permissions. This process will be exploited in the creation of reliable and secure QoS contracts as described in Section 5.

4   Virtualization Software

Virtual Machines (VM) [14] is a technology that enables the user to run several different operating systems concurrently on one machine. Using the VM, the user can initialize a new operating system on a given machine that runs in a sandbox, oblivious to any other operating system that may be running on that machine. VM is easily configurable

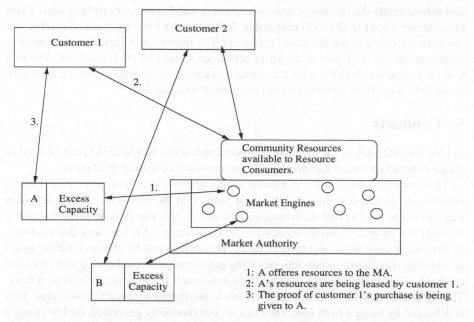

Fig. 1. The market engines negotiate contracts for resources between users with excess capacity, *resource providers*, to customers needing resources, *resource consumers*. The resource providers offers resources by sending the market engines credentials based on the amount of spare resources offered. Based on these credentials, the market engine then writes new credentials for consumers, in exchange for payment. Consumers then present these credentials to their respective providers.

in terms of available hard drive space, RAM, number of CPUs and CPU speed, and other local hardware. More importantly, it creates a layer of separation between the underlying operating system and the newly instantiated VM, preventing unauthorized access both to and from the VM. VM enables the user to tailor it to required usage and need. This includes but is not limited to, the choice of operating system, legacy application support, user and user administration rights, and full control of the operating system in the VM [15].

The concept of virtualization is integrated into the Pleiades system and the sharing of resources among participating machines. Users of the system are divided into (a) *resource providers*, those with excess capacity, shown in Figure 1 as A, and B, and (b) those who need resources, *resource consumers*, shown in Figure 1 as customers 1 and 2.

A Market Authority (MA) will oversee, negotiate contracts, and provide the necessary tools to support a sharing and trading of resources. Subsequently, the MA is responsible for distributing the necessary tools to permit this process. A VM tool will be developed for resource providers. Users wanting to provide resources are required to download and install this tool before the sharing of resources can commence. This tool enables the MA to oversee the state of any VM that is contracted out to resource consumers, enabling it to take any necessary steps to ensure that users are provided with the expected QoS. When the tool is not in use, it sits idly on the user's machine. The tool is enabled by the introduction of a valid contract. To enable the creation of VMs and subsequently the sharing of spare resources, a valid contract must be loaded. Once the contract is loaded, the tool ensures that the required VMs are generated to allow the resource consumer to use the leased resources. The information present in the contracts generates the basis of how much spare resources should be contracted out. The tool will only generate the VMs with the resources requirements specified in the contracts, preventing users from receiving more resources than requested.

5   Contracts

In [16] it is shown how the trust management application KeyNote [13] can be used to create contracts between merchants and customers with a trusted third party.

The core of the solution lies in a users' ability to prove that the customer has a secret known only to that customer and the third party, that the merchant can use at a later stage to claim validity that the transaction occurred. This can then be presented to the trusted third party to claim the money for the transaction. This has some prerequisites. A third party must be trusted by both users. This party must be able and willing to act as a middle man, issuing contracts, receiving payments, and reimbursing users for used contracts. This trusted third party therefore acts much in the same fashion as a bank. The bank must provide some means for users to prove that a transaction occurred. This is achieved by using a hash function and a secure randomly generated seed to create a hash chain. A hash function must be computationally inexpensive to compute the hash value of any given value, but computationally infeasible to recreate the original value given the computed hash value. More formally, assuming $\mathbf{h}()$ is a cryptographic one-way hash function, performing $\mathbf{h}()$ on $\mathbf{x}$ yields $\mathbf{y}$. Given $\mathbf{y}$, it should not be feasible to compute $\mathbf{x}$.

The bank creates a contract containing the value of computing the hash of a secure random generated seed value. The $\mathbf{h}^{n+1}(\mathbf{x})$ gives the coin visible in the contract, and $\mathbf{h}^1(\mathbf{x})$ is the last coin on the chain [16]. This gives the buyer $\mathbf{n}$ number of coins that can be spent. The merchant is able to check the coin by computing the hash of the coin until the hash value in the contract is reached. The seed and contract are sent securely to the customer in return for payment for the wanted services. The customer provides the contract and the correct coin on the chain to the merchant, who based on the trust management check of the contract and a hash check of the coin, can be certain that the buyer has paid for the services.

The resources are then given to the customer, and when expired, the merchant is able to prove to the bank that the transaction occurred by producing the last coin value obtained from the customer. Using this approach, our resource providers are the merchants, the resource consumers are customers, and the MA represent the trusted third party.

The MA keeps track of resources that have been made available by resource providers. The MA also is responsible for issuing rules on how contracts should be written, which is discussed further in Section 6. The resource provider writes a credential for the resources it wishes to sell, which is handed over to the MA. The credential is stored by the market engine, which will try to find a consumer for the available resources. If a consumer is found, the MA writes a new credential based on the provider's credential. The credential also contains the hash chain described above.

This new credential and seed coin are then delivered to the consumer upon a confirmation of payment having been received. The consumer presents this credential and proves that it has paid for the contract by providing the coin from the MA to the provider, who based on a trust management check will decide if the consumer is authenticated and authorized. If the consumer is authorized, the resources will be made available. Once the transaction is complete, the provider can be reimbursed by the MA, discussed further in Section 6.

This solution has a number of desirable features. Because the resource provider will trust the MA that it is willing to sell the resources to, it also will trust the consumer which purchased said resources. This trust is further strengthened by the consumer's ability to provide some proof that it obtained the contract legally, e.g., purchased the right to use the resources from the MA, by presenting the coins to the provider. This establishes a trust relationship between two otherwise unknown principals.

The resource provider is able to continue to use resources until it is presented with a valid contract. The virtualization software that is downloaded and installed on the provider's machine should only lay dormant, or preferably only execute until a potential contract arrives. Once approached with a contract, the provider is quickly able to decide if the contract is valid, based on the trust management check. As the consumer must provide a public key upon submission of the credential, the provider is assured that the consumer has purchased the contract from a trusted MA. The resource provider can not deny having allowed the spare resources to be leased out, as the contract is signed by its private key. Some form of time stamp must be incorporated to address the freshness of the contract. This topic is discussed in Section 7.

To address contract durations, we extend the contracts to incorporate the notion of time. A resource provider will explicitly denote in the contract the cost using resource set A for a pre-set duration. The consumer pays the MA a lump sum, which can be used to purchase contracts. A consumer specifies what kind of resources are needed, and for how long it is needed. The MA provides the contract for the resources with the required number of coins for the requested time duration. Once the contract is initialized, the resources will last for the pre-set duration given in the contract. Once the time is up, the provider requests a new coin before the consumer is allowed to continue work. This is done until the consumer either runs out of coins or no longer has any more use for the resources. This prevents the need to regenerate contracts when the pre-set time duration expires. The provider will only get reimbursed for the duration of services provided, and the consumer can elect to use the remaider of the money at the MA on another resource provider. It should be noted that the MA should lock the total value of the contract to the payment lodged by the consumer. This ensures that the consumer can only get contracts worth what was lodged, and the resource provider gets paid for its provided resources whether or not the contract is completed.

The MA or the resource consumer can delegate purchased resources to other MAs or consumers [17]. As the nature of trust management allows for the delegation of trust, the principal contract holder needs only write a new credential to the necessary peer, and hand off the credentials to the third party. This allows anyone to purchase resources in bulk, and then dividing them up and reselling them as they see fit. However, mechanisms are in place to ensure that this can be denied should the provider deem it necessary.

Scenarios where principals wish to form their own market authorities for collaboration might arise. These scenarios, where trust is complete among all participating principals, allow for the granularity of the contracts to be reduced for the purpose of increases in overall speed and administration. It is still important to make sure that the correct principals have the correct access to resources.

6 Trust Management Contracts and Reimbursements

Implementing support for payments using trust management credentials is not a new approach. References [16] and [10] both show how this can be successfully achieved and implemented. Furthermore, it shows how payments are made to a bank, and how the resource provider is reimbursed when the contract has been successfully completed. This solution comes at a price in form of performance degradation because all requests for computation must be checked by the trust management engine. This requires cryptographic computations that are inherently expensive. Reference [10] gives examples of this expense when computing *fine grained jobs* in WebCom. In parallel systems granularity is defined as the ratio of processing to communication. When this ratio is low, the computation is **said** to be fine grained, when high, the computation is **said** to be coarse grained. In effect granularity describes how frequently a computation is punctuated (that is, interrupted) by, in this case, a communication action. In a similar manner, the punctuation of code with TM checks defines granularity from that perspective.

The performance degradation on coarse grained jobs is less, because the queries to the trust management engine are less frequent and fewer. This puts pressure on the programmer to develop as many coarse grained jobs as possible, which might not always be feasible. It is clear that having the virtual machine query the trust management engine for every request is not feasible, as the shared amount of queries in terms of access to I/O, read and write calls to memory and hard drive, and so on, would severely impact the performance of the system.

Our solution addresses two critical questions. "How to reduce the performance degradation generated by querying the trust management engine?", and "how to convince the consumer that the resources it purchased are guaranteed to be supplied by the provider?" First, we deal with the trust management overhead by reducing the number of times the trust management engine has to be queried. This is achieved by creating a virtual machine. The application provided by the market authority only allows virtual machines to be activated with a valid contract. Once the resource provider has the contract and is willing to offer the resources in the terms stated in the contract, this contract is given to the application. The application, based on these terms, creates new virtual machines and subsequently deploys these to create redundancy across the system.

Once the virtual machines have been created, they must exist under the rule of the contract, which specifies requirements such as available hard drive space, memory availability, hardware resource access, and even time limits for hardware access. When the contract has expired, the application kicks in, and freezes the state of the virtual machines. If the resource provider is no longer willing to offer its services, the virtual machines will be removed from the system. If a new contract is loaded, the application will enable the virtual machine again, or should new terms arise, create new virtual machines based on said terms. It will then subsequently move the state of the old virtual machines into the new ones, thus preserving all modifications and changes made by the consumer during execution. By using a virtual machine, we address concerns on both the provider's and the consumer's side. Because the virtual machine operates in a sandbox, users cannot modify and make changes outside their sandbox. The trust management engine is not queried until a new contract appears, and security is achieved from the virtual machine sandbox and the operating system loaded in it. Implementations where the trust management is used to check the validity of contracts, the consumer is forced to pay first, before receiving the goods. If the consumer is using an unscrupulous provider, the provider might elect to not give the consumer the goods, and cash in on the contract before the consumer is able to report the fraud to the bank. The provider is subsequently punished for this, by banning it from the system, however the damage has already been done. If the resources provided are not what the consumer purchased, the market authority is notified, and can therefore elect to refuse payment to the provider. Our extension coupled with the implementation from Section 5 provides proof of a valid consumer, in form of a contract and a coin; proof for the provider to get reimbursed, in form of the coin produced by the consumer; and finally proof for the consumer that the resources paid for are provided, by the virtual machines made available and the notification to the MA if said resources drop below a threshold.

```
Authorizer: ResourceProvider
Local-Constants: "ResourceProvider"
                 "MA"
Conditions: SERVICE == "Pleiades" &&
            ((@TOTAL_CPUS+@USER_CPUS <= 4) &&
            (@TOTAL_CPU_CORES+@USER_CPU_CORES <= 8) &&
            (@TOTAL_MEM+@USER_MEM <= 4096));
Licensees: MA
Signature: ResourceProvider
```

Fig. 2. Credential from Resource Provider to an MA, leasing resources in form of CPUs, Cores and RAM. By keeping track of requests made by users, and storing these into a variables, e.g., @TOTAL_CPUS, @TOTAL_CPU_CORES and @TOTAL_MEM, the Resource Provider prevents the MA, by accident, issuing to many contracts based on the actual resources provided.

Figure 2 and 3 shows samples of possible TM contracts, specifying the amount of resources the resource provider is willing to lease out from Figure 2 (Public keys and signatures has been omitted in these examples). The total amount of available leased resources are addressed in the contracts to the MA to prevent faults where the MA leases too many resources out to consumers. A request for resources will thus be denied from the resource provider. It requires the resource provider to keep track of total amount of resources leased out.

Figure 3 is a standard contract, where the available resources are denoted in the contract, together with lease time, type of duration, available coins and the last coin on the chain as discussed in Section 5. The expressiveness of KeyNote will allow us to write credentials that are dynamic, thus instead of explicitly denoting a fixed set of

Authorizer: MA
Local-Constants: "MA"
                "ConsumerA"
Conditions: SERVICE == "Pleiades" &&
            @USER_CPUS <= 2 &&
            @USER_CPU_CORES <= 4 &&
            @USER_MEM <= 2048 &&
            @Duration == 60 &&
            DurationType == "min" &&
            @NumberOfCoins <= 10 &&
            Coin == "SomeValue";
Licensees: ConsumerA
Signature: MA

Fig. 3. Credential from MA, to a Consumer, denoting available resources that can be requested

resources, e.g., as maximum available memory, maximum available cores, contracts can be written as percentage of the total available system resources. This is ideal in a situation where users may from time to time need all available resources on the system, but where the system in larger time is idle. Scenarios like this, might be a corporation with workstations that are in use from 8-6 but not from 6-8.

Reimbursement is provided by the MA. The resource provider will present the contract and the last coin that it received from the consumer. If the MA has a record of creating the contract and the contract and coin are deemed valid by the trust management engine, the resource provider is reimbursed. The coin is checked by simply hashing the value of the coin until the hash value equals that in the contract. This also provides the basis for how much the provider should be reimbursed. At this point, the contract should be marked as paid, thus preventing the resource provider from trying to get paid several times. The resource consumer is notified by the MA to enable it to give feedback on the transactions [18]. This helps to thwart attempts to cheat the system by unscrupulous resource providers. Mechanisms should be in place to enable the cooperation between different market authorities sharing the negotiation of price and reimbursements of contracts to different users. This is subject for further research.

7   Summary and Future Work

This paper describes a way of providing a sustainable and secure economy in Pleiades. The solution utilizes trust management, an established secure system, to create contracts for consumers and providers. Using trust management, users are allowed to write, share, and use trust management assertions to issue, buy and consume resources. However, the way the trust management has been combined to create contracts, and the way it is used for trust management checks, reduces the cryptographic overhead associated with the general trust management process. An additional benefit for the consumer, is increased level of quality of service. The system scales well for future development, and also is suitable for the distributed nature of the MA.

Details of how the software provided by the MA is created, how contract freshness is maintained, and a set of pre-defined rules on how to correctly write the credentials, i.e., in terms of variable names, is needed.

Simulations of the system in order to show, amongst others, tradeoffs between instantiating short lived VMs and its coupling with the creation and usage of KeyNote credentials, how well the system scales when being exposed to evolving organisations, and more importantly the effectiveness between different organisations in relation to communication overheads, requires further investigation. Crossing different organisations poses other problems too, especially in terms of user's data security. Since this could be an inhibitor when sharing resources beetwen different organisations, though potentially not an issue when contained within the organization itself, it warrants the investigation into a separate component, that would address this issue, for the Pleiades system.

Revocation has been addressed by the creators of KeyNote in [19]. Revocation may be used, when addressing the subject of freshness of contracts, it relies on the synchronization of clocks between principals, which may be difficult to achieve.

The work done in [10] show what would appear to be, an inevitable increase in compute time when making trust management checks on fine grained jobs, due to the number of TM checks needed. A major contribution of the system described here is that this performance degradation is not inevitable. In fact, since the solution described here is general, it could be applied to systems other than Pleiades.

Acknowledgments

Christoffer Norvik and John P. Morrison acknowledges the support provided by the Science Foundation Ireland. Dan C. Marinescu expresses his thanks to the Science foundation of Ireland for the support provided by a Walton award. H. J. Siegel was supported by the US National Science Foundation under grant number CNS0615170 and by the Abell Endorsement.

The helpfull comments received from the reviewers are greatfully acknowledged.

References

1. Marinescu, D.C., Morrison, J.P., Siegel, H.J.: Pleiades: a Self-Organizing Service-Based Architecture (2007), http://condgraf.ucc.ie/Pleiades
2. Gelsinger, P., Gargini, P., Parker, G., Yu, A.: Microprocessors circa 2000. IEEE Spectrum 26(10), 43–47 (1989)
3. Intel Tera-scale: Computing Research Program,
   http://techresearch.intel.com/articles/Tera-Scale/1421.htm
4. Folding@Home: Distributed computing, http://folding.stanford.edu/
5. SETI@Home: Search for extraterrestrial intelligence,
   http://setiathome.berkeley.edu/
6. Fu, Y., Chase, J., Chun, B., Schwab, S., Vahdat, A.: Sharp: an architecture for secure resource peering. In: SOSP 2003: Proceedings of the nineteenth ACM symposium on Operating systems principles, pp. 133–148. ACM, New York (2003)
7. TrustCoM: Project, http://www.eu-trustcom.com/

8. Dimitrakos, T.: et al: Trustcom - A Trust and Contract Management Framework enabling Secure Collaborations in Dynamic Virtual Organisations. ERCIM News No. 59, 59-60 Sophia Antipolis, France (2004) (Accessed April 2008), http://www.ercim.org/publication/ercim_news/enw59/dimitrakos2.html
9. Wilson, M.D., Chadwick, D., Dimitrakos, T., Doser, J., Arenas, A., Giambiagi, P., et al.: The trustcom framework v0.5. In: Proc. 6th IFIP Working Conference on Virtual Enterprises (PRO-VE 2005), Valencia, Spain (September 26-28, 2005)
10. Patil, A., Norvik, C., Power, D.A., Morrison, J.P.: Implementing fine and coarse grained payment mechanisms using webcom. In: Proceedings of the he 8th Hellenic European Research on Computer Mathematics and its Applications Conference (HERCMA 2007), Athens, Greece (September 20-22, 2007)
11. Foster, I.: The anatomy of the grid: Enabling scalable virtual organizations. In: CCGRID 2001: Proceedings of the 1st International Symposium on Cluster Computing and the Grid, Washington, DC, USA, p. 6. IEEE Computer Society, Los Alamitos (2001)
12. Blaze, M., Feigenbaum, J., Ioannidis, J., Keromytis, A.D.: The role of trust management in distributed systems security. In: Vitek, J. (ed.) Secure Internet Programming. LNCS, vol. 1603, pp. 185–210. Springer, Heidelberg (1999)
13. Blaze, M., Feigenbaum, J., Ioannidis, J., Keromytis, A.: The KeyNote Trust-Management System Version 2, Request for Comments 2704 (1999)
14. Meyer, R.A., Seawright, L.H.: A virtual machine time-sharing system. IBM Systems Journal 9(3), 199–218 (1970)
15. Figueiredo, R.J., Dinda, P.A., Fortes, J.A.B.: A case for grid computing on virtual machines. In: ICDCS 2003: Proceedings of the 23rd International Conference on Distributed Computing Systems, Washington, DC, USA. IEEE Computer Society, Los Alamitos (2003)
16. Foley, S.N., Quillinan, T.B.: Using trust management to support micropayments. In: Proceedings of the Second Information Technology and Telecommunications Conference, Waterford Institute of Technology, Waterford, Ireland., TecNet, pp. 219–223 (2002)
17. Foley, S.N.: Using trust management to support transferable hash-based micropayments. In: Proceedings of the 7th International Financial Cryptography Conference, Gosier, Guadeloupe, French West Indies (2003)
18. Marinescu, D.C., Yu, C., Marinescu, G.M., Morrison, J.P., Norvik, C.: A reputation algorithm for a self-organizing system based upon resource virtualization. In: 17th Heterogeneous Computing Workshop (HCW 2008); accepted to appear in the proceedings of the 22nd International Parallel and Distributed Processing Symposium (IPDPS 2008), Miami, FL (April 2008)
19. Blaze, M., Ioannidis, J., Keromytis, A.D.: Experience with the keynote trust management system: Applications and future directions. In: Trust Management: First International Conference, iTrust, Heraklion, Crete, Greece (2003)

A Semantic Foundation for Trust Management Languages with Weights: An Application to the RT Family*,**

Stefano Bistarelli[1,2], Fabio Martinelli[2], and Francesco Santini[2,3]

[1] Dipartimento di Scienze, Università "G. D'Annunzio" di Chieti-Pescara, Italy
bista@sci.unich.it
[2] Istituto di Informatica e Telematica (CNR), Pisa, Italy
{stefano.bistarelli,fabio.martinelli,francesco.santini}@iit.cnr.it
[3] IMT - Institute for Advanced Studies, Lucca, Italy
f.santini@imtlucca.it

Abstract. In this paper, we present a variant of Datalog language (we call it Datalog^W) able to deal with weights on ground facts and to consequently compute a feedback result for the goal satisfaction. The weights are chosen from a proper c-semiring. In our context, our goal is to use this language as a semantic foundation for languages for expressing trust relationships. As a matter of fact, many of them have a semantics given in terms of crisp constraints: our approach is to extend them to cover also the soft case. Thus, we apply Datalog^W as the basis to give a uniform semantics to declarative RT^W (Trust Management) language family. The approach is rather generic and could be applied to other trust management languages based on Datalog, as a semantic sublayer to represent trust management languages where the trust level is relevant.

1 Introduction and Motivations

Trust is a very interesting and relevant notion in modern pervasive computer systems. It lies at the heart of human interactions and thus as soon as these interactions happen through (and among) digital devices, such trust relationships must be represented, specified, analyzed, negotiated and composed in those systems [11]. As a matter of fact, when one wants to mechanize the reasoning in certain situations, a formalization is necessary. If one wants also to achieve a common understand and comparison among different trust management system, a semantic mechanism would be extremely useful.

To make a concrete example, a Trust Management (TM) language is required to have the expressivity power to represent the trust-related facts of the considered dominion and a method to derive new assessments and decision starting from these base facts. Current trust management languages based on credentials

---

* The first and third authors are supported by the MIUR PRIN 2005-015491.
** The second author is supported by the EU projects GRIDtrust and SENSORIA.

C. Rong et al. (Eds.): ATC 2008, LNCS 5060, pp. 481–495, 2008.
© Springer-Verlag Berlin Heidelberg 2008

(for both expressing facts and access policy rules) uses several foundational approaches. However, facts and access rules are not so crisp in the real complex world. For example, each piece of information could have a confidence value associated with it and representing a reliability estimation, or a fuzzy preference level or a cost to be taken in account. The feedback final value, obtained by aggregating all the ground facts together, can be then used to improve the decision support system by basing on this preference level instead of a plain "yes or no" result (e.g, see [15,6,5]). In this scenario, a credential could state that the referred entity is a "student" or a "bright student" with a probability of 80% because her/his identity of student is based on what an acquaintance asserts (thus, it is not as certain as declared in IDs), or, in the second case, because the received marks need to be globally evaluated. In literature there are many examples where trust or reputation are computed by aggregating some values together [11], for example in PGP systems, or for generic trust propagation inside social networks. We think that similar quantitative measurements are useful also for trust languages, in order to have a more informative result.

For this reason, we describe a weighted version of Datalog (i.e. Datalog^W) where the rules are enhanced with values taken from a proper c-semiring structure [1,3], in order to model the preference/cost system; then, we use it as the basis to give declarative semantics to a Role-based Trust-management language according to the principles of RT_0 [14], and called here RT_0^W: the statements of RT_0^W are "soft", i.e. have a related c-semiring value. A similar improvement can be accomplished also for RT_1 [14], i.e. RT_0 extended with parameterized roles. Similar variations for RTML family languages were defined and implemented by using different formal tools in [15]. There, an initial comparison (and integration) between rule-based trust management (RTML) and reputation-based trust systems has been performed and a preliminary (ad-hoc) implementation RTML weighted presented in [8] for GRID systems. However, having a uniform semantics approach to model these languages (as Datalog^W) could be very useful to provide a common understanding as well as a basis for systematic comparison and uniform implementation.

Indeed, there are good reasons to prefer a language that is declarative and has a formal foundation. In this sense, we are following a similar approach as done in [13] for RTML trust management languages, where Datalog with constraints have been proposed as a formal semantics for trust management languages. Since trust is not necessarily crisp, Datalog^W could be used to give formal semantics to this kind of languages with "soft credentials". In this paper we show an approach for RTML that can be further extended to other Datalog-based languages. The main contribution of this paper is thus to provide a formal semantics for such languages that could also bring to a uniform implementation approach, as well as to a comparison among these languages . Giving weights to facts and rules contributes also towards bridging the gap between "rule-based" trust management (i.e. hard security mechanisms) and "reputation based" trust management [11] (i.e. soft security mechanisms).

It is also worth noticing that c-semirings are a valuable mechanism to model and solve optimization problems in several contexts. With our proposal of mixing credential based languages with soft-constraints based on c-semiring in a systematic way, we pave the way for linguistic mechanisms for making optimization decision related to the trust domain. Indeed, this domain could be also coupled with other parameters and thus creating a much more complex (self) optimization mechanisms. For instance, one could use a cost/preference parameter associated with the trust level. The composition of the trust semiring and the preference one is yet amenable of mechanization and this yet leads to a similar treatment we describe here.

In this paper we extend the ideas presented in [2] by giving a weighted semantics to all the RT languages presented in [14]. In Sec. 2 we describe the background notions about trust languages and c-semirings. In Sec. 3 we present a weighted version of Datalog, i.e. $Datalog^W$, while Sec. 4 features the weighted RT language family based on $Datalog^W$, i.e. RT_0^W, RT_1^W, RT_2^W, RT^{WT} and RT^{WD}. At last, in 5 we present the final conclusions.

2   Background

Datalog was originally developed as a query and rule language for deductive databases and is syntactically equivalent to a subset of the Prolog language. Several TM languages are based on Datalog, e.g., Delegation Logic [12], the RT (Role-based Trust-management) framework [14], SD3 (Secure Dynamically Distributed Datalog) [10] and Binder [9]. These are some of the languages that can benefit from the semantic basis presented in this paper, even if we will focus only in the RT language family.

The RT framework is a family of Role-based Trust-management languages [14], whose most basic part is RT_0 which has been then extended to RT_1 with parameterized roles: $University.professorOf(student)$ is a statement that can be used to name the professor of a student. An *entity* (or *principal*, e.g. A or B) in RT is a uniquely identified individual or process, which can issue credentials and make requests. RT assumes that an entity that issued a particular credential or a request can be determined through the use of public/private key pairs. A *role* in RT takes the form of an entity followed by a role name (e.g. R with subscripts), separated by a dot. A role defines a set of entities who are members of this role: each entity A has the authority to define who are the members of each role of the form $A.R$. Each statement defines one role to contain either an entity, another role, or certain other expressions that evaluate to a set of entities. More details will be given in Sec. 4.

An important extension that significantly enhances the expressivity of this kind of languages is presented in [13]. In that work, the authors present Datalog extended with constraints (denoted by $Datalog^C$) in order to define access permissions over structured resources as trees.

Several approaches advocated the usage of trust levels w.r.t. attributes, also stated directly in digital credentials. In addition to the works on the extension of

RTML with weights and its relationships with other trust models as the Josang one already mentioned [15,8], there is also the work on policy and reputation done in [5]. Here the PROTUNE policy language is extended to deal with trust and reputation levels. Also role based access control has been extended with trust levels in [6]. All these works use specific logics and approaches.

C-semirings. A c-semiring S [1,3] (or simply semiring in the following) is a tuple $\langle S, +, \times, \mathbf{0}, \mathbf{1} \rangle$ where S is a set with two special elements $(\mathbf{0}, \mathbf{1} \in S)$ and with two operations $+$ and $\times$ that satisfy certain properties: $+$ is defined over (possibly infinite) sets of elements of S and thus is commutative, associative, idempotent, it is closed and $\mathbf{0}$ is its unit element and $\mathbf{1}$ is its absorbing element; $\times$ is closed, associative, commutative, distributes over $+$, $\mathbf{1}$ is its unit element, and $\mathbf{0}$ is its absorbing element (for the exhaustive definition, please refer to [1,3]). The $+$ operation defines a partial order $\leq_S$ over S such that $a \leq_S b$ iff $a + b = b$; we say that $a \leq_S b$ if b represents a value *better* than a. Notice that the partial order can be defined since the $+$ operator is commutative, associative and idempotent. Other properties related to the two operations are that $+$ and $\times$ are monotone on $\leq_S$, $\mathbf{0}$ is its minimum and $\mathbf{1}$ its maximum, $\langle S, \leq_S \rangle$ is a complete lattice and $+$ is its lub. Finally, if $\times$ is idempotent, then $+$ distributes over $\times$, $\langle S, \leq_S \rangle$ is a complete distributive lattice and $\times$ its glb.

Varying the set S and the meaning of the $+$ and $\times$ operations, we can represent many different kinds of problems, having features like fuzziness, probability, and optimization. Moreover, in [3] the authors have shown that the cartesian product of two c-semirings is another c-semiring, and this can be fruitfully used to describe multi-criteria constraint satisfaction and optimization problems, e.g. the *path semiring* presented in Sec. 3.

3   A Weighted Extension of Datalog

Datalog is a restricted form of logic programming with variables, predicates, and constants, but without function symbols. Facts and rules are represented as Horn clauses in the generic form $R_0 :\!- R_1, \ldots, R_n$. A Datalog rule has the form $R_0(t_{0,1}, \ldots, t_{0,k_0}) :\!-R_1(t_{1,1}, \ldots, t_{1,k_1}), \ldots, R_n(t_{n,1}, \ldots, t_{n,k_n})$, where $R_0, \ldots, R_n$ are predicate (relation) symbols and each term $t_{i,j}$ is either a constant or a variable $(0 \leq i \leq n$ and $1 \leq j \leq k_i)$. The formula $R_0(t_{0,1}, \ldots, t_{0,k_0})$ is called the head of the rule and the sequence $R_1(t_{1,1}, \ldots, t_{1,k_1}), \ldots, R_n(t_{n,1}, \ldots, t_{n,k_n})$ the body. If $n = 0$, then the body is empty and the rule is called a fact. Moreover, each program P in Datalog (i.e. a finite set of rules) must satisfy two *safety* conditions: *i)* all variables occurring in the head of a rule also have to appear in the body, and *ii)* every fact in P must be a ground fact.

We can now define our *Weighted Datalog*, or Datalog^W based on classical Datalog. While rules have the same form as in classical Datalog, a fact in Datalog^W has the form: $R_i(x_{i,1}, \ldots, x_{i,k_i}) : - s$. Therefore, the extension is obtained by associating to ground facts a value $s \in S$ taken from the semiring $\langle S, +, \times, \mathbf{0}, \mathbf{1} \rangle$. This value describes some properties of the fact, depending on the chosen semiring: for example, we can add together all these values by using the *Weighted*

Table 1. A simple Datalog^W program

```
s(X) :- p(X,Y).        q(a) :- t(a).
p(a,b) :- q(a).        t(a) :- 2.
p(a,c) :- r(a).        r(a) :- 3.
```

semiring $\langle R^+, min, +, \infty, 0 \rangle$, trying to minimize the overall sum at the same time. Otherwise, we can find the best global preference level by using the *Fuzzy* semiring $\langle [0,1], max, min, 0, 1 \rangle$ or we can retrieve the highest resulting probability when we compose all the ground facts, by using the *Probability* semiring $\langle [0,1], max, \times, 0, 1 \rangle$.

Table 1 shows an example of Datalog^W program, for which we suppose to use the *Weighted* semiring. The intuitive meaning of a semiring value like 3 associated to the atom $r(a)$ (in Table 1) is that $r(a)$ costs 3 units. Thus the set N contains all possible costs, and the choice of the two operations min and $+$ implies that we intend to minimize the sum of the costs. This gives us the possibility to select the atom instantiation which gives the minimum cost overall. Given a goal like $s(x)$ to this program, the operational semantics collects both a substitution for x (in this case, $x = a$) and also a semiring value (in this case, 2) which represents the minimum cost among the costs for all derivations for $s(x)$. To find one of these solutions, it starts from the goal and uses the clauses as usual in logic programming, except that at each step two items are accumulated and combined with the current state: a substitution and a semiring value (both provided by the used clause). The combination of these two items with what is contained in the current goal is done via the usual combination of substitutions (for the substitution part) and via the multiplicative operation of the semiring (for the semiring value part), which in this example is the arithmetic $+$. Thus, in the example of goal $s(X)$, we get two possible solutions, both with substitution $X = a$ but with two different semiring values: 2 and 3. Then, the combination of such two solutions via the min operation give us the semiring value 2.

To compute trust, in Sec. 4.1 we will use the *path semiring* [16]: $S_{trust} = \langle \langle [0,1], [0,1] \rangle, +_p, \times_p, \langle 0, 0 \rangle, \langle 1, 1 \rangle \rangle$, where

$$\langle t_i, c_i \rangle +_p \langle t_j, c_j \rangle = \begin{cases} \langle t_i, c_i \rangle & \text{if } c_i > c_j, \\ \langle t_j, c_j \rangle & \text{if } c_i < c_j, \\ \langle max(t_i, t_j), c_i \rangle & \text{if } c_i = c_j. \end{cases}$$

$$\langle t_i, c_i \rangle \times_p \langle t_j, c_j \rangle = \langle t_i t_j, c_i c_j \rangle$$

In this case, trust information is represented by a couple of values $\langle t, c \rangle$: the second component represents a trust value in the range $[0,1]$, while the first component represents the accuracy of the trust value assignment (i.e. a *confidence* value), and it is still in the range $[0,1]$. This parameter can be assumed as a *quality* of the opinion represented instead by the trust value; for example, a high confidence could mean that the trustor has interacted with the target for a long time and then the correlated trust value is estimated with precision.

Finite Computation Time. Being the Datalog^W language a subset of the *Soft Constraint Logic Programming* language [4] with no functions, we can can use the results in [4] to prove that, considering a fixed Datalog^W program, the time for computing the value of any goal for this program is finite and bounded by a constant. The reason is that we just have to consider a finite subclass of refutations (i.e. *simple refutations*) with a bounded length. After having considered all these refutations up to that bounded length, we have finished computing the semiring value of the given goal. Given a refutation tree, a path from the root to a leaf is called *simple* if all its nodes have different labels up to variable renaming. A refutation is a simple refutation if all paths from the root to a leaf in its refutation tree are simple. The proof of Theo. 1 is given in [4].

Theorem 1 (Finite Set of Simple Refutations). *Given a Datalog^W program P and a goal C, consider the set $SR(C)$ of simple refutations starting from C and building the empty substitution. Then $SR(C)$ is finite.*

4 Extending the *RT* Family with Datalog^W

We describe four kinds of credentials for defining roles in a TM language family, here called RT^W, which is based on Datalog^W (see Sec. 3). This family uniformly extends the classical *RT* family [14] by associating a weight, or better, a semiring value to the basic role definition. Therefore, all the following credentials must be parameterized with a chosen $\langle S, +, \times, \mathbf{0}, \mathbf{1} \rangle$ semiring in order represent preference/cost or fuzzy information associated to the statements. For every following RT_0^W credential, we describe how it can be translated in a corresponding Datalog^W rule. Then we will suggest how to extend RT_0^W with parameterized roles, obtaining the RT_1^W language.

Rule 1. $A.R \longleftarrow \langle B, s \rangle$ where A and B are (possibly the same) entities, and R is a role name. This means that A defines B to be a member of A's R role. This statement can be translated to Datalog^W with the rule $r(A, B)$:- s, where s is the semiring value associated with the related ground fact, i.e. $s \in S$.

Rule 2. $A.R \longleftarrow B.R_1$ This statement means that A defines its R role to include (all members of) B's R_1 role. The corresponding Datalog^W rule is $r(A, x)$:-$r_1(B, x)$.

Rule 3. $A.R \longleftarrow A.R_1.R_2$, where $A.R_1.R_2$ is defined as *linked role* [14] and it means that A defines its R role to include (the members of) every role $B.R_2$ in which B is a member of $A.R_1$ role. The mapping to Datalog^W is $r(A, x)$:-$r_1(A, y), r_2(y, x)$.

Rule 4. $A.R \longleftarrow B_1.R_1 \cap B_2.R_2 \cap \cdots \cap B_n.R_n$. In this way, A defines its R role to include the intersection of the n roles. It can be translated to Datalog^W with $r(A, x)$:-$r_1(B_1, x), r_2(B_2, x), \ldots, r_n(B_n, x)$.

The semantics of a program using these rules will find the best credential chain according to the $+$ operator of the chosen semiring, which defines a partial order

$\leq_S$. Notice that only the basic role definition statement (i.e. **Rule 1**) is enhanced with the semiring value $s \in S$, since the other three rules are used to include one role into another or to obtain the intersection of different roles.

Notice that having a semiring value associated only with ground facts does not prevent us from giving a weight also to rules. This can be accomplished by slightly changing the syntax of the credentials used to compose the roles together (i.e. **Rules 1-2-3**), by associating a semiring value also to them. Then, in the Datalog translation, a new ground fact can be added in the body of the rule, whose weight models the use of that specific rule. For example, **Rule 2** becomes $A.R \longleftarrow \langle B.R_1, s \rangle$ (where s is a value taken from the same S semiring set), and its Datalog translation is $r(A, x)$:-$r_1(B, x), rule\_weight$, where $rule\_weight$:- s is the ground fact that gives a weight to the rule. Clearly, nothing changes from the computational point of view (see Sec 3).

It is easy to extend this language in order to enhance it with parameterized roles, thus obtaining a RT_1^W language following the hierarchy presented in [14]. This parametrization can be used to represent relationships among entities, e.g. *University.professorOf(student)* to name the professor of a student, but also to represent attributes that have fields, e.g. the number of exams or the enrollment academic year and so on. With respect to the previous four rules, in RT_1^W the *head* of a credential has the form $A.R(h_1, \ldots, h_n)$, in which A is an entity, and $R(h_1, \ldots, h_n)$ is a role name (R is a role identifier). For each $i \in 1 \ldots n$, h_i is a data term having the type of the ith parameter of R. For example, **Rule 1** can be rewritten in RT_1^W as $A.R(h_1, \ldots, h_n) \longleftarrow \langle B, s \rangle$, and mapped to Datalog^W as $r(A, B, h_1, \ldots, h_n)$:- s. Our intention is to extend the RT^W family according to the guidelines explained in [14] (see Sec. 5).

Since Datalog is a subset of first-order logic, the semantics of a TM language based on it is declarative and unambiguous. While The $\times$ operator of the semiring is used to compose the preference/cost values associated to the statements, the $+$ is used to let the framework select the best derivation with more chances to authorize the requester (among all the credentials revealed by her/him).

In the next theorem we claim that our weighted language family can be used to represent also classical RT credentials [14]. In this sense, the RT^W languages can be considered as a foundation layer for all the classical RT languages (RT_2^W will be instead presented in Sec. 4.2).

Theorem 2 (Language Family Inclusion). *For each S set of statements in the RT_0, RT_1 or RT_2 language, we can find a corresponding S^W set of statements respectively represented in RT_0^W, RT_1^W or RT_2^W, and whose semantics is the same. This can be accomplished by using Datalog^W together with the Boolean semiring.*

In Fig. 1 we show the result of Theo. 2, i.e. the vertical inclusions; the horizontal ones are explained in [14] (for RT) and in this paper (for RT^W). Theorem 2 can be proved by using the *Boolean* semiring $\langle \{0, 1\}, \vee, \wedge, 0, 1 \rangle$ and by assigning a weight of 1 (i.e. the *true* value) to all the ground facts. In this way we obtain a set of crisp statements and the semantics returns all the possible derivations, as the corresponding RT set of statements would do.

$$RT_0 \subseteq RT_1 \subseteq RT_2$$
$$\cap \qquad \cap \qquad \cap$$
$$RT_0^w \subseteq RT_1^w \subseteq RT_2^w$$

Fig. 1. A hierarchy of RT^W languages, compared with the classical RT one

In Sec. 4.3 and Sec. 4.4 we respectively introduce other two RT-based languages: RT^{WT} and RT^{WD} can be used, together or separately, with each of RT_0^W, RT_1^W, or RT_2^W. The resulting combinations are written as RT_i^W, RT_i^{WT} and RT_i^{WD} for $i = 0, 1, 2$.

4.1 Some Examples with Levels of Trust

We can start by adding levels to the classical RT_0 example presented in many RT related papers (e.g. [14]). To solve the example in Table 2, we use a *Fuzzy* semiring $\langle [0, 1], max, min, 0, 1 \rangle$, where the elements in $[0, 1]$ represents the truth degree connected to a credential and evaluated by the entity which signs and issues it: for example, StateU.highMarks $\longleftarrow$ $\langle$ Alice, 0.8 $\rangle$ in Table 2 certifies that Alice has obtained a good number of high marks (since the value is 0.8) for the exams completed at the StateU university (the credential is issued by StateU).

Table 2. An example in RT_0^W, with fuzzy values associated to the credentials

```
     EPub.disct ⟵ EPub.preferred ∩ EPub.brightStudent.
 EPub.preferred ⟵ EOrg.highBudget ∩ EOrg.oldCustomer.
EPub.brightStudent ⟵ EPub.goodUniversity.highMarks.
EPub.goodUniversity ⟵ ABU.accredited.
     ABU.accredited ⟵ ⟨ StateU, 0.9 ⟩.
  StateU.highMarks ⟵ ⟨ Alice, 0.8 ⟩.
   EOrg.highBudget ⟵ ⟨ Alice, 0.6 ⟩.
  EOrg.oldCustomer ⟵ ⟨ Alice, 0.7 ⟩.
```

The example in Table 2 describes a fictitious Web publishing service, *EPub*, which offers a discount to anyone who is both a preferred customer and a bright student. EPub delegates the authority over the identification of preferred customers to its parent organization, *EOrg*. In order to be evaluated as a preferred customer, EOrg must issues two different types of credentials stating that the customer is not new (i.e. *EOrg.oldCustomer*) and has already spent some money in the past (i.e. *EOrg.highBudget*). EOrg assigns a fuzzy value to both these two credentials to quantify its evaluation. EPub delegates the authority over the identification of bright students to the entities that are accredited universities. To identify such universities, EPub accepts accrediting credentials issued by the fictitious *Accrediting Board for Universities* (*ABU*). ABU evaluates a university with a fuzzy score and each university evaluates its enrolled students. A student is bright if she/he is both enrolled in a good university and has high marks. The final fuzzy score, obtained by composing together all the values of the used credentials, can be compared with a threshold to authorize the discount: e.g. only entities whose set of credentials produced a score greater than 0.7 are authorized. Otherwise, the final fuzzy result can be used to derive a proportional discount amount: for example a score of 0.8 could authorize a discount that is twice the discount allowed with a score of 0.4. The following credentials prove that Alice is eligible for the discount with a score of 0.6, determined by the fact that she has not a very high budget spent at EOrg (i.e. her *EOrg.highBudget* credential has a value of 0.6).

Table 3. An extension of the example in Table 2, using the *path semiring*

$$
\begin{aligned}
&\texttt{EPub.disct} \longleftarrow \texttt{EPub.preferred} \cap \texttt{EPub.brightStudent}.\\
&\texttt{EPub.disct} \longleftarrow \texttt{EOrg.famousProf.goodRecLetter}.\\
&\texttt{EPub.preferred} \longleftarrow \texttt{EOrg.highBudget} \cap \texttt{EOrg.oldCustomer}.\\
&\texttt{EPub.brightStudent} \longleftarrow \texttt{EPub.goodUniversity.highMarks}.\\
&\texttt{EPub.goodUniversity} \longleftarrow \texttt{ABU.accredited}.\\
&\texttt{EOrg.famousProf} \longleftarrow \langle \texttt{ProfX}, \langle\ 0.9,\ 0.9\ \rangle\rangle.\\
&\texttt{ProfX.goodRecLetter} \longleftarrow \langle \texttt{Alice}, \langle\ 0.9,\ 0.8\ \rangle\rangle.\\
&\texttt{ABU.accredited} \longleftarrow \langle \texttt{StateU}, \langle\ 0.9,\ 0.8\ \rangle\rangle.\\
&\texttt{StateU.highMarks} \longleftarrow \langle \texttt{Alice}, \langle\ 0.8,\ 0.9\ \rangle\rangle.\\
&\texttt{EOrg.highBudget} \longleftarrow \langle \texttt{Alice}, \langle\ 0.6,\ 0.5\ \rangle\rangle.\\
&\texttt{EOrg.oldCustomer} \longleftarrow \langle \texttt{Alice}, \langle\ 0.7,\ 0.7\rangle\rangle.
\end{aligned}
$$

In Table 3 we extend the example of Table 2 in order to represent also a case where the authorization can be accomplished by following different derivations. For example, a customer could be allowed to have a discount even if she/he presents a good recommendation letter written by a famous professor (i.e. *EPub.famousProf.goodRecLetter*). In Table 3 we use the *path semiring* presented in Sec. 3, thus a semiring value consists in a couple of trust/confidence feedbacks. The best derivation corresponds to the criteria defined by the $+_p$ (i.e. confidence is more important).

4.2 RT_2^W: Logical Rights

Trust languages can be used to grant some permissions, i.e. to represent access modes over some specific objects. For this reason it useful to group logically related objects (e.g. the files inside the same directory) and access modes, and to give permissions about them in a correlated manner. As proposed in [14], we introduce in our language the notion of *o-sets*, which are used to group together this kind of objects: o-sets names are created by associating an o-set identifier to a tuple of data terms. Moreover, an o-set identifier has a base type τ, and o-set names/o-sets created by using an o-set identifier have the same base type as the o-set identifier. Finally, the value of an o-set is a set of values in τ.

An o-set-definition credential is similar to the role definition credential that we have defined in Sec. 4 for RT_1^W: the difference is that the members of o-sets are objects that are not entities. Admin.Documents(read) $\longleftarrow$ ⟨FileA, 0.9⟩, for example, states that the administration office grants to *FileA* the permission to be read only for the 90% of it; *FileA* and the *Documents* o-set id are associated with the *file* type.

O-set-definition credentials can be translated in Datalog exactly as proposed for RT_1^W in Sec. 4: the *head* of a credential has the form $A.O(h_1, \ldots, h_n)$, where $O(h_1, \ldots, h_n)$ is an o-set name of type τ, while the body can be a value of base type τ, another o-set $B.O_1(s_1, \ldots, s_m)$ of base type τ, a linked o-set $A.R_1(t_1, \ldots, t_l).O_1(s_1, \ldots, s_m)$, in which $R_1(t_1, ..., t_l)$ is a role name and $O_1(s_1, \ldots, s_m)$ is an o-set name of base type τ, or an intersection of k o-sets of the base type τ (see Sec. 4.3 for the intersection of roles and o-sets).

Therefore, a credential in RT_2^W is either a role-definition credential or an o-set-definition credential. For more details on types and properties of RT_2^W credentials (w.r.t. RT_1^W), please refer to [14].

Example 1. In this example, the *AlphaCompany* allows the members of a project team to work on the documents of this project: each of the credentials representing the documents, e.g. a *fileA* file, are associated with a couple of values, e.g. ⟨0.9, 0.5⟩, which grant a member of the project the right to read 90% of the file and to modify 50% of it. This restriction on files can be explained by copyright or *Concurrent Versioning System* limitations, or due to the different position taken by employees. Even the credentials concerning the members of the project (e.g. *Bob*) are weighted with the same percentages, in this case related instead to the role of the entity (i.e. there are generic read/modify rights associated to *Bob*): in this way, it possible to combine all these levels of rights together, and to finally know how much a given entity can read and modify a given object. As we presented in Sec. 2, the cartesian product of two c-semirings is still a c-semiring and, therefore, it is not a problem to have multiple weights (more details are given in [3]); for this reason we use the vectorization of two *Fuzzy* semirings, i.e. ⟨⟨[0, 1], [0, 1]⟩, ⟨max, max⟩, ⟨min, min⟩, ⟨0, 0⟩, ⟨1, 1⟩⟩, in order to maximize (i.e. with ⟨max, max⟩) the composition of the values representing the rights, (i.e. with ⟨min, min⟩): in practice, we use the *Fuzzy* semiring to find the maximum read/modify percentages, obtained by keeping the worst value among all the composition percentages. The credentials to represent this scenario are the following ones, from which we can obtain AlphaCompany.fileAc(read, modify, fileA) $\longleftarrow$ Bob with a value of ⟨0.8, 0.5⟩:

AlphaCompany.fileAc(read, modify, AlphaCompany.documents(x)) $\longleftarrow$

AlphaCompany.team(x).

AlphaCompany.documents(proj) $\longleftarrow$ ⟨fileA, ⟨0.9, 0.5⟩⟩.

AlphaCompany.team(proj1) $\longleftarrow$ ⟨Bob, ⟨0.8, 0.7⟩⟩.

4.3 RT^{WT}: Threshold and Separation-of-Duty Policies

Threshold structures are satisfied by the agreement of k out of a set of entities that satisfy a specified condition, while *separation of duty* instead requires that two or more different people be responsible for the completion of a sensitive task, such deciding the result of an exam. With **Rule 4** (see Sec. 4) it is possible to implement simple threshold structures by using the intersection of roles; for example, the policy stating that a student is considered bright (bS) by her/his university (Uni) only if two out of three professors ($P1$, $P2$ and $P3$) say so, can be represented by the three rules $Uni.bS \longleftarrow P1.bS \cap P2.bS$, $Uni.bS \longleftarrow P1.bS \cap P3.bS$ and $Uni.bS \longleftarrow P2.bS \cap P3.bS$.

However, with this kind of intersections we are not able express complex policies: for example if we need to represent the fact that A says that an entity has attribute R if two different entities having attribute R_1 says so. For this reason we need to introduce the RT^{WT} language, in order to properly work with sets of entities. More specifically, RT^{WT} adds to the RT^W languages the notion of *manifold roles*, which generalizes the notion of roles [14]. A manifold role has a value that is a set of entity collections. An entity collection is either an entity, which can be viewed as a singleton set, or a set of two or more entities. Notice that, as the RT^{WD} language presented in Sec. 4.4, RT^{WT} can be used together with each of RT_i^W languages (see Sec. 4). In RT^{WT} we introduce two more types of credentials w.r.t. Sec. 4:

Rule 5. $A.R \longleftarrow B_1.R_1 \odot \cdots \odot B_k.R_k$. As we introduced before with words, the meaning of this credential is $members(A.R) \supseteq members(B_1.R_1 \odot \cdots \odot B_k.R_k) = \{s_1 \cup \cdots \cup s_k | s_i \in members(B_i.R_i) \text{ for } 1 \leq i \leq k\}$. Given $w_1, \ldots w_k$ as the actual weights of the derivations respectively rooted in $B_1.R_1, \ldots B_k.R_k$, the global weight of this clause is then composed as $w_1 \times w_2 \times \cdots \times w_k$, where $\times$ depends on the chosen $\langle S, +, \times, \mathbf{0}, \mathbf{1} \rangle$ semiring.

Rule 6. $A.R \longleftarrow B_1.R_1 \otimes \cdots \otimes B_k.R_k$. The formal meaning of this credential is instead given by $members(A.R) \supseteq members(B_1.R_1 \otimes \cdots \otimes B_k.R_k) = \{s_1 \cup \cdots \cup s_k | (s_i \in members(B_i.R_i) \wedge s_i \cap s_j = \emptyset) \text{ for } 1 \leq i \neq j \leq k\}$. Given $w_1, \ldots w_k$ as the actual weights of the derivations respectively rooted in $B_1.R_1, \ldots B_k.R_k$, the global weight of this clause is then composed as $w_1 \times w_2 \times \cdots \times w_k$, where $\times$ operator depends on the chosen $\langle S, +, \times, \mathbf{0}, \mathbf{1} \rangle$ semiring.

As usual, the Datalog engine will select the best derivation according to the $+$ operator of the semiring. Considering RT^{WT}, the translation to Datalog rules for **Rule 1**, **Rule 2** and **Rule 4** is the same as the one presented in Sec. 3. For **Rule 3**, **Rule 5** and **Rule 6** rules, the translation is instead the following one:

Rule 3. $A.R \longleftarrow A.R_1.R_2$ can be translated to $r(A, x) :\!\text{-}r_1(A, y), r_2(y, x)$ when $size(r_1) = 1$, or can be translated to $r(A, y) :\!\text{-}r_1(A, x), r_2(y, x_1), \ldots r_2(y, x_k)$, $set_k(x, x_1, \ldots, x_k)$ when $size(r_1) = k > 1$. Each role identifier has no a $size$: the size of a role limits the maximum size of each of its member entity set (see [14] for further details). The new set_k predicate takes $k + 1$ entity collections as arguments, and $set_k(s, s_1, \ldots, s_k)$ is true if and only if $s = s_1 \cup \cdots \cup s_k$; if s_i is an entity, it is treated as a single-set element.

Rule 5. $A.R \longleftarrow B_1.R_1 \odot \cdots \odot B_k.R_k$ can be translated to $r(A, x) :\text{-} r_1(B_1, x_1)$, $r_2(B_2, x_2), \ldots, r_k(B_k, x_k), set_k(x, x_1, \ldots x_k)$.

Rule 6. $A.R \longleftarrow B_1.R_1 \otimes \cdots \otimes B_k.R_k$ can be translated to $r(A, x) :\text{-} r_1(B_1, x_1)$, $r_2(B_2, x_2), \ldots, r_k(B_k, x_k), nset_k(x, x_1, \ldots x_k)$. The $nset_k$ predicate takes $k + 1$ entity collections as arguments and it is true only when $s = s_1 \cup \cdots \cup s_k$ and for any $1 \le i \ne j \le k, s_i \cap s_j = \emptyset$

Example 2. Suppose that for a university office a student is "bright" (i.e. $Uni.bS$) if one member of $Uni.evalExtAdvisor$ (i.e. an external advisor) and two different members of $Uni.EvalProf$ (i.e. a professor who teaches in that university) all say so. This can be represented using the following credentials (where A, B, C and D can be external advisors and/or professors):

$$\text{Uni.bS} \longleftarrow \text{Uni.evaluators.bS.}$$

$$\text{Uni.evaluators} \longleftarrow \text{Uni.evalProfs} \odot \text{Uni.evalExtAdvisor.}$$

$$\text{Uni.evalProfs} \longleftarrow \text{Uni.evalProf} \otimes \text{Uni.evalProf.}$$

$$\text{Uni.evalExtAdvisor} \longleftarrow \langle A, 0.9 \rangle. \quad \text{Uni.evalExtAdvisor} \longleftarrow \langle B, 0.7 \rangle.$$

$$\text{Uni.evalProf} \longleftarrow \langle A, 0.8 \rangle. \quad \text{Uni.evalProf} \longleftarrow \langle C, 0.8 \rangle.$$

$$\text{Uni.evalProf} \longleftarrow \langle D, 0.6 \rangle.$$

If we adopt the *Fuzzy* semiring $\langle [0, 1], max, min, 0, 1 \rangle$, the best authorization corresponds to the set $\{A, C\}$ with a value of 0.8 (i.e. the min between 0.9 and 0.8): we remind that A is both a professor (i.e. A teaches at the university) and an external advisor (i.e. A can be a visiting professor) and therefore only two entities can satisfy the request. Therefore, with this program we retrieve the best combination of evaluators for a student: the student is supposed to present her/his signed credentials and to request how much she/he is considered bright: the evaluations of different evaluators are composed by selecting the worst score (with the min operation of the semiring), but at the end the best derivation is selected (by using the max operator).

4.4 RT^{WD}: Delegation of Role Activations

The RT^{WD} language is finally added to our weighted family in order to handle delegation of the capacity to exercise role memberships. The motivations are that, in many scenarios, an entity prefers not to exercise all his rights. For example, a professor could want to log as a simple university employee, thus not having the rights to insert or change the student exam results, but only having the rights to check the number of canteen tickets. With a weighted extension (i.e. RT^{WD}) we are now able to state "how much" the rights are delegated to another entity (e.g. a session or a process). Therefore it is possible to quantify the "amount" of delegated rights, e.g. to modify a document, but only for the 80% of it, which is for example less than the rights held by the delegating entity (e.g. 100%). The delegation takes the following form: $B_1 \xrightarrow{D \ as \ A.R} B_2$, which means that B_1 delegates to B_2 the ability to act on behalf of D in D's capacity as a member of $A.R$.

For the definition of the RT^{WD} rules we introduce the *forRole* predicate as in [14]: $forRole(B, D, A.R)$ can be read as B *is acting for "D as $A.R$"* and it means that B is acting for the role activation in which D activates $A.R$. The delegation rules can be translated in the following way: $B_1 \xrightarrow{D \ as \ A.R} B_2$ $forRole(B_2, D, A.R) \longleftarrow forRole(B_1, D, A.R)$. This rule means that B_2 is acting for "D as $A.R$" if B_1 is doing so. Other kind of delegation rules that can be formulated are presented in [14].

Clearly, even the other rules presented in Sec. 4 and Sec. 4.3 must be modified according to the introduction of the *forRole* predicate. For example, $A.R \longleftarrow \langle D, s \rangle$ becomes $forRole(D, D, A.R) :\text{-} s$ and $s \in S$ is the associated weight taken from the $\langle S, +, \times, \mathbf{0}, \mathbf{1} \rangle$ semiring. Therefore we have presented only the **Rule 1** translation and, for sake of brevity, we omit all the other rules translation with the *forRole* predicate (from **Rule 2** to **Rule 6**); however the translation is similar to the one proposed in the RT^D design in [14]. A request is translated in the same way as a delegation credential; the request is replaced by the dummy entity corresponding to it. For example, the $B_1 \xrightarrow{D \ as \ A.R} req$ request is translated to $forRole(ReqID, D, A.R) \longleftarrow forRole(B_1, D, A.R)$, where $ReqID$ is the dummy entity for req.

Example 3. In this simple example we show how different delegation acts can lead to different costs. We use the *Weighted* semiring, i.e. $\langle R^+, min, +, \infty, 0 \rangle$, since we suppose the authorizer wants to minimize the cost associated with the credentials used for the authorization (the $+$ of the semiring is instantiated to min in the *Weighted* semiring): the costs are elements of R^+ (i.e. the set of positive real numbers) and are composed with the arithmetic $+$ (i.e. the $\times$ of the *Weighted* semiring). The total cost value can be considered, for example, as the cost charged to the authorizer in order to satisfy the requester. For example, the authorizer is represented by a university budget office, and the cost associated with the credentials represents the money cost to manage them (i.e. phone calls, faxes, travel expenses, etc). In the example, we have a university (i.e. *Uni*), where any conference organization event has to be proposed and approved before it is allowed to be practically organized. Any professor can propose such an event. A member of the "approval commission" can instead approve an event. A member of this commission is also a professor (i.e. the commission is made up of professors); however, a professor cannot approve his own proposed event. Therefore, the aim of the university budget office is to minimize the cost for the organization of the events. This can be represented as follows:

$$Uni.organizeEvent \longleftarrow Uni.propose \otimes Uni.approve.$$
$$Uni.propose \longleftarrow Uni.prof.$$
$$Uni.approve \longleftarrow Uni.appCommission.$$
$$Uni.prof \longleftarrow Uni.appCommission.$$

Suppose also that A and B professors are both in the approval commission and the cost of these two credentials is the same (e.g. 1 euro is a basic cost to manage a member of the approval commission): Uni.appCommission ⟵ ⟨A, 1⟩ and Uni.appCommission ⟵ ⟨B, 1⟩.

Both of them wish to propose and clearly accept the same event (named *bigConf*) and they present the following credentials. Moreover, we extend the syntax of the delegation rules as already explained in Sec 4: now they can have an associated semiring value (the cost) taken from R^+.

$$A \xrightarrow{\text{A as Uni.appCommission}} \langle \text{event}(\text{bigConf}), 6 \rangle.$$

$$A \xrightarrow{\text{A as Uni.prof}} \langle \text{event}(\text{bigConf}), 5 \rangle.$$

$$B \xrightarrow{\text{B as Uni.appCommission}} \langle \text{event}(\text{bigConf}), 8 \rangle.$$

$$B \xrightarrow{\text{B as Uni.prof}} \langle \text{event}(\text{bigConf}), 2 \rangle.$$

Given the request $forRole(reqID, \{A, B\}, Uni.organizeEvent)$ (and $reqID$ is the dummy entity), the system will choose B as the proposer (with a cost of 2) and A as the entity who approves the event (with a cost of 6), since it is the cheapest solution to the problem. The total cost of all the credentials is 10 euro, obtained by summing also 1 euro for each credential related to a professor. Notice that the other possible solution, with A proposer and B approver of the event, costs 15 euro, i.e. 5 euro more.

5   Conclusions and Future Work

We have proposed a weighted extension of Datalog (i.e. Datalog^W) and a trust language family based on it. These languages can be used to deal with vague and imprecise security policies or credentials, and preference or costs associated to each rule or fact. In practice, we can manage and combine together differ-ent levels of truth, preference or costs associated to the statements and finally have a single feedback value on which to authorize a trust request. We have extended the RT family [14] and we we have shown that the classical RT_0 and RT_1 languages are respectively included in our RT_0^W and RT_1^W languages. It is worthy to notice that our extension is completely orthogonal w.r.t. the RT extension proposed in [13], i.e. RT^C, where the supporting Datalog^C language allows first-order formulas in tractable constraint domains. The constraints are introduced to represent the access permissions over structured resources, e.g., tree domains and range domains. Our aim is instead the representation of trust levels modelling cost/preference or fuzziness of credentials. Our systematic ap-proach to give weights to facts and rules, contributes also towards bridging the gap between "rule-based" trust management (i.e. hard security mechanisms) and "reputation based" trust management [11] (i.e. soft security mechanisms).

On future improvement could be to leave to the programmer the opportunity to take more decisions inside the rules, for example based on the current ag-gregated semiring value (the process is called *reification* of the values, i.e. make them visible to the programmer); from its evaluation, some rules could be en-abled and others could be ignored, influencing the derivation process and the final result. Therefore we want to extend the language in this sense.

We plan to investigate the complexity of tractable soft constraints classes [7] in order to cast them in a Datalog-based language. Therefore, we want to extend also the RT^C language [13] (based on Datalog enhanced with crisp constraints) in its soft version.

References

1. Bistarelli, S.: Semirings for Soft Constraint Solving and Programming. LNCS, vol. 2962. Springer, Heidelberg (2004)
2. Bistarelli, S., Martinelli, F., Santini, F.: Weighted datalog and levels of trust. In: Advances in Policy Enforcement. IEEE, Los Alamitos (to appear, 2008)
3. Bistarelli, S., Montanari, U., Rossi, F.: Semiring-based constraint solving and optimization. Journal of the ACM 44(2), 201–236 (1997)
4. Bistarelli, S., Rossi, F.: Semiring-based constraint logic programming: syntax and semantics. ACM Trans. Program. Lang. Syst. 23(1), 1–29 (2001)
5. Bonatti, P., Duma, C., Olmedilla, D., Shahmehri, N.: An integration of reputation-based and policy-based trust management. In: Semantic Web Policy Workshop (2005)
6. Chakraborty, S., Ray, I.: TrustBAC: integrating trust relationships into the rbac model for access control in open systems. In: SACMAT 2006: Proc. of Access control models and technologies, pp. 49–58. ACM Press, New York (2006)
7. Cohen, D.A., Cooper, M.C., Jeavons, P.G., Krokhin, A.A.: The complexity of soft constraint satisfaction. Artif. Intell. 170(11), 983–1016 (2006)
8. Colombo, M., Martinelli, F., Mori, P., Petrocchi, M., Vaccarelli, A.: Fine grained access control with trust and reputation management for globus. In: OTM Conferences (2), pp. 1505–1515 (2007)
9. De Treville, J.: Binder, a logic-based security language. In: SP 2002: Proceedings of the 2002 IEEE Symposium on Security and Privacy, Washington, DC, USA, p. 105. IEEE Computer Society, Los Alamitos (2002)
10. Jim, T.: SD3: A trust management system with certified evaluation. In: SP 2001: Proceedings of the 2001 IEEE Symposium on Security and Privacy, Washington, DC, USA, p. 106. IEEE Computer Society, Los Alamitos (2001)
11. Jøsang, A., Ismail, R., Boyd, C.: A survey of trust and reputation systems for online service provision. Decis. Support Syst. 43(2), 618–644 (2007)
12. Li, N., Grosof, B.N., Feigenbaum, J.: Delegation logic: A logic-based approach to distributed authorization. ACM Trans. Inf. Syst. Secur. 6(1), 128–171 (2003)
13. Li, N., Mitchell, J.C.: Datalog with constraints: A foundation for trust management languages. In: Dahl, V., Wadler, P. (eds.) PADL 2003. LNCS, vol. 2562, pp. 58–73. Springer, Heidelberg (2002)
14. Li, N., Mitchell, J.C., Winsborough, W.H.: Design of a role-based trust-management framework. In: SP 2002: Proc. of Security and Privacy, p. 114. IEEE Computer Society, Los Alamitos (2002)
15. Martinelli, F., Petrocchi, M.: A uniform approach for the modeling of security and trust on protocols and services. In: ICS 2006: International Workshop on Computer Security (2006)
16. Theodorakopoulos, G., Baras, J.S.: Trust evaluation in ad-hoc networks. In: WiSe 2004: Workshop of Wireless security, pp. 1–10. ACM, New York (2004)

Annotation Markers for
Runtime Replication Protocol Selection

Hein Meling

Department of Electrical Engineering and Computer Science,
University of Stavanger, N-4036 Stavanger, Norway
hein.meling@uis.no

Abstract. This paper presents an architecture enabling developers to easily and flexibly assign replication protocols simply by *annotating* individual server methods. This avoids using costly replication protocols for all object methods, e.g. read-only methods can use less costly protocols, reserving the costly replication protocols for update methods. The architecture has been implemented in the Jgroup/ARM middleware, and enables addition of new replication protocols without modifying the core toolkit. It also supports runtime selection of replication protocol for individual methods. This can be used to support self-optimization of protocol selection by optimizing for the most appropriate configuration under a given system load.

1 Introduction

Middleware for building dependable distributed applications often provide a collection of *replication protocols* supporting varying degrees of consistency. Typically, providing strong consistency requires costly replication protocols, while weaker consistency often can be achieved with less costly protocols. Hence, there is a tradeoff between cost and consistency involved in the decision of which replication protocol to use for a particular server. But, perhaps more important is the behavioral aspects of the server. For instance, the server may be intrinsically non-deterministic in its behavior, which consequently rules out several replication protocols from consideration, e.g. atomic multicast.

This paper presents an architecture for Jgroup/ARM [11] enabling software developers to easily and flexibly select their replication protocol of choice for each individual server method. The principal motivation for the architecture is to improve the flexibility in choice of replication protocols, so as to reduce the resource consumption of dependable applications as much as possible. In many fault-tolerant systems, different replication protocols are supported at the *object level* [14, 15], meaning that all the methods of a particular object must use the same replication protocol. Jgroup [11] takes a different approach: when implementing a dependable service, the invocation semantics of each individual method can be specified separately using Java annotations [2, Ch.15]. This allows for greater flexibility as various methods may need different semantics. Hence, developers may select the appropriate invocation semantics at the *method level*, and even provide different implementations with alternative semantics. The presented architecture makes it very easy to add new replication protocols to the system, with no changes to the core toolkit. Protocol implementations are picked up automatically.

C. Rong et al. (Eds.): ATC 2008, LNCS 5060, pp. 496–506, 2008.

The current implementation supports four different replication protocols, or invocation semantics: *anycast, reliable multicast, atomic multicast* and *leadercast*. The latter is a variant of passive replication and permits servers with non-deterministic behavior, whereas atomic multicast can be viewed as a kind of active replication, and hence does not tolerate servers being non-deterministic. The architecture can also accommodate adaptive or runtime protocol selection based on runtime changes in the environment. A common example in which application semantic knowledge can be exploited is a replicated database with read and write methods. Often a simple *Read-One, Write-All* (ROWA) replication protocol [17] can then be used and still preserve consistency. A ROWA replication protocol can easily be implemented using anycast for read methods and either multicast, atomic, or leadercast for write methods. On the other hand, replication protocols which operate at the object level require that also simple read-only methods use the *strongest* replication protocol required by the object to preserve consistency. However, assigning appropriate invocation semantics to the methods of a server do require careful consideration to ensure preservation of consistency as well as reducing the resource consumption needed. Hence, a guideline is provided in [11], based on [8]. For example, if two methods of the same server modify intersecting parts of the shared state, they should use the same replication protocol.

By exploiting knowledge about the semantics of distributed objects, the choice of which replication protocols to use for the various methods can be used to obtain a performance gain over the traditional object level approach. Similar ideas were proposed by Garcia-Molina [9] to exploit semantic knowledge of the application to allow nonserializable schedules that preserve consistency to be executed in parallel as a means to improve the performance for distributed database systems. OGS [6, 7] also allows each method of a server to be associated with different replication protocols, but this must be explicitly encoded for each method through an intricate initialization step. The approach presented herein is much easier to use as it exploits Java annotations to mark methods with the desired replication protocol. The Spread [1] message-based group communication system can also be used to exploit semantic knowledge, since each message can be assigned a different replication protocol. JavaGroups [3] on the other hand would have required separate channels for each replication protocol. Unlike Jgroup however, neither of these two systems are aimed at RMI based systems.

Organization: In Section 2 the architecture is presented, while in Section 3 the protocol selection mechanism is covered. The leadercast replication protocol is covered in Section 4, and Section 5 covers the atomic replication protocol. Finally, Section 6 discusses potential enhancements to the architecture that would enable support for adaptive runtime selection of protocols.

2   The EGMI Architecture

The external group method invocation (EGMI) architecture of Jgroup/ARM [11] aims to provide: (a) flexibility and efficiency using to a customized RMI layer; (b) flexibility to add new replication protocols; (c) runtime adaptive selection of replication protocol (Section 6); (d) improved client-side view updating (covered in [12]).

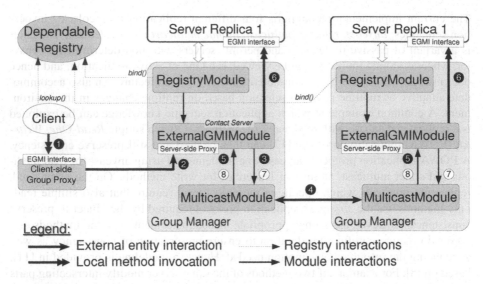

Fig. 1. The external GMI architecture

Fig. 1 illustrates the high-level interactions of the EGMI architecture. The figure illustrates interactions involved in a multicast invocation. Clients communicate with an object group through a *two-step* approach, except for the anycast semantic. Two communication steps are required for multicast interactions. The ExternalGMIModule acts as the *server-side proxy* (representative) for clients communicating with the object group, and is also responsible for protocol selection. The server representing the group is called the *contact server*. The choice of contact server is made (on a per invocation basis) by the *client-side proxy*, and different strategies can be implemented depending on the requirements of the replication protocol being used. The general strategy used by both anycast and multicast is to choose the contact server arbitrarily, while leadercast always selects the group leader. However, in the presence of failures an arbitrary server in the group is selected.

As shown in Fig. 1, before a client can invoke the object group, each member of the group must bind() its reference (client-side proxy) in the dependable registry. The client can then perform a lookup() to obtain the client-side proxy encompassing all group members. The client-side proxy provides the same EGMI interface as the server, enabling the client to invoke local methods on it (❶). The proxy encodes invocations into remote communications (❷), and ultimately complete the invocation by returning a result to the client. The ExternalGMIModule exploits the MulticastModule to send multicast messages (❸,❹,❺) to all group members. This is followed by the invocation of the encoded method (❻) on all members, and returning the results back to the contact server (⑦,⑧). The contact server is responsible for returning a selected result back to the client.

2.1 The Client-Side and Server-Side Proxies

The client-side and server-side proxies are implemented as a customized version of the Jini Extensible Remote Invocation (JERI) protocol stack [16]. All layers in JERI

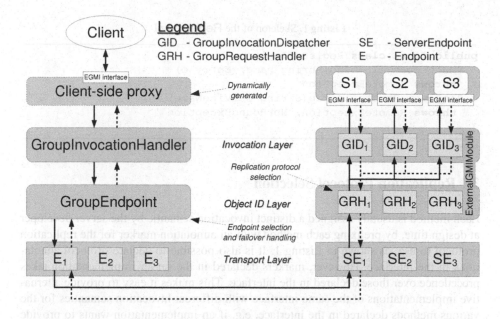

Fig. 2. The EGMI protocol stack

protocol stack have been retrofitted with group support, except for the transport layer, as shown in Fig. 2. Currently, a TCP transport is used between clients and the contact server, whereas multicast is used internally in the group.

The GroupInvocationHandler shown in Fig. 2 is responsible for marshalling and un-marshalling invocations. When invoked by the client-side proxy, internal tables are queried to determine the semantics of the method being invoked. Knowing the semantics on the client-side improves efficiency, as the contact server can forward the invocation to the group without unmarshalling it until received by the GroupInvoca-tionDispatcher at the destination server.

The GroupEndpoint maintains the current group membership lazily synchronized with the server-side membership [12]; it stores a single Endpoint for each member of the group. Each Endpoint object represents the transport between the client and the corresponding ServerEndpoint. GroupEndpoint also selects the endpoint to use for a particular invocation, based on the semantics of the method.

When the GroupRequestHandler (GRH) receives an invocation, the invocation se-mantic is extracted from the data stream. Depending on the invocation semantic, the in-vocation is passed on to a protocol-specific invocation dispatcher (see Section 3). Here the protocol dispatcher is assumed to be multicast (as in Fig. 2). Hence, the stream is passed on to the MulticastModule, and finally to the GroupInvocationDispatcher (GID) which takes care of the unmarshalling and invocation of the method on the remote server objects. As Fig. 2 shows, the results are returned to the contact server, which finally returns the result(s) to the client.

Listing 1. Skeleton of the RegistryImpl

```
public final class RegistryImpl {
  @Multicast IID bind(String name, Entry e)
   throws RemoteException
  @Anycast Remote lookup(String serviceName)
   throws RemoteException, NotBoundException
}
```

3 Replication Protocol Selection

Each method is usually assigned a distinct invocation semantic by the server developer at design time, by prefixing each method with an annotation marker for the replication protocol to use, as shown in Listing 1. It is also possible to declare protocol annotations in the interface. However, markers declared in the server implementation takes precedence over those declared in the interface. This makes it easy to provide alternative implementations of the same interface with different invocation semantics for the various methods declared in the interface, e.g. if an implementation wants to provide stronger consistency for some methods.

Fig. 3 depicts the protocol selection mechanism of the ExternalGMIModule. Each protocol must implement the ProtocolDispatcher interface through which invocations are passed before they are unmarshalled. This allows the protocol to multicast the invocation to the other group members before unmarshalling is done in the GroupInvocationDispatcher. However, the stream received by the GroupRequestHandler is partially

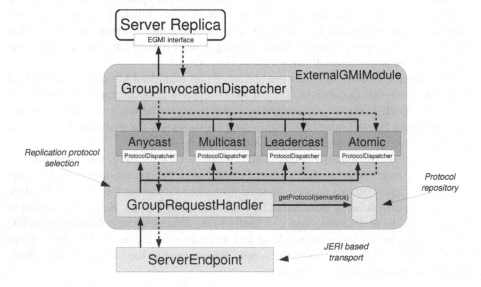

Fig. 3. EGMI replication protocol selection

Listing 2. The @Atomic annotation marker

```
@Retention(RetentionPolicy.RUNTIME)
@Target(ElementType.METHOD)
@interface Atomic { }
```

Listing 3. The ProtocolDispatcher interface

```
public interface ProtocolDispatcher {
  InvocationResult dispatch(InputStream in)
    throws IOException;
  void addListener(Object listener);
}
```

unmarshalled to obtain information necessary to *route* the message to the appropriate protocol dispatcher instance. The *protocol repository* holds a mapping between the annotation marker (a method's invocation semantic) and the actual protocol instance. The repository is queried for each invocation of a method.

3.1 Supporting a New Protocol

To support new replication protocols, two additions are required: (i) a new annotation marker must be added, allowing servers to specify the new protocol and (ii) the actual protocol implementation. Listing 2 shows the annotation marker for the @Atomic replication protocol. To support runtime protocol selection, the retention policy of the marker must be set to RUNTIME to allow reflective access to the marker. Furthermore, the target element type is set so that the marker only applies to METHOD element types. For details about the Java annotation mechanism see [2, Ch.15].

A new protocol implementation must implement the ProtocolDispatcher interface (see Listing 3), and placed in the protocol package location. The latter is configured using a Java system property. Replication protocols are constructed on-demand based on reflective [2, Ch.16] analysis of the server implementation (or its EGMI interfaces) to determine the invocation semantics of its methods. Methods whose invocation semantic is unspecified defaults to @Anycast. Only required protocols are constructed. This analysis is done in the bootstrap phase, and the information is kept in internal tables for fast access during invocations.

3.2 Concurrency Issues

Note that a protocol instance may be invoked concurrently by multiple clients, and care should be taken when developing a replication protocol to ensure that access to protocol state is synchronized. Furthermore, the EGMI architecture is designed for multithreading, and hence it does not block concurrent invocations using the same or different protocols. It is the responsibility of the server developer to ensure that access to server state is synchronized. However, invocations received while a new view is pending are blocked temporarily and delivered in the next view. This is necessary to avoid that invocations modify the server state while the state merge service [13] is active.

4 The Leadercast Protocol

The leadercast protocol presented in this section is a variant of the passive replication protocol [10]. The principal motivation to provide this protocol is the need for a strong consistency protocol that is able to tolerate non-deterministic operations. The main difference between leadercast and the passive replication protocols described in the literature [10] is optimizations in scenarios where the leader has crashed. That is how to convey information about the new leader to clients, and how to handle failover. These optimizations are possible due to the client-side view updating technique described in [12]. Fig. 4(a) illustrates the leadercast protocol, when the client knows which of the group members is the leader. In this case, the protocol is as follows:

1. The client sends its request to the group leader.
2. The leader process the request, updating its state.
3. The leader then multicasts an update message containing ⟨Result, StateUpdate⟩ to the followers (backups).
4. The followers modify their state upon receiving an update message, and replies with an Ack to the leader.
5. Only when the leader has received an Ack from all live follower replicas, will it return the Result to the client.

Result is the result of the processing performed by the leader, while StateUpdate is the state (or a partial state) of the leader replica after the processing. A partial state may for instance be the portions of the state that have been modified by the leadercast methods. Notice the compare() method performed at the end of the processing. This is used to compare the server state before and after the invocation of method(), and if the state did not change, there is no need to send the update message, as shown in Fig. 4(b).

The Result part of the update message is necessary in case a follower is promoted to leader, and needs to emit the Result to the client in response to a reinvocation of the same method. This can only happen if the leader fails, causing the client to perform a failover by reinvoking the method on another group member, as shown in Fig. 4(c). Hence, the followers needs to keep track of the result of the previous invocation made by clients. A result value can be discarded when a new invocation from the same client is made, or after some reasonable time longer than the period needed by the client to reinvoke the method. As depicted in Fig. 4(c), the failure of the leader causes the membership service to install a new view. Client invocations may be received before the new view is installed, however, they will be delayed until after the view has been installed, as discussed in Section 3.2. The follower receiving the reinvocation of a previously invoked method will simply return the result to the client along with information about the new leader.

If the follower receiving a reinvocation of a previously invoked method is not the new leader, the invocation is forwarded to the current leader, as shown in Fig. 4(d). This

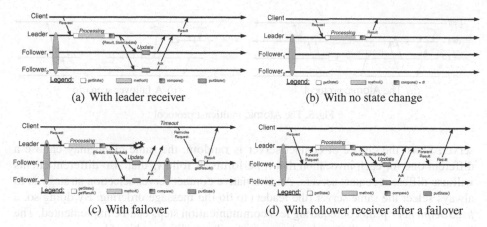

(a) With leader receiver

(b) With no state change

(c) With failover

(d) With follower receiver after a failover

Fig. 4. The Leadercast protocol

can happen if the leader failed before the followers could be informed about the original invocation. This forwarding to the current leader will only occur once per client, since the result message contains information about the new leader, and hence the client-side proxy can update its contact server.

As discussed above, the client-side proxy is responsible for selecting the contact server. For the leadercast protocol, the group leader (primary) is selected unless it has failed. The server selection strategy is embedded in the invocation semantic representation associated with each method. When the client detects that the leader has failed, the choice of contact server is random for the first invocation; the new leader is then obtained from the invocation reply and future invocations are directed to the current leader.

5 The Atomic Multicast Protocol

The atomic multicast protocol implemented in the context of this thesis is based on the ISIS total ordering protocol [4], hence only a brief description is provided herein. The protocol is useful to ensure that methods that modify the shared server state do so in a consistent manner. Methods using the atomic protocol must behave deterministically to ensure consistent behavior. The protocol is a *distributed agreement protocol* in which the group members collectively agree on the sequence in which to perform the invocations that are to be ordered. Fig. 5(a) shows the protocol. In the first step, the client sends the request to a contact server, who forwards the request to the group members, each of which respond with a *proposed sequence number*. The contact server selects the *agreed sequence number* from those proposed and notifies the group members; the highest proposed sequence number is selected. Finally, when receiving the agreed sequence number each member can perform the invocation and return the result(s) to the contact server, which will relay it to the client.

The contact server selection strategy is random for load balancing and fault tolerance purposes. The contact server acts as the entity that defines the ordering of messages, and serves this function for all invocations originated by clients using it as the contact

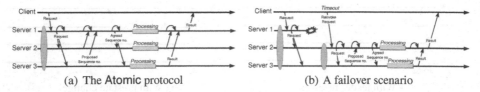

(a) The Atomic protocol   (b) A failover scenario

Fig. 5. The Atomic multicast protocol

server. Since the choice of contact server is random, the same client may choose a different one for each invocation that it performs. It follows that also different clients will use different contact servers. An alternative contact server selection strategy is to always select the same server (the leader) to do the message ordering. By doing so, a *fixed sequencer* protocol requiring less communication steps can be implemented. The fixed sequencer and other total ordering protocols are discussed in [5].

Fig. 5(b) illustrates one scenario in which the contact server fails before completing the current ordering. The client detects the failure of the contact server, and sends the request to an alternative server. In this particular scenario, the remaining servers needs to rerun the agreement protocol. However, had the contact server failed after completing the agreement protocol, but before emitting the result to the client, the new server must emit the previous result in response to a reinvocation.

The two-step communication approach used for EGMI between the client and the group members precludes the provision of a true active replication scheme. In particular, the client-side proxy will not receive replies directly from all the servers, and thus cannot mask the failure of the contact server towards the client-side proxy. Hence, if the contact server fails during an invocation, the client-side proxy is required to randomly pick another server and perform a reinvocation. The failure of the contact server, however, is still masked from the client object. But the disadvantage is that the failover delay of the atomic approach is equivalent to that of the leadercast approach when the contact server fails. However, one way to provide true active replication is to let clients become (transient) members of the object group prior to invoking methods on it, allowing clients to receive replies from all members and not just the contact server. It is foreseen that the client-side proxy can hide the fact that it has joined the object group, from the client object before performing an invocation, e.g. by annotating the method with @Atomic(join=true). An optional leaveAfter attribute could also be provided indicating the number of invocations to be perform before the client-side proxy requests to leave the group. This way true active replication can be provided also to clients.

6   Runtime Adaptive Protocol Selection

Another useful mechanism that can easily be implemented in this architecture is support for *dynamic runtime protocol selection*. Dynamically changing the replication protocol of methods at runtime is useful for systems that wish to dynamically adapt to changes in the environment. For instance, a server may decide to change its replication protocol for certain methods to improve its response time, if the system load increases. One might also imagine a special module that can configure the replication protocols of a server group remotely from some management facility (e.g. ARM [11]) to adapt to changing requirements. For example, if moving to more powerful hardware, one can simply migrate replicas to the new hardware, followed by a change of the replication protocol to use for certain methods. This section briefly outlines how this feature can be implemented.

First, a @Dynamic marker is needed, which must be added to methods that should support dynamic reconfiguration. Next, the Dynamic replication protocol must be implemented, which is simply a wrapper for the other supported protocols. The Dynamic protocol must maintain a mapping for each @Dynamic method and its currently configured invocation semantic. By default, methods that declare @Dynamic should be configured with the @Anycast semantic, unless the marker is parametrized with the desired default protocol, e.g. @Dynamic(protocol=@Leadercast). A DynamicReplication-Service interface can be provided that enables the server (or other protocol modules) to dynamically change the invocation semantics of the server's methods at runtime. A protocol module may then implement update algorithms that can seamlessly reconfigure the replication protocol of individual methods at runtime. One scheme could be to change the replication protocol of certain methods based on the size of the group. For example, if the group only has three members or less then @Atomic is used; if it has more than three members then @Leadercast is used.

Another, more subtle use of this feature relates to a client designed for testing the performance of various replication protocols. The server can then simply implement a set of test methods, each declaring the @Dynamic marker, whereas the client can invoke a special method to set the appropriate replication protocol to be tested, before invoking the actual test methods on the server. To allow clients to reconfigure the replication protocol of methods, the server (or a module) must provide a remote interface (e.g. by exporting the DynamicReplicationService interface) through which clients can update the invocation semantics of the server-side methods.

7   Conclusions

This paper presented an architecture and accompanying implementation of a dynamic protocol selection mechanism that makes it flexible and easy to improve the resource utilization of replicated services, by taking advantage of application semantics. The features of this architecture may also be used to support self-optimization by runtime reconfiguration of replication protocols for each individual server method.

References

1. Amir, Y., Danilov, C., Stanton, J.: A Low Latency, Loss Tolerant Architecture and Protocol for Wide Area Group Communication. In: Proc. Int. Conf. on Dependable Systems and Networks (June 2000)
2. Arnold, K., Gosling, J., Holmes, D.: The Java Programming Language, 4th edn. Addison-Wesley, Reading (2005)
3. Ban, B.: JavaGroups – Group Communication Patterns in Java. Technical report, Dept. of Computer Science, Cornell University (July 1998)

4. Birman, K.P., Joseph, T.A.: Exploiting Virtual Synchrony in Distibuted Systems. In: Proc. 11th ACM Symp. on Operating Systems Principles (1987)
5. Défago, X.: Agreement-Related Problems: From Semi-Passive Replication to Totally Ordered Broadcast. PhD thesis, École Polytechnique Fédérale de Lausanne, Switzerland, Number 2229 (August 2000)
6. Felber, P.: The CORBA Object Group Service: A Service Approach to Object Groups in CORBA. PhD thesis, École Polytechnique Fédérale de Lausanne, Switzerland (January 1998)
7. Felber, P., Défago, X., Eugster, P., Schiper, A.: Replicating CORBA Objects: a Marriage Between Active and Passive Replication. In: Proc. 2nd Int. Conf. on Dist. Applic. and Interop. Systems (June 1999)
8. Felber, P., Jai, B., Smith, M., Rastogi, R.: Using semantic knowledge of distributed objects to increase reliability and availability. In: Proc. 6th Int. Workshop on Object-Oriented Real-Time Dependable Systems (WORDS) (January 2001)
9. Garcia-Molina, H.: Using semantic knowledge for transaction. Processing in a distributed database 8(2), 186–213 (1983)
10. Guerraoui, R., Schiper, A.: Software-based replication for fault tolerance. IEEE Computer 30(4), 68–74 (1997)
11. Meling, H.: Adaptive Middleware Support and Autonomous Fault Treatment: Architectural Design, Prototyping and Experimental Evaluation. PhD thesis, Norwegian University of Science and Technology, Dept. of Telematics (May 2006)
12. Meling, H., Helvik, B.E.: Performance Consequences of Inconsistent Client-side Membership Information in the Open Group Model. In: Proc. 23rd Int. Performance, Computing, and Comm. Conf. (April 2004)
13. Montresor, A.: System Support for Programming Object-Oriented Dependable Applications in Partitionable Systems. PhD thesis, Dept. of Computer Science, University of Bologna (February 2000)
14. Moser, L.E., Melliar-Smith, P.M., Narasimhan, P.: Consistent Object Replication in the Eternal System. Theory and Practice of Object Systems 4(2), 81–92 (1998)
15. Ren, Y., et al.: AQuA: An Adaptive Architecture that Provides Dependable Distributed Objects. IEEE Trans. Comput. 52(1), 31–50 (2003)
16. Sommers, F.: Call on extensible RMI: An introduction to JERI (December 2003), http://www.javaworld.com/javaworld/jw-12-2003/jw-1219-jiniology_p.html
17. Tanenbaum, A.S., van Steen, M.: Distributed Systems – Principles and Paradigms. Prentice Hall, Englewood Cliffs (2002)

Enhanced Three-Round Smart Card-Based Key Exchange Protocol

Eun-Jun Yoon and Kee-Young Yoo*

Department of Computer Engineering, Kyungpook National University,
1370 Sankyuk-Dong, Buk-Gu, Daegu 702-701, South Korea
Tel.: +82-53-950-5553; Fax: +82-53-957-4846
ejyoon@tpic.ac.kr, yook@knu.ac.kr

Abstract. In 2007, Kwon et al. proposed a three-round protocol, SKE, for smart card-based key exchange in the three-party setting which provides both key independence and forward secrecy. This paper demonstrates the vulnerability of the SKE protocol and then presents an improvement to repair the security flaws of the SKE protocol.

Keywords: Cryptography, Authentication, Password, Key exchange, Smart card, Cryptanalysis.

1 Introduction

A key exchange protocol between two communication entities, allows participants to identify each other and establish a common session key, which is used to encrypt transmitted messages between them over an insecure channel. In general, the key exchange protocols can be classified into three types: public key, symmetric key, and password. The public key or symmetric key based key exchange protocols need to share long-term secret keys between each user. However, it is difficult for a human to memorize long random strings used as secret keys. In contrast, the password based key exchange protocol allows users to establish a session key using only human-memorable passwords. However, because of low entropy of the password space, the password based key exchange protocol should be designed to be secure against password guessing attacks or dictionary attacks [1].

Recently, three-party key exchange protocol [2][3][4][5][6][7][8][9] is an important cryptographic technique in the secure communication areas, by which two clients, each shares a long-term secret key or a human-memorable password with a trusted server, can agree a secure session key. Especially, smart card-based key exchange in the three-party setting [8][9] allows two users to establish a session key between them using smart cards, where each user uses a human-memorable password to gain access to his/her smart card.

In 2007, Kwon et al. [9] proposed a three-round protocol, SKE, for smart card-based key exchange in the three-party setting which provides both key

---

* Corresponding author.

C. Rong et al. (Eds.): ATC 2008, LNCS 5060, pp. 507–515, 2008.
© Springer-Verlag Berlin Heidelberg 2008

independence and forward secrecy and security against DoS attacks. Because the SKE protocol only needs three-round to share a session key between two clients, it provides both round and communication efficiency and is suitable for mobile applications in which session keys have to be exchanged frequently.

Nevertheless, this paper demonstrates the vulnerability of the SKE protocol. Using our attacks, we have shown that the SKE protocol is insecure to an impersonation attack and is vulnerable to an integrity violence of the session key from illegal modification. We also present a simple improvement to repair the security flaws of the SKE protocol.

This paper is organized as follows: In Section 2, we briefly review the SKE protocol. Section 3 shows the security flaws of the SKE protocol. In Section 4, we present a simple improvement of the SKE protocol and discusses the security of the proposed protocol. Finally, our conclusions are presented in Section 5.

2   Review of SKE Protocol

This section reviews Kwon et al.'s SKE protocol [9]. The SKE protocol is composed of three phases: registration, session key agreement, and password updating. In the SKE protocol, all parameter choices depend on a security parameter l. Abbreviations used in this paper are as follows:

- A, B, S: two users and a trusted server.
- $MAC_k(m)$: the MAC of message m under key k.
- $E_k(M)$: the symmetric encryption of a plaintext M under key k.
- $D_k(C)$: the symmetric decryption of a ciphertext C under key k.
- $PE_y(M)$: the public key encryption [10][11] of a plaintext M with public key y.
- $PD_x(C)$: the public key decryption [10][11] of a ciphertext C under private key x.
- $H(\cdot)$: a secure hash function such that $H(\cdot) : \{0,1\}^* \to \{0,1\}^l$.
- x_s: a master secret of the server S.

2.1   Registration Phase

1. When a new user A wants to register, A gives a password pw_A to S.
2. Upon receiving a request from A, S computes $PW_A = H(A||pw_A)$, $v_A = H(A||x_s)$ and $w_A = v_A \oplus PW_A$.
3. S stores (A, v_A, w_A) in a smart card and gives the smart card to A.

2.2   Session Key Agreement Phase

When A wants to establish a session key with B, A inserts his/her smart card into a card reader, and types a password pw'_A. The smart card then computes $PW'_A = H(A||pw'_A)$ and $v'_A = w_A \oplus PW'_A$, and checks if $v'_A = v_A$ holds. If the number of failing tries exceeds a predefined threshold, the smart card deactivates

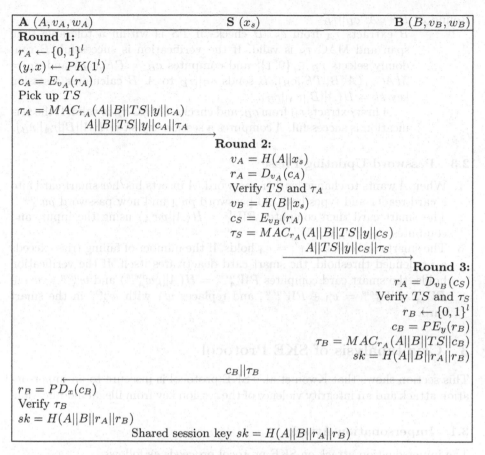

Fig. 1. Kwon et al.'s SKE protocol

itself to prevent on-line dictionary attacks. B also authenticates itself to his/her smart card as A does.

After the above authentication of users by the smart cards, A and B (in fact, the smart cards of A and B) execute the following protocol. An execution of session key agreement phase is shown in Fig. 1.

Round 1. $A \rightarrow S$: $A||B||TS||y||c_A||\tau_A$

  A randomly selects $r_A \in \{0,1\}^l$ and a pair of one-time public/private keys (y, x). A computes $c_A = E_{v_A}(r_A)$ and $\tau_A = MAC_{r_A}(A||B||TS||y|| c_A)$, where TS is a time stamp. A then sends $A||B||TS||y||c_A||\tau_A$ to S.

Round 2. $S \rightarrow B$: $A||TS||y||c_S||\tau_S$

  The server S computes $v_A = H(A||x_s)$ and extracts r_A from c_A. S checks if TS is within a tolerable time span and MAC τ_A is valid. If the verification is successful, S computes $v_B = H(B||x_s)$, $c_S = E_{v_B}(r_A)$, and $\tau_S = MAC_{r_A}(A||B||TS||y||c_S)$. S sends $A||TS||y||c_S||\tau_S$ to B.

Round 3. $B \to A$: $c_B || \tau_B$

B extracts r_A from c_S. B checks if TS is within a tolerable time span and MAC τ_S is valid. If the verification is successful, B randomly selects $r_B \in \{0,1\}^l$ and computes $c_B = PE_y(r_B)$ and $\tau_B = MAC_{r_A}(A||B||TS||c_B)$. B sends $c_B||\tau_B$ to A. B calculates a session key $sk = H(A||B||r_A||r_B)$.

A first extracts r_B from c_B, and checks if MAC τ_B is valid. If the verification is successful, A computes a session key $sk = H(A||B||r_A||r_B)$.

2.3 Password Updating Phase

1. When A wants to change his/her password, A inserts his/her smart card into a card reader and types both old password pw_A and new password pw_A^{new}.
2. The smart card then computes $PW_A' = H(A||pw_A)$ using the input, and computes $v_A' = w_A \oplus PW_A'$.
3. The smart card checks if $v_A' = v_A$ holds. If the number of failing tries exceeds a predefined threshold, the smart card deactivates itself. If the verification holds, the smart card computes $PW_A^{new} = H(A||pw_A^{new})$ and $w_A^{new} = w_A \oplus PW_A'$. $PW_A^{new} = v_A \oplus PW_A^{new}$, and replaces w_A with w_A^{new} in the smart card.

3 Cryptanalysis of SKE Protocol

This section shows that Kwon et al.'s SKE protocol is insecure to an impersonation attack and an integrity violence of the session key from illegal modification.

3.1 Impersonation Attack

The impersonation attack on SKE protocol proceeds as follows:

1. $A \to S$: $A||B||TS||y||c_A||\tau_A$
   A performs Round 1 of the session key agreement phase.
2. $E(B) \to A$: $c_B^*||\tau_B^*$
   Upon intercepting $A||B||TS||y||c_A||\tau_A$ sent by A, the attacker E lets $c_B^* = y||c_A$ and $\tau_B^* = \tau_A$. Finally, E sends $c_B^*||\tau_B^*$ to A for impersonating user B.

Upon receiving $c_B^*||\tau_B^*$ from $E(B)$, A will decrypt c_B^* by computing $PD_x(c_B^*)$. Then, A will check if MAC τ_B^* is valid. Because MAC τ_B^* is $MAC_{r_A}(A||B||TS||c_B^*)$, where $c_B^* = y||c_A$, the verification is successfully passed by A. Finally, A will compute a session key $sk = H(A||B||r_A||PD_x(c_B^*))$ and use it to perform the subsequent communication with B.

As a result of this impersonation attack, A will assure that he/she is communication with B by verifying MAC τ_B^* and believe the responding party is a legal user B. However, the user B did not perform the SKE protocol to agree the session key sk. Thus, B will always reject A's sending message. It means that the SKE protocol dose not provide *explicit authentication* unlike Kwon et al.'s security analysis. An example of the impersonation attack on SKE protocol is shown in Fig. 2.

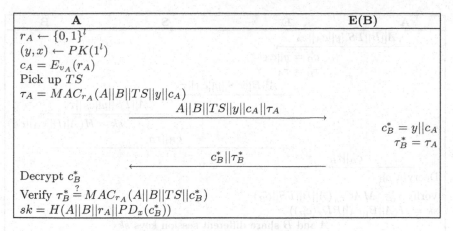

Fig. 2. Impersonation attack

3.2 Integrity Violence of the Session Key from Illegal Modification

SKE protocol is also vulnerable to an integrity violence of the session key from illegal modification. Suppose that attacker E interposes the communication between A, S, and B. Then, attacker E can perform the illegal modification attack as follows:

1. $A \to S$: $A||B||TS||y||c_A||\tau_A$
   A performs Round 1 of session key agreement phase.
2. Upon intercepting $A||B||TS||y||c_A||\tau_A$ sent by A, the attacker E forwards it to S, and lets $c_B^* = y||c_A$ and $\tau_B^* = \tau_A$.
3. $S \to B$: $A||TS||y||c_S||\tau_S$
   S performs Round 2 of session key agreement phase.
4. $B \to A$: $c_B||\tau_B$
   B performs Round 3 of session key agreement phase.
5. Upon intercepting $c_B||\tau_B$ sent by B, the attacker E replaces c_B with c_B^* and τ_B with τ_B^*, respectively. Finally, E sends $c_B^*||\tau_B^*$ to A.

After all, as described in the above impersonation attack, A will compute the wrong session key $sk = H(A||B||r_A||PD_x(c_B^*))$. However, A cannot detect the generation of this wrong session key because he/she authenticate $c_B^*||\tau_B^*$ by verifying MAC τ_B^*. From now, A and B shall use mutually different session keys in encrypting/decrypting their messages.

Unlike Kwon et al.'s security analysis, because all communicating parties check the validity of the received messages using the MAC, SKE protocol cannot detect this illegal modification attack and cannot prevent communicating parties from maintaining the invalid sessions.

Through this illegal modification attack, attacker E can neither obtain the wrong session key nor the correct session key sk but can make two parties believe and use an unintended session key. Therefore, an illegal modification attack is a serious attack, since it can prevent the two communication parties from reaching

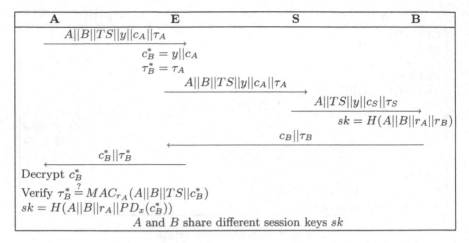

Fig. 3. Integrity violence of the session key from illegal modification

a common secret key. An example of the integrity violence of the session key from illegal modification on SKE protocol is shown in Fig. 3.

4   Enhanced SKE Protocol

This section proposes an improvement of Kwon et al.'s SKE protocol [9] to prevent above two attacks. The enhanced SKE protocol is also composed of three phases: registration, session key agreement, and password updating. The registration phase and the password updating phase are same as Kwon et al.'s SKE protocol. Our enhanced session key agreement phase performs as follows.

4.1   Enhanced Session Key Agreement Phase

When A wants to establish a session key with B, A inserts his/her smart card into a card reader, and types a password pw'_A. The smart card then computes $PW'_A = H(A||pw'_A)$ and $v'_A = w_A \oplus PW'_A$, and checks if $v'_A = v_A$ holds. If the number of failing tries exceeds a predefined threshold, the smart card deactivates itself to prevent on-line dictionary attacks. B also authenticates itself to his/her smart card as A does.

After the above authentication of users by the smart cards, A and B (in fact, the smart cards of A and B) execute the following protocol. An execution of enhanced session key agreement phase is shown in Fig. 4.

Round 1. $A \rightarrow S$: $A||B||TS||y||c_A||\tau_A$

  A randomly selects $r_A \in \{0,1\}^l$ and a pair of one-time public/private keys (y, x). A computes $c_A = E_{v_A}(r_A)$ and $\tau_A = MAC_{r_A}(A||B||TS||y||c_A)$, where TS is a time stamp. A then sends $A||B||TS||y||c_A||\tau_A$ to S.

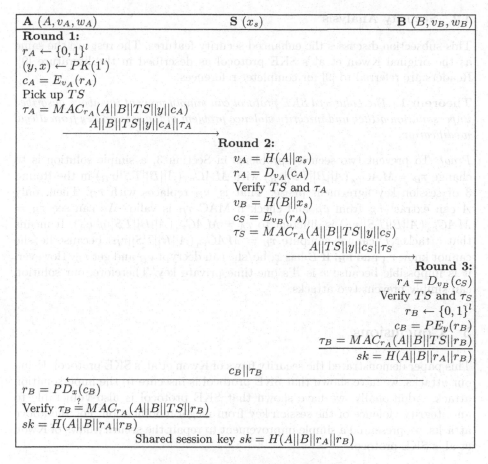

A (A, v_A, w_A)	**S** (x_s)	**B** (B, v_B, w_B)

Round 1:
$r_A \leftarrow \{0,1\}^l$
$(y, x) \leftarrow PK(1^l)$
$c_A = E_{v_A}(r_A)$
Pick up TS
$\tau_A = MAC_{r_A}(A\|B\|TS\|y\|c_A)$
$$A\|B\|TS\|y\|c_A\|\tau_A \longrightarrow$$

Round 2:
$v_A = H(A\|x_s)$
$r_A = D_{v_A}(c_A)$
Verify TS and τ_A
$v_B = H(B\|x_s)$
$c_S = E_{v_B}(r_A)$
$\tau_S = MAC_{r_A}(A\|B\|TS\|y\|c_S)$
$$A\|TS\|y\|c_S\|\tau_S \longrightarrow$$

Round 3:
$r_A = D_{v_B}(c_S)$
Verify TS and τ_S
$r_B \leftarrow \{0,1\}^l$
$c_B = PE_y(r_B)$
$\tau_B = MAC_{r_A}(A\|B\|TS\|r_B)$
$sk = H(A\|B\|r_A\|r_B)$
$$c_B\|\tau_B \longleftarrow$$

$r_B = PD_x(c_B)$
Verify $\tau_B \overset{?}{=} MAC_{r_A}(A\|B\|TS\|r_B)$
$sk = H(A\|B\|r_A\|r_B)$

Shared session key $sk = H(A\|B\|r_A\|r_B)$

Fig. 4. Enhanced SKE protocol

Round 2. $S \rightarrow B$: $A\|TS\|y\|c_S\|\tau_S$
   The server S computes $v_A = H(A\|x_s)$ and extracts r_A from c_A. S
   checks if TS is within a tolerable time span and MAC τ_A is valid. If the
   verification is successful, S computes $v_B = H(B\|x_s)$, $c_S = E_{v_B}(r_A)$,
   and $\tau_S = MAC_{r_A}(A\|B\|TS\|y\|c_S)$. S sends $A\|TS\|y\|c_S\|\tau_S$ to B.
Round 3. $B \rightarrow A$: $c_B\|\tau_B$
   B extracts r_A from c_S. B checks if TS is within a tolerable time
   span and MAC τ_S is valid. If the verification is successful, B ran-
   domly selects $r_B \in \{0,1\}^l$ and computes $c_B = PE_y(r_B)$ and $\tau_B = MAC_{r_A}(A\|B\|TS\|c_B)$. B sends $c_B\|\tau_B$ to A. B calculates a session
   key $sk = H(A\|B\|r_A\|r_B)$.
   A first extracts r_B from c_B, and checks if MAC τ_B is valid. If the ver-
   ification is successful, A computes a session key $sk = H(A\|B\|r_A\|r_B)$.

4.2 Security Analysis

This subsection discusses the enhanced security features. The rest are the same as the original Kwon et al.'s SKE protocol as described in the literature [9]. Readers are referred to [9] for completer references.

Theorem 1. *The enhanced SKE protocol can simply prevent the above described impersonation attack and integrity violation problem of the session key from illegal modification.*

Proof. To prevent two security problems in Section 3, a simple solution is to change $\tau_B = MAC_{r_A}(A||B||TS||c_B)$ with $MAC_{r_A}(A||B||TS||r_B)$ in the Round 3 of session key agreement phase. That is, c_B replaces with r_B. Then, only A can extract r_B from c_B and check if MAC τ_B is valid. We can see $\tau_B = MAC_{r_A}(A||B||TS||r_B)$ is different to $\tau_A = MAC_{r_A}(A||B||TS||y||c_A)$. It means that attacker E cannot compute $\tau_B = MAC_{r_A}(A||B||TS||r_B)$ because he/she cannot know r_A and r_B. If E has x, he/she can decrypt c_B and get r_B. However, it is impossible because x is A's one-time private key. Therefore, our solution can simply prevent two attacks.

5 Conclusions

This paper demonstrated the security flaws of Kwon et al.'s SKE protocol. Using our attacks, we have shown that SKE protocol is insecure to the impersonation attack. Additionally, we have shown that SKE protocol is also vulnerable to an integrity violation of the session key from illegal modification. For the above attacks, we presented a simple improvement to repair the security flaws of Kwon et al.'s SKE protocol.

Acknowledgements

This research was supported by the MKE(Ministry of Knowledge Economy) of Korea, under the ITRC support program supervised by the IITA(IITA-2008-C1090-0801-0026). This work is partially supported by the 2nd Brain Korea 21 Project in 2007.

References

1. Ding, Y., Horster, P.: Undetectable on-line password guessing attacks. ACM Operating Systems Review 29(4), 77–86 (1995)
2. Bellare, M., Rogaway, P.: Provably secure session key distribution: The three party case. In: 27th ACM Symposium on the Theory of Computing.STOC 1995, pp. 57–66. ACM Press, New York (1995)
3. Steiner, M., Tsudik, G., Waidner, M.: Refinement and extension of encrypted key exchange. ACM Operating Systems Review 29(3), 22–30 (1995)

4. Lin, C.L., Sun, H.M., Steiner, M., Hwang, T.: Three-party encrypted key exchange without server public-keys. IEEE Commun. Lett. 5(12), 497–499 (2001)
5. Chang, C.C., Chang, Y.F.: A novel three-party encrypted key exchange protocol. Computer Standards and Interfaces 26(5), 471–476 (2004)
6. Lee, S.W., Kim, H.S., Yoo, K.Y.: Efficient verifier-based key agreement protocol for three parties without server's public key. Appl. Math. Comput. 167(2), 996–1003 (2005)
7. Sun, H.M., Chen, B.C., Hwang, T.: Secure key agreement protocols for three-party against guessing attacks. Systems and Software 75, 63–68 (2005)
8. Jaung, W.S.: Efficient three-party key exchange using smart cards. IEEE Trans. Consum. Electron. 50(2), 619–624 (2004)
9. Kwon, J.O., Jeong, I.R., Lee, D.H.: Three-round smart card-based key exchange scheme. IEICE Trans. Commun. E90-B(11), 3255–3258 (2007)
10. Abdalla, M., Bellare, M., Rogaway, P.: DHAES: An encryption scheme based on the Diffie-Hellman problem, Submission to IEEE P1363 (1998)
11. Abdalla, M., Bellare, M., Rogaway, P.: The oracle Diffie-Hellman assumption and an analysis of DHIES, CT-RSA01, pp.143–158 (2001)

Assertions Signcryption Scheme in Decentralized Autonomous Trust Environments

Mingwu Zhang[1], Bo Yang[1], Shenglin Zhu[1], and Wenzheng Zhang[2]

[1] Department of Computer Science and Engineering, College of Informatics,
South China Agricultural University, Guangzhou, 510642, P.R. China
{zhangmw,byang,zhusl}@scau.edu.cn
[2] National Laboratory for Modern Communications, Chengdu, 610041, P.R. China
wzzhang@163.com

Abstract. Trust management is a crucial approach to authenticate user and protect resource in distributed systems. Trust between two unknown parties in different autonomous domain is established based on the parties properties, by which are proven their qualifications through the disclosure of appropriate credentials. Assertion, described as well-defined uniformly semantic structure entities such as credentials, policies and requests, is encrypted by issuer or authority's public key. In this paper, we propose an efficient assertion security protect model based on signcryption scheme for multiple autonomous domain managers and privacy key generators(PKGs). We proved its security including confidentiality, unforgeability, public verifiability, and ciphertext anonymity under the DBDH assumption in the random oracle model, where the proposed scheme has comparable advantage in security and efficiency to other previous ID-based signcryption schemes in multiple PKGs.

Keywords: Trust management, assertion, signcryption, autonomous trust domain, privacy.

1 Introduction

In distributed systems, such as P2P, Ad hoc, wireless sensor network and ubiquitous computing systems, authorization and access control are the process by which a security enforcement point determines whether an entity should be allowed to perform a certain action. Authorization takes place after entity has been authenticated. Furthermore, authorization occurs within the scope of an access control policy.

Trust management, introduced by Blaze et al. [4] as a unified approach to specifying and interpreting security policies, credentials, and relationships which allows direct authorization of security-critical actions, is an important approach to design authorization and delegation systems in decentralized environments, such as business partnerships or coalition operations, and open decentralized systems. This allows for increased flexibility and expressibility, as well as standardization of modern, scalable security mechanisms [20, 11].

C. Rong et al. (Eds.): ATC 2008, LNCS 5060, pp. 516–526, 2008.
© Springer-Verlag Berlin Heidelberg 2008

Trust between two unknown parties in different autonomous domain is established based on the entities' properties, by which are proven their qualifications through the disclosure of appropriate credentials. All requests, credentials and interactive policies are described as assertions, by which use a uniform structure and semantic to describe exchanging information in distributed networks [4, 11, 15, 1]. Assertion confers authority on keys that states the assertion source trusts the public key in the authority structure to be associated an action.

In general, assertions are encrypted by issuer or authority public key. However, in self-organized networks such as ubiquitous systems, ad hocs, and wireless sensor networks, there have neither pre-established infrastructures, nor centralized control servers. Especially, there are inadequate for assertions encryption in autonomous domain trust environments because inter-domain entities cannot obtain the other side's public key without the help of pre-establish trust relationship. At the same time, for the dynamic and decentralized, it is impossible to set up the infrastructure such as PKI in large decentralized autonomous self-organized environments.

Signcryption, first proposed by Zheng [22], is a cryptographic primitive that performs signature and encryption simultaneously, at a lower computational costs and communication overheads than the traditional systems like PGP that executes signing and encryption a message in sequential procedures. ID-based cryptography, user's public key can be any binary string that can identify the user's identity, is supposed to provide a more convenient alternative to conventional public key infrastructure. Many ID-based signcryption schemes that have been proposed are based on a single PKG [16, 19, 8, 2, 21], which is inadequate for multiple autonomous environments [10, 17]. In large scale decentralized networks, nodes and entities can be organized as autonomous domains, on which each domain has its key manager and private key generator.

Assertions will be exchanged between negotiation entities in trust system. Especially, in autonomous trust environment, assertions may be resent one by one on multi-hop networks. In order to protect assertion security, Blaze et al. [4] suggested that assertion should be signed in PKI infrastructure. Park et al. [17] described a security model on fast mobile grid services based XML signcryption component. Bagge and Molva [3] proposed a policy-based encryption and signature schemes based on bilinear pairings, whereas it has lower efficiency in computing. In [18], Wang and Cao proposed an IBE scheme in multiple PKGs environment which is based on Boneh-Franklin encryption scheme [5]. Lal and Sharma [13] provided that Wang and Cao scheme [18] encryption scheme does not have chosen ciphertext security in mDBHP assumption [12].

Li et al. [14] proposed an ID-based signcryption scheme based on multiple PKGs in Ad hoc networks. The proposed scheme might leak the privacy because of middle node can verify the ciphertext and know the message originality of trust entities. In [9], author proposed a signcrption scheme that provide public ciphertext authenticity and is forward and provably secure as well as publicly verifiable in simple PKG model.

In this paper, we propose an efficient assertions protecting scheme in autonomous trust environments, which is derived from ID-based signcryption in multiple PKGs. Proposed scheme has the following security properties: confidentiability, unforgeability, ciphertext anonymity, and public verifiability. We also give its security proof under DBDH assumption in the random oracle model and give a comparison with recent literatures in security, computing complexity and ciphertext size.

The rest of this paper is organized as follows: Section 2 reviews the basic concepts of bilinear map groups, the hard problems underlying our proposed scheme, and gives a formal ID-based assertion signcryption scheme and its security notions. We describe our concrete scheme in section 3 and prove its security in section 4. We give the performance and security comparison with recent literatures in section 5 and draw our conclusion in section 6.

2   Cryptographic Blocks

2.1   Pairings and Complexity Assumptions

Definition 1 (Bilinear pairings). *Let* $\mathbb{G}_1$ *be a cyclic additive group, whose order is a prime* q, P *be a generator of* $\mathbb{G}_1$. $\mathbb{G}_2$ *be a cyclic multiplicative group of the same order. Let* $\hat{e} : \mathbb{G}_1 \times \mathbb{G}_1 \to \mathbb{G}_2$ *be a admissible bilinear mapping which satisfies the following three properties:*

- *Bilinearity: If* $P, Q \in \mathbb{G}_1$ *and* $a, b \in Z_q$, *then* $\hat{e}(aP, bQ) = \hat{e}(P, Q)^{ab}$.
- *Non-degeneracy: There exists* $P, Q \in \mathbb{G}_1$ *such that* $\hat{e}(P, Q) \neq 1$.
- *Computability: For all* $P, Q \in \mathbb{G}_1$, *one can compute* $\hat{e}(P, Q)$ *in an efficient polynomial time.*

Definition 2 (CDHP). *Given* (P, aP, bP) *for* $a, b \in Z_q^*$, *to compute* abP.

Definition 3 (BDHP). *Given* (P, aP, bP, cP) *for* $a, b, c \in Z_q^*$, *to compute* $\hat{e}(P, P)^{abc}$.

Definition 4 (DBDH Problem). *Given* (P, aP, bP, cP, h) *for* $a, b, c \in Z_q$, *and an element* $h \in \mathbb{G}_2$, *to decide whether* $h = \hat{e}(P, P)^{abc}$ *holds.*

Let IG be a DBDH parameter generator. We say that an algorithm $\mathcal{B}$ has advantage $Adv_{IG,B}(k)$ in solving the DBDH problem for IG in time at most $t(k)$ if for sufficiently large k:

$$Adv_{IG,B}(k) = \left| P_{a,b,c \in_R Z_q, h \in G_2}[1 \leftarrow \mathcal{B}(aP, bP, cP, h)] - \right.$$
$$\left. P_{a,b,c \in_R Z_q}[1 \leftarrow \mathcal{B}(aP, bP, cP, \hat{e}(P, P)^{abc})] \right|$$

2.2   Assertions Signcryption Scheme

An assertion signcryption scheme is specified as five randomized algorithms: *System-setup, Issuer-setup, Extract, Signcrypt, and Designcrypt.*

- *System-setup*: It takes a security parameter k as input and returns systm parameters *Params*. The system parameters include three cryptographic hash functions.
- *Issuer-setup*: Each autonomous domain manager PKG_i takes the *Params* as input and returns his public/private key pair (P_{pub}^i, s_i) where he only publishes his public key to group members.
- *Extract*: This algorithm is the same to ID-based key extract algorithm [7,6], where the difference is in that a user should register in and extract from his autonomous domain manager PKG_i in multiple autonomous trust domain environments.
- *Signcrypt*: To send an assertion a to Bob identified by Q_B, sender Alice obtains the ciphertext C by this algorithm on input of (a, S_A, Q_B).
- *Designcrypt*: User Bob with secret key S_B uses this algorithm to decrypt the ciphertext and verify the valid of the signature.

2.3   Security Notions

The security of our proposed scheme satisfies *semantics security*, *unforgeability*, *public verifiability*, and *ciphertext anonymity*.

1. Assertion confidentiality: The recipient of a message learns nothing about the assertions he would need to possess in order to decrypt the message, unless he actually has them. The game $IDASC$ for semantic security in our scheme is described as:

   - Initial: The distinguisher $\mathcal{D}$ runs the $System-setup$ and $Issuer-setup$ algorithms with a security parameter k and sends the public parameters *Params* to adversary $\mathcal{A}$.
   - Proceeding query 1 adaptively: Adversary $\mathcal{A}$ performs key extract queries, signcrypt queries, designcrypt queries adaptively. These queries are the same as ID-based signcryption schemes [6](the different in that it can make queries in multiple PKGs in proposed scheme).
   - Challenge:$\mathcal{A}$ chooses two assertion a_0, a_1 and two identities ID_A, ID_B on which he wants to be challenged. In this stage $\mathcal{A}$ cannot perform the key extract query corresponding to ID_B. $\mathcal{D}$ picks a random b from $\{0,1\}$ and computes $\sigma = \mathbf{Signcrypt}(m_b, S_{ID_A}, ID_B)$ and sends σ to $\mathcal{A}$.
   - Query 2 adaptively: The adversary $\mathcal{A}$ can ask a polynomially bounded number of queries adaptively again as in the first stage with the restriction that he cannot make the key extraction query on ID_B and designcrypt query on σ.
   - Response: Finally, adversary $\mathcal{A}$ returns a bit b' and wins the game if $b' = b$.

Definition 5. *The assertion signcryption scheme is semantic security (IND-IDASC-CCA) if adversary $\mathcal{A}$ obtains the advantage $Adv^{IND-CCA}(\mathcal{A})$ $= |Pr[b' = b] - 1/2|$ is negligible in IDASC game.*

Note that the scheme about confidentiality is insider security since the adversary has the ability to query the private of the sender of a signcrypted assertion. It ensures the forward security that the confidentiality is preserved even if the sender's private key is compromised.

2. Unforgeability: An signcryption scheme based on multiple PKGs is existentially unforgeable against chosen-message insider attack (EUF-IDASC-CMA2) if no PPT forger $\mathcal{F}$ has a non-negligible advantage in the following game:
    - Challenger runs $System - setup$ and $Issuer - setup$ just like in IDASC game.
    - Forger $\mathcal{F}$ adaptively performs a number of queries just like in IDASC game.
    - $\mathcal{F}$ produces a ciphertext (σ, ID_A, ID_B) in the sense that the key is the range of key extract algorithm, and wins the game if: (a) $Designcrypt$ $(\sigma, ID_A, ID_B) \neq \perp$; (b) σ is not produced by $Signcrypt$ oracle.

3. Ciphertext anonymity: Ciphertext anonymity means that ciphertexts contain no third-party extractable information that helps to identity the sender or the intended recipient. The game about ciphertext anonymous against chosen-ciphertext insider attack (ANON-IDASC-CMA2) if no PPT distinguisher $\mathcal{D}$ has a non-negligible advantage in the following game:
    - Challenger runs $System - setup$ and $Issuer - setup$ just like in IDASC game.
    - The adversary $\mathcal{A}$ performs the queries just like in IDASC game. At the end of this stage, $\mathcal{A}$ outputs a message a, and two senders ID_{A_0}, ID_{A_1}, and two recipient identities ID_{B_0}, ID_{B_1}, where $\mathcal{A}$ must not have the key extract queries on ID_{B_0}, ID_{B_1}.
    - Challenger picks a random b, b' from $\{0, 1\}$ and computes a ciphertext $\sigma = Signcrypt(a, ID_{A_b}, ID_{B_{b'}})$ and send σ to $\mathcal{A}$.
    - $\mathcal{A}$ adaptively makes a number of queries just like in IDASC game with the restriction that it must not make designcrypt queries on σ. Finally, $\mathcal{A}$ outputs the bits (d, d') and wins the game if $(d, d') = (b, b')$.

Adversary $\mathcal{A}$'s advantage in anonymous game ANON-IDASC-CMA2 is defined as:

$$Adv^{ANON-CMA}(\mathcal{A}) = |Pr[(d, d') = (b, b')] - 1/4|.$$

4. Public verifiability: Public ciphertext verifiability means that any third party should be able to verify the origin of the ciphertext without knowing the content of the message and getting any help from the intended recipient.

3   Proposed Scheme in Multiple Autonomous Trust Domain

In this section, we describe our proposed ID-based assertion signcryption scheme. The proposed scheme consists of five algorithms as following.

1. System-setup: Given a security parameter k, generate $(G_1, G_2, \hat{e}, q, P)$ as in definition 1. Choose three hash functions $H_1 : \{0,1\}^* \to G_1$, $H_2 : \mathbb{G}_1 \times \{0,1\}^l \to \mathbb{Z}_q^*$, $H_3 : G_2 \to G_1^2 \times \{0,1\}^l$, where l is the number bits of message ciphertext.

2. Issuer-setup: Each assertion issuer PKG_i (Trust domain managers or PKGs) picks at random a secret master key $s_i \in \mathbb{Z}_q^*$, and publishes the corresponding public key $P_{pub}^i = s_i P$.

3. Extract: In an autonomous trust domain, a user selects a corresponding PKG to register in and extracts his/her private key. Suppose that Alice registers with PKG_i and extracts his privacy key by $S_A = s_i Q_A$, where $Q_A = H_1(ID_A)$.

4. Signcrypt: Suppose that Alice, identified by ID_A in trust domain PKG_1 (domain public key is P_{pub}^1), wants to send an assertion A to user Bob in trust domain PKG_2(domain public key is P_{pub}^2), she carries out the following:

   – Chooses $r \leftarrow_R \mathbb{Z}_q^*$, and computes $U = rQ_A$;
   – Computes $h = H_2(U||a)$, and $V = (r+h)S_A$;
   – Computes $t = \hat{e}(S_A, Q_B)^r$, and $W = H_3(t) \oplus (V||Q_A||a)$;
   – Sets the ciphertext as $C = (U, W)$.

5. Designcrypt: On received the signcrypted assertion $C = (U, W)$ from ID_A, Bob follows the steps below to obtain the plaintext assertion a:

   – Computes $t = \hat{e}(U, S_B)$;
   – Computes $(V||Q_A||a) = W \oplus H_3(t)$, and $h = H_2(U||a)$;
   – If $Q_A \notin G_1$ or $V \notin G_1$ holds, returns $\perp$; otherwise
   – Accepts the assertion a and returns $\top$ iff the following equation holds:
   $\hat{e}(P_{pub}^1, U + hQ_A) = \hat{e}(P, V)$

It is easy to see that the above algorithms are consistent. Indeed, if C is a valid ciphertext, then

$$\hat{e}(P, V) = \hat{e}(P, (r+h)S_A) = \hat{e}(P, S_A)^r \hat{e}(P, hS_A)$$
$$= \hat{e}(P_{pub}^1, U)\hat{e}(P_{pub}^1, hQ_A) = \hat{e}(P_{pub}^1, U + hQ_A)$$

Note that we accept the assumption in [7] that multiple PKGs share common system parameters. Furthermore, Every PKGs has different master secret key s_i. Different from [14] in multi-domain communication that needs two domains public key, our scheme only needs the signcypter trust domain's public key, and it can pass through the inter-domains resend message without mid-domain PKGs's public key . That is, if a message is sent to the target node that pass across multiple trust domain secretly, it decrypts the ciphertext using source domain public key P_{pub}^1 and target node private key.

4   Security Analysis

Theorem 1 (Confidentiality). *If there is an adversary $\mathcal{A}$ can succeeds with probability ϵ in IDASC game, then there is a distinguisher $\mathcal{D}$ can solve the DBDH problem with advantage at least*

$$\epsilon' \geqslant \epsilon \cdot \frac{1}{q_{H_1}} - \frac{1}{2^k} \cdot \frac{q_U}{q_{H_1}}$$

Proof. Assuming that the distinguisher $\mathcal{D}$ receives a random instance$(P_{pub}^1,$ $aP_{pub}^1, bP_{pub}^1, cP_{pub}^1, h)$ of the DBDH problem. His goal is to decide whether $h = \hat{e}(P_{pub}^1, P_{pub}^1)^{abc}$ or not. $\mathcal{D}$ will run $\mathcal{A}$ as a subroutine and act as $\mathcal{A}$'s challenger in the IND-IDASC-CCA2 game. We assume that $\mathcal{A}$ will ask for $H_1(ID)$ before ID is used in any other queries. We also assume that $\mathcal{A}$ never makes an Designcrypt query on a signcrypted assertion obtained from the Signcrypt oracle, and he can only make Designcrypt queries for observed ciphertext assertions.

To maintain consistency and avoid collision between queries made by $\mathcal{A}$, $\mathcal{D}$ keeps the following lists: L_i for $i = 1, 2, 3$ that are initially empty and are used to keep track of answers to queries asked by $\mathcal{A}$ to oracles H_1, H_2, H_3, respectively.

At the beginning of the game, $\mathcal{D}$ gives $\mathcal{A}$ the system parameters with $P_{pub}^1 = aP$, The value a is unknown to $\mathcal{D}$ and simulate the master key of the P_{pub}^1.

H_1 queries: $H_1(ID_i)$

- At the j-th query, $\mathcal{D}$ answers by $H_1(ID_j) = bP$(Assume that the identity ID_j belongs to P_{pub}^1, otherwise exchange P_{pub}^1 for P_{pub}^2)
- For $i \neq j$, if ID_i already appears on the L_1, then $\mathcal{D}$ responds with $H_1(ID_i) = b_iP$, otherwise
- $\mathcal{D}$ chooses $b_i \in_R Z_q^*$, puts the pair (ID_i, b_i) in list L_1 and answers $H_1(ID_i) = b_iP$.

H_2 queries: $H_2(U||a)$

- If $(U||a, h) \in L_2$ for some h, returns h.
- Else chooses $h \in_R Z_q^*$, adds the pair $(U||a, h)$ in list L_2 and answers $H_2(U||a) = h$.

H_3 queries: $H_3(t)$

- If $(t, z) \in L_3$ for some z, returns z.
- Else chooses $z \in_R G_1 \times G_1 \times \{0,1\}^l$, adds the pair (t, z) in list L_3 and answers $H_3(t) = z$.

Key extract queries: $Extract(ID_i)$

- If $ID_i = ID_j$, $\mathcal{D}$ aborts the simulation.
- Else searches the list L_1 for the entry (ID_i, b_i) corresponding to ID_i and answers b_iP.

Signcrypt queries: $Signcrypt(a, ID_A, ID_B)$

We have the following cases to consider:

- Case 1: $ID_A \neq ID_j$. $\mathcal{D}$ finds the entry (ID_A, b_A) in L1, and computes the private key S_A by running the key extraction query; then $\mathcal{D}$ returns the result by query $Signcrypt(a, S_A, Q_B)$.
- Case 2: $ID_A = ID_j$ and $ID_B \neq ID_j$. Chooses $r, h \in_R Z_q^*$; computes $U = rP - hQ_A, V = rP_{pub}^1$; adds $(U||a, h)$ to L_1; computes $t = \hat{e}(S_A, Q_B)^r$ ($\mathcal{D}$ could obtain S_A from the key extraction algorithm because $ID_B \neq ID_j$); finds $H_3(t)$ in L_3 with $r' \neq r$ and computes $W = H_3(t) \oplus (V||Q_A||a, r')$ (In this case, $\mathcal{D}$ will repeat the process with $r' \neq r$ at most $q_S + q_{H_3}$ times as L_3).

- Case 3: $ID_A = ID_j$ and $ID_B = ID_j$. Following the three steps of Case 2; chooses $h^* \in_R G_1 \times G_1 \times \{0,1\}^l$ and computes $W^* = h^* \oplus (V||Q_A||a)$; Adds tuple $(ID_A, ID_B, U, V, W^*, r, h^*)$ to L_s and returns (U, W^*).

Designcrypt queries: $Designcrypt(U', W')$

For a designcrypt query on a ciphertext $C' = (U', W')$ between identities ID_A and ID_B, we have the following two cases to consider:

- Case $ID_B = ID_j$. $\mathcal{D}$ always returns a symbol $\bot$ that notifies $\mathcal{A}$ the ciphertext $\sigma' = (C', U', W')$ isn't a valid one.
- Case $ID_B \neq ID_j$. $\mathcal{D}$ computes $t' = \hat{e}(U', S_B)$; obtains the $(V||Q_A||a) = W \oplus H_3(t)$ from L_3; extracts $t = H_2(U||a)$ from L_2; finally, returns a' if equation $\hat{e}(P, W') = \hat{e}(P^1_{pub}, U' + hQ_A)$ holds, otherwise rejects the ciphertext.

After a polynomially bounded number of queries, $\mathcal{A}$ picks a pair of identities on which he wishes to be challenged. Note that $\mathcal{D}$ will fail and stop if $\mathcal{A}$ has asked a key extraction query on ID_j. The probability of $\mathcal{A}$ will not fail in this stage is $(q_{H_1} - q_K)/q_{H_1}$. Furthermore, with a probability $1/(q_{H_1} - q_K)$, $\mathcal{A}$ can choose the pair (ID_i, ID_j) with $i \neq j$ to be challenged. Hence the probability that $\mathcal{A}$'s response is helpful to $\mathcal{D}$ is $1/q_{H_1}$.

$\mathcal{A}$ chooses two plaintext $m_0, m_1 \in \mathcal{M}$. Challenger $\mathcal{D}$ chooses $b \in_R \{0,1\}$, lets $U = cP^1_{pub}$ and $t = h$ to signcrypt message m_b in **Signcrypt** algorithm. Here h is a candidate for the DBDH problem. $\mathcal{D}$ sends the signcrypted assertion C to $\mathcal{A}$. $\mathcal{A}$ performs a polynomially bounded number of queries just like in the first stage. Neither can he request a key extraction about ID_i and ID_j, nor ask the **Designcrypt** query on C. At the end of the queries, $\mathcal{A}$ produces a bit b' for which he believes the relation $C = Signcrypt(m_{b'}, S_{ID_i}, Q_{ID_j})$ holds. At this moment, if $b' = b$, distinguisher $\mathcal{D}$ outputs $h = \hat{e}(U, S_{ID_j}) = \hat{e}(cP^1_{pub}, abP) = \hat{e}(P^1_{pub}, P^1_{pub})^{abc}$ which solves the DBDH problem for the previous random instance, otherwise $\mathcal{D}$ stops and answers "failure".

Now we consider the probabilities in queries phases, challenge phase and response phase. The probability that $\mathcal{A}$ choose the pair (ID_i, ID_j) with $i \neq j$ to be challenged on the pair (ID_i, ID_j) is $1/q_{H_1}$. The probability that $\mathcal{D}$ can give a correct **Designcrypt** query is $\epsilon + 1/2 - q_U/2^k$. Finally, the advantage of $\mathcal{D}$ that solving the DBDH problem is

$$\epsilon' \geq \frac{1}{q_{H_1}} \cdot (\epsilon - q_U/2^k) = \frac{\epsilon \cdot 2^k - q_U}{q_{H_1} 2^k} = \epsilon \cdot \frac{1}{q_{H_1}} - \frac{1}{2^k} \cdot \frac{q_U}{q_{H_1}}$$

Theorem 2 (Ciphertext anonymity). *If there is an adversary $\mathcal{A}$ can succeeds with probability ϵ, then there is a simulator $\mathcal{B}$ can solve the DBDH problem with advantage at least*

$$\epsilon' \geqslant \epsilon \cdot \frac{1}{q_{H_1}} - \frac{1}{2^k} \cdot \frac{q_U+1}{q_{H_1}(q_s+2)}$$

Theorem 3 (Unforgeability). *The proposed scheme is existentially unforgeable against adaptive chosen-message attacks(EUF-IDASC-CMA2).*

Proof. The unforgeability against adaptive chosen messages attacks of our scheme is derived from the signature security of Cha and Cheon [6] under the CDH assumption. If an attacker $\mathcal{F}$ can forge a signcrypted message, he can forge a Cha and Cheon's signature as following:

- Sign: Given an assertion a, computes $U = rQ_A, h = H_2(U||a)$, and computes $V = (r + h)S_A$, The signature on a is $\sigma = (U, V)$.
- Verify: When receiving $\sigma = (U, V)$, it performs the proposed verify algorithm. Computes $h = H_2(U||a)$, checks whether the equation holds: $\hat{e}(P, V) = \hat{e}(P^1_{pub}, U + hQ_A)$.

Due to the hardness of CDH problem in Cha and Cheon's scheme, our proposed scheme is unforgeable against chosen message attacks.

Theorem 4 (Public verifiability). *The proposed scheme provides the public authenticity.*

Proof. One may be convinced that the ciphertext is came originally from Q_{ID_A} by computing and verifying as follows:

- computes $h = H_2(U||a)$
- checks whether the equation $\hat{e}(P, V) = \hat{e}(P^1_{pub}, U + hQ_A)$ holds.

5 Efficiency Analysis

We compare the security with recent literatures providing encryption and signature schemes in multiple PKGs environments in Table 1. In [14], it provides the semantic security, unforgeability and public verifiability. In [18], it is identical to that of Galindo's BF-IBE encryption variant, which cannot provide unforgeability. Ciphertext anonymity in [14, 18] hasn't been proposed, whereas it only provides encryption scheme security proof in multiple PKGs in [18].

Table 1. Security comparison with related schemes

scheme	security			
	confidentiality	unforgeability	public verifiability	ciphertext anonymity
[14]	y	y	y	?
[18]	y	n	n	n
our scheme	y	y	y	y

Table 2. Comparison of computing costs and ciphertext size

scheme	sigcrypt/sig			desig/verify			ciphertext size
	G_1	G_2	$\hat{e}$	G_1	G_2	$\hat{e}$	
[14]	3	1	1	0	1	4	$2|G_1| + |m|$
[18]	1	1	1	1	0	1	$|G_1| + 2|m|$
our scheme	3	0	1	1	0	3	$3|G_1| + |m|$

In Table 2, we compare the computing complex and ciphertext size. Because the scheme in [18] cannot provide unforgeability, it has the least ciphertext size. Compared with [14], we can see that our scheme has higher efficiency in computing costs.

6 Conclusion

We have proposed an efficient assertion protect scheme based on ID-based signcryption scheme. Our scheme can work in multiple autonomous domain environments such as decentralized self-organization network, autonomous P2P, and large scale distributed trust management environment etc. We have proved that our scheme satisfies the confidentiality, unforgeability, public verifiability, and ciphertext anonymity with higher security than recent literatures. However, our scheme is only loosely related to DBDH problem, which raises an open problem to provide a tight security proof for multiple trust domain security in standard security assumptions. Furthermore, it is interesting in protecting assertion privacy in multiple trust autonomous domain environments.

Acknowledgement

We would like to thank the anonymous reviewers for their valuable comments and feedbacks. This work is supported by the National Natural Science Foundation of China under Grants 60573043 and 60773175, the Foundation of the Key Lab for Guangdong Electronic Commerce Application Technology under Grant 2007gdecof002, and the Foundation of National Laboratory for Modern Communications under Grant 9140c1108010606.

References

1. Agudo, I., Lopez, J., Montenegro, J.A.: A representation model of trust relationships with delegation extensions. In: Herrmann, P., Issarny, V., Shiu, S.C.K. (eds.) iTrust 2005. LNCS, vol. 3477, pp. 116–130. Springer, Heidelberg (2005)
2. Baek, J., Steinfeld, R., Zheng, Y.: Formal proofs for the security of signcryption. Journal of cryptology 20, 203–235 (2007)
3. Bagga, W., Molva, R.: Policy-based cryptography and applications. In: S. Patrick, A., Yung, M. (eds.) FC 2005. LNCS, vol. 3570, pp. 72–87. Springer, Heidelberg (2005)
4. Blaze, M., Feigenbaum, J., Lacy, J.: Decentralized trust management. In: Proc. of the 17th Symposium on Security and Privacy, pp. 164–173. IEEE Computer Society Press, Los Alamitos (1996)
5. Boneh, D., Franklin, M.: Identity-based encryption from the weil pairing. In: Kilian, J. (ed.) CRYPTO 2001. LNCS, vol. 2139, pp. 213–229. Springer, Heidelberg (2001)
6. Cha, J., Cheon, J.: An identity-based signature from gap Diffie-Hellman groups. In: Desmedt, Y.G. (ed.) PKC 2003. LNCS, vol. 2567, pp. 18–30. Springer, Heidelberg (2002)

7. Chen, L., Kudla, C.: Identity based authenticated key agreement protocols from pairings. In: Proceedings. 16th IEEE Computer Security Foundations Workshop, 2003, pp. 219–233 (2003)
8. Chen, L., Malone-Lee, J.: Improved Identity-Based Signcryption. In: Vaudenay, S. (ed.) PKC 2005. LNCS, vol. 3386, pp. 362–379. Springer, Heidelberg (2005)
9. Chow, S.S., Yiu, S., Hui, L.C., Chow, K.: Efficient forward and provably secure id-based signcryption scheme with public verifiability and public ciphertext authenticity (Springer-Verlag). In: Lim, J.-I., Lee, D.-H. (eds.) ICISC 2003. LNCS, vol. 2971, pp. 352–369. Springer, Heidelberg (2004)
10. Kidston, D., Robinson, J.: Distributed network management for coalition deployments. In: MILCOM 2000. 21st Century Military Communications Conference Proceedings, Los Angeles, CA, USA, vol. 1, pp. 460–464 (2000)
11. Krukow, K., Nielsen, M.: Trust structures: denotational and operational semantics. International journal of information security 6, 153–181 (2007)
12. Lal, S., Kushwah, P.: Security proof for shengbao wangs identity based encryption scheme. Cryptology ePrint Archive, Report 2007/316 (2007), http://eprint.iacr.org/
13. Lal, S., Kushwah, P.: Multi-pkg id based signcryption. Cryptology ePrint Archive, Report 2008/50 (2008), http://eprint.iacr.org/
14. Li, F., Hu, Y., Zhang, C.: An identity-based signcryption scheme for multi-domain ad hoc networks. In: Katz, J., Yung, M. (eds.) ACNS 2007. LNCS, vol. 4521, pp. 373–384. Springer, Heidelberg (2007)
15. Li, N., Winsborough, W.H., Mitchell, J.C.: Distributed credential chain discovery in trust management. Journal of Computer Security 11, 35–86 (2003)
16. Malone-Lee, J.: Identity-based signcryption. Cryptology ePrint Archive, Report 2008/098 (2002), http://eprint.iacr.org/
17. Park, N., Moon, K., Chung, K., Won, D., Zheng, Y.: A security acceleration using xml signcryption scheme in mobile grid web services. In: Lowe, D.G., Gaedke, M. (eds.) ICWE 2005. LNCS, vol. 3579, pp. 191–196. Springer, Heidelberg (2005)
18. Wang, S., Cao, Z.: Practical identity-based encryption (ibe) in multiple pkg environments and its applications. Cryptology ePrint Archive, Report 2007/100 (2007), http://eprint.iacr.org/
19. Yang, G., Wong, D.S., Deng, X.: Analysis and improvement of a signcryption scheme with key privacy. In: Zhou, J., López, J., Deng, R.H., Bao, F. (eds.) ISC 2005. LNCS, vol. 3650, pp. 218–232. Springer, Heidelberg (2005)
20. Yao, D., Tamassia, R.: Cascaded authorization with anonymous-signer aggregate signatures. In: Proc. of 2006 IEEE workshop on Information Assurance, pp. 21–23 (2006)
21. Yu, Y., Yang, B., Huang, X.Y., Zhang, M.W.: Efficient identity-based signcryption scheme for multiple receivers. In: Xiao, B., Yang, L.T., Ma, J., Muller-Schloer, C., Hua, Y. (eds.) ATC 2007. LNCS, vol. 4610, pp. 13–21. Springer, Heidelberg (2007)
22. Zheng, Y.: Digital signcryption or how to achieve cost (signature & encryption) ≪ cost(signature)+cost(encryption) (Springer-Verlag). In: Kaliski Jr., B.S. (ed.) CRYPTO 1997. LNCS, vol. 1294, pp. 165–179. Springer, Heidelberg (1997)

A Study of Information Security Practice in a Critical Infrastructure Application

Martin Gilje Jaatun[1], Eirik Albrechtsen[2], Maria B. Line[1], Stig Ole Johnsen[2], Irene Wærø[2], Odd Helge Longva[1], and Inger Anne Tøndel[1]

[1] SINTEF ICT, NO-7465 Trondheim, Norway
{Martin.G.Jaatun,Maria.B.Line,Odd.H.Longva,
Inger.A.Tondel}@sintef.no
[2] SINTEF T&S, NO-7465 Trondheim, Norway
{Eirik.Albrechtsen,Stig.O.Johnsen,Irene.Waro}@sintef.no

Abstract. Based on multiple methods we have studied how information security practices, and in particular computer security incident response practices, are handled in the Norwegian offshore oil and gas industry. Our findings show that there is still insufficient awareness regarding the importance of information security in the offshore industry, and that increased vigilance is required in order to respond to mounting threats of tomorrow.

Keywords: Incident Response Management, Information Security, Process Control, Security Practice.

1 Introduction

During the last years the concept of Integrated Operations (IO), i.e. use of information technology and real-time data to operate petroleum processes, has been implemented in the oil and gas industry on the Norwegian Continental Shelf [1]. This implies that new technologies and new ways of working and communicating are implemented to create remote operations, control and support; e.g. through merging ICT systems and Supervisory Control And Data Acquisition (SCADA) systems. This development is still in progress, and the integration of industrial processes, technology and different actors is likely to continue and even tighten up in the years to follow. On the one hand, integrated operations represent a major opportunity for increased and more efficient production and reduced operational cost as well as improved safety performance [1]. On the other hand, implementation of new and supplementary information systems increases the systems' vulnerability to breakdowns due to information security breaches. Breaches can lead to consequences such as production stops; disabling of critical safety barriers and problems of providing oil and gas to customers [2]. It is thus necessary for the petroleum industry to implement adequate information security measures to contribute to a stable production and sale as well as safety for its employees.

This paper gives a picture of information security practices in the Norwegian oil and gas industry by presenting empirical findings from the research project "Incident

C. Rong et al. (Eds.): ATC 2008, LNCS 5060, pp. 527–539, 2008.
© Springer-Verlag Berlin Heidelberg 2008

Response Management" (IRMA), funded by the Research Council of Norway and the Norwegian Oil Industry Association.

The IRMA research project developed a framework for incident response management [3]. The management framework includes the following three phases (see Fig. 1): prepare (planning and preparation of incident response); detect and recover (detection of incidents and restoration to normal operation); and learn (experience sharing and learning afterwards). There are several standards and good practice documents that describe incident handling (e.g. [4, 5]). The management system developed in IRMA differs from the traditional incident handling approaches in two ways: It focuses on both reactive and proactive learning; and it is tailored to the oil and gas industry.

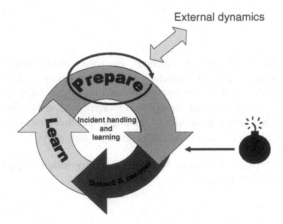

Fig. 1. Incident Response Management Phases

The complex processes of oil and gas producing installations are monitored and controlled by Supervisory Control And Data Acquisition (SCADA) systems which are traditionally operated by personnel with a different background than administrators of traditional computer systems. This implies that there is a situation of disparate cultures that also results in information security challenges.

The paper is structured as following: Section 2 presents the empirical sources and methods we have used, section 3 presents our findings, which are discussed further in section 4, while section 5 concludes and summarises our study.

2 Empirical Sources and Methods

The development of the incident response management (IRMA) framework for the petroleum industry presented in Jaatun et al. [3] required a combination of different empirical sources of information security practices in this industry:

- An interview study with key personnel in the Norwegian oil and gas industry
- A case study of incident response management practice at an oil and gas installation in the North Sea

- A risk and vulnerability assessment of infrastructure and work processes at an offshore installation
- A study of cultural aspects of information security by using a tool for assessing information security culture at a particular installation
- A workshop on information security and integrated operations
- A workshop on the main findings of IRMA in the Norwegian offshore industry
- System dynamic workshops

In addition, the IRMA project team has been represented in Norwegian Oil Industry Association's (OLF) workgroup on information security for the entire duration of the project. The workgroup meetings have provided the project with important background information and firsthand access to operator and contractor personnel who are actively involved with offshore safety and security work. The workgroup meetings have also been used to discuss preliminary results from IRMA, and have provided us with useful feedback. Furthermore, the fact that we had contributed to the workgroup meetings made it significantly easier to recruit participants for our workshops and interviews.

Although the empirical studies had a main emphasis on incident handling, other parts of information security were also uncovered during the study, which are presented in the subsequent sections.

The bulleted list above also shows that a combination of different qualitative social science methods was used for collecting information about information security practices in the oil and gas industry. Information security practices in this particular industry have previously not been the subject of many research attempts. In that way, qualitative research methods proved to be a good methodological approach due to the explorative nature of qualitative research. In general, qualitative research provides understandings of social phenomena by proximate studies of the local contexts of the study [6]. By close interaction between researchers and informants, the researchers will get an understanding of the processes studied rather than only a description of the processes [7], which proved to be useful for the present study.

Qualitative research results should not be treated as generalized facts, but understandings of processes in the particular context of the study [6]. As a consequence, the findings presented in this paper are not necessarily generalized facts, but a representation of information security practices in the Norwegian oil and gas industry.

3 Findings

This section presents the main findings from the different data sources mentioned in the previous section.

3.1 Interviews

Nine interviews of personnel with knowledge and experience of information security in the oil and gas industry were conducted by phone in the period of March-June 2007. The interviews aimed at exploring how incidents were handled in the Norwegian oil and gas industry, and were approached by looking at how incidents were practically dealt with and how the informants believed a best practice for incident response management should look like. The interviews were analyzed according to [8] by structuring the information in matrices and looking for patterns in the structured data (see [9] for a detailed result matrix).

In general, the interviews showed that the informants experienced very few information security incidents that have impact on production. It was assumed that it could be between one and two years between each incident.

Information security measures tend to have a main focus on technology. Technical issues are often covered exclusively, while there are seldom discussions of defenses in breadth; covering organisational and human factors in addition to technical issues.

There are many plans for different parts of incident response in the studied organisations, with different level of details. A short and common plan, documenting specific incident response management incorporated in the organisation, is missing among most of the interviewees. Scenario training, which is widely used in other loss prevention areas in the industry, for handling information security breaches is seldom performed. Furthermore, the interviews showed that individual awareness and proactive unrest related to information security could be improved. Knowledge and understanding of information security could be improved among employees, especially among suppliers.

The learning phase after an incident has occurred is considered to be important. However, some informants were worried whether learning actually had any effect for future activities, and feared that learning was quickly forgotten. The learning is thorough. Root causes are not always identified, discussions do not always involve information and communication technology (ICT) and process professionals together, and lessons learned are not published.

The interviewees' organisations' reporting systems are seldom tailored to information security, and there are often many different reporting systems, leading to a lack of a unified system for reporting incidents. The interviews also indicate a lack of frankness about real incidents. A change of focus is demanded in the industry to make experience transfer both inside the organisation and to external organisations possible.

3.2 A Case Study at an Oil and Gas Installation in the North Sea

In the early stages of the IRMA project, a case study at an oil and gas installation was performed. The case study aimed at describing how incident response management was performed in practice at a selected offshore installation. Interviews, meetings and document studies were used in the case study.

In general, the incident response management at the studied installation has a potential to be more systematic and planned, as the current management approach seemed scattered and randomly made. The study showed that the only incident handling procedure at the installation was a procedure for handling virus infections[1]; there were no other relevant procedures for incident response. There were some awareness-creating activities at the installation, which among other subjects also

---

[1] This procedure was not immediately available at the start of the case study, and might actually have been developed as a result of our inquiry.

included information security. Our findings indicate that if there is a virus infection in the SCADA systems, it might take weeks before the infection is detected; even if the system is not operating normal.

When incidents happen, there is limited learning in the organisation from these incidents, and there is moderate communication within the organisation about real incidents.

3.3 Risk and Vulnerability Assessment

To gain more insight into ICT-related risks involved in integrated operations, a risk and vulnerability assessment was conducted based on the work process of daily production optimization of an offshore installation. Small-scale workshops with managers were performed to identify incidents and assess the risk of these incidents.

This assessment and the knowledge attained by analyzing the coupling and dependencies of ICT systems, vulnerabilities, responsibilities, possible consequences of various incidents and how incidents are usually detected and recovered, gave a basis for further work as well as implications for the assessed installation.

The most critical incidents identified in the risk assessment were: the operation centre goes down jamming the SCADA system; the SCADA system goes down; a virus/worm infects the system from external sources; and missing situational awareness from central control room operator.

The risk assessment suggested the following risk reducing measures relevant for incident response management: monitoring the stability of the SCADA equipment when it is integrated with ICT infrastructure; external PCs should be scanned and checked prior to being allowed in technical network or offshore network, or supplier should guarantee that the equipment are without viruses; incident reporting and learning from incidents should be improved; the responsibilities related to technical network and the integration of ICT/SCADA systems should be unambiguous and monitored; awareness, safety and security culture should be improved onshore and offshore; common risk assessment among the actors in the organisational network should be established and sustained; and emergency response plans should incorporate information security incidents.

3.4 Assessment of Information Security Challenges at an Installation

A tool for assessing organisational aspects of information security, Check-IT [10, 11], was used to identify some key challenges related to an integrated operation installation in a half-day workshop with ten managers and staff members. CheckIT consists of a set of questions regarding organisational aspects of information security, including alternatives for answers. Although it is a questionnaire, the questions are so open-ended that they function well for group discussions as well, which results in both an assessment of the current status as well as improved awareness among discussion partners.

The study showed that information security is not satisfactorily integrated in projects and new installations. Furthermore, suppliers and service providers are not satisfactorily involved in incident planning, detection and learning. The identification of critical ICT systems is not satisfactorily in developing integrated operations; HAZOP analysis [12] (risk analysis) of ICT/SCADA systems is seldom done.

Productivity goals are sometimes prioritized ahead of information security requirements, as rules and procedures related to information security are sometimes ignored in situations with conflicting demands.

In general, the personnel on offshore installations have a low level of awareness related to information security (e.g. regarding spyware and virus). This is partly explained by lack of communication of information security issues in the organisation. This lack of communication is also reflected in unsatisfactorily sharing of information security incidents between organisations in the industry.

3.5 Workshop on Information Security and Integrated Operations

A workshop on information security in integrated operations was arranged by the Norwegian Petroleum Directorate, the Petroleum Safety Authority Norway, The Norwegian Oil Industry Association (OLF) and SINTEF in November 2006 [13]. The workshop aimed at 1) creating awareness on information security in integrated operation among different organisational groups (ICT, Health, Safety, Security and Environment (HSSE), automation and operations); 2) creating an arena for experience transfer and networking; and 3) identifying possible measures. About fifty participants from the oil and gas industry, the power supply industry; public agencies and research institutions attended the workshop.

Several information security issues in integrated operations were discussed in parallel groups, including topics on incident response management. One result of the workshop was that there is a need for more measurement of information security (key performance indicators) to evaluate whether the security level corresponds to policies and regulations; to evaluate effects of measures and to integrate information security with other business areas. Such measurements should be with some kind of reference point, e.g. the OLF Information Security Baseline Requirements (ISBR) [14].

There is a lack of willingness to report incidents in the industry; as a consequence more work is needed to study how to develop a reporting culture; how to inform about incidents; and how to develop a best practice regarding reporting and handling of incidents. Routines for reporting, including feedback on the reports, should be simplified.

Training and preparedness for ICT-related incidents is lacking. The industry has traditionally trained on defined hazard and accident situation scenarios in other loss prevention areas. Such scenarios are however lacking for ICT-related incidents. Furthermore, the workshop indicated that there is a gap in communication between different groups of professionals offshore, i.e. HSSE, ICT and process. This is reflected by ICT routines that are not adjusted to the offshore reality.

3.6 Workshop on Main Findings from IRMA

In October 2007 some of the main findings on IRMA project in the offshore industry were discussed at a workshop. 15 participants from the industry, governmental agencies, consulting companies and research institutions participated at the workshop.

Regarding the plan phase of incident response management it was emphasized that incident response management must appear as a proactive management approach in order to be prepared to handle and learn from whatever incidents that may occur. In this proactive approach, performing risk analysis should be the foundation for providing decision support to how incident response management should be planned and performed.

In the detect and recover phase, it is important that those who discover or suspect an incident know who to notify. One must define possible incidents and then see which channels for reporting are the most efficient for those incidents, e.g. perform a risk analysis.

To be able to learn from incidents, structures for reporting incidents must be in place. A module for information security incidents is needed in applied software for reporting incidents. Contractors fill out a form, which is registered in the incident reporting tool Synergi[2] by someone else. It is a challenge that different parts of the organisation have different traditions for reporting incidents. For example that control room operators do not report incidents, since they only handle the consequences of incidents, not the incident itself.

The workshop participants felt that an information security forum for experience transfer in the oil and gas industry is an interesting idea, but the industry must decide what such a forum should be used for. It is important to include different professions in such a forum.

The workshop also discussed whether historical data on incidents is relevant for IRMA in integrated operations. New technology and new ways of organizing work may change the relevance of historical data.

3.7 System Dynamics Workshops and Cooperation with the AMBASEC Project

In 2005 the IRMA project team in collaboration with the AMBASEC[3] research project team, carried out two system dynamic workshops, The objective of the workshops were to reach a deeper understanding of present risks in the transition to integrated operations and the implications for incident handling in this transition. The processes included building a system dynamic model for a particular integrated operation installation.

The results from the workshops and the collaboration between IRMA and AMBASEC are documented in two reports [15, 16] and several scientific publications [17-20]. The areas of discussion included identifying key indicators and dynamic system stories to anticipate change in a system's state over time.

In the first workshop, a preliminary version of a system dynamics model for the transition to integrated operations was established, and a set of stakeholders[4] and their influences on possible outcomes for security in IO were identified. Two dynamic stories were developed with the intent to show the relationship between operational

---

[2] http://www.synergi.com

[3] AMBASEC (A Model-based Approach to Security Culture) is a project funded by the Research Council of Norway, anchored at Agder University College (AUC – now University of Agder). AMBASEC has had a formal collaboration with IRMA.

[4] Examples of stakeholders are oil company (system owner), chief executive officer, platform chief, control room manager, incident response team manager, Ptil, media etc.

change, security and the stakeholders: "Virus exposure in virtual organisations" and "The effect of the introduction of compliance mechanisms to suppliers and contractors."

Workshop attendees discussed a risk and vulnerability analysis for the work process "daily production optimization", and came up with different views on how work processes will develop in the future of IO.

Findings from the first workshop included:

- Monitoring risk change should be given high priority when developing new policies in the industry related to incident reporting, creating CSIRTs[5] and raising awareness.
- Transitions from traditional to integrated operations create vulnerabilities. The timing of these vulnerabilities may depend on how well the organisation is able to change its operating processes, train its staff and contractors, and gain acceptance of the transition.
- Successful implementation of collaborative arenas reinforces their effectiveness. On the other hand, limited success will likely slow acceptance of this innovation, and increase the resources required for subsequent rollouts, or possibly derail the project.
- The transition from existing to new work processes will introduce new security issues and potential for security lapses. These problems, if not detected and mitigated, are expected to increase the resistance to further change and adoption.
- Delays in learning and reflection may reduce the migration to integrated operations. Development of a capacity to detect problems and learn from them may facilitate future transitions. Conversely, a limited capacity to detect problems as they occur will obstruct change and delay corrections, increase risk, and put the project at greater peril.

The second workshop was focused on the implementation of a new workprocess in the Brage oilfield. Simulation on the SD-model where the parameters were adjusted by the experts from Hydro brought forward a set of hypotheses:

- Maturation and adoption of technology enables work processes and transformation.
- Introduction of new technologies and work processes can create knowledge gaps and vulnerabilities.
- More communication off-platform reduces resistance to change, which enables adoption of mature processes.
- Incident reporting creates a stock of knowledge of incidents, which allows us to bring on mature work processes and improves rate of getting mature technology online, reducing vulnerabilities, incidents and damage.

While the effects of this work on the proposed integrated operations migration are not by any means clear, the group model building process achieved several important outcomes for the participants. The qualitative models identified several problematic areas in the transition. The potential for a Knowledge Gap and a Work Process gap

---

[5] Computer Security Incident Response Team.

reinforced the importance of timing and knowledge sharing. The long-term effectiveness of CSIRT activity on the ability of the firm to develop a strong security culture is dependent upon a move beyond damage repair and into active learning.

From a methodical perspective, the results had two additional important outcomes: Group model building engaged and focused a diverse set of experts and modellers to develop a holistic, systems view of a problem. This was particularly gratifying given the initial skepticism expressed during the planning of the meeting. Through the feedback models, a wide set of interrelationships emerged that influence the success or failure of both the integrated operations and the CSIRT initiatives. Though little hard data was available, the participants' knowledge of the general structures and behaviours in their environment was sufficient for credible and understandable causal modelling. This is a crucial finding in high-threat environments, as little data is ever made available outside the secure environment of the firm.

The state of information security in this domain is still relatively immature when compared to the state of safety. In the realm of safety there are numerous reporting systems, often mandated by law or if not directly by law, by high political pressure. Perhaps we will not see well-functioning incident reporting systems for information security before government intervenes or threatens to do so. Another reason for the relatively slow adaptation of incident reporting systems may be the singular focus on information security as a technical issue. Non-security personnel are often kept completely out of the loop and are instead presented with a set of prescribed rules. However, this is a limited approach to user education. Users must be kept 'in the loop'; only then will they see the necessity and usefulness of following the rules prescribed by information security specialists.

Simulation runs on the SD-model illustrate the potential for a successful incident reporting system. However, they also show that there is potential for partial or even complete failure if important factors, such as the quality of investigations and motivation, are not handled well.

4   Discussion

Traditionally, there has been, and still is, a greater focus on *safety* than on *security* in the offshore industry. This is due to the fact that the process control systems used to be proprietary, and the set of security threats applicable was clear and not very large, while working conditions for the people posed a greater overall threat to their lives.

4.1   Few Incidents are Observed

A general view in the industry is that there are few information security incidents occurring. A majority of employees therefore do not see why having a plan for incident response is important. It is perceived more as an unnecessary and expensive hassle than an efficient measure which may save lots of time and money the day something happens.

It is claimed within the industry that loss of money is acceptable as long as no lives are lost. However, an offshore installation in full production generates so much money, that it is hard to believe that loss of money really is of no concern.

Because of the lack of a complete method for incident response, how can it be stated that not many incidents occur? In meetings where IT staff and process control staff have been together, we have seen several times that one of the groups have revealed stories about incidents that up till then was unknown by the other one. Communication of incidents seems to be absent, and also the ability to discover incidents can be questioned. This leads us to conclude that improved indicators for information security are needed.

4.2 Combining Two Different Worlds

Regarding the two groups IT staff and process control staff, there is clearly a gap between them which may pose great security challenges. This is especially relevant now when process control systems change from being nearly completely proprietary, or at least not connected to any external networks, to include more commercial off-the-shelf hardware and software and being connected to the Internet, although with several layers of security mechanisms. Where process control staff used to be in total control and manage their systems without any help from IT staff, there is now need for a close interaction where IT staff need to manage and maintain systems in production. This requires a mutual understanding for each other's fields of expertise. In the world of the IT staff, computers crashing from time to time are normal; rebooting is sometimes necessary and often this also fixes the problem; and installing patches can usually be done at any time. In the world of the process control staff, keeping the production systems running without interruption is crucial, as a system crash may result in stop in production, which again leads to loss of money. This means that patches should not be installed before there is a 100% certainty they will work without any compatibility problems. Rebooting computers may be the same as stop of production as well as disable safety systems. And backup systems are rarely tested, if at all, because what if they do not work? These different mindsets can be explained by different objectives in the loss prevention approaches [21]. The IT world typically sees confidentiality and data integrity as the main objective, while the industrial control systems aim at system availability and data integrity to ensure plant safety and occupational injury prevention.

It is a challenged to combine the mindsets of IT staff and process control staff is a in a successful way, but collaboration between them is necessary. This means that there is a need for communication and skills development for both groups of people. To integrate different perceptions of risk and risk mitigation, Klinke and Renn [22] suggest a discourse-based management approach where the involved actors interact and discuss risk issues. Workshop methods such as seek conferences and focus groups might prove useful for this purpose.

4.3 Learning Based on Few Incidents

As long as we do not have proof of anything else, we need to base our work on the perceived fact that few incidents actually occur. However, as we believe that this will change in the near future, with the ongoing transition to integrated operations and the use of new technologies, we see a clear need for improvement of incident response management. First and foremost, having a plan for how to deal with different kinds of incidents, including reporting procedures and responsibilities, is a good starting point. A greater challenge is how to implement learning of incidents as there are so few to learn from.

Sharing experiences and knowledge between companies within the same industry is a good way of gathering information about incidents which again can be used as a basis for learning. It is important that the employees can relate to the referred incidents, which can be achieved by collecting information from similar companies. A challenge in such cross-organisational learning is openness about the incidents. Embarrassing and threatening aspects is known to be major obstacles for learning [23] , most security incidents are in its nature threatening and embarrassing, so a a key challenge in future sharing of inexperience and learning is to create an environment for openness on these incidents. We see that the work group organized by OLF has succeeded in this type of information exchange. This group has now existed for three years, and is based on trust and openness. This has been a good first-step-on-the-way in improving communication about information security within the industry. However, in the long run it is not sufficient that only Chief Information Security Officers (CISOs) communicate. Information needs to be spread throughout a larger part of each company, and there must be communication present across company limits on several layers.

5 Conclusion

We have presented the findings of an empirical study of information security practices in oil and gas operations on the Norwegian Continental Shelf, with a special focus on computer security incident response. Our findings show that there is still insufficient awareness regarding the importance of information security in the offshore industry, and that increased vigilance is required in order to respond to mounting threats of tomorrow.

Further work is required in order to instill this sense of vigilance on the oil and gas industry. We believe that increased effort should be put into developing information security indicators that proactively can measure (lack of) security for these installations, including near-miss type of indicators. If the industry allows itself to get lulled into a sense of security based on the currently small number of perceived incidents, it risks getting swamped by a future deluge of attacks.

Acknowledgements

This research was supported by the Research Council of Norway and the Norwegian Oil Industry Association (OLF). The authors thank all participants of OLF's workgroup on information security, and in particular StatoilHydro, for their cooperation.

References

1. OLF, Integrated Operations on NCS, Norwegian Oil Industry Association (2004),
   `http://www.olf.no/?22894.pdf`
2. Albrechtsen, E., Hovden, J.: Industrial safety management and information security
   management: risk characteristics and management approaches. In: European Safety and
   Reliabilty Conference 2007 (ESREL 2007), Stavanger, Norway (2007)
3. Jaatun, M.G., et al.: Incident Response Management in the oil and gas industry, SINTEF
   Report A4086, Trondheim (December 2007),
   `http://www.sintef.no/upload/10977/20071212_IRMA_Rapport.pdf`
4. ISO/IEC TR 18044:2004 Information technology – Security techniques – Information
   security incident management (2004)
5. Grance, T., Kent, K., Kim, B.: Computer Security Incident Handling Guide, NIST Special
   Publication 800-61 (2004),
   `http://csrc.nist.gov/publications/nistpubs/800-61/sp800-61.pdf`
6. Thagaard, T.: Systematikk og innlevelse: en innføring i kvalitativ metode (in Norwegian)
   [Systematic and insight: introduction to qualitative methods] Bergen: Fagbokforlaget
   (2003)
7. Kvale, S.: Det kvaliative forskningsintervju (in Norwegian) [Interviews: an introduction to
   qualitative research interviewing]. Oslo: Ad Notam Gyldendal (1997)
8. Miles, M.B., Huberman, A.M.: Qualitative Data analysis: an expanded sourcebook. Sage,
   Thousand Oaks, Calif (1994)
9. Albrechtsen, E., et al.: IRMA - Interviews on incident response in the oil and gas industry,
   SINTEF MEMO (November 22, 2007)
10. Nordby, Y., Hansen, C.W.: Informasjonssikkerhet – atferd, holdninger og kultur (in
    Norwegian) [Information security – behaviour, awareness and culture] NTNU-rapport
    ROSS(NTNU)200504 (2005)
11. Johnsen, S.O., et al.: CheckIT – A program to measure and improve information security
    and safety culture. International Journal of Performability Engineering 3(1 Part II), 174–
    186 (2007)
12. Hazard and operability studies (HAZOP studies) - Application guide, IEC 61882 (2001)
13. Jaatun, M.G. (ed.): Arbeidsseminar om IKT-sikkerhet i Integrerte Operasjoner: Referat (in
    Norwegian) [Minutes from workshop on ICT Security in IO] (2007),
    `http://www.sintef.no/upload/10977/sluttrapport.pdf`
14. Information Security Baseline Requirements for Process Control, Safety and Support ICT
    Systems (2007), `http://www.olf.no/hms/retningslinjer/?50182.pdf`
15. Rich, E., Andersen, D.F., Richardson, G.P.: OLF IRMA-AMBASEC Group Modeling
    Report I, University at Albany, Albany, NY (2006)
16. Rich, E., Andersen, D.F., Richardson, G.P.: OLF IRMA-AMBASEC Group Modeling
    Report II, University at Albany, Albany (2006)
17. Rich, E., Gonzalez, J.J.: Maintaining Security and Safety in High-threat in E-operations
    Transitions, presented at 39th Hawaii International Conference on System Sciences,
    Hawaii (2006)
18. Rich, E., et al.: Emergent Vulnerability in Integrated Operations: A Proactive Simulation
    Study of Risk and Organizational Learning, presented at 40th Hawaii International
    Conference on System Sciences, Hawaii (2007)
19. Sveen, F.O., Rich, E., Jager, M.: Overcoming organizational challenges to secure
    knowledge management. Information Systems Frontiers 9(5), 481–492 (2007)

20. Sveen, F.O., et al.: Toward viable information security reporting systems. Information Management & Computer Security 15(5), 408–419 (2007)
21. Stouffer, K., Falco, J., Kent, K.: Guide to SCADA and Industrial Control Systems Security (draft), NIST Special Publication 800-82 (2006),
    http://csrc.nist.gov/publications/drafts/800-82/Draft-SP800-82.pdf
22. Klinke, A., Renn, O.: A New Approach to Risk Evaluation and Management: Risk-Based, Precaution-Based, and Discourse-Based Strategies. Risk Analysis 22(6), 1071–1094 (2002)
23. Argyris, C., Schön, D.A.: Organisational learning II: Theory, method and practice. Addison-Wesley, Reading (1996)

Web Search Results Clustering Based on a Novel Suffix Tree Structure

Junze Wang, Yijun Mo, Benxiong Huang, Jie Wen, and Li He

Institude of Communication Software and Switch Technology, Huazhong
University of Science and Technology, Wuhan 430074, Hubei, China
wangjunze@smail.hust.edu.cn

Abstract. Web search results clustering are navigator for users to search needed
results. With suffix tree clustering (STC), search results can be clustered fast,
automatically, and each cluster is labeled with a common phrase. Due to the large
memory requirement of suffix tree, some other approaches have been proposed,
with lower memory requirement. But unlike other algorithms, STC is an
incremental algorithm and a promising approach to work on a long list of
snippets returned by search engines. In this paper we proposed an approach for
web search results clustering and labeling, based on a new suffix tree data
structure. The approach is an incremental and linear time algorithm, with
significantly lower memory requirements. This approach also labels every final
cluster a common phrase, thus it is suitable for quickly browsing by users.
Experimental results show that the new approach has better performance than
that of conventional web search result clustering.

Keywords: Search results organization, document clustering, incremental
clustering, a new suffix tree, lower memory requirement.

1 Background and Related Work

Existing search engines often return a long list of search results, so users have to go
through the list to identify their required results. The goal of a clustering algorithm on
our domain is to group each document with others sharing a common topic, thus helps
users to find relevant results.

Most traditional clustering algorithms cannot be directly used for web search results
clustering because of some practical issues. For example, the clustering algorithm
should be fast enough for online calculation; and the generated clusters should have
readable descriptions for quick browsing by users, etc. Zamir and Etzioni [1][2] gave a
detailed analysis on these issues. They also proposed an algorithm named STC, which
finds clusters based on the common phrases shared by snippets.

In recent years several web search results clustering algorithms have been proposed
[3-8]. But they are not incremental clustering algorithm. Unlike them, the STC
algorithm is an incremental algorithm, so web search result clustering based on this
algorithm is a promising approach to work on a long list of snippets returned by search

C. Rong et al. (Eds.): ATC 2008, LNCS 5060, pp. 540–554, 2008.

engines. However the original STC algorithm often constructs a long path of suffix tree and suffers from large memory requirements.

Hau-Jun Zeng and etc. [9] introduced an improved suffix tree with N-gram to deal with the problem of the original suffix tree. However, the suffix tree with N-gram can discover only partial common phrases when the length of N-gram is shorter than the length of true phrases. For example, given a true phrase "suffix tree clustering algorithm", a suffix tree with 3-gram can discover partial phrases: "suffix tree clustering" and "tree clustering algorithm". In this case, STC with N-gram labels a cluster with a partial phrase (probably unreadable), and gives too many candidate clusters. Thus, it may hurt the final cluster quality.

In response to this situation, Jongkol Janruang [10] proposed a new partial phrase join operation, which can join the partial phrases, combine the candidate clusters, and generate more readable labels.

Additionally, STC algorithm extracts all right-complete substrings of the true phrase (including the true phrase itself). Take the phrase "suffix tree clustering algorithm" for example, all the right-complete substrings of it, such as "tree clustering algorithm", "clustering algorithm" and "algorithm", will be discovered, and all these partial phrases are regarded as candidate phrases. In this condition STC algorithm gives too many candidate clusters and may hurt the final cluster quality too. On this issue [11] has given a good analysis on this issue.

We will analyze the shortcomings of STC with N-gram further more in section 2; In section 3, we will propose a new suffix tree data structure, named suffix tree with X-gram, along with a improved STC algorithm which overcomes the shortcomings of conventional STC algorithms, and still maintains the advantages; At last the experimental results show that our new approach has better performance than that of conventional STC algorithms.

2 Suffix Tree with N-Gram

Original suffix tree is a very efficient way to identify true common phrases in snippets, but suffers from large memory requirements. Suffix tree with N-gram performs the similar function, and has lower memory requirements. "With N-gram" means the suffixes fed to the suffix tree is limited no more than N. If a suffix is longer than N, only the first N chars will be fed to the tree and the chars after the Nth char will be discarded. As an example, an original suffix is shown in Figure 1, and a suffix tree with N-gram (N=3) is shown in Figure 2, given the snippet [suffix, tree, clustering, algorithm, x1, x2, x3] for building the two suffix trees. The expression $\{x_1, x_2, ..., x_i\}$ (m, n) means the word sequences "$x_1, x_2, ..., x_i$" present in snippet m, at position n. So in Figure 2, {suffix, tree, clustering} (1, 1) means "suffix tree clustering" presents in snippet 1, at position 1; {tree, clustering, algorithm} (1, 2) means "tree clustering algorithm" presents in snippet 1, at position 2.

Obviously suffix tree with N-gram maintains fewer words than original suffix tree. In this way it has lower memory requirements. Maintaining fewer words also implies it spends less time in building the tree.

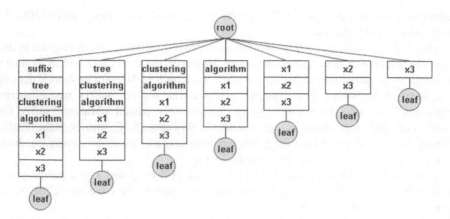

Fig. 1. The original suffix tree building depends on the snippet [suffix, tree, clustering, algorithm, x1, x2, x3]

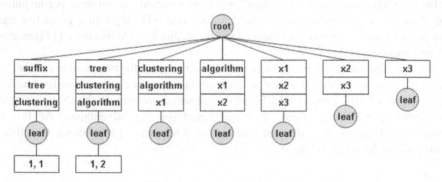

Fig. 2. The suffix tree with 3-gram building depends on the snippet [suffix, tree, clustering, algorithm, x1, x2, x3]. The maximum depth of this suffix tree is 3.

However, suffix tree with N-gram discovers only partial common phrases when the length of N-gram is shorter than the length of true phrases. For example, give a true phrase "suffix tree clustering algorithm", a suffix tree with 3-gram can discover partial phrases: "suffix tree clustering" and "tree clustering algorithm".

A new partial phrase join operation is proposed in [10]. The candidate cluster combining technique uses the join operation to define a new common phrase of a new cluster when merging a pair of similar candidate clusters. For example, the candidate cluster A = {suffix, tree, clustering} (1, 1) and B = {tree, clustering, algorithm} (1, 2) shown in Figure 2, a new common phrase is defined as

$$A + B = \{suffix, tree, clustering, algorithm\} \ (1, 1)$$

This new phrase can be discovered in snippet [suffix, tree, clustering, algorithm, x1, x2, x3].

The partial phrase join operation generates the true common phrases which are more readable, but still can not overcome the shortcomings of "right-complete" [12]. Given the true phrase "suffix tree clustering algorithm", STC discovers all its right-complete substrings, such as "tree clustering algorithm", "clustering algorithm", "algorithm" and the phrase itself, and considers all of them as candidate clusters. But in all of them, only the phrase itself is useful for clustering! Given a phrase with length L, there are at most L right-complete substrings. Generate so many useless candidate clusters will increase the consumption of STC algorithm and hurt the final cluster quality.

In addition, there is still some redundant data in the suffix tree with N-gram. In the next section we will introduce a new data structure named suffix tree with X-gram, which can be constructed with less memory space; and we will introduce a complement operation to eliminate the useless "right-complete" substrings of the true phrases.

3 The Clustering Algorithm Based on Suffix Tree with X-Gram

In order to lower the memory requirement, the maximum length of suffixes fed to the suffix tree should be limited. In STC with N-gram, it is no more than a constant variable N. But in fact, we want the true phrases fed to the tree as a whole one, even it is longer than N; and the noisy word sequences fed to the suffix tree as short as possible, even it is already shorter than N.

In the clustering algorithm based on suffix tree with X-gram, we use X to denote the maximum length of suffixes fed to the suffix tree. We make X an adaptive variable. The suffix tree with X-gram also limits the length of the suffixes which fed to the tree, but is more reasonable than with N-gram. With this data structure, the word sequences which are presented more frequently are considered more likely to be true common phrases, and will be fed to the tree as a whole one; but the noise word sequences fed to tree will be limited, even it is not so long. In this way suffix tree with X-gram discovers the true common phrases, and maintains fewer words than suffix tree with N-gram. Now we show the construction process of suffix tree with X-gram.

A suffix tree with X-gram for the word sequences S[1...m] can be built like this: first enters the first word S[1] into the tree as a leaf node. Then it successively enters the suffix S[i...j] into the growing tree, for i increasing from 2 to m, and S[i...j] is the longest prefix of suffix S[i...m] matched the conditions. The details of this construction method are presented as follow:

1. Initialize a tree only has a root node. Add the first word S[1] to the tree and then generate the suffix tree T_1, which only has a leaf node denotes the word S[1].

2. Tree T_{i+1} is constructed from T_i. The steps are as follows:

2.1. Starting at the root of Ti the algorithm finds the longest path from root whose label matches a prefix of S[i+1...m]. This path is found by successively comparing and matching words in suffix S[i+1...m] to words along a unique path from the root, until no further matches are possible.

2.2. When no further matches are possible, the algorithm must arrive at a node, say N_{cur}. Now the match part between the path in the tree and the suffix S is S[i+1, j]. The algorithm creates a new leaf node labeled S[j+1], which is a child node of N_{cur}.

For instance, given the snippet [suffix, tree, used, in, suffix, tree, clustering], this algorithm first feeds the word "suffix" to the tree (step 1 in the algorithm), then feeds the words "tree", 'used', "in" to the suffix tree ordinal. Then it is turn to the word "suffix", and "suffix" already exists in the tree as a path from root to a leaf node. So add word "tree" to tree, as a child node of "suffix" (step 2.2 in the algorithm). The suffix tree generated at last is shown in Figure 3.

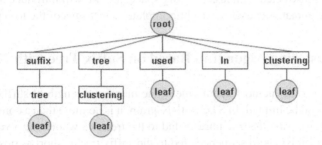

Fig. 3. An Example of Suffix Tree with X-gram. Building depends on the snippet [suffix, tree, used, in, suffix, tree, clustering]. Step 1: feed "suffix" to tree; step 2: feed "tree" to tree; step 3: feed "used" to tree; step 4: feed "in" to tree; **step 5: feed "suffix tree" to tree; step 6: feed "tree clustering" to tree;** step 7: feed "clustering" to tree.

The suffix tree with N-gram limited the depth of suffix tree with a constant variable N; but with X-gram, the depth of suffix tree will be limited with a variable X, which is not constant but an adaptive variable. So if a word sequences present several times in snippets, it will be fed to the tree wholly, even it is longer than N; and if a word sequences present little times, it will be feed to the tree partial, even it is shorter than N.

Given the snippets set show in Table 1:

Table 1. Snippets set

D1	suffix, tree, clustering, x1, x2
D2	y1, suffix, tree, clustering, y2
D3	z1, z2, suffix, tree, clustering

Build the original suffix tree, suffix tree with 3-gram and suffix tree with X-gram, which are shown in Figure 4(a), Figure 4(b) and Figure 4(c). The number of nodes maintained by respective suffix tree is show in Table 2. We use Ukkonen's algorithm [13] to construct the suffix tree and every node denotes a word.

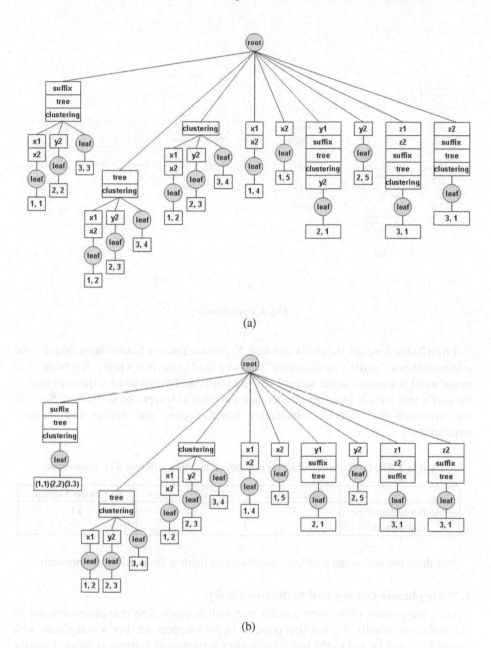

Fig. 4. (a) Example of original suffix tree. Building with the snippets set shown in Table 1.
(b) Example of suffix tree with 3-gram. Building with the snippets set shown in Table 1.
(c) Example of suffix tree with X-gram. Building with the snippets set shown in Table 1.

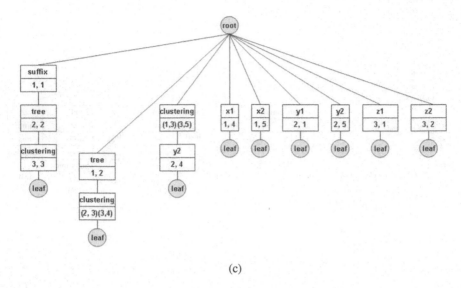

(c)

Fig. 4. (*continued*)

From Table 2 we see the suffix tree with X-gram maintains fewer nodes, and the true common phrase "suffix tree clustering" has been feed to the tree wholly. It is because of many word sequences in the snippet sets are noise, and noisy word sequences feed to the suffix tree with X-gram are shorter than the other two types of suffix tree. So, with our approach the algorithm maintains fewer nodes, and lowers the memory requirements.

Table 2. The total number of nodes maintained by three different STC algorithms

	Original STC	STC with 3-gram	**STC with X-gram**
number of nodes be maintained	33	24	**13**

But there are still some problems needed to be dealt with in this new approach.

1. Some phrases can not feed to the tree wholly.

Review the process of building a suffix tree with X-gram. The true phrase can not be fed to the tree wholly when it first presents in the snippets set. For a true phrase with length L, it will be fed to the tree wholly after it presented L times at most. Take the example of the phrase "suffix tree clustering" in snippets set shown in Table 1. When it presents at the first time in D1, the substring "suffix" was fed to the tree; when it presents at the second time in D2, the substring "suffix tree" was fed to the tree; when it presents at the third time in D3, the whole phrase "suffix tree clustering" was fed to the tree.

It need to be noticed that in application, most true common phrases no longer than 4 (almost 80% [14]). It means most true common phrases can be fed to the tree as a whole phrase, after they present 4 times at most.

On the other hand, the word sequences with frequency no greater than threshold T are considered as noise and should be filtered out in clustering process. Suppose T is 4, then the word sequences with frequency less than 4 will be considered as noise and should be filtered out.

In a word, if a word sequence with frequency no less than threshold T (suppose T is 4), it will be considered as a true phrase, and it probably can be fed to the tree as a whole one; and if a word sequence with frequency less than the threshold T, it should be a noisy word sequences and need not to be feed to the tree as a whole one.

Review the snippets set shown in Table 1, the word sequence "suffix tree clustering" presents 3 times and fed to the tree wholly at last, so it should be a true phrase; and the word sequence "x1 x2" can not be fed to the tree as a whole one, and it obviously a noise.

In addition, the vast majority of the true common phrases with length no more than 6 (more than 90% [14]), so we limited the most depth of suffix tree with X-gram no more than 6. In this case, the vast majority of the true common phrases can still be found wholly.

Undoubtedly there are still some true phrases be broken up and can not fed to the tree wholly. In this condition, we adopt the partial phrases join operation, and then the true common phrase can be discovered.

Although join operation still needed in STC with X-gram, due to more true phrases can be fed to the suffix tree wholly, so fewer partial phrases are needed to be joined, than that in STC with N-gram.

2. A phrase can be fed to the tree wholly, but not all snippets contain this phrase can be discovered in the suffix tree with X-gram.
The snippets set are given in Table 3, we build a suffix tree with X-gram which is shown in Figure 5. We give only 3 branches (branch A, B, and C) and omit other branches. Here we use Ukkonen's algorithm. The dotted lines denote the suffix links.

Table 3. Snippets set

D1	suffix, tree, clustering, x1, x2
D2	y1, suffix, tree, clustering, y2
D3	z1, z2, suffix, tree, clustering
D4	suffix, tree, clustering, v1, v2
D5	w1, suffix, tree, clustering, w2

The true phrase "suffix tree clustering" presented in D1, D2, D3, D4 and D5, but in the suffix tree we can only find it presented in D3, D4 and D5. In the suffix tree with X-gram, we merely discover D1 contains "suffix", D2 contains "suffix tree", but we can not discover D1 or D2 contains the phrase "suffix tree clustering". It means that not all the snippets contain this phrase can be discovered in the suffix tree with X-gram.

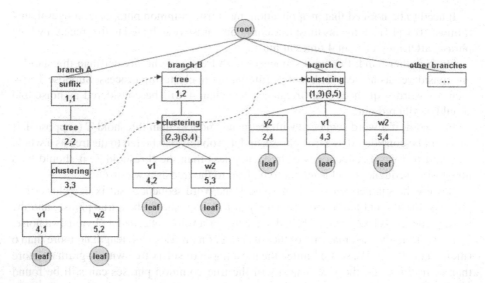

Fig. 5. The suffix tree with X-gram building with the snippets set shown in Table 3. The dotted lines denote the suffix links.

In this condition, we can not select the candidate clusters depending on the frequency of a word sequences in the suffix tree directly. We should complement this branch first. In this step, the successive word sequences followed "suffix" in D1 and successive word sequences followed "tree" in D2, will be fed to the tree, in order to complement the branch. The length of these word sequences is limited; ensure the depth of the tree no more than 6. Because we used the Ukkonen's algorithm to construct the suffix tree, so the successive word sequences can be located with suffix links.

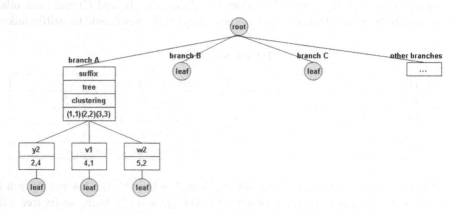

Fig. 6. The suffix tree with X-gram after complement

After complement operation, the suffix tree is shown in Figure 6.

Now we can get a candidate cluster {suffix, tree, clustering} (1, 1)(2, 2)(3, 3)(4,1)(5, 2) from the tree. And after complement operation, all the merely "right-complete" substring of true phrase "suffix tree clustering", such as "tree clustering" and "clustering" are all filtered out.

In the branch A shown in Figure 5, the word sequences followed "suffix" in D1, the word sequences followed "suffix tree" in D2, the word sequences followed "suffix tree clustering" in D3, are all uncertainty. These parts may form "suffix tree clustering v1" 3 times, or "suffix tree clustering w2" 3 times, or "suffix tree clustering" 3 times. Suppose the threshold T of the frequency is 3, this branch may contain candidate clusters, so it needs to be complemented.

It should be emphasized that not all the branches need to be complemented. Take the branch C shown in Figure 7 for example, it can not contain phrase with frequency greater than 2. Suppose T is 3, then this branch can not contain candidate clusters. This branch needs not to be complemented.

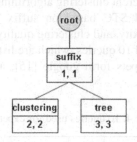

Fig. 7. A branch which need not to be complemented

Suppose a branch contains such a phrase, which with frequency C in the suffix tree, and with length L. If C+L is greater than T, this branch should be complemented.

In fact, the phrase of length L and with frequency C may presents L-1 times before it can be fed to tree as a whole one. It means this phrase may present C+L-1 times in whole snippets set. When C+L > T, this phrase may be a candidate cluster. So the branch which contains this phrase should be complemented.

Take the example of the phrase "suffix tree clustering" in snippets set shown in Table 3. In Figure 5 we discover this phrase presents 3 times in branch A ([suffix, tree, clustering] (3, 3)(4, 1)(5, 2)), and its length is 3. C is 3, L is 3, so this phrase should presents 5 times in the snippets set (C+L-1=5). Actually this phrase presents 5 times (in D1, D2, D3, D4, and D5).

The steps of search results clustering algorithm based on suffix tree with X-gram are as follows:

1. The document cleaning stage. For most text-based document clustering algorithms, this stage is very similar. The HTML tags, punctuation and other similar non-informative text are removed; a set of stop words removed; stemming is applied to reduce words to their root form.

2. In the second stage, a suffix tree with X-gram is created using the word sequences in the snippets set. Then complement the braches which may contain the candidate clusters. In this process we filter out all the merely "right-complete" substrings of true common phrases, and get the candidate phrases.

3. The candidate clusters are merged, scored and sorted. Then generate the final clusters. To keep the cost of this last step constant, we do not check all the candidate clusters, but only with the k highest scoring ones (we take k to be 100 in our experiments).

4 Experiments

4.1 Experiment Setup

We now show a few experimental results to give the user a feel for the cluster performance of STC with X-gram.

We first compare three different clustering algorithms (original STC, STC based on suffix tree with 3-gram, and STC based on suffix tree with X-gram) for space complexity, then time complexity, and clustering quality at last.

For this purpose we defined 10 queries, which are listed in Table 4. For every query we collect search result snippets form google [15], and feed the snippets to three different algorithms.

Table 4. 10 queries used for experiment

type	queries
ambiguous queries	apple, jaguar, java, matrix
entity names	data mining, information retrieval,
general terms	salsa, resume, music, yellow page

It should be noticed that in STC based on suffix tree with N-gram, N valued 2, 3, and 4 respectively, to evaluate this algorithm more comprehensive. If N valued 1, this algorithm is just like "bag of word", can not generate more readable labels for final clusters, or taking $O(n^2)$ time complexity to generate the frequent sets; and if N valued too big, this algorithm becomes to original STC, and will suffer from large memory requirement.

4.2 Space Complexity

The original STC algorithm can often construct a long path of suffix tree, and suffers from large memory requirements. The improved suffix tree with N-gram performs the same function but has lower memory requirements. Our approach has also significantly reduced memory requirements. We use the total number of nodes maintain by three different algorithms to compare the space complexity.

Table 5. The total number of words maintained by each algorithm

	total number of nods be maintained
Original STC	10767
STC with 4-gram	8178
STC with 3-gram	5765
STC with 2-gram	3315
STC with X-gram	**2803**

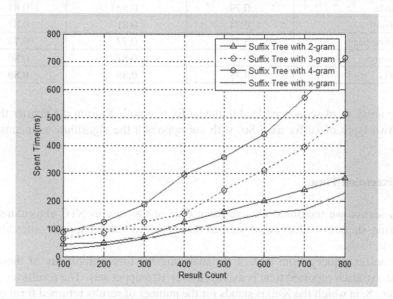

Fig. 8. Time complexity analysis

Table 6. Example cluster labels for "data mining" that is query word

A New STC	STC+N-gram	Original STC
Data Mining and Knowledge Discovery	Data Mining and Knowledge	Data Mining and Knowledge Discovery
Principles of Data Mining and Knowledge Discovery	Principles of Data Mining	Principles of Data Mining and Knowledge Discovery
data mining concepts and techniques	data mining concepts	data mining concepts and techniques
data mining with sql server 2005	data mining with sql	data mining with sql server 2005

For each query listed in Table 4, every algorithm collects first 200 search results form google and building a suffix tree. The total number of nodes maintained by three approaches is shown in table 5.

Table 7. Average precision of all clusters

query	STC with 3-gram	STC with X-gram	Original STC
apple	0.81	0.80	0.81
jaguar	0.89	0.88	0.87
java	077	0.76	0.80
Salsa	0.80	0.78	0.80
data mining	0.73	0.76	0.75
information retrieval	0.71	0.79	0.76
matrix	0.79	0.84	0.81
music	0.74	0.81	0.81
yellow page	0.71	0.77	0.77
Resume	0.73	0.81	0.80
AVG	**0.77**	**0.80**	**0.80**

The noisy word sequences feed to the suffix tree with X-gram are shorter than the other two types of suffix tree. So, with our approach the algorithm maintains fewer nodes.

4.3 Execution Time

In this section we measured the execution time of the various STC algorithms while clustering snippets collection of various sizes (100 to 1000 snippets, collected form google).

We select a query from table 4 for analyzing the time complexity of these three algorithms. Each reported time is averaged over 10 snippet sets. The results are shown in Figure 8, in which the X-axis stands for the number of results returned form original search engine, and the Y-axis is the time spent in the whole algorithm. It should be emphasized that the times values are not total processing time, excluding snippets downloading, parsing time.

In this experiment we search only for maximal frequent sets, not for all frequent sets. And we use a 3% threshold, start at 3 (100 * 3%) and end with 30 (1000 * 3%).

The result of the execution time is shown in Fgure 8.

It is plain that the time complexity of all three approaches are approximately linear, but our approach, based on suffix tree with X-gram, is the fastest. It is because suffix tree with X-gram maintains fewer words than that of suffix tree with N-gram or original STC algorithm, so fewer words are feed to the tree and fewer nodes to be pruned. And STC with X-gram can fed more true phrases to the tree wholly than that of with N-gram, so there are less partial phrases need to be joined. In this way suffix tree with X-gram can be faster than other two.

4.4 More Readable Description

Our cluster labels are true common phrases and more readable than conventional STC technique. As shown in Table 6, that is example of "data mining" is query words.

4.5 Clustering Precision

Due to lacks of standard dataset for testing web search result clustering, we have to build a small test dataset. For this purpose, we have defined a set of queries for which search results were collected from Dmoz.com [16]. The average of precision of the three approaches is shown in Table 7.

Form the Table we can see the average difference in precision performance using the STC+X-gram is litter better than using STC+N-gram.

5 Conclusion

STC based on suffix tree with X-gram significantly lower the memory requirements than the original STC and it generate more readable label than STC+N-gram, nearly the same precision as original STC, and still an incremental and a linear time algorithm, and faster than other types of STC algorithm.

We also proposed a complement operation to complement the suffix tree with X-gram, which filter out all the merely right-complete substrings of the true phrase, and can generate more reasonable candidate clusters.

So, our web result clustering algorithm based on the two novel approaches get better performance than conventional web result clustering algorithms so it is very suitable for online application.

References

1. Zamir, O., Etzioni, O.: Grouper: A Dynamic Clustering Interface to Web Search Results. In: Proceedings of the Eighth International World Wide Web Conference (WWW 8), Toronto, Canada (May 1999)
2. Zamir, O., Etzioni, O.: Web Document Clustering: A Feasibility Demonstration. In: Proceedings of the 19th International ACM SIGIR Conference on Research and Development of Information Retrieval (SIGIR 1998), pp. 46–54 (1998)
3. Osinski, S., Weiss, D.: A Concept-Driven Algorithm for Clustering Search Results. IEEE Intelligent Systems 20(3), 48–54 (2005)
4. Weiss, D.: Carrot2: Design of a Flexible and Efficient Web Information Retrieval Framework. In: Szczepaniak, P.S., Kacprzyk, J., Niewiadomski, A. (eds.) AWIC 2005. LNCS (LNAI), vol. 3528, pp. 439–444. Springer, Heidelberg (2005)
5. Weiss, D., Stefanowski, J.: Web search results clustering in Polish: Experimental evaluation of Carrot. In: Proceedings of the New Trends in Intelligent Information Processing and Web Mining Conference, Zakopane, Poland (2003)
6. Osinski, S., Weiss, D.: Conceptual Clustering Using Lingo Algorithm: Evaluation on Open Directory Project Data. Institute of Computing Science, Poznan University of Technology (2004)
7. Osinski, S., Stefanowski, J., Weiss, D.: Lingo: Search Results Clustering Algorithm Based on Singular Value Decomposition. Institute of Computing Science, Poznan University of Technology (2003)

8. Dell, Z., Yisheng, D.: Semantic, Hierarchical, Online Clustering of Web Search Results. In: Yu, J.X., Lin, X., Lu, H., Zhang, Y. (eds.) APWeb 2004. LNCS, vol. 3007, Springer, Heidelberg (2004)
9. Hua-Jun, Z., et al.: Learning to Cluster Web Search Results. In: SIGIR 2004, Peking University (2004)
10. Janruang, J., Kreesuradej, W.: A New Web Search Result Clustering based on True Common Phrase Label Discovery. In: Computational Intelligence for Modeling, International Conference on Computational for Modeling Control and Automation, 2006 and International Conference on Intelligent Agents, Web Technologies and Internet Commerce, p. 242 (November 2006)
11. Dong, Z.: Towards Web Information Clustering, doctoral dissertation. Southeast Univ., Nanjing (2002)
12. Chang, C.H., Lui, S.C.: IEPAD: Information Extraction based on Pattern Discovery. In: Proceedings of the tenth International Conference on World Wide Web, Hong Kong, May 2-6 (2001)
13. Ukkonen, E.: On-line construction of suffix trees. Algorithmic 14(3), 249–260 (1995)
14. Zamir, O.: Clustering Web Document: A Phrase-Based Method for Grouping Search Engine Results. Doctoral Dissertation, University of Washington (1999)
15. Google search engine (2008), http://www.google.com
16. Open Directory Project (2008), http://dmoz.org

Di-GAFR: Directed Greedy Adaptive Face-Based Routing

Tao Yang[1], Ye Huang[1], Jianxin Chen[1], Geng Yang[1], and Chunming Rong[2]

[1] College of Computer Science, Nanjing University of Posts and
Telecommunications(NJUPT)
yangg@njupt.edu.cn
[2] Department of Electrical and Computer Engineering, University of Stavanger

Abstract. In this paper, we present Di-GAFR, a novel WSN geometric routing algorithm containing greedy, face and directed routing. In Di-GAFR, forwarding decisions merely depend on information about a node's immediate neighbors in the network topology, which made the algorithm absolutely local and highly scalable. Additionally, we have proved that Di-GAFR was asymptotically optimal. Simulations demonstrate that Di-GAFR sufficiently outperforms other prominent algorithms, such as GPSR and GOAFR, in the "critical" region.

Keywords: Geometric routing, face routing, directed routing, Di-GAFRs.

1 Introduction

With the growing availability of global positioning systems (GPS, Galileo, etc.), an increasing number of applications have deployed them in Wireless Sensor Networks. Thus, it can easily be imagined for each wireless node to understand its own location. Then geometric routing, which makes forwarding decisions using only the information through the control messages of the traversing(current) packets and the positions of immediate adjacent nodes in the network topology, and is free from establishing or maintaining the router table for the whole network, has been proved as an effective mechanism of reducing storage, communication and computation overheads. Hereby it is gaining popularity for efficient and large-scale routing scheme for WSNs.

The first geometric routing algorithm that guarantees delivery is Face Routing algorithm (Compass Routing II), proposed in a seminal paper by Kranakis, Singh, and Urrutia [1]. Let n denote the number of nodes in the network, the algorithm guarantees that the message will arrive at the destination and terminates in $O(n)$ steps, while a very simple flooding algorithm can also terminate in $O(n)$ steps. Later, there comes AFR (Adaptive Face Routing)[2], a pure face routing and terminating with cost $O(c^2)$ in the worst case, where c is the cost for a optimal route. However, Lacking of greedy forwarding method, AFR does not perform well on modern large-scale wireless networks.

B. Karp and H. Kung[3] proposed GPSR(Greedy Perimeter Stateless Routing) C a combination of greedy routing and face routing. It consumes pretty low overheads, as the simulation demonstrates. Although GPSR outperforms previous

C. Rong et al. (Eds.): ATC 2008, LNCS 5060, pp. 555–566, 2008.

routing schemes in average-case, yet it's not a worst-case optimal one, due to switch back to greedy routing algorithm excessively.

On the basis of AFR, F.Kuhn et al. [4] introduced GOAFR, the first ad-hoc algorithm to be both asymptotically optimal and average-case efficient. If GOAFR fails, however, it has to restart in order to return to the source and to enter the next new turn, which is independent of the current turn. In such case, the redundant computation consumes extra inter-node communication overheads.

Our geometric routing algorithm Di-GAFR(Directed Greedy Adaptive Face Routing)combines greedy routing, face routing and directed routing. It implements the tradeoff between storage and computation, by adding some fields in each node's buffer to avoid redundant searches and guarantees worst-case optimality as well.

2   Previous Work

we use the unit disk graph (UDG) and $\Omega(1)$-model defined by F.Kuhn and R.Wattenhofer in [2]. Let $G = (V; E)$ denote an Euclidean graph, where V denotes the set of nodes and $E \subseteq V$ denotes the set of edges. And let $n := |V|$ be the number of nodes. The Euclidean graph with edges between all nodes with distance at most 1 is called the unit disk graph. If the distance between any two nodes is bounded from below by a term of order $\Omega(1)$, i.e. there is a positive constant d_0 such that d_0 is a lower bound on the distance between any two nodes, this is referred to as the $\Omega(1)$-model.

We employ the GG(Gabriel Graph)[5] to simplify the network topology. In GG, an edge $d_{(u;v)}$ exists between vertices u and v iff no other vertex w is present within the circle whose diameter is $d_{(u;v)}$. Since GG is locally generated consuming little computation overheads, furthermore, As [4] has proved, when there is an optimal route in UDG, equivalent results can be achieved in $UDG \cap GG$, Thus, we establish our model in $UDG \cap GG$.

Throughout the paper we assume that:

1. Nodes have the same transmission range R. Two nodes with distance greater than R can communicate by relaying their messages through a series of intermediate nodes which is called multi-hop routing;
2. Nodes is equipped with a location service, i.e. each node knows its Euclidean coordinates;
3. Nodes knows all the adjacent nodes (nodes within transmission range R) and their coordinates by exchanging the"*hello*"-messages. The sender of a message knows the coordinates of the destination;
4. The control fields are restricted within $\emptyset(1)$ step, only keeping relevant information of messages.

With these assumptions our algorithm is rigorously local. And the nodes are free from maintaining the global topology information and link states, which reduces the storage and computation overheads dramatically, and enhances adaption as well.

3   Di-GAFR Algorithm

3.1   Node Storage and Message Format

Each node is equipped with a location service, for example, each node knows its Euclidean coordinates. Then adjacent nodes exchange one-hop "HELLO"-messages. When receiving a "HELLO", the coordinates and expire time fields are filled in. And the node distributes a random ID to the adjacent node from m-integer poor, where '0' denotes the node itself. Hereby, the m neighbors could be uniquely identified.

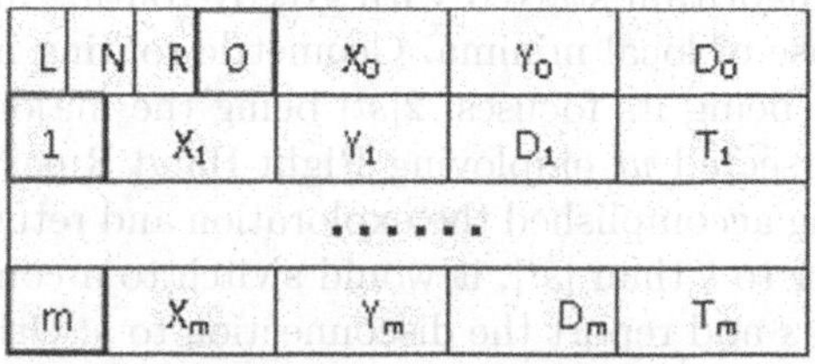

L	N	R	0	X_0	Y_0	D_0	
			1	X_1	Y_1	D_1	T_1
				⋯⋯⋯			
			m	X_m	Y_m	D_m	T_m

Fig. 1. Node Storage

Additionally, we add 3 extra fields: L(ID for last hop), N(ID for next hop), and R (restart flag). L and N are initialized as 0 (the node itself as predefined), and N is cleared initially (initialized $FALSE$). L and N are selectively modified when routing. And R is set when the node traces back after face routing failing at the 1st round, so that it can restart from this node next time. We present the main buffer format in figure 1, besides L, N and R, X and Y denote the node-location, D denotes valid time and T denotes the time receiving the message. Re-initializing the L, N and R fields when D is expired implements the adaptability in dynamic networks. It is obvious that the information storage of R costs only 1 bit ($TRUE,FALSE$), with L and N $\lfloor log_2 m \rfloor$ bit(0,1,2,,m) separately.

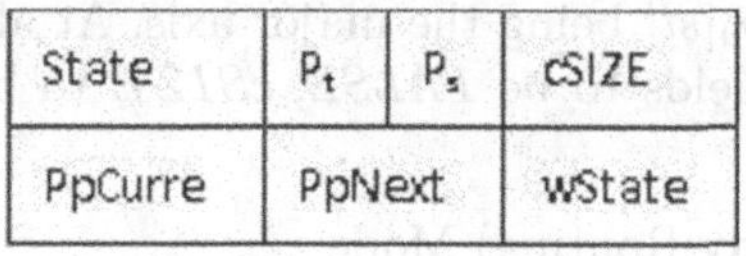

State	P_t	P_s	cSIZE
PpCurre	PpNext		wState

Fig. 2. Message Format

Then, let s denote the source node, t denote the destination node, P_s be the source location, P_t be the destination position, $cSIZE$ denote the current elliptic major axis and $|st|$ denote the minor axis. When traversing geometric routes, $PpCurrent$ stores the switch node ID from which the current planar shifts, while $PpNext$ stores the one to which the current face shifts. State field denotes the message state, which contains $FACE$, $AFTERFACE$ and $FORWARD$. $FACE$

demonstrates the algorithm steps into face routing; $AFTERFACE$ demonstrates the traversal has crossed the boundary for the 1st time; and $FORWORD$ demonstrates that the traversal has crossed the boundary again or crossed all over the boundary. $wState$ stands for global state, which also has 3 optional value, i.e. $NORMAL, FAIL$ or $DISCONNECT$. $FAIL$ demonstrates t's reachability at the $1^s t$ round, then modifying $cSIZE$ to restart; $DISCONNECT$ demonstrates disconnection; and $NORMAL$, which is set as default value, demonstrates the other cases.

3.2 Di-GAFR

In GOAFR[4], the algorithm started with greedy routing and switched to geometric routing in case of local minima. Geometric routing initialized an elliptic bound with s and t being its focuses, $2|st|$ being the major axis. GOAFR traversed the face intersected ut employing Right-Hand Rule[3], where u denoted local minima. Having accomplished the exploration and returned to u, if it failed to find a point closer to t than $|st|$, it would switch to a complete new GOAFR algorithm from u to s and report the disconnection to s; Otherwise, if it crossed the boundary for the $1^s t$ time, it would traverse reversely at the same route; if it crossed the boundary for the $2^n d$ time and still failed to find a point closer to t than $|ut|$, it would switch to a new GOAFR algorithm from u to s, double the radius and restart again at s; if it managed to find a point v closer to point t than $|ut|$, it would forward to point v and employ greedy routing.

GOAFR guarantees both reachability from s to t and worst-case optimal, if s is connected to t. This algorithm, however, increases overheads by returning to s when failing every round and recalling GOAFR when restarting from s.

In our Di-GAFR, we continue to use the denotation in section 3.1, where s denotes the source, t denotes the destination, s knows the coordination of t, with two pre-set constants $\rho \geq \rho_0 \geq 1$. Additionally, we assume that the nodes are temporarily stationary in the WSN, which is finite networks.

$Di\text{-}GAFR$:

0. Initialization: starting at s, an elliptic bound ξ is initialized with s and t being its focuses, $c := \rho_0|st|$ being the major axis. At all nodes, the L, N fields are initialized as 0, R fields to be $FALSE$, $cSIZE$ to be c, and $PpCurrent = PpNext = NULL$.

1. DGR(Direct Greedy Routing) Mode
Start: if $N \neq 0$ {
        forward the message to Node the N-field indicated
        }Else {
           If ID == t
               Finished successfully, stop!
           Else if meeting local minimum
               Go to step 2
               Else {
                    {Forward to the adjacent node i geographically closest to t

if crossed ξ
$c := \rho c$}
Fill in N-field with ID-i
Fill in L-field with last node's ID
Go to *Start*
}
}

2. DAFR(Direct Adaptive Face Routing) Mode

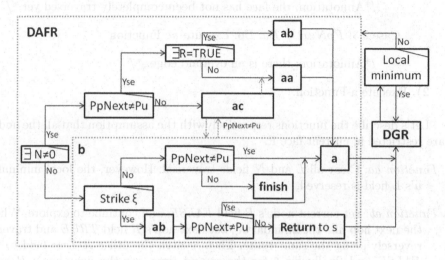

Fig. 3. Node Storage

Let u denote local minimum, Pu denote u's geographic location, with the initialization value $PpNext = Pu$.

Traverse face F at the intersection of current face and ut employing right-hand rule and check a node whose N field is non-zero and R field is *TRUE*.

The algorithm *finished* successfully when meeting t, or:

1). Two cases:

Case 1: no such node whose N field is not 0:

Do: Start to traverse face F and execute Function b.

/*Annotation: if R== FALSE, the face has not been traversed last round; Else if R==TRUE, the face has been proved failed last round and traced back.*/

Case 2: There exists a node whose N field is not 0:

Do: Fill in $PpNext$ field with the node whose position is closest to t and $N \neq 0$, Then;

Case 2.1: $PpNext \neq Pu$ and no such node whose R field is TRUE:

Do: Execute *aa* Function

/*Annotation: the face has been traversed completely.*/

Case 2.2: $PpNext \neq Pu$ and there exists a node whose R field is $TRUE$:

Do: Execute *ab* Function

/*Annotation: the face has not been completely traversed yet.*/

Case 2.3: $PpNext = Pu$: Do: Execute *ac* Function

/*Annotation: there is an overlaid edge. */

2). Execute a Function.   *

Let's describe the functions respectivelywith the assumption that all the nodes are restricted in current face F.

Function aa: Clear all L and N fields traversed. However, the local minimum u's L field is reserved.

Function ab: Set current node's R field *FALSE*, and continue to explore. When the next hop hits the boundary ξ, Set next hop's R field *TRUE* and traverse reversely along the same route. Then, switch the other *R-True*-field to be *FALSE*, and finally hit ξ for the second time, set the next hop's R field *TRUE*. During the exploration, if it finds a closer node to t than *pNext*, update *PpNext* field with current node's IDs.

Function ac: Execute Function *b*. Afterwards, If $PpNext \neq Pu$, traverse back to entry point according to L field, denote *pNext* to *u*, and then execute Function *aa*.

Function a: Fill in the L and N fields with relevant IDs along $u \rightarrow pNext$ route, and then return to step 1 at the *pNext* node.

Function b:
Case 1: Having traversed all F's edges without hitting ξ, if $PpNext = Pu$,
Do: traverse back to s according to u's L field, report disconnection and end the algorithm; else,
Do: execute Function *a*.
Case 2: Hitting ξ during exploration, execute Function *ab*. After that, If $PpNext = Pu$
Do: traverse in opposite direction using u's L field back to s, reset the elliptic boundary by renewing the major axis $c := \rho c$, and go to *step 1*;
Else Do: execute Function *a*.

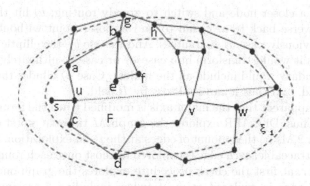

Fig. 4. Message Format

As figure 4 described, our algorithm initialized at source s, with the initial elliptic boundary ξ_1, employing greedy forwarding to u, where u denoted the local minimum. Then it Switched to DAFR mode at u and continued to traverse employing Right-Hand Rule. If the nodes' N fields are all 0(cleared), execute Function b, i.e. $u \to a \to b$. Hittingξ_1 for the first time during $a \to b$, then set a's R field *TRUE* and traverse in the opposite direction, i.e. $b \to a \to u \to c \to d$. Hitting$\xi_1$ again during $c \to d$, then set c's R field *TRUE*. Verify that $PpNext = Pu$, where $|at| > |ut|$ and $|ct| > |ut|$, and traverse back from u to s according L fields. Renew $c := \rho c$ at s, thus we establish a new elliptic boundary ξ_2, and forward using N fields. Reaching u again without appropriate node whose $N \neq 0$, execute Function b. Arriving at a, update R field as *FALSE* and continue to explore $a \to b \to e \to f \to b \to g$ by Right-Hand Rule.Hitting ξ_2 for the first time during $b \to g$, set b's R field *TRUE* and traverse in the opposite direction, and continue to traverse backwards at c after renewing c's R to *FALSE*. Hitting ξ_2 again during $h \to g$, set h's R field *TRUE*. Since $PpNext = Pv \neq Pu$, execute Function a, i.e. fill in the L and N fields with relevant IDs along $u \to pNext$ route. Afterwards, Switch to DGR Mode at $v(pNext)$ along $v \to w \to t$. Thus, the algorithm succeeds at reaching t.

3.3   Di-GAFR's Asymptotical Optimality

We prove the Di-GAFR to be asymptotically optimal, i.e. our algorithm is worst-case optimal.

THEOREM 3.1: Di-GAFR always terminates in $O(n)$ steps, where n is the number of nodes. If s and t are connected, Di-GAFR reaches t; otherwise, disconnection will be detected.

PROOF: Let us first prove our algorithm present a closer node to t every round, in whatever cases.

Greedy mode naturally ensures that the message is always forwarded to the adjacent node which is closest to the destination. In DAFR routing, there are 3 cases: *a)* find a closer node and switch to greedy routing; *b)* hit the boundary twice and traverse back to *s*; *c)* fail to find a closer point without hitting the boundary. Obviously, case *a)* guarantees. And in case *b)*, the elliptic boundary is enlarged, thus it would transform into case *a)* or case *c)* ultimately (in extreme case, the boundary would include all the nodes). Case *c)* alludes that the graph is disconnected, and thus it can lead to *s* by *L* field.

Then, it is apparent that the major axis is modified when the former boundary is hit twice. Thus, Di-GAFR explores the graph *M* times at worst case.

Let E_i (i=1,2,M) be the amount of edges at the $i-th$ exploration. Since greedy routing is irretraceable, each edge is explored at most once each round. In DAFR mode, however, at first the check procedure explores the graph once. Thus, for case *a)*, each edge is explored at most twice, including a tracing back when hitting the boundary; for case *b)*, each edge is explored at most three times(2 times as case *a)* does, plus another tracing back using *L* field). Consequently, each edge is explored at most four times every face. While two edges coincide at 2 faces, the edge is explored at most 8 times. To sum up, each edge is explored at most 9 times at the $i-th$ round (once in DGR mode, another 8 times in DAFR mode). Together with the Euler polyhedral formula $(n - m + f = 2)$ and planar feature $(2m \geq 3f)$, it yields that the number of edges *m* is bounded by $m \leq 3n - 6$(where *f* denotes the amount of the faces, and *m* is the amount of the edges).

Hence, our algorithm has searched *E* edges totally:

$$E = \sum_{i=1}^{M} E_i \leq \sum_{i=1}^{M} 9m = 9M(3n - 6) \leq (27M) \cdot n \equiv O(n)$$

THEOREM 3.2: Di-GAFR is asymptotically optimal, i.e. reaches the destination with cost $O(c^2(p^*))$, where p^* is an optimal path from s to t.

PROOF: [2] has defined Asymptotical Optimality, i.e. worst-case optimality, and has proved the lower boundary of geometric routing cost to be $O(c^2(p^*))$. Hence if Di-GAFR reaches the destination with cost $O(c^2(p^*))$, it is Asymptotically Optimal. Generally, we use the Euclidean distance metric(see [2]) as the cost model.

Theorem 3.1 has proved Di-GAFR reaches the destination in $O(n)$ steps. In UDG environment, with each edge costing $c(e) \leq 1$, the total cost is less than $O(n)$, where *n* denotes the number of nodes after the $M - th$ exploration.

As the elliptic boundary enlarges, there should be $c_(k - 1)c(p^*)c_k$, where k is a constant and $1 \leq k \leq M$. Together with $\Omega(1)$ -model definition, i.e. arbitrary two nodes has a distance no less than d_0, thus, any rotundity with radius $d_0/2$ will not intersect with each other and the elliptic area is less than πc_{M^2}. Hence,

$$n \leq \frac{\pi \cdot c_{M^2}}{\pi(d_0/2)^2} \equiv O((\rho^{M-(k-1)}c(p^*))^2)) \equiv O(c^2(p^*))$$

Thus, Di-GAFR is Asymptotically Optimal.

4   Algorithm Analysis

In our simulations, we mainly chose GPSR[3] and GOAFR[4] as the referenced algorithms, not only because they were classic and dominant in the geographic routings but also because they were significantly similar to our Di-GAFR. In order to acquaint ourselves with GPSR and GOAFR, we described the family tree of GPSR, GOAFR and Di-GAFR. For comparing the algorithms more conveniently, we give a alias to *Di-GAFR*, that is *DGAFR*.

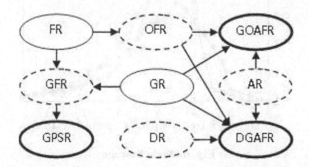

Fig. 5. The family tree of GPSR, GOAFR and Di-GAFR

As it was shown in figure 5, GR(Greedy Routing) and FR(Face Routing) denoted the primitive greedy and face algorithms respectively; AR(Adaptive Routing) mean that the routing needed preset a bound and constantly modify the bound when meet the failure routing in one turn; DR(Directed Routing) mean that the routing needed some flash memories to store the path which had just traversed; OFR was explained detailedly in [4], which selected another forwarding strategy differed from the primitive FR. Finally, since GFROFRAR and DR didn't exist actually, we described them in dashed ellipses.

Following the Setdest Function presented by CMU in NS environment, we generated networks scenario on square fields of side length 20 units by distributing network nodes randomly and uniformly in $UDG \cap GG$ topology. For every simulation series the number of nodes was determined according to the chosen *network density(D)*, where network density was the density of nodes in the UDG. For each considered network the source s and the destination t were also chosen randomly. To determine Di-GAFR's performance in network layer, the collisions in MAC layer was ignored here. In order to judge the average practicability of an algorithm we followed the definition *mean performance $Perf_A$* (N) of an algorithm A on a network N in [4] with m randomly simulated environment:

$$Perf_A \equiv \frac{1}{m} \sum_{i=1}^{m} (perf_A(N_i, s_i, t_i)) \equiv \frac{1}{m} \sum_{i=1}^{m} \frac{S_A(N_i, s_i, t_i)}{S_p(N_i, s_i, t_i)}$$

Where N_i denoted the i-th network simulated; s_i and t_i denoted the source and destination node respectively; $S_A(N_i, s_i, t_i)$was the number of steps algorithm A performed on network N finding a route from s to t (which is in

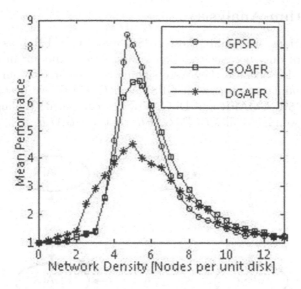

Fig. 6. Node Storage

our case, with all simulated algorithms, equal to the number of sent messages); $S_p(N_i, s_i, t_i)$ denoted the (hop) length of the shortest path (with respect to the hop metric[2]) between the s_i and the ti on N. And let$\rho_0 = 1.4, \rho = \sqrt{2}$,which proved to be good for practical purposes in [4]. Finally, grounding on our hardware surroundings, we let m be 1000 for facility which is reasonable.

Using the triples (N_i, s_i, t_i) as network densities ranging from 0.2 to 12 nodes per unit disk, with the step 0.5, we obtained Figure 6 ($meanperformance - networkdensity$). In low network density, i.e. $D \to 0$, s_i and t_i were neighborhood or disconnected (the statistics exclude disconnection cases). Thus, the mean cost was one hop that equals with the cost of the shortest path. And so $perf \approx 1$; When $1D3.5$ Di-GAFR performed worse than the other two algorithms, due to an extra face search and relevant control information overheads. Since the geometric topology was rather simple, the actual operations of GPSR and GOAFR were almost the same with the same forwarding criteria. Hence, they shared the performances; When $3.5D7$, which was the peak distribution value interval(critical region), algorithm performed diverge here. Di-GAFR dramatically reduced the traversing overheads by using L and N fields, thus outstripped the other two schemes tremendously. GPSR behaved worst since it earliest returned to greedy mode, and thus it lost the Asymptotical Optimality; When $D7$, which mean in dense networks, as greedy routing's proportion increased, Di-GAFR and GOAFR got weakened by searching the whole face. When $D12$, greedy routing dominated with little failure and all the 3 algorithms normalize.

Figure 7 described the mean performance results obtained in simulations on networks generated in square fields of side length ranging from 4 to 40 units with the step 4 units, where network density was preset 4.71(the critical density particularly described in [4]). It was apparent that in small-scaled network, different

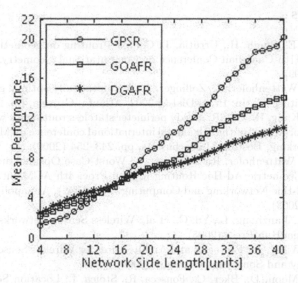

Fig. 7. Message Format

algorithms displayed incomparable performance curses. In such condition, they varied occasionally (highly depending on the choice of s and t). As the network size extended, the lack of a bounding ellipse resulted in a fast growing curve for GPSR, since it would cost far more if unlucky. To the contrary, Di-GAFR restricted the boundary and had recorded the routes, which reduced the overheads of restarting. Besides, the overheads proportion by adding fields and pre-searching lessened gradually comparing with the scale of the networks. Thus, Di-GAFR's performance values grew relatively slowly for all simulated network sizes. Especially, when side length is over 24 units, Di-GAFR outperforms GPSR by almost 50% and continues to widen. Hence Di-GAFR is practically feasible in large-scaled networks.

5 Conclusion

We introduce Di-GAFR in this paper. Di-GAFR is free from repeated search when exploration fails by adding L, N and R fields which simplify the search effectively. Through rigorous analysis, we have proved that Di-GAGR is worst-case optimal. And simulation results present that Di-GAFR almost outperforms GPSR by 40%, GOAFR by 30% in the "critical region". Meanwhile, as network size extends, Di-GAFR is sub-linearly increasing, advancing to GPSR and GOAFR overwhelmingly. In wireless sensor network, geometric routing underlay the distributed storage and query. Hence the implementation of Di-GAFR in distributed data management is a nontrivial work. And the data storage and query employing integration of Di-GAFR and geometric hashing function would be challenging and practical.

References

1. Kranakis, E., Singh, H., Urrutia, J.: Compass routing on geometric networks [C]. In: Proc. 11th Canadian Conference on Computational Geometry, Vancouver, pp. 51–54 (1999)
2. Kuhn, F., Wattenhofer, R., Zollinger, A.: Asymptotically optimal geometric mobile ad-hoc routing [C]. In: Proc. Dial-M 2002, Atlanta, Georgia, pp. 24–33 (2002)
3. Karp, B., Kung, H.: GPSR: greedy perimeter stateless routing for wireless networks [C]. In: Proceedings of the 6th annual international conference on Mobile computing and networking, Boston, Massachusetts, pp. 243–254 (2000)
4. Kuhn, F., Wattenhofer, R., Zollinger, A.: Worst-Case Optimal and Average-Case Efficient Geometric Ad-Hoc Routing [C]. In: Proc. 4th ACM Int. Symposium on Mobile Ad-Hoc Networking and Computing (MobiHoc.), Annapolis, Maryland, pp. 267–278 (2003)
5. Liming, S., Jianzhong, L., Yu, C., et al.: Wireless Sensor Networks [M], pp. 89–94. Beijing TsingHua Press (2005)
6. Karl, H., Willig, A.: Protocols and Architectures for Wireless Sensor Networks [M]. John Wiley and Sons, Inc., Germany (2005)
7. Ortiz, J., Moon, D., Bker, C., Fonseca, R., Stoica, I.: Location Service for Point-to-Point Routing in Wireless Sensor Networks [C]. In: IPSN 2007: Proceedings of the Sixth International Symposium on Information Processing in Sensor Networks, pp. 166–175 (2007)
8. Nath, S., Gibbons, P.B.: Communicating via Fireflies: Geographic Routing on Duty-Cycled Sensors [C]. In: IPSN 2007: Proceedings of the Sixth International Symposium on Information Processing in Sensor Networks, pp. 440–449 (2007)
9. Milosavljevic, N., Nguyen, A., Fang, Q., Gao, J., Guibas, L.: Landmark Selection and Greedy Landmark-descent Routing for Sensor Networks [C]. In: Proceedings - IEEE INFOCOM 2007: 26th IEEE International Conference on Computer Communications, pp. 661–669 (2007)
10. Tsai, M., Yang, H., Huang, W.: Axis-Based Virtual Coordinate Assignment Protocol and Delivery Guaranteed Routing Protocol in Wireless Sensor Networks [C]. In: Proceedings - IEEE INFOCOM 2007: 26th IEEE International Conference on Computer Communications, pp. 2234–2242 (2007)
11. GPSR code [EB/OL], http://www.cs.cmu.edu/~bkarp/gpsr/gpsr-ns-2.1b6.tar.gz

Cooperative Management Framework
for Inter-domain Routing System*

Ning Hu, Peng Zou, PeiDong Zhu, and Xin Liu

Computer School, National University of Defense Technology,
P.R. China
Ning_Hu@163.com
http://www.nudt.edu.cn

Abstract. The inter-domain routing system consists of many interconnected Autonomous Systems (ASes) which are independently operated and usually have different routing policies. Due to lack of effective coordinative mechanism, policy conflicts may arise, which can cause various problems in performance, security and robustness. To facilitate the collaboration among ASes, we propose an ISP-oriented inter-domain routing system cooperative management framework CMF based on the self-organization method. CMF provides fundamental support to the ISP's cooperation which includes organization structure, mechanisms and applications. CMF can help ISPs alleviate the side effect caused by the autonomy and selfishness of AS. The framework is generic solution, which can be used not only in inter-domain routing operation, but also in other related fields such as intrusion detection and network measurement.

1 Introduction

The inter-domain routing system of the Internet includes many interconnected Autonomous Systems (ASes) which are operated by different administrative domains such as Inter Service Providers (ISPs), companies and universities. An ISP operates its routing policy independently and tries to maximize its benefit. This leads to two characteristics of an AS: autonomy and selfishness. The Internet is a cyberspace full of tussle [1]. Some studies show that route convergence delay and persistent route oscillation may occur if there are conflicts among ASes [2], [3]. Since BGP [4] does not supply a validation mechanism to confirm the correct of the routing message, misconfiguration, software bug and malice are inevitable. The security and robustness of the Internet routing are becoming hot topic [5], [6], [7], [8].

In our opinion, the key reason of these issues is lack of cooperation among ASes. Firstly, ISPs behave adversely and competitively, which impacts the optimization of Internet routing. Secondly, there are no effective mechanisms for information sharing or cooperation. Thirdly, ISPs lack the ability to cooperate. Finally, there is no cooperation-oriented organization form to manage the ISP's cooperative behavior. K. Claffy

---

* Research supported by the National Grand Fundamental Research 973 Program of China under Grant No.2003CB314802 and National High-Tech Research and Development Plan of China under Grant No.2006AA01Z213 and National Natural Science Foundation of China Grant No.60673169.

C. Rong et al. (Eds.): ATC 2008, LNCS 5060, pp. 567–576, 2008.

indicated the ISPs' coordination is the top problem of internet management and the root cause is not technical factor but economic, owner-ship, and trust [9]. The cooperation among ISPs needs effective mechanisms to resolve the issues such as organization form, information sharing, privacy preserve and incentive etc. To the best of our knowledge, there is no mature architecture or platform used to ISP's operation.

Our contributions can be summarized in three aspects. We refine ISP's common requirements for the cooperative operation in inter-domain routing system and design some fundamental mechanisms which are necessary to ISP's cooperation. This paper proposes a Cooperative Management Framework for inter-domain routing system (CMF), which includes self-organization, reputation, information sharing and incentive mechanism. We also develop two cooperative operating applications to evaluate the validity of the cooperative mechanisms based on CMF, which are routing policies consistency checker and route monitor.

The rest of this paper is organized as follows. In Section 2, we provide a brief background of inter-domain routing system and motivate the need for better cooperation. Some design considerations and a cooperative framework are described in Section 3. In Section 4, two applications based on CMF are developed. We discuss related works in Section 5, and conclude in Section 6.

2 Background and Motivation

Due to its large scale, intensive structure, complex connectivity and diverse policies, the inter-domain routing system is exposed to challenges in its performance, security and robustness. The lack of cooperation among ISPs intensifies the frangibility of inter-domain routing system.

For the autonomy, an AS always selects best route according to its local information. This can lead to path inflation. In hot potato routing algorithm, an AS uses the closest link (early-exit) for transferring traffic to the downstream ISP as it minimizes resource usage in the upstream network without considering resource usage in the downstream. Some ASes construct route loop or prolong the AS_PATH property of a BGP route to deceive other AS not to use their route to transfer traffic.

Because the privacy of ISPs can be inferred from the routing policy such as network topology, IP address assignment and commercial relationship with other ISP, ISPs are unwilling to reveal their local policy to others. The original design of BGP allowed only AS-PATH reachability information to be shared, this proved to be not enough. Since there is no cooperative monitor mechanism, the internet routing has to rely on a large part on trust. Many security issues in BGP, such as black-hole routing, route spoofing, prefix hijacking, are inevitable in current circumstances. In fact, it is very difficult to detect or locate these problems only by analyzing single AS routing policy or BGP route table.

There are very few methods for cooperative monitor or configure the ISP's routing policy. Because ISP's routing policy can be expressed by router configurations, conflicts between ISPs can be detected by contrasting multi-AS routing policy. But there is no tool available to do this work.

The commercial relationships of ISPs provide constraints to policy configuration. Similar to this, we need a cooperation-oriented organization model to guide the ISP's cooperative behavior. The model needs solve the questions of partner selection, cooperation negotiation and behavior management.

Our goal is to refine the essential requirements for operating inter-domain routing system and implement a platform which supplies the fundamental cooperative mechanisms to ISPs. By using these mechanisms, ISPs can collaborate more efficiently. Within CMF we focus on the works as follow: (a) Propose an organization form AS alliance to support the cooperation among ISPs. (b) Design a reputation mechanism to evaluate the ISP's routing behavior. (c) Design an information sharing mechanism to protect ISP's privacy.

3 Cooperative Management Framework

3.1 Design Considerations

The cooperation among ASes has some particularity and requirements. First, the cooperation among ASes must be self-organization behavior because there is no control center. Each AS must select the cooperative partner independently. Second, be-cause an AS need prevent their commercial secrets such as internal topology, route decision and neighbor relationship from leaking during the cooperation, the information sharing mechanism must be based on semi-honest model [10]. Third, the behavior of an AS need to be supervised and evaluated. Finally, incentive is needed.

3.2 Architecture

According to considerations in section 3.1, we design a cooperative management framework with triple-layer which provides support to ASes cooperation. The structure of it is shown in Fig. 1. The morphology layer describes the relationships among ASes. Because the cooperative relationship between ASes can be built upon their commerce relationship, we use the existing models such as provider-customer and peering-peering to describe the relationship among ASes. We also propose a new model which is called AS alliance to describe the cooperative relationship between ASes which is built by some self-organization algorithm. The morphology layer resolves the issues of partner selection, collaborative negotiation and cooperation mode. The mechanism layer provides some essential mechanisms which include self-organism mechanism, reputation management, information sharing mechanism and incentive mechanism. The self-organism mechanism controls the behavior of AS such as alliance building, evolvement and negotiation. Reputation mechanism can be used to supervise and evaluate the malice or selfishness of AS. Information sharing mechanism enables ASes to exchange information with privacy preservation. Incentive mechanism provides strong incentive to cooperation. We develop some cooperative applications at the base on the fundamental mechanisms described upon. These applications can improve the ability of monitor and operation on inter-domain routing system.

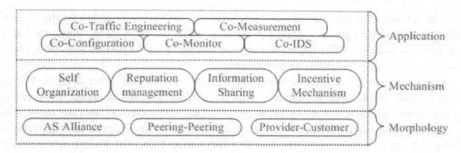

Fig. 1. Architecture of CMF

3.3 AS Alliance

AS alliance supplies a practical organization form for guide the cooperation among ASes, which has an ability of self-organization and self-evolvement. AS can join or leave some alliance freely. AS alliance is a logical structure. Members of AS alliance can be connected by physical link or some collaboration relationship.

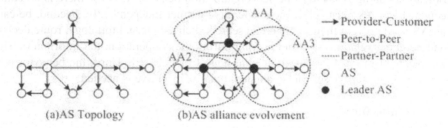

Fig. 2. AS topology and AS alliance

In Fig. 2(b), there are three AS alliances which are AA1, AA2 and AA3. Every alliance has a leader node selected by members. The leader node has the power of arbitrator. The AS alliance building algorithm can be very flexible but the essential rule is self-organization. The establishing process of AS alliance is similar to the social behavior of human. At the initial phase, AS selects partner randomly. During the cooperation, AS can reselect other node as its partner. Only the good cooperative relationship is long-term stable. After a period of time, the relationship will be convergence.

3.4 Reputation Mechanism

CMF provides a reputation model in sociology to evaluate the reliability of AS's behavior and information [11]. PKI is a useful technique to anti-spoof but it is not a good selection for CMF. First, ASes are operated by different ISPs or governments which have different benefits and political positions. It is impossible to force every ISP to trust a unique third part such as s-BGP [12]. Second, PKI usually costs much CPU resource and impact the performance of routing system [13]. CMF uses a weighted summary function to calculate the AS's reputation instead. The parameter of the function includes AS relationship, AS tier, statistics of the history routing information and other ASes' recommendation. Reputation mechanism supplies a reference to AS when it selects routing information from other neighbor.

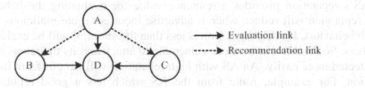

Fig. 3. Reputation evaluation model

In Fig. 3, the formula below is used to calculate AS-D's reputation evaluation from AS-A.

$$Rep(A, D) = \alpha * r(A, D) + \beta * t(D) + \gamma * p(D) + \delta * q(B, C) \tag{1}$$

Table 1. Functions and variables used in formula 1 description

Name	Description
Rep (A,D)	AS-D's reputation from AS-A
r(A,D)	Commercial relationship between AS-A and AS-D
t(D)	AS-D's tier in the internet
p (D)	Fault probability of the history route from AS-D
q(B,C)	Recommendation from AS-B and AS-C
α, β, γ, δ	Weighted gene

3.5 Information Sharing Mechanism

To detect the policy disrupt or invalid route, an AS needs to do some collaborative operation such as query or comparison with other ASes. For example, an AS can send its query of confirm to other ASes whether a route from its neighbor is valid. These operations need share information such as route, policy or link status with other ASes. For protecting its commercial benefit, an ISP does not share its privacy with others. This is the main cause that prevents the ISP from cooperating. BGP does not supply a mechanism for information sharing. IRR [14] implements centralized information sharing model, but the model dose not resolve the questions of incentive and privacy preservation. IRR only collects routing policy and dose not provide guarantee to the accuracy of the data in its database. The information sharing mechanism of CMF makes two improvements. First, the scope of information sharing is limited in AS alliance. Be different from IRR, AS only exchange information with cooperative partner in CMF. CMF implements a privacy sharing protocol across private database based on the study of Secure Multi-party Computation problem (SMC) in the literature [15]. By using the protocol, ISP can share information without privacy leaking.

3.6 Incentive Mechanism

The incentive mechanism of CMF facilitates ISP's coordination through three facets. First, ASes build their cooperative relationship by the way of self-organization without any compulsive reason. Every member of the alliance will benefit from it. Second, the AS's reputation provides a reference value for evaluating the behavior of AS. AS's reputation will reduce when it advertise incorrect route malicious or has some selfish behaviors. If AS's reputation is less than threshold, it will be excluded by other members. So the AS will be more vulnerable to attack and its malicious behavior will be detected more easily. An AS with high reputation will benefit from its good manifestation. For example, route from the AS which has a good reputation will be selected priority and this means more traffic and revenue. Finally, the service of cooperative monitor and cooperative configure are deployed on the base of AS alliance. Only join the alliance can AS use these services. As mentioned before, AS must restrict its selfishness and coordinate with other AS friendly to maintain its good reputation. If every AS behaves as upon, the security and robustness of the whole system can be enhanced, so all the member will benefit from it. The incentive mechanism can promote the aggregation of ASes as their needed. It is favorable to the evolvement toward equality and multipolarization of Internet architecture.

3.7 Simulation

To validate the incentive mechanism, we constructed a simulation experiment which is shown as Fig. 4. To simplify the complexity, we define an intension function ξ which is used to denote the need of the AS node, the intension function ξ : Prefix$\times$ASn $\rightarrow$ [0, N] calculates a intension value which obeys poisson distribution. The parameter prefix is IP address prefix which belongs to address range **R** and the parameter ASn is AS's number. We also define an intension matching function ψ : IntensionX$\times$IntensionY $\rightarrow$ {0,1} . If the difference value between the two intensions is less than the threshold T, the function ψ returns 1, otherwise it returns 0. We defined a selection function θ : Reputation$\times$Intension $\rightarrow$ [0, M] which returns a selection from AS-0 to AS-M according to their reputation as decrease order. If all the reputation is 0, it selects an AS randomly. We define a cooperative function o : IntesionX$\times$ASN $\rightarrow$ [0, L] , which returns a cooperation result evaluation from 0 to L. The evaluation also obeys poisson distribution. The value 1 represents the best and 0 represents the worst.

We create an AS set with **M** nodes randomly. Each node maintains a reputation matrix which contains other node's reputation value. At the initial, the reputation matrix is cleared. In each loop, every node selects an IP_Prefix from **R**, calculates its intension with function ξ , selects partner with function θ and send its request to the selection node. When node receives a request from other node, it uses function ψ to decide whether accept this request. If the function ψ returns 1, the node sends an agreement ACK with a cooperation evaluation result which is calculated by function o back to the initiator. If the function ψ returns 0, the cooperation evaluation result is 0. Every time when node receives the ACK from others, it recalculates the reputation matrix according to the evaluation. After each node has got an ACK, the loop is over. After a period of time, when we collect the cooperation relationship of the nodes, we find the nodes with similar intension and friendly cooperation are aggregated.

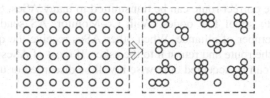

Fig. 4. ASes' aggregation under the influence of incentive

4 Application

4.1 Cooperative Configuration

By the way of ISP's collaboration, we can remove the inconsistency existed in routing policy. The inconsistent configuration happens in following cases: a) Policy conflict leaded by misconfiguration. Configuring a network of BGP routers is like writing a complex program. Many configuration files of border router have more than a million lines. As a result, router configurations tend to have faults. Routing policy can be expressed by using route filter. If one AS's route export policy is mismatched with its neighbor's route import policy, some routing information will be discarded. b) Path inflation arisen from routing algorithm. Some routing algorithms might lead to path inflation such as Hot-Potato routing. Griffin's research works show that persistent route oscillation is possible. c) Incorrect policy by malice. For the malicious targets such as attack and hijacking, some ASes configure their policies which violate the commercial relationship constraints deliberately.

We implemented a policy consistency analysis tool Co-RCC (Cooperative Router Configuration Checker) which can be used to detect the inconsistency among multi-ASes' policies. Be different from RCC, Co-RCC doesn't analyze ASes' policy directly, this is because many ISPs may be unwilling to reveal their local policy to others. Co-RCC uses routing information to infer the consistency of policy. Given AS A and AS B, we use the notation import_from(B) to describe the route set that A is importing from B. Similarly, export_to(B) is the set of route that A exports to B. First, A build the export_to(B) according to its route table and export filter. Second, by using the information sharing protocol that is provided by CMF, A calculates the intersection of export_to(B) and import_from(A) with B. If the intersection contains export_to(B), there is no conflict. In the procedure described upon, A can only know the routes that are shared with B. For any route belongs to B but not to A, A know its existence but not know its value. So it is impossible for A to infer B's import policy.

4.2 Cooperative Monitor

The security of routing information is the key issue of the security of inter-domain routing system. Due to AS's autonomy, there is no cooperative monitor and validation mechanism among ASes. For this weakness, the malicious nodes hijack and spoof routing information. We develop a cooperative route monitoring tool which is called Co-Monitor. Co-Monitor takes the advantage of the rich connectivity of the internet to monitor and validate the correctness of routing information. For the rich connectivity of the internet, the correct route can be transmitted to many ASes. So it is insufficient for the attacker to spoof few nodes. With Co-Monitor, AS sends route validation query to other member of alliance. When other ASes receive the query, they vote to the validation of the route and return it to the asker. If most of ASes assure the route is correct, the route can be accepted otherwise it will be discarded or under suspicion.

5 Related Work

Inter-domain routing system is the fundamental infrastructure of Internet and BGP is the inter-domain routing protocol used in the Internet today. Most research works about operation of inter-domain routing system is aimed at the management of BGP.

Ramesh et al. find that AS routing policy is established without coordination and such independently established policies can adversely impact the stability and analyzability of internet routing [16].They proposed an architecture for routing policy coordination. The architecture is composed of three components include RPSL (Routing Policy Specification Language), IRR (routing registry) and analysis tools. Because of ISP's selfishness and autonomy, the accuracy and integrity of information from IRR is uncertain [17], [18]. MIT developed a router configuration checker – RCC [19]. RCC is a router configuration check tools that finds faults in the BGP configurations of routers in single AS without considering multi-AS policy conflict. With Internet's richly connected topology, false routing and prefix hijacking can be detected through ISP's cooperation [20], [21]. In these works, AS sends a confirmation query for the route which is received from BGP update message to other ASes. Every AS received the query returns an acknowledgement to the querying AS. So the querying AS can validate the route according to the acknowledgement. ENCORE is a multi agent-based inter-AS diagnostic system [22]. ENCORE deploys intelligent agents in multiple ASes and performs collective observation and analysis. AISLE is a multi-agent-based framework which is used to policy-based routing adjustment system for transit ISPs and their customer ASes [23]. In AISLE, many Virtual Router (VR) are deployed in different ASes, these VR cooperate each other and control the border router of AS to select the best route. Kerio-Bygyo Project implemented a coordination platform to detect, recover and protected the network address prefix hijacking [24].

6 Conclusion

Inter-domain routing system is a complex decentralized system without a central control center. Due to the selfishness and autonomous, it is very hard to manage the behavior of AS's. Most research works on inter-domain routing system management is focused on single AS without considering cooperation. How to operate the Inter-domain routing system has become a question got a lot attention from ISPs. In order to facilitate the collaboration among ISPs, this paper proposes an ISP-oriented cooperative management framework CMF. CMF is based self-organization method. It implements AS's collaboration by the form of AS alliance and provides corresponding mechanisms to facilitate the cooperation. We also developed two tools, Co-RCC and Co-Monitor, to evaluate the effectiveness of cooperation. CMF is a generic tool. Its application is not limited to inter-domain routing system management. It also facilitates cooperative network measurement and intrusion detection. The research on how to improve the coordination among autonomous systems is becoming a driving force behind the robustness and efficiency of the next-generation Internet.

References

1. Clark, D.D., Wroclawski, J., Sollins, K.R., Braden, R.: Tussle in Cyberspace: Defining Tomorrow's Internet. In: SIGCOMM 2002, August 19-23, 2002 (2002)
2. Griffin, T.G., Wilfong, G.: An Analysis of BGP Convergence Properties. In: Proc. ACM SIGCOMM (1999)
3. Varadhan, K., Govindan, R., Estrin, D.: Persistent Route Oscillations in Inter-domain Routing. Computer Networks 32(1), 1–16 (2000)
4. Rekhter, Y., Li, T.: A Border Gateway Protocol 4 (BGP-4), RFC1771 (1995)
5. Mahajan, R., Wetherall, D., Anderson, T.: Understanding BGP misconfigurations. In: Proc. of ACM. SIGCOMM (August 2002)
6. Chi-ken, C.: Policy-based Routing with Non-strict Preferences. In: ACM SIGCOMM 2006, September 11-15, 2006 (2006)
7. Haowen, C., Dash, D., Perrig, A., Zhang, H.: Modeling Adoptability of Secure BGP Protocols. In: SIGCOMM 2006, September 11-15, 2006 (2006)
8. Ballani, H., Francis, P., Xinyang, Z.: A Study of Prefix Hijacking and Interception in the Internet. In: ACM SIGCOMM, August 27-31, 2007 (2007)
9. Claffy, K.: Top problems of the Internet and how to help solve them (2003), http://www.caida.org/outreach/presentations//netproblems_lisa03
10. Lindell, Y., Pinkas, B.: Privacy preserving data mining. Journal of Cryptology 15(3), 177–206 (2002)
11. McKnight, D.H., Chervany, N.L.: The meanings of trust. MISRC Working Paper Series, Technical Report 94-04, arlson School of Management, University of Minnesota (1996)
12. Kent, S., Lynn, C., Mikkelson, J., Seo, K.: Secure border gateway protocol (sbgp). IEEE JSAC Special Issue on Network Security (2000)
13. Meiyuan, Z., Smith, S.W., Nicol, D.M.: Evaluating the Performance Impact of PKI on BGP Security. In: The 4th Annual PKI Research and Development Workshop (April 2005)
14. Internet Routing Registries, http://www.irr.net/
15. Yao, A.C.: Protocols for secure computations. In: Proc. of the 23rd Annual IEEE Symposium on Foundations of Computer Science (1982)
16. Govindan, R., Alaettinoglu, C., Eddy, G., Kessens, D., Kumar, S.: An architecture for stable, analyzable Internet routing. IEEE Network 13(1), 29–35 (1999)
17. Battista, G.D., Refice, T., Rimondini, M.: How to extract BGP peering information from the internet routing registry. In: ACM SIGCOMM 2006 workshops, September 11-15, 2006 (2006)
18. Siganos, G., Faloutsos, M.: Analyzing BGP policies: Methodology and tool. In: INFOCOM 2004 (2004)
19. Feamster, N., Balakrishnan, H.: Detecting BGP configuration faults with static analysis.In: Proc. Networked Systems Design and Implementation (May 2005)

20. Goodell, G., Aiello, W., Griffin, T., Ioannidis, J., McDaniel, P., Rubin, A.: Working around bgp: An incremental approach to improving security and accuracy of Inter-domain routing. In: NDSS (2003)

21. Yu, H., Rexford, J., Felten, E.W.: A Distributed Reputation Approach to Cooperative Internet Routing Protection. In: 1st IEEE ICNP Workshop on Secure Network Protocols, 2005 (NPSec) (2005)

22. Akashi, O., Hirotsu, T., Sato, K., Kourai, K., Maruyama, M.: Sugawara: Agents Support for Flexible Inter-AS Policy Control. In: Proc. of the 2003 Symposium on Applications and the Internet Workshops (SAINT-w 2003) (2003)

23. Akashi, O., Fukuda, K., Hirotsu, T., Sugawara, T.: Policy-based BGP Control Architecture for Autonomous Routing Management. In: SIGCOMM 2006 Workshops, Pisa, Italy, September 11-15, 2006 (2006)

24. Mizuguchi, T., Yoshida, T.: Inter-domain Routing Security BGP Route Hijacking. In: APRICOT 2007 (2007)

Performance Problem Determination Using Combined Dependency Analysis for Reliable System*

Shunshan Piao, Jeongmin Park, and Eunseok Lee**

School of Information and Communication Engineering Sungkyunkwan University
Suwon, 440-746, South Korea
{sspiao,jmpark,eslee}@ece.skku.ac.kr

Abstract. Performance problems such as Service Level Objective violations are determined by specific approach are particularly important since it can significantly improve system reliability. In this paper, we propose an improved performance problem determination mechanism by using combined dependency analysis. Using the proposed preprocessing in prior research, a compact model is created hierarchically. We use temporal inference which associates time with the created models and occurring symptoms, then post symptom into created model to provide probabilistic reasoning. The results of dependency reasoning are combined with the closeness evaluation between symptom and created model. Combined inference is applied according to the characteristic of environment knowledge. Using the improved combined approach enables us to extend problem localization in various situations and it provides much accurate and efficient problem determination technique for reliable system. Performance problem determination using the combined dependency analysis is illustrated to prove the availability and accuracy for improving system reliability.

Keywords: Combined Dependency Analysis, Temporal Inference, Performance Problem Determination.

1 Introduction

Performance problem management becomes the main issue of gradually innovatory and distributed service providing system. At the user level, it should guarantee end-to-end response time and throughput for different types of user transactions [1]. A complex system may be fail at a given task or encounter performance problem during running time with the cause that the rapid growth in size and complexity in distributed computing systems nowadays. Thereby, problem determination techniques are adopted to solve performance problem such as Service Level Objective (SLO) violations in an IT infrastructure especially in Ubiquitous computing environment, devoting to autonomic computing [2] which assumes less human intervention during system operations. Self-healing systems provide resiliency by discovering and preventing disruptions as well as

* This research was supported by MKE, Korea under ITRC IITA-2008-(C1090-0801-0046), Grant No. R01-2006-000-10954-0, Basic Research Program of the Korea Science & Engineering Foundation, and the Post-BK21 Project.
** Corresponding author.

C. Rong et al. (Eds.): ATC 2008, LNCS 5060, pp. 577–587, 2008.
© Springer-Verlag Berlin Heidelberg 2008

recovering from malfunctions. For solving system performance accurately and hence improving reliability, performance problem determination based on combined dependency analysis are required in large scale systems, providing rapid and accurate inferences using huge data volumes [3].

Whatever the problem domain is, most problems are unobservable but existed, considering the reliability of system, the system has to determine their locations from collected information via monitoring. When using probabilistic dependency analysis techniques for performance problem determination, some problems should be solved at first becomes the main issue. 1) For collected information, how to define them based on criteria, 2) For network topology, how to determine the connections between nodes and the structure of the model. 3) For created model, how to determine the conditional relationships between each pair of nodes. The structure can be fixed by experts based on domain knowledge, whereas it also can be fixed via learning from data. Thereby, various machine learning methods are used in problem determination to provide automated approach instead of human intervention [4].

From above issues, much accurate problem determination based on dependency analysis, is critical to designing an effective automated system management to repair performance problems. In this paper, we propose an approach to performance problem determination using combined dependency analysis that adapts to various situations, which enables us to determine the locations of problems under given observations. Based on probabilistic dependency analysis, a hierarchical Bayesian network is created via learning from data automatically. For overcoming the deflections derived from time delay in specific situation, we use temporal inference to increase the accuracy of problem determination, which associates time with the created models and the occurring symptoms. Observed symptoms are posted into the created model to provide dependency reasoning. The results of dependency reasoning are combined with the closeness evaluation between collected symptom and created model. Moreover, combined dependency analysis methods are applied adapting to the characteristics of knowledge of current situations to improve the accuracy. Using the improved combined approach enables us to extend problem determination in various situations of dynamic domains and it provides much accurate and efficient problem determination technique for improving reliable system. Performance problem determination using the proposed combined dependency analysis with temporal inference is illustrated to prove the availability and accuracy of the proposed approach in improving system reliability.

The rest of this paper is structured as follows. First, we provide related work on problem determination introduced in various fields, especially using various techniques that belong to probabilistic dependency analysis. Second, we give a detail description of the proposed approach to performance problem determination for reliable system, including the process of Bayesian network modeling and combined dependency analysis that adapts to various situations in problem domains. Third, an application based on performance evaluation is given to show the course and results of inferences using the proposed approach. In the end, we give the conclusion and the future work.

2 Related Work

There are already some research efforts on problem determination techniques in various problem domains, and it conducts large scope of machine learning approaches in automated system management. The topics of problem determination such as root cause analysis and proactive prediction techniques remain an open research problem since the inherent variety and the increasing complexity of computing systems.

An adaptive diagnostic technique called active probing uses probabilistic reasoning techniques combined with information-theoretic approach [3]. The fault diagnosis is implemented based on intelligent probing techniques which impose a cost because of the additional network load and the probe results must be collected, stored and analyzed. An event prediction for proactive management was proposed in [5] to build a proactive prediction and control system for large clusters. An approach for event correlation that uses a dependency graph to represent correlation knowledge is introduced in distributed system management. The event correlator searches through the dependency graph to localize managed objects whose failure would explain a large number of management events received [6]. An extended symptom-fault-action model was proposed to incorporate actions into fault reasoning process to tackle lost and spurious symptoms [7]. Architecture to capture the changes in dependencies and a temporal correlation algorithm to perform fault diagnosis with the dynamically changing dependency information are proposed [8]. A probabilistic event-driven fault localization technique uses a probabilistic symptom-fault map as a fault propagation model to isolate the most probable set of faults through incremental updating of a symptom-explanation hypothesis [9].

Problem determination techniques based on the results of various measurements are widely used, including root cause analysis, problem prediction, and fault diagnosis. Existing problem determination approaches can be divided into groups, including deterministic approach and probabilistic approach. In probabilistic approach, most of them rely on explicit fault propagation model representing causal relationships among events (event correlation) or dependencies among communication system entities (conditional dependency analysis) [7]. Such approaches are quite generic and are applicable to a wide variety of problem domains.

In this paper, we can consider performance problem determination starting with representing a probabilistic dependency model among system elements rather than considering them mutually independent in large scale domains. However, although many machine learning algorithms that are appeared on existing researches make great efforts on structure modeling for probabilistic dependency analysis, they are mostly applicable to specific domain and approaches are designed according to the specific characteristic of the domain. For more complex system which includes various states, it needs adaptive problem determination mechanism that adapts to different situations.

3 Performance Problem Determination

Problem diagnosis and prediction are the main functions in support of performance problem determination in the fields of autonomic computing in large scale systems.

A combined approach to performance problem determination based on probabilistic dependency analysis and temporal inference is introduced that adapting to specific problem domains. Such approach contributes to automated system management which let system deal with problems that occur without any anticipation and prevents system from unexpected loss via pretreatments.

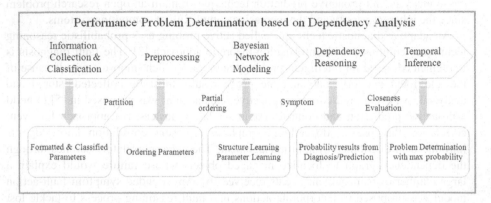

Fig. 1. Performance Problem Determination using Combined Dependency Analysis

Information is collected from the target system and classified, formatted and classified parameters are then partitioned for creating several models. Before modeling, preprocessing is executed which extracts an ordering parameters. The ranking parameters are input as partial ordering when making Bayesian network modeling. A hierarchical network is completed after structure learning and parameter learning. Probability results are given from diagnosis and prediction through dependency reasoning which is based on the created network. Combining with the closeness evaluation from temporal inference, the final result of problem determination is decided with max probability. The whole process of performance problem determination using dependency analysis is described in Fig. 1.

In this paper, Bayesian network algorithm is used as a dependency modeling method to provide approaches to problem determination for improving system reliability. Probabilistic dependency analysis throughout the whole network is able to localize root causes of problems. For various characteristics of problem domains, combined dependency analysis is applied using temporal inference.

3.1 Probabilistic Dependency Analysis Based on Bayesian Network

Formally, Bayesian network are directed acyclic graphs (DAG), which is a probabilistic graphical model to represent a set of variables and their dependencies. The connections between nodes only imply a direct influence of parent node over child node in the sense that the probability of child node is conditional on the value of parent node [10]. Bayesian network can propagate probabilities via extending Bayes' Rule throughout the whole network automatically for more complex problems. Instead of full joint distribution only the product of the local distributions of each node is required. Bayesian network is widely used in uncertainty domains with vague, incomplete, and conflicting information, and it can be run in multiple directions.

We use Bayesian network algorithm to execute probabilistic dependency analysis. Thereby, the method of modeling a hierarchical network structure by following an improved process should be focused. Structure learning plays an important role in using Bayesian network method. As manual created Bayesian model [11] may be disputed it is unalterable and unable to reflect to the real-time changes of data. Learning structure from data automatically became main issue as it searches a structure that captures a true distribution, and it can deal with missing data and hidden variables. Probabilistic dependency analysis is executed based on a learned structure which gives insight into the performance domain to provide performance problem determination. Many existing researches use machine learning to provide automated structure learning. Thereby, overfitting and generalization problems should be solved when using machine learning. In order to solve such problems and provide efficient structure learning, we add a preprocessing which ranks parameters before learning.

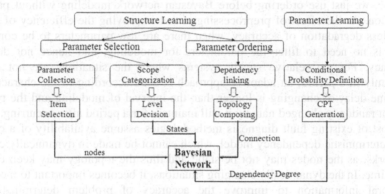

Fig. 2. Modeling Composition

There are mainly two learning phases that includes structure and parameter learning in the whole process of Bayesian network modeling (Fig.2). To create an efficient and accurate model, a preprocessing step which provides ordering parameters is prepared by using information theory method based on analyzing mutual relationships for structure learning that is difficult to find relationships between nodes in diverse domains. In the preprocessing phase, we can narrow down the size of parameters, and rank these selected factors in an order to contribute to structure learning.

The collected parameters are divided into observing parameters and problematic parameters at first. Information gains are computed between a problematic parameter and an observing parameter. For each problematic parameter, all computed information gains are ranked with descendent order in a list. Considering the lists of all problematic problems, observing parameters with mean information gains which exceeds defined threshold are selected and returned as a list including all problematic parameters. Two parameters are selected from the head of the observing list. Then two parameters are stored in a set with order according to the results of mutual information by exchanging directions of two parameters. The operation is stopped when meeting a close loop and continued to run until all parameters are considered. All parameters in pairs are ranked again in a single list. Problematic parameters are not considered when ranking selected parameters. It implies that all problematic parameters are independent of each other when learning. As the ordering shows that the anterior parameter may have direct influence on the posterior one in the order, it can determine the direction of arrow in the network when analyzing two nodes have conditional dependency relationship.

3.2 Combined Dependency Analysis Using Temporal Inference

In order to improve the availability and efficiency of the proposed approach, we can apply different mechanism of the approach according to the characteristics of application domain. For the dynamically changing systems, we can group the situations into two cases, including one case with many parameters considered and the other one with few parameters. In the case of including many parameters, we use selection and ordering in preprocessing and then create the Bayesian network model; or else, we just use ordering before Bayesian network modeling without parameter selection. As the effect of preprocessing is that improving the efficiency of learning with less degradation of accuracy, when there are few parameters to be considered, there is no need to filter the parameters for modeling, and hence not degrading accuracy. For the relative steady systems where the situations are not changed randomly in a period, an adaptive approach is used according to the characteristics: the time delay of changing is longer than the interval of modeling and the problems are not randomly changed namely it will maintain for a period after occurring.

Most of existing fault diagnosis methodologies assume availability of a complete and deterministic dependency model, which cannot be made in dynamically changing networks, as the nodes may not be static and thus the topology may keep changing with time. In the dynamically changing situations, it becomes important to incorporate temporal information to improve the accuracy of problem determination. An improved dependency analysis combined with temporal inference is proposed to associate time with created model and associate time with occurring symptom to adapt to periodic changing situations.

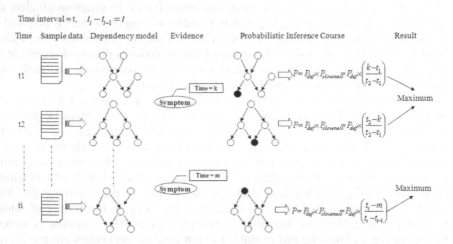

Fig. 3. Combined Dependency Analysis using Temporal Inference

Fig. 3 shows that the final result of combined dependency analysis is derived from the inference output of probabilistic dependency analysis and the closeness between the creating time of model and the occurring time of symptom. The interval of creating model can be fixed properly according to the features of the target systems. We can compute using following formulas.

$$P_{result} = P_{dep} \times P_{closeness}$$

$$P_{result} = P_{dep} \times \frac{t_{net.after} - t_{sym.occur}}{|t|_{net.interval}} \text{ or } P_{result} = P_{dep} \times \frac{t_{sym.occur} - t_{net.before}}{|t|_{net.interval}}$$

P_{dep} stands for reasoning result of probabilistic dependency analysis from using Bayesian network model, $P_{closeness}$ means the closeness for occurring symptom and creating model, $t_{sym.occur}$ is the occurring time of symptom and $t_{net.interval}$ is the interval of creating model. As the dependency model is updated periodically with interval time, the occurring symptom can be posted into the model created before the symptom arrival ($t_{net.before}$) or the one that is created after symptom occurred ($t_{net.after}$), considering the relevance of them which is weighed on the basis of the closeness. Then after computing based on the mechanism mentioned above, we can determine the maximum one as the final result.

Probabilistic dependency analysis combined with temporal inference is able to be used efficiently for determining root cause of performance problem after problem detection, and hence improving the reliability of system.

4   Illustration on Performance Evaluation

Based on the characteristics of probabilistic model, a complex system can be represented by a probabilistic dependency graph to combine various components via links which represent physical or logical connections [3]. Internet service infrastructures in ubiquitous environment requires automated performance problem determination to guarantee high quality of services for different types of user transactions, it brings a challenging task in system performance evaluation. Service Level Objectives (SLOs) including response time and request throughput are related to high quality of service. Performance problem determination can find which system metrics is the exact root cause of problems. Multivariate distributions such as system performance metrics derived from monitoring can be integrated to provide a compact factorized representation for probabilistic dependency inferences. For improving system reliability, we also consider system metrics and use them to analyze performance problem using problem determination based on combined dependency analysis. Each parameter in the collected information is classified into several levels according to given criteria at first, as listed in Table 1.

Table 1. System performance metrics classification

Attributes	Classes
CPU Utilization	High, Medium, Low
RAM Utilization	High, Medium, Low
Disk Utilization	High, Medium, Low
Bandwidth	High, Medium, Low
Packetvolume	High, Medium, Low
Clientcount	High, Medium, Low
Responsetime	Error, Warning, Normal
Throughput	Error, Warning, Normal

In preprocessing, system metrics are returned as ordering list for efficient modeling. According to the meaning of ordering list and the assumptions, the anterior one in the ordering list can be the parent of posterior one. Problematic parameters like response time and throughput have no relationship in the network.

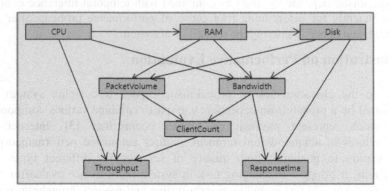

Fig. 4. Hierarchical Structure

In the case of including several parameters, we can directly use ordering on collected parameters without parameter selection in preprocessing. Using the ranking parameters and training data to support network modeling, a compact hierarchy model is constructed. The hierarchical structure using ordering parameters as input is shown in Fig. 4. Comparing with traditional simple Bayesian network, not only the relationships between causes and effects are found, it also discovers internal dependency relationships among causal parameters in the network. Based on the topology of Bayesian network, parameter learning is executed to determine conditional probability table (CPT) for each node.

Probabilistic dependency analysis including top-down and bottom-up reasoning is executed via probabilities propagation in the network after posting observed symptom as evidence, which represents the states of several observed parameters with full belief. After the probabilities of the rest parameters are dynamically changed, the results of reasoning can be determined. For overcoming the deflections derived from time delay in dynamically changing dependency model, our approach addresses this issue by combing probabilistic dependency analysis with temporal inference. Associating time with dependency model helps to represent the topology and relationships changed with time and to provide the relevance of dependencies while processing a symptom which occurred at a particular time. Similarly, associating time with occurring symptom contributes to reasoning the relevance of symptom and problem dependencies for processing the temporal inferences.

In order to prove the effort and requirement of preprocessing, we consider various estimations on experiments by whether using the preprocessing or not.

The evaluations on time consumption and accuracy are given whether using parameter selection and ordering in preprocessing or not according to the characteristics of problem domains. When using parameter selection and ordering of preprocessing in domains with many parameters, although the accuracy is little lower than that only using ordering of preprocessing, the time consumption is much better than that not using parameter selection in preprocessing. Moreover, comparing the case of that not using preprocessing, parameter ordering plays an important role for structure learning in probabilistic dependency analysis. However, in the problem domains with less parameter, both parameter selection and ordering are used in preprocessing makes that the result is not optimal. Although the parameter selection in the preprocessing can reduce the learning time, the accuracy is dropped distinctly, which tell us that only using parameter ordering in preprocessing for problem domains with less parameters can make effort on accuracy and reduce time consumption. We can find the comparison results from Table 2.

Table 2. Comparisons with diverse situations

Problem domains	Dimensions	Time consumption (sec)	Accuracy (%)
Domains with many parameters	Selection and Ordering in preprocessing	14.62	88.1
	Only ordering in preprocessing	15.66	90.7
	Without Preprocessing	16.84	91.5
Domains with less parameters	Selection and Ordering in preprocessing	9.12	73.6
	Only ordering in preprocessing	10.03	91.8

In order to prove the effort of using temporal inference for decreasing the deflection from time delay, we evaluate the final results of inferences between that only using probabilistic dependency analysis and that using combined dependency analysis using temporal inferences. When using dependency analysis to combine probabilistic reasoning result derived from dependency model with computation of closeness, the average accuracy of final results is better than that only considering probabilistic dependency analysis, as showed in Table 3.

Table 3. Evaluation on Temporal Dependency Analysis

Inference	Mechanism	Average accuracy
Probabilistic Dependency Analysis	Reasoning results from dependency model	84%
Combined Dependency Analysis	Results of probabilistic dependency analysis * Temporal inference	89%

Various tests under different conditions account for that taking selected ordering parameters that derived from preprocessing as input of structure learning is much efficient for modeling, and using combined dependency analysis make great effort on the accuracy of problem determination in various problem domains with dynamically changing dependency topology and problematic situation maintaining.

5 Conclusion

In this paper, we propose an improved mechanism of performance problem determination that adapts to various problem domains via using combined dependency analysis. We use the preprocessing approach to execute parameter selection and ordering according to different characteristics of situations to provide efficient and accurate learning for probabilistic dependency analysis. We also use temporal dependency analysis to increase the accuracy of problem determination, which has a notion of time while performing probabilistic reasoning. Moreover, a mechanism of combined dependency analysis is applied adapting to the characteristic of knowledge of existing domain in order to improve the efficiency and accuracy. With the improved performance problem determination, it enables us to extend the scope of problem localization and permit it applicable in various situations of domains, which provides much accurate and efficient problem determination technique for improving the reliability of system.

Future work will be continued to consider an efficient approach different from existing one based on fault type learning, providing proper repair strategy after determining the type of occurring problem.

References

1. Agarwal, M.K., Kar, G., Mahindru, R., Neogi, A., Sailer, A.: Performance Problem Prediction in Transaction Based e-Business Systems. IBM Research Report Computer Science, RC24286(W0706-065) (June 2007)
2. Jeffrey, O., Kephart David, M., Chess IBM Thomas, J.: Watson Research Center, The Vision of Autonomic Computing. IEEE Computer Society (January 2003)

3. Rish, I., Brodie, M., Ma, S., Odintsova, N., Beygelzimer, A., Grabarnik, G., Hernandez, K.: Adaptive Diagnosis in Distributed Systems. IEEE Transactions on Neural Networks (March 2005)
4. Steinder, M., Sethi, A.S.: A Survey of Fault Localization Techniques in Computer Networks. Science of Computer Programming, Special Edition on Topics in System Administration 53(2), 165–194 (2004)
5. Sahoo, R.K., Oliner, A.J., Rish, I., Gupta, M., Moreira, J.E., Ma, S., Vilalta, R., Sivasubramaniam, A.: Critical event prediction for proactive management in large-scale computer clusters. In: Proceedings of the ACM SIGKDD, Intl. Conf. on Knowledge Discovery and Data Mining, pp. 426–435 (August 2003)
6. Boris, G.: Integrated Event Management: Event Correlation Using Dependency Graphs. In: The Tenth IFIP/IEEE International Workshop on Distributed Systems: Operations & Management, Zurich, Switzerland, IEEE Computer Society Press, Los Alamitos (1999)
7. Tang, Y., Al-Shaer, E.S., Boutaba, R.: Active integrated fault localization in communication networks. Integrated Network Management, 543–556 (May 2005)
8. Natu, M., Sethi, A.S.: Using temporal correlation for fault localization in dynamically changing networks. International Journal of Network Management (2007)
9. Steinder, M., Sethi, A.S.: Probabilistic Fault Diagnosis in Communication Systems through incremental hypothesis updating. Computer Networks 45(4), 537–562 (2004)
10. Alpaydm, E.: Introduction of Machine Learning. © Massachusetts Institute of Technology, pp. 39–59 (2004)
11. Ding, J., Kramer, B., Bai, Y., Chen, h.: Backward Inference in Bayesian Networks for Distributed Systems Management. Journal of Network and Systems Management 13(4) (December 2005)

A Free-Roaming Mobile Agent Security Protocol
Based on Anonymous Onion Routing and
k Anonymous Hops Backwards

Xiaogang Wang[1], Darren Xu[2], and Junzhou Luo[3]

[1] School of Computer Science and Engineering, Southeast University, Nanjing, P.R. China
wxiaog@seu.edu.cn
[2] YRC Worldwide Technologies, Overland Park, Kansas, USA
yongnan.xu@yrcw.com
[3] School of Computer Science and Engineering, Southeast University, Nanjing, P.R. China
jluo@seu.edu.cn

Abstract. Security and anonymity are vital for free-roaming mobile agent-based applications. Based on anonymous onion routing, this paper proposes a security protocol to defend truncation attacks for free-roaming mobile agent-based applications. This protocol uses "two hops forwards and k anonymous hops backwards" chain relation to implement the generally accepted mobile agent security properties. Security analysis proves that this protocol can defend known attacks, especially multiple colluded truncation attacks and provide privacy protection to previously visited servers. Performance evaluation shows this protocol requires limited communication overhead if right parameters are chosen.

Keywords: Mobile Agent, Colluded Truncation, Anonymous Onion Routing.

1 Introduction

Mobile agents are executable codes which can migrate from originating hosts to intermediate servers to generate and collect data, and return to the originators to submit results after completing scheduled tasks. Free-roaming agents are those mobile agents that are free to choose their next hops dynamically at each hop based on initial requirements and current conditions.

While mobile agents roam, malicious servers may expose, modify, insert, or truncate data the agents have collected from other previously visited servers to benefit themselves. One of the attacks is the colluded truncation attack in which two or more servers may collude to delete a part of the results collected by an agent from previously visited servers. Security protocols are needed to protect mobile agents, collected data and identities of visited servers. An effective approach to defending colluded truncation attacks is to design chain relation based security protocols which link results from the currently visited server to results generated at the previously visited servers and the identities of the next hops.

Karjoth et al. [1] proposed a set of security protocols which uses digital signatures and hash functions to protect chain relations. A chain relation links a result from the

C. Rong et al. (Eds.): ATC 2008, LNCS 5060, pp. 588–602, 2008.
© Springer-Verlag Berlin Heidelberg 2008

currently visited server to a result generated at the previous server and the identity of the next hop. By using different combinations of cryptographic mechanisms, each scheme of the protocol family provides different security properties. However, none of the protocols can defend two-colluder truncation attacks.

Karnik et al. [2] introduced the Append Only Container scheme. It is a compact case of the KAG protocol family. The protocol uses an encrypted checksum to build a backward chain relation to link an agent's previous result with the agent's data generated at the currently visited host. The backward chain relation guarantees that only new data can be added to the results the agent collected and no data can be deleted from them. This scheme cannot defend two-colluder truncation attacks.

Corradi et al. [3] integrated the Multiple-Hops Protocol in their mobile security project. Similar to the KAG protocols, this protocol uses a chain relation which includes both backward and forward chaining. At each server, the protocol runs a hash function to compute a cryptographic proof of a result from the previous server, a result generated at the current server, and the identity of the next hop. Like other protocols, this protocol cannot defend two-colluder truncation attacks.

Xu et al. [4] proposed an improved free-roaming mobile agent security protocol to address all the issues found in the previously discussed protocols, especially defend two-colluder attacks. The protocol uses "one hop backwards and two hops forwards" chain relation as the protocol core to implement the generally accepted mobile agent security properties. Although this protocol can defend two-colluder attacks, it is vulnerable to some special cases of multiple-colluder truncation attacks in which two or more of the attackers are adjacent.

We propose an improved security protocol aiming on colluder truncation attacks while addressing all the security requirements. The rest of this paper is organized as follows. In Section 2, the commonly accepted mobile agent security properties, notations and assumptions used in protocol description are presented. In Section 3, we discuss the protocol in detail. In Section 4.1, the general security properties of the new protocol are analyzed. In Section 4.2, multiple-colluder truncation attacks and other special cases are discussed. In Section 5, the performance of the protocol is analyzed based on implementation and simulation. In Section 6, the highlights of the protocol are concluded.

2 Notations and Security Properties

When a free-roaming agent completes its actions on server S_{i-1}, it selects and visits next server S_i to generate and collect data. While the agent migrates to server S_i, S_i encapsulates an offer o_i with other related data to generate its encapsulated offer O_i, and then appends the encapsulated offer O_i to the partial results carried by the agent from the preceding servers. After completing its itinerary $S_0, S_1,..., S_i,..., S_m,..., S_0$, the agent completes its trip and returns to its originator S_0. S_0 then extracts and verifies the encapsulated offers from each visited servers.

We define the model and cryptographic notations used in the paper in table 1 and 2 respectively. The notations used here are similar to those in other security protocols, such as [4] for comparison.

Table 1. Model Notation

Notation	Definition
$S_0=S_{n+1}$	Originator
S_i, $1 \leq i \leq n$	Servers
o_0	Token from S_0 to identify the agent instance on return
h_i, $1 \leq i \leq n$	Integrity check value associated with O_i
$O_0, O_2, ..., O_n$	Chain of encapsulated offers from $S_0, S_1, ..., S_n$
$BackR_i$, $1 \leq i \leq n$	Backward anonymous onion used for traveling from S_i to S_{i-k}
$CountK_i, 1 \leq i \leq n$	Number of backward servers at S_i

Table 2. Cryptographic Notation

Notation	Definition
r_i	Random number generated by S_i
(Pr_i, Pb_i)	Private and public key pair of S_i
(tPr_i, tPb_i)	Temporary private and public key pair of S_i
$Enc_{Pbi}(m)$	Message m encrypted with the public key Pb_i of S_i
$Sig_{Pri}(m)$	Signature of S_i on message m with its private key Pr_i
$H(m)$	One-way, collision-free hash function
$A \rightarrow B:m$	Server A sends message m to server B
$\perp$	End mark in an onion
$rtBackR$	Backward onion used from S_i to S_{i-k}
$rtReturnR$	Prepared forward onion generated from S_i to S_{i-k}
$ftReturnR$	Forward onion used from S_{i-k} to S_i
$ftBackR$	Prepared backward onion generated from S_{i-k} to S_i

The generally accepted security properties are described in many other papers [4, 5, 6, 7]. We will pay close attention to Public Verifiable Forward Integrity and Truncation Resilience properties.

3 The Protocol

Based on anonymous onion routing, our protocol builds a chain relation to link the current server S_i backwards to k previously visited servers (S_{i-k} $S_{i-k+1}, ..., S_{i-1}$) and the identity of the next hop S_{i+1}. The protocol aims on defending all known attacks, especially multiple-colluder truncation attacks while supporting privacy protection. The protocol also fixes some weaknesses found in other protocols. We describe the protocol as follows.

3.1 Anonymous Onion Routing

Anonymous onion routing [9] is an infrastructure for private communication over a public network. It provides anonymous connections that are strongly resistant to both eavesdropping and traffic analysis. Any identifying information such as the identities and temporary public keys of visited servers is encrypted in layers that can only be decrypted by a chain of onion routers using their respective private keys. An onion is a data structure that is treated as the destination address by intermediate onion routers. Each layer of the onion defines the next hop in a route. An onion router that receives an onion peels off its layer, identifies the next hop, and sends the embedded onion to that onion router. Thus, the onion can be used to establish an anonymous connection. In our protocol, servers act as onion routers, and four different types of onions are designed for constructing backward and forward onion routing.

In order to make a chain relating current server S_i and next hop S_{i+1} to backwards k previously visited servers S_{i-1}, S_{i-2}, ..., S_{i-k}, the necessary chain message must first be transferred backwards making use of the backward onion and then be transferred forwards making use of the forward onion.

First, S_i gets its backward onion $rtBackR_i$ by receiving backward anonymous onion $BackR_{i-1}$ carried with the mobile agent which migrates from S_{i-1} to S_i.

$$BackR_{i-1}=Enc_{tPbi-1}(\cdots(Enc_{tPbi-k+1}(\perp,S_{i-k},tPb_{i-k})\cdots),S_{i-2},tPb_{i-2})$$
$$rtBackR_i=BackR_{i-1}$$

By using its temporary private key tPr_{i-1}, the first backward server S_{i-1} can decrypt backward onion $rtBackR_i$ received from S_i and get the identity of the second backward server S_{i-2} and corresponding embedded onion $rtBackR_{i-1}$ for S_{i-2}.

$$rtBackR_{i-1}=Enc_{tPbi-2}(\cdots(Enc_{tPbi-k+1}(\perp,S_{i-k},tPb_{i-k})\cdots),S_{i-3},tPb_{i-3})$$

Similarly, in order to be able to return from S_{i-k} to S_i, S_i must also construct prepared forward onion $rtReturnR_i$ by encryption while the message is being transferred from S_i to S_{i-k}. The prepared forward onion $rtReturnR_i$ is constructed by S_i as follows.

$$rtReturnR_i=Enc_{tpbi-1}(\perp,S_i,tPb_i)$$

By decrypting $rtBacR_i$ received from S_i, S_{i-1} can also get tPb_{i-2} and use tPb_{i-2} to construct $rtReturnR_{i-1}$ so as to be able to return from S_{i-k} to S_{i-1} on later stage.

$$rtReturnR_{i-1}=Enc_{tpbi-2}(rtReturnR_i,S_{i-1},tPb_{i-1})$$

Then, S_{i-1} passes the backward and prepared forward onion $rtBackR_{i-1}$, $rtReturnR_{i-1}$ and necessary data together to S_{i-2}. To prevent eavesdropping, all information transferred between servers must be encrypted by the recipient's temporary public key.

The intermediate server S_x (i-k$\leqslant$x$\leqslant$i-2) acts like S_{i-1} successively. When S_{i-k} receives end mark $\perp$ as $rtBackR_{i-k+1}$, S_{i-k} use prepared forward onion $rtReturnR_{i-k+1}$ as forward onion to start message transferring from S_{i-k} to S_i in reverse direction.

It is obvious that any intermediate server S_x (i-k$\leqslant$x$\leqslant$i) only knows the identity of its adjacent severs, so the privacy of previously visited servers can be preserved.

3.2 Agent Starting at S_0

By extending Xu et al. [4] protocol, we also assume that the originator S_0 first starts the agent and encrypts the offer by using its public key to produce a cryptographically protected encapsulated offer $ProtectedO_o$. Then the agent selects and migrates to its next hop S_1 with $ProtectedO_o$.

S_1 generates offer o_1 and a random number r_1. S_1 first signs its own offer, and then encodes the offer by using the originator's public key to produce S_1's protected encapsulated offer $ProtectedO_1$. The server S_1 also generates a pair of temporary digital signature keys $[tPr_1, tPb_1]$ for signing its own final encapsulated offer later. The agent then selects its next hop S_2. Based on simple anonymous onion routing, S_1 can make a chain relating S_0, S_1 and S_2. Then the agent migrates to S_2 with the final encapsulation offer O_0 from S_0, the protected encapsulated offer $ProtectedO_1$, the number of backward servers $CountK_1$, backward anonymous onion $BackR_1$ from S_1, and the temporary public key of S_1.

$$Back_1 = Enc_{tPb1}(\perp, S_0, tPb_0)$$

3.3 Agent Migrating at S_i

3.3.1 Offer Provision

The agent migrates to S_i with all previous encapsulated offers O_0, O_1,..., O_{i-2}, plus the protected encapsulated offer $ProtectedO_{i-1}$ from S_{i-1} (instead of the finial encapsulated offer O_{i-1}), the number of backward servers $CountK_{i-1}$, the temporary public key of S_{i-1} and the backward anonymous onion $BackR_{i-1}$. The typical structure of the mobile agent migrating to S_i can be shown in figure 1.

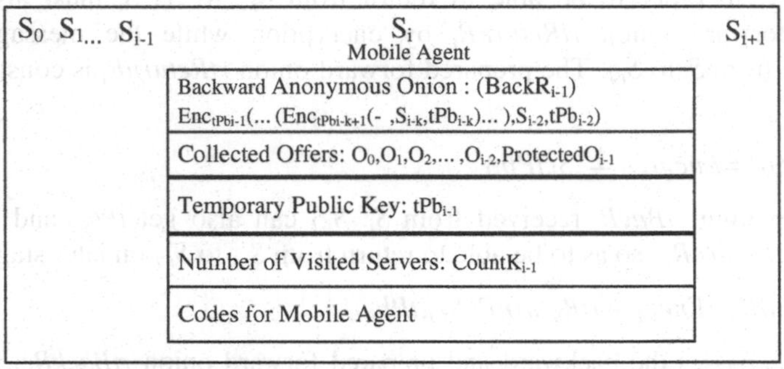

S_0 S_1... S_{i-1}	S_i Mobile Agent	S_{i+1}
	Backward Anonymous Onion : ($BackR_{i-1}$) $Enc_{tPbi-1}(... (Enc_{tPbi-k+1}(-, S_{i-k}, tPb_{i-k})...), S_{i-2}, tPb_{i-2})$	
	Collected Offers: $O_0, O_1, O_2,..., O_{i-2}, ProtectedO_{i-1}$	
	Temporary Public Key: tPb_{i-1}	
	Number of Visited Servers: $CountK_{i-1}$	
	Codes for Mobile Agent	

Fig. 1. Structure of the mobile agent migrating to S_i

After generating a random number r_i and a pair of temporary digital signature keys $[tPr_i, tPb_i]$, S_i computes its protected encapsulated offer $ProtectedO_i$ and the number of backward servers $CountK_i$ based on the predefined parameter k. To prevent reusing of the one time digital signature keys [4], a recording and checking function can be added to the agent.

S_i: Receive $O_0, O_1,..., O_{i-2}, ProtectedO_{i-1}, CountK_{i-1}, tPb_{i-1}, BackR_{i-1}$ from S_{i-1}
   Compute $CountK_i = min (k, CountK_{i-1}+1)$
          $ProtectedO_i = Enc_{Pb0} (Sig_{Pri}(o_i), r_i)$
   Generate $[tPr_i, tPb_i]$
   Select S_{i+1}

3.3.2 Interactive Offer Encapsulation

In order to generate a chain relation of the k hops backwards previously visited servers and two hops forwards S_i and S_{i+1}, S_i first computes its hash value tH_i, generates corresponding backward onion $rtBackR_i$ and prepared forward onion $rtReturnR_i$. Then S_i informs its previous server S_{i-1} with the next hop identity S_{i+1}. In order to prevent revealing S_{i+1}'s identity to S_{i-1}, S_i only passes an encoded identity $Enc_{pb0}(S_{i+1})$ to S_{i-1} to build the chain relation. S_i first computes and transmits $tH_i = H(S_{i+1}, S_i)$ to S_{i-1}. To prevent potential self-loop attack, S_{i-1} compares $Enc_{pb0}(S_{i+1})$ with $Enc_{pb0}(S_i)$, and refuses to return its final encapsulated offer O_{i-1} and reports the incident if $Enc_{pb0}(S_{i+1})$ and $Enc_{pb0}(S_i)$ are the same.

S_i: Compute $tH_i = H(S_{i+1}, S_i)$
  $rtBackR_i = BackR_{i-1}$
  $rtReturnR_i = Enc_{tPbi-1}(\perp, S_i, tPb_i)$
$S_i \rightarrow S_{i-1}$: $Enc_{pb0}(S_{i+1}), tH_i, rtBackR_i, rtReturnR_i, CountK_i$

S_{i-1} is now able to build a chain relation h_{i-1} of its previous offer O_{i-2}, the k hops backwards previously visited servers and its next two hops S_i and S_{i+1}. The protected encapsulated offer $ProtectedO_{i-1}$ has been computed when the agent was at S_{i-1}. In order to build the chain relation concerning k hops backwards servers, currently visited server S_i and next hop S_{i+1}, S_{i-1} must continue to inform $k-1$ hops backwards servers to generate corresponding chain hash values. S_{i-1} first computes its hash value tH_{i-1} and transmits backwards by using anonymous onion routing.

S_{i-1}: Compute $tH_{i-1} = H(tH_i, S_{i-1})$ (if $Enc_{pb0}(S_{i+1}) \neq Enc_{pb0}(S_i)$)
  $rtBackR_{i-1}, S_{i-2}, tPb_{i-2} = Dec_{tPri-1}(rtBackR_i)$
  $rtReturnR_{i-1} = Enc_{tpbi-2}(rtReturnR_i, S_{i-1}, tPb_{i-1})$

  Now, S_{i-1} can get $rtBackR_{i-1}$ as $Enc_{tPbi-2}(\cdots (Enc_{tPbi-k+1}(\perp, S_{i-k}, tPb_{i-k}) \cdots), S_{i-3}, tPb_{i-3})$ and get $rtReturnR_{i-1}$ as $Enc_{tPbi-2}(Enc_{tPbi-1}(\perp, S_i, tPb_i), S_{i-1}, tPb_{i-1})$.
$S_{i-1} \rightarrow S_{i-2}$: $tH_{i-1}, rtBackR_{i-1}, rtReturnR_{i-1}, CountK_i$

This process continues successively backwards until S_{i-k+1} receives $rtBackR_{i-k+2}$ from S_{i-k+2}.

S_{i-k+1}: Receive $tH_{i-k+2}, rtBackR_{i-K+2}, rtReturnR_{i-k+2}, CountK_i$ from S_{i-k+2}
  Compute $tH_{i-k+1} = H(tH_{i-k+2}, S_{i-k+1})$
  $rtBackR_{i-k+1}, S_{i-k}, tPb_{i-k} = Dec_{tPri-k+1}(rtBackR_{i-k+2})$
  $rtReturnR_{i-k+1} = Enc_{tPbi-k}(rtReturnR_{i-k+2}, S_{i-k+1}, tPb_{i-k+1})$

By now the backward onion $rtBackR_{i-k+1}$ should be the end mark $\perp$.

$S_{i-k+1} \rightarrow S_{i-k}$: $tH_{i-k+1}, rtBackR_{i-k+1}, rtReturnR_{i-k+1}, CountK_i$

S_{i-k}: Compute $tH_{i-k} = H(tH_{i-k+1}, S_{i-k})$
  $ftReturnR_{i-k}, S_{i-k+1}, tPb_{i-k+1} = Dec_{tPri-k}(rtReturnR_{i-k+1})$
  $ftBackR_{i-k} = Enc_{tPbi-k+1}(\perp, S_{i-k}, tPb_{i-k})$ (if $CountK_i < k$)
  $ftBackR_{i-k} = \perp$ (if $CountK_i = k$)

By now the forward message transmitting process must be followed.

$S_{i-k} \to S_{i-k+1}$: $tH_{i-k}, ftReturnR_{i-k}, ftBackR_{i-k}$

S_{i-k+1}: Compute $tH_{i-k+1}=tH_{i-k}$
$ftReturnR_{i-k+1}, S_{i-k+2}, tPb_{i-k+2}=Dec_{tpri-k+1}(ftReturnR_{i-k})$
$ftBackR_{i-k+1}=Enc_{tPbi-k+2}(ftBackR_{i-k}, S_{i-k+1}, tPb_{i-k+1})$

$S_{i-k+1} \to S_{i-k+2}$: $tH_{i-k+1}, ftBackR_{i-k+1}, ftReturnR_{i-k+1}$

S_{i-k+2}: Compute $tH_{i-k+2}=tH_{i-k+1}$
$ftReturnR_{i-k+2}, S_{i-k+3}, tPb_{i-k+3}=Dec_{tpri-k+2}(ftReturnR_{i-k+1})$
$ftBackR_{i-k+2}=Enc_{tPbi-k+3}(rtBackR_{i-k+1}, S_{i-k+2}, tPb_{i-k+2})$

This process goes on successively forwards until S_{i-1} receives $ftReturnR_{i-2}$ from S_{i-2}.

$S_{i-2} \to S_{i-1}$: $tH_{i-2}, ftBackR_{i-2}, ftReturnR_{i-2}$
S_{i-1}: Compute $tH_{i-1}=tH_{i-2}$
$ftReturnR_{i-1}, S_i, tPb_i=Dec_{tpri-1}(ftReturnR_{i-2})$
$ftBackR_{i-1}=Enc_{tPbi}(ftBackR_{i-2}, S_{i-1}, tPb_{i-1})$
$h_{i-1}=H(ProtectedO_{i-1}, tH_{i-1})$ (if $ftReturnR_{i-1}= \perp$)
$O_{i-1}=Sig_{tPri-1}(ProtectedO_{i-1}, h_{i-1}, H(S_{i-1}), tPb_i)$

S_{i-1} finally signs and finalizes the finial encapsulation offer O_{i-1} by using its secret key tPr_{i-1}.

$S_{i-1} \to S_i$: $O_{i-1}, ftBackR_{i-1}$

3.3.3 Offer Verification
Now S_i has all previous offers including the final encapsulated offer O_{i-1} from S_{i-1}. S_i recovers all previous $ProtectedO_k$, h_k and tPb_{k+1} ($1 \leq k \leq i-2$) recursively from O_0, O_1, ..., O_{i-2} to verify the offers O_1, O_2,..., O_{i-1} with corresponding public keys. The protocol confirms the $ProtectedO_{i-1}$ encapsulated in O_{i-1} by S_{i-1} in Step 3.3.2 is the same $ProtectedO_{i-1}$ carried over by the agent in Step 3.3.1 to prevent S_{i-1} from changing its mind to use a different offer o_{i-1} after the agent migrates.

S_i: $Ver(O_0, Pb_0)$, recover $ProtectedO_0$, h_0, $H(S_0)$ and tPb_1
     $Ver(O_k, tPb_k)$, recover $ProtectedO_k$, h_k, $H(S_k)$ and tPb_{k+1}, $1 \leq k \leq i-2$

The protocol confirms the $H(S_k)$ encapsulated in O_k is unique among the previously visited servers by comparing $H(S_k)$ ($1 \leq k \leq i-2$), S_i will report the incident if there are same values among $H(S_k)$.

3.3.4 Agent Migration
S_i forwards all previous offers and its protected encapsulated offer to S_{i+1} if all previous encapsulated offers are verified as valid.

S_i: Compute $BackR_i =ftBackR_{i-1}$
$S_i \to S_{i+1}$: $O_0, O_1,..., O_{i-1}, ProtectedO_i, CountK_i, tPb_i, BackR_i$

3.4 Agent at S_{i+1}

Agent migrating at S_{i+1} has the similar processes as at S_i. We outline the protocol at sever S_{i+1} for comparison with steps at S_i.

S_{i+1}: Receive $O_0, O_1, \ldots, O_{i-1}$, ProtectedO$_i$, CountK$_i$, tPb$_i$, BackR$_i$ from S_i

Compute $CountK_{i+1} = min\ (k,\ CountK_i + 1)$

$ProtectedO_{i+1} = Enc_{Pb0}(Sig_{Pri+1}(o_{i+1}), r_{i+1})$

Generate $[tPr_{i+1},\ tPb_{i+1}]$

Select S_{i+2}

Compute $tH_{i+1} = H(S_{i+2}, S_{i+1})$

$rtBackR_{i+1} = BackR_i$

$rtReturnR_{i+1} = Enc_{tPbi}(\perp, S_{i+1}, tPb_{i+1})$

$S_{i+1} \rightarrow S_i$: $Enc_{pb0}(S_{i+2})$, tH_{i+1}, $rtBackR_{i+1}$, $rtReturnR_{i+1}$, $CountK_{i+1}$

S_{i+1} waits for k hops backwards servers to generate tH_i.

$S_{i-1} \rightarrow S_i$: tH_{i-1}, ftBackR$_{i-1}$, ftReturnR$_{i-1}$

S_i: Compute $tH_i = tH_{i-1}$

$ftReturnR_i$, S_{i+1}, $tPb_{i+1} = Dec_{tpri}(ftReturnR_{i-1})$

$ftBackR_i = Enc_{tPbi+1}(ftBackR_{i-1}, S_i, tPb_i)$

$h_i = H(O_{i-1}, tH_i)$ $(if\ ftReturnR_i = \perp)$

$O_i = Sig_{tPri}(ProtectedO_i,\ h_i,\ H(S_i),\ tPb_{i+1})$

S_i finally signs and finalizes the final encapsulation offer O_i by using its secret key tPr_i.

$S_i \rightarrow S_{i+1}$: O_i, ftBackR$_i$

S_{i+1}: Ver(O_0, Pb_0), recover ProtectedO$_0$, h_0, and tPb_1

Ver(O_k, tPb_k), recover ProtectedO$_k$, h_k, and tPb_{k+1}, $1 \leq k \leq i$

Compute $BackR_{i+1} = ftBackR_i$

$S_{i+1} \rightarrow S_{i+2}$: $O_0, O_1, \ldots, O_i$, ProtectedO$_{i+1}$, CountK$_{i+1}$, tPb$_{i+1}$, BackR$_{i+1}$

3.5 Agent Returns to S_0

When the agent returns to the originator S_0, it has all the encapsulated offers O_0, $O_1, \ldots, O_n$. The agent creator S_0 begins to decrypt the offers and extract the data. It uses its public key Pb_0 to recover ProtectedO$_0$, $H(O_0)$ and temporary public key of tPb_1 from O_0, and then uses the temporary public key tPb_1 to recover ProtectedO$_1$, $H(O_1)$ and tPb_2 from the next encapsulated offer. By using these temporary public keys S_0 can extract all the ProtectedO$_i$. The ProtectedO$_i$ can then be decrypted by using the public key Pb_0 of S_0 and the offers $o_1, \ldots, o_n$, $S_1, \ldots, S_n$ can be obtained. S_0 can also detect colluded truncation attacks by verifying h_0, $h_1, \ldots, h_n$.

4 Security Analysis

We prove our protocol achieves the generally accepted security properties in this section. Let's assume the agent's itinerary is S_0, $S_1, \ldots, S_{i-2}$, S_{i-1}, $S_i \ldots, S_m, \ldots, S_0$, and collected encapsulated offers are O_0, $O_1, \ldots, O_{i-2}$, O_{i-1}, $O_i, \ldots, O_m, \ldots, O_n$ correspondingly.

4.1 General Security Properties

Xu et al's protocol [4] satisfies all general security properties including defending the two-colluder truncation attack and many of its special cases, such as growing a fake stem attacks, revisiting attacks and interleaving attacks. Our protocol can obviously satisfy the security properties as well as an extension on the protocol.

Our protocol aims on not only defending multiple-colluder attacks, but also providing privacy protection. Privacy protection is a vital demand in real applications. In our protocol, the privacy is preserved by using anonymous onion routing. No intermediate server is able to acquire any information about other previously visited servers except its adjacent servers.

4.2 Colluded Truncation Attacks

As Xu et al. [4] analyzed that in only one-hop forwards protocol, S_i can modify its next hop in its own chain relation, S_i is able to collude with S_m to truncate the offers between them and append new offers without being detected. This is why the one-hop forwards chain relation based protocols cannot defend colluded truncation attacks without other protection mechanisms.

In "one hop backwards and two hops forwards" protocol proposed by Xu et al. [4], S_{i-1} builds the chain relation $h_{i-1}=H (O_{i-2}, r_{i-1}, S_i, S_{i+1})$ with next two hops S_i and S_{i+1}. Although the inclusion of S_i and S_{i+1} guarantees that the truncation attacks against O_i and/or O_{i+1} will be detected, the chain relation h_{i-1} may not be able to prevent S_i and S_{i+1} from changing their own chain relations by collusion.

In our "two hops forwards and k hops backwards" protocol, the chain relation h_{i-1} can prevent S_i and S_{i+1} from changing their own chain relations, it guarantees that only O_i from S_i and O_{i+1} from S_{i+1} and O_{i+2} from S_{i+2} until O_{i+k+1} from S_{i+k+1} can follow O_{i-1}.

It is possible that multiple (three or more) colluders exist. Assume S_m holds partial encapsulated offers from $S_0,...,S_{i-1}, S_i, S_{i+1},..., S_x, S_{x+1},..., S_{m-1}$. S_i and S_m ($i<x<m$) leave O_{i-1} intact and collude to truncate O_x and/or afterwards. As Xu et al. [4] analyzed that "one hop backwards and two hops forwards" protocol can defend two nonadjacent colluder truncation attack, but can't detect two or more adjacent colluder truncation attacks. Assume S_i and S_{i+1} are two adjacent colluders. The protocol proposed by Xu et al. [4] is vulnerable to such attack. But in our protocol, although S_i and S_{i+1} are adjacent and may collude with S_m to truncate offers collected between S_{i+1} and S_m, such attack can be detected by our protocol. As S_{i-1} builds the chain relation $h_{i-1}=H(O_{i-2}, H(...(H(S_{i+1}, S_i), S_{i-1})..., S_{i-k}))$ relating next two hops S_i and S_{i+1} and k hops backwards servers, only S_i and S_{i+1} can append O_i and O_{i+1} after O_{i-1}. If O_i and/or O_{i+1} are truncated, the server identities of the new offers after O_{i-1} cannot satisfy the chain relation $h_{i-1}=H(O_{i-2}, tH_{i-1})$ without violating the collusion-free hash function assumption. So the truncation against O_i and O_{i+1} cannot happen or the action will be detected. Similarly, if O_{i+2} is truncated, the server identities of the new offers after O_{i+1} will not satisfy the chain relation h_i. In general, as long as the number of adjacent colluders is not bigger than k, our protocol can effectively detect such truncation attacks. Our protocol extensively extends "one hop backwards and two hops

forwards" protocol and can be used to defend various kinds of multiple-colluder truncation attacks for free-roaming mobile agent.

5 Implementation and Evaluation

We have implemented the protocol in a local 100Mbps Ethernet to evaluate the protocol and it's effectiveness of our security protocol.

We use the Java Agent Development Framework system (JADE) developed by Telecom Italia (formerly CSELT). JADE is a Java software platform that provides basic middleware-layer functionalities which are independent of specific applications and simplifies the realization of distributed applications that exploit the software agent abstraction. JADE is also a very efficient agent platform with agent containers that can be distributed over the network. Agents live in containers which are the Java process that provides the JADE run-time and all the services needed for hosting and executing agents [11].

5.1 Implementation

5.1.1 Implementation Platform

We implemented our security protocol based on JADE [11] platform. The hardware platform used for the implementation includes eight computers with Intel Pentium 4 on a local 100Mbps Ethernet. The CPU and Memory of each computer are 3GHz and 512MB respectively. The software used for the implementation includes the operating system Windows XP and JADE (3.5) multi-agent platform. We use JAVA as the programming language, and the Java™ 2 Platform, Standard Edition (J2SE™) version 1.6.0 as the essential Java tools and APIs for implementing the security protocol.

The common functionality includes creating initial data on the originator, updating the data of the agent, and verifying the integrity of the agent on the originating host. We first develop Java agents which are resided at every host respectively. The residing agent at each host is on behalf of the host server and responsible for communicating with the free roaming agent when the free roaming agent migrates to the host. Then, we design a free roaming agent which starts at originator S_0, visits each succeeding host and collects corresponding offers.

In order to implement k anonymous hops backwards protocol based on anonymous onion routing, we utilize 512 bits RSA encryption mechanism coming with Java Cryptography Architecture (JCA) which includes the Java Cryptographic Extension (JCE)) based on JDK1.6.0. The system timestamp technique in Java is used for measuring response time metrics.

5.1.2 Performance Metrics

In order to evaluate the performance of security protocol, we measure the total time and the total volumes of transferred messages caused by free-roaming agent's traveling from originated host S_0 and returning to S_0. Both the time and volume of messages are mainly concerned with N, the number of visited hosts and the value of k hops backwards parameter. The total processing time includes the computing complexity cost for privacy and security processing in anonymous onion routing construction.

5.2 Results and Evaluation

5.2.1 Attack Pattern Simulation

In order to find an optimal balance point of the required numbers of hops backwards to satisfy both security and performance, we have done the research on the probability of the multiple-colluded truncation attacks occurred in various scenarios. In a typical scenario, the free-roaming agent at each hop may choose the next host according to its intention, but the probability of choosing malicious node is relating to the percentage of malicious nodes in the network. The length of adjacent multiple-colluded attackers can be simulated as a typical attacking model against our security protocol. By simulation, we get the distribution of the probability of the multiple-colluded truncation attacks existing in a network. Under different percentage of malicious nodes in the network, the distribution of multiple-colluded attackers with 20 random selected hosts among 50 relating hosts is shown in figure 2 by simulation.

Based on the simulation result, the probability of the multiple-colluded truncation attacks increases correspondingly with the increase of m the percentage of malicious nodes in the network. However, the probability of adjacent multiple-colluded nodes is very small in practical scenarios. This implies that in order to defend against multiple-colluded truncation attacks in our security protocol the k hops backwards parameter may be set smaller according to different application scenarios.

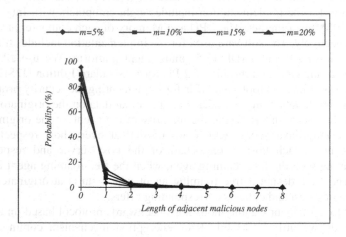

Fig. 2. Distribution of multiple-colluded attackers

5.2.2 Communication Overheads

Like other chain based protocols with ability of defending colluder truncation attacks, our protocol requires communications between servers after agent's migration and may increase communication overhead.

Communication includes the overhead for the mobile agent's migration and k hops backwards message transmission over the LAN to build a chain. Using the Sniffer tool in JADE, we can get the volume of total transferred messages according to different parameter k for 16 hosts in our environment. In our implementation, each host generated two residing agents to simulate two different hosts such that less simulating computers are required to simulate more hosts. Table 3 and figure 3 show the communication results. We can find that the volume of k hops backwards message transmission varies with different k parameters. The size of mobile agent is 117 kilo bytes and is not included in the messages table 3.

Table 3. Messages under N Hosts and k Hops Backwards (Kbytes)

Messages		k hops backwards					
		1	2	3	4	5	6
N hosts	4	2.3	6.1	12.2			
	8	5.5	16.1	43.2	101.5	213.6	405.1
	12	8.6	26.1	74.2	188.3	441.5	983.9
	16	12.1	36.2	105.2	275.1	669.3	1562.7

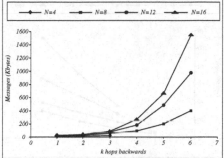 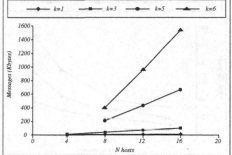

Fig. 3. Messages under k hops backwards   **Fig. 4.** Messages under different N hosts

Figure 4 depicts the relation between the volume of message transmission and the number of visited hosts under certain k hops backwards.

From the testing results, we know that mobile agent's migration communication overhead is necessary and is proportional to the servers that the mobile agent visited in all with various k hops backwards. But the total volume of message transmission is not proportional to the k value. The relation between the total volume of message transmission and the value k is exponential. So, we need to find a suitable value k for various application environments to avoid huge communication overheads. The volume of messages transmission is mainly caused by the encryption of RSA public keys.

5.2.3 Response Time Evaluation

In order to defend the multiple-colluded truncation attacks, we prefer to integrate more hops backwards to the chain in the security protocol. However, more hops backwards will cause more communication overhead, more processing time and eventually downgrade the protocol performance. The response time includes the time for message transmission, mobile agent migration time and the processing time for each related host. The response time can be shown in table 4 and figure 5. We can find that the total response time varies with different k parameter and the total number of visited hosts.

Figure 6 depicts the relation between the total time and the number of visited hosts under certain k hops backwards.

Table 4. Total Time under N Hosts and k Hops Backwards (Seconds)

Total time		k hops backwards					
		1	2	3	4	5	6
N hosts	4	5	6	7			
	8	12	16	18	23	28	37
	12	19	26	29	32	44	69
	16	31	35	41	53	70	116

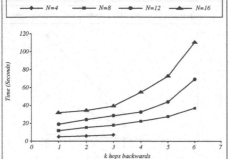 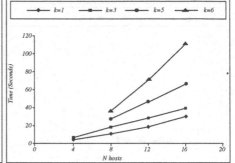

Fig. 5. Total Time under k hops backwards   **Fig. 6.** Total Time under different N hosts

From the testing results, we know that the total time for mobile agent's traveling is proportional to the servers under various k hops backwards. But the relation between the total time and the value k is exponential. So, we need to find a suitable value k practical application to avoid large response time.

5.2.4 Optimal Configuration
Based on implementation and simulation results, the balance point of the numbers of hops backwards to satisfy both security and performance should be and can be identified. As the distribution of multiple-colluded attackers indicated in 5.2.1, the length of adjacent multiple-colluded attacker is very small in practical environment, so the value of k hops backwards can be chosen between 2 and 5, such that both security and performance requirement can be satisfied.

6 Conclusion

Based on anonymous onion routing, our protocol uses a "two hops forwards and k hops backwards" chain relation to build a free-roaming agent security protocol to implement all of the generally accepted security properties while supporting privacy protection. The protocol is designed especially to defend multiple-colluder truncation attacks and many of its special cases. The solution based on anonymous onion routing satisfies the privacy protection requirements.

Compared with other free-roaming agent security protocols, this protocol has no requirements for confidential channels and co-signs on encrypted contents. By using anonymous onion routing information, no host is required to preserve such connection status information such as its successor, predecessor. This feature is very important in practical applications to simplify the implementations. Like other protocols with ability of defending colluder truncation attacks [4, 8], this protocol requires communications between servers after agent migrations and may increase communication overhead or cause the process fail if the backwards visited server are not available. This problem can be addressed by using some re-encryption mechanism for replacing those relay nodes which fail. The result shows that by choosing right k hops backwards parameter this protocol will satisfy communication overhead and response time and meet both the generally accepted mobile agent security and anonymity requirements. This protocol offers many unique and attractive features to protect free-roaming agents in a distributed environment. In the future, we plan to simulate the protocol through and deploy it in a larger test environment.

Acknowledgments. This work is supported by National Natural Science Foundation of China under Grants No. 90604004, Jiangsu Provincial Natural Science Foundation of China under Grants No. BK2007708, Jiangsu Provincial Key Laboratory of Network and Information Security under Grants No. BM2003201, Key Laboratory of Computer Network and Information Integration (Southeast University), Ministry of Education under Grants No. 93K-9 and International Science and Technology Cooperation Program of China.

References

1. Karjoth, G., Asokan, N., Gülcü, C.: Protecting the computation results of free-roaming agents. In: Rothermel, K., Hohl, F. (eds.) MA 1998. LNCS, vol. 1477, pp. 195–207. Springer, Heidelberg (1998)
2. Karnik, N.M., Tripathi, A.R.: Security in the Ajanta Mobile Agent System. Technical Report TR-5-99, University of Minnesota, Minneapolis, MN 55455, USA (1999)
3. Corradi, A., Montanari, R., Stefanelli, C.: Mobile agents Protection in the Internet Environment. In: 23rd Annual International Computer Software and Applications Conference (COMPSAC 1999), Phoenix, AZ, USA, pp. 80–85 (1999)
4. Xu, D., Harn, L., Narasimhan, M., Luo, J.: An Improved Free-Roaming Mobile Agent Security Protocol against Colluded Truncation Attacks. In: 30th Annual International Computer Software and Applications Conference (COMPSAC 2006), Chicago, USA, pp. 309–314 (2006)
5. Cheng, J., Wei, V.: Defenses against the truncation of computation results of free-roaming agents. In: 4th International Conference on Information and Communications Security, Singapore, pp. 1–12 (2002)
6. Yao, M., Foo, E., Dawson, E.P., Peng, K.: An Improved Forward Integrity Protocol for Mobile Agents. In: 4th International Workshop on Information Security Applications (WISA 2003, Jeju Island, Korea, pp. 272–285 (2003)

7. Songsiri, S.: A New Approach for Computation Result Protection in the Mobile Agent Paradigm. In: 10th IEEE Symposium on Computers and Communications (ISCC 2005), Cartagena, Spain, pp. 575–581 (2005)
8. Zhou, J., Onieva, J., Lopez, J.: Protecting Free Roaming Agents against Result-Truncation Attack. In: 60th IEEE Vehicular Technology Conference, Los Angles, USA, pp. 3271–3274 (2004)
9. Reed, M.G., Syverson, P.F., Goldschlag, D.M.: Anonymous connections and onion routing. IEEE Journal Selected Areas in Communications 16(4), 482–494 (1998)
10. Gomez-Martinez, E., Ilarri, S., Merseguer, J.: Performance analysis of mobile agents tracking. In: 6th international workshop on Software and performance, Buenes Aires, Argentina, pp. 181–188 (2007)
11. Chmiel, K., Gawinecki, M., Kaczmarek, P., Szymczak, M., Paprzycki, M.: Efficiency of JADE agent platform. Scientific Programming 13(2), 159–172 (2005)

Secure Ethernet Point-to-Point Links for Autonomous Electronic Ballot Boxes

Armando Astarloa, Unai Bidarte, Jaime Jiménez, Jesús Lázaro,
and Iñigo Martinez de Alegría

Department of Electronics and Telecommunications, Faculty of Engineering,
University of the Basque Country
Urquijo s/n, 48013 Bilbao - Spain
{jtpascua,jtpbipeu,jtpjivej,jtplaarj,jtpmamai}@bi.ehu.es

Abstract. Rapid growth of computer networks and advances in cryptographic techniques allow new approaches of electronic voting systems. In this research, we present a System-on-Programmable-Chip crypto-bridge module that enables secure ethernet point-to-point connections between electronic ballot boxes and the remote host of the central electoral office through insecure Ethernet networks. The proposed crypto-bridge is implemented using reconfigurable devices, and two implementations are presented: a single channel module and multi-channel module. HDL source code of the AES cipher, Ethernet MAC controller and tiny processor embedded in the crypto-bridge is public and open enforcing the confidence in the system.

1 Introduction

In order to explain the motivation of the presented research, two fields must be contextualized: the electronic ballot boxes and the widely use of Ethernet standard for network communications.

Taking into account the rapid growth of computer networks and advances in cryptographic techniques, electronic polling over the Internet is now becoming a real option for voters who have access to the Net. However, electronic democracy must be based on electronic voting systems that have the following properties as described by Cranor et al. [1]: accuracy, invulnerability, privacy, verifiability, and convenience. Internet voting systems are still under development, it seems that it will take time before they can become widely available to all citizens [2,3]. But in this context, there are available new electronic voting system that are accurate, invulnerable, private, verifiable, convenient, and compatible with electoral traditions. One example is the electronic ballot box presented in [4,5] that uses OCR techniques to automatically read paper ballots and digital communication techniques to transmit electoral results to the central electoral office, where results coming from all voting boxes will be counted. This electronic ballot is an embedded system (ARM CPU core based) with Ethernet communications capabilities.

C. Rong et al. (Eds.): ATC 2008, LNCS 5060, pp. 603–614, 2008.

Ethernet networks are widely implemented in Local Area Networks (LANs). However, the use of this well known standard is being extended to Metropolitan Area Networks (MANs). In the context of broadband services providers are introducing new point-to-point Ethernet services [6]. Some of the keys for this success are summarized as follows:

- It is a well known technology and the consumer devices can include very low cost 10/100/1000 Mbps Ethernet links.
- Nowadays, the Internet Protocol (IP) is used world-wide for data, voice and video transport. This evolution helps the Ethernet expansion because it is not a connection-oriented network and it is optimized for IP packets traffic.
- Ethernet technology, in conjunction with switching, full duplex and autosensing, allows users to adjust the required performance within the network to their exact requirements. This feature is favoring the expansion of Ethernet in industrial networks used for production and automation. Industrial Ethernet can be easily linked with the company Intranet and Internet.
- The simplicity of the Ethernet frame structure eases 'on-the-fly' communication packet hardware processing. This high-speed computation scheme is necessary in many scenarios for example, when applying intensive cryptographic algorithms to high speed channels [7].

Taking into account the expansion of Ethernet networks, the need for secure Ethernet solutions is rapidly growing [8,9]. And this growth is not only related to personal computers or servers, but to a heterogeneous group of machines as well. Good examples are casino gambling machines, digital scale networks or electronic ballot boxes. In those contexts, the need for secure communications with autonomous means is mandatory. The challenge in securizing communications networks is to obtain flexible means which are able to deal with the intensive computation needed by the cryptographic algorithms. But, in general, the control of these machines is carried out by embedded systems. And embedded systems are fundamentally processor-based devices operating under resource-constrained conditions, like the electronic ballot box described in this research. The embedded systems pose severe resource constraints on terms of computational capacity and memory [10]. The cryptographic algorithms computation requirements are so high for a conventional embedded processor device, that most of its computation capacity would be needed if that computation was performed by software. For many embedded systems, this situation is not affordable.

In order to deal with this drawback, processors most commonly used for industrial applications such as ColdFire, have embedded cryptographic cores (crypto-cores) in the same device [11]. Using this approach, the frame encryption and decryption is performed by hardware, freeing the main processor core from this task. The main drawback of this approach is the limited flexibility that it shows. These embedded processors are ASIC technology. Thus, the crypto-core is fixed on terms of algorithm implementation and interfaces; both for the software interface and for the communication media controller peripheral or core.

Besides the ASIC processor-based embedded systems solution, the industry is massively adopting the core-based design methodology for system integration using Field-Programmable-Gate-Arrays (FPGAs), which leads to the appearance of the System-on-Programmable-Chip (SoPC) platforms [12]. Taking into account the fact that FPGAs do not incur in non-recurring engineering charges due to their reconfigurable nature, the number and diversity of the available IP cores for digital systems composition has heavily increased [13,14]. The SoPCs are very flexible in different ways: number and type of IP cores and processors, bus architecture, hardware and software co-processing, etc. This flexibility allows very short time-to-market and facilitates custom device design for every industry and application. The SoPC technology faces the secure communication paradigm with the maximum flexibility: Depending on the application, different crypto-cores and communication media controller cores can be included in the FPGA device. For the secure communication section of the SoPC, the designer is in charge of finding the best FPGA resource occupation-data throughput trade-off and the optimum IP licence cost as well.

The research that we present in this paper, aims to find a solution to establish point-to-point secure Ethernet links between electronic ballot boxes and a central electoral office through insecure Ethernet networks (for example, through an Ethernet MAN). The proposed solution is focused on the SoPC technology and methodology, and integrates Open Source cryptographic algorithms hardware engines and Open Source Ethernet controllers [15].

The remainder of this paper is organized into five sections. In section 2 the network scenario for this application is presented. Sections 3 and 4 detail the proposed architecture for the single channel and for the multichannel versions of the crypto-bridge respectively. In Section 5, the implementation results for both versions are summarized. The paper ends in Section 6, with the conclusions and future work.

2   Secure Electronic Ballot Box

Figure 1 shows the connection scheme to secure the connection among two electronic ballot boxes (SECURED E-BALLOT BOX 0 and SECURED E-BALLOT BOX 1) and the host computer of the central electoral office.

Each SECURED E-BALLOT BOX integrates an embedded CPU with Ethernet capabilities. So, each CPU has its own Ethernet MAC address. For example in the network scenario represented in Figure 1, MAC ADDR 0 is the MAC address for the SECURED E-BALLOT BOX 0, and MAC ADDR 1 and REMOTE HOST MAC ADDR are the addresses for the SECURED E-BALLOT BOX 1 and for the central electoral office host computer respectively. The connection with the remote host is done through a non-secure Ethernet net.

In order to provide a secure point-to-point link between electronic ballot boxes and the remote host, each SECURED E-BALLOT BOX integrates an OSCRYB module (OSCRYB 0 and OSCRYB 1) [16]. The OSCRYBs run as Ethernet bridges between different physical Ethernet networks, but apart from this task, they are able to filter Ethernet frames for a given MAC address pair. If the Ethernet frames do not match these addresses, they are transferred transparently between the Ethernet networks. If a frame matches, it is processed attending to the order that the MAC addresses have into the packet address fields.

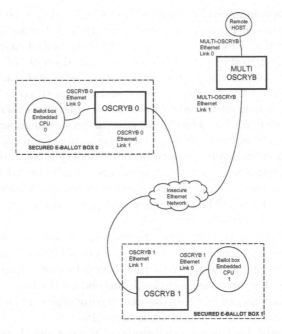

Fig. 1. Secure electronic ballot boxes network integration

In the central office remote host side, a multi-channel OSCRYB (MULTI-OSCRYB) module is located between the insecure Ethernet Network and the secure Ethernet LAN of the central electoral office where the remote host is stated. As will be detailed in Section 4, each MULTI-OSCRYB SoPC embeds OSCRYB modules as many SECURED E-BALLOT BOX are connected to the insecure Ethernet network. This redundancy offers an unique point-to-point secure link with an specific key pair for each ballot box and ensures the necessary computation power for the network analysis and cryptographic tasks.

For example, the point-to-point link between the SECURED E-BALLOT BOX 0 and the central office remote host will work at follows: In the OSCRYB 0 Ethernet Link 0, if MAC ADDR 0 matches the Ethernet local address packet field, and REMOTE HOST MAC ADDR matches the Ethernet remote address packet field of an incoming packet, then it is encoded and transferred ciphered to the MULTI-OSCRYB 1 Ethernet Link 1. If the OSCRYB 0 Ethernet Link 1 receives a ciphered packet with the MAC ADDR 0 in the remote address packet field and REMOTE HOST MAC ADDR in the local address packet field, then it is deciphered and transferred to the Ballot box embedded CPU 0. The MULTI-OSCRYB channel that is in charge of ciphering the Ethernet point-to-point connection between SECURED E-BALLOT BOX 0 and the central office remote host works in a similar manner, but with the matching MAC addresses reversed.

Using this mode of operation, the establishment of secure channels between heterogeneous devices connected to Ethernet networks is an easy and little intrusive task. However, as all the necessary computation is performed in the

OSCRYB crypto-bridges, these must be designed with a powerful architecture that provides the means to ensure the necessary dataflow.

3   OSCRYB SoPC Architecture

Figure 2 summarizes the internal dataflow in an OSCRYB. Two Open Source Ethernet IP Medium Access Controllers IP cores [17], ETHERNET MAC IP 0 and ETHERNET MAC IP 1, are in charge of controlling the OSCRYB Ethernet Links 0 and 1. The incoming network traffic through the OSCRYB Ethernet Link 0 is transferred to the cryptographic SEC-enc core by the ETHERNET IP 0. This SEC core is configured to perform encoding operations, and it is in charge of filtering, ciphering and padding the frames with destination Device 1. These packets are transmitted to the ETHERNET MAC IP 1. The traffic received through the ETHERNET MAC IP 1 controller is filtered by a second SEC core (SEC-dec) configured to filter and decipher the frames with destination Device 0.

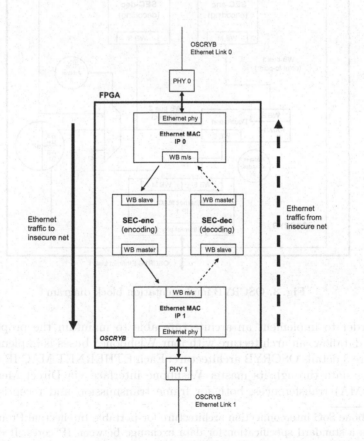

Fig. 2. OSCRYB block diagram

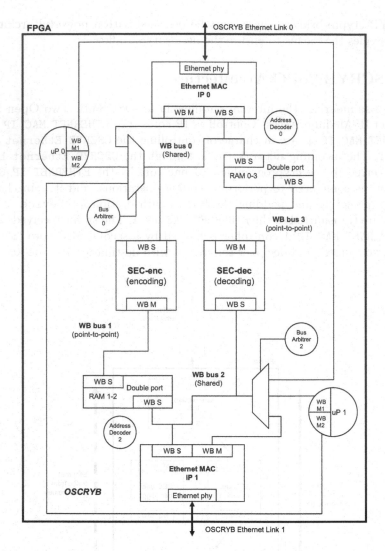

Fig. 3. OSCRYB implementation block diagram

In order to implement an architecture able to maintain the proposed full-duplex dataflow, an architecture with four Wishbone[1] buses is implemented.

Figure 3 details OSCRYB architecture: Each ETHERNET MAC IP controller transfers data through its master Wishbone interface via Direct Memory Access (DMA) transferences, both for frame transmission and reception. These

---

[1] Wishbone SoC interconnection architecture for portable Intellectual Property cores [18] is a standard specification for data exchange between IP cores. It defines the interfaces, what bus topologies are allowed and signaling. It is absolutely royalty free and is used to share open projects [19]. It provides high levels of robustness and flexibility.

transferences must be configured in the ETHERNET MAC IP cores' registers through their slave Wishbone interfaces using a configuration blocks called 'Buffer Descriptors' [17]. In the same way, SEC modules have configuration registers, as the cryptographic KEY and packet length before and after the ciphering, that must be accessed to configure the data transfers.

Two tiny control microcontrollers, uP-0 and uP-1, have been included in each OSCRYB module to control the dataflows and to configure these registers for each transfer. uP-0 is in charge of controlling data transfers to the insecure Ethernet network and the uP-1 configures the transferences received from this network. These control processors are based on the tiny soft 8 bit processor PicoBlaze [20]. The software is stored in the internal dedicated memory of the FPGA and the processors are implemented using general purpose FPGA logic. For this application, each processor has been provided with two master Wishbone interfaces (WB M1 and WB M2).

uP-0 using its WB M1 interface configures ETHERNET MAC IP 0 to transfer the frames received from the OSCRYB Ethernet Link 0 to the SEC-enc. These frames after having been filtered and if it is the case, ciphered, are temporally stored in intermediary RAM memory (Double port RAM 1-2). uP-0 through its WB M2 interface configures a ETHERNET MAC IP 1 'Buffer Descriptor' to initiate the DMA transfer that moves the ciphered frame from Double port RAM 1-2 to the OSCRYB Ethernet Link 1. uP-1 works in a similar way but controlling the dataflow from ETHERNET MAC IP 1 to ETHERNET MAC IP 0.

To implement the described operativity some auxiliary elements are necessary in the architecture. Wishbone bus 0 has a shared bus interconnection topology that links three slaves interfaces ETHERNET MAC IP 0, SEC-enc (encoding) and one port of Double port RAM 0-3 with three master interfaces: ETHERNET MAC IP 0 master interface, uP0 WB M1 and uP1 WB M2. In a similar way, Wishbone bus 2 carries the transferences to ETHERNET MAC IP 1, to SEC (decoding), to the second intermediary double port RAM memory (Double port RAM 1-2), from ETHERNET MAC IP 1 and from both tiny control microcontrollers.

Wishbone bus 1 and Wishbone bus 3 are Wishbone point-to-point buses that link SEC cores with double port RAM memories implemented using FPGA dedicated memory [21]. The aim of these memories is to provide an intermediary storage space necessary to synchronize all the transfers.

OSCRYB crypto-bridge uses the SEC core to process Ethernet frames 'on-the-fly'. The heart of the SEC module is a frame processor that embeds a frame filter logic and cryptographic algorithm hardware. It offers flexible means able to deal with the intensive computation needed by the cryptography algorithms. The selected algorithm is the Rijndael [22,23]. This is one of the widest cryptography algorithm. It was selected by The National Institute of Standards and Technology (NIST) for the Advanced Encryption Standard (AES) [24]. NIST adopted Rijndael algorithm with 128 bit block size. It combines a 128 bit key and a 128 bit unencrypted data block to get a 128 bit block of ciphered data, and applying the same operations in reverse order using the same key, the plaintext data may be recovered from the ciphered vector. To process messages or packets into blocks it is necessary to define the block cipher's mode of operation. NIST has a list of 16 different modes [25]. A detailed description of the SEC module is presented in [16].

4   MULTI-OSCRYB SoPC Architecture

Thanks to the high density level of the modern FPGAs and to the modularity of the OSCRYB, it is viable to integrate many OSCRYBs in a single high capacity FPGA device.

Each OSCRYB module embedded on a MULTI-OSCRYB SoPC secures one point-to-point Ethernet link. Depending on the size of the reconfigurable device, the MULTI-OSCRYB will be able to connect a different number of SECURED E-BALLOT BOXs to the insecure Ethernet network. Figure 4 represents a simplified block diagram of a generic MULTI-OSCRYB SoPC for n SECURED E-BALLOT BOX. Because of OSCRYB module has not only its SEC modules but two Ethernet MAC controllers as well, different network topologies can be adopted for a given scenario. As an example, in the model depicted in Figure 4, all the physical Ethernet links are joined using a HUB.

5   Implementation Results

A single OSCRYB SoPC, like the proposed for the SECURED E-BALLOT BOX is a 'Single channel' implementation. For this module, the low cost Xilinx Spartan-3 family has been selected.

For the MULTI-OSCRYB (a 'Multiple Channel' implementation), the high capacity Xilinx Virtex-4 family is the best option for the required resources. For all of the implementations considered, the two intermediate double port RAM memories have 128 Kbytes of capacity. Taking into account this size, for each memory 8 internal BlockRAMs are necessary. The AES implementation that we have used in this development, the R. Usselmann Open Source HDL AES high speed one [26], uses 7 BlockRAMs. Moreover, each control tiny processor stores its program in one memory BlockRAM, so, two more consumed RAM memory blocks must be taken into account for each OSCRYB module instantiation.

Table 1 summarizes the implementation results for a single OSCRYB. If we take into account that the Ethernet controller IP core embedded in each OSCRYB is capable of operating up to 100 Mbps, and that the real dataflow obtained for the internet OSCRYB ciphering and filtering engine (the SEC module) is higher than 100 Mbps, we can ensure that the system will be able to process the channel optimally.

The implementation results after synthesis, mapping and routing stages of a MULTI-OSCRYB are detailed in Table 2. The Virtex-4 xc4vlx160-11ff1513 FPGA is used as reference. This device embeds 152.064 Logic Cells and 5.184 Kbits of dedicated RAM memory. The maximum number of OSCRYB modules for this device is 8.

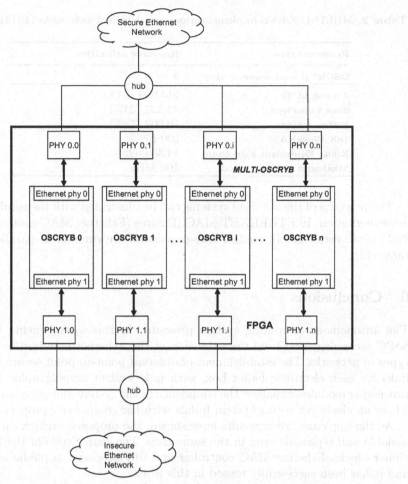

Fig. 4. MULTI-OSCRYB implementation block diagram

Table 1. Single channel OSCRYB SoPC implementation on a Spartan-3 xc3s1500-5fg320 FPGA

Resources type	Resource utilization
4 input LUTs	13.990 (20%)
Slice Flip-Flops	5.555 (52%)
Spartan-3 Slices	8.957 (67%)
18K BlockRAM	21 (65%)
Xilinx Equivalent gate count	1.552.007
Maximum running speed	75 MHz
SEC max. data throughput	139 Mbit/s

Table 2. MULTI-OSCRYB implementation on a Virtex-4 xc4vlx200-11ff1513 FPGA

Resources type	Resource utilization
OSCRYB modules on-a-chip	8
4 input LUTs	114.929 (64%)
Slice Flip-Flops	43.227 (24%)
Virtex-4 Slices	70.002 (78%)
18K BlockRAM	200 (59%)
Xilinx Equivalent gate count	14.366.622
Maximum running speed	100 MHz

The powerful of the obtained systems can be illustrated with the results of this implementation: 16 ETHERNET MAC IP cores (Ethernet MAC controllers), 16 SEC crypto-cores and 16 control tiny-processors are running in parallel in the same chip.

6 Conclusions

The autonomous computing system presented in this work benefits from the SoPC technology and from the extension of the Ethernet standard in different types of networks. The establishment of different point-to-point secure Ethernet links for each electronic ballot box, with independent cryptographic keys and processing modules, enhances the confidence in the system and offers an scenario where an electronic voting system fulfills with the compulsory properties.

As the implementation results have shown, the proposed architecture is fully scalable and replicable even in the same chip. The source code of the two AES cipher blocks, Ethernet MAC controller and tiny processor is public and open; and it has been successfully reused in this work.

This research promotes the integration of secure communications in electronic ballot boxes. The future work in this line is multidisciplinary: Future tasks related with electronic design will be focused on the integration of the new high-speed encryption, authentication algorithms and enhancement of the control software for the tiny processors. In the same way, telematic research will be needed in order to propose optimized protocols for dynamic key interchange between OSCRYB modules.

Acknowledgment

This work is developed in the framework of the project 'Embedded crypto-bridge for electronic voting applications' (EJIE07/03), a public research project funded by the agreement of the University of the Basque Country and EJIE S.A. (UPV/EHU-EJIE 2007).

References

1. Cranor, L.F., Cytron, R.K.: Sensus: A Security-Conscious Electronic Polling System for the Internet. In: Proceedings of the Hawaii International Conference on Systems Sciences, pp. 7–10 (1997)
2. MTI. Voting, what is what could be, caltech mit voting technology project (July 2001), http://web.mit.edu/voting/
3. California Internet Voting Task Force. A report on the feasibility of internet voting (January 2000), http://www.ss.ca.gov/executive/ivote/final_report.htm
4. Goirizelaia, I., Espinosa, K., Martin, J.L., Lázaro, J., Arias, J., Igarza, J.J.: An Electronic Secure Voting System Based on Automatic Paper Ballot Reading. In: Sanfeliu, A., Martínez Trinidad, J.F., Carrasco Ochoa, J.A. (eds.) CIARP 2004. LNCS, vol. 3287, pp. 470–477. Springer, Heidelberg (2004)
5. Espinosa, J.K., Goirizelaia, I., Igarza, J.J.: OCR Applied to an Electronic Voting System. Pattern Recognition and Image Analysis 17(4), 457–461 (2007)
6. IEEE-SA Standards Board. IEEE 802.1XTM. IEEE Standard for Local and metropolitan area networks – Port-Based Network Access Control. IEEE-SA Standards (2004)
7. Chodowiec, P., Gaj, K., Bellows, P., Schott, B.: Experimental Testing of the Gigabit IPSec-Compliant Implementations of Rijndael and Triple DES Using SLAAC-1V FPGA Accelerator Board. In: Proceedings of the Information Security Conference, pp. 220–234 (October 2001)
8. IEEE-SA Standards Board. IEEE 802.11iTM. IEEE Standard for Information Technology – Telecommunications and information exchange between systems – Local and metropolitan area networks – Specific requirements – Part 11: Wireless LAN Medium Access Control (MAC) and Physical Layer (PHY) specifications – Amendment 6: Medium Access Control (MAC) Security Enhancements. IEEE-SA Standards (2004)
9. Sáiz, P.: A model for establishing secure sessions at the link layer between endpoints in Ethernet networks. PhD thesis, Faculty of Engineeering. UPV/EHU (October 2007)
10. Hwang, D.D., Schaumont, P., Tiri, K., Verbauwhede, I.: Securing Embedded Systems. IEEE Security and Privacy 4(2), 40–49 (2006)
11. Inc. Freescale Semiconductor. ColdFire Security: SEC and Hardware Encryption Acceleration Overview. Freescale Semiconductor Application Note 2788 (2003), http://www.freescale.com/files/32bit/doc/app_note/AN2788.pdf
12. Martin, G., Chang, H. (eds.): Winning the SoC Revolution: Experiences in Real Design. Kluwer Academic Publishers, Massachusetts (2003)
13. Zorian, Y., Gupta, R.K.: Introducing Core-Based System Design. IEEE Design & Test of Computers 14(4), 15–25 (1997)
14. Bergamaschi, R.A., Bhattacharya, S., Wagner, R., Fellenz, C., Muhlada, M.: Automating the Design of SOCs Using Cores. IEEE Design & Test of Computers 18(5), 32–45 (2001)
15. OpenCores Comunity. OpenCores: Free open source IP Cores and Chip Design (2004), http://www.opencores.org
16. Astarloa, A., Bidarte, U., Lázaro, J., Arias, J., Olaguenaga, E.: OSCRYB: Open Source CRYpto-Bridge for Secure Ethernet point-to-point Industrial Communications. In: Proceedings of the 33nd Annual Conference of the IEEE Industrial Electronics Society (IECON 2007) (November 2007)

17. Nguyen, K., Mohor, I., Markovic, T.: OpenCores Ethernet MAC 10/100 Mbps: Overview (2006),
    http://www.opencores.org/projects.cgi/web/ethmac/overview
18. Silicore Corporation. Wishbone System-on-Chip (SoC) Interconnection Architecture for Portable IP Cores Revision: B.3 (September 2002),
    http://www.opencores.org
19. Rudolf Usselmann. SoC Bus Review, http://www.opencores.org
20. Chapman, K.: PicoBlaze 8-Bit Microcontroller for Virtex-E and Spartan II/IIE Devices. Xilinx Application Notes (February 2003), http://www.xilinx.com
21. Xilinx Corp. Using Block SelectRAM+ Memory in Spartan II FPGAs. Xilinx Application Notes (December 2000), http://www.xilinx.com
22. Daemen, J., Rijmen, V.: Rijndael: Algorithm Specification (2001),
    http://csrc.nist.gov/encryption/aes/rijndael/
23. Astarloa, A., Sáiz, P., Lázaro, J., Jacob, E., Bidarte, U.: Multi-architectural 128 bit AES-CBC Core based on Open-Source Hardware AES Implementations for Secure Industrial Communications. In: Proceedings of the 10th International Conference on Communication Technology (ICCT2006), pp. 221–226 (November 2006)
24. Gaj, K., Chodowiec, P.: Comparison of the Hardware Performance of the AES Candidates Using Reconfigurable Hardware. In: Proceedings of The Third Advanced Encryption Standard Candidate Conference, pp. 40–54 (April 2000)
25. National Institute of Standards and Technology. Cryptographic Toolkit. Modes of Operations. Computer Security Resource Center (2005),
    http://csrc.nist.gov/CryptoToolkit/tkmodes.html
26. Usselmann, R.: AES (Rijndael) IP Core (2002),
    http://www.opencores.org/projects.cgi/web/aes_core/overview

Wireless Sensor Network Assisted Dynamic Path Planning for Transportation Systems

Yue-Shan Chang[1], Tong-Ying Juang[1], and Chen-Yi Su[2]

[1] Department of Computer Science and Information Engineering, National Taipei University
151, University Road, Sanhsia, Taipei County, 237, TAIWAN, R.O.C.
{ysc,juang}@mail.ntpu.edu.tw
http://web.ntpu.edu.tw/~ysc/
[2] Institute of Information Management, National Taipei University
151, University Road, Sanhsia, Taipei County, 237 TAIWAN, R.O.C.
brojac@gmail.com

Abstract. The static path planning of transportation network is only considering the shortest-path from source to destination. The approach cannot adjust the path dynamically when the predetermined path is obstructed. It could increase the traveling time to destination and could not effectively plan the path with shortest time. In this paper we propose a Wireless Sensor Network (WSN) assisted framework for dynamic path planning for transportation systems, which collects the traffic information dynamically using sensor nodes and plan the path of transportation network with shortest time using Satellite Navigation System. The WSN can be used for calculating the estimated traveling time and looking for a shortest-time path by way of fusing the traffic information, such as average speed and number of vehicles in a timeframe, collected from the candidate path. Users can thus use handheld device, such as PDA, with GPS (Global Position System) and GIS (Geographic Information System) to dynamically plan the path via requesting the WSN to collect traffic information. It can perform better than the static path planning approach.

1 Introduction

With advances in computing hardware/software and wireless communication, the Satellite Navigation System (SNS) can be embedded into a handheld device, such as PDA (Personal Digital Assistant), by merging with GPS (Global Position System) and GIS (Geographic Information System) to assist users with planning their travel path. Such technology can also be adopted in monitoring the location of mobile equipment, searching scenic resort, and navigating to destination with shortest path.

Wireless Sensor Networks (WSN) [1] comprise a great volume of sensor nodes that are fully autonomous with many inherent characteristics, such as limited computation power and resources, energy constraints, limited reliability, and lower communication capabilities. They can be used to monitor environmental information [2], target detection, object tracking, and traffic network monitoring [3, 5, 8, 9] via deploying massive and inexpensive sensor nodes. These sensor nodes may have multiple sensing elements

C. Rong et al. (Eds.): ATC 2008, LNCS 5060, pp. 615–628, 2008.
© Springer-Verlag Berlin Heidelberg 2008

for collecting and responding to environmental information by collaborating internal part of network such as data/value fusion [6, 7], routing algorithm [4], data gathering, and data aggregation. The system based on WSN can thus make a real time decision by collecting and fusing the information from sensor nodes.

The path planning of transportation network in the Satellite Navigation System is in general using static path planning approach. It is mainly considering the distance from source to destination. The approach to users may not be efficient because it cannot adjust the path dynamically when the predetermined path gets obstructed. It might increase traveling time to destination and could not effectively plan the path with shorter time.

Finding a shortest-time path requires estimating the traveling time of each possible link and then computing the possible shorter-time paths. Obviously, the efficient path to destination is not based on the distance but rather the time to destination. The vehicle should dynamically change the route when the time to destination is larger than other paths. For example, in the Fig. 1, path 1-2-5-7-8 result in shortest time (3+4+4+4=15 time units) to destination 8 at first time instance, and this path is hence chosen by the driver. But, when the vehicle is at link 1-2, the time of link 2-5 is changed to 15 time units due to some obstruction at link 2-5. The shortest time to 8 is now 2-4-5-7-8 (7+4+4+4=19) which is less than the previous path 2-5-7-8 (15+4+4 = 23). And, when the vehicle is at link 2-4, the time of link 4-5 is changed to 6 time units and link 5-7 is changed to 6 time units due to obstructions at link 4-5 and 5-7, respectively. The shortest time to 8 is the path 4-7-8 (10+5=15) which is less than the previous path 4-5-7-8 (6+6+5 = 17).

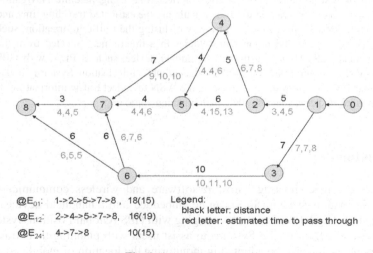

@E_{01}:   1->2->5->7->8 ,   18(15)   Legend:
                                          black letter: distance
@E_{12}:   2->4->5->7->8,   16(19)   red letter: estimated time to pass through
@E_{24}:   4->7->8   10(15)

Fig. 1. An example scenario

In this paper we propose a Wireless Sensor Network (WSN) assisted framework for dynamic path planning for transportation systems. The framework can dynamically adjust and suggest the traveling path for moving vehicle for improving the problem of static path planning approach by collecting the traffic information dynamically using sensor nodes and planning path of transportation network in Satellite

Navigation System. The WSN can be used to calculate the possible traveling time and look for a shortest-time path by way of fusing the traffic information, such as average speed and number of vehicles in a timeframe, collected from the candidate path. Users can thus use handheld devices, such as PDA which with GPS (Global Position System) and GIS (Geographic Information System), to dynamically plan the path via requesting the WSN to collect traffic information.

The system is assumed that the handheld device can automatically issue the request to the WSN for re-looking for possible shorter-time path from the candidate paths when the vehicle is closing to an intersection. In the framework, we model the traffic network utilizing the *Macroscopic Model* and compute the possible shorter-time path by *on-demand heuristic algorithm* when the traveling time of each link calculated in the candidate paths. The simulation result shows the framework can effectively adjust the traveling path and improve the problem of static path planning problem.

The remainder of the paper is organized as follows. Section 2 presents the traffic network model. We examine assumptions, system parameters, and sensor nodes configuration. Section 3 shows the time estimation approach of traffic path and link. Section 4 shows and examines the simulation result. Section 5 reviews some related works. Finally, we give conclusion in Section 6.

2 Traffic Network Model

2.1 Network Components and Assumptions

Here we define the network architecture and make some assumptions used in the system. Fig. 2 shows the components and network architecture of the system. The system consists of GPS, handheld device with GPS receiver and GIS, and WSN. The WSN comprises a sensing node (SN) and a cross node (CN). The CN is deployed on intersection and SN is deployed along with the link between two intersections. The network architecture of WSN is cluster-based WSN [14].

All links connected to an intersection can be viewed a cluster, and CN is a cluster head in the WSN. SN is responsible for sensing the number of passing vehicles and calculating their average speed, while CN is responsible for forwarding request to related sensor of link, and getting and fusing the information from SNs. Each CN is also an SN but CN has more power than SN in the computing and communication. Every node has a node ID and a link ID. Each CN has all neighbors CNs' ID and physical location. The location can be the GPS's coordinate, which is used to determine the direction a request forwarded to.

When a vehicle that has a handheld device of the system approaches to an intersection, the handheld device can automatically contact to a CN and issue a request to look for next path to destination. The contacted CN (CCN) will issue the traveling time estimation procedure in order to look for next path. In addition, we make the same assumption as [10] that each sensor the energy can be supplied from roadside or streetlamp.

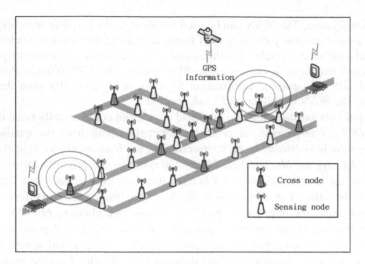

Fig. 2. Network architecture and components

2.2 Network Model

The network is simply assumed as an acyclic graph G = (V, E); here V is a set of vertices and E is a set of edges between vertices. A vertex can be a CN. E_{ij} represents a link from V_i to V_j. In order to without loss generality, the E_{ij} is different from E_{ji} because the traffic at the two directions is independent. In addition we define the parameters used in the model as follows:

- Link distance- L_{ij}: represents the length from E_i to E_j.
- Link speed limitation- α_{ij} : default limited speed of E_{ij}.
- Default link traveling time- λ_{ij} : the traveling time from E_i to E_j without any obstruction in the E_{ij} and the vehicle can pass through in the speed α_{ij} . The λ_{ij} is equal to L_{ij}/α_{ij} .
- Sensing Node ID (SN_ID)- S_k^{ij} : represents k^{th} sensing node in the E_{ij}.
- Cross Node ID (CN_ID)- Cm: the mth cross node in the network.
- Number of SN- N_{ij}: the number of sensing node in the E_{ij}.
- Distance of sublink- $R_{(k,\,k+1)}$: the length from S_k^{ij} to S_{k+1}^{ij}. The length can be computed from the location of S_k^{ij} and S_{k+1}^{ij} as follow.

$$R_{(k,\,k+1)} = \eta \times \sqrt{(X_k - X_{k+1})^2 + (Y_k - Y_{k+1})^2}$$

where (X_k, Y_k) is the GPS's coordinate of S_k^{ij} and (X_{k+1}, Y_{k+1}) is the GPS's coordinate of S_{k+1}^{ij}. η is a constant to map from coordinate to physical length.

To estimate the traveling time of a link we also need to define the parameter n_k that is the number of vehicle in a link in a time period. SN will count the number of vehicle that passing through the link during the time slot.

3 Traveling Time Estimation

In this section we present the time estimation approach used in the paper.

3.1 Time Estimation of Sub-link

The traveling time of a sub-link can be estimated by means of collecting the number of vehicle and their average speed between two sensing nodes. The time of a sub-link is an essential time we can evaluate. It can be estimated by computing the traffic information collected from two neighbor sensing nodes. The time of a link is the summation of all sub-links, such as C_m-$S_1^{m,m+1}$, $S_1^{m,m+1}$-$S_2^{m,m+1}$, ..., and $S_k^{m,m+1}$-C_{m+1}. The time of a sub-link can be estimated by using the traffic information sensed by sensing nodes. Then we can use *Macroscopic Model* [13] that is usually used in traffic network to computing the traveling time of the sub-link.

According to the Macroscopic Model, the relationship between traffic and density of sub-link can be modeled as a continuous fluid model, as shown in Fig. 3. We can thus compute the average speed and traveling time based on these two terms. The Macroscopic Model is as follow:

$$\frac{\partial}{\partial R} f(R,t) = \frac{\partial}{\partial t} d(R,t) \tag{1}$$

f : Traffic (Number of vehicle/Time)
d : Density (Number of vehicle/Length)
R : Location
t : Time

then

$$f = d \times \varepsilon \tag{2}$$

$$\varepsilon = \frac{f}{d} \tag{3}$$

where ε : Average speed in the sub-link

And the traveling time of the sub-link can be estimated as follow.

$$\lambda = \frac{\Delta R}{\varepsilon} = \frac{\Delta R}{f/d} = \frac{\Delta R.d}{f} = \frac{\Delta R.\{d_{(k+1)} + d_{(k)}\}}{\{f_{(k+1)} - f_{(k)}\}} \tag{4}$$

where λ : estimated traveling time

ΔR : sub-link length

$f_{(k)}(t)$: detected traffic of sensing node k at time t

$d_{(k)}(t)$: density of node k at time t

Traffic in a sub-link. The detected traffic in the SN S_{k+1}^{ij} at the time t can be represented as $f_{k+1}^{ij}(t) = \dfrac{(n_{k+1}^{ij} - n_k^{ij}) + C}{t}$, the C is a constant representing the number of vehicle resided in the sub-link between S_k^{ij} and S_{k+1}^{ij} before detection.

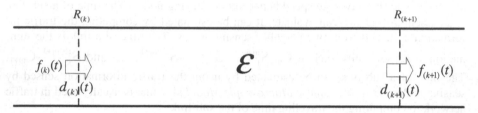

Fig. 3. Macroscopic Model

Density in a sub-link. The density of vehicle in the sub-link between SN S_k^{ij} and S_{k+1}^{ij} at time t can be represented as $d_{k+1}^{ij}(t) = \dfrac{(n_{k+1}^{ij} - n_k^{ij}) + C}{R_{(k+1,k)}}$. The C is same as above definition.

Average speed in sub-link. According the formula (3), we can compute the average speed in the sub-link between SN S_k^{ij} and S_{k+1}^{ij} as follow:

$$\varepsilon_{k+1}^{ij} = \frac{f_{k+1}^{ij}}{d_{k+1}^{ij}} = \frac{(n_{k+1}^{ij} - n_k^{ij}) + C}{t} \times \frac{\Delta R_{(k+1,k)}}{(n_{k+1}^{ij} - n_k^{ij}) + C} = \frac{\Delta R_{(k,k+1)}}{t} \qquad (5)$$

Traveling time of sub-link. The traveling time of sub-link k in the link i to j can be computed by the S_k^{ij} according to the formula (4) as follows.

$$\lambda_k^{ij} = \frac{\Delta R_{(k,\,k-1)}}{\varepsilon_k^{ij}} \qquad (6)$$

3.2 Time Estimation in a Link

The traveling time of a link is the summation of traveling time of all sub-links in the link. The requesting CN can fuse the collected result from all of SNs in the link and compute the traveling time of the link and reply the result to the requesting CN. We can represent the traveling time of a link as follows:

$$T_{ij} = (\lambda_1^{ij} + \lambda_2^{ij} + ... + \lambda_N^{ij}) = \sum_{k=1}^{N} \lambda_k^{ij} \qquad (7)$$

If a CN has more than one possible links to destination, the CN will fuse and compute the two traveling time of links respectively. For example, on an intersection CN_i, there are two possible links to destination that are CN_j and CN_k respectively. The CN_i will receive two replies from the two CNs. The CN_i so that will need to fuse the result of link i-j and i-k, and then reply the result to last CN. The detail requesting and forwarding algorithms will be presented in the next section.

3.3 Time Estimation of Traveling Path

The shortest path in general can be found using Dijkstra algorithm due to constant distance between two nodes. There are location-aware routing algorithms in sensor networks and ad hoc networks [15] researches to look for routing path. But the shortest-time routing path is possible of dynamical change and is associated with traveling time of link. Here we use an *on-demand heuristic algorithm* with GPS assisted to look for the shortest-time path to destination.

In order to without loss generality, we assume that the CN only have neighbor CN's ID and their physical location, and do not have any GIS information to destination. When a vehicle approaches a CN, the SNS in the mobile device will send the approached CN (CCN) a request to look for shortest-time path to destination. CCN will forward request and sensed traffic information to next CNs that approaching destination via near SN. SN and CN will compute cooperatively the traveling time of link.

For example, as shown in Fig. 4, when a vehicle approaches the CN_1, the mobile device with SMS send CN_1 (CCN) a request to look for the shortest-time path to

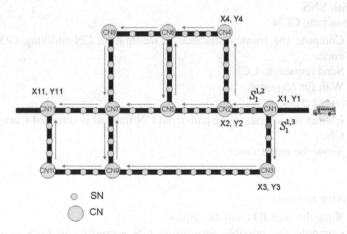

Fig. 4. Request forwarding flow

CN11. CN1 will forward the request with sensed information to CN_2 and CN_3 via $S_1^{1,2}$ and $S_1^{1,3}$ respectively. CN_2 will forward the request to CN_4 and CN_5, and CN_5 will also forward it to CN_6 and CN_7. Similarity, CN_6 forwards the request to CN_5 and CN_8. The request will finally be forwarded to destination (CN_{11}).

Obviously, the request might be forwarded repeatedly in some links. This problem can easily be solved by applying following two criteria while CN forwarding the request to destination.

$$Df <= c * Dsp$$

where   Df: accumulated forwarding distance.
                Dsp: the shortest distance from source to destination
                c: constant, assumed 1.5

The forwarding angle $\angle CN_p\text{-}CN_n\text{-}CN_d$ is large than $\pi/3$, where CN_d is destination CN, CN_p is current CN, and CN_n is next CN. That is:

$$\sin^{-1}\frac{\sqrt{(Y_d - Y_n)^2 + (X_d - X_n)^2}}{\sqrt{(Y_d - Y_p)^2 + (X_d - X_p)^2}} > \frac{\pi}{3}$$

First criterion can avoid looking for longer path in forwarding phase and reduce the number of forwarding. Second criterion is in order to ensure that forwarding direction. The context in the request is a five tuple, there are *CN list* from CCN to current CN, next CN, accumulated traveling time, accumulated distance, and shortest distance.

3.4 Algorithms

According to approach mentioned above, here shows the algorithms run on various nodes.

Vehicle with SNS
  a). approaching CCN:
    1. Compute the shortest distance to destination CN utilizing GIS for reference.
    2. Send request to CCN.
    3. Wait for response.
  b). receiving response:
    1. Extract the shortest-time path from CN list that is returned from destination CN.
    2. Show the path to user.

CCN
  a). receiving request:
    1. Keep the user ID from the request.
    2. Compute the possible forwarding CN according to GPS coordinates of neighbor CN, and add its own CN_ID to CN list.

    3. Send the request that involve the sensed data by CCN to possible forwarding CNs via neighbor SN in that direction.
    4. Wait for response.
  b). receiving response:
    1. Retrieve the CN list and forward it to user.

SN
  a). receiving request:
    1. SN will compute the sub-link traveling time λ_k^{ij} according to average vehicle speed and traffic of S_{k-1}^{ij} and S_k^{ij} and the sub total traveling time T_{ij}.
    2. Ccompute the accumulated distance.
    3. Send the request with sensed average speed, number of vehicle, accumulated distance, and T_{ij} to next SN.
  b). receiving response:
    1. Forward response to next SN.

Intermediate CN
  a). receiving request:
    1. Execute first two steps of SN in receiving request.
    2. Discard this request if accumulated distance is greater than c* Dsp. or continue step 3.
    3. Compute the possible forwarding CN according to GPS coordinates of neighbor CN, and add its own CN_ID to CN list.
    4. Send the request that involve the sensed data by the CN to possible forwarding CNs via neighbor SN in that direction.
    5. Wait for response.
  b). receiving response:
    1. Retrieve next CN from the CN list and forward the response to that CN.

Destination CN
  a). receive request:
    1. Wait for all requests from same user a time period.
    2. Select shortest-time path from the requests of same user and retrieve the CN list.
    3. Send back the response to CCN via shortest-time path shown in retrieved CN list.

4 Simulation

This simulation is using Matlab to simulate the traffic density and catch partial map from online e-map Urmap1. Fig. 5(a) shows the partial map that is from Zhongshan district to Da-an district in Taipei city.

---

[1] Urmap: http://www.urmap.com/

Each CN is placed on intersection. This simulation the starting point and ending point certainly are the intersection. The starting point is at intersection 6, and the ending point is at intersection 34. Fig. 5(a) shows the shortest distance path in the map.

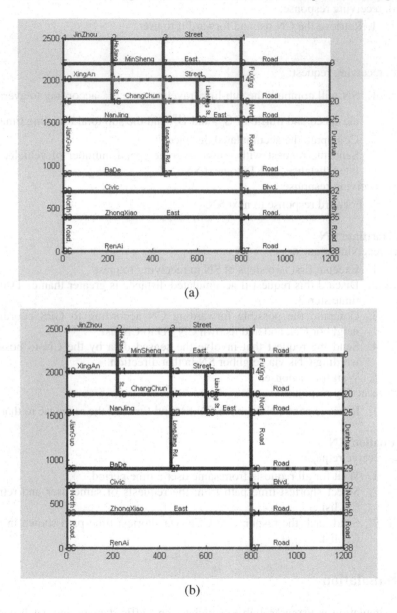

(a)

(b)

Fig. 5. The map in this simulation and the shortest distance path. (a) The shortest-path. (b) Dynamic path planning at t=0. (c) Dynamic path planning at t=5.1288 (link 29→28 traffic jam) (d) Dynamic path planning at t=7.1607 (link 32→31traffic jam).

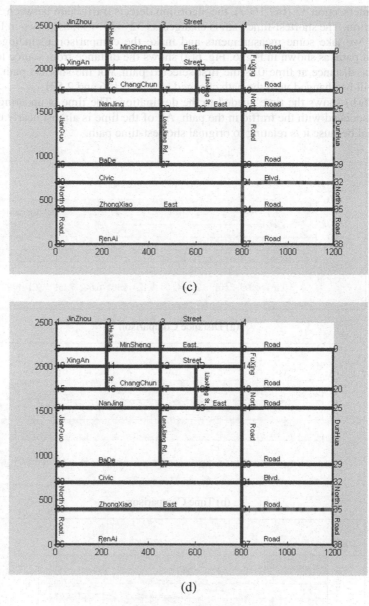

Fig. 5. (*Continued*)

The traffic in each link is generated randomly. Fig. 5(b) shows the shortest-time path estimated at t_0 using proposed algorithms. The estimated path is the sequence of intersection: $6 \to 7 \to 8 \to 9 \to 20 \to 25 \to 29 \to 28 \to 31 \to 34$ and traveling time is 5.3584 minute. When the vehicle run to intersection 20 (t=5.1288), the algorithm estimates the shortest-time path is changed to $20 \to 25 \to 29 \to 32 \to 31 \to 34$ because there are traffic jam between 29 and 28 intersection, as shown in Fig. 5(c). When the vehicle run to intersection 32 (t=7.1607), the algorithm detects traffic jam between 32 and 31 intersection. The shortest-time path is changed as 32→35→34, as shown in Fig. 5(d).

Next we take some measurements and make the comparison including distance, time and path, as shown in Fig. 6. Fig. 6(a) shows the distance from source to destination. The distance at time 0 is the first selected path, not the shortest path. The distance will be changed with the path changed at time 0.186 and 2.501.

Fig. 6(b) shows the time needed to the destination. The time is updating dynamically associated with the traffic in the path. All of the time is almost nearly except for the initial because it is relating to original shortest-time path.

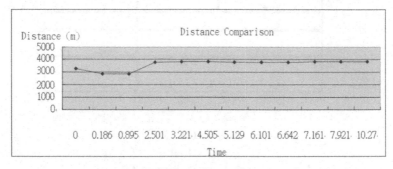

(a) Distance Comparison

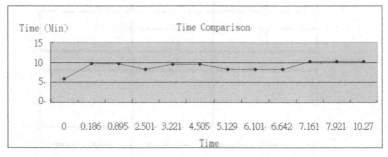

(b) Time Comparison

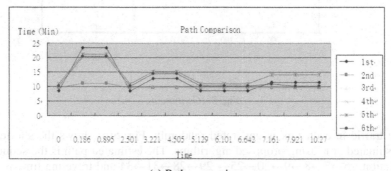

(c) Path comparison

Fig. 6. Measurement and comparison

Fig. 6(c) shows the path comparison of six measurements. The time at initial of 1st measurement has the shortest time because it is relating to original shortest-time path. When the vehicle approaches the second intersection (t= 0.186), the vehicle makes 2nd measurement and receives the response from the network showing next link obstructed. The vehicle turns to other link to avoid the obstruction. When the t= 2.501, the vehicle makes 3rd measurement and receives the response from the network also showing that the next link obstructed. The vehicle can make a decision to turn to other link. Finally, at the 6th measurement, the simulation shows that the time to destination is closing to the initial.

5 Related Works

In this section we depict some related works in the topic.

Chen et al. [5] proposed architecture based on WSN technology for Intelligent Transportation System (ITS) of a transportation network. With the help of WSN technology, the traffic information of the network can be accurately measured in real time. Based on this architecture, an optimization algorithm is proposed to minimize the average traveling time for the vehicles in the network.

Jun [11] discussed the problem of finding the minimum-cost path in the network of multi-modes of public transportation. The study used the GA-based approaches in finding the minimum total time path. In order to use GIS data, some reorganizations and relationships centering on the transfer areas were necessary. In this preliminary study, an imbedded script language called AML was used to automate the whole process because the language contains many built-in functions that handle the coverage-format data. This resulted in somewhat slow performance than expected.

Sawant et al. [10] addressed the approach of sensor networks to increase the safety of road traveling. The scheme does not require any changes to the existing highway infrastructure. Authors showed, using various examples, that the exchange of sensed data among vehicles can be beneficially used to avoid accidents. Isotropic and non-isotropic sensors were studied with respect to the coverage area and the probability of detection. Authors considered a typical highway intersection and plotted the sensor coverage area and the probability of detection for various vehicles equipped with non-isotropic sensors.

6 Conclusions and Future Work

We have proposed a framework for dynamic path planning of transportation system based on the Wireless Sensor Network (WSN). The framework can dynamically adjust and suggest the traveling path of moving vehicle for improving the problem of static path planning approach by collecting the traffic information dynamically using sensor nodes and planning path of transportation network in Satellite Navigation System. In this paper, we use Macroscopic Model that is usually used in traffic network to computing the traveling time of the sub-link and link, and use an *on-demand heuristic algorithm* with GPS assisted to look for the shortest-time path to destination. In addition, we explain the simulation result. The simulation result shows the framework can effectively adjust the traveling path and improve the problem of static path planning problem. The future work will develop the algorithm into sensor network and physically deploy the framework to the transportation system to evaluate the performance.

References

1. Akyildiz, I.F., Su, W., Sankarasubramaniam, Y., Cayirci, E.: Wireless sensor net-works: a survey. Computer Networks 38(4), 393–422
2. Suri, A., Iyengar, S.S., Cho, E.: Ecoinformatics using wireless sensor networks: An overview. Ecological Informatics 1(3), 287–293
3. Matsuo, T., Kaneko, Y., Matano, M.: Introduction of intelligent vehicle detection sensors. In: IEEE/IEEJ/JSAI International Conference on Intelligent Transportation Systems, pp. 709–713 (1999)
4. Akkaya, K., Younis, M.: A survey on routing protocols for wireless sensor networks. Ad Hoc Networks 3(3), 325–349
5. Wenjie, C., Liqiang, G., Zhilei, C., Zhanglong, C., Shiliang, T.: An intelligent guiding and controlling system for transportation network based on wireless sensor network technology. In: IEEE The Fifth International Conference on Computer and Information Technology, pp. 810–814 (2005)
6. Chin-Der, W., Ming-Hui, L.: Data fusion methods for accuracy improvement in wireless location systems. In: Wireless Communications and Networking Conference, pp. 471–476 (2004)
7. Durrant-Whyte, H.: Data fusion in sensor networks. In: Fourth International Symposium on Information Processing in Sensor Networks, April 15, 2005, pages 2 (2005)
8. Coleri, S., Cheung, S.Y., Varaiya, P.: Sensor Networks for Monitoring Traffic. In: Forty-Second Annual Allerton Conference on Commuinication, Control, and Computing, U. of Illinois (September 2004)
9. Wenjie, C., Lifeng, C., Zhanglong, C., Shiliang, T.: A Realtime Dynamic Traffic Control System Based on Wireless Sensor Network. In: 2005 International Conference on Parallel Processing Workshops (2005)
10. Sawant, H., Tan, J., Yang, Q.: A Sensor Network Approach for Intelligent Transportation Systems. In: 2004 IEEE International Conference on Intelligent Robots and Systems, September 28-October 2004, pp. 1796–1801 (2004)
11. Jun, C.: Route Selection in Public Transportation Network Using GA, http://gis.esri.com/library/userconf/proc05/papers/pap1874.pdf
12. Koutsonikolas, D., Das, S., Charlie Hu, Y.: Path Planning of Mobile Landmarks for Localization in Wireless Sensor Networks. In: Proceedings of the ICDCS Interna-tional Workshop on Wireless Ad Hoc and Sensor Networks (IEEE WWASN 2006), Lisboa, Portugal (July 4-7, 2006)
13. van den Berg, M., Hegyi, A., De Schutter, B., Hellendoorn, J.: A macroscopic traffic flow model for integrated control of freeway and urban traffic networks. In: 42nd IEEE Conference on Decision and Control, Maui, Hawaii, pp. 2774–2779 (December 2003)
14. Younis, M., Youssef, M., Arisha, K.: Energy-aware management for cluster-based sensor networks. Computer Networks 43(5), 649–668 (2003)
15. Ko, Y.-B., Vaidya, N.H.: Location-aided routing (LAR) in mobile ad hoc networks. In: 4th annual ACM/IEEE international conference on Mobile computing and networking MobiCom 1998, October 1998, pp. 66–75 (1998)

A Recoverable Semi-fragile Watermarking Scheme Using Cosine Transform and Adaptive Median Filter

Shang-Lin Hsieh, Pei-Da Wu, I-Ju Tsai, and Bin-Yuan Huang

Department of Computer Science and Engineering, Tatung University, Taipei, Taiwan
slhsieh@ttu.edu.tw

Abstract. The paper proposes a novel semi-fragile watermarking scheme capable of detecting and recovering tampered regions to protect the integrity of images. The proposed scheme generates the features from the host image itself and uses them as the watermark, which is then embedded into the frequency domain of the host image. Additionally, the scheme uses an adaptive median filter to distinguish between common image processing operations and malicious attacks so that it can react properly. Moreover, the scheme can locate tampered areas and recover these areas. According to the experimental results, the scheme is robust to common image processing operations, including JPEG compression, and is capable of detecting malicious attacks, such as counterfeiting.

Keywords: Semi-fragile watermarking, integrity of images protection, discrete cosine transform, adaptive median filter, tampered detection and recovery.

1 Introduction

Ensuring the integrity of critical images is important when they are being transferred on the Internet because they may be modified by some malicious party. Some techniques such as fragile and semi-fragile digital watermarking schemes have been developed to protect the integrity of images. The fragile watermarking scheme first embeds a pattern, called a watermark, into a host image. Later, the receiving party can verify the integrity of the host image according to the extracted watermark because the watermark will break if there is any change done to the image. The changes may result from common image processing operations or malicious image attacks. Image attacks, such as counterfeit attack, are unacceptable because they destroy the information in images. On the contrary, image processing operations, such as compression, brightness adjustment, and contrast adjustment etc., are normally used to improve the quality or enhance the features of images, and therefore they should be regarded as legitimate and acceptable. However, the fragile watermarking scheme cannot distinguish legitimate operations from malicious attacks. On the other hand, in the semi-fragile watermarking scheme, the watermark will only break when the image suffers malicious attacks. Therefore, it is more suitable than fragile watermarking to protect the integrity of images. Moreover, some semi-fragile watermarking schemes not only can verify the image integrity but also recover the tampered areas.

In recent years, several papers on fragile or semi-fragile watermarking [1-8] have been published. Lu et al. [1] proposed a fragile watermarking scheme that is sensitive

C. Rong et al. (Eds.): ATC 2008, LNCS 5060, pp. 629–640, 2008.

to any changes. Izqierdo and Guerra [5] and Liu et al. [6] proposed schemes that can verify the integrity of the protected image. However, they cannot locate the tampered regions and do not have the recovery ability. The scheme proposed by Liu and Hsieh [7] can recover the tampered areas, but it is not convenient because the original watermark must be sent to the receiving party, which is sometimes impossible. Lin et al. [8] proposed a scheme that can recover tampered areas without the help of the original watermark. However, the recovery information may be destroyed without much difficulty because it is embedded into the spatial domain.

In the paper, a recoverable semi-fragile watermarking scheme without the need of the original watermark is proposed. The scheme generates the features from the host image itself and uses them as the watermark. Then the watermark is embedded into the frequency domain rather than the spatial domain. Additionally, the scheme uses adaptive median filter to distinguish between common image processing operations and malicious attacks so that it can react properly. Moreover, the scheme can locate the tampered areas and recover them with satisfactory quality.

The rest of this paper is organized as follows. Section 2 describes related background. Section 3 presents the proposed scheme in detail. The experimental results are shown and discussed in Section 4. Finally, the conclusion is drawn in Section 5.

2 Related Background

The proposed scheme uses Torus automorphism to obtain the position for embedding and adopts an adaptive median filter to increase the ability to discriminate between common operations and malicious attacks. The following subsections introduce the related background.

2.1 Torus Automorphism

To achieve the recovery ability, features generated from a certain block need to be embedded to another block. The scheme uses Torus automorphism to obtain the position for embedding. Torus automorphism [11] is one class of dynamic systems that can be expressed as follows:

$$\begin{pmatrix} x_{t+1} \\ y_{t+1} \end{pmatrix} = \begin{pmatrix} a_{11} & a_{12} \\ a_{21} & a_{22} \end{pmatrix} \begin{pmatrix} x_t \\ y_t \end{pmatrix} \bmod N \tag{1}$$

where a_{11}, a_{12}, a_{21}, and $a_{22} \in Z$, and N is the size of the given image. The new coordinates (x_{t+1}, y_{t+1}) can be generated from the current coordinates (x_t, y_t) by the transform function.

2.2 Adaptive Median Filter

The proposed scheme uses an adaptive median filter that can adjust the size of the mask according to the manipulation type the image suffered. In general, common image processing operations cause some variations on the pixels of the images while malicious attacks result in the scrap regions. A median filter [13] can be used to remove the effect of variations caused by image processing. The filter moves the filter mask from point to point in an image and considers its nearby neighbors to decide whether it is representative of its surroundings or not. The median filter works by first sorting all the pixel values from the surrounding neighborhood of the central pixel and then replacing the value of the pixel with the median pixel value. Fig. 1 [13] illustrates an example. The neighboring values are 115, 119, 120, 123, 124, 125, 126, 127, and 150. Thus the median value is 124. The central pixel value 150 is replaced with 124.

3 The Proposed Recoverable Semi-fragile Watermarking Scheme

The proposed scheme includes two phases: *watermarked image generation* phase and *integrity verification* phase. In the former phase, the scheme first generates the features from the host image. The features are then used as the watermark and embedded to the host image for image verification and tamper recovery. In the latter phase, the scheme first extracts a watermark and next generates features from the suspect image. It then compares the features with the extracted watermark. If the scheme detects that the suspect image has suffered malicious attacks, it will locate the tampered areas and recover them using the extracted features which constitutes the watermark. Fig. 2 shows the block diagram of the scheme.

Fig. 1. An example of the median filter

3.1 Main Stages in the Proposed Scheme

The scheme includes several stages, which will be described in detail in the following subsections.

3.1.1 Preprocessing
The host image is divided into several non-overlapping blocks of size 8×8 pixels as shown in Fig. 3.

3.1.2 DCT
The scheme applies 2D-DCT to each block and then obtains 64 coefficients for each block.

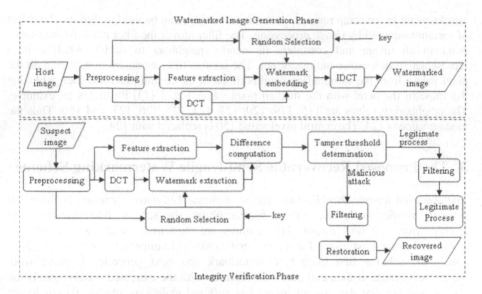

Fig. 2. The block diagram of the proposed scheme

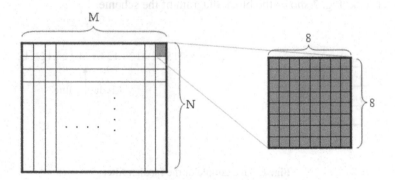

Fig. 3. The size of each block

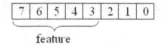

feature

Fig. 4. The bit positions for feature extraction

3.1.3 Feature Extraction

The stage first computes the average of each block obtained from the *preprocessing* stage. Next, the bits 3-7 of the eight binary bits of the average are selected as the feature F of each block (Fig. 4).

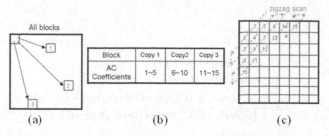

Fig. 5. The positions for embedding (a) three randomly selected blocks (b) the coefficients of each block for embedding each copy (c) the embedding positions of each block in the zigzag scan order

3.1.4 Random Selection

In order to resist malicious attacks, the features of a certain block must be embedded into another block. The scheme adopts Torus Automorphism to randomly select the block for embedding features.

3.1.5 Embedding

The proposed scheme embeds the features of a block to three different blocks. Moreover, the first 15 AC coefficients in zigzag order of DCT domain of a block are chosen for embedding the features. The scheme obtains three positions for embedding by applying Trous Automorphism three times. For the first time, the features of the source block are embedded into the 1st to 5th AC coefficients of the selected block. For the second time, the features are embedded into the 6th to 10th coefficients, and for the last time, the 11th to 15th coefficients.

Next, the features are embedded by modifying the DCT coefficients [14]. Two values are calculated for modification rules.

$$Q = \frac{|C|}{M}, \quad S = \begin{cases} 1, & if \ C \leq 0 \\ -1, & otherwise \end{cases} \tag{2}$$

where M is obtained by experiments and used to modify the coefficients, and C is a modified coefficient. The modification rules are given as follows:

$$
\begin{aligned}
&If \quad w = 0: \\
&\quad r = \frac{M}{4} \\
&\quad C\_low = S(Q \times M + r) \\
&\quad C\_high = S((Q+1) \times M + r) \\
&\quad C = \begin{cases} C\_low, & if \ |C\_low - C| \leq |C\_high - C| \\ C\_high, & if \ |C\_low - C| > |C\_high - C| \end{cases}
\end{aligned}
\tag{3}
$$

$$If \quad w = 1:$$
$$r = \frac{3M}{4}$$
$$C\_low = S((Q-1) \times M + r)$$
$$C\_high = S(Q \times M + r) \qquad (4)$$
$$C = \begin{cases} C\_low, & if \ |C\_low - C| \leq |C\_high - C| \\ C\_high, & if \ |C\_low - C| > |C\_high - C| \end{cases}$$

According to the embedding data $w \in \{0,1\}$, the remainder r is set to be $M/4$ or $3M/4$ if watermark bit value w is 0 or 1 respectively. Fig. 6 shows the ranges of tolerance for the watermark bits. It is important to set the value M appropriately because a larger M will affect the original image quality while a smaller M will result in erroneous watermark extraction.

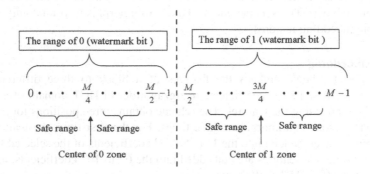

Fig. 6. the ranges of tolerance for the watermark bits

3.1.6 Watermark Extraction
In this stage, the three previously embedded watermark copies mentioned in Section 3.1.5 are extracted. The first copy is extracted from the 1st to 5th AC coefficients of the first selected block, the second one from the 6th to 10th AC coefficients of the second block, and the third one from the 11th to 15th AC coefficients of the third block. The scheme then uses the following rules to extract the features from the three copies.

$$b = \begin{cases} 0, & if \ (\ |C| \ \bmod \ M \ ) < M/2 \\ 1, & otherwise \end{cases} \qquad (5)$$

where b is the extracted watermark bit, M is the mode value, and C is the AC coefficient of previously embedded watermark.

3.1.7 Difference Computation
After the three copies of the previously embedded watermark are obtained, the proposed scheme then adopts the following voting rule to construct the final watermark. The voting rule is described as follows.

$$PF'_i = \begin{cases} 1, & PF_i^1 + PF_i^2 + PF_i^3 \geq 2 \\ 0, & otherwise \end{cases} \tag{6}$$

where PF'_i represents the ith ($i = 1, 2, ..., 5$) bit of the extracted feature set PF', and PF_i^j the ith bit of the previously embedded jth ($j = 1, 2,$ and 3) copy. After PF' is determined, it is used with the corresponding block feature F (generated from the suspect image) to calculate a difference value D according to the following equation.

$$D_i = (F_i \oplus PF'_i) \tag{7}$$

where $\oplus$ is the exclusive OR operation, D_i, F_i, and PF'_i represent the ith bit of the difference value D, the corresponding block feature F, and extracted feature PF' respectively. Finally, the scheme calculates the difference rate DR according to the following equation.

$$DR = \frac{D}{2^7 + 2^6 + 2^5 + 2^4 + 2^3} \tag{8}$$

If DR is greater than 0.5, then the block is regarded as a tampered block and the number of the tampered blocks denoted as N is increased by one.

3.1.8 Tamper Threshold Determination

The semi-fragile watermarking scheme must be able to distinguish between common image processing operations and malicious attacks. Therefore, a *tamper threshold determination* stage is designed to detect the manipulation type of image processing. In general, common image processing operations cause many variations on the pixels of the images while malicious attacks result in scrap regions. To judge whether an image has been manipulated by image processing operations or malicious attacks, a tamper threshold (T_{tatal}) is used to determine the manipulation type. The value of the threshold T_{tatal} is set to one eighth of the number of the total blocks. When the number of the tampered blocks (N) is greater than T_{tatal}, the manipulation type is regarded as a common operation. Otherwise, it is considered a malicious attack. According to the manipulation type, T_{tatal} is set to a different value, which will be used to detect if a block is tampered or not in different situations. The rules are given as follows.

$$T_{tamper} = \begin{cases} 0.8, & if \ \ N \geq T_{total} \\ 0, & otherwise \end{cases} \tag{9}$$

According to the experimental results, the threshold is set to 0.8 for common image processing operations, or 0 for malicious attacks. Finally, the binary difference image DI is obtained by comparing T_{tamper} with the difference rate DR of each block. The binary value of each pixel in DI is determined according to the following rule.

1. If $DR > T_{tamper}$, then the binary value of the corresponding pixel in DI is set to 1.
2. Otherwise, the binary value is set to 0.

The value 1 in DI means the block is tampered while the value 0 means the block is not.

3.1.9 Filtering

The scheme adopts an adaptive median filter to remove the pepper and salt noise resulting from common image processing. It adjusts the window size of the median filter according to the manipulation type. The window size is 3×3 for malicious attacks (i.e., T_{tamper}=0), and 5×5 for legitimate operations (i.e., T_{tamper}=0.8). The adaptive median filter is applied to DI to obtain a binary tamper region image RI, which contains only 1 and 0 (since DI is a binary image).

3.1.10 Restoration

The stage restores the tempered region according to the pixel value in RI. If the value is 1, which means the corresponding block is tampered, the scheme will replace the pixel values of the tampered block (of size 8×8) with the corresponding feature (which is the average of the original block) in the previously embedded watermark.

3.2 The Algorithms of the Two Phases

The proposed scheme contains two phases. One is *watermarked image generation* phase, and the other is *the integrity verification* phase. The algorithms of the two phases are presented as follows.

3.2.1 The Watermark Image Generation Phase

First, the host image is divided into several non-overlapping blocks by *preprocessing* stage and then the features are extracted from the host image in the *feature extraction* stage. At the same time, the scheme also applies DCT to each block. Next, the *random selection* stage randomly selects the blocks for embedding. Finally, the *embedding* stage combines the original image with the watermark to generate the watermarked image. The following procedure lists the steps of the *watermarked image generation* phase.

Input: an original gray level image $H(512×512)$.
Output: a watermarked image $W(512×512)$.

1. Divide the original image H into 64×64 non-overlapping blocks of size 8×8.
2. Obtain the feature of each block according to the description in Section 3.1.3.
3. Apply DCT to each block.
4. Select embedding positions from the DCT blocks according to the description in Section 3.1.4.
5. Embed the feature of each DCT block into the selected positions according to the rules described in Section 3.1.5.
6. Apply IDCT to each DCT block to obtain the watermarked image $W(512×512)$.

3.2.2 The Integrity Verification Phase

The main goal of this phase is to locate tampered regions. First, the suspect image is divided into several non-overlapping blocks by the *preprocessing* stage. Next, the *feature extraction* stage generates the current features from the suspect image. At the same time, the *watermark extraction* stage extracts the watermarks, i.e., embedded features from the suspect image. In the *difference computation* stage, the current features are compared with the embedded features and then the difference image between them is obtained. After the *tamper threshold determination* stage, the scheme can determine the correct manipulation type. In the *filtering* stage, the adaptive median filter is used to remove irrelative noise. Finally, the tampered regions are restored by the embedded features in the *restoration* stage. The steps of the *integrity verification phase* are given in detail as follows.

Input: a suspect gray level image $S(512 \times 512)$.
Output: a recovered image $R(512 \times 512)$.

1. Divide the suspect image S into 64×64 non-overlapping blocks of size 8×8.
2. Determine the previously embedding positions according to the description in Section 3.1.4.
3. Generate the new feature F of each block in S according to the description in Section 3.1.3.
4. Apply DCT on each block and then extract the feature set PF' from each DCT block according to the rules described in Section 3.1.6.
5. Calculate the difference rate of each block by comparing F and PF' according to the description in Section 3.1.7.
6. Determine the tamper threshold T_{tamper} and then obtain the difference image DI according to the rules described in Section 3.1.8.
7. Apply the adaptive median filter to DI according to T_{tamper}, and obtain the tampered region image RI.
8. Restore the tampered region according to RI and the description in Section 3.1.10 to obtain the recovered image R.

4 Experimental Results

Some experiments have been conducted to prove that the scheme can resist some common image processing operations and detect malicious attacks. The image processing software *"Ulead PhotoImpact 11"* was used in the experiments to simulate several kinds of image processing.

Four pictures, including "Lena", "Baboon", "F16", and "Peppers" (as shown in Fig. 7), have been tested by the proposed scheme. The PSNRs between the watermarked images and the host images are given in Table 1. According to the experimental results, the PSNRs are all greater than 40dB, which shows the qualities of the watermarked images are satisfactory.

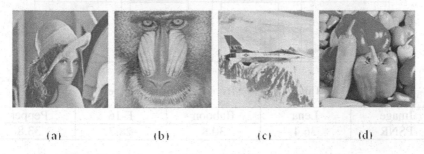

(a)   (b)   (c)   (d)

Fig. 7. The test images (a) Lena (b) Baboon (c) F-16 (d) Pepper

Table 1. The PSNRs of the watermarked images

Image	Lena	Baboon	F-16	Pepper
PSNR	44.2	44.7	44.1	44.3

Table 2. The results of the images after image processing operations

	Lena		Baboon		F-16		Pepper	
JPEG								
Brigntness adjustment								
Contrast adjustment								

Table 3. The results of the proposed scheme for the images after malicious attacks

Suspect image	Difference	After filter	Recovered image

Table 4. The PSNRs of the recovered images

Image	Lena	Baboon	F-16	Pepper
PSNR	36.4	30.8	28.7	33.8

4.1 Common Image Processing Operations

According to the experimental results, the proposed scheme can resist the JPEG compression, brightness adjustment, and contrast adjustment. After the *filtering* stage, Most of the pepper and salts noise in the difference image caused by those operations were removed. The images suffered the operations were still regarded as untampered images. Table 2 shows the results of the images after image processing operations.

4.2 Malicious Attacks

According to the following experimental results, the proposed scheme can detect malicious attacks, such as counterfeit attack, and then restore the tampered area effectively. Table 3 shows the suspect images, the difference images, tamper region images, and the recovered images. Table 4 shows the PSNRs of the recovered images. Most of the PSNRs are greater than 30, which means that the proposed scheme can recover the tampered image with satisfactory quality.

5 Conclusions

This paper proposed a novel recoverable semi-fragile watermarking, which is able to detect and recover tempered areas. Additionally, the proposed scheme has following two features:

1.   It can remove the pepper and salt noises caused by common image processing operations, such as JPEG compression, brightness adjustment, and contrast adjustment.
2.   It can appropriately decide the manipulation type (legitimate image processing operations or malicious attacks) and accordingly discover the tempered areas.

According to the experimental results, the scheme can effectively resist common image processing operations and detect malicious attacks. Moreover, it can locate the tampered areas correctly and recover them accurately.

References

1. Lu, H., Shen, R., Chung, F.-L.: Fragile watermarking scheme for image authentication. Electronics Letters 39(12) (2003)
2. Dittmann, J., Steinmetz, A., Steinmetz, R.: Content-based digital signature for motion pictures authentication and content-fragile watermarking. In: IEEE International Conference on Multimedia Computing and Systems, vol. 2, pp. 7–11 (1999)
3. Wu, C.W.: On the design of content-based multimedia authentication systems. IEEE Transactions on Multimedia 4(3) (2002)
4. Lu, C.-S., Liao, H.Y.M.: Structural digital signature for image authentication: an incidental distortion resistant scheme. IEEE Transactions on Multimedia 5(2) (2003)
5. Izquierdo, E., Guerra, V.: An Ill-Posed Operator for secure Image Authentication: IEEE Transactions on Circuits and Systems for Video Technology. 13, 842–852 (2003)

6. Liu, Y., Gao, W., Yao, H., Liu, S.: A Texture-based Tamper Detection Scheme by Fragile Watermark. In: The 2004 IEEE International Symposium on Circuits and Systems, ISCAS 2004, Vancouver, CA, pp. 177–180 (2004)

7. Lin, C.H., Hsieh, W.S.: Applying Projection and Bspline to Image Authentication and Remedy. IEEE Transactions on Consumer Electronics 49, 1234–1238 (2003)

8. Lin, P.L., Huang, P.W., Peng, A.W.: A Fragile watermarking Scheme for Image Authentication with Localization and Recovery. In: IEEE Sixth International Symposium on Multimedia Software Engineering (MSE 2004), Florida, USA, pp. 13–15 (2004)

9. Khayam, S.A.: The Discrete Cosine Transform (DCT): Theory and Application1: Department of Electrical & Computer Engineering Michigan State University (2003)

10. Pennebaker, W.B., Mitchell, J.L.: JPEG – Still Image Data Compression Standard. Int. Thomsan Publishing, New York (1993)

11. Chang, C.C., Hsiao, J.Y., Chiang, C.L.: An Image Copyright Protection Scheme Based on Torus Automorphism. In: First International Symposium on Cyber Worlds, pp. 217–224 (2002)

12. Voyatzis, G., Pitas, I.: Chaotic Mixing of Digital Images and Applications to Watermarking. In: Proceedings of European Conference on Multimedia Applications, Services and Techniques, vol. 2 (1996)

13. Hypermedia Image Processing Reference, http://www.cee.hw.ac.uk/hipr/html/hipr_top.html

14. Lin, S.D., Kuo, Y.-C., Huang, Y.-H.: An Image Watermarking Scheme with Tamper Detection and Recovery. In: International Conference on Innovative Computing, Information and Control, Beijing, P.R.O.C, vol. 3, pp. 74–77 (2006)

15. Semantics-sensitive Integrated Matching for Picture Libraries, http://wang.ist.psu.edu/docs/related/

Intelligent VoIP System in Ad-Hoc Network with Embedded Pseudo SIP Server

Lin-huang Chang[1,2], Chun-hui Sung[2], Shih-yi Chiu[2], and Jiun-jian Liaw[2]

[1] Department of Computer and Information Science
National Taichung Univ., Taichung, Taiwan, R.O.C.
lchang@ntcu.edu.tw
[2] Graduate Institute of Networking and Communication Engineering
Chaoyang Univ. of Technology, Taichung, Taiwan, R.O.C.

Abstract. Wireless networks and the voice over Internet protocol (VoIP) have recently been widely adapted. VoIP services over Ad-hoc network can be accomplished by middleware embedded in mobile devices. In this study, we have implemented an intelligent VoIP system with embedded pseudo session initiation protocol (SIP) server in an Ad-hoc network. We employed the standard SIP protocol and integrated SIP presence to handle SIP signaling and user discovery mechanism. The embedded pseudo SIP server, acting as the middleware between transport and application layers, was compatible with common VoIP user agents (UAs) using SIP. Our testbed shows acceptable VoIP quality of service (QoS) level in transmission delay for both signaling and voice packets.

1 Introduction

There are many Internet applications, such as voice over Internet protocol (VoIP), which involves heavy multimedia transmission over high-speed networks. Acceptable quality of service (QoS) is one of the top issues that need to be addressed in VoiIP applications.

To transfer VoIP packets over the Internet, it is important to conduct the signaling exchange in advance. The Internet Engineering Task Force (IETF) defined the Session Initiation Protocol (SIP) to solve the signaling issues. The SIP can initiate, modify, and terminate voice session. It differs from H.323 in that SIP is a simple and flexible protocol which integrates RTP with RTCP for voice transfer in an infrastructure network.

Currently, many Internet applications or services adhere to the client/server architecture. The client/server architecture requires the user to obtain the IP address of the counterpart prior to establishing a connection. On the other hand, the Ad-hoc network is designed for temporary and/or emergent situations, such as battlefield, temporary post-disaster reconstruction, and conferencing center. The Ad-hoc network with free installation and without fixed infrastructure allows single mobile device or workstation directly to carry out the point-to-point communication without relays via access point (AP). However, the client/server architecture used for common VoIP applications, is hard to realize in an Ad-hoc network environment.

C. Rong et al. (Eds.): ATC 2008, LNCS 5060, pp. 641–654, 2008.

In this study, we present a distributed VoIP architecture based on pseudo SIP servers across an Ad-hoc network. The designed architecture embeds the pseudo SIP server in all end devices such that users can talk to others intelligently without a well-defined infrastructure. The proposed pseudo SIP server utilizes SIP presence to discover the mobile device and exchange the signaling over the Ad-hoc network.

The rest of this paper is organized as follows. We will briefly introduce the Ad-hoc, VoIP systems and related works in Section 2. Section 3 presents the system architec-ture, functionalities and designs followed by the detailed implementation and analysis in Section 4. Finally, the paper is concluded in Section 5.

2   Backgrounds and Related Works

2.1   Ad-Hoc Network

The emergence of wireless technology has encourages people to use all sorts of mobile devices. People can connect to the network at any time and any location to access the Internet. When two devices want to communicate, they rely on the wireless base station such as an AP to transmit data. There are a number of problems with the centralized model which may be overcome by peer-to-peer technology.

The Mobile Ad-hoc Network (MANET) is a network that uses wireless communication technology comprising many wireless devices. It allows single devices or workstations to directly communicate point-to-point without the relay via AP as long as the device or workstation has installed an 802.11 wireless network interface. Because the node in the wireless network can be moved freely at any time without the restriction on direction or range, the network topology may change at any time.

In general, routing protocols can not adjust routes due to the addition or removal of nodes during the communication between two mobile nodes. Therefore, new protocols, such as Ad hoc On-Demand Vector Routing (AODV) and Optimized Link State Routing Protocol (OLSR), are required for these mobile nodes to communicate with each other given a dynamic network topology. Wireless mobile device on the Ad-Hoc network therefore possess routing functionality similar to that found on routers, although the routing protocol may be different.

2.2   Ad-Hoc VoIP System

In VoIP applications, the signaling and voice data are delivered using packet switching from client(s) to client(s) via switches, routers, and/or servers, such as SIP register or SIP proxy servers. The registration and forwarding of the signaling via SIP servers employ the client/server architecture. The client/server architecture, however, is complicated to deploy in Ad-hoc network environment. Therefore, the integration of SIP functionality with clients would be one of the solutions to conduct Ad-hoc VoIP applications.

On the other hand, due to the frequent changes in network topology in an Ad-hoc network, the discovery service for users becomes even more important. Some studies has focused on the research of VoIP over Ad-hoc network using modified SIP protocol [7] or other protocol, such as service location protocol (SLP) for service discovery [8]. However, modified SIP protocol may not be compatible with SIP user agents

(UAs). In this paper, we used a pseudo SIP server [1] to handle the SIP signaling which maintained the originality of the SIP protocol. The pseudo SIP server was designed based on the standard SIP protocol and compatible with SIP UAs. It is therefore more suitable for Ad-hoc VoIP realizations.

2.3 Related Works

Chang et al. [2][9] designed the pseudo SIP Server combined with universal plug and play (UPnP) for Ad-hoc VoIP applications. They conducted the user registration and remote user discovery by UPnP processing phases. Figure 1 shows the process flow of the Ad-hoc VoIP using UPnP protocol. Any user, for instance User 1, entering the Ad-hoc network will advertise itself and then get a detailed description from each of the available devices.

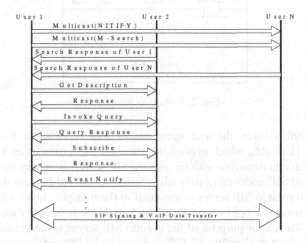

Fig. 1. The process of the UPnP over Ad-Hoc VoIP

Unlike previous studies [7-8], they did not modify the standard SIP protocol to accomplish VoIP service over Ad-hoc network. Their proposed pseudo SIP server with UPnP architecture is compatible with all SIP UAs. However, the overhead issue by using UPnP protocol for user discovery and registration may not be the best solution for Ad-hoc VoIP signaling. Therefore, in this paper, we employed the all-SIP idea by using SIP presence to discover the mobile device and exchange the signaling over the Ad-hoc network.

3 System Design

This section discusses the detailed design of our Ad-hoc VoIP system. The pseudo SIP server based on the standard SIP protocol also included the SIP presence functionality. Unlike designs using SLP or UPnP, our design accomplished the all-SIP signaling with user discovery support. Additionally, the proposed design further deals with the instant mobility issue by introducing the mobility management functionality.

This allowed the mobile device to move freely in the Ad-hoc network while instanta-neously maintaining the user information.

3.1 System Architecture

Figure 2 shows the system architecture, which includes four parts: (1) SIP UA, (2) pseudo SIP Server embedded in transport layer, (3) Internet Protocol version 6 (IPv6), and (4) 802.11 layer.

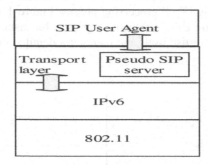

Fig. 2. System architecture

In the application layer, the user agent can be any version, for example Kphone [19], Linphone [15], etc., which applies the standard SIP protocol as VoIP signaling. The UA will then communicate with the pseudo SIP server. By using the conven-tional UA with standard SIP, users can easily talk to others in the Ad-hoc environ-ment.

The proposed pseudo SIP server is designed in the transport layer which acts as the middleware to serve the application layer, such as UAs. It is easily embedded in the mobile device. The major purpose of the pseudo SIP server is the management of SIP signaling. With the functionality of SIP registrar and SIP proxy servers, the pseudo SIP server accomplishes the ability to discover users and exchange signaling in Ad-hoc VoIP applications.

In the network layer, we employed the IPv6 protocol to accomplish auto-configuration for the Ad-hoc mobile nodes. We also used the IEEE 802.11b/g in the data-link layer for media access control (MAC) and radio signaling. This architecture will provide the mobile nodes the VoIP ability under Ad-hoc environment. The de-tailed design of the system and process flows are discussed in the next sub-sections.

3.2 Mobility Management Functionality

In the Ad-hoc network, users can join or leave the group and/or the Ad-hoc network freely which will cause a problem for user member update and/or instant user discov-ery. This issue can be divided into two categories: service initiation timing and mov-ing in/out of mobile nodes. In our pseudo SIP server, we designed the functionality of mobility management to handle these problems.

When a user initiates the VoIP service using a pseudo SIP server, it will not realize the existing user message due to the asynchronous process initiation. For the client/server infrastructure, this can be done by a SIP proxy server during the registration process. In Ad-hoc network, however the user needs to wait until the SIP expires.

To solve the synchronous delay issue, the pseudo SIP server conducts registering as shown in figure 3. First, user A initiates the pseudo SIP server and caches its REGISTER message. Then, when user B initiates the pseudo SIP server and multi-casts its REGISTER message, user A updates user B REGISTER message and uni-casts its own message to user B. The REGISTER messages for different users there-fore remain consistent and the user lists will be synchronized in the Ad-hoc network.

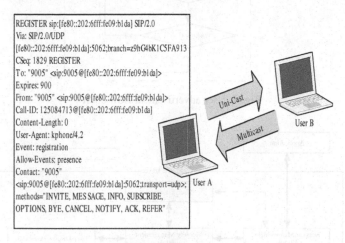

Fig. 3. REGISTER mechanism

On the other hand, when a mobile node moves into the transmission range of the Ad-hoc network, it needs a trigger mechanism to avoid the long wait for the SIP to expire. In our pseudo SIP server, we set a trigger mechanism for user advertisement and discovery instantly, as shown in figure 4. The pseudo SIP server searches the user list upon receiving the INVITE message from UA. If the user is found in the cache it will forward the INVITE message, otherwise, it will multicast a REGISTER message. After the timeout, if the pseudo SIP server is still can not find the user, it will reply a 404 Not Found message back to UA.

Through the REGISTER mechanism for asynchronous initiation and discovery and advisement process, the embedded pseudo SIP server being compatible with SIP UA can provide the VoIP service in the Ad-hoc network without complex design and too much overhead.

3.3 System Module Design

Different from the client/server VoIP architecture in the infrastructure network, the distributed Ad-hoc mobile nodes embedded with pseudo SIP server should provide some fundamental properties of SIP registrar and proxy/redirect servers to accomplish the discovery, user list update, mobility management and signaling for session estab-lishment and tear-down. Figure 5 depicts the system module design, consisting of the Session Management module, the Mobility Management module, the User Discovery module, the SIP Presence module, as well as the User-list cache.

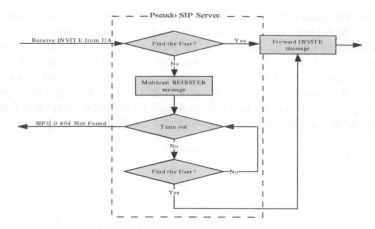

Fig. 4. User advertisement flow chart

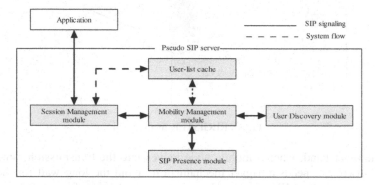

Fig. 5. System module design of the Pseudo SIP Server

The Session Management module was designed to receive and parse the SIP signaling, and then respond to different SIP Methods. To handle the movements of the mobile users in the Ad-hoc network, we designed the Mobility Management module to synchronize the user lists. The user lists are updated and stored in the User-list cache. On the other hand, if one user is not in the User-list cache, the User Discovery module is called to locate the user followed by the update in the User-list cache. Finally, the SIP Presence module applied the Subscribe and Notify mechanisms in RFC 3856 [11] to update and synchronize the user lists during registration.

3.4 System Flow Chart

It is important to take into accounts the memory space and resource dispatch of the pseudo SIP server, because it is middleware embedded in the mobile devices. Moreover, we need to maintain the ability of mobility management for Ad-hoc VoIP services. Therefore, we retrench the unnecessary process and refine the signaling process flow of the pseudo SIP server. Also, pseudo SIP server takes only the most common

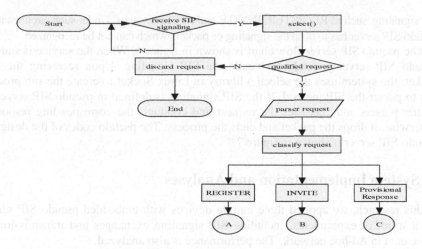

Fig. 6. The Pseudo SIP Server flow chart

```
do{
    //listening port 5060, wait for SIP signaling
    recvfrom(sip_signaling);

    //determine qualify SIP signaling or not
    if(qualified_request(sip_signaling) == FALSE){
            drop_packet(sip_signaling);
            return;
    }
    //parser SIP method
    method = parser_method(sip_signaling);
    //allocate function
    switch(method){
            case "REGISTER":
            register(sip_signaling);//REGISTER function
            break;
            case "INVITE":
            invite(sip_signaling);//INVITE function
            break;
            case "Provision":
            //Provisional response function
            provision(sip_signaling);
            break;
} }
```

Fig. 7. The Pseudo SIP Server pseudo code

SIP signaling, such as REGISTER, INVITE and ACK messages. Under such circumstance, pseudo SIP server has to drop the signaling or packets which can not be recognized.

The pseudo SIP server flow chart is shown in figure 6. When the service is started, pseudo SIP server is ready to handle the SIP signaling. Upon receiving the SIP packet, the system uses the select( ) library in Linux Socket to create the sub process and to parser the SIP method. If the SIP signaling is defined in pseudo SIP server, it further parsers and classifies the request and conducts the corresponding response. Otherwise, it drops the packet and ends the process. The pseudo codes of the designed pseudo SIP server is shown in figure 7.

4   System Implementation and Analyses

In this research, we applied three mobile devices with embedded pseudo SIP server for a series of experiments, including SIP signaling exchanges and transmission of voice data in Ad-hoc network. The performance is also analyzed.

4.1   Experimental Environments

The experimental environments for Ad-hoc VoIP was set up as shown in figure 8 where every node conducted the Ad-hoc mode as independent basic service set (IBSS) to connect to other nodes. In the experimental design, the User 1 signal covered User 2 and User 3, but User 2 signal did not cover User 3 and vice versa. The communica-tion between User 2 and User 3 was relayed via User 1. In the networking layer, we employed the IPv6 auto-configuration for link-local addressing.

The network topology was set up to analyze the performance of the embedded pseudo SIP server in Ad-hoc network as well as to measure the influence of perform-ance in Ad-hoc hopping issue.

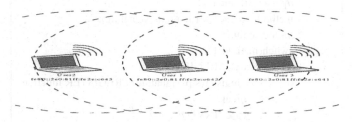

Fig. 8. Ad-Hoc network topology

4.2   System Implementation

The system was implemented using Ubuntu Linux 6.10 [18] as the operating system, and applying Kphone 4.2 [15] to be the UA on top of the embedded pseudo SIP server. For the Ad-hoc network routing protocol, we also employed the open source codes to realize the OLSR [16][17] routing mechanism. By using iwconfig command in our implementation setup, the designed Ad-hoc VoIP system with embedded pseudo SIP server was accomplished. The configuration of the experimental setup is shown in figure 9.

```
#!/bin/bash

iwconfig eth1 mode ad-hoc
iwconfig eth1 essid x32
iwconfig eth1 channel 6
ifconfig eth1 up
ifconfig eth1 192.168.10.22 netmask 255.255.255.0 up
route add -net 224.0.0.0 netmask 240.0.0.0 dev eth1
```

Fig. 9. Ad-Hoc network configuration

Table 1. The detail of experimental hardware

Notebook:	
Version	IBM ThickPAD x32
CPU	Pentium 1.8 GHZ
Memory	512 Mbytes
Wireless card	Intel PRO/Wireless 2200
Operating System	Obuntu 6.10
Access Point:	
Version	ASUS WL-HDD 2.5

We used three laptops acting as mobile device for embedded pseudo Sip server development and Ad-hoc VoIP implementation. Table 1 shows the detail of the hardware.

4.3 Performance Analysis

For the Ad-hoc VoIP performance analyses, one of the most important parameters is the delay issue. Therefore, we aimed at the delay of signaling exchange and voice data transmission. The experimental results of Ad-hoc VoIP with embedded pseudo SIP server were also compared with those in the infrastructure architecture. The hopping issue at Ad-hoc network will play an important role in delay. We conducted the experiments for Ad-hoc VoIP with two hops. The experimental results and analyses discussed below will exhibit the feasibility of Ad-hoc VoIP using embedded pseudo SIP server.

4.3.1 Local Host Registration Delay

In this experiment, we measured the registration delay from local host UA to the embedded pseudo SIP server. In order to map to the practical operating environment, the mobile nodes were executing video games and streaming videos at the same time while conducting the local host registration. The experimental result is shown in figure 10. We measured the signaling delay between the registration initiated from local host UA and 200 OK response received by UA. The measurement was conducted continuously 1000 times and then we averaged the data and determined the one-way registration delay. In figure 10, the x-axis represents the number of measurements. The y-axis represents the measured registration delay in microseconds. According to our experimental results, the average registration delay when simultaneously

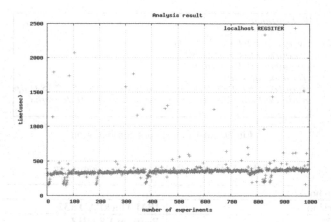

Fig. 10. The delay for the local host register

executing video games and streaming videos for the embedded pseudo SIP server is around 0.301 ms which is negligible compared to other delays.

4.3.2 Registration Delay for Different Architectures

In this experimental scenario, we compared the registration delay from caller to callee in different network architectures. The network architectures with embedded pseudo SIP server in Ad-hoc mode and standalone VoIP server in the infrastructure topology are shown in figures 11(a) and 11(b), respectively. In the standalone VoIP architecture, we connected the access point (AP) to the infrastructure SIP server.

The experimental result is shown in figure 12 where we conducted the experiments for 100 times, labeled at x-axis. The delay time in second, labeled in y-axis, is measured the period from sending out the registration request to receiving the 200 OK response by the remote UA.

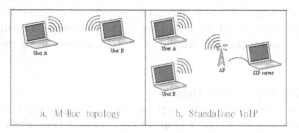

Fig. 11. The REGISTER time with different architectures

The average registration delays for standalone VoIP architecture and Ad-hoc VoIP with embedded pseudo SIP server are 0.0016 and 0.0012 seconds, respectively. Although the CPU resources are shared by embedded pseudo SIP servers and other processes, the distributed peers with SIP server functionality communicate with each other directly. This results in a lower registration delay.

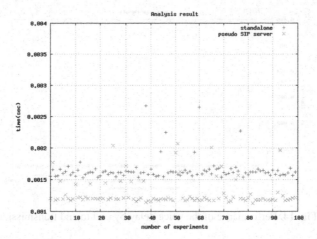

Fig. 12. Performance of the delay time with the different architectures

4.3.3 Signaling Delay in Ad-Hoc VoIP

The delay due to calling process by using INVITE method is contributed from the processes of INVITE, TRYING, RINGING, 200 OK and ACK signals, which corresponds to the signals from pushing the dial tone by caller to the ringing back by callee. We conducted the Ad-hoc VoIP experiments with two hops. User 2 calling User 3 hopped via User 1, as shown in figure 8.

We conducted 100 measurements with this scenario and the results are illustrated in Figure 13. The average signaling delay was 0.022 seconds and it varied from 0.016 to 0.04 seconds which represents excellent signaling quality for VoIP services.

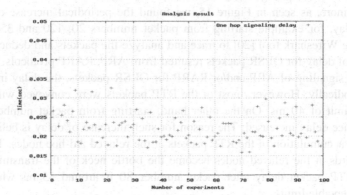

Fig. 13. Performance of the signaling delay with two hops

4.3.4 Voice Data Delay in Ad-Hoc VoIP

Besides the signaling delay conducted earlier, we measured the delay of RTP packets to provide information for realization of Ad-hoc VoIP services.

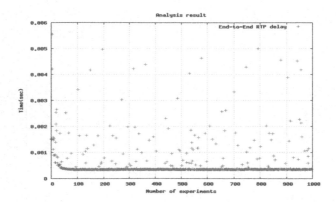

Fig. 14. Performance of the voice delay by end to end transmission

The first experiment was set up to be one hop only and measured the one-way RTP packet delay for 1000 times. The performance of the voice delay for end to end trans-missions is illustrated in Figure 14. The average voice data delay with no hopping is about 0.5 ms and it varied from 0.3 ms to 5.6 ms which are relatively low. According to G.711 [6] defined by ITU-T, this delay belongs to excellent VoIP service.

The second experiment was set up to be a two-hop Ad-hoc VoIP and we measured 1000 one-way RTP packet delays. The result is shown in Figure 15. The average voice data delay with two hops is around 19 ms and it varied from 1 ms to 136 ms in which about 90% of the RTP packets are conveyed within 40 ms. This belongs to acceptable level according to ITU-T standard.

Furthermore, as seen in Figure 15, we found the periodical increase of the RTP packet delay, for example starting from packet numbers 20, 120 and 350, etc. We applied the Wireshark tool [20] to trace and analyze the packets and deduced that the increases of delay for OLSR packets resulted from ARP, RARP protocols. Due to the periodical signaling of ARP and/or RARP for OLSR packets, the delay increase existed periodically. However, most of the RTP packets were conveyed within an acceptable limit of 40 ms. On the other hand, starting from packet number 800, the overall voice delay increased. The reason for such increase of delay is believed to be due to the accumulation of the RTP packets at the relayed Ad-hoc nodes. The buffers of NIC cards at the relayed nodes become the bottle neck of the transmission. The average RTP packet delay after packet number 80 is around 35 ms which is still within acceptable limits.

From the experimental results discussed above, we have provided a primary realization of Ad-hoc VoIP system with embedded pseudo SIP server. The designed system is suitable for two hop of Ad-hoc VoIP service. The embedded pseudo SIP server is also compatible with all UAs.

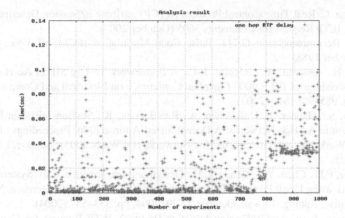

Fig. 15. The VoIP hop delay

5 Conclusions

In this paper, we have implemented an intelligent VoIP system with embedded pseudo SIP servers in an Ad-hoc network. We employed the standard SIP protocol and integrated SIP presence to handle SIP signaling and discovery mechanism for Ad-hoc VoIP services. The embedded pseudo SIP server, acting as the middleware between transport and application layers, is compatible with common SIP-based VoIP UAs. Our testbed demonstrated acceptable VoIP QoS levels in terms of transmission delays for both signaling and voice packets.

Acknowledgements

This research is partially supported by the National Science Council of Republic of China, Taiwan under contracts, NSC 96-2221-E-142-007 and NSC 95-2221-E-324-020. The authors would also like to thank the comments of professor Sandnes from Oslo University College, Norway.

References

1. Chang, L.H., Chuang, P.D., Chen, Y.J., Yang, C.Y.: The Innovation of Pseudo SIP Server on Ad-Hoc VoIP System. In: Proceeding of World Wireless Congress 2005(WWC 2005), United States, May 25-27, 2005, pp. 313–317 (2005)
2. Chang, L.H., Chuang, P.D., Chen, Y.J.: An Ad-Hoc VoIP System Implementation using UPnP Protocol over IPv6. In: Proceedings of International Computer Symposium (ICS), Taipei, Taiwan, December 15-17, 2004, pp. 265–270 (2004)
3. Day, M., Rosenberg, J., Sugano, H.: A Model for Presence and Instant Messaging, IETF Request for Comments 2778 (February 2000)
4. Day, M., Aggarwal, S., Mohr, G., Vincent, J.: Instant Messaging / Presence Protocol Requirements, IETF Request for Comments 2779 (February 2000)

5. Huitema, C.:Real Time Control Protocol (RTCP) attribute in Session Description Protocol (SDP), IETF Request for Comments 3605 (October 2003)
6. ITU-T Recommendation G.711, Pulse Code Modulation (PCM) of Voice Frequencies (November 1988)
7. Khlifi, H., Agarwal, A., Grégoire, J.-C.: A Framework To Use SIP in Ad-Hoc Networks. In: Proceedings of IEEE 2003 Canadian Conference on Electrical and Computer Engineering, pp. 985–988 (May 2003)
8. Leggio, S., Manner, J., Hulkkonen, A., Raatikainen, K.: Session Initiation Protocol Deployment in Ad-Hoc Networks: A Decentralized Approach. In: Proceedings of the International Workshop on Wireless Ad-Hoc Networks (IWWAN 2005), London, UK (May 23 - 26, 2005)
9. Chuang, P.D., Chen, Y.J., Chang, L.H.: Design and Implement a VoIP System on Ad-Hoc Network using UPnP Protocol. In: Proceedings of TANET 2004 Conference, National Taitung Univ., Taitung, Taiwan, October 27-29, 2004, pp. 533–537 (2004)
10. Resenberg, J., et al.: SIP:Session Initiation Protocol. IETF Request for Comments 3261 (June 2004)
11. Rosenberg, J.: A Presence Event Package for The Session Initiation Protocol (SIP), IETF Request for Comments 3856 (August 2004)
12. Rosenberg, J.: A Session Initiation Protocol Event Package for Registrations, IETF Request for Comments 3680 (March 2004)
13. Schulzrinne, H., Casner, S., Frederick, R., Jacobson, V.: RTP: A Transport Protocol for Real-Time Application, IETF Request for Comments 3550 (July 2003)
14. CPU Usage Limiter for Linux, http://sourceforge.net/projects/cpulimit/
15. Kphone, http://sourceforge.net/projects/kphone
16. OLSR Multicast Forwarding Plugin, http://sourceforge.net/projects/olsr-bmf/
17. olsr.org, http://www.olsr.org
18. Ubuntu Linux, http://www.ubuntu.org.tw
19. WIRLAB Network Research Lab, KPhone, http://www.wirlab.org/kphone
20. WireShark, http://www.wireshark.org/

A Weighted Routing Protocol Using Grey Relational Analysis for Wireless Ad Hoc Networks

Hung-Chi Chu*, Yi-Ting Hsu, and Yong-Hsun Lai

Graduate Institute of Networking and Communication Engineering,
Chaoyang University of Technology,
Taichung, 41349, Taiwan
Fax: 886-4-23305539
{hcchu,s9530603,s9530616}@cyut.edu.tw

Abstract. Issues relating to routing protocols are important in wireless ad hoc network research. In this paper we present a weighted ad-hoc routing protocol that exhibit low cost and high efficiency. In our method, important factors including hop count, end-to-end delays, and nodes' residual energy are considered. Grey Relational Analysis is utilized for discovering the importance of these factors and to decide their weighted values. Simulation result shows that the performance of our method is better than traditional wireless ad hoc network routing protocols.

Keywords: Routing protocol, grey relational analysis, wireless ad hoc networks.

1 Introduction

With the rapid progress of wireless communications technology, wireless networks are being applied to the military, agriculture, commerce, and so on. Mobile devices such as notebooks, personal digital assistants, cell phones, etc, make it convenient for us to communicate any time and any place.

The IEEE 802.11 wireless network standard describes two communication modes: namely the infrastructure mode and the ad hoc mode. The former utilizes the access point to help establish a connection to the internet. Access points act as intermediate nodes that connect wired and wireless networks. The latter mode relies on mobile nodes within direct communication range to communicate directly with each other. Each mobile node in an ad hoc mode also forwards the message from one to another neighboring node. Wireless communication models that do not rely on access points are known as Mobile Ad Hoc Networks [1].

One of important challenge in wireless networks is the routing problem. We know that routing is the process of selecting paths in a network along which to send data. In infrastructure mode, the routing problem can be solved by traditional routing techniques. Typically, each access point can be seen as a router that has a priori knowledge of its neighboring nodes. According to this information, a routing table can be created to deal with the routing problem. In ad hoc mode, each mobile node is

---

* Correponding author.

C. Rong et al. (Eds.): ATC 2008, LNCS 5060, pp. 655–663, 2008.

responsible for packet routing that can be seen as a router without a priori knowledge of the network topology. In this scenario, each mobile node listens to the broadcast announcements from its neighbors to establish its local network topology. The announcements may contain the neighbors of mobile node and the ways to reach them. Over time, it is possible for mobile nodes to uncover the entire network topology via announcement messages.

One challenge in ad hoc routing is that the routing mechanism may fail to work when the network topology changes with the movement of mobile node. To overcome the challenge and to keep the quality of service (QoS), an ad hoc routing protocol should be designed by considering the changed of network topology, energy consumption and end-to-end delay and so on. In this paper, we present a weighted routing protocol for wireless ad hoc networks that yields low cost and is highly efficient. The decision of important factors with suitable weights is determined by the grey relational analysis. A brief description of grey relational analysis is presented in section 3.

2   Related Work

Routing in wireless ad hoc network is different from routing in traditional wired network. Ad hoc routing is achieved by sending data from a source node to the target node via neighboring nodes. That is, neighboring nodes receives data that from others and relays it to another. This is called ad hoc routing. However, routing mechanism for traditional wired network is not suitable for ad hoc network, because the router that is responsible for data routing is not present. Therefore, ad hoc routing for wireless ad hoc network should be considered carefully.

Generally speaking, wireless ad hoc routing [2] can be divided into three major classes, active routing, passive routing, and hybrid routing. The basic operations of these classes are summarized in the following subsections.

2.1   Active Routing Methods

In active routing, also called as table driven routing, a routing table is created on the mobile nodes. When the network topology changes, the routing table should be updated immediately. A typical table driven routing method is Destination Sequenced Distance Vector (DSDV) [3] routing. In DSDV, each mobile node maintains its routing table via exchanging the routing information between its neighboring nodes periodically. This is an intuitive routing method that select the lowest cost (or minimal hop count) routing path to be the best route. An improvement of DSDV routing method, Cluster-head Gateway Switch Routing (CGSR) [4], has been proposed. In CGSR, a clustering technique for data aggregation is used to reduce the power consumption and communication overhead. In general, the active routing methods have simple operation mechanism, but exhibit high control overheads and high power consumption.

2.2   Passive Routing Methods

The basic concept of passive routing is on-demand routing. When a necessary routing request occurs, the routing path will be established by utilizing control packets. A typical on-demand routing method is Ad-hoc On-demand Distance Vector (AODV)

[5]. The AODV routing method had become a Request for Comments (RFC) that is released by Internet Engineering Task Force (IETF) in July, 2003. When necessary, a source node sends the control packets of Route Requests (RREQs) to destination node. After receiving the RREQs, the destination node replies with Route Reply (RREPs) control packets. Finally, the on-demand routing path can be created via these control packets. One of the enhancement routing methods of AODV is Dynamic Source Routing (DSR) [6]. In DSR, a source node sends control packets to establish an on-demand routing path and stores the other possible routing path in its cache memory. When a communication link on the routing path fails, the source node can select another routing path from its cache and transfer data packets immediately. In general, the passive routing methods have lower routing table maintenance costs, but have high packet delays.

2.3 Hybrid Routing Methods

Hybrid routing methods combine active and passive routing. A typical hybrid routing method is the Zone Routing Protocol (ZRP) [7]. In ZRP, the entire network topology is divided into several smaller routing zones. When source node and destination node are within the same zone, the active routing method is applied to rapidly provide a routing path. When source node and destination node are located in different zone, the passive routing method is applied on demand to establish a routing path between zones. The Fisheye Zone Routing protocol (FZRP) [8] is also a hybrid routing method. It uses the view point of fisheye to divide the entire working area into two zones, basic zone and extended zone. In FZRP method, an active routing method is used in basic zone and a passive routing method is used in extended zone. In general, the Hybrid routing method has short routing delay for an intra-zone routing, low control overhead for an inter-zone routing, and high system complexity.

Active routing methods have low packet delays but high control overheads and the passive routing methods have low control overheads but high packet delays. By considering the tradeoff between packet delays and control overheads, the hybrid routing methods try to find the balance between active and passive routing methods that can maximize the system performance. However, hybrid routing methods just only reduce the defect of active and passive routing method slightly. In recent years, on-demand routing is proposed for improving the system performance such as packet delays or energy consumption. It is obvious that several factors such as nodes' residual energy, end-to-end delay, hop count, and so on affect the performance of routing method [9-11]. By considering some important routing factors, the routing method will be more reliable and outstanding. Therefore, this paper proposes a grey relational routing (GRR) method that considers important routing factors using grey relational analysis. The GRR is a passive weighted routing method that is modified by AODV.

3   Grey Relational Routing

Grey relational analysis is useful for finding the importance of factors for a system with limited sampling data. In this section, we introduce the basic concept of grey theory and grey relational analysis. And then the detail of the weighted routing method is proposed.

3.1 Grey Theory

Grey theory [12] was introduced in 1982 by Julong Deng. A grey system comprises partially known information and partially unknown information. In general, the analysis of system characteristics is based on the statistical model which finds the statistical properties between data in a large sample set. However, a large sample set may not be readily available; therefore, many systems are said to be in a state of poor information. The characteristic of a grey system is that it can utilize only a few known data through accumulated generating operation (AGO) to establish a prediction model. Grey system has been widely applied to control, medical, agriculture, military, and engineering problems [13, 14].

3.2 Grey Relational Analysis

Based on grey theory, the grey relational space (GRS) was originally proposed to relate the main factor to the other reference factors in a given system. We applied this technique here to select some input variables which show stronger impact to the system output. Let $\gamma(y_0(k), x_i(k))$ be the grey relational coefficient at point k between output sequence y_0 and input sequence x_i. The followings describe the four basic axioms for the grey relational space:

(1) $\gamma(y_0(k), x_i(k)) \in (0, 1]$, $\forall k$.
(2) $\gamma(y_0(k), x_i(k)) = \gamma(x_i(k), y_0(k))$ if and only if it is a single-input and single output system.
(3) $\gamma(y_0(k), x_i(k)) \neq \gamma(x_i(k), y_0(k))$ almost holds if and only if it is a multi-input and single-output system.
(4) $\gamma(y_0(k), x_i(k))$ decrease with the increase of $\Delta(k)$, where $\Delta(k) = | y_0(k) - x_i(k)|$

From the above axioms we can understand that if an input sequence shows a higher similarity than the others to the output, then this input variable can be said to be more important to the output. To calculate the grey relational degrees between the output and input variables and then to compare the relative importance, the following procedures are usually used:

Step 1: Let the output sequence be $y_0 = (y_0(1), y_0(2), \ldots, y_0(n))$, where n stands for the number of data.

Step 2: Denote the m sequences to be compared by $x_i = (x_i(1), x_i(2), \ldots, x_i(n))$, $i=1$, 2, ..., m.

Step 3: Calculate

$$\gamma(y_0(k), x_i(k)) = \frac{\min_j \min_k | y_0(k) - x_j(k)| + \xi \max_j \max_k | y_0(k) - x_j(k)|}{| y_0(k) - x_j(k)| + \xi \max_j \max_k | y_0(k) - x_j(k)|}$$

Where $\xi \in (0, 1]$ is the distinguishing coefficient. $j=1, 2, \ldots, m$. $k=1, 2, \ldots, n$. $\gamma(y_0(k), x_i(k))$ is called the grey relational coefficient at point k. Note that a normalization operation on the data sequences is normally required since the range or unit in one data sequence may differ from the others. Aggregating the grey relational coefficient calculated at each point, we can obtain the grey relational grade for an entire sequence.

Step 4: The grey relational grade between the output and a specific input sequence is derived as follows:

$$\gamma(y_0, x_i) = \frac{1}{n} \sum_{k=1}^{n} \gamma(y_0(k), x_i(k))$$

Here $\gamma(y_0, x_i)$ represents to what degree of influence the sequence x_i can exert on the output sequence y_0. In other words, the system output can grasp some useful information about the variation of data points from input sequence. Thus, the analysis of grey relational grade provides us an alternative to decide which input variables show the crucial effect to the output.

According to the grey relational analysis, we consider the impact factors about end-to-end delay, nodes' residual energy, and hop count from source to destination in the network topology with uniform distribution. Then the relational degree about hop count, end-to-end delay, and nodes' residual energy are 26%, 36% and 38%, respectively.

3.3   Weighted Evaluation Function

Recent research [9-11] present a routing method that only considers one factor for improvement. We know that many factors influence the performance of the routing protocol. Therefore, we propose a Grey Relational Routing (GRR) method using a weighted evaluation function. The weighted value of the impact factors is decided by grey relational analysis that we mentioned in previous section. Our method will choose the routing path with the smallest value of weighted evaluation function. Assume that one of a routing path has t intermediate nodes $n_1, n_2, \ldots,$ and n_t. The source node is n_0 and the destination node is n_{t+1}. The weighted evaluation function E_{va} is:

$$E_{va} = W_E (1 - \sum_{i=1}^{t} E_i) + W_D \sum_{i=0}^{t} D_{i,i+1} + W_H H$$

Where E_i presents the normalization of residual energy of node i, $D_{i,i+1}$ presents the normalization of end-to-end delay from node i to node $i+1$, and H presents the normalization of hop count of this routing path. The symbol of W_E, W_D, and W_H present the weighted value of nodes' residual energy, end-to-end delay, and hop count, respectively.

As shown in Fig. 1, some data packets will be sent from source node S to destination node D. In this scenario, we have four possible routing paths P_1 ($S \rightarrow A \rightarrow B \rightarrow C \rightarrow D$), P_2 ($S \rightarrow E \rightarrow F \rightarrow G \rightarrow D$), P_3 ($S \rightarrow H \rightarrow I \rightarrow D$), and P_4 ($S \rightarrow A \rightarrow F \rightarrow G \rightarrow D$). The value on the link between two adjacent nodes is the end-to-end delay and the value above the node is its residual energy. By using a routing protocol with the shortest delay, the maximal residual energy and the minimal hop count, the path P_1, P_2 and P_3 will be selected, respectively. However, our method considers these factors via weighted evaluation function to choose the path P_4. The factors are listed in Table 1.

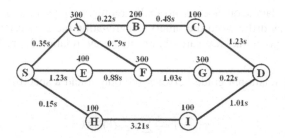

Fig. 1. An example of routing path with different factors

Table 1. The factors from path P_1 to path P_4

Path	Hop count	Delay	Energy	Eva	Routing protocol
P_1	4	**2.28**	600	0.73	Minimal delay
P_2	4	3.76	**1000**	0.78	Maximal residual energy
P_3	3	4.37	200	0.88	Minimal hop count
P_4	4	2.39	900	**0.68**	Our method (GRR)

3.4 Grey Relational Routing Method

The energy issue is very important in wireless networks. As we mentioned in section 2, the passive routing method has the advantage of low energy consumption. Therefore, the grey relational routing (GRR) method that we proposed is based on the traditional passive routing method such as AODV relies on hop count, nodes' residual energy and end-to-end delays. We use the weighted evaluation function to choose a suitable routing path. Our GRR method contains the two main phases.

In the first phase, we need to perform a route discovery process. As shown in Fig. 2(a), a source node S broadcasts Route Request (RREQ) control packets to discovery a path to destination node D. The RREQ control packet contains the following information:

{*Source ID, Destination ID, Total Hop count, Total Delay, Total Residual Energy*}

For each intermediate node, it computes the weighted evaluation function E_{va} from source node to it, updates the RREQ control packet in the fields of Total Hop count, Total Delay, and Total Residual Energy, stores this modified RREQ packet and its E_{va} in cache memory, and forwards the modified RREQ to its neighboring nodes. To avoid the overabundant of RREQ control packets, the intermediate node discards the redundant RREQ packet without the smallest E_{va} value. When destination node receives the RREQ packet, the path with the smallest E_{va} will be selected to be the routing path.

In the second phase, we need to perform a route reply process to establish the discovered routing path. As shown in Fig. 2(b), according to the smallest E_{va}, destination node D sends the Route Reply (RREP) control packet to intermediate node I and to confirm the routing path. For each intermediate node, it always selects the path that has the smallest E_{va} and forwards the RREP packet by unicast. When the source node S receives the RREP control packet that reply from destination node D, the on-demand routing path is established by weighted evaluation function.

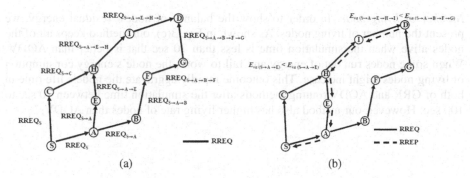

Fig. 2. (a) Route Discovery Process. (b) Route Replay Process.

4 Simulation Result

We evaluated the proposed method by using the Network Simulator version 2 (NS2) [15]. IEEE 802.11 MAC protocol and energy model are considered. In initial state, the bandwidth was 2M bits per second. The simulation consisted of 10, 20, 30, 40, and 50 nodes distributed randomly in a 1000m×1000m square field. For each node, its transmission range was 250m. For each traffic flow, we generated 512 bytes User Datagram Protocol (UDP) data packet with constant bit rate per second. As the number of nodes increased, two, four, six and eight packet traffic flow were considered. Assuming that each node's initial energy was 1000J, the transmitted power dissipation was 15J, the received power dissipation was 10J, the power dissipation of idle state was 5J and the duration of simulation was 100 seconds. Average end-to-end delay, average energy variance and number of living node were considered in our simulation.

Average end-to-end delay: The end-to-end delay measures the time for source node to send a data packet to destination node. This measurement shows the total latency that includes the routing path discovery, routing path reply and one packet propagation time. As shown in Fig. 3(a), the end-to-end delay of our method is better than AODV when the number of nodes in the network is larger than 30. On the contrary, ours is worse than AODV when the number of nodes is less than 30. This is because that in sparse network, the distance between two adjacent nodes is large that incurs long point-to-point delay. In this scenario, the factor of hop count is more important than others. The defect will be considered by using dynamic GRR method to immediately update the weighted value.

Average energy variance: Energy is one of important factors in wireless ad hoc networks. When a node run out of energy, it will lose its functionality and fail to work. Therefore, we consider the variance of average energy consumption to show that our method has lower energy consumption than AODV. In Fig. 3(b), the x-axis indicates the simulation time (sec) and y-axis indicates the variance of energy consumption. Because the factor of nodes' residual energy is considered in our method, the proposed method can reduce the energy consumption compared to AODV.

Number of living node: In order to show the balance of nodes' residual energy, we present the number of living nodes. As shown in Fig. 3(c), our method keeps all of the nodes alive when the simulation time is less than 70 sec that is better than AODV. When some nodes run out of energy and fail to work, the node's energy consumption of living nodes might increase. This outcome rapidly aggravate the node's life time in both of GRR and AODV routing methods after the simulation time between 70 sec to 100 sec. However, our method also has higher living rate of nodes than AODV.

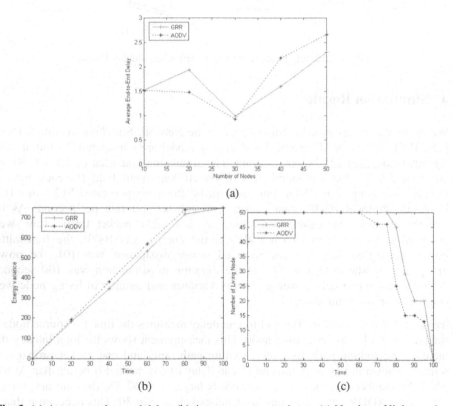

Fig. 3. (a) Average end-to-end delay. (b) Average energy variance. (c) Number of living node.

5 Conclusion

Considering some impact factors of routing mechanism such as end-to-end delay, nodes' residual energy, and hop count, a passive routing method, Grey Relation Routing (GRR), is presented. For each factor, we assign a weighted value that is decided by grey relational analysis to indicate its importance. By simulation results, the GRR method is better than traditional passive routing method such as AODV. Our method can effectively reduce the energy consumption, reduce the end-to-end delay and prolong the network lifetime.

References

1. Corson, M.S., Macker, J.P., Cirincione, G.H.: Internet-Based Mobile Ad Hoc Networking. IEEE Internet Computing, 63–70 (July/August 1999)
2. Lee, S.J., Hsu, J., Hayashida, R.: Selecting a routing strategy for your ad hoc networks. Computer Communications 26, 723–733 (2003)
3. Perkins, C.E., Bhagwat, P.: Highly Dynamic Destination-Sequenced Distance-Vector Routing (DSDV) for Mobile Computers. In: Proc. of the ACM SIGCOMM, vol. 24(4), pp. 234–244 (Octiber 1994)
4. Chiang, C.C., Wu, H.K., Winston, L., Mario, G.: Routing in Clustered Multihop, Mobile Wireless Networks With Fading Channel. In: IEEE International Conference on Networks, pp. 197–211 (1997)
5. Perkins, C.E., Belding-Royer, E.M., Das, S.R.: Ad Hoc On-Demand Distance Vector (AODV) Routing., IETF Mobile Ad Hoc Networks Working Group, RFC 3561 (July 2003)
6. Johnson, D.B., Maltz, D.A., Hu, Y.C.: The Dynamic Source Routing Protocol for Mobile Ad Hoc Networks. Internet- Draft, draft-ietf- manet-dsr-10.txt (July 2004)
7. Zhang, X., Jacob, L.: Multicast zone routing protocol in mobile ad hoc wireless networks. In: Proc. Of the 28th Annual IEEE International Conference on Local Computer Networks, pp. 150–159 (2003)
8. Yang, C.C., Tseng, L.P.: Fisheye Zone Routing Protocol: A Multi-Level Zone Routing Protocol for Mobile Ad Hoc Networks. Computer Communications 30, 261–268 (2007)
9. Lin, X.H., Kwok, Y.K., Lau, V.K.N.: BGCA: Bandwidth Guarded Channel Adaptive Routing for Ad Hoc Networks. In: Wireless Communications and Networking Conference, pp. 433–439 (March 2002)
10. Kim, D., Lee, W., Park, B.N.: A Power Balanced Multipath Routing Protocol in Wireless Ad-Hoc Sensor Networks. In: IEEE International Conference on Computer and Information Technology, pp. 222–227 (2006)
11. Li, L., Li, C., Yaun, P.: Performance evaluation and simulations of routing protocols in ad hoc networks. Computer Communications 30, 1890–1898 (2007)
12. Deng, J.-L.: Introduction to grey system theory. The Journal of Grey System 1, 1–24 (1989)
13. Deng, J.-L.: Control problems of grey systems. System and Control Letters 5, 228–294 (1982)
14. Huang, Y.-P., Huang, C.-C.: The integration and application of fuzzy and grey modeling methods. Fuzzy Sets and Systems 78, 107–119 (1996)
15. The Network Simulator 2, http://www.isi.edu/nsnam/ns/index.html

Author Index

Lecture Notes in Computer Science

Sublibrary 2: Programming and Software Engineering

For information about Vols. 1– 4408
please contact your bookseller or Springer